Malaparte
A Biography

MAURIZIO SERRA

Translated by Stephen Twilley

nyrb **New York Review Books** New York

This is a New York Review Book
published by The New York Review of Books
207 East 32nd Street, New York, NY 10016
www.nyrb.com

Copyright © 2011 by Éditions Grasset & Fasquelle
Translation copyright © 2025 by Stephen Twilley
All rights reserved.

First published in the French language as *Malaparte: vie et légendes* in 2011.

Library of Congress Cataloging-in-Publication Data
Names: Serra, Maurizio, 1955– author. | Twilley, Stephen, translator.
Title: Malaparte, lives and legends / by Maurizio Serra; translated by Stephen Twilley.
Other titles: Malaparte, vies et légendes. English
Description: New York: New York Review Books, 2024. | Series: New York Review Books | Includes bibliographical references and index. | Identifiers: LCCN 2024008794 (print) | LCCN 2024008795 (ebook) | ISBN 9781681378701 (paperback) | ISBN 9781681378718 (ebook)
Subjects: LCSH: Malaparte, Curzio, 1898–1957. | Authors, Italian—20th century—Biography. | LCGFT: Biographies.
Classification: LCC PQ4829.A515 Z8613 2024 (print) | LCC PQ4829.A515 (ebook) | DDC 853/.92 [B]—dc23/eng/20240511
LC record available at https://lccn.loc.gov/2024008794
LC ebook record available at https://lccn.loc.gov/2024008795

ISBN 978-1-68137-870-1
Available as an electronic book; ISBN 978-1-68137-871-8

Printed in the United States of America on acid-free paper.

10 9 8 7 6 5 4 3 2 1

Contents

Acknowledgments and a Note on Texts and Sources............ ix
Malaparte's Principal Works xv

Introduction: The Woes of Narcissus........................ 1

1. The Beginnings of a Bonaparte (1898–1924)

First Steps 25
"Unable to Do Otherwise, We Performed Miracles"......... 51
A Young Man in Revolt.................................. 71
In Search of a Role..................................... 79
With the Black Bands of the Revolution 86
A Squalid Affair.. 97

2. Fascism and High Society (1925–1933)

Fascist, but Not Like the Others 111
Country and City....................................... 126
Duce and Chameleon 138
FIATS for the Soviets!.................................. 158
Flaminia... 181
The Technique of Self-Promotion 193
The Jar Returns to the Well... 221

3. Kremlin and Swastika (1934–1943)

Oh, What a Lovely Confinement! 233
Galeazzo and Edda...................................... 257

Virginia 267
Excellent Prospects 287
Lawrence of Ethiopia 299
No Entry 308
From the Alps to Piraeus 321
On Eastern Fronts 337
Finnish Interlude 362

4. Chronicles of the Plague (1944–1946)

"It's of No Importance Whether What Malaparte Relates
    Is True or False" 381
In Which Is Told the Story of a Chamber Pot and a Cigar ... 400
Music and Gallows 411
On the Side of the Goose 419
Skin and Mud 428
No Such Thing as Bad Publicity 447
In Praise of Rottenness 464

5. From Paris to Mao (1947–1957)

Paris Is No Longer Worth a Mass 477
The Two Straw Hats of Italy 491
Theater 506
Cinema 523
"But I Loved You, Damned!" 535
From Music Hall to the Long March 545
"This Suburb of Prato Called Peking…" 574
"To My Dear and Most Devoted Friend… Gianni Schicchi!" ... 591

Conclusion: Capri, or The Bird That Swallowed Its Cage 613

Notes 631
Index 699

I shall lose at Austerlitz and win at Waterloo.

—Malaparte

Acknowledgments and a Note on Texts and Sources

A BIOGRAPHY IS, first of all, the sum total of the debts contracted by a biographer, which in the present case are especially numerous.

I was able to count on the full and active cooperation of the principal biographers and specialists of Malaparte, with a few exceptions, most notably of Franco Vegliani, who passed away before my own work began. I hope I have managed to repay their trust. The conclusions I have come to here are largely in keeping with the results of their research. In this group I would like to thank first of all my lifelong friends Giordano Bruno Guerri and Francesco Perfetti.

Many of the testimonies quoted herein come from figures who directly or indirectly knew Malaparte. In some cases, I have substituted names with initials, at the request of the person concerned, or out of discretion. I offer my very heartfelt thanks to all of them. I would like to express my particular gratitude to Countess Maria Sole Agnelli Teodorani Fabbri, Lino Pellegrini (1915–2013), and the Hon. Giorgio Napolitano, Italian president of the republic from 2006 to 2015, for their precious testimony, previously uncollected by biographers or researchers.

In different ways, I am also indebted to the following: Paolo Balbo, Franco Baldasso, Giovanni Belardelli, Mauro Canali, Andrea

ACKNOWLEDGMENTS AND NOTE

Capra, Edmonde Charles-Roux, Michel Déon, Renzo De Felice, Anne de Lacretelle, Diane de Margerie, Beatriz de Moura, Cyprienne del Drago, Bernardino di Campello, Jorge Edwards, Alain Elkann, Bengt Jangfeldt, Ludovico Incisa di Camerana, François Laudenbach, Gianni Letta, François Livi, Loredana Luciolli, Félicien Marceau, Emmanuel Mattiato, Alvise Memmo, Fernando Mezzetti, Beatrice Monti von Rezzori, Roberto Morozzo della Rocca, George L. Mosse, Jean Neuvecelle, René Novella, Michel Ostenc, Giuseppe Pardini, Antonello Pietromarchi, Claudio Quarantotto, Nello Quilici, Ruggero Ranieri di Sorbello, Waldo Rojas, Daniele Rulli, Onofrio Solari Bozzi, Anna Teodorani Fabbri, and Guy Tosi.

It is thanks to Matteo Noja, then the director of the Fondazione Biblioteca di via Senato, in Milan, that I was able to examine the Archivio Malaparte contained there. This impressive collection of documents did not modify on any essential point the idea that I had come to of the man and his work, but it allowed me to clarify some specific points and to correct or complete many pieces of secondhand information. Likewise, thanks to the hospitality of the writer's grandnephew Niccolò Rositani Suckert and his wife, Alessia, I was able to sojourn briefly at Malaparte's famous house on Capri, Casa Come Me, the "house like me," where I drafted the book's conclusion. One of the writer's grandnieces, Laura Ronchi Abbozzo, also kindly provided me with useful information.

I would also like to mention, among those who generously made unpublished material and correspondence available to me, Claude Nabokoff Joxe, granddaughter of Daniel and Marianne Halévy; Daniele Rulli, who sent me the letters Malaparte wrote to his parents over the course of twenty years; and Monique Grossin, Orfeo Tamburi's heir. Prof. Didier Musiedlak and his assistant, Nicolas

Patin, sent me a copy of Malaparte's personal file held at the Paris Prefecture of Police. Romania's ambassador to UNESCO, Prof. Nicolae Manolescu-Apolzan, and his deputy, Lilian Zamfiroiu, permitted me to access the Romanian Foreign Ministry records relevant to Malaparte's stays in Bucharest and Jassy in 1941. Finally, I thank the personnel of the Italian Central Archive of the State and of the Archive of the Ministry of Foreign Affairs, in Rome, particularly Federica Onelli, for the professionalism and efficiency with which they followed up all my requests.

Father Ferdinando Castelli, SJ (1920–2013), a man of great erudition and great kindness, allowed me free, unlimited access to the library of the Vatican-vetted Jesuit magazine *La Civiltà Cattolica*, in the splendid surroundings of Villa Malta in Rome, which contains many first editions of Malaparte as well as other rare works pertaining to my research.

I am greatly indebted to all my previous translators of this book. But no one could succeed in adapting it for the English-speaking reader with more talent, meticulousness, and insight than Stephen Twilley, with whom I have worked closely and with the greatest pleasure. He therefore deserves, in my eyes, the Dantesque title of "il miglior fabbro" that Eliot famously accorded to Ezra Pound.

Other acknowledgments of testimonies and clarifications received have been indicated in the text or in the notes. There are certainly still unknown sources to explore, given the extent of Malaparte's contacts in political, diplomatic, literary, journalistic, and, last but not least, society circles of his time; but I do not believe they would substantially change the image offered here, and I trust that the most important documentation has been examined and presented in this book.

ACKNOWLEDGMENTS AND NOTE

Edda Ronchi Suckert, one of the writer's two sisters, dedicated much of the last years of her life to the chronological edition of Malaparte's papers and letters, amounting to roughly ten thousand pages in twelve volumes.[1] Initially printed privately in Città di Castello, the project was continued by the Florentine publisher Ponte alle Grazie and completed in 1996. Such devotion on the part of someone already well advanced in years to the memory of an admired and adored brother is certainly moving and should inspire the gratitude of all scholars. This prodigious selection, which also includes variants of well-known works, numerous unpublished texts, uncollected articles, and fragments of the writer's *Giornale segreto* (Secret journal), is therefore an indispensable tool. But one needs to know how to use it. Edda displays an unshakable faith in *all* of Malaparte's assertions, some of which are, however, belied by the documents in her edition (sometimes truncated and more often copied in typescript without the originals being preserved) and by what can be established from other sources. Furthermore, she garnishes everything with long commentaries and digressions, often confusing dates and episodes, in addition to making factual mistakes, especially concerning foreign letter writers.* Let us say that some sections are very rich, others much less so, and that certain matters of no little significance for an understanding of Malaparte, among them his romantic life, are treated in a rather synthetic manner.

If we cannot speak of true censorship, then, as in the case of famous sister-editors such as Isabelle Rimbaud or Elisabeth Förster-Nietzsche, the fact remains that the examination of the chronolog-

---

*Thus, for example, a letter attributed to Albert Camus is in reality from the French doctor Clément Camus, a friend and confidant of both Malaparte and Céline.

ical edition must be undertaken in the light of the totality of the Archivio Malaparte (indicated here in the notes with the abbreviation "AM"). It is an imposing amount of material, notwithstanding the many omissions due to negligence and to veritable sackings: the correspondence alone comprises nearly a thousand known interlocutors and a few hundred unidentified ones. Now in the able hands of curators Carla Maria Giacobbe and Federico Oneta, the archive has finally been inventoried and is, as of this writing, undergoing a systematic reorganization of its contents. It is therefore on the basis of a comparison across this documentation, sometimes incomplete for the reasons expressed, that I have undertaken my studies.

One last observation, addressed to the kind attention of the English-language reader: This biography was born from the proposal of a French publisher, and it was written in French, with the aim of addressing an international, nonspecialist audience. France was a second homeland for Malaparte, and he gladly let others think him a bilingual writer, à la Beckett, Cioran, or Semprún, or even a multilingual one, like Eliade and Nabokov.[2] He might have become one, too, because he had a facility with languages, but he lacked persistence and the sense of fully expressing himself in French, and after a few pages he would return to Italian. All his books that appeared first in France and then in Italy were edited or revised by professional translators, with whom he regularly quarreled. He composed directly in French only two ill-fated plays, which some of his Parisian friends offered, in vain, to rewrite; some polemical or journalistic texts; a small part of *Diary of a Foreigner in Paris*; some contentious prefaces, like the one to the French version of *The Volga*

ACKNOWLEDGMENTS AND NOTE

Rises in Europe; and numerous articles, interviews, sketches, fragments, et cetera, some notable, with which one could assemble a small but appealing anthology. In the same language—sometimes, after the Second World War, in decent English, as well—he also wrote many letters that, though careless in their syntax and spelling, bear his unmistakable imprint.* In this new, English-language version of the book, necessarily abridged but true to the spirit of the original, you will accordingly find indicated in a note where appropriate: "Original in French [or English]."

Maurizio Serra
Rome-Paris, April 2023

---

*Malaparte, who got irritated with anyone who did not know how to write his German surname correctly, did not pay much attention to the spelling of foreign names, as evidenced by his correspondence and by unpublished texts, aside from the errors his sister Edda often added in recopying them.

Malaparte's Principal Works

AFTER DECADES OF NEGLECT, dispersion, and partially faulty versions, Adelphi in Milan has started to republish the author's major works in new critical editions, under the impulse of its former director Roberto Calasso and that of Giorgio Pinotti, a noted scholar of the writer. Wherever possible here, published English-language translations have been used. The abbreviations indicated before the titles below are employed in citations of passages in the book, followed by the corresponding page numbers. In the absence of a previously published translation, the passages have been translated here for the first time.

Works by Malaparte Published in English

CT	*Those Cursed Tuscans*, translated by Rex Benedict. Athens: Ohio University Press, 1964.
DFP	*Diary of a Foreigner in Paris*, translated by Stephen Twilley. New York: NYRB Classics, 2020.
K	*Kaputt*, translated by Cesare Foligno. New York: NYRB Classics, 2005. First published 1948 by Alvin Redman (London).
KB	*The Kremlin Ball*, translated by Jenny McPhee. New York: NYRB Classics, 2018.

MALAPARTE'S PRINCIPAL WORKS

S   *The Skin*, translated by David Moore. New York: NYRB Classics, 2013. First published 1952 by Alvin Redman (London).

T1   *Coup d'État: The Technique of Revolution*, translated by Sylvia Saunders. New York: Dutton, 1932. Based on *Technique du coup d'État*, translated by Juliette Bertrand (Paris: Grasset, 1931).

V   *The Volga Rises in Europe*, translated by David Moore. London: Alvin Redman, 1957.

W   *Woman Like Me*, translated by Robin Monotti Graziadei. Leicester, UK: Troubador Publishing, 2007.

Works by Malaparte Unpublished in English

AB   "Autobiografia," text of 1944 published for the first time in *Rinascita* (Rome), August–September 1957.

AR1   *L'arcitaliano*. Florence: La Voce, 1928.

AR2   *L'arcitaliano e tutte le altre poesie*, definitive edition of AR1. Florence: Vallecchi, 1963.

AV   *Avventure di un capitano di sventura*. Rome: Edizioni de La Voce, 1927.

BA1   *Battibecco (1953–55)*. Milan: Garzanti, 1955.

BA2   *Battibecco (1953–57)*, definitive edition of BA1. Florence: Vallecchi, 1967.

BI   *Benedetti italiani*. Florence: Vallecchi, 1961.

CB   *Coppi e Bartali: I due volti dell'Italia*. Milan: Adelphi, 2009.

CD   *I custodi del disordine*. Turin: Buratti, 1931; Venice: Aria d'Italia, 1957.

MALAPARTE'S PRINCIPAL WORKS

CP   *Il Cristo proibito* (*The Forbidden Christ*), screenplay and dialogues for the film, critical edition by Luigi Martellini. Naples: ESI, 1992.

CV   *Il compagno di viaggio*. Milan: Excelsior 1881, 2007.

DC   *Deux chapeaux de paille d'Italie*. Paris: Denoël, 1948.

DK   *Das Kapital*, French version by the author. Rome-Milan: Aria d'Italia, 1951.

DONC   *Don Cameleo*. Florence: Vallecchi, 1946.

DOP   *Anche le donne hanno perso la guerra*. Bologna: Cappelli, and Rome-Milan: Aria d'Italia, 1954; repr. in *Sipario*, July–August 1958.

DP   *Du côté de chez Proust*, French version by the author. Rome-Milan: Aria d'Italia, 1951.

EV   *L'Europa vivente: Teoria storica del sindacalismo nazionale*. Florence: Edizioni de *La Voce*, 1923.

FP   *Fughe in prigione*. Milan: Treves, 1936; Florence: Vallecchi, 1943.

GS   *Giornale segreto*. Extracts in *Malaparte*, vols. 4, 5, etc.

IB   *Italia barbara*. Turin: Gobetti, 1925; Rome: Edizioni de *La Voce*, 1928.

IL   *Intelligenza di Lenin*. Milan: Treves, 1930.

IP   *L'inglese in paradiso*. Florence: Vallecchi, 1960.

LB   *Lenin buonanima*. Florence: Vallecchi, 1962. First Italian edition of *Le Bonhomme Lénine* (1932).

ME   "Memoriale 1946" (a.k.a. "1946 statement of defense"). Extracts in *Malaparte*, vols. 1–5.

MM   *Mamma marcia*. Florence: Vallecchi, 1959.

MU   *Muss* and *Il grande imbecille*, edited by Francesco Perfetti. Milan-Trento: Luni, 1999.

MALAPARTE'S PRINCIPAL WORKS

RC   *Io, in Russia e in Cina*. Florence: Vallecchi, 1958.

RI   *Racconti italiani*, definitive edition, edited by Enrico Falqui. Florence: Vallecchi, 1959.

S   *Sangue*. Florence: Vallecchi, 1954.

SC   *Il sole è cieco*. Milan: Tempo, 1941; Florence: Vallecchi, 1947.

SD   *Storia di domani*. Milan-Rome: Aria d'Italia, 1949.

SG   *Sodoma e Gomorra*. Milan: Treves, 1931.

T2   *Tecnica del colpo di Stato*. Milan: Bompiani, 1948. First Italian edition of *Technique du coup d'État* (1931).

VC   *Viva Caporetto!* Prato: Stabilimento Lito-Tipografico Martini, 1921. Republished as *La Rivolta dei santi maledetti* (Rome: La Rassegna Internazionale, 1921) and then as *La rivolta dei santi maledetti e altri saggi politici (1921–1931)* (Florence: Vallecchi, 1961). The edition cited here is in *Opere scelte*, edited by Luigi Martellini (Milan: Mondadori, 1997).

VE   *Viaggio in Etiopia e altri scritti africani*, edited by Enzo R. Laforgia. Florence: Vallecchi, 2006.

VP   *Vita di Pizzo-di-Ferro detto Italo Balbo*, with Enrico Falqui. Rome: Libreria del Littorio, 1931.

VT   *Viaggi fra i terremoti*, edited by Enrico Falqui. Florence: Vallecchi, 1963.

Introduction
The Woes of Narcissus

A narcissist... *me*? And he fiercely denied it.
—Giancarlo Vigorelli, 1980

There are many reasons, all of them excellent, not to like him. But none to deny him a prominent place among the most singular interpreters of a twentieth century whose anxieties live on into our own. Curzio Suckert, known as Malaparte (1898–1957), this "cursed Tuscan" of genuinely international stature, represents an inescapable model of the contemporary intellectual, one that many after him have sought to imitate without matching his substance, style, or icy presence. The time has come to clear the field of the commonplaces and clichés that have, often with the help of the man himself, obscured our view of him. Mythomaniac, exhibitionist, raconteur, Malaparte was not—at least not entirely—the turncoat who abandons one lost cause after another to run to the winners, whoever they may be. A personality bristling with contradictions and frequently conflicting needs, he was guided or dominated, in every choice, more by his temperament than by events. His internal coherence may not please the beautiful souls, but it would seem indisputable, as does his courage. If his chameleon nature allowed

INTRODUCTION

him to adapt to any and all circumstances, his vocation as a D'Annunzian "armed aesthete" successfully protected him from the worst kinds of complicity and raised him above fashions, including those he created himself. He was a special correspondent to the awfulness of history, passing fresh and untouched from salon to trench, revolutions to diplomatic conferences, factories to forced marches, Mussolini to Hitler, Stalin to Mao, anarchists to the pope. An "antihero of our times," he breathed the air of totalitarian ideologies without becoming infected. Malaparte sought to present a vision of modern man modeled on the ancient Greek tragedians—a mixture of grandeur and cynicism, ideals and servitude—in which, as a good narcissist, he saw himself reflected. Nearly seventy years after his death, he has won the wager. Like him or not, he is still here, alive and well, in Italy and, perhaps to an even greater extent, abroad.

If he chose to bemire himself with the "blood, pleasure, and death" extolled by Maurice Barrès in the preceding generation, Malaparte nevertheless straddled all the currents of his age without immersing himself in any. He never lost sight of the fact that he was a writer first, a militant second, and that above all his task was to *witness*—in his own way, of course. No profession of faith could impose limits on his talent, because no cause deserved to be taken too seriously. This shows his ambivalence, but also his need for freedom, his refusal to fall into line with any party, no matter how seductive. Malaparte was caught in a whirlwind of continually reinvented lives and legends, into which we shall seek to follow him and discover his subterfuges. This man, who seemed to live for an audience, sought silence in order to find himself. A born provocateur, ideologically unserviceable, he made repeated attempts at the one career that truly did not suit him, that of the politician. This is doubtless why today neither the Right nor the Left recognize him as one of their own. Running to the winners, Malaparte almost always ended up on the wrong side, with a love for lost causes (if not losers) that is hard not to admire. All his life he was obsessed by a taste for exhibitionism and scandal, veering toward paranoia in his final years. "What negative judgment has struck you most?" he was asked one day. "Silence," came the reply, of rare sincerity.[1]

If Malaparte often spouted nonsense, and happily lied, he never betrayed the mocking ghosts of his idols: the Greek tragedians, Saint-Simon, Chateaubriand, Byron, Baudelaire, Foscolo, D'Annunzio. The reason is obviously not a moral one. He was incapable of distorting reality, because he would have first had to accept it, to admit that the real existed before its representation. History interested him only to the extent to which he could dye it like cloth, according to the innovations that his father, an excellent technician from Germany, had introduced to the spinning mills of his hometown of Prato, in Tuscany. Malaparte disdained history, even as it dominated his books. It was the true subject of an author for whom everything else, everything that is generally the substance of literature—loves and losses, separations and reunions, memories of childhood, sunsets, metaphysical anguish—was decidedly secondary. With politics, pursued with the same ardor as literature but with much less success, he came and went as he pleased, taking what he needed and discarding it when done. History, he wrote more than once, is death; but this equivalence inspired in him no morbid attraction, no *cupio dissolvi*. We should rid ourselves here of another misconception, because Malaparte was one of the least decadent and most vitalistic authors in all of literature. In him, vocation unfailingly prevailed over emotion. Even in his most theatrical effects, in his most violent descriptions, he remains impassive before a mirror that reflects the world around him; and there is always the suspicion that he delighted in the horrified reactions of his readers. Of *Kaputt*, his masterpiece, he wrote that "inside there is nothing but soldiers, corpses, dogs, sunflowers, horses, and clouds."[2] It is the elements that interested him, in their primordial decomposition and disaggregation, as in a painting by Francis Bacon, the artist who perhaps most resembles him in that central phase of his work. But beware of being taken in by those scenes of torture, of really believing in them. For him, history was to be "Malapartized" like everything else.

His choice around 1925 of an "Italian" pseudonym, following the directive of Mussolini, testifies to a precocious talent for self-promotion. Where would he have ended up with that albatross of a last name, Suckert, that not even police headquarters or OVRA, the Fascist secret police, ever managed to spell correctly? "Malaparte," on the other hand, represents a passport to the world over, and the assonance with *male* (evil) allowed him to attract and frighten bourgeois audiences everywhere. It was the official birth of a writer who already had two or three dazzling books to his credit, the germ of those to come. From that point on it would be impossible to distinguish the writing from the life. This man of ice would seek among his readers only unconditional accomplices or adversaries, and that is generally just what he would obtain.

Hence the error of reproaching him for endless opportunism, amoral flexibility, an innate flair for slipping through the cracks and emerging unscathed in every instance, whereas what prevailed in him was a kind of mineral indifference to the passions of most men. In this light, his sawtooth trajectory appears perfectly rational, obliging us to pay tribute to the stoicism—the word does not seem excessive—he displayed in cultivating his persona right to the end. Malaparte may have been a condottiere without troops, an eternal contrarian, a minority man forever seeking consensus and frustrated not to find it, but he was never a genuine adventurer. Like Truman Capote, he was always ready to lose a friend for the sake of a joke, but also to respond to someone else's joke with an insult or a challenge to a duel. All his life, though he could be a supple diplomat when he needed to be, he was obsessed by an immoderate taste for polemic and display. Money never really mattered to him; power, which he often coveted but never obtained, would have held his interest for all of five minutes. And even his taste for fame never managed to erode his supply of good old Tuscan cunning and suspicion.

Malaparte was, after D'Annunzio, the most Renaissance of twentieth-century Italian—and possibly not only Italian—writers. He aspired to an inimitable existence that nonetheless was *not*, as happens to amateurs, his masterpiece: it was rather notes for, or a first draft of, his real work. "I can only write about things I have seen and lived"[3]—naturally, but in his own way, usually without bothering to distinguish between reality and fiction.* The performance for him counted much more than the result, and this explains the constitutive human frigidity, the solitude of the dandy, but also the incapacity to pursue a goal with the tenacity of a real man of power: having set off on one path, ten more opened up before him, and he

---

*The problem was raised anew with the appearance of a demystifying biography of a "disciple" of Malaparte, the prominent Polish writer and reporter Ryszard Kapuściński. See Artur Domosławski, *Ryszard Kapuściński: A Life*, trans. Antonia Lloyd-Jones (Brooklyn: Verso, 2012), 396.

didn't want to give up any of them. It was not (entirely) a pose, if to the company of his fellows he preferred the faithfulness of animals, especially his beloved dogs. One after another, women succumbed to his charm, which was hard and smooth, inert and feline, even as he granted them little of himself in return. For Daniel Halévy, his faithful French mentor, "to all foreigners he seemed like the consummate exemplar of the Italian race."[4] This is perhaps why they have appreciated him, and do so to this day, more than his compatriots have.

Nationalist and cosmopolite, pacifist and bellicist, elitist and populist, blunt chronicler and baroque narrator, arch-Italian and anti-Italian, at times also a charlatan, Malaparte never ceases to confound in his modernity, in his challenge to conventions and to anything that stinks of the politically correct. Precocious in all things, the fourteen-year-old Curt Erich Suckert had already found in the classrooms of the Cicognini boarding school and in the labor and socialist unrest of Prato the ideal to which he would always remain bound: republican, antibourgeois, and—notwithstanding his alleged deathbed conversion—anticlerical. The next step was interventionism, which led him to flee home to join the Garibaldi Legion of volunteers in France in 1914. Even if it is doubtful that he experienced his baptism of fire at the time, it was certainly no picnic: as a subject of the kaiser, not yet a naturalized Italian, he risked the firing squad if captured by the Germans. Between 1915 and 1918, he was on the front line of the horrifying White War in the Dolomites, first as a soldier and later as an officer. In June/July 1918, he returned to the French front, to Bligny, where the "magnificent mad farmers" of the Alpine Brigade, left without provisions or munitions, "incapable of anything else, performed a miracle," blocking the storm

INTRODUCTION

troopers' offensive in the Argonne for two days and two nights. Bayonet charges and flamethrower assaults, mass graves and corpses clinging to barbed wire are a constant in his work, and it is hard to say he exaggerated: he grasped everything of which man is capable, for good or ill. His participation in the Great War was exemplary, as it was for the infantrymen Marinetti, Sant'Elia, Barbusse, Ungaretti, Remarque, Owen, and many others. We could easily imagine the fanciful but entirely plausible encounter, in the "storm of steel," between Curzio and his contemporary and fellow infantryman Ernst Jünger. It was the most authentic page of his life, maybe because he was not *yet* Malaparte, just an anonymous combatant; and nostalgia for that masculine rite of passage would echo throughout his work. Forty years later, an ailing Malaparte would return from China to be struck down by a lung cancer traceable to damage suffered in 1918 from German gas.

The war over, modernism advanced at an even more furious pace, driven by "the heroic wind of speed" proclaimed by D'Annunzio in his 1910 novel *Forse che sì forse che no* (Maybe yes, maybe no). And the modernism of literary Europe in the first postwar period went by the names of Tzara, Breton, Joyce, Hemingway, Eliot, Pound, Ehrenburg, Morand, Brecht, Toller, Dos Passos, Khlebnikov, Blok, and so on. Its epicenter was Paris, while in Italy it masqueraded as Fascist revolution, swallowing up the few avant-garde experiences on the peninsula, from the Futurists to the Florentine magazine *La Voce* of Papini and Prezzolini. Curzio, unwilling to be left out of the course of events, showed little interest in writing as a solitary, ivory-tower pursuit. Back in Italy, following a diplomatic interlude at the Paris Peace Conference and as a junior member of the Italian legation to Warsaw, he struggled, like so many impatient young people, to find his path, and before finding it, more or less tried them all. To make an impression in Rome's bohemian circles, he created a short-lived literary movement, Oceanism, and began to cultivate the image of the brooding artist (not least because, already tall and slim by nature, he often had to skip meals). He published a provocative and in parts beautiful book, *Viva Caporetto!*, which earned him the first of many succès de scandale and forced him to leave the army and public administration. But as would often be the case with his books, the text affirms the opposite of what the title proclaims: if indeed he rails against the foolishness of the high command, Curzio shows no sympathy for the masses of stragglers and fugitives incapable of turning protest into the conquest of power. To do that, revolt must be guided by a core of clear-eyed and determined leaders, the officials and noncommissioned officers who saved the country before and *after* Caporetto. At this point—and we are already on the path that would lead, ten years on, to *Technique du coup d'État* (*Coup d'État: The Technique of Revolution*)—Curzio's options could not be other than Bolshevism or Fascism. But his roots were and would remain nationalist, and for him Italy would always be, for better or worse, the measure of everything. And so he chose the latter.

Curzio entered the ranks of Fascist syndicalism and threw himself into the battle of ideas in support of squadrism, giving life to one of the most radical magazines of the movement, *La Conquista dello Stato*. But he did not participate in the March on Rome, a fact that would be held against him by party hard-liners and purists, prompting him to assert the contrary, up until when he reestablished the truth in his defense affidavits of 1944–46: an example of the numerous falsifications, nested one inside the other like Russian dolls, which to this day make the discussion of Malaparte and Fascism so slippery. The reality was laid out in the pioneering biography by Giordano Bruno Guerri and confirmed by more recent research: like many other Italian intellectuals of the period, Malaparte was indisputably, genuinely Fascist until the start of the 1930s.[5] To be sure, he had always been a political rebel, by nature but also out of conviction. He showed as much already in 1929, when, newly installed at the head of *La Stampa* of Turin, one of the main newspapers in Italy, owned by FIAT, he rushed to describe the Soviet reality in a series of dispatches that outraged bien-pensant readers. And there is no doubt that during his 1931–33 sojourn—*not* exile—in France, his provocative behaviors nourished the conspiracy theories that informers and spies spread about him. Il Duce, who knew his men (who for him were all chumps), paid the rumors no mind and spared the writer a referral to the Special Tribunal for the Defense of the State. Malaparte did *not* resign from the party in 1931, as he later claimed, and anti-Fascist activity was *not* the reason he was arrested and sent into *confino* (confinement in a remote area) in 1933–34; instead it was for having maligned his former protector Italo Balbo, whose immense popularity, thanks to his daring aviation feats, had become a thorn in Il Duce's side. He remained on the island of Lipari for a few months, rather than the five years he was meant to serve, before being transferred to Ischia, then to Forte dei Marmi, and in the end was pardoned by the dictator. At that point he tried to reacquire his National Fascist Party (PNF) membership card, in order to marry Virginia Agnelli and become "the boss of FIAT"—yet another castle in the air, in which he succeeded only in making other powerful enemies. His failed return to party ranks did not prevent him from once again becoming one of the most influential and highly compensated of Italian journalists, writing not exactly candid reports on the war in Spain and Italy's invasion of Greece, remaining in the Fascist orbit until the fall of Mussolini, on July 25, 1943. Meanwhile, he had gone from would-be protagonist to witness. The boy Curzio could risk his life; the professional writer Malaparte had to preserve it: "I was born to write beautiful pages, not to die in war," he declared at the outbreak of the new conflict.[6] It was the price to pay to stay in the saddle and, thanks to a magazine like *Prospettive*, which he founded and edited, to allow youth stifled by Fascist autarky to drink of the great intellectual currents, from psychoanalysis to surrealism, forbidden at the time from crossing the Italian border. But between that and being an internal opponent of the regime, there's some distance, to say the least.

These are, in brief, the facts that many readers outside Italy, even the most lucid and sensitive, still struggle to accept.[7] When this biography appeared in France, in 2011, there was a great deal of consternation over "revelations" that, for many reviewers, made Malaparte out to be worse than he was in reality.* However, what often goes missing in such righteous indignation—which harks back to old tropes of Italian Fascism as opera buffa and a conspiracy of gangsters, and not as the "modern" dictatorship it unquestionably was till the outbreak of war—is the will to understand that Malaparte was not motivated *solely* by opportunism. From beginning to end, one finds in him a fascistic strain that he never belied under any regime, in particular a taste for force, the only real ideology of a man who disdained all ideologies. For him, when it comes to a leader, it

---

*Typical in this respect was the largely inappropriate comparison made in the press to the case of Céline, fed by the polemics that marked, in 2011, the absence of official celebrations of the fiftieth anniversary of the French author's death.

doesn't matter whether he is of the Right (Mussolini) or of the Left (Lenin, Stalin, Mao); when it comes to a leading state, whether it is totalitarian (the Soviet Union, the Third Reich) or democratic (France, the United States). What's important is to stamp the authority of a powerful will on those whose job it is to follow: nations, peoples, individuals. Malaparte may be moved occasionally by the defeated, but it is much more the case in his work than in his life. At times they compel his respect, such as when the old princess Radziwill, in *Kaputt*, standing in the rain at the bombed-out Warsaw train station, her makeup ruined, refuses the chair offered her by a German officer. But they don't inspire him for long: Malaparte did not always love winners, but he almost always disdained losers.

Fascist, then, but also with Marxist and anarchist tendencies, and always a rebel, Malaparte would remain such out of mistrust, even repugnance, toward parliamentary democracy. If he cries profusely in his books, and if his exposed heart gives the illusion that it is always beating for someone or something, Malaparte sheds no tears for the fate of the Old Continent or the end of its influence in the world. He pillories "the new Europe rising from the corpse of dead old Europe" (MM, 11), like the true soldier who knows he must accept the amputation of a gangrenous limb. Late in life, he would declare himself a supporter of "European nationalism," but this commitment should not be overestimated. It is possible to see a compensation for Fascism, too, in his attraction to the Soviet Union that swept aside Hitler's armies, and for Mao's China. Few intellectuals of his era predicted with as much precision or decried with more vigor the decline of the West. As for the United States, credit to the winners, whose flag features a piece of the stained cloth of the Old Continent. Malaparte, among the first to understand what it means for a muscular and uninhibited democracy to "export" its own values to the world, was fascinated by American society and tried desperately to be recognized in the New World. And 9/11, had he survived to see it, would surely have taken its place in an "American Kaputt."

Fascist, again, but close to revolutionaries and as far as possible from conservatives, nostalgics, monarchists, reactionaries. His ideological underpinnings can be found, then, in the sphere of *fascismo rosso*, the Fascism of the Left, a current officially suppressed after the 1922 seizure of power, but one that reappears with the generation of the 1930s, and that shaped many intellectuals who subsequently moved on to communism. Starting in the winter of 1941, the tone of Malaparte's war correspondence became increasingly hostile toward the Axis. This fact alone would suffice—without forgetting that he never signed a line of anti-Semitic propaganda—to demonstrate that, in the course of the so-called *ventennio* (the two decades of the Fascist regime), Malaparte had less to be forgiven for than many of his colleagues, who were generally more capable of reinventing themselves after the war. But it was he himself, with his incessant and often superfluous transformations, who fed the worst rumors, shamelessly denying everything that the loved and hated *padre padrone* Mussolini had done for him.

In fact, Malaparte is as atypical a writer of the "right" as Pavese and Pasolini are writers of the "left." One does not find in him the delirious invective and xenophobia of a Céline, the fear of contagion and usury of a Pound, the veneration for throne and altar of a Maurras. His republican roots, suffused with the values of 1789, never withered. His love for the working class, if sometimes floridly expressed, was authentic. Nevertheless, in Italy Malaparte continues to be generally considered an intellectual of the Right, and on the Left is met with prejudice if not complete ostracism. Blacklisted by the Italian Communist Party (PCI) against the advice of its leader, the astute Palmiro Togliatti, Malaparte would fall into the anti-Communist camp at the beginning of the Cold War, assailed by many of those he had benefited and derided by fellow travelers.

Efforts in postwar Italy to punish Fascists targeted Malaparte as a prominent figure under the regime. Investigations into his activities by the High Commission for Sanctions against Fascism dragged on for a few years before being shelved, probably following the personal intervention of Togliatti. But the purge process inspired bitter pages from him: "What a disappointment these anti-Fascists are! They're Fascists without the black shirt!"[8] Afterward, he chose to "exile" himself for the second time—and neither was this actual exile—in Paris, whence he hoped to return home laden with literary and worldly fame, like D'Annunzio in 1915. The disappointment would sting, notwithstanding the success of *Kaputt*, *The Volga Rises in Europe*, and *The Skin*. Comforted by the friendship of a few old greats like Cocteau and Cendrars, and of the young rebels who shared his romantic view of a nation deprived of its patriotic destiny, Malaparte was excluded from the vogue of existentialism and committed literature: Sartre, Camus, Aragon, Éluard, and Malraux, new stars of the Parisian firmament, deliberately ignored him. He then decided to challenge them on their own terrain, staging two plays written in French. All he achieved was to narrowly avoid yet another duel with a critic, one who had compared the public leaving the theater early to those fleeing in the exodus of 1940, "machine-gunned by Malaparte's old friends" in the Fascist air force:[9] a legend that unfortunately survives north of the Alps to this day. But it was above

INTRODUCTION

all the revelations about his past—fed by Italian "deep throats," which never go lacking in such cases—that pushed him to pack his bags and return to Italy, where he would spend the last decade of his life essentially as an exile in his own country.

As soon as he could, he began to travel again: he would have liked to return to Russia, but the Communists remained broadly suspicious of him. He consoled himself with Chile and Uruguay and announced he would pedal across the United States, with the sponsorship of Coca-Cola, to join the then still single Grace Kelly in Hollywood and offer her a vial of the water of Capri, finding a backer to gift him a deluxe bicycle. At this point he seemed, in fact, to be spinning his wheels, while his narcissism became ever more tinged with paranoia. He quarreled with everybody: in order to bring out his books he had to create his own modest publishing house; radio and the nascent television industry ignored him; he declared war on literary prizes after *The Skin* was passed over for the Strega Prize in 1950, in favor of Cesare Pavese's *Beautiful Summer*. He decried the faults of the cultural system as if he had never been part of it. He placed his hopes in the cinema, and he cruised the length of Via Veneto, as yet undiscovered by *la dolce vita*, in a large American convertible. But after completing his only film, *The Forbidden Christ*, which many today salute as a masterpiece, he no longer found money for the storylines and scripts he was constantly churning out. He tried the theater again, in Venice and Milan, with *Anche le donne hanno perso la guerra* (The women lost the war too), and a clever critic wrote that he had lost a good occasion to keep quiet. He threw himself into social satire with a variety show, *Sexophone*, performing in clubs in Versilia, a resort town on the Tuscan coast, flanked by dancers in feather boas, taking in more boos than receipts. He served as a jury member for beauty contests; recounted in installments for a weekly publication the suicide of an American starlet who had had the terrible idea of falling in love with him; pitched, in an oil company magazine, the idea of an auto race on Capri, he who had built a unique and inaccessible house there. He tracked his appearances in the fashion or gossip magazines more than in the literary press, as many writers without an ounce of his talent do today. Some wondered if these bit parts were not the consequence of a loss of means, not only financial but intellectual. He now published little and attracted an audience only for a minor book, the portrait sketches of *Those Cursed Tuscans*. And yet his desk drawers overflowed with works in progress, two of which, while incomplete, are worthy of him: *Mamma marcia* (Rotten mama) and *The Kremlin Ball*. Perhaps he understood that, in a byzantine age like ours, literature no longer sufficed to nourish the fame of a writer.

The only activity he carried on until his death was his first love, journalism. In the weekly magazine *Tempo*—not to be confused with the similarly named Roman daily, to which he also frequently contributed—he had a column, Battibecco, in which he followed his inspiration and vented his spleen on a wide variety of topics, as a precursor in that still-reigning national pastime that is *tuttologia* (the belief that one knows everything). Some of these pieces are lucid and biting, heralding the Pasolini of *Scritti corsari* (Corsair writings). Malaparte, even if for opposite reasons, also mythologized a pre-bourgeois Italy: a "beautiful and poor," peasant and aristocratic-proletarian country, in which, unlike Pasolini, deep down he did not believe at all. And naturally he practiced the other national pastime—indiscriminate protest against the current powers that be—in a readers' letters column called Write to Me and You Will Have Justice, where he winked at *qualunquismo*.* He still hoped for a return to politics. He stood for election in Prato as a member of the Italian Republican Party, the only party that had listed him: the result was a majestic failure, and to celebrate the loss he quarreled with the organizers, guilty of having sent him to defeat.

Thus we come to his travels in Russia and China, undertaken in the last year of his life (the US trip, continually deferred, never happened). The occasion was Malaparte's reconciliation with some young Communist intellectuals who did not agree with the banishment of the writer decreed by the most reactionary cadres of the PCI. Malaparte set out for Moscow, by way of Sweden, in the fateful October of 1956, as the Hungarian Uprising was breaking out. He would not write a word about the events, even as he spoke vaguely about the "errors of Stalin," recognized by the Soviets themselves. The Soviet Union held little interest for him at this point, and, via Siberia, he hurried to arrive in the still mysterious China of Mao. From the start he loved everything about the Chinese people—their courtesy, their kindness, their straightforward manners—and did not seem to notice the brutal dictatorship of the Great Helmsman as he prepared to launch the mad industrialization drive of the Great Leap Forward. He was already unwell, but he still had time to be received by Mao, whom he apparently asked to free the monks and nuns imprisoned by the Chinese state, obtaining reassurances on the

---

*Qualunquismo was a right-wing populist movement of the immediate postwar years in Italy, devoted to *l'uomo qualunque* (the common man) and associated with cynical political disinterest. It has remained synonymous with cynical and demagogic social or political views.—Trans.

matter (*apparently*, because Malaparte's version of the meeting is the only one available to us). After which, he was rushed to the hospital in Hankow (Wuhan), almost 750 miles from Peking. The Chinese doctors' diagnosis, notwithstanding the rudimentary equipment at their disposal, was the correct one: cancer of the bronchial tubes.

He was a goner and he knew it. His letters leave little room for doubt. He was a courageous man, who came from a culture stronger than our own, a peasant culture in which death is a matter of course. But death throes can also abet the spectacularization of a work-life. In the long months of hospitalization, first in China, then in a Roman clinic, Malaparte would succeed in mounting an extraordinary farewell ceremony, one in which everyone in Italy who mattered—politicians and journalists, socialites, priests, and artists—marched to his sickbed in the legendary room 32.

"To judge a man, one must carefully examine his portraits," wrote Malaparte (KB, 29). This man had a mouth as thin as a sheet of paper. His deep-set eyes would explore ceaselessly in every direction, then stop suddenly, as if vitrified, leading some interlocutors to think he was an opium enthusiast: "When he squints, this prodigious visionary has the tiny but precise eye of a lens."[10] He would apply the same rule to his surroundings; people and things had value in his eyes only for the connections his imagination suggested to him. Otherwise he ignored them, or forgot them immediately. It's an approach that can also be detected in his passion for photography, with often notable results.[11]

His rounded and regular head plugged into a rather long neck, as captured in the Modiglianesque portrait of him that Massimo

INTRODUCTION

Campigli, one of the best painters of his generation, made in 1933. His hardiness and stature (a shade over six feet), tall for an Italian of the period, did not come from his German father, as might be supposed, but from his Lombard mother, from whom he also took his fair complexion, slender limbs, and straight nose. He was devoted to the cult of the body and physical fitness, pursued with the discipline of an athlete and the refinement of a runway model. In his "Leninist" youth, he flaunted a beard and mustache, but later only rarely returned to a look that did not suit him. He meticulously shaved his legs, underarms, chest, and the backs of his hands; he attended to his hairstyle such that not a single lock could ruin the oval of his face, the line of his profile. His raven hair, slicked back at the top and sides, accentuated the pallor of his forehead, the immobility of his features, the dark-rimmed eyes. His favorite photo from his time in East Africa shows him shaving in the savanna, standing before a mirror held up for him by an Eritrean askari in uniform. He was proud of his taut cheeks, to which he would nightly apply, legend has it, raw steaks; the freshness of his skin; and the cleanliness of his fingernails. His suits were always impeccable, down to the knot of his tie and the silk handkerchief sprouting from his breast pocket, with slacks perfectly creased: everything to establish the persona, while concealing the man. This edifice, so well maintained, eventually gave way to something soft and indecisive, which a spiteful witness ascribed to the "pudding" effect. He put on weight in later years, in part due to medications, squeezing himself into too-tight and outdated suits, which made him look a bit like the fin de siècle characters in the play he would unsuccessfully debut in Paris in 1948, *Du côté de chez Proust*.

To claim that Malaparte was obsessed with his appearance is only

INTRODUCTION

partially true. He rejected the languorous poses of the aesthete, in favor of a willful, assertive modernity. It could be said he developed for the middle classes the idea of personal hygiene as a daily, even hourly, struggle. Like D'Annunzio—the "divine" Gabriele—Malaparte disdained the cheap pleasures of tobacco, alcohol, and drugs, as he explained (in English) in a letter adapted to the puritan taste of an American correspondent:

> Judging from the photograph published in the *New York Herald Tribune*...you must certainly believe that I am a fervent pipe-smoking addict. Instead, I am glad to inform you that the pipe was empty and that I merely used it as a companion in solitude, when I spent two years as a war-correspondent in Finland and Lapland.
>
> This picture was taken after an operation I had to undergo in a Finnish hospital. Then doctors told me that I owed it to my clean way of living and complete abstinence of coffee, tobacco, and, before all, alcoholics, if I could at all pull through such a serious illness...
>
> I always believed that a clean life is the best way to preserve a clean mind and physical health helps moral health. Ordinarily I don't live in town and pass most of the year in the Tuscan countryside, in the vicinity of Florence, my birthplace, or on the island of Capri, many miles away from any human dwelling place. This is not a sign of egotism, but a way of keeping off from the corrupt life so fashionable these days. I live alone, in the sole company of many dogs, which teach me very much. In my house there is not a single bottle of wine, and I do not remember to ever have had blurred thoughts due to alcoholic influence. If I blurred at times, it was because of the spectacle of human depravity and cruelty which I had to observe during this war.[12]

In the same period, witnesses reveal him instead to be an occasional smoker of Gauloises or a pipe and a connoisseur of champagne. Life in Casa Come Me, the "house like me," on Capri, could be spartan to the point of asceticism, with the larder often empty, but the cellar never lacked for grand crus from the best vineyards, to impress guests to whom he rarely offered them.[13] He loved the luxury of five-star hotels and the beauty of flatware, much more than the comfort of furnishings or the rich variety of meals. In love, attention to toilette and scenery seemed to count more than physical satisfaction, which was swift, not to say brutal, and not infrequently avoided. Makeup, which he employed less and less discreetly with the years, brought "an insignificant adjustment"—as the barber in *Death in Venice* has it—to what the advance of time was taking from him.[14] Among all the countries he visited, the absence of Japan is striking; maybe he ran out of time to discover a place in which he would predictably have felt at home, with its cult of order and protocol, the pursuit of appearances to the point of renunciation and self-erasure, the cult of the shadow. A 1949 photograph that shows him barefoot, dressed up in a sailor's shirt and worn breeches, in a pose evocative of a ritual dance, gripping two large, curved swords, is the most surprising homage that Malaparte ever made without knowing it to the country of his peers Kawabata and Tanizaki. Like the samurai who knows how to be himself in his opposite, Malaparte sought to pursue strength even into its ultimate weakness. Testifying to this is another exemplary image, in which, his face stubbly, distraught but once again self-possessed, he expires in the clinic under the spotlights, among the votive candles and flower bouquets.

In his private life he proved for the most part neither violent nor irritable like his father, something incompatible with the cult of good manners, even if he occasionally failed to repress an angry outburst or fit of pique. He loved appearing in public but shunned physical contact. He was too squeamish, too delicate, faced with "dirty hands," with the repulsion that contact with the crowd entails. Malaparte changed collaborators and followers like others change their linen; and you could count on one hand those who remained close to him to the end (mostly old classmates or fellow soldiers, socialites or diplomats, rather than literary types). His generosity was unpredictable, capricious like his anger, and little known, because the beneficiaries often forgot to thank him for it. He was capable of rushing to the aid of friends and relatives, but also of actors just starting out or no longer getting cast, of school friends and brothers-in-arms, of disgraced colleagues, even of strangers who wrote to him from a hospice or prison. But these real gestures of humanity were kept secret in order to promote his image of coldness and distance.

Perhaps no one displayed such scorn for his compatriots, while being so similar to them. Reading and rereading Malaparte, including hundreds of pages of letters and unpublished material, becomes an almost incestuous experience. In his classification of national types, he offers us a family portrait, a "certain idea" of the Italians, without modifying it much over the course of years, alongside his vision of the French, the English, the Russians, the Germans, the Polish. You can be taken aback by such arrogance and by the derisive undertone that would never leave him; irritated by his manipulations, by the unbearable Italian tendency to play the misunderstood victim of persecution; exasperated by how he would reuse the same passage from one text to the next. Sometimes you just can't take it anymore, and you toss the book out the window. But then you go down into the street or courtyard and get it back.

INTRODUCTION

Aside from the many lives, too many legends about him still linger. Where can we find the key to a plausible interpretation, in a writer who bent over backward to obscure his traces? I've tried to sift through the innumerable anecdotes about the man to leave only those that preserve at least an appearance of truthfulness. It is typical of the mythomaniac to provoke a contagion effect in those near him, and about Malaparte it was easy to say everything and its opposite: After all, who would or could deny it?[15] Accordingly, one of the most incisive portraits of Malaparte comes to us from the poet Umberto Saba, in a letter written to his daughter shortly after the writer's death. In a few pages, displaying the mix of *pietas* and cattiness of the best Saba, he runs through the many signs of affection and egotism he received from his friend, above all at the moment of the racial laws, and observes:

> So-called bad faith is not—as is believed—common. To conduct a life—I mean a whole life—thinking one thing and writing another (all the while remaining "afloat") requires, in addition to a truly extraordinary (almost staggering) intelligence, a coherence, a self-control, an equally (if not more) extraordinary courage. (I would hazard to say also a "moral seriousness," however concentrated on one's own interests.) Was this perhaps, at least in part, Curzio Malaparte's "genius," his trump card? I repeat: I don't know; and "judging" is not in my nature.... In any event, even though I'm not what is commonly called a believer, I prayed to a Jesuit Father to say a mass for the peace of the soul of Curzio, who, even while being my antithesis, helped me, or sought to help me, in my misfortune.[16]

A fine way to conclude without concluding, we might say, among parentheses, quotation marks, and allusions. But I'd like at least to underline that "coherence," which will become the guiding thread of the interpretation on offer here. Let us return, thus, to the Malaparte mystery. The hypertrophic cult of the self reveals too many cracks to the careful observer not to obscure its coherent image and, in some way, "de-Malapartize" it. Yes, it is precisely here that we must depart from. It is here that Malaparte exposes himself, notwithstanding the masks and the subterfuges. Like every great author, he survives not only his defects and his contradictions but also his traps and his tricks. Because he had, powerful and unconfessed, a taste for defeat. And so this is his story: Malaparte, or the woes of Narcissus.

1. The Beginnings of a Bonaparte
(1898–1924)

I miss History desperately…
—Romain Gary, *La nuit sera calme*

First Steps

What does the languid yet determined face of this adolescent tell us? What does Kurt Erich / Curzio, long before he becomes Malaparte, tell us? At the beginning, it is impossible to separate the wheat from the chaff. Everything is tightly intertwined in this rebel in the making, with the insolent prowess of a Rimbaud reborn: we are immediately forced to play his game if we want to flush him out. Malaparte expressed differing, contradictory assessments of his own childhood. He spoke of "anguish" and "humiliation"; he wrote that "as a child I was sad, profoundly unhappy" ("Morte delusa," in S, 77; then in RI, 309); he recalled "my poor and sad and humiliating and insurgent childhood" (MM, 3). And yet nothing proves that it was so dramatic, still less exceptional. What is surprising, rather, is the emotional intensity that bound him to his relationships, blood or elective, to the point that he never felt the need to establish his own family, this act of adult responsibility par excellence. If he was the only unusual character in his family and was quick to win the admiration of those around him, he retained to the end a particular affection for his older brother, Sandro, the first of the five Suckert children. Sandro and his other brother, Ezio, radiated a physical splendor worthy of the Riace bronzes, while Curzio, according to his sister Edda, was "a handsome, elegant young man, but what especially attracted everyone was his way of talking. You would try to listen to him because he entertained people, especially at home; you wouldn't realize how late it was getting. He would describe imaginary, impossible things, or things that did happen, but transformed by art."[1] He had invented a terrible divinity, Auramada, before which all his siblings had to kneel and make offerings, under pain of incurring a dreadful punishment: their eyelashes would be curved down into their eyes to pierce, even perforate them.[2] Which is already a very Malapartian idea.

Born June 9, under the sign of Gemini, in the decade governed by Mars and Mercury, he carried within himself the traits of flexibility, inquisitiveness, inconstancy, eternal youth. And duplicity. Much later, a journalist would express surprise: "He retained such a youthful appearance that everyone wondered how it was possible that that man was already so rich in adventures, exploits, memories."[3] At the time of his birth, in Prato, his family still lived in a nice fourth-floor apartment at 416 Via Magnolfi, which people called Via Nuova, because it connected the old station to Piazza del Duomo. Three years later, Erwin Suckert, a restless and troublemaking soul, as his son would be, decided to go live in Coiano, on the outskirts of Prato on the lovely road running through the Bisenzio Valley. And here Curzio had a premonition of his vocation: one fine day, as the children are packing up their things for the move, he is unable to find a toy sailing ship, "my favorite." This ship exists only in his imagination: he has never owned one. But his tones of desperation are so "sincere" that his family members, even as they have never seen such a ship in the house, join in the search, scouring all the rooms and all the closets. They toil without success, while Curzio continues to provide them with new details about the phantom object: it's called Fida like his dog, the name is written in red on the prow, "and everyone was almost convinced that I was telling the truth, *as I myself was*."[4] In this ability to believe in his own reality—perception interwoven with fabrication, because things exist only if they are spoken of, and on the sole condition that they are spoken of—lies the driving force of his personality.

Surrounded by much-loved brothers and sisters—another two children died in infancy—and raised in the spacious home of well-to-do, cultured parents, what more could he have asked for? Of course, regular quarrels between the rigid and irritable Erwin and both his bosses and his workers led on a few occasions to his dismissal. He even had to retreat to Piedmont and Lombardy for a few years, in search of better fortune. But the family does not seem to have endured much hardship as a result. Nor does Curzio seem to have suffered from the monotony of provincial life; the land fascinated him, in fact, and inspired that need for identification that would always go together with the desire to be elsewhere: an existential contradiction that represents a promising departure point for a writer. In a lovely passage of his maturity, he recalled the outings the five children would make near Prato to savor the land of the surrounding districts: to *savor* in the literal sense of the word; that is, to smell it, to sniff it out, to fill one's mouth with it, distinguishing its flavors and scents, as one would with a fruit or vegetable. This land devoured with bliss and satisfaction was the land that would, in its turn, devour those who loved it, transforming them into land just as rich and healthy, down the centuries:

> Now and then I would bite into those thin herb roots, seeming to have in my mouth the flavor, the smell, the voice, and the gaze of Ezio, Maria, Edda, Sandro. And thus would I happily pass the time of eternity, feeding on the same land of which my flesh and bones are made. ("Terra come me," in RI, 369)

Let's not fool ourselves. As always in Malaparte, too many truths pile up without merging into one, thus inviting ambiguity. He wanted to be buried in that land, yes, and he would be; but he did not have the least intention of living there. He would remain forever faithful to it, and there he would maintain perhaps his most sincere friendships, along with those born of military service, but he would distance himself from it as soon as possible. As an adult he would sometimes return there to restore himself, only to leave immediately after. Prato very quickly became too small for him, and he never wished to live there permanently, or even own property, a house, a garden. He would make do with a tomb, far from the city, on the dramatic heights of Mount Spazzavento, where he could "lift [his] head every now and then to spit in the face of the cold gale that sweeps down the mountain passes" (CT, 96). The land, the territory, would never represent for him immutable values or obligatory reference points, functioning instead as an antidote: the anti-*Kaputt*, anti-*Skin*, anti-putrefaction; the motherland, "sweet Venus who makes the fruitful earth teem," to whom his beloved Lucretius dedicated his immortal poem. It is indeed the power of nature to reintegrate man into the cycle of life, to have him draw strength within the *axis* of creation. This is the source of his refusal of decadence, of any condition *off axis* with respect to life: a not inconsiderable paradox for an author so often portrayed as one of the last great decadents of the twentieth century. There emerges, too, an antihistoricist reflex. But we already know that, as far as the history of his times was concerned, he would take into consideration only what pleased and what served him, remaining indifferent to the rest.

As an adult, Malaparte richly embroidered his precocious sense of being different, misunderstood within his family and without. This is all rather to be expected. He also invented for himself a proletarian identity *honoris causa*, thanks to his foster family, the Baldis, to whom he was entrusted for long periods; he would remain very attached to the father, Milziade (or Mersiade), as he would to his milk brother, Baldo. The latter, who years later would become a successful entrepreneur and leather exporter in France under the name Jacques Baldi, would be his accomplice in some fantastic failed attempts to strike it rich. In this way, it's been said, he wanted to compensate for his father's failure. There is nothing very original in this, either: reversals of fortune were frequent in the period, and often much more dramatic than those suffered in the Suckert household. All it took was for a family head to fall ill or suddenly die to precipitate an often irreparable tumble down the social ladder. The fear of demotion and proletarianization was the great obsession of the European middle classes prior to the catastrophe of 1914, and in a certain sense paved the way for it. But the concept of *middle class* was not expressed solely in the census. It was one's cultural level that opened career opportunities, the possibility of rising in a professional context. From this point of view, the real loser was Erwin

Suckert, who struggled to adapt to changes in the job market; not his son, whose education was excellent.

All his life, Malaparte would refuse to consider himself a bourgeois, and yet he was trained to become one. He and Sandro, despite their father's financial difficulties, were enrolled at an elite boarding school, the Collegio Cicognini; founded by Jesuits in 1692, it became a state institution near the end of the nineteenth century, with a reputation for great rigor. Other writers to emerge from the school include Ranieri Calzabigi (1714–95), the author of the libretto for Gluck's *Orfeo ed Euridice*; Gabriele D'Annunzio (1863–1938); and Tommaso Landolfi (1908–79), whose debut work Malaparte would praise. Curzio's talent was soon recognized by his instructors and classmates. His voice, precociously confident, already a bit theatrical in tone, left no one indifferent. His first texts were extemporaneously composed, in handwriting that is well spaced, slender, and legible, and which would change relatively little in the course of years. In 1912, when another glory of the Collegio, the playwright Sem Benelli (1877–1949), dubbed "the cast-off slipper of D'Annunzianism" by his detractors, made his triumphant return to Prato, it was Curzio who was called on to offer him the school's homage; the speech also became his first text to be brought out by a local publisher,[5] with a second one appearing the following year. At this point he had become the Collegio's official orator, producing compositions in verse and prose more or less on his own.

What do we know about this nervous adolescent, about his need to get away and to stand out? Not a lot. But is there much more that would be worth the trouble to find out? It seems unlikely. If legend quickly took hold of D'Annunzio, starting to weave around this slender figure with the blond curls and dreaming eyes the thread of destiny, nothing in Curzio announces with certainty a similar vocation. What they shared was the need to create an exceptional life for themselves, lacking the power to live it immediately. D'Annunzio fought for his entire youth, if not for all his life, to free himself of his father's less-than-exalted roots, while Curzio searched for an adoptive father and found him in Milziade Baldi, then in Bino Binazzi, a local poet, who introduced him to the French Romantics and expressionists. Fate, if that's what it was, had it that Erwin Suckert died a few months before his son, who, already hospitalized, never found out, and that Milziade Baldi followed him to the grave a week after his funeral.

The gradual name change started in childhood. The other Suckert siblings have Italian, or at least Italian-sounding, names, whereas *Kurt Erich* rapidly became *Curt, Curtino*, then *Curzio*, at school and even at home. Now he was the one who *wanted* to be known that way. Without having a single drop of Tuscan blood in his veins, he would lay claim to a sort of Tuscan genetic code, of Pratese parochialism, even. It was an unconscious negation of the authority of that ignorant, unpleasant father imposed by chance and biology, who, what is more, expressed himself in the language of command par excellence, German, destined to remain forever incomprehensible to his son. Traces of the origins of the Suckerts are scarce.[6] Curzio wanted to know more, undertaking a pilgrimage with Ezio to Zittau, but it's doubtful they found much. The Saxon city, called Żytawa in Polish, had formerly been the site of Polish and Czech settlements: the name Suckert can still be found in the city and nearby areas. Erwin—who also went by an Italianized version of his name, Ervino—never spoke his mother tongue at home or taught it to his children; but he wanted them to see and respect in him all the virtues associated with the power of imperial Germany. If the Bel Paese inclined traditionally toward French literature and poetry, the scientific, commercial, and industrial sectors of the peninsula harbored a cult of the Reich that had swept away the Second French Empire of Napoleon III in 1870 and imposed itself as the leading power of continental Europe. The other original element—Erwin's adherence to the Protestant religion—does not seem to have left deep traces in the children, who would later convert to Catholicism and would never be part of the small, but close-knit and influential, Tuscan Protestant community.[7] And yet:

> It took very little to make that neo-classical facade collapse... An uncharacteristic voice resounded in the house, and we children would seek refuge in the vegetable garden, telling each other: "The German has woken up." (W, 70)

German and, more broadly, Nordic culture, mythology, and technology always appealed in some distant way to Malaparte, whom we tend too often to consider an elective Frenchman, because of his works published directly in French and his numerous stays in Paris. In this home environment, already quite open to international life, books made for good company. The first works that Curzio found in the paternal library were in Gothic letters: medieval storytellers, the Brothers Grimm, Goethe and the poets of Sturm und Drang. He discovered the great Greek tragedies in the editions established by the philologists of Dresden and Heidelberg. Conversely, the choice to enlist as a volunteer in 1914 against the German inside him would arise from the thirst for adventure, but also from a desire to avenge himself against the domineering father who had tried to impose his values on him. Their relationship would always remain adversarial. In fact, Erwin Suckert, too, had chosen Italy at the time of the Great War: according to an unconfirmed anecdote, when his sons were leaving for the front in 1915, he took them to the train station. All his life, the attraction to and horror of blood, as well as the startling chiaroscuros emerging from his pages, would recall the German aspect of Malaparte. "It's impossible to understand or accept me if you forget that in me there is all the madness and romanticism of the Germans," he wrote to his friend Giancarlo Vigorelli in 1940. It's true that at the time the Wehrmacht looked to be getting on rather well...

The foregoing is enough to divide father and son, and there is no need to listen to the gossip according to which his genitor was not Erwin, whom Curzio resembled so little—"an unassuming little man, who seemed to sink back into himself"[8]—but a well-known Prato lawyer.[9] What importance can it have, if a father wants to dominate a son who denies him any moral right to paternity? It was claimed that in his later life the adult Malaparte no longer wanted to see Erwin, because he was ashamed of him. "He hated homosexuals and his own humdrum background," wrote Bruce Chatwin, with scant empathy.[10] As for this presumed hatred for homosexuals, we will return to it at length. As for the rest, Malaparte, appearances notwithstanding (and unlike Chatwin), was not truly a snob; or he was only occasionally, in reaction to some humiliation suffered or, when it served him, to obscure his provincial background. And he concealed few things about his life less than his origins, which were in any case not all that humdrum. No, he was not ashamed of Erwin, even as he hated the latter's fits of rage, his reactionary attitudes, and his mood swings, and perhaps feared that they were a sign of "bad blood" that could be passed down to him. In the 1930s, he wrote a few pages of reminiscences about his family, in which a certain affection for his father comes through. But he could not forgive him for representing the authority figure that failed, unable to fulfill his primary task. And here we are struck by the analogy, but also the difference, with a near contemporary of his, the writer Stefan Zweig, another son of an inventor and textile manufacturer: a domineering and authoritarian father like Erwin, but a successful entrepreneur who *never* failed, and who therefore maintained the devoted respect of his son till the end.[11]

Curzio's case recalls that of the adolescent who turns into a rebel because his father is not a *natural* authoritarian. Perhaps he feared that Erwin's nervous breakdowns, leading to his parents' separation in 1923, were provoked by the onset of madness. And he had developed very early on a phobia of everything that was not governed by the will and by physical and moral health, an aversion that would guide him throughout his life. In the conflict between Tuscany and Germany, then, the one to yield would be the latter[12]—a choice that precedes and determines the one the rebellious son would make soon after, fleeing and enlisting, shortly after the outbreak of the Great War, in the Garibaldi Legion in France, then in the Alpine Brigade, upon his return to Italy. This renunciation of his German roots is true on an emotional level, as it is in terms of models. He was immediately attracted by a human type we could define, forcing the terms a bit, as "old Bolshevik": no-nonsense workers, honest men of few words, marked by the spirit of sacrifice and dedication, allegory of a people on the march for their own redemption, as depicted in Pellizza da Volpedo's famous painting *The Fourth Estate* (1901). Milziade Baldi, the "exemplary Tuscan" (FP, 220), is the first example of that proletarian aristocracy that Malaparte would respect all his life, without identifying with it. He would remain fascinated by this ingenuous probity, in which eternal man is reflected, close to nature and uncorrupted by history, the lust for profit, or bourgeois indolence. It is the Baldi household, humble but impeccably clean (revisited forty years later onscreen, in *The Forbidden Christ*), even more than the dormitories of the Cicognini, where Curzio learns the sense of good form that would never leave him: to not tolerate on his person the smallest stain or a single loose button, to avoid the cheap pleasures of alcohol and gambling, to abstain from curses and blasphemy (which for a farmer is truly not easy). No one would ever see him unkempt or unshaven, and when that finally did happen on his deathbed, Malaparte managed to turn it into an equally compelling counteraesthetic. Before he was a dandy, Curzio was the tiny Lombard lookout in *Cuore*, or *The Heart of a Boy*—the hugely popular children's novel by Edmondo De Amicis, first published in 1886, the urtext of an Italian civic religion—a young explorer, a sentinel of order and virtue, a little pioneer, a little Red Guard.

The struggle against his father via national proxies contains an element of doubling. Not even the Cicognini, strictly speaking, was a purely Pratese institution: the school attracted gifted students from all over Italy, especially the south. Curzio slept at the Baldis', but the atmosphere he breathed in class was less provincial than in town. So where did he draw his blood, his nature, his profound strength from? Where did he put down roots? How could he reconcile himself with the legacy of paternal grandfathers who had fought for German independence at Sadowa and Sedan? It was the German Romanticism that pulsed in his veins, driving him to cut them to see the blood, equated with nectar: "From the wound flowed a thin vermilion stream, and I thought of the mysterious power that coursed through my veins, of that dense, purplish, ardent river that beat at my wrists" ("Primo sangue," in S, 29). At the same time, "Italy is not a Romantic country; it doesn't have any kind of madness" (BI, 231). Curzio perceived very early on the divide between Latin realism—and no Latin is more realist than the Italian, and, among Italians, than the Tuscan—and the need, characteristic of the Nordic spirit of the nineteenth century, to go beyond reality: the *Wanderer und Seher*, the pilgrim and seer, mystically and erotically attracted by the south, which we find in the paintings of the Nazarenes, the early nineteenth-century brotherhood that gathered in Rome to revive the great models of Christianity.

This split identity would never be entirely overcome. The German path would weigh on his inspiration in a way that has few equivalents in Italian letters: in Pirandello, for example, it derived not from his blood, but from his studies of philosophy and philology in Bonn. In the last years of his life, Malaparte would often go to the Black Forest in the summer to restore himself, preferring to spend winters in Capri and Forte dei Marmi: for that matter, what Latin could have conceived, without Nordic influences, the carceral dimension of Casa Come Me? He had a thirst for solitude, certainly, which he would never manage to satisfy; but it's not by chance that he traveled these routes against the current. Abroad, there continue to circulate outlandish stories to the effect that Malaparte was born in Italy to German parents, or to German Jewish migrants, or that he should be considered an Italian-German writer. How many times did I hear, during the various presentations of the French edition of this book, that Malaparte "was not really Italian"? There is, conversely, in Malaparte's obstinately asserted Tuscanism a strident, artificial aspect, which does not entirely convince. Even in his last writings, we find wordplay and turns of phrase, largely lost in translation, that to an Italian ear sound a bit dated, like the verses of his teacher Bino Binazzi. The Tuscany of Curzio's contemporaries, on the other hand, had already decisively entered modernity. The intellectuals established in Florence—such as the raving, impetuous poet Dino Campana, author of the *Canti orfici* (Orphic songs), dedicated to the kaiser on the eve of the outbreak of the Great War; or the group of Giuseppe Prezzolini, Giovanni Papini, Ardengo Soffici, and Aldo Palazzeschi, who would bring out two magazines of international importance, *La Voce* (1908–16) and *Lacerba* (1913–15)—were open to the great international currents of Bergsonism, idealism, mysticism, orientalism, and so on. Compared with these expressions, Malaparte's tendency toward a backward-looking pastiche betrayed a lack of naturalness similar to that of the urbanite who puts on his best suit to go play the gentleman in the countryside. Artifice represented an integral part of his persona right from the beginning, something that must inspire circumspection in the reader of his many autobiographical disclosures. Nonetheless, this artificiality expresses an authentic wound, along with a taste for performance, which would remain true of him from the beginning to the end of his life. But he didn't cheat. Malaparte was always a mythomaniac, inclined to storytelling because for him reality had no objective, verifiable value. A rhetorician at times, an impostor never.

Thus he began to be and, at the same time, *saw* himself to be. When and how does the narcissistic condensation of Kurt Erich, becoming Curzio around the time of puberty, emerge? In a reminiscence entitled "Primo amore" (First love)—the object of this first exclusive love, obviously, is himself—he would maintain that "in the life of every man there is nothing more secret and more mysterious than the innocence and chastity of childhood" (RI, 301). But the day he loses this plank of salvation in the torrent of life, he refuses to renounce his overinvestment in the "I," which is typical of both the child and the artist. To the legend of the beautiful being (lovingly, sorrowfully reproduced in the reflection of his unattainable and inaccessible double), to this precocious acquaintance with unhappiness, the boy adds the will to create himself. Where could desire alone, without inner discipline, otherwise lead? To total disaster. But Curzio doesn't want to fail, doesn't want to take refuge in an elsewhere far from reality, to succumb to the psychotic conflict between reality and fantasy. He is, right from the beginning, an angelic little war machine, fully equipped to live and survive, an admirer of success through self-mastery. Nothing that constitutes the daily life of regular people seems to interest him. He doesn't know, would never know, the meaning of a birthday, a holiday or day of rest, a family memorial service. He doesn't participate in the events that punctuate social life, especially in a small town: baptisms, weddings, funerals. "His conversation, or rather his monologues, always revolved around himself; other people were like billiard balls he loved to strike in a complicated carom shot," wrote someone who knew him well.[13] Having again and again seen his father choked with rage, embroiled in wretched labor disputes, he would become an expert navigator, able to sense the way the wind was blowing and boldly change tack at the right time, only to then ruin everything through an irrepressible need to grandstand. Perhaps that's when the German in him would reawaken. But on the whole, he would remain faithful to these two linked elements—respect for strength and the ability to adapt himself to events—and it is impossible to deny the coherence of this approach, which would turn Curzio into Malaparte.

It is fair to wonder how an adolescent endowed with such an energetic vision of life became a writer rather than an entrepreneur, banker, or politician. The fact is that his sensibility was overwhelming from the start, and he felt moved to express it in every circumstance. From the moment he bent over a sheet of paper he knew, like anyone else called to writing, that it was there and only there that his destiny lay; writing is not necessarily happiness, but for the real writer nothing else can take its place. Nonetheless, if literature was the main business of his life, literary men appealed to him only if, from Saint-Simon to Chateaubriand, from Byron to D'Annunzio, by way of Boccaccio and Goethe, they were with equal success *something else*; that is, they produced something that would justify their stay on earth, and not only collect dust in libraries. Exasperated by ivory towers, he wanted to go into the streets and fight. Like his great models, he would be by turns a soldier, man of action, diplomat, and expert courtier; and even when he was no longer one of them, he would remain closer to the soldiers, men of action, diplomats, and courtiers than to most of his writer colleagues.

From early on, women played only a marginal role in the construction of his personality. Unlike most of his peers, Curzio disdained brothels, which on the contrary provoked in him a phobic revulsion: one of the rare brothel scenes to appear in his work, the Soroca girls episode in *Kaputt*, serves as a prelude to the slaughterhouse scene, in which the unfortunate women await an atrocious fate. No admission of autoerotic practices has come to light, neither then nor later, even as they might be explained by his narcissistic personality. According to his first biographer, who rushed to Prato at a time when the city still teemed with more or less trustworthy witnesses, "No one remembers the boy before he left for the war ever having a sweetheart, or him strolling of an evening in the company of some girl."[14] His sister confided the name of a local beauty, with whom Curzio fell in love at fourteen and for whom he had written a novel, of which some fragments remain, with an unflattering, but very telling, title: "La puzza delle donne" (The stench of women). Here are the first lines, in the form of a (romantic?) letter: "You are the most beautiful creature to bloom under the sun... But you stink!"[15] A sign of hidden homosexuality? No, Curzio's tastes led him exclusively to women, but he would find ways to throw off inconvenient admirers with little compunction, something that friends and witnesses attributed, once again, to his "German cruelty." It has been speculated that he was impotent, then, and wanted to avenge himself for this complex. There does not appear to be any evidence for this. Malaparte's sexuality did not lurk in the "erogenous zones of passivity" that Sartre attributed to Flaubert.[16] As a lover he was completely "normal." But sex, like food and alcohol, held little attraction for him; he distrusted it, seeing in it something low and harmful to creative energy. Ever since childhood—under what influences, one wonders—he seemed obsessed with not dissipating his energies, not squandering his lifeblood, the seed that gives life, even if he later refused to pass it on and create other life. There was no metaphysical or religious conditioning in this conviction. He did not want to stay pure, a notion he would have found hilarious. He wanted to be strong, self-confident, and dominant. This particular antibourgeois was very petit bourgeois in his attitudes: if one of his lovers paraded around in a too-revealing swimsuit, scoldings and slaps would rain down; if another rested her bare feet on the dashboard, he would cry out in shock: "This wench is ruining my car!"[17]

Pretending to a vigorously virile nature, melancholy at times but free of sentimentalism, always in control of a love life rich in variety, Malaparte displayed the aversion of a prudish spinster to any idea of filiation. The most obvious example of his phobias is in the episode of *The Skin* where he attends the fake pregnancy of a so-called invert who, in the course of a semiorgiastic pagan rite, "delivers" a bloody doll. The allegory is clear: homosexuals, toward whom he always displayed—as a human category, not as individuals—an almost pathological aversion, something that often inspired them to (incorrectly) believe he was one of them, simulate a slavery that is already dismal enough when it occurs naturally. To reproduce is the task of common mortals. The exceptional being avoids perpetuating what must remain unique, inimitable, without peers or posterity. Resistant to intimate connections, he nonetheless found disciples throughout his life and captivated many of the young people who came in contact with him. But he had no official heir, in art or in life. Which is to say: no Malaparte before me, no Malaparte after me.

The French writer Raymond Guérin, a regular guest on Capri in the 1950s and a witness complicit in the creation of the Malapartian legend, had the right intuition here: "He would have felt offended in his virility if he had to passively accept certain caresses. He's a man whose carnal relations have to be simple and healthy. Which makes him the opposite of a true lover."[18] Such an attitude was common in his milieu and in his generation, where sensuality was considered a form of weakness. If he was not exuberant and could permit himself the luxury of long periods of celibacy throughout his life, he fornicated easily, without foreplay, or decadent gymnastics *alla* *francese*, as the expression went at the time. The idea that intercourse is manly and caresses are feminine, or that abstinence forges the soldier and lasciviousness dissipates him, can be found in Malaparte from beginning to end. It's the kind of copulation—brief and intense like the explosion of a bomb—hailed by Marinetti and taken up by Mussolini's Fascism, even if Malaparte would pair it with his obstinate refusal of procreation, contrary to the demographic policies of the regime encouraging large families and ostracizing "unproductive" bachelors.* "He had a prime pair in the right place," wrote Biancamaria Fabbri,[19] whose judgment we can trust, and the vulgar expression, deliberately chosen by a woman who was not vulgar in the least, should underscore the health of this man who could be sweet and attentive to his companion, but for whom things finished there, with the fulfillment of his "duty" (and not always). He preferred to sleep alone, to avoid being surprised in the abandonment of slumber, not to mention the bathroom, where he would barricade himself in for his ablutions. If the body is vulnerable or subjected to physiological functions, it is necessary to hide it, out of fear that it will reveal us in our most prosaic, least contrived nature. And as far as nudism—discovered in Finland, where it was a sanitary practice—is concerned, he never made the exhibitionistic use of it that was attributed to him, and no reliable witness saw him sunbathe nude, dripping with oil, in Forte dei Marmi or on Capri. When, near the end of his

---

*A revealing case is that of Carlo Emilio Gadda in one of his most emblematic texts, *Eros e Priapo* (1945). Gadda was at least at the beginning of the Fascist period a true believer; at the same time he was a repressed and self-punishing homosexual. The retrospective repulsion on display here against the "priapic" dictator is the reflection of his estrangement at the time from the current values of the regime. In this sense, the text can be likened to Malaparte's *Muss*, as a manifestation of subversive love-hate.

life, Malaparte willingly submitted to the gentle care of his Chinese nurses, it was not only on account of his state of physical prostration, but also because the nurses ceased, in that moment, to be women.

Sex aside, where did this lack of interest in female companionship spring from? Neither his familial context nor his surroundings were suffused with erotophobia or sanctimony. It is inevitable, nonetheless, to wonder about the role of his mother: Did she represent perhaps an unattainable feminine ideal? It is from her, Elvira (also known as Evelina or Eugenia), née Perelli, that the Suckert children derived their good looks, along with their strength of character. Elvira came from a wealthy family, and the rare photos that have come down to us attest that she was eminently possessed of "that beauty at once soft and majestic that shines in the Lombard blood," lauded by Manzoni in *The Betrothed*. At the age of sixteen Elvira had posed for Paolo Troubetzkoy, an artist of Russian origin who became the official painter of Florentine polite society. It was in Florence, too, where she met Erwin:

> My father and mother met for the first time in the early 1890s... one Sunday in June, near sunset. The municipal band was playing slow Viennese waltzes, between the trees of the avenues strolled the Florentine beauties, their arms in black gloves up to the elbow, their throats enclosed in a high lace ruff.... My father had been the first to travel the length of Via Tornabuoni on a bicycle (a German Phaenomen velocipede, at the time the best in the world). And it was an escapade and a scandal.[20]

Erwin had fallen at her feet, in a scene that recalls a bit too closely a page of Stendhal's *Lucien Leuwen* to be entirely credible. And thus was born the idyll between the beauty and the inventor, in reality separated by too much. Elvira dominated her husband through her deportment, personality, and social background, through the sweet firmness of her character and her impeccable household management. Does this suffice to attribute to her an exclusive role in the emotional life of her son? One day a journalist asked Malaparte if he had ever thought of killing someone, and he responded firmly: "Yes, my mother, when I was a child, out of jealousy."[21] Elsewhere he recounts that Elvira continually scolded him, that she refused to read his books, that she preferred one or another of his siblings, and so on. And it was perhaps in order to settle scores with her that he wrote, "Italian women are worth more as women than as wives or mothers" (BI, 232). But let us be careful not to take these quips at face value: Malaparte loved to astonish his interlocutors to feed his own legend. Besides, who could reproach a woman, however "feudal and conformist,"[22] or simply bourgeois, at the mercy of such a husband, for having desired a stable life and a good job for her children? In theory, one could trace back to this conflict with his mother the rumor according to which Malaparte "selects his lovers one by one, with a preference for older women."[23] But this is, precisely, a rumor: if Roberta Masier, "Flaminia," and Virginia Agnelli were rich, they were not older than him, and, after 1945, Malaparte went with women half his age, of good families but of little means, like Jane Sweigard, Biancamaria Fabbri, and Rebequita Yáñez.

Must we, then, evoke the attempt at maternal castration, the momism of the male persecuted by the adoration of a dominating mother, destined to erect a wall between him and *real* women? From Proust to Tanizaki, by way of Romain Gary and Philip Roth, the examples abound. And yet Curzio emancipated himself very early on, fleeing the paternal (and maternal) roof at sixteen, never to return. Over the years he would sign photos and letters to his mother, "Your *figliaccio*" (bad son), or employ bizarre formulas like "to Mommy, with doting spite." But nothing suggests any great intimacy between them, except perhaps in the moment of his political undoing and confinement on Lipari. Can we speak, in his case, of symbiosis anxiety, as conceived by psychoanalysis as the "fear that one will not be able to remain separate from mother"?[24] Malaparte invited his mother to Forte dei Marmi and Capri, but he confined her to a room as far as possible from his own; even regular guests, like Orfeo Tamburi and Guérin, never met her.[25] Elvira appears just as infrequently in his work, even if he did pay her a heartrending and cruel tribute in *Mamma marcia*, describing her death throes. And yet, according to Biancamaria Fabbri, "He kept the memory of his mother intact. Malaparte adored beauty, and she was beautiful."[26] Would he have loved her less if she had been ugly? Would he have loved his two brothers less if they had not been so handsome? Conversely, he loved his father rather less, not only because of his failures but also because he was ugly and graceless; he represented the darkness and heaviness of the Teutonic forests, as against the splendor of Mediterranean civilization. Many aesthetes of the Right and the Left, especially in France, from Brasillach to Genet, were in the 1930s and 1940s attracted to the Hitlerian vision of a blond Nietzschean dolichocephalic, whereas Malaparte was not the least bit interested. The Italians, he would write during the Rome-Berlin honeymoon period, hiding himself for the purpose behind Stendhal, "were without a doubt, and are to this day, a superior race, even if they don't have blond hair" (BI, 258).[27]

From this double inheritance, paternal and maternal, also comes his remarkable capacity for work. From beginning to end, with hardly a break or crisis of inspiration, through productivity highs and lows, but more highs than lows, Malaparte, like D'Annunzio, was a slogger with few equals, assisted nearly to the very end by an iron constitution, unacquainted with disgust, vertigo, or the horror of the blank page. He had little patience for discussions of formal values, debates about art and literature, or theoretical analyses, and when he nonetheless had a go, you could feel the effort. He loved, very much, the craft. None of his books involved fewer than four or five versions, sometimes even more over the course of years. He always sought to tailor according to what was useful for the given moment. The smallest episode, the slightest anecdote, the most insignificant encounter—dutifully embellished—all were born of meticulous preparation, facilitated by a prodigious capacity for assimilation. The journalist and special correspondent Lino Pellegrini, who saw him at work at the front, told me that "he would absorb everything like a sponge." It was the sign of an erudition more broad than deep, of a need to astonish and to make a good impression at any cost; often, the journalist prevailed over the man of learning. But if, for example, he wielded seven or eight languages evidently without knowing them, native-speaking readers have been struck by the precision of the terms chosen to evoke the call of a Finnish explorer in the tundra or the tale of a Moldavian deserter.

No, it was not passion for his *mamma* and the luxury of *grands hôtels*, gratuitous malice from an erstwhile friend, the writer and humorist Leo Longanesi,[28] that would make Malaparte a being capable of mastering his own desires, closed off to passion, impermeable to feeling. It is self-love, love of the "I" that is loved and fulfilled insofar as it loves itself. And he who loves his reflection loves contact less, as Rilke has it in a beautiful poem, *Narziss* (1913). The poet's disgust at "dirty hands," even female ones, was certainly shared by Curzio. "I have a horror of vice," the latter wrote. "On Capri, like anywhere else on earth, vice is always something banal, a sign of stupidity."[29] From Jünger to Borges, Saint-Exupéry to Malraux, the list is long of major twentieth-century authors, all confirmed heterosexuals, for whom women played a negligible role. Such was the case for Malaparte. In his work, in the thousands and thousands of pages he left us, published or unpublished, there is not a single story, a single scene, of true love. And of all the women in his life, none inspired him to create a single major female character, except in a few minor stories. The love affair sketched out in *Das Kapital* or in *Anche le donne hanno perso la guerra* serves only to clarify the ideological content of the play. We find neither eroticism nor amorous cruelty of a Proustian sadomasochistic sort in the "impromptu" he based on the *Recherche*. In *The Forbidden Christ*, Bruno is obsessed with the murder of his brother Giulio but remains unmoved when his fiancée confesses to him that she gave herself to Giulio during Bruno's absence. In Malaparte's hundreds and hundreds of letters, I did not find the least allusion to any jealousy inspired in him by a woman; meanwhile, they overflow with envy and ill will toward journalists better paid, politicians more successful, colleagues more appreciated by publishers or the public.*

Was such narcissism incompatible with a taste for women? Not at all, provided that he might "love her like I would love myself, if

---

*However, the Chilean poet Waldo Rojas told me that Rebequita Yáñez, who was a friend of his, gave him a thick packet of letters from Malaparte, written in a mixture of Italian, French, and Spanish, of strong erotic content, "so much so that I blushed." The letters were lost after Rebequita's death.

I were a woman" (W, 4–5). A tacit confession of emotional sterility? Not necessarily, as long as the woman accepted the subaltern role he reserved for her, bearing in mind that a woman "like me" does not exist, and seeing as how *she* is *him*, and he is not a woman! There is no way out of this tautology. Malaparte sprinkled his work with outwardly sincere homages to the courage, intelligence, and self-sacrifice of women. He believed in their emancipation, was surrounded by women all his life, and gave evidence on a thousand occasions of a sensibility we could define as feminine. But deep down he remained impervious to union with a woman, notwithstanding the very Latin excesses of possessiveness with which he deviled the female companions who shared a longer or shorter period of his life. He did not, in the manner of Drieu La Rochelle or Pavese, see women as the representative of an enemy people, but rather of a different people, with whom relations are conducted more out of interest than out of mutual understanding.[30] He never managed to merge with a woman, nor did he try. After all, to his eyes, this is not characteristic of man:

> Men and women belong not only to two different sexes but to two different races. The race of women has its traditions, its customs, its sentiments, its moral, intellectual, and material interests, all quite distinct from those of the male race. There is greater resemblance, greater understanding, between an Italian woman and a French (English, German, Russian, Spanish) woman than between an Italian woman and an Italian man. The two races in those countries are no longer, as is the case with us, in the ancient relationship between victors and defeated, slave to the antiquated, stupid, ridiculous, immoral masculine mythology: they are free beings, belonging to a

race that has finally found the equality that men, the victors, have always denied, in Italy, to the defeated race.³¹

Not only equivalence of the "distinct races," then, but superiority of the woman in terms of sacrifice and dedication. This is the sincerely feminist side of Malaparte, even if it can be misunderstood. In *Benedetti italiani* we find the metaphor, often hinted at in his work, of Italy in the form of a woman, straddled by male ardor, followed by a salute to the "great compassion of Italian women, obliged to applaud the ridiculous comedy of the man in heat" (BI, 229). Elsewhere, he would relate how, in 1944, traveling up the Italian peninsula, heading for Rome with an American division, he saw in a pit a dozen dead women, which other women were dressing for the wake:

> Only women's hands were worthy of touching those dead women's faces. Maybe it was the persistence of an ancient religious rite. But I preferred to interpret that behavior as a revolt, as a protest against the race of men, against masculine brutality, against savage, bloody Mars. No man's hand was worthy of touching those waxen faces, that long, soft hair, those half-closed eyelids.³²

Even in his "loves," from the flaunted and theatrical to the more discreet, Malaparte almost never took the initiative. He adored being courted, and his refined seduction technique was based on his capacity to remove himself, confounding his admirers (of both sexes). He never entered into an exclusive relationship, not even in his longer-term ones: not out of machismo, given that he was a parsimonious steward of his own forces and a somewhat cold calculator of pleasure received or granted; but simply because he was incapable of it. Occasionally, especially toward the end, he would confide to a certain devoted companion his intention to settle down, and he even talked about possible "candidates": a touch of human, probably sincere confession, very different from the public Malaparte—but the matter stopped there. With children and adolescents, especially boys, he was capable of giving more of himself. He could tell them incredible, fascinating tales of adventures, bring them gifts from his travels (which he rarely brought to women), follow them in their studies, read and comment on their naive poetry without arrogance, or drag them on long walks to discover nature: all behaviors indicative of a surrogate paternity. As he wrote to the publisher Roland Laudenbach:*

> The boxer's little letter gave me immense pleasure, so adorable was the language in his mouth. I would like you to be poor, so poor that you were unable to raise your children, and you were obliged to give one up to me. I would be an extraordinary father; I would imitate you.[33]

Otherwise, the company of animals, especially dogs, sufficed for him. His home life was spartan, overseen by a housekeeper or maid: the most faithful was an energetic peasant from Pordenone, Maria Montico, who remained—or rather, survived—in his service for nearly two decades, from 1937 to 1955, and divulged no secrets about her employer. And, naturally, he basked in the admiration of his

---

*The "boxer" was one of Laudenbach's children, François, who to this day recalls Malaparte's great friendliness toward him. I have received identical testimonies from other sons or daughters of Malaparte's friends (or lovers), who were then children or adolescents, including Maria Sole Agnelli, Daniele Rulli, Onofrio Solari Bozzi, Antonello Pietromarchi, and Beatrice Monti von Rezzori. All remember him with a nostalgia and affection I have rarely (if ever) found in "adult" witnesses.

intimates, who became his preferred public, until such time as he quarreled and broke with them. For the most part, he meant to be alone, and he was. In good times and in moments of crisis it was ever thus, and he would have it no other way.

"Unable to Do Otherwise, We Performed Miracles"

Prato may be a provincial city, but it is not a dead one, far from it. Like nearly all Italian municipalities, it has been shaped by a long, important local history. A worldwide center for the production, treatment, and trade of cloth in the Middle Ages, it declined in the Renaissance as a fief of Florence, a mere dozen miles away. The decline was a relative one, given that Prato Cathedral is an architectural jewel of the twelfth century, containing the relic of the "holy belt" of the Virgin Mary and adorned with sculptures by Giovanni Pisano and frescoes by Filippo Lippi, Paolo Uccello, and Agnolo Gaddi. Its churches and palazzi are of a refined opulence, with two-toned decorations employing the distinctive green serpentine marble that, alternated with white Carrara marble, adorns nearly all the facades of Tuscan Renaissance churches. In the vicinity, in Poggio a Caiano, a favorite destination of the pack led by young Curzio, can be found one of the most beautiful Medici villas, which inspired the architecture of the Château de Vaux-le-Vicomte. After Italian unification, Prato experienced considerable economic and demographic revitalization; today it is the second-largest city in Tuscany, with more than 190,000 inhabitants and a thriving Chinatown.*

---

*A candidate in the 2009 municipal elections plastered city walls with the slogan "Prato ai Pratesi / Fuori i Cinesi" (Prato for the Pratese / Out with the Chinese).

THE BEGINNINGS OF A BONAPARTE (1898–1924)

But already in the period when the Suckert and Baldi boys were discovering the city, traversing its length and breadth by day and night, Prato was literally breaking out of the walls with which Robert of Anjou had fortified it in the fourteenth century, to expand into the surrounding area. With nearly all of its fifty thousand inhabitants—men, women, and adolescents (officially over the age of fourteen, at times even younger)—working in the new mechanized textile and spinning industry, Prato became known as the "Manchester of Italy."[34] It was a working-class city but one rooted in the countryside, prosperous and welcoming, where everyone knew one another and the conditions of life could be considered, for the period, satisfactory. Even social relations were, on the whole, untroubled. There were few large estates and few great landowners, a fairly wide distribution of small properties, a cultured and rather open bourgeoisie. As Malaparte recounted in a 1952 radio interview:

> I consider myself very fortunate, as a writer, to have been born in a working-class city. Because Prato is one of the few Italian and European cities that is completely working-class: the bourgeoisie is small, such that, in the evenings, it strangely resembles one of the Soviet cities of southern Russia. You can say anything about me, except that I am a provincial writer. And I owe this to Prato, a city that is working-class and thus also modern and European.[35]

But the situation was rapidly evolving. The Italian Socialist Party, founded in 1892, could already count on a solid base of disciplined militants. To its left operated a nebulous collection of anarchists, republicans, and Mazzinians that had come together in Tuscany starting with the wars of independence against foreign occupiers, but also against the Savoy monarchy and the central government in Rome. On the other side of the barricade—an apt phrase, because fistfights, if not firefights, were by then the order of the day—the nationalists found one of their champions in Paolo Giorgi, headmaster of the Cicognini.[36] The nationalists soon became interventionists, because they considered it inevitable that Italy would enter the war to complete the project of national unity, liberating Trento, Trieste, and the other territories still in the hands of Austria-Hungary. Poetic myths were superimposed on the crisis of ideologies. The time had come for Italians to prove they were the worthy descendants of Dante and to lay claim to a great imperial and colonial destiny.

The patriotic fever rose, despite warnings by the major figures of "Italietta,"* starting with the long-serving liberal prime minister Giovanni Giolitti, who, armed with the statesman's first gift, realism, sought in vain to explain that the country had an interest in preserving a prosperity-bringing neutrality in the impending conflict between the Central Powers and the Triple Entente. Attesting to this in the first decade of the century was the development of the banking system and entrepreneurial infrastructure in sectors such as construction, chemistry, textiles, and the automobile industry. But Giolitti felt obliged nonetheless to launch a colonial expedition: the war against Turkey of 1911–12, which ended with the occupation of Tripolitania and Cyrenaica, in present-day Libya. The military operation was modest but strengthened the bellicist party.

And yet, *intervene* against whom? Italy was bound by the defensive

---

*Lit., "little Italy," a derogatory term for the Italian state and society as small-minded, provincial, and petit bourgeois; during the Fascist *ventennio*, "Italietta" was used to indicate the part of society opposed to the regime and supportive of pacificist, democratic, and parliamentarian positions.—Trans.

Triple Alliance to Germany and Austria-Hungary. Its relations with the former, which had made considerable capital investments in the new country, were excellent, with no disputes about borders, such that Rome would reluctantly declare war on Berlin only in August 1916, fifteen months after switching allegiance to the Entente. Conversely, Rome and Vienna were so at odds that they could only be allies or enemies. The weight of the Holy See, as close to the most Catholic Habsburg crown as it was hostile to the House of Savoy, after the 1870 capture of Rome, hardly simplified things. Furthermore, the Triple Alliance was called into question by a part of public opinion attracted by the effervescence of modernity, by the values of democracy and progress represented by London and Paris.

In this agitated atmosphere, the barely adolescent Curzio could not be content with a secondary role. He already had the spirit of not only an orator but also a demagogue. "Once again I see you at fourteen, impassioned and self-confident, as you would be three years later when, wearing a red shirt, you spoke to the people of Prato, gathered around the monument to Garibaldi, in favor of Italy entering the war," one of his schoolmates would recall, in the course of funeral services for Malaparte in the city's cathedral.[37] And he was already a factionist: temperamentally, to express himself he would always need to be *for*, but above all *against*, someone or something. He could neither live nor write without attacking. Unanimity disgusted him; compromise mortified him. Physically, while no Hercules, he was tall, agile, and bold. His choice was soon made: in the street brawls he took the side of the interventionists against the humanitarian socialists and the pacifists, against the trade unions marching by with banners exalting the Second International. He was often the one carrying the tricolor flag at patriotic demonstrations. But he was disliked by the bien-pensants, the clergy, and the forces of public order, because he supported the Italian Republican Party (PRI), heading up its youth section, and refused to participate in any religious ceremony. Sometimes he blended in with other groups, just to get into the middle of the protest, and he was even arrested at anarchist strikes. Curzio placed himself on the right out of nationalist commitment and a natural sense of hierarchy, but on the left out of a rejection of the established order and an attraction to the proletariat of both workers and peasants. He wanted war to complete the project of national unity, but not to defend the Savoy dynasty. And he knew immediately what side to be on: against Germany, for France. He already spoke the latter's language and had devoured the texts of Romantic and Symbolist authors, which he was acquainted with thanks to Bino Binazzi.

This precocious commitment, viewed in the light of his future itinerary, attests to an undeniable underlying coherence in the "chameleon" Malaparte. What attracted him immediately was the strength that arose from the young nation, and he would despise Italy (that is, the Italians) any time that it and they were not strong, in the same way he would always admire strong nations and peoples, independent of the regime: the France of 1914 (but not of 1934 or 1940), the Soviet Union, the United States, China. Only much later would Malaparte's antiwar and antinationalist positions emerge, at the time of *Kaputt* and *The Skin*. For now, let us look at the appearance of the first contradictions, which would in time lead him to invent for himself—and ably antedate—rebellions or aversions. But he never disavowed the choices he made in his early years. Struggle, the nation, the people, and above all else strength represented values he would never distance himself from. Anticlericalism would remain an almost constant polemical reference, even as along the way he would pluck out a noble fruit—the imitation of Christ—that became central to his work, as his existential pessimism gradually grew. With regard to socialism, his disappointment at seeing it so little put into practice in Fascist Italy or in Lenin's and Stalin's Soviet Union would ultimately incline him, in the twilight of his life, toward the Chinese experience. Let's skip over for the moment the utopian aspect of this last profession of faith: Malaparte was always more at ease in destruction than in construction. He was an often prophetic writer and an agitator for ideas, capable of tremendous acuity. Yet he was not, and never would be, a systematic thinker, or a detached political scientist. If there is something of Sartre in him, in his intuitive capacity and polemical outbursts, he would never be an Aron in the rigor of his analysis. But let us recognize straightaway that, contrary to widespread opinion, he expressed a basic coherence in his life and work that, be it in paradoxical forms, he would never belie.

The Austrian ultimatum to Serbia did not oblige Italy to intervene, given the defensive nature of the Triple Alliance, and in this case, Austria was the aggressor; nor had Vienna shared in advance its bellicose intentions with Rome, which it distrusted, as it secretly had with Berlin. Hence the government declared its neutrality in August 1914, giving the English and the French, whose historiography has rarely recognized as much, a measure of breathing space—because the first phase of the war was not in their favor, with Belgium and Serbia promptly invaded, France threatened, Russia on the verge of collapse, and the British Empire menaced by the Turks in the Aegean Sea. Meanwhile the pro-French, democratic side in Italy was strengthened; it was a heterogenous group, but one well represented in the leading intellectual milieus. There we find the Reformist Socialists of Leonida Bissolati, Marinetti's Futurists, the Florentine group around *La Voce*, and progressive spirits like Guglielmo Ferrero and Arturo Toscanini. The pro-German position, on the other hand, was traditionally strong among industrialists and bankers and in academic milieus, and inclined, with the influential philosopher Benedetto Croce, mostly toward neutrality. The neutralist faction, led by Giolitti, also remained prevalent in parliament, in the business world, and in the press.

Then two figures who would tip the scales in favor of the democratic Entente came to prominence. The first was Gabriele D'Annunzio. Returned from exile (for debt) in France, he threw himself into an unprecedented speaking tour. According to one account, "The effect of that dazzling speech from the balcony of the Hotel Regina, in front of 150,000 Romans, was extraordinary. After that, official Italy no longer had any choice but between entering the war immediately, or revolution."[38] The other figure, still relatively unknown outside the socialist movement, represented the left wing of the party. He firmly opposed the war in his columns for *Avanti!*, of which he was the editor in chief. But, from one day to the next, he radically changed his opinion, after receiving a financial contribution from the French Socialists, who had just entered a government of national unity in Paris. Expelled from the Italian Socialist Party, he created a new daily newspaper, *Il Popolo d'Italia*, and threw himself into the interventionist campaign. His name was Benito Mussolini.

In the first weeks of the conflict, the chief of the Great German General Staff, Helmuth von Moltke the Younger, unleashed a risky offensive on the Marne. Fortunately, the German generalissimo did not possess the strategic genius displayed by his uncle, Field Marshal

Moltke the Elder, in 1870–71, and Paris was safe for now. Meanwhile, volunteers flowed in from every part of Italy and Europe to defend republican France. One of them bore an illustrious name: Peppino Garibaldi was a nephew of the "Hero of Two Worlds," a title that the populist democrat Giuseppe Garibaldi shared with the aristocrat Marquis de Lafayette. Peppino was worthy of such blood: he had roamed the globe fighting for the oppressed, from South Africa to Guyana, from Mexico to the Balkans. Now he rushed to the besieged French capital with his five brothers to create the Garibaldi Legion, incorporated as the Fourth Marching Regiment of the Foreign Legion, but composed entirely of Italian forces. There were roughly 2,500 men and a few dozen officers, recruited from among the Italian immigrants in France and the idealists who poured in from its "sister nation": republicans, Mazzinians, revolutionary syndicalists, all "to fulfill Dante's prophecy, the supreme vow of Giuseppe Mazzini, Giuseppe Garibaldi, and Giosuè Carducci...against *la barbarie*!" commented one enthusiastic witness.[39] They were entitled to wear the famous red shirt clearly visible beneath their unbuttoned green jackets, creating an excellent target for the snipers of the German army.

Following cursory training at the base in Montélimar, the regiment underwent its baptism of fire on Christmas night at Belle Étoile, near the Bois de Bolante. It was a massacre, in which one of the Garibaldi brothers, Bruno, fell. They made a second attack, in scarcely better conditions, on January 5, in the Argonne, where a second Garibaldi brother, Costante, fell. This is from a French war bulletin:

> On January 8, 1915, the survivors of the Garibaldi Legion had been sent as reinforcements to the Haute-Chevauchée in the Meurissons

zone, where the situation was critical: their heroic charges allowed for the situation to be restored and for a part of the territory that had been lost to be retaken. On January 11, 1915, the Garibaldians, whose forces had been depleted by death and injuries as well as by sickness, were sent on rest leave.[40]

Peppino was the prototype of those men—honest, simple, and straightforward in their strength and convictions, like Milziade Baldi—who would always hold a particular fascination for Malaparte, maybe because he was so different from them. He decided to leave the family home in great secrecy to enlist with a group of friends in the regiment. When exactly? Here is what he would recount thirty years later:

> I was at school, and Mr. Destrée, the Belgian MP who was making a propaganda tour for heroic Belgium during the period of Italian neutrality, that is in 1914, immediately after the summer of 1914, truly moved us, the young people of my generation, to the point that several fled the school, myself among them. I crossed the frontier on foot, at Ventimiglia, and I enlisted in the 408th French Regiment. I fought the war at the beginning in madder-red pants. I was wounded twice on the French front and twice cited in the army's daily reports.[41]

The truth is a bit less lyrical. Malaparte likely enlisted between mid-February and mid-March of 1915, as shown by his service record and as attested by his sister Maria.[42] According to his other sister, Edda, he would have returned home in "March or April 1915"; the date of his departure from Prato, however, was not specified.[43] It is thus improbable he participated in the battles of the Argonne, as he later maintained.⁴⁴ He was more likely restricted, after his training period, to accompanying the Garibaldians to their new garrison, in Avignon. Does that mean his first undertaking was already a fiction? Absolutely not. For starters, he could not have known when he left Prato that the Garibaldians would no longer be sent to the front line. In the second place, if he had been captured by the enemy, his German nationality would have exposed him to the fate of traitors: the firing squad. It was a risk he would continue to run for the entire war. However we look at it, then, the flight to France was a vitally important turning point, and it is not by chance that he would call it "the most beautiful page of my life, the purest page."⁴⁵ But he would also say of the Garibaldi Legion that "for me it was the prelude to Fascism."⁴⁶ As it was for others as well.

In March 1915, the regiment was dissolved. Peppino Garibaldi and his two surviving brothers, Ezio and Sante, returned to Italy, where they campaigned for the country's now imminent entry into the war, which would take place on May 24. The Italian army and that of the empire known throughout central Europe as *k. und k.*—"*kaiserlich und königlich*," imperial and royal—would clash for three and a half years in one of the most deadly theaters of the Great War, the "White front," which went from the South Tyrolean Alps to the Adriatic.⁴⁷ The front followed roughly the borders between present-day Italy, Austria, Slovenia, and Croatia: that is, nearly 375 miles of mostly uplands and mountain ranges, where trenches were not dug out of the earth and the mud, but had to be carved from bare rock, at an altitude of almost ten thousand feet. A predominantly Mediterranean people thus found itself fighting in the mountains, and what mountains! The imperial army was less numerous, because half its forces had already for the previous ten months been fighting alongside the Germans in Austrian Galicia and in Poland, against Russia. But it was better equipped, better prepared for highland combat, and enjoyed the considerable advantage in every case of dominating the mountain ridge, against which the Italians were obliged to launch assaults, for fear of being pushed back down to the plains of Lombardy and the Veneto. The Alpine region is the geostrategic key to all the invasions the peninsula has historically witnessed from the northeast and northwest. Here began shortly, as on the western front, a war of position, in absolute ignorance of the lessons of Napoleon and Clausewitz. The eleven battles that took the name of the Isonzo River were one immense bloodbath that, like at Verdun or on the Somme, would cut down on either side hundreds of thousands of innocent young lives for the conquest or loss of virtually insignificant portions of ground. Thirty years later, Malaparte would still seethe with anger at the "glorious, gory, moronic, and useless offensives of Cadorna, the only general in history to have won eleven offensive battles, remaining in the same place the whole time."[48] Luigi Cadorna, nicknamed "the Butcher" and even worse, was indeed hated by his troops, nor has he found greater understanding among military historians. But it is legitimate to wonder who, without an iron hand like his, could have kept the army together in the conditions of flagrant unpreparation in which Italy had entered the war.

At the time, Sandro Suckert was already in the service; Curzio had just turned seventeen. Having triumphantly returned to Prato from the French front, he resumed his studies, but the academic year was coming to an end. He left as a volunteer with fellow members of the PRI youth group, two years before the draft. For the second time he demonstrated uncommon strength of character and courage. He was assigned to the Fifty-First Infantry Regiment of the Alpine Brigade, a descendant of the Hunters of the Alps corps raised by Giuseppe Garibaldi for the Second Italian War of Independence, under the command of Peppino. (Later, Malaparte would become the standard-bearer of the Fifty-Second.) Peppino, who had been thanked for his heroic exploits in France by the president of the republic in person, upon his return to Italy had been made a simple battalion commander, given the career military officers' mistrust of the Garibaldians.* Peppino's exceptional courage nevertheless earned him a rapid rise, and in August 1917, on the eve of the disaster of Caporetto, he was finally named commander of the Alpine Brigade, a unit boasting a strong esprit de corps. Recruitment was limited to Tuscans and Umbrians, supplemented by other rough mountain men hailing from Abruzzo, Calabria, and Sardinia.

The encounter with his former comrades was brotherly, and the still beardless Curzio, of a beauty so fragile in appearance, once again became the group's mascot. The training was as hard as the living conditions. At dawn, they had to rush to cut the blocks of ice that would satisfy the encampment's water needs that evening, after grueling marching and combat simulation drills lasting the entire day. A few hours of rest, after some watery soup, and at dawn the next day it started all over again. And yet Curzio the individualist, the loner, would for his entire life maintain a profound, almost nostalgic affection for that unrepeatable experience, in which the life of each soldier was bound to that of his comrades. Before long he

---

*Colonel Del Mancino was responsible for the command of the unit. The Fifty-First Regiment, together with the Fifty-Second (Colonel Trulla), constituted the Alpine Brigade, under the command of General Teodorico Serra. See the excellent website https://www.frontedolomitico.it/.

would come under enemy fire, and in fact he would serve as a common soldier for two years of fierce fighting on the Dolomite front: the Col di Lana (Buchenstein), dubbed the "col of blood," which the Italians occupied on April 17, 1916, after having set off an eleven-thousand-pound mine there, producing an immense crater still visible today; the Marmolada massif, where the Austrians (in fact, mostly Hungarians and Croats) dug out a veritable city under the glacier, with dozens of miles of underground tunnels; as well as Pescoi, Monte Sief, Cengia Martini on Lagazuoi, the Falzarego Pass, Son Pauses, Monte Piana, the Tre Cime di Lavaredo, the Croda Rossa, and the Sentinella Pass.

Today you can in fair weather hike most of the front line, leaving early in the morning from Cortina d'Ampezzo and returning in the evening, at cocktail hour, to the luxurious lodges of that ski paradise. Along the way, you can make stops at the numerous cemeteries lovingly cared for by inhabitants of the valley and military associations and always blanketed with fresh flowers, sending a thought and leaving a flower to the veterans of both sides who, just over a century ago, were frozen, amputated, overwhelmed by snowstorms, buried by avalanches, flattened in ravines under mules and baggage trains, torn apart by explosions, poisoned by water from corpse-infested streams, blinded by the winter sun, driven crazy or to suicide by the never-ending slaughter, reconciled only in the "fraternity of death."

Curzio was one of them, one of the most anonymous: few traces have come down to us of that period that was perhaps the most extraordinary, because the most *normal*, of his life. We know only that he was always impeccable in appearance, "neat as a pin."[49] His first experiences were terrible, however, the same as for all his fellow soldiers, as he wrote to his brother Sandro:

How can I, with the two postcards they give us, write to everyone? You will, of course, ask me how the war is going up here. Very well. Naturally, given the very difficult conditions presented by the terrain, our progress is slow. By force of bayonet. From time to time the Austrians attempt to counterattack, but we always repel them, with tremendous losses. The trouble is they have so many, too many machine guns. The other day I left the trench to try to recover an engineer corps lieutenant's corpse. It was infernally dark, but as soon as they saw me they started firing with machine guns. Bullets whistled inches from my head. Then the colonel called me back, saying he didn't want to sacrifice me. It would have to be done some other time. And now I sign off with a kiss. Write to me. Your brother Curtino.[50]

The soldier clung daily to the hope of surviving; but the writer cut his teeth on the margins of battle. Curzio sent brief journalistic dispatches to military papers and wrote some rather middling patriotic poems.[51] Was it then that he began to make notes for his first real book? Nearly all the significant testimonies of the Great War were born in this way, from Marinetti to Hemingway, by way of Barbusse, Montherlant, Jünger, Ungaretti, Trakl, Remarque, Aldington, Graves, and so many others.[52] But how can we explain the intimate transformation of a promising student, still caught up in school speech contests, into a mature, fully formed writer, alive to his own merits and defects, endowed with an originality of tone he would maintain for the rest of his career? In the absence of a sufficient explanation, let us point out just two events that would play a crucial role: the breakthrough on the Italian front, in October 1917, and his new departure for France, the following spring.

"UNABLE TO DO OTHERWISE, WE PERFORMED MIRACLES"

In early fall 1917, Cadorna conquered, at the cost of unprecedented losses and sacrifices, a few strategic peaks and two-thirds of the Friulian plain. But this progression dangerously extended communication lines between corps. For the imperial army it was at this point essential to reverse the situation. If all the warring parties had already been weakened by epidemics, desertions, and mutinies, the Austrians for their part had to confront another mortal threat. The propaganda of the irredentist parties of all the nationalities in the empire had intensified, with the support of the Entente countries. The Czechs and the Croats, above all, who had created governments-in-exile in Paris, called openly for the dissolution of the empire; meanwhile, Bolshevik propaganda flooded into the West, after the collapse of czarist Russia in the February Revolution. The strategic situation likewise evolved at the expense of the Central Powers, notwithstanding the victories in East Prussia, Galicia, and Romania, because the naval economic blockade had shut off supplies from the Atlantic. The United States' entry into the war, which would drag nearly all of Latin America with it, was by now inevitable and brought Entente victory into view. The French commander in chief, Pétain, understood it well: after the disaster of his predecessor, Nivelle, in the Second Battle of the Aisne, in April 1917, he decided to move as little as possible, in anticipation of American reinforcements, thus becoming the most popular, not to say the only popular, Allied commander among the troops.*

The Italians, too, thought the war of position could transform into a war of attrition, but it was a miscalculation, one that threatened

---

*A reputation that would prove useful to him a little over twenty years later, when, in June 1940, he became the man of the armistice and of collaboration with the Germans, in a France once again on the brink of collapse.

to ruin them. The Austro-Hungarian army had as a matter of fact passed under German control. Hindenburg and Ludendorff, the "Orientalists" who had crushed Russia, managed to gain the trust of the German emperor Wilhelm II. From 1916 on they ran the General Staff with an iron fist, after having pushed aside "Occidentalists" like Falkenhayn, responsible for the setback at Verdun. They knew that their Habsburg ally, especially after the death of the venerated emperor Franz Joseph and the accession to the throne of the timid and pious Charles I (later beatified), had become the weak link in the alliance. They then turned to the Italian front as a proving ground for the "win or perish" offensive that they would launch the next year in France. Unified command was entrusted to Ludendorff's deputy, Otto von Below, architect of the Masurian Lakes triumph over Russia and perhaps the greatest strategist of the entire First World War.

On October 24, 1917, the Austro-German Fourteenth Army swept over the Italian Second Army, a bloated and ill-disposed organism on an excessively fragmented front running through Caporetto, today Kobarid, in Slovenia. It was the twelfth and final battle of the Isonzo. Below's plan was simple, of truly Napoleonic audacity: to strike a mortal blow at the center, followed by the advance of two lateral cupping movements to collect the spoils, like the pincers of a gigantic crab. It was a disaster aggravated by adverse weather and by the collapse of the back lines, all the more unforgivable since some Croatian deserters had revealed the broad strokes of the enemy action. The ambulance driver Ernest Hemingway, who was not there, knew how to provide a sufficiently truthful description of it, in *A Farewell to Arms*, that the book was banned in Fascist Italy. Having lost the Isonzo and all of Friuli, the Italians managed to consolidate their positions on the Piave, the "river sacred to the fatherland," at the conclusion of a retreat that allowed them to save the essential part of the Third and Fourth Armies. But the Second, the backbone of the entire deployment, was annihilated. If the numbers of dead and wounded were roughly the same on each side and represented only a fraction of the victims of the Second Battle of the Aisne or Verdun (thirty thousand men for the Italians, versus twenty thousand for the attackers), the losses in deserters, prisoners, and matériel were enormous.

It was what we would call today a humanitarian crisis, with almost thirty thousand civilians fleeing before the enemy or chased from their villages. Panic, fed by an obsession with presumed enemy atrocities—like those of the German Uhlans, who skewered women and children in Belgium and France, almost entirely "fake news" but widely believed at the time—was an ancillary cause of the disaster, because it contributed to blocked roads and interrupted the remaining communication lines. The Austro-Germans obtained the advantage they had pursued in vain for over two years, penetrating more than ninety miles into Italian territory. They arrived at the entrance to the Po Valley and threatened to sever the Milan–Venice axis. One more push and Italy would be out of action. In the collective memory Caporetto thus became "the mother of all defeats," in an exaggeration to which the socialists, the Communists, and even the Fascists contributed from time to time to discredit the old ruling classes—this without taking into account the war of the generals, who for years pathetically blamed each other for the defeat, from one committee of inquiry to another. In reality, the episode was just one of a series of colossal errors committed by all the commands involved in the Great War, some sooner, some later, from Ypres to Gallipoli, from the Yser to the Somme, pointlessly sacrificing their troops. All this would have a notable influence on the moral decadence and disorder of the postwar period and on the rise of radical movements on the extreme right and extreme left.

Curzio, who would later often be accused of inventing episodes in which he did not participate, was a trustworthy observer of these events, and indeed a minor protagonist. The Alpine Brigade achieved marvels of daring, losing almost half of its forces. For its trouble, as soon as the brigade had taken up its position on the new lines, it had to immediately return to the attack to repel another enemy breach. Curzio participated in all these actions and once again did his part with courage, honoring his newly obtained rank of lieutenant. But the worst—or the best—was yet to come.

In April 1918, when the Italian front had finally stabilized after a further two battles to hold the line, attention shifted again to the western front. The Germans had just launched the spring offensive "Operation Michael." Below, urgently recalled from the Italian theater, was charged by Ludendorff with repeating the triumph of Caporetto. In late May, the German attack near Reims opened up a wide gap in the Franco-British lines: the nightmare of September 1914 was happening again; Paris was threatened once more. The Italian government sent an expeditionary force of twenty-five thousand men, under the command of General Albricci, which took up a position between Reims, Épernay, and Châlons-sur-Marne, substituting for a British army group decimated by fighting. Included in the force were the soldiers of the Alpine Brigade. They did not even have time to prepare fortifications before the Germans attacked, on June 23 and 24, in the forests of Bligny, near the mouth of the river Ardre. The attacks were repelled by Italian special forces wielding bayonets, but the respite would be brief. On July 15, following a violent barrage, the enemy assault troops, the famous *Sturmtruppen*, which counted Ernst Jünger among their most wounded and decorated members, went on the offensive in the Bois des Éclisses. It was hand-to-hand combat, according to the description Curzio would give of it twenty years later, in the notes accompanying the poem "I morti di Bligny giocano a carte" (Bligny's dead are playing cards). It is a deeply moving text, throbbing with sincerity, as indeed is nearly everything Malaparte dedicated to "his" war, scattered across several volumes, from *Fughe in prigione* (Escapes in prison) to *Mamma marcia*. If the style is already typically Malapartian, all the details, for once, are authentic and verifiable:

> During the night of July 14–15 a horrible firestorm was unleashed upon our lines. Von Mudra, *der Argonnengeneral*, had concentrated against us, across a front barely three miles wide, more than two thousand shells. It was a massacre. Sitting on the grass, leaning against tree trunks, in a terrain without trenches, without communication paths, without shelters, we got ourselves killed out in the open, smoking one cigarette after another. At dawn, when the *Sturmtruppen* attacked the Bois des Éclisses pass with tanks, our forces were reduced by half. All the battalion commanders were dead. Of every two machine guns, one was out of commission. The French, English, and Americans had antitank rifles. We Italians had none. Unable to do otherwise, we performed miracles. Eventually we had the idea of setting fire to the woods in front of the tanks, which were then forced to turn around, for fear of the gas tanks exploding. We fought amid the flames. We waited for reinforcements that couldn't reach us because the Germans, having broken the line held by two battalions of Senegalese on our left flank, had sneaked in behind us.

Cut off and taking fire in the back from all sides as we were, our soldiers held out courageously, nonetheless. We hadn't eaten for twenty-four hours. It was impossible to evacuate the wounded without them falling into German hands. As evening came on we had almost no cartridges left, and no hand grenades. The St. Étienne machine guns lacked belts; the FIATS' magazines were empty. The battle dragged on through the night. The morning of the 16th, new German troops entered the fray, determined to finish the job, preceded by a violent mustard-gas bombardment. Our masks, old and all in poor condition, couldn't protect us, and soon all that could be heard in the immense forest was the gasps of the dying. From two to four in the afternoon we repelled nineteen German assaults and made seven counterattacks with bayonets. In command of the Ninety-Fourth flamethrower section, I managed to do a bit of good. The hand grenades hanging from the German soldiers' belts, in contact with the flames, exploded. Around sunset, Anglo-French artillery arrived in reinforcement, and, forgetting that we too wore gray-green, like the Germans, started firing upon us. Notwithstanding everything, we held fast, and the Germans did not pass. The next day, when a Scottish army corps finally showed up to give us a hand, Ludendorff's offensive was already broken, von Mudra's troops falling back on Fère-en-Tardenois.[53]

The battle continued until July 24. The final toll was heavy: an entire division wiped out, almost five thousand dead, four thousand wounded. The Italian soldiers' conduct was cited as exemplary by Pétain: "On July 15, 1918, on the flanks of Reims Mountain, the Second Italian Corps contributed with its heroics to barring the Germans from the road to Épernay." Curzio was decorated by the

Italians with the bronze medal and by General Guillaumat, commander of the French Fifth Army, with the Croix de Guerre with palms. He also earned a pulmonary lesion, which would seal his fate, thirty-nine years later, in a Roman clinic. But he was through with the trenches.

In the early 1950s, however, Malaparte returned there to show a seventeen-year-old family friend the woods where he had fought. Once there he could not resist recounting one of the fabulous stories in his repertoire:

> When I was injured and brought, nearly unconscious, to the infirmary, a dog followed me, a mongrel in which I spotted the descendant of the purest breed of Afghan greyhounds. The dog remained faithfully at my bedside for days, gazing at me with such intense and pure love that once the doctor asked me, exasperated, "But for God's sake, Suckert, why is this dog staring at you from morning to dawn?" To which I replied: "But can't you see, Captain, the dog is blind, and its eyes have been replaced by two lapis lazuli given to me by an Indian maharaja."[54]

A Young Man in Revolt

The German offensive would finally be halted in mid-August; meanwhile, General Albricci named Curzio his adjutant, subsequently entrusting him, at war's end, with writing the official history of the Italian expeditionary force. He set to work in Saint-Hubert, Belgium, where the Italian forces were stationed to await repatriation, in late January 1919—all of them except the Alpine Brigade, which would be sent to the Rhineland, in accordance with interallied agreements, to remain until August. Upon his arrival in Germany, however, Curzio managed to get himself assigned to the Italian delegation to the Supreme War Council and left for Paris and Versailles. The long and complex peace negotiations were a privileged vantage point for a bright young man on the make. The soldier quickly became a budding diplomat. He refined his French, studied English and also Russian, which he would always boast of knowing better than he really did. Later, he would claim to have met the Big Four—Wilson, Clemenceau, Lloyd George, and Orlando—whom he probably saw only from a distance, maintaining as well that he attended the signing of the Treaty of Versailles (as long as he was there, why didn't he sign it himself?). In any case, he soon grew tired of military history; his preparatory work would be brought to completion a few years later by a staff officer, in a piece of work already poisoned by Fascist rhetoric.[55] The real book that Curzio would draw from his experience of the front has nothing edifying or commemorative about it; if anything, it's the opposite, starting with the title, or with the two titles that he would choose in 1921: *Viva Caporetto!* for the private edition, which appeared in Prato at his own expense; then, with a mite more prudence, *La rivolta dei santi maledetti* (The revolt of the cursed saints), for the commercial edition, published immediately afterward in Rome, which was nonetheless impounded.[56]

Viva Caporetto!—which Malaparte would after World War II describe as a "quite unfortunate" title[57]—is a text that struck readers then, and still strikes us today, for its rejection of bellicist rhetoric, especially when we recall that the author was a twenty-year-old who had known nothing but boarding school and war. The leap in quality with respect to the conventional efforts of a few years earlier is startling: a writer was born, with his anger, his expressive violence, his

Célinian turpitude at times. It was also an epochal phenomenon. The conflict caused an entire generation to grow up too fast: its members, having survived the trenches, would sink into a dismay that the most extremist postwar tendencies would feed on. Millions of young recruits discovered, behind the rhetorical veil of a purportedly patriotic war, that "it's the truth of things that's mad."[58] From this would come an abundant literature, confessional and aggressive in the extreme, pitiless in its hatred for shirkers and profiteers, viscerally "other" and "anti-," estranged in its every fiber from the Europe that had launched itself with shameful heedlessness into the "wicked dance," as magisterially evoked by Thomas Mann at the end of *The Magic Mountain*. Be this literature pacifist or bellicist, socialist or nationalist, realist or surrealist, idealist or mechanist, it finds its common denominator in the rejection of bourgeois certainties, seeing as how the middle classes, holders of political power and arbiters of moral values in the pre-1914 society, had failed miserably.

After the Great War the cleavage became even more pronounced. The Versailles system—in which neither defeated Germany, nor Bolshevik Russia, nor even, soon, the neo-isolationist United States, saw its interests reflected—quickly revealed its cracks. A fearful, improvised diplomacy failed to offer a solid basis for a continental peace, one that, according to historian and witness Jacques Bainville's prophetic formula, would quickly turn out to be "too harsh in its mild aspects, too mild in its harsh aspects." The old politicians, lacking the genius for mediation displayed a century earlier at the Congress of Vienna by Talleyrand and Castlereagh, Humboldt and Metternich, sought in vain to stem the rage of the young and the hunger for justice among peoples. As Wilson, Lloyd George, and Clemenceau bent over the map to determine the fate of Anatolia, a young English diplomat with a brilliant future, Harold Nicolson, shook with impotent fury: "It is appalling, those three ignorant and irresponsible men cutting Asia Minor to bits as if they were dividing a cake... Isn't it terrible—the happiness of millions being decided in that way?" he wrote to his wife, Vita Sackville-West. It would be one of the reasons he abandoned the career to dedicate himself to journalism and literature, even as later he often lamented his choice.[59]

Rebellion manifested itself in Curzio with a striking clarity of contour: he already knew how to juggle opposing elements, discomfiting readers even as he attracted them.[60] Often cited is the precedent of Henri Barbusse's *Under Fire*, winner of the 1916 Prix Goncourt, which Curzio read closely either in Belgium or at Versailles. There are entire passages in the Italian's book that recall Barbusse, or another pacifist writer like Arnold Zweig, two authors who would soon gravitate into the Communist orbit.

> When the infantryman realizes he doesn't hate the enemy and isn't hated by him, when he notices that in each camp aversion to the war is equally fierce... a profound change occurs in his primitive mentality... his hate turns back against those who had cried, "Bring on the war!" and then holed up in the interior of the country... all those who, neutralists, interventionists, or quietists, did not share with him the labors and dangers of the trenches. (VC, 50)

This hypocrisy prompted in him mordant, mocking brushstrokes, heralding the nightmares of *Mamma marcia*, thirty years later:

> The people of the trenches hated the ladies of the Red Cross, all ribbons and smiles and picture postcards and little flags... who,

every time an infantryman thanked them for a cup of broth or coffee and a postcard with the king or Cadorna on it, would exclaim, happy and moved, "Poor little soldier!" without knowing that the good, sweet little soldier, returning to his troop train cattle car, would say to the others: I found two whores in that shack who gave me some broth and a postcard! (VC, 78–79)

But *Viva Caporetto!* also shows an affinity with another book coming out of the war, from a completely different perspective. In *Storm of Steel*, another twenty-year-old, Ernst Jünger, proudly affirms the sacrifice of an entire generation. A detailed comparison between the two works would be revealing. The two young "veterans" are the same age and have the same ingenuousness or fundamental chastity before existence, the same disgust with those remaining on the sidelines, the same detachment from suffering humanity, and the same need to belong to a group, to feel in solidarity with a higher cause. We will return to this analogy between them, regarding the analysis of totalitarianism that Malaparte would sketch out in the 1930s. But other things separate them. The German did not question the men and the values that guided the conduct of the war, even if it ended in defeat. He directed his contempt at the democratic, socialist, or republican "internal enemy," who had not allowed the soldier to carry out his task to the full.[61] The Italian railed instead against the politicians and generals who had sent soldiers to be massacred, even if the war ended in victory, and denounced the sclerotic hierarchies, the lying appeals that had deceived young men and played upon the purity of their ideals. If Curzio saluted the self-sacrifice of his comrades and described their silent, surly, or resigned heroism, above all he wanted to pay homage, as Malraux would say in *The Walnut Trees of Altenburg*, to those "who had waged war without loving it."[62] This desire to save the soldier, the alive and thinking simple man, from the "mechanized death that indifferently continues its work" (VC, 35) contrasts with the absolute, automated, mechanistic duty of a Jünger or, in another vein, a Marinetti. It contrasts as well with the Nietzschean and D'Annunzian superman, with the Barresian cult of blood, pleasure, and death. Lacking deep humanistic values, Curzio already expressed himself as a realist, and this realism, if often deformed by an irrepressible imagination, would remain one of the strongest characteristics of his style.[63]

Why, then, these provocative titles, and who are the "cursed saints" in question? For starters: out of a taste for mockery and to get himself talked about. Curzio had already become Malaparte, a few years ahead of his official choice of pseudonym. It wasn't enough for him to stir the pot and attract attention; he aimed, from his first book, for a succès de scandale. He glorified the revenge of the "army's proletariat" against the obtuse order and discipline imposed by an inept high command, unable to redeem the sufferings and sacrifice of their troops with a great victory over the enemy. The deserters, plunderers, and fugitives who threw away their rifles to head back down into the Po Valley become paradoxically the victorious masses; they want "to smash everything" in order to transform the imperialist war into a rebellion against the ruling classes. They've not suffered a defeat, they've provoked it, and now they're truly about to turn the tide of the conflict, by seizing power. But this mortal danger leads the reactionary forces to close ranks; on the brink of collapse, the dying Italy of the past regains strength and with its last reserves of energy crushes the insurgents, who have not been guided by a sufficient number of authentic revolutionary leaders. The conflict, however, is only deferred: a fresh blow and the system will shatter.

Here Curzio is combining two phenomena that did not have a direct causal connection: the Bolshevik Revolution took place in early November, according to the Gregorian calendar, while the breach of the Italian front occurred, as discussed, on the preceding October 24. In the latter case, there was a military rout provoked by panic before an enemy of crushing technical superiority, rather than by political motivations; in the former, the ancien régime had collapsed like rotten fruit and an elite of professional revolutionaries was on the point of imposing itself on the masses and taking over as leaders. When Malaparte was writing his book, Russia was still in the midst of a civil war whose outcome remained uncertain. Already this revealed his taste for forcing the historical evidence to his own ends, in accordance with a tendency he would display from then on. Because the lesson of Caporetto was exactly the opposite. The dimensions and suddenness of the defeat provided the jolt the country needed to rise again, finally changing its approach to the war. The commander in charge, General Diaz, applied the lesson of Pétain: save the greatest possible number of men, avoiding deadly and useless frontal attacks. Diaz was able to patiently consolidate the new positions, on a front that was both smaller and easier to manage—the plains, finally, instead of the mountains!—in essentially defensive maneuvers, forcing the enemy to attack in the open, wearing it down with deep counterattacks. The country came together in a spirit entirely unknown in its recent history, one that it would no longer be able to draw on during the Second World War. Not only did "the revolt of the cursed saints" not provoke the collapse of the home front, but the stampede toward the back lines was stopped at a relatively contained human cost, contrary to the ruthless repression described in the book.* Two-thirds of the 750 executions carried out in accordance with military justice between 1915 and 1918, in an army numbering more than five million men, took place before, and not after, Caporetto, even as one must add numerous summary executions in cases of looting, mutiny, and so on.

The misunderstanding is even more evident if we consider just who were the heroes exalted by the young author. His true protagonists, the true "cursed saints," were not the soldiers left to fend for themselves in a disorderly flight, which as an ex-combatant he could not, despite everything, fail to judge severely. They are the frontline officers, like him, who really held the line's fate in their hands; they are "the valiant officers of the trenches, the good Franciscans, the shepherds of the people" (VC, 109), who witnessed the rout with heavy hearts, swearing it would be the last. Without them, without a new type of aristocracy to take the place of the one deposed by history, the revolutionary ardor was destined to die out. The masses would become once again the inert cannon fodder of before Caporetto. And it is here that we see emerge the social pessimism that would pervade Malaparte up through Fascism and beyond. In the face of the myth of proletarian internationalism exalted by the Bolshevik revolution, Curzio turned to the nation. The book's last page is already a veritable manifesto of Fascist insurrection, not against the fatherland, but in the name of its redemption:

*Or in a film like Francesco Rosi's *Many Wars Ago* (*Uomini contro*, 1970), based on a memoir by the former volunteer officer Emilio Lussu, in which antiwar ideology prevails over historical truth and alters the message and content of the book.

This shall be the encounter of two revolutions: Italy's, dominated by individualism, and Russia's, dominated by collectivism. Fascism versus Bolshevism. I have faith in our Christ: Italian, Catholic, armed with cross and sword. Our Christ knows how to resist evil. He will prevail. (VC, 109)

And thus, with this dialectic reversal, a work born of the dissolution of the established order closes with an apologia for a new national order: militarized, pure and hard, even more implacable than its predecessor. Curzio, the erstwhile young republican who refused to enter Prato Cathedral with the tricolor, throws in Christ's banner to boot, skipping over the entire anticlerical tradition of the Risorgimento, over the nation's unity obtained by tearing Rome away from the pope. We could almost believe he already had in mind a reconciliation with the church, achieved by Mussolini with the Concordat of 1929... But for now our attention turns to the development of the Fascist movement, because it is here that the "cursed saints" would contend with the technique of the coup d'état.

In Search of a Role

At the close of the peace conference, Curzio managed to obtain a new transfer, this time to Warsaw. He was made an attaché to the Italian legation in the Polish capital, which was once again independent but now threatened by the Red Army of Marshal Tukhachevsky. It was a doubly exciting choice, offering him not only another chance to see history up close; by this point, he had also acquired a taste for the diplomatic life. It could even be called an infatuation, and later he would gladly pass himself off as "the youngest Italian diplomat."[64]

THE BEGINNINGS OF A BONAPARTE (1898–1924)

Diplomats are cited often in his work, generally in rather flattering ways, and the feeling was mutual—as long as he remained outside their ranks, as would be seen later, when Malaparte sought to be named an ambassador. But let us return to Warsaw: What exactly were his duties? Malaparte always claimed to have occupied a diplomatic post, which we would happily grant him, as the majority of his biographers have, but which, alas, does not show up in the Ministry of Foreign Affairs' annual report. Even if Curzio had been removed from office following the publication of *Viva Caporetto!*— he came to claim this as well[65]—his service record and the date of his layoff or retirement should appear in the aforementioned report, known affectionately as the "book of books" by career officials, who are probably its only and at the same time its most careful readers. Nor does his name appear in records of the competitive examination for officials he claimed to have won in September 1919. The more prosaic reality is that "the reserve infantry lieutenant Erisch Suchert [*sic*], after gaining authorization from the Presidency of the Council of Ministers, was placed at the disposal of the Royal Ministry of Foreign Affairs and dispatched to Warsaw" for a year, from September 25, 1919, to September 29, 1920, on which date he signed the standard statement of cessation of duties.[66] His job, according to the report in his service record, was that of secretary to the mission leader, "tasked with ciphering and copying." It follows that he would not subsequently be in a position to either resign or be barred from a career into which he had never entered.*

---

*Many years later he would tell a young family friend not to hesitate to enter diplomatic service, if he liked it: "I too liked that life, that atmosphere that, however, I breathed for too short a time" (testimony of Onofrio Solari Bozzi to the author).

The thing has little importance in itself, but it betrays a certain snobbism, a taste for high society, that seems hardly to accord with the call to egalitarianism and antibourgeois revolution he preached in his writings. But it is also proof of that capacity to live and evolve in different contexts, to be one thing and its opposite, which would be at the base of his reputation as a "chameleon." In the Polish capital he discovered there was not only war and beautiful death; there was also the good life. Warsaw was the test bed for his first loves—was he still a virgin at the time? It's possible—and for his first duels, which, however, had nothing to do with women. He also found time to apply himself in the hall of arms with the athletic apostolic nuncio, Monsignor Ratti, the future Pope Pius XI. Curzio had an aptitude for fencing, and his powerful but agile musculature, rapid reflexes, supple joints, courage, and discipline would for twenty years make him a formidable swordsman. It would be the only sport he truly pursued, along with a bit of cycling and mountaineering; soccer, on the contrary, would always leave him cold. Even more remarkable: he did not seem attracted to flight and aviation, which had swiftly caught on among the "valiant knights" of the Great War. And if in the 1950s he could be seen driving American sports cars, it was essentially to cultivate his fleeting reputation as a man of the cinema.

Malaparte would always remain tied to Poland, in part perhaps thanks to the possible Polish origins of his paternal family. Did he actually witness, as he would later claim, the "miracle on the Vistula" that allowed Piłsudski's troops to chase away the Red Army from the doors of the capital in August 1920? Was it really then that he first saw the Bolshevik war machine in action, ready to storm into the West with "oceanic" impetus? It is difficult—or rather, as it stands, impossible—to confirm such a thing. Back in Rome, he returned to service in the Ministry of War and enrolled in a law program, having earned his secondary-school degree during the war, in a session set up specially for combatants. But he found his legal studies much less interesting than journalism and politics, even if he didn't yet know which direction to pursue. In 1921 he left the army for good: all roads were open to him, and none.

It was a period of hesitation, uncertainty, and illusions, as it was throughout Europe for millions of other demobilized young men who no longer knew how to orient themselves in civilian life. He would subsequently speak about the time only rarely, as if it were a bad memory. It was also a period of straitened circumstances, every day a matter of weighing lunch against dinner. His diet was already the one he would remain faithful to later, even when he could afford to move on from neighborhood trattorias to upscale restaurants: hardly any pasta or other starchy food, to which he preferred Tuscan minestras, fish if available, or a little bit of meat (he had a weakness for roast suckling pig, in spite of his love for animals), salads generously dressed with garlic and olive oil, fruit, everything washed down with a glass of Chianti, which he generally left unfinished, or mixed with water. No bread, sweets, coffee, or spirits.

At the cost of sacrifices in his diet, about which he cared little, he managed to look after his appearance, about which he already cared a great deal: slicked-back hair, face smooth as marble, thin mustache that came and went, a disenchanted attitude, the pose of the dandy typical of the carefree 1920s, after the austerity of war: thus we find him in a famous portrait by the Italo-Hungarian Ghitta Carell, the most celebrated society photographer between the two wars. Malaparte was pleased to cite the anecdote of the king of Spain, Alphonse XIII, known for his slovenliness and tobacco use, who one day asked a gentleman of his court: "Tell me, how much time do you require for your morning routine?" "Two hours, *Señor*." "Strange. It takes me twenty minutes." "It shows, *Señor*." He would later employ up to three hours.[67] He lived, and would do so for years, in furnished rooms, owned just two suits ("one of camel hair, the other of gray flannel,"[68] always perfectly ironed), and very carefully chose his ties, for which he had a genuine passion.*

With his good looks and elegant reserve, he stood out among the regulars of the third room of the Caffè Aragno on the Corso, a gathering spot for intellectuals of the capital. It was his brief but far from insignificant Roman bohemian period. There Curzio met two soon-to-be-separated brothers, Giorgio de Chirico and Alberto Savinio, becoming attached especially to the latter, of whose work he would become an avid collector. In one corner would sit Pirandello, sipping his insomniac's glass of cold milk and awaiting the dawn, surrounded by his actors, for him the only reality of a world that didn't exist. He'd bump into the marquess painter Filippo de Pisis, gentle and rouged, in search of a sailor or bricklayer to brutalize him; or Vincenzo Cardarelli, "the greatest dying poet," sunk day and night in the same armchair, wrapped in his coat, hat on head, two blankets on his lap, under the searing Roman sun. And then there was Anton Giulio Bragaglia, inventor of the "theater of the revolution" and "synthetic theater," who had already authored the legendary *Index Rerum Virorumque Prohibitorum*, ridiculing the list of books prohibited by the Holy Office, and his two brothers, the actor Arturo and the filmmaker

---

*He confided a strange theory of his to Biancamaria Fabbri: "Woe to anyone wearing a new tie; your friends won't forgive you." Perhaps for this reason, he was one of the first, in the second postwar period, to wear a turtleneck under a jacket.

THE BEGINNINGS OF A BONAPARTE (1898–1924)

Carlo Ludovico, who would die a centenarian after having anticipated the spaghetti western and shot memorable films in other genres, including *The Queen of Babylon*, *The Loves of Hercules*, and *Desert Furlough*. Plus models, dancers, suffragettes, fortune tellers, prophets of the occult and vegetarianism, transvestites, and some of the first out lesbians, dressed in masculine attire and sporting monocles.

Among them moved a smiling, chubby young man who tried to adopt a military bearing in homage to his father, a sea dog and war hero, and who spent his nights filing news items or proofreading for the capital's newspapers. Curzio sympathized with this "Toscanello" from Livorno, who would never forget him. His name was Galeazzo Ciano. Both of them dreamed of becoming great playwrights and both religiously gathered the indecipherable pieces of paper that Pirandello tossed away with his cigarette butts. At the Aragno, Curzio rediscovered older friends from the Florentine group like Prezzolini, Palazzeschi, and Soffici, but not Dino Campana, who was already shut up in the psychiatric hospital where he would die twenty years later. He read a great deal, refined his style, wrote dutifully bad poetry that he would later disavow, tried to launch his own *ism*, "Oceanism," complete with manifesto and a magazine predictably called *Oceanica*, studded with citations drawn from all over the map and pompous proclamations such as "We are against the bourgeoisie and against every manifestation of that bourgeois spirit that introduced into men's lives the democratic concept of mediocrity." And, imitating the Marinettian oracles but shifting to the left, he proclaimed in all modesty:

> Oceanism is the most modern artistic-philosophical movement in Europe; in every country, in Paris, in Germany, in Czechoslovakia,

in Poland, and in Russia, our group already has a great many active followers who, gathered in Groups, are working on the reconstitution of the socialist international: in France, the Clarté group, captained by Henry [*sic*] Barbusse, is nothing if not a manifestation of Oceanism.[69]

No one, or almost no one, took him seriously. The Futurists, above all, understood that deep down he didn't give a damn about artistic coteries and avant-garde theories. What he wanted was to win over the wider public. Malaparte would always have the greatest contempt for "ivory towers" and for the devotees of art for art's sake, even if he loved to play, when necessary, the misunderstood-and-persecuted-artist card. To earn a living and to make a name for himself, he wrote for every possible outlet. Through the intermediary of Alberto Cianca, one of the rare anti-Fascist intellectuals who would always remain friendly to him, he contributed to *Il Mondo*, founded by the liberal Giovanni Amendola, who three years later would become one of the regime's most famous victims.* Politically he was fumbling in the dark: still a member of the Italian Republican Party, his gaze strayed left to *L'Ordine Nuovo*, founded by Antonio Gramsci, who would be the first to saddle him with the chameleon label. He also met another agitator of ideas, coming from the liberal left, Piero Gobetti, a young prodigy from Turin. We'll talk about him again in the next chapter. But in the end Fascism won out: on

---

*Amendola was married to a polyglot Russian activist, writer, and translator, Eva Kühn, who later played a role, still debated by historians, in the complex relations between Fascist Italy and the Soviet Union in the 1920s. One of their sons, Giorgio, was until his death, in 1980, the acknowledged leader of the pro-Soviet wing of the Italian Communist Party.

THE BEGINNINGS OF A BONAPARTE (1898–1924)

September 20, 1922—a symbolic date, the anniversary of the Bersaglieri entering the Porta Pia breach and ending the popes' temporal power—just a month before the March on Rome, Curzio enrolled in the Florence branch of the Fascist Party.

With the Black Bands of the Revolution

After the Second World War, Malaparte tried to justify this choice, attributing it to his bewilderment and anger at the "anti-nation" of the socialists and Communists. His gesture would have represented a kind of resurgence of faith—naive and soon disappointed—in the future of the fatherland. Such an explanation is plausible, but insufficient. As with so many other young people disoriented by the war, it was above all a taste for adventure and a conviction that Fascism was going to win out that motivated his decision. And yet, he had never considered himself a classic man of the Right, and in fact he neither was then nor would ever be. His immediate choice was focused on Fascist syndicalism, the most radical and left-leaning wing of Mussolini's movement. If, like most of the young men who had come through the war, he wanted to turn his back for good on the "ruins of Giolittism" and the passivity of "Italietta," he no longer believed in the possibility of doing so while staying within the established order. One of his first poems dedicated to his fellow soldiers ends with a threat: "Be silent, Red Song, / and sit tight; it's time for / the fight-back."[70] Camaraderie with brothers-in-arms also played an important role here. In terms of the earliest Fascism, Curzio embraced the Jacobin—not to say revolutionary—tendency that attracted Futurists, republican syndicalists, former D'Annunzian

Fiume legionnaires, the marginalized, rebels, and the dissatisfied of every stripe, from former officers to anarchists, from the petite bourgeoisie to the underclass. Mussolini, in his audacity, was able to maneuver this heterogeneous mass to frighten the bien-pensants and convince them that he and he alone represented a bulwark between teetering order and rising revolution—whether from the Right or from the Left didn't matter. If it's true that early Fascism defended, generally speaking, agrarian and industrial interests against the socialist-Communist push, the phenomenon was considerably more complex than the image of simple street violence that has remained stuck to it.

The first, irregular Fascist militias, the *squadre d'azione* (literally, "action squads"), represented a reaction to the insurrectional climate favorable to Bolshevism not only in Italy but also in Germany, Austria, Hungary, and the rest of central Europe during the Biennio Rosso, the two "red" years (1919–20), leading most notably to the factory occupations in Turin, Milan, and Genoa in August–September 1920. What's more, the squads were composed largely of ex-combatants, ready for anything, the *Arditi* shock troops (whose distinctive black uniforms they would adopt as their own) and the *trinceristi*, or trench fighters (while on the left emerged formations of *Arditi del popolo*, or *Arditi* of the people). These weren't the fugitives of Caporetto, then, but the victors of the Piave, who rejected the postwar spirit of demobilization and antimilitarism, as if their sacrifice had been worse than useless, even blameworthy. These men had been formed by combat, and in many cases they hadn't known anything else; to ask them to return to classes or menial jobs, while getting spit on in the streets or having medals torn from their chest, was really too much. It's not by chance that the spread of the squads

THE BEGINNINGS OF A BONAPARTE (1898–1924)

was greatest in regions devastated by the war (Friuli, Veneto) and in those where elite troops had been recruited, such as Lombardy, Emilia, Romagna, Abruzzo, and of course Tuscany and Umbria, which had supplied the men of the Alpine Brigade. Conversely, squadrism was weakest in the regions most closely tied to the crown (Piedmont, Liguria, and, in part, Sardinia) and in southern Italy, less directly touched by the conflict, with the exception of Puglia. It was primarily owing to squad actions that two years of "black" reaction (1921–22) followed the Biennio Rosso, in an atmosphere of latent civil war. If, for Curzio, the squadrists became the new "cursed saints," it was because they were ready to take up arms again, this time to go all the way.

The squads' revolutionary—not to say openly insurrectional—tendency was proclaimed publicly by most of the squadrist leaders (called *ras* in picturesque homage to the Ethiopian feudal lords) at the rally of San Sepolcro, held on March 23, 1919, in the eponymous piazza in Milan, marking the birth of a party originally called, not for nothing, the Italian Fasces of Combat. The terminology may seem laughable now, but Fascism was a very serious phenomenon, determined to draw on a former glory it did not have and to establish its values in opposition to current ones. Before long the country counted two thousand branches of the Fasces, with three hundred thousand members. Gramsci was the first to warn against a schematization according to which Fascism was nothing but the henchman of reaction and capital, to which it owed its triumph and later its ruin. To see things in these terms is to disregard the undeniable originality and, in many respects, the primacy of Italian Fascism among antidemocratic movements of the twentieth century, and not only of the Right. It is to avoid historicizing Fascism and, in the case that interests us here, to risk not understanding Curzio's route from republicanism to Fascism, and later to anti-Fascism, by way of the trenches. Without the war, and its enormous cost to Italian society, there would have been no Fascism.

Is it overblown to see Curzio's choice as a new revolt against his father and against his provincial, bourgeois origins? In that still-fluid phase, he could have Fascist sympathies without falling into extremism, along with many of the officers and diplomats he mixed with, who saw in the Mussolinian movement a sort of muscular patriotism, which could be integrated into the traditional, monarchical order. They would become Fascists only when the king, after long hesitation, finally called Il Duce to government, becoming anti-Fascists when the king pushed him out of government, on July 25, 1943. But that wasn't the case for Curzio. What attracted him to Fascism was a profound social transformation in which he saw himself reflected and, at the same time, a need to run out to meet history.

We cannot retrace here, except in broad strokes, the itinerary that would transform Fascism from a movement rebelling against the system into an instrument for preserving and controlling the system. This took place in two roughly equal stages. The first went from 1919 to 1922, the year of the March on Rome, and would pave the way for the establishment of the regime and the gradual dissolution of parliament. The second centers on the crucial moment between the end of 1925 and the beginning of 1926, when Mussolini, having overcome the crisis provoked by the Matteotti murder (about which more soon), oversaw passage of the laws known as *fascistissime* (very Fascist), abolishing the last democratic safeguards. The squads, with few exceptions, would be disbanded or incorporated into the official Voluntary Militia for National Security between 1923 and 1925. The

THE BEGINNINGS OF A BONAPARTE (1898–1924)

Fasces' first platform, published on June 6, 1919, in *Il Popolo d'Italia*, Mussolini's new daily, was oriented decidedly toward the left. It spoke of nationalizations and job protections, denounced war profiteers, laid claim to an "anti-imperialist" foreign policy, and expressed a preference for the republican option. The platform was very committed to young people and the popular masses, calling for lowering the voting age to eighteen and for universal suffrage, with proportional representation and voting by list. But if the left-wing faction was essential in street battles, Mussolini quickly understood that he could not win power without shifting right, ensuring the support of the establishment—the army, the police, the landed estates—and reassuring capital and the Savoy dynasty. The electoral debacle of November 1919 made him understand the need to radically modify the San Sepolcro platform, break off negotiations with the socialists and syndicalists, and tactically seek out allies on the opposite side —in short, to normalize the movement. As early as the Second Congress of the Fasces, in June 1920, the republican option was abandoned and Mussolini publicly exalted the "colossal power" of the Vatican and the worldwide influence of Catholicism, clearing the way for the Concordat some ten years later. The National Fascist Party was born in November of the next year to rein in and abolish the Fasces, by which time the opposition had already been rendered harmless.

The struggle between Mussolini and the *ras* would last for another two or three years, but one after the other, they would be isolated and subjugated. Pragmatism, dynamism, and opportunism, instinct, passion, and calculation: these were the resources of the nascent Duce. But they were tactical resources, unaccompanied, behind the facade, by a long-term strategic vision. Ideology was nothing but a screen for conquest, then for the consolidation of power. Nonetheless, the ex-Socialist Mussolini, having become a *national* socialist in the proper sense of the term, would never change completely; he never became a reactionary, or even a hard-line conservative, in the vein of Franco, Salazar, or Horthy. He remained, deep down, an overambitious and potentially totalitarian revolutionary, even if, unlike Stalin or Hitler (whom he envied in this respect), he never wielded absolute power. On several occasions in the 1930s he would seek in more or less committed ways to recover the ideals of the movement—proletarian, collectivist, antibourgeois—to rebuild Italian society, but all these efforts would founder, even before the disastrous new war. Unlike the air force, in large part a creation of the regime, and the militia, the core of the nation's military—the army, navy, and carabinieri—would remain essentially, if secretly, monarchist rather than Fascist. This "dyarchy" of command would have lethal consequences on the conduct of the war between 1940 and 1943 and prepare the ground for the royal coup of July 25, 1943.

Mussolini also launched a program of "social hygiene," to combat the paralyzing influence of the family and "virilize" the new Italian men (while women remained marginalized). To this end he repeatedly returned to the watchwords of Futurism and of the Fiume legionnaires.[71] One example is how, in 1934, he authorized Alessandro Blasetti, a great precursor of neorealism and a friend to Malaparte, to shoot the official epic history of the squads: *The Old Guard*, a film strongly influenced by the Soviet cinema of Eisenstein and Pudovkin, was a tribute to national reconciliation, behind the still-current ideals of the Fascist revolution. Likewise, Mussolini entered the global conflict in 1940 aiming for a compromise peace—a bit as he had done in Munich two years earlier—between Hitler and the democracies, under the illusion that even a partial success could allow him to definitively install the regime and "Fascistize" Italy once and for all: an absurd bet, lost as soon as the war began, because the country refused to follow him.

Mussolini returned to the republican, statist, anticapitalist option, becoming the nearly powerless hostage of the resuscitated Blackshirts, "the old, faithful guard of the Fascist revolution,"[72] in the bitter epilogue of civil war (September 1943–April 1945) and the Italian Social Republic (a.k.a. the Republic of Salò), which some of its followers would have liked to have called the "Proletarian Fascist Republic." Salò had a short-lived constitution, the Verona Charter, which recuperated the essential points of the San Sepolcro platform, and so the circle closed, at the cost of great suffering and much fratricidal blood spilled in the war of liberation from Nazi Fascism. But we mustn't mistake Salò for a collaborationist postscript like any other, nor Mussolini for a Quisling, or even a Pétain. If it's true that it could not have lasted eighteen months without the military support of Hitler's Germany, its de facto master, neither can we speak of a regime born *solely* out of enemy occupation, as elsewhere in German-controlled Europe. Its roots were entirely Italian and Fascist. Thus Salò represented a sinister but genuine product of national history, whose logic resided not *solely* in the alliance with Nazi Germany but also in a return to the latent civil war of 1919–22.[73]

It's important to keep all this in mind in order to follow Curzio's trajectory. He determined with notable alacrity how to distance himself from Fascism-as-movement and yet travel the entire parabola of Fascism-as-regime, abandoning it at the moment of the Salò epilogue: a bit out of conviction, but also because loyalty was for him a very relative concept. For the moment, though, we are still at the beginning of this journey. His relatively minor role and his youth, far from harming him, represented an ace up his sleeve in the game being played: he could honestly present himself as the prototypical new man, born of the war and the first postwar age. Squadrism tempted him more for the battle of ideas than for the street brawls, and we already know that his taste for force was always accompanied by realism, allowing him to respond to the various scenarios that emerged along the way. In the face of Mussolini, uncontested leader not only of the party but also of the new Italy, D'Annunzio rose up, then backed down, by now fossilized and politically useless, although he did give Il Duce, some years later, his best advice: avoid the devil's pact with Hitler. Marinetti abandoned the party, then backtracked and became mired in academicism. Others were swept away. Malaparte, for his part, quickly learned to adapt to events.

In 1922, when Curzio opted for Fascist syndicalism, whose supporters clashed daily in the piazzas with leftist unions and working-class Catholics, he ran a considerable risk. He found adversaries inside as well as outside the party. Promised the leadership of Florence's Chamber of Labor, he was ousted after barely a month and a half, leading him to challenge the man allegedly responsible to a duel.[74] The D'Annunzian, republican, and socialist syndicalists prevailed, at a moment when Fascism needed above all to reassure the traditional ruling classes. Patriots and military men never forgave Malaparte for insulting the army in his first book, which he subjected to a few cuts in the 1923 edition, according to a practice that would become habitual for him. Was this a matter of substantive alterations, or simple stylistic touch-ups? Opinions differ.[75] In any case, he convinced neither yesterday's friends nor those he wished to make now. For the former he was a turncoat, while for the latter he was not sufficiently trustworthy. He was also shut out of the movement's control room, which saw the rise of men like Giuseppe Bottai, the future ideologue and minister of education, who would become perhaps the only "organic" intellectual of the Fascist era. The doors of newspapers, publishing houses, and theaters remained closed to him. He had energy, courage, and audacity in abundance, but struggled to find a place of his own. What's more, he had not participated in the March on Rome of October 28, 1922, and the first-person account he would give in *Technique* would be created out of whole cloth (T1, 183–90). For the time being, he settled for exalting it in overwrought, bombastic language:

> We Italians have created the Earth. We are the heroes of Genesis. The history of our national life is the history of the world. We are the fruit of all races. As Italy is the land of arrival and of fusion of all peoples, thus we are the perfected form, the vessel chosen to accommodate all bloods. We know now that we are great and mighty, capable of every glory and every cowardice, condemned to an irreparable and magnificent destiny. But that is not enough for us. We want to know whom we are born of, of what God or what beast, we who feel capable of every greatness and every infamy.[76]

In this way he sought to live down an absence that party hard-liners and purists would long hold against him.* His failure to participate

---

*The certificate, complete with band and dagger, of participation in the march ought to have marked out, in theory, the aristocracy of Fascism: "Fascist since the March on Rome" could be read on wedding invitations and death notices, a status that assured no material advantages, but a certain prestige. How many

in the march was all the stranger in that he took orders from Tullio Tamburini, among the most inveterate of squadrists. The Fascism of Emilia and Tuscany, and of Florence in particular, was perhaps the most violent in Italy, behind the refined and cosmopolitan image that the city evokes across the world. Often detached, ironic, anti-sentimental, the Tuscan can become cruel when the time comes: Tamburini, future police commander at Salò, would be living proof of this, while the "bloody poet" Alessandro Pavolini, the party's last secretary, would go down fighting, weapons in hand, against the partisans, and the Pisan Guido Buffarini Guidi, interior minister, would be executed at Liberation. Curzio quickly learned how to navigate in waters teeming with sharks and where today's ally could become tomorrow's enemy. Score settling was not uncommon among the different squads. On a few occasions he avoided a beating, if not worse, from his own comrades, and he kept a set of brass knuckles in his pocket, just in case.

In 1923, according to the first police reports, Curzio also enrolled in a Roman Masonic lodge, after having been rejected in two previous affiliation attempts.[77] Was this another way to step out of obscurity, out of the political fringes? His employment as a modest Fascist official would provoke no greater interest in us than that of the even more obscure Communist official Aragon in Moscow, some years later, if it had not been accompanied by an intense production

---

actual participants were there? Around twenty-six thousand, according to the historian Renzo De Felice. But the regime increased the number by several thousand individuals, often posthumously, to demonstrate the strength and prevalence of Fascism from its very beginnings. The fact that Malaparte did not obtain even an "honorary" credential of this sort was a sign of the enduring resistance to him in the party.

of articles, editorials, and appeals, today forgotten, and yet indispensable for understanding his evolution.[78] It was also the time when a profusion of newspapers, magazines, and sheets of all sorts (often short-lived) echoed the political conflicts inflaming the public from one end of the peninsula to the other. In this overheated atmosphere, with the piazzas filled with insults and accusations, as well as cudgel blows and, increasingly, pistol shots, Curzio stood out for his virulence in the hard-line press. The elegant, learned evocations of what went on behind the scenes of the peace conference or the Battle of Warsaw were forgotten, or rather set aside. Was it a way to get himself noticed by party leaders, to reassure its hard-liners? Certainly, but not only. From the moment he left the family home, in 1914, Curzio had never, as it were, laid down his arms: in a natural way, writing became a new kind of weapon for him, and so it would remain. If I have so far expressed reservations about Malaparte's commitment, the fact remains that, from beginning to end, writing was for him synonymous with combat, and only in combat did he feel alive. Even when he seemed to surrender to the life of the gentleman and to a luxury experienced without real pleasure, Curzio remained fundamentally a warrior and an ascetic: two terms that often provoked derision and incredulity in his time, and that perhaps do so even more today, and that nonetheless we cannot manage to separate from his person. For this man who despised normal feelings, who disdained the "derangement of the senses" of a Rimbaud, and who was fated to see fail, one after the other, all his attempts to obtain, or to maintain for long, a position of power, only the fusion of writing and combat would remain to justify an intensely savored existence.

A Squalid Affair

In the split within Fascism between hawks and doves, hard-liners and pragmatists, Curzio continued to line up stubbornly with the former. He took to the streets rarely, but he flooded the movement press with his writings, endorsing the most radical positions. The first government formed by Mussolini, after the March on Rome, included only three Fascist ministers: a reassuring gesture aimed at the other parties and at public opinion, which Hitler would imitate a dozen years later. But it was only a gesture. Day by day, Fascism eroded what remained of the parliamentary system. Mussolini, who had reserved for himself the portfolios of the Ministry of the Interior and of Foreign Affairs, directed the security forces to suppress, without involving himself personally, the last manifestations of opposition. He was conscious of still being politically fragile, because the party had only about twenty members of parliament; so close to the goal, he didn't want to squander his success through excessive haste. If the socialists and Communists were in decline by then, it was still necessary to reassure that gray zone of bien-pensants he had yet to win over, also for social reasons. Corporal Benito was—and would remain—at the margins of polite society and convention, like Lance Corporal Adolf. The king, Victor Emmanuel III, did not love him. That cold, ungrateful, intelligent little man, who for that matter did not love anyone, had accepted Fascism as the lesser evil; he had not forgotten that it had been an anarchist who killed his father, Umberto I, in 1900. On the other hand, he feared that his Aosta cousins, very popular since the Great War and separated from the Savoy by an old dynastic grudge, could arrange with the Fascists to seize the throne. Mussolini, then, had to keep the moderates from coalescing against him, and the monarchists from devouring Fascism, rather than the contrary. This is the reason he had yet to resolve to disband the squads.

That said, we mustn't interpret (too) literally certain written contributions by Curzio, notably in the columns of *La Conquista dello Stato*, the magazine he founded and edited from June 1924 to December 1928, in which he called for the greatest severity against adversaries and the undecided, in the name of "necessary extremism."[79] The question of this publication's financing is still controversial. Was there a discreet subvention from Mussolini, who according to Malaparte had even selected the magazine's title? It is possible, even probable, but not proven.[80] What is certain is that Il Duce already followed him with the distant and slightly contemptuous interest he reserved for all his collaborators. We don't know when the two met for the first time, but they were made to understand each other, within the limits to be pointed out in the next chapter. These violent, fanciful articles, in which Curzio plays at being a strategist and an ideologue, shed little light on what he was really looking for in Fascism. Certainly, to write incendiary texts without taking part in the worst episodes of violence is not necessarily an extenuating circumstance. *La Conquista dello Stato* was not, for that matter, a simple movement paper, but a proving ground for young talents, some of whom would later pass over to communism, such as Elio Vittorini, the future author of such anti-Fascist books as *Conversations in Sicily* (1941), who would not be kind to his benefactor in the postwar period.[81] Curzio had already revealed himself to be a remarkable talent scout, a role he would insist on claiming, with less and less success, nearly to the end of his life. But his work here was above all political, offering unconditional support to Mussolini in the form of constant nagging, an amorous shadowing that verged on threats. Just scan the editorial headlines: "Mussolini Declares Himself an Integralist. But When Will We Achieve Integral Fascism?" "Fascism against Mussolini?" "Everyone, Even Mussolini, Must Obey the Warning of Integral Fascism."[82] And so on.

The magazine's first issue appeared just as a major crisis struck Fascism and the head of government, carrying both to the brink. The Matteotti affair erupted in the wake of the April 6, 1924, elections that had marked a tactical triumph for Il Duce. Indeed, Mussolini had led to victory the "national list": a grand coalition of right-wing parties, in which the Fascists, while still a minority, controlled all the key positions. A Socialist deputy, Giacomo Matteotti, a humanitarian pacifist, hence doubly hated by the squadrists, meticulously gathered evidence of electoral fraud and embezzlement by the Fascists and the police force, which went all the way up to the interior minister himself. He presented his evidence on May 30, 1924, before a chamber filled to overflowing and an immobile Mussolini, livid with rage on the government bench, thus signing his own death warrant. What happened immediately afterward has generated an immense literature, continuing to this day, fed by periodic new revelations.[83] One thing is beyond doubt: Matteotti was kidnapped outside his house on the Lungotevere in Rome by five Fascist thugs on June 10, around four thirty p.m. Perhaps it was supposed to have been just a "good beating," to give him a clear warning. But Matteotti, an athlete, fought courageously for his life and was knifed to death. His rotting corpse would be found in the Roman countryside only in mid-August. Did Mussolini personally give the order to eliminate him, or merely intimate to his acolytes that they needed to ensure their adversary could do no harm? Was it a "simple" squadrist-type attack gone bad, or an out-and-out execution? Such an order has never been found, but it was not indispensable, from the moment free rein was given to the Ceka, a group organized and financed by Giovanni Marinelli, the party administrator, and directed by an American-born hooligan, Amerigo Dumini, under the command of Mussolini's personal secretary, Cesare Rossi. The sinister name of this criminal gang derives from the Cheka, the first Bolshevik secret police organization, chief instrument of the Red Terror. The public's indignation was enormous; the moderates in the "national list" also distanced themselves from Mussolini. It was one thing for the squads to bludgeon a few striking workers, but to slaughter an honest, respected deputy was not (yet) conceivable. What would the king do? His scant affection for his head of government was well known. The investigation quickly revealed the perpetrators and even identified the instigators, stopping just short of Il Duce's door. Mussolini seemed to be on the verge of collapse. It was said he kept a pistol at hand, ready to blow his brains out if the carabinieri came to arrest him.*

What role did Curzio play in this vile sequence of events? A very ugly one. For starters, in the matter of his friendships: he was well acquainted with Dumini, known as *Dumini, nove omicidi* ("Dumini, nine homicides") and *il sicario del duce* ("Il Duce's hit man"), even if he claimed otherwise. He had also been his second in a duel. Dumini was a slab of a man, with a scarred face and the small, bright, cruel eyes of an assassin. Born and raised in the United States, the

---

*Yet when the carabinieri actually came to arrest him, twenty years later, upon leaving the royal audience on July 26, 1943, he offered not the slightest resistance, seeming almost relieved.

son of an English mother and an Italian father, he discovered his patriotic vocation during the Great War, becoming soon thereafter one of the most ferocious of squad organizers. He and Curzio came from the same reservoir of Florentine extremism, and it was in this environment that they had met. Certainly, for Curzio when he led the Fascist unions of Florence, it was difficult not to enter into contact with Dumini, but there's a big difference between that and binding yourself to him. And here we arrive at a not unimportant psychological crux. Malaparte not only declared himself attracted to blood, from the day when, as a boy, "getting a deep cut in the palm of my hand, the sight of my blood gave me a stunned, happy shock" ("Primo sangue," in S, 23; then in RI, 277). He was also undeniably fascinated by ruffians. Another character of this sort, whom we'll meet later, is Arconovaldo Bonaccorsi, "the butcher of the Balearic Islands" during the Spanish Civil War. The tendency of certain intellectuals in search of virility to make common cause with thugs is well known. Drieu La Rochelle, who suffered from this attraction, gave it an almost psychoanalytic interpretation in his late novels *Les Chiens de paille* (Straw dogs) and *Journal d'un délicat* (Diary of a sensitive man). But it's difficult to understand what mechanisms could provoke it in a healthy man, indifferent to vice, like Curzio, who had already sufficiently proved his physical and moral strength in the Great War. And yet slumming it with lowlifes seduced him. Perhaps the camaraderie of the squads was the continuation of the camaraderie of the trenches? If there were naifs and fanatics among the squadrists, it is difficult to ascribe either category to Dumini, who made several attempts to blackmail Mussolini and would distinguish himself twenty years later, at Salò, as a smuggler and arms trafficker. Was the attraction an aesthetic one, then, a chance to transform a piece of ugly humanity into writing? But the fascination with horror wouldn't really take hold in Malaparte's work until later. And so? Aside from a good dose of exhibitionism, always present in him, the most likely explanation is that Curzio counted *also* on men like Tamburini and Dumini to lay the foundations for his political rise, not with the aim of competing with Il Duce, but to prevail over other local party *ras*. It was the Renaissance aspect—if one wished to so dignify it—of his personality: the superior man surrounded by Caesar's "villains and robbers," prepared to do anything. The choice of a nom de plume, which was also a nom de guerre, would soon confirm this vision, which—fortunately—would always remain only on paper.

We should mention here Curzio's numerous stays in Paris between 1923 and 1925. What did he go there to do? There was an official reason and a real reason. The former was tied to his new role as general secretary of Fascist unions abroad and National Fascist Party inspector: a high-flown title masking a rather modest job, seeing as how for the moment such unions were almost entirely theoretical; later, when they would take shape, he would no longer be responsible for them. This allowed him, at Liberation, to deny having ever held such a position. "For this latest accusation, I'll have to cite you as a witness for both the nonexistence of any sort of Fascist unions abroad and the nonexistence of the post," he would write to his lifelong friend Guglielmo Rulli, then ambassador in Oslo. "If you want to avoid being interrogated by a letter rogatory in Norway, give me a statement."[84] The inspection tour was a chance to temporarily escape Rome, where he had vainly attempted to insert himself into the party's press office. In the French capital he entered into contact with various intellectual circles, above all those linked to Charles Maurras and Léon Daudet's far-right French Action movement, in view of a possible and rather vague collaboration. But he was also excited about the "social Fascism" of Georges Valois, which presented several points in common with his vision. It was Malaparte who accompanied a Valois-led French Action delegation to Rome, received by Mussolini at Palazzo Venezia on January 10, 1924.[85]

The other, less noble reason was to discreetly follow the activity of the first anti-Fascist groups forming in France, especially in the capital: the *fuoriusciti*, or political refugees. In addition to his weakness for hoodlums, Malaparte had one for conspiracies, the two readily going hand in hand. The Fascist secretary in Paris, Nicola Bonservizi, tried to represent the moderate wing of the Fascist movement, going so far as to establish contact with anti-Fascist republicans. Curzio struck up a friendship with him. But early 1924 saw the arrival of Dumini in Paris, acting as an agent provocateur. The impression in Rome was indeed that Bonservizi was too soft. The result of Dumini's action was to compromise Bonservizi, who would be assassinated in February 1924 by an anarchist waiter, Ernesto Bonomini, immediately identified by the French authorities. Curzio, who to protect Bonservizi had moved to his house and slept the night on a couch that was too small for him, was unable to thwart the attack.[86] A dirty business. Did Bonomini, a weak, shiftless character, really act alone? Some witnesses had seen him in the company of foreigners with Tuscan accents (Dumini's father was Florentine), never identified. In any case, the Fascist government brought a civil action in the proceedings against Bonservizi's assassin, which would take place in Paris: the accused, as a minor, would be sentenced to just eight years in prison. At that point Curzio made an audacious decision, one that was not at all "chameleonlike." In a moment when so many rats were abandoning a ship that seemed destined to sink, he reaffirmed his own unconditional support for Il Duce, not only with his pen but with his deeds. It was a cold, unscrupulous, entirely unsentimental political calculation, betting on the ultimate victory of Mussolini when he seemed about to lose everything, as a speculator buys shares in a distressed company he knows is destined to recover.

In another plot twist, Curzio showed up to testify during the investigation of Matteotti's killers, on September 22, 1924, and subsequently at the first trial, which would take place not in Rome but, as a precaution, in the central Italian town of Chieti, in March 1926. According to his deposition, Dumini had confided to him, the very evening of the kidnapping and murder of the Socialist deputy, that they had meant to give him a lesson, yes, but not to kill him. His death was accidental, then.[87] The testimony would carry considerable weight: Dumini, who had until that moment denied having any part in the crime, took up this version to his own benefit, understanding immediately that it could mean merely a conviction for manslaughter. But there was worse: Curzio became the key witness in a scheme, in which Mussolini himself participated, to prove Matteotti's responsibility for the assassination of Bonservizi, an event that would have explained, and in a certain measure justified, Dumini's act. In this account, Dumini, having come across Matteotti "by chance," confronted him to demand an explanation man to man, in the course of which the Socialist deputy, who suffered from lung problems, died after coughing up blood. Reprehensible behavior, to be sure, but there was no conspiracy or premeditation. Two years later, at his trial, Dumini would cite in support of this version a report sent to the party at the time by comrade Suckert, according to which the Socialist deputy had inspired the attack on Bonservizi. Curzio would essentially confirm this version before the court, declaring, however, to have met Dumini only in March 1924, after the death of his "dear friend" Bonservizi, which was false and easy to prove as such.[88] Moreover, if their acquaintance had been so recent and superficial, why would Dumini have revealed the details of Matteotti's death to *him*, and to no one else? In his autobiography, published in 1950, Dumini would slip in a single deceitful sentence aimed at Malaparte, where he claims that the party administrator, Marinelli, entrusting him with the mission to France, had added: "Your friend Curzio Suckert has been, and continues to be, very useful to us. I don't know how he obtained the information, but it's held up to all our scrutiny. Matteotti is the man we identified as responsible for these events."[89]

Matters stopped there, but Curzio's testimony could have cost him dearly if justice had not already had her hands tied. The evidence against Dumini was overwhelming, but the outcome of the trial was inevitable. The rest is well known. Mussolini, his initial distress having passed, overcame the political crisis, demonstrating extraordinary cynicism and sangfroid. The opposition split, courting ruin; moderates and opportunists quickly returned to the victor, while the king, ever fearful of losing his throne, sanctioned the situation, refusing to dissolve parliament. The accused were acquitted or, like Dumini, given light sentences and amnestied a few months later. Dumini underwent a new trial at Liberation and was given a life sentence. But he left prison following an amnesty proclaimed by the Communist justice minister Togliatti. After a long life full of vicissitudes, he died in poverty in a hospital bed, cared for by the Sisters of Mercy and a devotee of Saint Rita, claiming in

THE BEGINNINGS OF A BONAPARTE (1898–1924)

his autobiography to have "never done harm to anyone and, on the contrary, I have been happy whenever I have been able to do good."[90] Which confirms only that we are not always the best judge of our own actions.

Matteotti would be quickly forgotten, notwithstanding the bunches of flowers that would from time to time, during the twenty years of the regime, be deposited under cover of night at the site of the kidnapping and that the police would make disappear at dawn. The Matteotti affair had swept away his final hesitations, and Mussolini could move decisively into the establishment of the dictatorship. On January 3, 1925, he openly challenged the parliament, assuming political and moral responsibility for the event, while denying the existence of the Ceka and state terrorism. At the same time, if his hold on power was at this point secure, he no longer needed accomplices. Curzio was part of a delegation that had gone to Mussolini the day before to reassure him of party cohesion, but also to make sure their leader had no hesitations. It was the last moment—until Salò—when Il Duce was hostage to the Blackshirts. Shortly thereafter, he officially moved toward their dissolution; but he would never be able to do without them, to his undoing. It remains unclear whether Mussolini, after his fall in July 1943, was not resigned to exiting the political game. Freed by the Germans, kept under watch by the diehards of the first and the last hour, he would be forced to take up the reins of a puppet state, all the way to the miserable end.

But the Mussolini who had just overcome the most difficult test of his career was not a man on his last legs, anything but. Was he perhaps grateful to his followers, once the danger had passed? To imagine so means not to know the man, and yet Curzio believed it, displaying the kind of naivety that doomed his political career. After the war and the fall of Fascism, Malaparte maintained that his deposition, considered an accusation against "Domini" [sic], had drawn the ire of the lawyer defending the Fascist hit man: none other than Roberto Farinacci, the *ras* of Cremona, recognized leader of the Blackshirts, secretary of the party from 1924 to 1926, and eternal rival of Mussolini. Farinacci was not only an extremist who frequented as well the milieus of capital and finance. He was also an astute political brain, endowed with a charisma and tactical skills second only to Il Duce's.* He was the man whom, in September 1943, the Germans planned to put at the head of a Fascist republic if they could not free Mussolini. The rivalry between the two would continue to the very end: Farinacci would be captured and shot by partisans on the same day that Mussolini's corpse would be hung from its feet in Piazzale Loreto.

The break between Suckert and Farinacci, like the one that saw him in conflict with other representatives of Fascist radicalism, such as the Futurists Mario Carli and Emilio Settimelli and their magazine, *L'Impero*, took place right around 1926, with the inevitable train of reciprocal accusations and duels. But it was only marginally provoked by the Matteotti trial, in which, according to every testimony, Curzio's deposition gave the impression, rather, of being "suggested" by Dumini's defense.[91] The truth is that Malaparte had at that point abandoned his illusions of revolutionary Fascism to align himself, quite dexterously, with Mussolini's policy of state Fascism.[92] In the columns of *La Conquista dello Stato*, he defined

---

*Until relatively recently there was no critical biography of Farinacci, despite the figure's undoubted importance. See now Giuseppe Pardini, *Roberto Farinacci ovvero della rivoluzione fascista* (Florence: Le Lettere, 2007).

Farinacci at the time with a withering quip that would never be forgotten or forgiven by its target: "a cross between a wolf and a sheep, where we don't know if the result is a cowardly wolf or a ferocious sheep."[93] Curzio, as audacious as he was, would never have exposed himself to such an extent vis-à-vis Fascism's no. 2 if he had not believed he could count on the benevolence of its no. 1. Mussolini, emerging triumphant after having narrowly escaped disgrace, could finally torpedo his feared and hated rival, forcing Farinacci to resign as party secretary the day after the trial in Chieti. It was a little like what Hitler would do a dozen years later, when he got rid of Röhm and the SA during the Night of the Long Knives, with one difference: the former would spare his internal opposition, leading twenty years later to his disastrous end. Curzio had no interest, after all the risks he had run to earn the trust of Il Duce, in siding with the losers. He continued to pump out articles on the direct or indirect order of the chief. As he would do later, in the conflict with Balbo, he counted on Mussolini's gratitude. This time, things went reasonably well for him; the next time, rather less so.

With regard to Curzio's actual responsibility for the Matteotti murder and its aftermath, opinions diverge.[94] But it's difficult to deny that his role was lamentable, to say the least. Thereafter, he spoke about it as little as possible, and with good reason. When he could not avoid doing so, as in the statement presented to the purge commission in 1946, he would limit himself to repeating the lie of having "testified against Dumini" and being persecuted by Farinacci.[95] The following year, invited to appear as a witness before the Rome Court of Assizes during the retrial, he was exonerated at the last moment.[96] Was this the result of a discreet intervention on the part of Togliatti, who continued to control the purge process through his men? We'll come back to that. In any case, Malaparte's absence in the Court of Assizes, far from being a negligible matter, was by far the most significant among those of former witnesses summoned for the new trial.[97] And the whole affair would remain the most serious stain on his reputation. Finally, to complete an already shameful picture, Curzio demonstrated an almost Stalinist zeal in maligning various former comrades in the Italian Republican Party. He acted this way to make people forget friendships that had grown cumbersome, but also maybe to punish them for not having offered him the leadership of the PRI at a moment when he might have been able to better negotiate his support for Fascism. Beyond calculations and resentments, the republican ideal would remain present to the end, like the first love you never forget.

The Matteotti murder represented a turn in his life from another point of view as well: Malaparte would never again sink so low, not even in the name of a purported political ideal. There would be other quite disturbing, even squalid episodes, and other unedifying friendships. But the self-image that he wanted to leave to posterity, as a man and a writer, by now counted much more in his eyes, and he would refuse to become the apparatchik, the spy, the profiteer of the regime that would hold his fellow countrymen in chains for two decades. It was literature that would bring some consolation in the oppressive atmosphere of those years. *Viva Caporetto!* was followed by two brief essays: a half-baked satire, "Le nozze degli eunuchi" (1922; The eunuchs' wedding), and a sort of theoretical manifesto, "L'Europa vivente" (1923; Living Europe), pompously subtitled "Teoria storica del sindacalismo nazionale" (A historical theory of national syndicalism); this would also be his first book translated into French, five years later, with the inspired title *L'Italie contre l'Europe* (Italy against Europe). They are hardly masterpieces, or even major works: the style bristles with convoluted philosophizing, without the striking capacity for synthesis of the future Malaparte. But in them you catch glimpses of an authentic writer, an original polemicist rather than a mere hack like the majority of his peers. The time had come for Curzio to step aside, to make room for the persona he had chosen to incarnate.

2. Fascism and High Society (1925–1933)

> We hate constancy, the heart's tyrant.
> —GIUSEPPE VERDI (libretto by Francesco Maria Piave), *Rigoletto*, I, 1

Fascist, but Not Like the Others

HENRY MILLER, in a page of his autobiography, remarked that behind his friend Stanley "I always visualized a line of warriors, diplomats, poets, musicians. Myself, I had no ancestry whatever. I had to invent one."[1] In 1925 Curzio had the same problem, which he solved in his own way, deciding it was time to reinvent himself and erase Suckert once and for all, in favor of Malaparte. Initially both names existed, as in the first edition of *Italia barbara* (Barbarous Italy), or else they alternated, in the torrential journalistic output of those years. It was a matter of habituating the reader to the new identity, a bit like how today a bank keeps the old logo for a time as part of a new brand it's preparing to launch. Let us note, meanwhile, this first display of Curzio's talents as a publicist, which he would refine in subsequent years.

Every Malaparte aficionado knows he chose the pseudonym—which would become his legal name only several years later[2]—after reading an anonymous pamphlet marking the hundredth anniversary of Napoleon's death. The author, a Catholic satirist and probably a Jesuit, had been inspired by a May 1858 article in *Le Moniteur universel*, according to which "the Bonapartes had an entirely different name, Malaparte," and were of noble Italian stock, like Malatesta, Malaspina, and so on. The author then played on the alternation Bonaparte/Malaparte to comment on the itinerary of Napoleon, "who acted as Bonaparte when he defended the pope and as Malaparte when he attacked him."[3] Forgotten for years in the library stacks, the text enjoyed a new popularity under Fascism, when a nationalist campaign tried to prove the Italian origins of Napoleon. This probably explains how it fell into Curzio's hands. Mussolini venerated the Corsican, before discovering Julius Caesar. The Napoleonic myth would return in his life's last moments, if it's true, as one of his executioners claimed, that Mussolini exposed his chest, crying, "Aim for the heart!"

Malaparte found it useful, then, at the first signs of the anticosmopolitan campaign, to publicly and solemnly assert his own national identity. In this period the regime imposed the forced Italianization of Germans from Alto Adige and Slavs from Venezia Giulia: Bauers became Contadini; Stupinichs, Stupingi; and Zateks, Zatecchi.* Now, as we'll see, the accusation of being a "German," and even a "German Jew," would become common among police informers and adversaries of the writer.[4] He was tired of seeing his name mangled, as Sukert, Suchert, Suhert, Suckery... Thus he would feel obliged to claim in 1938, in a statement of self-defense at the time

---

*History rarely teaches wisdom and tolerance: in 1945, Tito's Yugoslavia would begin forcibly slavicizing the old names in the surviving Italian community.

of the introduction of the racial laws: "I took the name of Malaparte at the suggestion of Il Duce, who in 1926 told me: 'A Fascist writer has to sign with an Italian name. Find yourself a pseudonym.'"[5]

With or without Il Duce's direct intervention, then, Curzio was in search of a pseudonym, which he also wanted to be high sounding, in the Renaissance style fashionable at the time. His predecessor at the Cicognini, Sem Benelli, had enjoyed great success with *The Jester's Supper*, a lavish drama of passion and blood at the court of Lorenzo the Magnificent.* But to opt for an authentic historical name like Borgia, Medici, or Farnese would have seemed too crass, the appropriation of a parvenu. The search, accordingly, was laborious, the solution not immediate. A sheet of paper preserved in the writer's archive contains a long list in his own hand of crossed-out names, each more fantastic than the last: Curzio Bonalancia, Curzio Colonna, Curzio Borgia-Suckert, and so on. But there are also attempts at simple Italianization (Curzio Sucherti, Curzio Suchertio), not to mention Curzio Baldi, in memory of his adoptive father, and even a Curzio Pratoforte, in honor of his native city.[6] According to another account, the pseudonym was the work of Pirandello, the great interpreter, not coincidentally, of the split personality; Malaparte, however, refused to confirm the anecdote, making it clear he owed nothing to anyone.[7] Furthermore, *Ma-la-par-te*, with or without the French-style silent final *e*, had the advantage of being easily pronounced in the major languages, like *Dante* or *Leonardo*; because he was already convinced he would one day

---

*In 1919 the play was staged to great acclaim in New York under the title *The Jest*, starring Lionel and John Barrymore. In 1942 Alessandro Blasetti would turn the play into an even more popular film, in which one glimpsed the first, unforgettable bare breast of Italian sound film, of the diva Clara Calamai.

become a key player on the international scene. The choice was an excellent one on several fronts, then: it mythologized his Tuscan side and abolished his German side for good, while also suggesting a certain reverential aura. He enjoined in a 1926 letter:

> And remember that I am no longer called Curzio Suckert, but Curzio Malaparte. I'm sick of this *t* ending. I want to be Italian not just in brain, in spirit, in body as I am, but also in the ending of my name. Malaparte is my standard.[8]

But he did not consider completing the job, by leaving the Protestant faith. Maybe because his flamboyant anticlericalism in the period was at odds with a conversion to Catholicism? In any case, from that moment on, until his last breath, he would be just Malaparte, a name to be worn like a uniform and a title of nobility: *Qui sibi nomen imposuit*, according to the Latin formula for announcing a new pontiff. Even the name Curzio would be used less and less, and almost exclusively in private; only family members and a select few close friends would continue to call him Curtino. Three decades later, Malaparte would pen a curious article on the topic, one of the last of his Battibecco columns, before his fatal voyage to China. Titled "Curzio Is Dead," it reads in part:

> The other day, Tuscan newspapers announced the death of my friend Curzio Palandri, the cook at Nilo Montanari's trattoria, in Pisa. He was an Italian of old, honest breed, a quick-witted, generous, loyal Tuscan. He is the first Curzio I've seen buried. One day it will be my turn. And I hope that I too one day will be able to rest in the peace of honest men, which my poor friend Curzio earned through

a lifetime of work, sacrifice, and goodness. But I don't know whether I will have earned that peace.[9]

Armed, it's appropriate to say, with his new patronymic, Malaparte renewed his drive for glory. And here we come to the first in a long series of disappointments. After having exposed himself through his missions in France and the cover he provided to Dumini in the Matteotti trial, he expected, with legitimate reason, to be compensated with a prominent role in the *nomenklatura* of the regime. He saw himself center stage, enjoying a direct relationship with the leader, who would guarantee his rise and protect him from the jealousy of other aspirants. Overflowing with energy and ambition, he nonetheless had no precise ideas about what he could do or ask for, because he wanted to do everything at the same time, from literature to journalism, politics to diplomacy. His appetite for life and success gave him wings; he was a Tuscan Rastignac, out to conquer the capital and its sites of power and pleasure. It was this insatiability that would lead him, as at so many other points in his life, to the brink of catastrophe.

March 1925 saw the publication of a manifesto of intellectuals in favor of Fascism, which gathered a considerable number of signatories. Its originator was Giovanni Gentile (hence the name "Gentile manifesto"), philosopher of the spirit passing over into action, who saw in the new movement the culmination of the nation's rebirth, erring spectacularly, with faultless good faith and immense personal generosity. Gentile would be the catalyst for the creation of some exceptional institutions, such as the Scuola Normale Superiore di Pisa, the *Enciclopedia italiana*, and the Italian Institute for the Middle and Far East of the great Orientalist Giuseppe Tucci (who awarded a scholarship to a then unknown young Romanian, Mircea Eliade), where numerous Jews and anti-Fascists would find a refuge and the possibility of expressing themselves almost freely.* The case of Gentile, which is not the only one, just the most important, demonstrates the eccentricity of Fascism in the panorama of twentieth-century totalitarianism. He would be killed in April 1944 by a command of partisans recruited from among his disciples; in this way he would pay for having dignified the dictatorship, and above all for having preached, in the Socratic manner, an impossible national reconciliation in an Italy torn by civil war. His old frenemy Benedetto Croce would note the event in his diary, with the cold philosophical detachment he imposed on everything. His wife, beside him, would burst into sobs. Wherein we see that the reactions of simple souls are often more human than those of the masters of thought...

Malaparte—still as Suckert—signed the Gentile manifesto, destined to provoke, two months later, a countermanifesto, initiated by Croce. These proclamations constitute the last time the country's two great political-intellectual currents confronted each other openly. If we run through those lists of names today, we see that the country's elite were at that moment still divided into two more or less equal camps. This was another factor pushing Mussolini to hasten the arrival of dictatorship. The situation would inevitably alter in the years to follow. The majority of the signatories of the "Croce manifesto" would have to find some accommodation with the

---

*Through his elder son, Giovanni Jr., a gifted physicist, Gentile helped establish the "school of Via Panisperna," a legendary laboratory of exceptional talents, including the future Nobel laureates Enrico Fermi and Emilio Segrè, who in 1938 both emigrated to the United States, and Bruno Pontecorvo, who after the war defected to the Soviet Union.

regime in order not to lose their job, or else leave the country. A prime example is the case of Sem Benelli, whose tortuous path displays certain affinities with the young Malaparte's.

Harassment of the regime's undaunted and ever more isolated opponents would rapidly take on squadrist characteristics. Matteotti's fate paved the way for that of Giovanni Amendola, the indomitable cofounder of the political newspaper *Il Mondo*, a baby-faced giant with fists the size of mallets, who would die in Cannes, in April 1926, of wounds sustained in a Fascist attack. Antonio Gramsci was arrested and put where he could do no harm. In his *Prison Notebooks* he would continue to mock Malaparte, without managing to get hold of his latest writings. Others would be sentenced to prison or *confino* by a special court for state security, an organ of judicial repression created in November 1926. The regime was born.

One of the remaining pockets of resistance was represented, once again, by a magazine. The weekly *Rivoluzione Liberale*—"the last refuge of militant intellectualism"[10]—had been founded in Turin by a twenty-year-old who seemed to have already read and understood everything, as is often the case with those destined for a brief and dazzling life. His name was Piero Gobetti, a promoter of an audacious synthesis of liberalism and socialism, in which the October Revolution played an essential role.* In his writings, Gobetti proposed a path from the Enlightenment to a highly idealized Bolshevism, as if it were a single long struggle against obscurantism and dogmatism. His anti-Fascism, conversely, was born from the idea

---

*Well studied today outside Italy, in France and Germany especially, Gobetti is rarely mentioned in American scholarship. See David Ward, *Piero Gobetti's New World: Antifascism, Liberalism, Writing* (Toronto: University of Toronto Press, 2010).

that, in a still profoundly conservative society after the war, Mussolini's movement would rapidly lose any revolutionary vocation; it would end up being used by religion and capital, and not using them as it proclaimed. We are not, then, too far from the analysis of Gramsci, another of Gobetti's primary interlocutors, with the difference that the latter displayed an unyielding devotion to the ideal of liberty, rather than to that of class struggle. The Greek motto printed on the frontispiece of his magazines (he had time to found two more in his brief life) and his books—"What have I to do with slaves?"—aimed to preclude any concession to totalitarianism, be it of the Right or the Left. Gobetti was also a great publisher, managing to bring out essential works at odds with the prevailing Fascist rhetoric, including *Dal Patto di Londra alla pace di Roma* (From the Treaty of London to the Peace of Rome), by the historian and economist Gaetano Salvemini, and, on the literary front, *Cuttlefish Bones*, Eugenio Montale's debut verse collection, both from 1925. Would Gobetti's somewhat utopian intransigence have evolved with age and experience? The question must remain unanswered, unfortunately. Some scholars today believe that the influence of his theses—too radical, insufficiently political—ended up weakening rather than reinforcing Italian democracy, before and even after Fascism. Both his direct and indirect disciples, who reunited for the most part in the ephemeral Action Party, would enjoy great prestige during the Resistance and at Liberation, but would soon be crushed by the pressure of the new mass parties of the postwar era.

Thus we understand what connects Gobetti and Malaparte, and at the same time what divides them. If their meeting was a kind of love at first sight, their friendship and ultimate estrangement played out according to a parable of separated brothers, as with Croce and

Gentile, but condensed into just three to four years. Suckert's contributions to *Rivoluzione Liberale* began, in fact, in August 1922—that is, on the eve of his enrollment in the Fascist Party—with an article titled "Le ultime eresie d'Occidente: Il desiderio anglosassone del divino" (The last heresies of the West: The Anglo-Saxon desire for the divine), a dead-on analysis of Puritanism and the religious impulse that dominated (and dominates to this day) American political life.[11] It was the beginning of a relationship unlike any other in Curzio's life. Here is how, twenty years later, he would describe their meeting:

> I quickly established a warm friendship with Piero Gobetti, who never failed to pay me a visit every time he came to Rome. We spent long hours together discussing every sort of social, literary, political, or religious problem. We disagreed on just one point: the war. He undervalued the moral importance of war for the young generations, I perhaps overvalued it. He was younger than me; he hadn't participated in the war and thus was colder, calmer, more objective. He was also much freer in his judgments. For me the war had been my first fundamental experience of life. I could not, therefore, be objective, nor free, in the face of war. And it was precisely the war factor that prevented me from being an anti-Fascist, *then*. Piero Gobetti was at the time, and remained so until his death, the recognized leader of anti-Fascist intellectualism. Many of my attitudes of the time are tied to him, as are my first literary achievements. Anyone wishing to judge my activity in those years must necessarily refer to this figure.[12]

This retrospective homage is not entirely trustworthy. The war was certainly not the only factor separating them; after all, Gobetti had enlisted voluntarily in 1918, in anticipation of his call-up, and did not take part in combat only because the armistice arrived first. The real difference was that Suckert considered Fascism the only possible response to Italy's national crisis, while Gobetti stubbornly refused to do so; he saw in it, just like Gramsci, nothing but a bump in the road for capitalism, the derailment of an embryonic society rendered even more fragile by the war. The fact remains, however, that "Gobettaccio," as Malaparte affectionately Tuscanized him, was one of two decisive influences in his life; the other, Mussolini, served as a counterpoint throughout his career, even after the fall of Fascism.

Outside these two cases, one struggles to identify a single interlocutor whom Curzio accepted as such, with whom he was willing to truly confront himself. What fascinated him about Mussolini was his success, the expression par excellence of strength, whereas Gobetti believed and acted according to values that Malaparte *would have liked* to recognize in himself. Everything about the frail young man struck him: his vast learning, with the inevitable eclecticism and lacunas of his twenty years; his capacity for synthesis; his resoluteness without sectarianism. In short, several characteristics that he lacked and *would have liked* to possess. Physically, too, they could not have been more dissimilar. Clumsy, inelegant, shaggy haired, with thick glasses and an ironic but sweet smile, Gobetti was disarmingly ugly, a look-alike of the Russian poet Aleksandr Blok, who nonetheless attracted men and women like flies. He scrutinized and absorbed everything without prejudice, passing it through the sieve of reason, then modifying and rejecting what did not work, or failed to convince him. Next to him, Curzio was incurious before the world; he was unable to contemplate it, occupied as he was with contemplating himself, in sovereign indifference to the objective causes of historical events, to economics, sociology, or other social sciences, an apathy that only his friend's eloquence managed sometimes to break through. Then he, in turn, would launch an attack, out of a lover's spite, as he would whenever a friend or an adversary backed him into a corner. A taste for provocation, too, pushed them toward each other, and at the same time set them against each other. They often quarreled, but not even Curzio's adherence to Fascism sufficed to separate them. Gobetti, indifferent to the advice of those wanting to warn him against Malaparte, invited him to contribute to his magazine again, as if it were nothing. In *L'Europa vivente*, Suckert had reprised the message formulated in the last lines of *Viva Caporetto!* to call for Fascism to develop into a new Counter-Reformation, breathing new life into the claim of an "eternal" Italy.* It was a message greatly encouraged at the time by Fascism, which was already preparing to select the Catholic Church as its only interlocutor, denying any Protestant (or even Jansenist) influence on the nation's history.[13] And let us not forget the psychoanalytic evidence emerging between the lines, of a settling of scores with his father, Erwin, in Curzio's attacks on the Reformation and Luther.[14]

He picked up the rejection of the French Revolution and its aftermath from Maurras's hard-line nationalism. Nonetheless, Curzio was, like Gobetti, a product of his time and of another generation.

---

*After the war, in France, he would invert the formula and become more Gobettian than the original: "Italy did not experience either the Reformation or the French Revolution. The source of its current malady is to have remained outside the great moral, social, and political movements that were the Reformation and the events of 1789" (DC, 3). The passage, with few variants, appears in the typescript of *Muss*, with an additional, even more explicit sentence: "In its essence, Fascism is merely the sum of the defects of Catholic civilization, the last aspect of the Counter-Reformation" (MU, 38, 40).

FASCISM AND HIGH SOCIETY (1925–1933)

Both men were shaped by the revolutions of 1789 and 1917 and shocked by the war. Both (and Gramsci as well) claimed the same point of departure: the limits and errors of a Risorgimento that imposed monarchy and centralization without the active participation of the masses, especially in the south. But it is here that, while Gobetti looked to the future for the key to a new social pact, Malaparte built castles in the air, falling into an outdated romanticism à la Maistre or Barrès. He invoked "tradition" and the "restoration" of values preceding the country's belated unification, as though they were manna from heaven. It takes a thoroughly Malapartian contempt for history to ask to return to a long, dark period of division and struggle, from the fifteenth to the nineteenth century, that transformed Italy from the cradle of European civilization to a colony of its powerful neighbors. And what happened to socialism and anticlericalism, essential factors in the birth of Fascism? He stopped talking about them. The reality is that, without openly troubling himself too much, taking on an extremist pose, Suckert rapidly adapted to the new national climate. Like Mussolini, he had understood that Fascism wouldn't survive unless it came to terms with the traditional influences in Italian society: the monarchy, the clergy, the still-feudal power of landowners in the south and the new class of capitalist industrialists in the north.

Gobetti did not limit himself to opening the doors of his magazines to Malaparte; in 1925 he published *Italia barbara*, which marked the culmination of a vision opposed to his own. Why did he do it? Out of a taste, once more, for provocation, albeit one wedded to an effort to rehabilitate the friend he sincerely cared about, to wrest him away from the Fascist temptation. Then again, the book is curiously preceded by a note by Gobetti that tears down its contents in fifteen lines. After calling the author "Fascism's most formidable pen," a definition that would stick to Malaparte for a long time, Gobetti claims that if he has decided to present "the book of an enemy to *his* audience," it is due precisely to the esteem and friendship he feels for him. But he adds that "he will not insult him with a confutation," given that Suckert-Malaparte's arguments spring from the "varicolored fantasy" and "whimsy" of the author, and do not deserve to be taken seriously even in the context of critical opposition. In private, Gobetti was even more explicit:

> Dear Suckert, now would be the time for you to get serious. Don't you understand that you're wasting time, that the Fascists are playing you, that in the party you're a fifth-class man, that your writings for the past year haven't been worth a damn? I think it's right that you stay in the Fascist Party, because you're a born Fascist, one of the authentic ones. But show some presence of mind: you are a born artist and must not lose yourself completely.[15]

An impeccable diagnosis, which Malaparte would come to endorse—after the fall of the regime. And yet, *Italia barbara* is a far from insignificant text. Its declaration of war—against "the scattered, cowardly family of intellectuals. Cowardly people. Malicious people. Desperately opposed to any upheaval that does not result in their immediate benefit, and that gives prominence to qualities they do not possess: courage, strength, will, ferocity" (IB, 192)—closely recalls the lesson of Gobetti. But what is most interesting about the book concerns its style, not its thinking. The author chose an almost Spenglerian argument—the revolt of the young generation ("barbaric," idealist, spiritualist, uncontaminated, and, naturally, Fascist) against the inert and outdated values of yesterday—but he spoils it with his usual defect of improvisation and with mood swings that upset the train of thought. The vehicle is powered by a fire feeding on brilliant and fanciful assertions, repurposed from his many articles of the period. But one understands, behind the expressive virtuosity, that he is the first not to believe fully what he is saying. The need to astonish the reader prevails, as it did in *L'Europa vivente*, over logical exposition, a tendency that we will find in almost all his work to come. He knew perfectly well that he had no authority to present his doctrine of "integral" Fascism, which Il Duce, for one, carefully avoided formulating. Malaparte's "barbarism," which was to have emerged as a sort of elixir of youth for the Italian people, thus remained suspended between an evocation of the (debatable) glories of a vague past and a premonition of an even more glorious, but just as vague, future. It was a blind alley similar to the one Marinetti would end up in when he sought to prove that the Second Futurism, created within Fascism, was an avant-garde different from European avant-gardes such as surrealism, and superior to them, because rooted in a national and anticosmopolitan heritage. Such self-evident nonsense would pave the way for academicism and regression in the Futurist movement in the 1930s and 1940s.

How did Malaparte react to Gobetti's critique, which laid bare his limits and contradictions? We do not know. Was there any clearing of the air between the two behind the scenes? It is possible, but no trace of it remains. A few months after the book appeared, Gobetti suffered the same fate as Matteotti and Amendola. He was attacked and beaten bloody by Blackshirts almost under the eyes of the police, an attack rendered only more cowardly by his poor health. His magazine and publishing house were closed shortly after.

Gobetti then decided to leave the country, but died shortly after his arrival in Paris, in February 1926, as a result of his injuries. To speak of his end was prohibited in Italy. Malaparte kept quiet as well, and the silence of a friend weighed twice as heavily. But what could he have done? His friendship with Gobetti was already bad enough in the minds of party members. Only after the fall of the regime did he try to make up for lost time. But his article "Obbiezione di coscienza" (Conscientious objection), a moving tribute to Gobetti, written in August 1943, never saw the light of day, thanks to political events. In 1946, in the preface to the first single-volume Italian edition of his pamphlet *Don Camaleo* (Mr. Chameleon), astutely dedicated to Gobetti, he described their last meeting in emotional terms:

> But as I was close to completing the manuscript, Piero Gobetti telegraphed me, begging me to come to him in Turin right away.... I reached Turin in the evening and went straight from the station to his house, where I had dinner with him and his wife. They had just had a child, and Gobetti, showing him to me, said: "And to think I'll have to leave him!" After dinner he announced that he had decided to abandon Italy, that he would be leaving the next day for Paris, where he would create an Italian publishing house around his *Rivoluzione Liberale*, to which I myself was a regular contributor; and he invited me to follow him to Paris to help him in his venture.... I responded that a political writer has many legitimate reasons to prefer exile to servitude, but that literary men, even if they have the same reasons to prefer exile to a servile life, cannot emigrate, as they are bound to their own language, their own land, their own people.... For this reason I chose to remain in Italy, and I preferred, and *had to prefer*, struggle to exile, because one day the Italian people's

moral resistance to tyranny would be judged not only by the political writings of its emigrants but, above all, by the literary works of the writers who remained in Italy. We discussed these and other problems at length, and we parted with the promise that I would get the manuscript of *Don Camaleo* to him as soon as I had finished the last chapter. We didn't say goodbye, just bye for now. He was paler than usual but smiling: I realized that his glasses were slightly fogged. Piero Gobetti left for Paris, where a few weeks later he very sadly died. (DONC, 14–16)

True, false, a bit true and a bit false? Would the friendship have survived had Gobetti survived the attack? It's hard to say. But the memory of this "little brother" who was capable of being his moral and intellectual superior never ceased to torment him. Gobetti's influence, nullified after 1925, would strongly guide his pessimistic reading of the Italian and European crisis after 1945. The end of Fascism and Nazism would not, in his eyes, entail the development of a true "liberal revolution," of a European federalism worthy of the name, transcending old nationalist divisions. Their conflicted friendship did at least end on a nice note. Shortly before his own death, Malaparte led a media campaign for the transfer of Gobetti's remains from Père-Lachaise in Paris to Turin's monumental cemetery[16]—a gesture contested, incidentally, by the martyr's disciples and family, as an attempt at belated reappropriation.

Country and City

Within the Fascist orbit, the idea of the moment was not Malaparte's, even if he would seek to exploit it to his own ends. The *Stra-*

paese (literally, "supervillage" or "supercountry") movement, little known today, nevertheless had a genuine significance between the wars. How to define it? It was a form of return to the land and tradition, to the values associated with the good old days, which "do not lie." The phenomenon was not an exclusively national one, notwithstanding Fascism's encouragement of it. It could be found, more or less contemporaneously, among land nostalgics in France and Spain, and above all in totalitarian countries that, while preaching industrialization and modernity, exalted ancestry and origins, not to mention race, be it Stalin's Soviet Union or, soon, Hitler's Germany. Italian Fascism had from the beginning a highly composite ideology, too rich for us to discuss here in detail.[17] Mussolini wrote a good deal (and well) in his life, in an essentially journalistic mode, but he left no theoretical treatise, no *Mein Kampf*, or even a history of the Fascist revolution, such as the one published in three volumes between 1937 and 1940 by Roberto Farinacci. Only after much hesitation did he agree, in 1932, to sign the entry on Fascism in the *Enciclopedia italiana*, edited by Gentile and the historian Gioacchino Volpe: the text is rambling, often obscure, and deliberately vague, leaving Il Duce ample room to maneuver. The immense body of literature published by the regime across twenty years to regulate all aspects of "Fascist life," from education to sports, nutrition to clothing, free time to the relationship between the sexes, is in general of little relevance on the theoretical level. Giuseppe Bottai was probably the only party official to have envisioned an organic implementation of Fascist ideology; he was also the only one Malaparte respected from an intellectual point of view. Upon the fall of the regime, Bottai would describe his frustrations with that "two-faced" Mussolini.[18] The reality is that Mussolini did not want Fascism to be conceivable without him: his person alone had to protect and guarantee the coherence and duration of the system. "Fascism," a caustic Pirandello was said to have exclaimed, "is an empty tube that anyone can fill up as they wish." That wasn't exactly the case, but behind the repetition of approved slogans, every official, from top to bottom in the hierarchy, sought to apply directives as he saw fit. Born with the aim of setting Italians' lives in order—and not just locking Italians up—Fascism would sink into anarchy and chaos, behind a patina of authoritarian conformity. But this state of things would emerge only with the war; for the moment, Mussolini was at the height of his power. If he remained convinced that life was a permanent struggle, in which the weaker must succumb to the stronger, he was still endowed with pragmatism and a gift for tactics that pushed him to interpret dogmas and principles in the most utilitarian manner possible. The moment when he would fall into ideological obsession, which he had always distrusted previously, was still to come.*

Two examples will suffice: despite his anticlerical origins, Mussolini did not hesitate, in 1929, to sign an agreement with the church, of great advantage to the latter, under the illusion of putting an end to the deep hostility that, since 1870, had continued to inspire the actions of the Holy See with regard to the Italian state. And in 1938, to seal the alliance with Nazi Germany and to give Italians a so-called national conscience, he introduced the racial laws, even though

---

*Mussolini was up until his last days a voracious reader and autodidact. His grounding owed much to French thinkers like Proudhon, Gustave Le Bon (*Psychology of Crowds*, 1895), and especially Georges Sorel, the creator of revolutionary syndicalism, who, virtually ignored by his compatriots, had a notable influence in Italy around the Great War. Sorel was read passionately by Gobetti, too.

he, like the vast majority of his compatriots, had never been an anti-Semite. To the extent that we may speak of an anti-Semitic prejudice in Italian society before 1938, it was essentially Catholic in origin, and some whiff of it would pass into Strapaese; the best-known Italian anti-Semite under Fascism was a defrocked priest, Giovanni Preziosi, who committed suicide at the fall of the Salò regime. But none of this played a role in forming Mussolini, who was influenced by prominent international figures like the Russian socialist Angelica Balabanoff and the Venetian Margherita Sarfatti, both of Jewish descent (and both his mistresses). Even after 1938, Mussolini would insist, in contrast to national socialism, on the nonbiological nature of "Italian racism." This does not change the fact that the anti-Semitic campaign orchestrated by the regime—to which its intellectuals, as we will see, lent themselves with slavish zeal—was despicable, preparing the ground for spoliations and deportations in the last period of the war.

Strapaese was a heterogeneous phenomenon, which had various initiators but one privileged site of origin, and once again it was Tuscany, with its countless parochial rivalries: the Florence of Giovanni Papini, who now drowned his syncretist mysticism in a sanctimonious Catholicism, and of a great painter and former Blackshirt like Ottone Rosai; the San Casciano of the "mean-minded" philosopher Domenico Giuliotti; Rignano sull'Arno, the refuge of Ardengo Soffici, who had disavowed his cubist season in prewar Paris; and finally, Colle Val d'Elsa, in the province of Siena. This is where, in July 1924, the painter and satirical cartoonist Mino Maccari, the probable inventor of the term *Strapaese*, launched a magazine whose title, *Il Selvaggio*, contained an entire program, and whose watchword would be "Savage provinces, awake!" (*Selvaggia provincia, svegliati!*). The only significant example in this genre emerging outside Tuscany, but still adjacent to it, concerns another magazine, *L'Italiano*, published by Leo Longanesi. He and Maccari would make an ideal pair, dubbed "the two dwarves in pursuit of Snow White," owing to their short stature and immoderate passion for women.*

Nor would the two disavow such inspiration after the war, continuing their work as peerless spoilers and enliveners of the cultural scene, up until the untimely passing of Longanesi (in September 1957, two months after Malaparte) and the rather later one (1989) of the ninety-year-old Maccari. If the anti-intellectualism displayed by writers like Papini and Soffici was more than suspect, *Il Selvaggio* represented something more modest but straightforward: the celebration of rural Italy, human reservoir of Fascism, against bourgeois submissiveness and against the working-class base of the northern industrial centers (Milan, Turin, Genoa), which would remain essentially left leaning under the regime. Along the way Strapaese caught the mood of the early hard-liners, marginalized and full of spite, whom the party seemed to have set aside and forgotten. All this may seem a bit simplistic, but the formula responded to the demands of the "barbaric" identity better than the lucubrations of Malaparte. Which did not prevent him from taking over the project with his customary nonchalance, not hesitating in 1927, shortly after the death of the anti-Fascist Gobetti, to republish *Italia barbara* just as it was—*without* the original preface—with the publishing house of the ultra-Fascist Longanesi.

This behavior is rather revealing of the modus operandi that Malaparte would maintain all the way to his deathbed, thirty years

---

*It is noteworthy that one of the few defenders of Strapaese in postwar Italy would be a man like Pasolini, attracted by its ruralism and anti-industrialism.

later, which consists in playing the field, often with opposing partners. Indeed, less than two years after his adoption of Strapaese came the plot twist, his sponsorship of the birth of a contrary movement, *Stracittà* (literally, "supercity"), associated with the quarterly magazine *"900": Cahiers d'Italie et d'Europe*. Malaparte headed up the publication with the writer Massimo Bontempelli, who, to better underline its international character, decided to have all texts appear in French. It certainly was a provocation for the followers of Strapaese, who cried treason and declared themselves ready to organize a punitive expedition to settle the score with those two traitors. But Malaparte-Suckert (he still signed his name thus) managed to convince them it was all a trick: this "Italianized French" magazine had the goal of spreading abroad the good word of Fascism. Beyond the Alps, *Les Nouvelles Littéraires* had just affirmed his claim, albeit going against the grain: "It is impossible to offer a better demonstration of the current state of the French language than by making it the Italian language's means of expressing the Fascist spirit."[19] At any rate, the censors imposed a return to Italian in 1928.

What caused this about-face? First of all, a calculation: in the long run, the anticonformism of Strapaese irritated party bosses, who no longer wanted revolution, just a well-compensated career under the shadow of the regime. The time had come for the Fascists to "put on some belly," Longanesi sarcastically remarked. Maccari added: "The Magi will end up in the manger." In proclamations Mussolini condemned this tendency toward bourgeoisification, but in practice he supported it, as it helped to disarm the now-inconvenient squads. At this point he needed not praetorians, but slaves, and all the better if they were corrupt, and thus easier to control. Malaparte, ever vigilant, did not take long to understand the need to change tack and align himself with the regime's new direction. He distanced himself from *Il Selvaggio* and *L'Italiano*, even as he continued to contribute to them, while *La Conquista dello Stato* languished and came to an end. A new project entered his head: to "sell" the regime abroad under the most seductive appearances. Indeed, the moment called for strong propaganda action: if Fascism had triumphed domestically, its international valuation remained low. Perhaps the trains arrived on time, but the press around the world remained generally hostile. From their exile in Paris, London, New York, or Moscow, the *fuoriusciti* loudly cried that Mussolini had taken over through violence and fraud, conveniently forgetting their own ineptitude and divisions—in other words, their own share of responsibility for the advent of Fascism. It was, then, a genuine battle of ideas that Malaparte wanted to wage against his adversaries. To do so, he needed a more sophisticated approach than a simple celebration of the land or the countryside. *Les Nouvelles Littéraires*, decidedly attentive to what happened in Italy, observed this intent in a comment of December 3, 1927:

> Two tendencies divide Italian literature today. The supporters of Strapaese are in reality ultranationalists who want to purge Italian literature of any relationship with foreign countries. It is a "peasants' revolution," says Curzio Malaparte, leader of Strapaese, and he praises his partisans for having "big shoes and fine minds," and for having produced a revolution in Italian letters that was, he claims, indispensable. "For too long, alas, the capital of so many Italians has no longer been Rome, nor Florence, Naples, Bologna, or Milan, but Paris..." He includes in his disdain and anger all the "Parisians of Stracittà." According to the latter, to remain faithful to national

traditions would be a sign of bad taste. And so they blindly adopt the petit bourgeois ideal of the fashionable writer who comes from Paris, Vienna, or New York.[20]

"900" was a product of refined bibliophilia, to this day appreciated and sought out by collectors, embellished by the art of Picasso, Campigli, Rosai, and the leading surrealist painters. The magazine opened its doors to the greatest names of international literature without apparent ideological distinctions, from the Anglo-Saxons Joyce and Woolf to the Soviet Ehrenburg, publishing chapters from fundamental works of the twentieth century like *Ulysses* and *Zeno's Conscience*. The particularly substantial French contingent counted Philippe Soupault, Yvan Goll, Max Jacob, Blaise Cendrars, Pierre Mac Orlan, and others. Indeed, *"900"* was clearly modeled on the Parisian *Nouvelle Revue Française*, and could be considered politically innocuous, in part for its limited output of three to four issues per year, with a small (and pricey) print run. The ironic, cultured Bontempelli—a fine mind, hardly a Fascist deep down, "the most European of Italian writers" (*Les Nouvelles Littéraires* again), passionate about all the isms, a pioneer of "magical realism"—was the ideal teammate for such an operation.* He was, from almost every point of view, the opposite of Curzio, even physically: "slim and slight, coquettish in his composure, in the almost geometric presence of his eye, his jaw, his salt-and-pepper hair, but truly seductive, with

---

*His essays, sketches, and short stories appeared in the 1920s and 1930s in *The Cornhill Magazine* and other English and American publications. Some of his novels are now available in recent translations, notably *The Chess Set in the Mirror* (Philadelphia: Paul Dry Books, 2007) and *The Faithful Lover* (Austin, TX: Host Publications, 2007), both translated by Estelle Gilson.

the hint of an always Platonic smile."²¹ It was precisely their differences that allowed them to understand each other. The friendship went back to their bohemian years in Rome, when they shared a wretched room with two beds behind Piazza del Popolo. It would remain strong enough that Malaparte, in a rare homage, described him after the war as "my master, and that of many writers, for the probity of his talent, culture, and style."²²

The results lived up to early expectations, but management of the publication soon proved troubled. To Strapaese adherents among the provincial Fascist press, Malaparte's explanations and professions of loyalty no longer sufficed. Attacks against the "xenophile" Bontempelli took aim at him as well; actually, there was even more anger at him, because the disappointment was greater. His incendiary writings of the early years of Fascism had earned him a certain popularity among the movement's base, and now he had thrown this capital down the drain. If we can identity a moment in which Malaparte lost out in the political game, this was it. It's no coincidence that the first reports by the political police that have come down to us date from this period, late 1927, even if it is likely there were earlier ones. An anonymous informer wrote from Paris that "Sukert [sic] arrived here looking for a publisher";* the head of

---

*The reports were essentially of two types, generally anonymous but recognizable thanks to certain characteristics. Reports by more or less spontaneous informers are often just a few lines long, whereas those by regular agents sometimes take up several pages and display a more psychological or political bent. The material is generally of a good and even an excellent professional level. It was especially after the 1930 establishment of OVRA that the political police armed itself with one of the most sophisticated information services in Europe. See the monumental work by Mauro Canali, *Le spie del regime* (Bologna: Il Mulino, 2004).

the political police, in Rome, added: "For the moment he is not undertaking political activity, intent as he is on creating as much publicity around his name as possible."[23] Nino Frank, a young cosmopolitan intellectual, Swiss citizen, and well-known anti-Fascist, was the magazine's very active editorial assistant in Paris, appointed by Bontempelli. Frank was at the origin of an incident that could have cost Malaparte dearly. The Fascist police discovered that Frank accompanied the writer on his Parisian rounds, and Malaparte, having caught wind of this, dumped him publicly, accusing him of defaming Mussolini and Fascism.[24] His case was not an isolated one; indeed, numerous other collaborators were designated or unmasked as opponents of the regime. Publication of the magazine, now in disrepute, was suspended in early 1929. Ultimately, *"900"* remains an alluring landmark in the panorama of ideas of the first half of the twentieth century. In its pages we find not only names of real importance but also an élan, a breathing space, a curiosity about major new international currents—currents soon stifled by a regime increasingly characterized by autarky and cultural retreat.

Malaparte does not appear to have suffered unduly on account of this failure and, unlike Bontempelli, would not experience any lasting effects. He had spent almost five years immersed in political battles; the time had come to return to literature. At the end of 1926 he went so far as to declare that he didn't believe (anymore?) in a "Fascist art," which didn't prevent him from hatching new ventures at his usual frenetic pace. At the start of 1927, he became editorial director of the publishing house Edizioni de *La Voce* in Florence. Its founder, Giuseppe Prezzolini, entrusted him with his baby at a moment when, without breaking with the regime, he had decided to accept a position in the League of Nations' International Committee on

Intellectual Cooperation (a sort of predecessor to UNESCO), in Paris, from whence he subsequently moved to New York. Prezzolini had understood that the battle-of-ideas era was over in Italy, something that Malaparte would still take some time to understand. The latter was then also given the reins to a somewhat faded publication, *La Fiera Letteraria*, which Fascism wanted to transform into a breeding ground for young talents, rechristened shortly after as *L'Italia Letteraria*. This time, *Les Nouvelles Littéraires* hastened to welcome his appointment:

> Curzio Malaparte has become the editor of *La Fiera Letteraria*: a good opportunity for the magazine to shed its embonpoint, because Malaparte has demonstrated extraordinary professionalism and literary courage. He has recently fought two or three duels and regularly contributes to *La Fiera* his "Pages of the Sibyl," among the liveliest and most caustic pieces written in recent years.[25]

All these ventures would rapidly fail, one after the other. Malaparte cried conspiracy, as usual, but the cause lay in his unbridled ambition, in his spasmodic need to draw attention to himself, to the point of irritating or frightening audiences and patrons. It was, in a certain sense, to his credit: Malaparte would never be a faithful hack, ready to fall in line. With Edizioni de *La Voce*, which published *"900"* as well, he had taken over a remarkable roster of Italian and foreign authors, some of them suspect or disapproved of. To respect contracts already signed, while avoiding issues with the censors, he often had to adapt the title and contents of the books he published, in accordance with a practice then fairly widespread. Thus the initial title of the otherwise excellent Italian translation of *Death in Venice* was the incongruous *Un sogno* (A dream), because the censor ruled that the allusion to death contained in the original title would have harmed the reputation (and tourist industry) of the lagoon city. Or else he had to precede the works with a warning from the publisher, distancing himself from the theses expressed therein, or tear apart in a review a work he himself had published. All this verges on the grotesque; but it was necessary to improvise, and Malaparte was already an expert player. And these experiences would at least have the merit of developing his fine taste as an intellectual agitator and talent scout.

But the work, *his* work? The question gnawed at him. Unrealized projects piled up, while his actual output was modest: no *Viva Caporetto!*, not even an *Italia barbara*. In Longanesi's magazine *L'Italiano* he published the first part of a rather trite amusement, *Il reame dei cornuti di Francia* (The kingdom of French cuckolds), which twenty years later would be dusted off by his opponents beyond the Alps to harm him. He followed up with a picaresque novel, *Avventure di un capitano di sventura* (Adventures of a soldier of misfortune), a final tribute to the ideals of Strapaese. Things went better with the ballads of *L'arcitaliano*, and here we should pause to consider Malaparte as a poet, a part of his oeuvre that has been ignored abroad and is now little known in Italy as well. And yet especially in rhyming satire, Malaparte left behind some memorable works. Certain refrains, like the one from the "Cantata dell'Arcimussolini" (Song of the arch-Mussolini)—"Spunta il sole e canta il gallo / Mussolini monta a cavallo" (The sun comes up and the cock crows / Mussolini climbs on his horse)—have become proverbial and are often cited without mention of the author. Behind the winking reference to Il Duce's sporting life can be read an exhortation to remain vigilant in the midst of triumph, something underlined in the preceding, more threatening verse: "Chi ha tradito paghera" (Traitors will pay). Yet Malaparte was also the author of many more poems with an intimist tone, which he continued to churn out at every stage of his life and to publish occasionally in magazines or anthologies.[26] Here, however, the results were bad, sometimes very bad, especially if we think about what Italian poetry was able to express in those years. And we can understand why. His temperament, realist to the point of harshness, and his inability to let go and really expose himself predisposed him to satire, not to lyrical outbursts. At most, he could find his feet in the more elegiac accents of compositions like "I morti di Bligny giocano a carte," but these were, precisely, exceptions.

In the same period, he published the first part of another satirical work, in prose this time, that represents a turning point in his oeuvre, to the extent that its title stuck to him like a second pseudonym: *Don Camaleo*.

Duce and Chameleon

To understand the origin of this new provocation, we must return to Malaparte's enduring hope of carving out a leading role for himself on the new Italian scene. He preferred to court heresy and go for broke rather than keep his head down, to be an enfant terrible rather than a liegeman. But everything has a price. The great career he dreamed of in the party and in the government continued to elude him; he had to make do with more or less honorary roles and the odd stipend. He'd tried everything, in every direction, but the doors he'd pried open closed again one after the other, leaving him outside. Everybody knew him, but everybody, or nearly everybody, distrusted him. The organs of radical Fascism, like *L'Impero*, founded by the Futurists Mario Carli and Emilio Settimelli, and *Il Tevere*, founded by Telesio Interlandi, future champion of the racial laws, continued to attack him, mocking the erstwhile braggart of *La Conquista dello Stato* ready to put the country to fire and sword. Whether he called himself Suckert or Malaparte, he was always a spoilsport. He was only thirty, but Fascism was a regime of young men, and one aged quickly on the system's fringes. He gladly acted the disenchanted cynic, feigning to look at the facts from on high, but it wasn't hard to see that for a pose. In reality, Malaparte was champing at the bit as, with a heavy heart, he watched eleventh-hour recruits, greenhorns, and daddy's boys like Galeazzo Ciano, who hadn't taken part in either the war or the squadrist movement, overtake him in the salons, corridors of power, and other places that counted in the capital. From this psychological—even more than political—motivation would spring *Don Camaleo*, the audacious pamphlet that would contribute so much to the fame of Malaparte, in life and in death. And do him so much harm.

The background of *Don Camaleo* was the establishment of the regime, following the gradual conquest of power in the three years after 1922. Mussolini was firmly installed as the leader of the nation but had not yet succumbed to the imperial megalomania and exaltation of the new caesar. If in parades he still wore his black shirt under the uniform of a First Honorary Corporal of the Fascist militia, without signs of rank or decorations, he had meanwhile discovered the frock coat and striped pants of the statesman and the diplomat. His character remained essentially the same: he had too much disdain for other men and too much belief in his own star to change his behavior or vision of the world. But as his power grew, so did his isolation. The only person to exert a moderating influence on him was his younger brother Arnaldo, to whom he entrusted the helm of *Il Popolo d'Italia* and the care of most of his speeches and writings.*

After Arnaldo died of a heart attack, in December 1931, Mussolini shut himself away in almost total solitude, which made him more vulnerable to a disastrous cult of personality. The *ras* and other early hard-liners were reduced to the role of vassals, substituted by a new class of functionaries, bureaucrats, industrialists, and military men, and by a crowd of clients who had rallied around the system as one rallies around the winner, ready to abandon him the moment Victory gazes elsewhere. Mussolini, at the beginning, knew this perfectly well; adulation had yet to weigh down his features and his gait. He exploited the weaknesses of his followers—all interchangeable—more than their strengths. Sometimes he chose the best, especially if they were young and enthusiastic, because they lacked experience and knew little or nothing of the history that preceded them. In this way, ably mixing power's various ingredients—corruption, ambition, idealism, intimidation, and, when required, violence—he could end up believing that he had established Fascism on durable foundations (if not "millenarian" ones, like his future

---

*Mussolini's *My Autobiography* (New York: Scribner's, 1928), written especially for the American public, was in fact drafted by Arnaldo and the then US ambassador in Rome, Richard Washburn Child, a convinced pro-Fascist who later tried in vain to establish a contact between Il Duce and President Roosevelt.

German comrade). Yet, faced with a new war, these foundations would crumble into dust.

Contrary to the image, simplified to the point of caricature, that one often encounters of Mussolini, especially abroad, he was probably the most complex and contradictory of all the twentieth-century dictators.* And yet his personality—so elusive, behind the appearances—was by then already the subject of several admonitory texts, which deserved more attention from his contemporaries. For the most part, these contributions were published abroad, by political refugees. Sometimes he commented on them in articles published under obvious pseudonyms—Mussolini boasted of reading everything about himself; his journalistic activity was relentless till the end—while the censors already ran rampant in the country. The French case is particularly interesting and prominently features the publisher Bernard Grasset. After the failed project of a Mussolini biography written by Malaparte, Grasset managed to publish two notable books in a row in 1932. The first, titled simply *Mussolini*, with a pensive-aggressive portrait of the dictator on its cover, was written by the playwright and novelist Antonio Aniante (1900–1983), a former follower of Gobetti who remained a man of versatile talent and little success throughout his long, unhappy life. The second was *Mussolini diplomatico*, by Gaetano Salvemini (1877–1953), an exemplary analysis of the first phase of Il Duce's foreign policy by a respected anti-Fascist politician, historian, and economist. Mussolini himself answered with a detailed and nominally anonymous confutation in the Italian press.

*Hence I have given to my biography of the dictator the title, in French, of *Le mystère Mussolini* (Paris: Perrin, 2021) and, in Italian, of *Il caso Mussolini* (Milan: Neri Pozza, 2022).

While Salvemini's volume is well known to specialists,* Aniante's sunk undeservedly into oblivion. Nonetheless, the latter is a finely nuanced portrait of the dictator and, at the same time, an autobiography of the generation of writers that passed almost directly from the trenches to Fascist revolution. Aniante absolves Mussolini of his most serious responsibilities, such as the Matteotti murder; but he does not hide from French readers, especially those who tended to find justifications for him, that Il Duce wanted to dominate Italy as an absolute ruler and would do anything to stay in power. It followed, Aniante observed, that "Fascist intellectuals like Malaparte are continually in conflict with the hierarchy."[27] As we'll see, Malaparte did not appreciate this recognition, which risked exposing him to reprisals from on high.

Compared with these two texts, *Don Camaleo*, somewhere between a political pamphlet and a literary divertissement, can give the impression of harboring more limited and above all more personal ambitions. Its reputation is generally based on the title, because even in Italy the book has been out of print for decades, and on the image it seems to offer of its author, rather than on the book's content. Nevertheless, one is struck to this day by the originality and impertinence of Malaparte's approach, simultaneously situating himself within the regime and outside (or above) it. It is not just satire but the laying bare of an archetypal complex. As we have seen, Mussolini was the only figure, along with Gobetti, who had truly impressed himself on Malaparte's nature and development. But his "separated

---

*Salvemini continued to organize and publish in Britain and the United States, before returning to Italy after the war. Among his many works: *Under the Axe of Fascism* (1936) and, with George La Piana, *What to Do with Italy* (1943). He remained till the last a resolute opponent of Malaparte.

brother" crushed him with his intransigence, while the presence of the *padre padrone*, so encumbering, so carnal, provoked a reaction in him that was—for once—human. The explanation was simple: Gobetti represented the country's elite; Mussolini incarnated its masses. "It is impossible to paint the portrait of Mussolini without painting the portrait of the Italian people" (MU, 67). Malaparte has been reproached for the pages of *Muss, Il grande imbecille*, and the other postwar writings in which he mocks the leader he had for so long adulated. And yet, if we just cast our mind back to the famous scene, which he did *not* witness, of Mussolini's hanging in Piazzale Loreto, as it appears in *The Skin*, we understand that only in his fallen state was the dictator truly dear to him; only reduced in his turn to the status of victim did he successfully provoke his pity, and not only his vanity. In *Muss* we find the sketch of an even more extraordinary (untrue) episode: his encounter in Rome's Piazza Colonna with Mussolini's alleged executioner.* The text, of which I offer here only the most relevant passages, is worth an entire psychoanalytic session:

> [Mussolini's assassin] walked slowly, eyes lowered. I passed before him once, twice, five times, to get a good look at him. He had a pale

---

*Who killed Mussolini and Clara Petacci? Where, and in what circumstances? Aside from the date (April 28, 1945), everything is still a subject of controversy in this sinister episode that has absorbed historians for more than three-quarters of a century. According to the much-debated official version, the death sentence (itself controversial) handed down by the Committee of National Liberation for Northern Italy was carried out on the direct order of the Communist partisan Walter Audisio (alias Colonnello Valerio), later a PCI member of parliament and senator. Malaparte, without naming him, included in his sketch the man's profession (accountant) and physical appearance (beret, trench coat, toothbrush mustache).

face, wrapped, like a piece of meat, in skin resembling butcher paper the color of skin.* The face of an idiot and a coward. I'm sorry to say he had the face of an idiot and a coward, because assassins are sacred, they have something sacred in them, which commands respect.... Assassins, when led to their execution, used to pass through a hushed crowd... On their left shoulder they would carry an invisible owl with the eyes of Athena, *Athena Glaukopis*, owl-eyed....

... I was overwhelmed by a profound disgust, by sad disappointment, thinking that this was the man who had slain Mussolini, who had had the sad honor of slaying Mussolini. And I wondered why fate had allotted such an endeavor to such a man, such a Brutus.... To die by the hand of one of his own [followers] seemed to me, and still does, the only end that he could have hoped for himself. If I had been one of them, I would have shot him without hesitation. His son was not beside him at that moment, nor any blood relation; it was the responsibility of one of his followers to shoot him. I would not have hesitated a moment.

... I said to myself: "He's a thief, not an assassin. He killed him not like you kill a man, but like you steal a bit of money from a drawer.... Then he stretched out his hands to rummage through the pockets of the dead man.... I would like to know how much that theft brought him. A few thousand lire, a seat in parliament, maybe a gold cigarette case (but Mussolini didn't smoke), maybe a watch. But Mussolini didn't wear a watch, never looked at a watch, didn't need to know what time it was. Or maybe, that day in Dongo, he had in his pocket the old silver watch the editors of *Avanti* had

---

*Malaparte, who loved John Dos Passos, may be recalling a passage he read on Lipari: "A man with a face like a raw steak walked up the steps." See *The 42nd Parallel* (1930; London: Penguin, 1973), 32.

presented him in 1912, the same watch he had with him in October 1922: stopped at 6 p.m. on October 28, 1922, when he rose to power.... The victors of 1945 were afraid of that watch, stopped at that hour. To get it, they would have slaughtered all of Italy, would have rummaged through the pockets of thousands, of millions of dead Italians...." So I said to myself: and I ran to the bus as it prepared to leave, leaped onto the platform, pushed my way through the throng of passengers, reached the assassin. He looked at me and blanched.

"Pardon me," I said to him in a low voice, "would you be so kind as to tell me the time?" The man pulled his left hand from the pocket of his trench coat, glanced at his wristwatch.

"I'm sorry," he said in an unsteady voice, "my watch has stopped." (MU, 71–75)

It's not surprising that Malaparte avoided making this text public, so revealing is it of his love-hate relationship with Mussolini's figure and even, carnally, with his body.* Il Duce becomes by turns Caesar,

---

*The sacralization of the leader's body, alive or dead, played an essential role in Fascist mythology; see Sergio Luzzatto, *The Body of Il Duce: Mussolini's Corpse and the Fortunes of Italy*, trans. Frederika Randall (New York: Henry Holt, 2014). In April 1945, Alessandro Pavolini, the party's last secretary, called for forty thousand diehards to come to the "Valtellina redoubt," to turn it into "Fascism's Thermopylae," around Mussolini. A few hundred in total, nearly all adolescents, followed him. A year later, Mussolini's remains, buried in an unmarked grave at Musocco Cemetery in Milan, were stolen and hidden for three months by a group of young "nostalgics" holding out for a more dignified burial. Eventually authorities recovered the body in a Franciscan monastery in Pavia and moved it to a Capuchin monastery northwest of Milan, where it stayed, in secret, for eleven years. On August 30, 1957, the body was buried in the Mussolini family vault in the cemetery at San Cassiano di Predappio.

FASCISM AND HIGH SOCIETY (1925–1933)

Napoleon, and "the great imbecile," a Shakespearian idiot, without any contradiction between these visions. He lived the life of the greats and deserved the death of the greats, better if by the hand of a blood relation or a disciple. One thinks of Mishima at the end, surrounded by the most ardent members of his personal army of suicidal praetorians; but also of the Salò diehards who would not have hesitated to strike down their leader if he had been so weak as to spare his son-in-law Ciano, the viper in the nest, the relative who betrayed him. That Malaparte draws here on the symbolic power of the parricide, which does not countenance the unclean hands of a common executioner,* is the best demonstration of his frustrations. He cannot liberate himself from the influence of the *padre padrone*, even when the latter lies muddy and disfigured at his feet.

It was the end point of a long and tortuous journey. But it does not constitute an umpteenth about-face. Over the course of the 1920s, up to and including *Don Camaleo*, Malaparte remained one of Fascism's most outspoken and least conformist voices, when the majority of his fellow intellectuals had already chosen the path of compliance, or of the "honest dissembling" of the seventeenth-century writer Torquato Accetto, revived by Benedetto Croce. The articles Malaparte continued to devote to Mussolini, the man of the Italian "October Revolution" (that is, the 1922 March on Rome), are highly representative of this attitude. For him, in a 1923 essay, the authentic, uncontested leader was the one who, "when he *realizes*

---

*From a Marxist perspective, the symbolism is just the opposite: the responsibility for killing the tyrant lies with the anonymous representative of the oppressed people and of the party leading the proletariat. Thus, and not only for security reasons, the PCI hid the name of the "official" executioner of the dictator for years, until it was publicly disclosed by investigating journalists.

he has betrayed his own nature, has become an Italian, an ordinary Italian like all the rest, revolts."[28] In 1925, celebrating the third anniversary of the March on Rome, he emphatically took up the theme again in the name of the hard-liners, whose mouthpiece he claimed to be. In an open letter, almost as if speaking to an equal, he enjoined Il Duce to "realize the revolution through constant, decisive government action [and] turn us sansculottes and veterans of the Fascist revolution into the intrepid grenadiers of future battles."[29] Two years later, he lampooned the deified "arch-Mussolini," and cited Madame de Staël to ask: "When will his old friends notice that Napoleon has replaced Monsieur Bonaparte?"[30] Audacious, certainly, and also prophetic. But all this counted for less than he hoped. The leader ignored him. Malaparte, with the Matteotti affair resolved, no longer mattered much in his eyes.

The two men met rather less often than Malaparte let on—probably not more than five or six times, face to face—and there is no evidence of a real friendship, much less an intimacy, between them. (But then, again, the dictator treated all his subordinates as mere instruments.) To the writer's devotion—rendered obligatory, of course, by the establishment of the regime, but fundamentally sincere until at least the early 1930s—Il Duce would respond in a detached manner, stoic but benevolent. The most obvious example, as we'll see, would be the alternation of the stick and the carrot throughout the *confino* affair. What Mussolini really thought of Malaparte is not hard to find out, as several sufficiently credible testimonies have come down to us. He appreciated his energy and ingenuity, and he didn't forget his support during the Matteotti affair, but that was as far as it went. Above all, he granted him no political role of any significance. Compared with the likes of Farinacci, Balbo, and Dino Grandi, and even to other, minor *ras*, with their local power bases, Malaparte was simply no match. Even on the intellectual level, Mussolini's esteem for him was relative and more concerned with him as a journalist or agitator than as a genuine thinker. He considered him not a true Fascist but an inveterate individualist, who used the revolution to get ahead—not that that bothered him, because Mussolini, in due time, appreciated talent more than loyalty. It is in these terms that he spoke of Malaparte to a young journalist, Yvon de Begnac, to whom Mussolini dictated his thoughts for posterity between 1934 and 1943. And it is significant that Il Duce entrusted to this merely diligent scribe the role of interlocutor stubbornly denied to Malaparte. Here is a representative sample of those entries:

> I know Malaparte is bitter because I haven't catapulted him into the [Italian] Academy. Malaparte is a clever man.... Don't tell me he's always sincere. He's had everything from us. And he doesn't know the danger that "man runs in wanting everything." The revolution cannot grant power to those who do not wield it at the service of the collective. Malaparte will always, and only, be at the service of himself.... He's a typical little D'Annunzian Tuscan.... It's the provinces, not the Collegio Cicognini, that brought him to Rome. That bit of good D'Annunzianism that slipped under his skin gives his prose and poetry a veneer of Europeanism.

Malaparte then tried to hook up with Begnac, to write the book on Il Duce. But the chief would scuttle the project:

> Malaparte looks to the novel. He was important for the culture of Fascism, as long as Prezzolini, at first, and Bottai, later, tempered his

impulses to fantasy. But there is something inhuman in his boasting and his desire to be considered outside the contemporary stream of fashion, not out of a need for isolation or solitude, but to present himself as an inimitable exemplar of his age. Malaparte has always talked about revolutions to carry out. Thanks to his immodesty, of which he is an exemplary product, he is unable to distinguish, in my revolution, between those who carry it out and the man who is its inspiration and leader.[31]

The last sentence here offers a good illustration of a relationship conceived in profoundly different, not to say opposed, ways by the two interlocutors. A voracious and disjointed autodidact, Mussolini would always be ill at ease with the luminaries of the Italian Academy (created in 1929, on the French model), to which Malaparte would never belong. The likes of Gentile, Pirandello, Marconi, and Respighi bored him to death, as did the institution's great archaeologists, scientists, and philologists. He found the ramblings of Marinetti or the honorary Fascist Ezra Pound unbearable, but he respected them for their international fame, and because they were idealists, a category he was little acquainted with. The same could be said of Nicola Bombacci, an ex-Communist with the look of a soothsayer, a bushy beard, and flashing eyes. He had swapped Lenin for Mussolini, never hurt a fly, and would share Il Duce's melancholy evenings in the last months of Salò, before being strung up by his feet beside him. Mussolini's relationship with D'Annunzio was more complicated. The poet hounded him with messages, exhortations, warnings, and a mountain of debts. But what to do? D'Annunzio was the regime's vestal virgin, before becoming its Cassandra at the moment of the tragic German alliance, which he had in vain opposed.

He was the sole rival who could threaten Il Duce at any given moment, due to his celebrity and authentic charisma. Better to mummify him in his hillside hermitage on the Lago di Garda, the Vittoriale degli Italiani, surrounded by informers of both sexes dressed as drivers, cooks, or shepherdesses, and wait patiently for the mummy to stop knocking on his door and throw open those of the beyond instead.

Malaparte, in comparison, had won himself a rather more modest space. But perhaps herein lies the source of the indulgence he inspired in the inhabitant of Palazzo Venezia, even inside the immense bare hall from which Mussolini surveilled, guided, and scolded the nation, from dawn to dusk, every day of the week, permitting himself increasingly rare interruptions to leave and see how the external world was getting on. Malaparte was a young, courageous, and intelligent young man, who had known how to shake off the extremists at the right moment and tried to make himself useful. Moreover, he was an excellent writer, of the type Mussolini liked—cold, acerbic, and nimble—who grabbed the reader and held on till the end of the sentence or article. He may have had a naturally rebellious character, which earned him many enemies and rivals, but for Il Duce, loyal to the golden rule of divide and conquer, that was actually an advantage. If he subsequently made Malaparte feel the weight of his ill humor, his benevolent and scornful attitude would never change. The reason is simple, and we have already alluded to it. In Il Duce's eyes, Malaparte never rose from bit player to interlocutor, never worried or threatened him. He was substantially innocuous: thus for him he existed, like 90 percent of Italians, only to the extent he proved useful to him. If he served him well, better to compensate him, but always judiciously; if not, kick him out the door, or into prison. In reality, Il Duce always displayed toward him a notable indulgence, even a rough affection, if the word can be applied to Mussolini. And he did so not only in the 1920s, but literally up until the day before his fall. But here the problem is reversed. Malaparte didn't want affection, not knowing what to do with it; he wanted respect and something more. He dreamed of a relationship at the top, like the one Malraux would have with de Gaulle, which he would never obtain, in terms either of form or of substance. At that moment Mussolini was truly—and would always remain—not a big brother (fifteen years separated them), but the *Vaterfigur* of his existence. He was the incontestable, untouchable, indisputable father, in a way that neither Erwin nor Milziade ever managed to be: a *natural* authority, in short. They had so much in common! A provincial childhood and a burning desire to escape it, Mussolini via Switzerland, he via France; a history of republicanism and anarchism in the family; a taste for solitude; contempt for the bourgeois; devotion to the cult of strength, pushed to the point of asceticism (no alcohol, tobacco, gambling...). After the Matteotti murder, Malaparte ran significant personal risks: the taint of complicity in a political killing was no small matter for a writer already attentive to the judgment of posterity. In exchange, he demanded to be treated as an equal: he knew he possessed a talent the other lacked, and he didn't intend to be a mere object in his hands. Malaparte suffered from the one-way nature of the relationship, because in the end this omnipotent father did not want anything to do with him, had no intention of making him his heir apparent, his favorite disciple.

Nearly all biographers of Malaparte have taken up the brilliant version he gives of their first face-to-face meeting, in 1923, at Palazzo Chigi, in Mussolini's office, when the latter was both prime minister and minister of foreign affairs. Comrade Suckert enters with his heart in his throat, convinced he's there to receive a reward. Nothing doing. Il Duce, after ignoring him for some time, without inviting him to sit down,* gives him a severe reprimand for publicly making fun of the ugly ties he wears. A contrite Malaparte acknowledges his fault, swears he will never do it again, and, on the point of taking his leave, humbly asks to say one last thing. "Go ahead," Il Duce replies grudgingly. "You're wearing an ugly tie today as well" (DFP, 154). The anecdote is malicious—all of Italy knew that Mussolini was taking lessons in etiquette and how to dress, to live up to his new role—and surely spurious, because no one in Italy, even in those early years, would have dared to address the dictator in such a way. But in it we can recognize the outline of *Don Camaleo* and the moral that inspired it. Of all his books, this is the only one Malaparte wrote, at least initially, to draw the attention of a single reader, who encompassed all the others. To mock a hero makes him more human, while also making oneself a bit heroic. Paradoxically, the book's title has lived on in the popular imagination to indicate not its protagonist, but its author. Later, a sharp-witted reader well acquainted with both, Giuseppe Bottai, would ask, "Was *Don Camaleo* perhaps an autobiography?"[32]

If Malaparte chose the satirical approach, which better accorded with his temperament, it was also because Il Duce was taken seriously by followers and adversaries, courtiers and zealots, who turned him into a monument rather than saw him for what he was. Surrounded

---

*Mussolini would subsequently perfect the protocol: only important guests, mostly foreigners, would be able to sit down opposite him. All others, including ministers and former comrades, would remain standing, at attention, and speak up only if authorized or questioned.

by universal reverence—which, with his successes, increased abroad as well—Il Duce withdrew into swirls of incense smoke.* It was a stroke of intuition, and sincere for once, but not enough to make Malaparte a historian or an impartial analyst. Compared with Aniante and especially with Salvemini, who sought to examine Fascism and its leader with greater objectivity, Malaparte chose a method that was entirely impressionistic; it recalls, without having its philosophical energy, the great precedent of *Gulliver's Travels*.† He was in thrall to this Mussolini, a "polymorphous being," who under his eyes evolved into a series of allegorical creatures endowed with easily recognizable human characteristics. And the book's moral, equally Swiftian, was entrusted not to Mussolini, but to a fictional character, Dr. Libero, representing the hated (hypocritical, skeptical, and sententious) pre-Fascist elite: "'A free man!' exclaimed Dr. Libero with deep disdain. 'The road to hell is paved with free men'" (DONC, 328).

Don Camaleo, whose first subtitle was "I raised a chameleon," had a disputed genesis, which was in fact typical of Malaparte's most important works, nearly all of which were subject to rewriting, at times significant, on various subsequent occasions. Thirty-two

---

*Around this time an ambassador of the old school was sent into early retirement. Received by Mussolini for a farewell visit, he gave him an extensive report on his last mission, to the Geneva disarmament conference. "The other countries do not have recourse to a toxic gas that we produce in great quantities," he concluded. "Which?" a surprised Mussolini retorted. "Incense, Duce." Unlike Malaparte's story about the ties, this anecdote is authentic. (Not incidentally, the outgoing ambassador had little to fear on this occasion, having just been made a senator by the king.)

†Malaparte greatly admired Swift. He would cite him in particular at the end of his preface to the first Italian edition of his coup d'état study, *Tecnica del colpo di Stato* (Milan: Bompiani, 1948).

episodes, roughly two-fifths of the book, were published in *La Chiosa*, a women's supplement to the *Giornale di Genova*, between July 1, 1926, and January 17, 1927. Why choose such a marginal, anodyne publication? Was it because he failed to find a more important venue? Or was it instead because it provided him with a cover? The book had been commissioned or prompted by Gobetti, which made it impossible to distribute... Whereas the dedication to Gobetti, dusted off for the occasion, would turn out to be very useful after the fall of Fascism. Malaparte furnished a somewhat different version of the book's origins in the preface to the first single-volume edition, published in Italy only in 1946, which provided the basis for the French translation appearing two years later.* But this seems less important than the rest: he claimed that the manuscript, which he kept in duplicate, was confiscated by the Genoa prefecture on Mussolini's orders, and that even *La Chiosa* was suspended, as a precautionary measure. None of this is very plausible, seeing as he would serenely publish some passages of it shortly after in Longanesi's still very official magazine *L'Italiano*.[33] It was hence most likely the dictator's haughty indifference that wounded Malaparte, more than his divine rage: let us recall his admission, one of the few that seemed heartfelt, according to which silence weighed more heavily on him than any attack. After the war, Malaparte would take advantage of the ostensible persecution he suffered on account of this book to exaggerate his anti-Fascist credentials, in France and elsewhere abroad. He would insist, as if on a point of honor, that "if I had not published *Don Camaleo* in 1928 [*sic*], when Mussolini was

---

*The Italian edition was illustrated by Riccardo Magni; the French, equally noteworthy, by Orfeo Tamburi. Both are much sought after by bibliophiles.

alive, I would perhaps forgo doing so today. It is unworthy of a writer to make a dead man look ridiculous, if it's true the dead cannot defend themselves" (DONC, 19).* *Excusatio non petita, accusatio manifesta*, as the ancients in their wisdom had it...

These distortions have done a disservice to the merits of the text, which are real. In this period, to present the omnipotent Duce not as the hero who had "sculpted" the revolution with his political genius and the force of his will, but as a high-wire performer who knew how to make use of all the politician's tricks to ascend to power and stay there, already required a certain bravery. Malaparte had continued his intellectual insurgency after the establishment of the dictatorship. But he had never dared represent the leader with the features of a mischievous little animal that gets by in all situations by adapting to its environment. To the imperatives imposed by Il Duce—such as "Live dangerously!" or "Cast your heart beyond the obstacle!"—which at this point covered the walls of all Italy, he countered with an eternally skeptical vision of national history, in which the strongman of the moment would collapse sooner or later under the weight of his personal flaws and the fickleness of public opinion. Thus the book was permeated with advice, often drawn from his *Conquista dello Stato* articles, which Mussolini had by no means asked for and which, following his triumph, could only irritate him:

> The Italian people has preserved, despite everything, its own moral consciousness, and this is precisely why it doesn't love victors. It

---

*In addition to this preface, the book includes a bio-bibliographical note—almost certainly by the author—that cites his contributions to *Energie Nuove* and *Rivoluzione Liberale*, Gobetti's two main magazines, without mentioning his editorship of or contributions to *La Conquista dello Stato*.

applauds them but doesn't esteem them. I would say it disdains them. And for the same reason, it does not love the defeated: it doesn't applaud them, because defeat already implies, in politics, a moral judgment, and because it would be naive to applaud the defeated; but neither does it jeer them, as other, more politically advanced peoples do. (DONC, 257)

We find here in embryonic form the thesis that Malaparte, always generous when it comes to unsolicited advice, would set forth in *The Skin* with regard to the Americans. It was definitely Gobetti's reading of Fascism, and especially of the man Mussolini, which Malaparte made his own. That said, the text could not pass for anti-Mussolinian in 1926–28, or even in 1946–48. The Chameleon, unscrupulous politician of a thousand faces, was the man able to successfully incarnate the national spirit, only to be struck down in a final defeat (presaged in the 1920s, confirmed in the 1940s), which is clearly the worst ending for any politician. Once again, it was not by the yardstick of an abstract ideal, à la Gobetti, but only by his defeat that Malaparte judged Mussolini after the war. It was the opposite of strength, the basis of his rise, then of his triumph, which Il Duce was unable to preserve at the moment of his fall. But when Malaparte wrote *Don Camaleo*, what he had before him was still Mussolini the conqueror. His "transformism" consists in a principle of cunning, in a mode of adaptation and political survival, not involving any moral judgment. And here ends the analogy with Gobetti, for whom the term had entirely negative connotations. It is thus easy to understand why Malaparte avoided finishing *Don Camaleo* at the time, whether or not Mussolini intervened to stop its publication. He had already run too many risks: not with respect to anti-Fascism, but because he allowed himself to give advice to a sullen dictator on what he should do to stay in power. It was a gesture not of insurrection or rupture, but of impertinence. In declining to complete and publish *Don Camaleo*, Malaparte largely gave up—umpteenth paradox—the well of innocence, insolence, and amusement that, notwithstanding his constant changes of tack, he had preserved in all his efforts from those years. If this father would not let Malaparte make fun of him anymore, speak plainly, or offer his devotion and advice, how could he still feel bound to him?

L'arcitaliano picked up the same theme in a more playful tone and less direct manner. In the last issues of *La Conquista dello Stato*, which had gone from being a weekly to appearing every two months, in anticipation of ceasing publication, Malaparte would try instead to impart a more strictly political message. From the moment that "Mussolinianism" took the place of integral Fascism, "we find ourselves today in the same situation as the new post-1821 European generations and the post-1871 French generation"; it was therefore necessary to follow the way of "patience" and "interior discipline" to strengthen faith in the future.[34] Are we seeing Malaparte here displaying humility and obedience, falling in line? Must we evoke the internal exile of so many German and Soviet intellectuals under dictatorship? It seems excessive. Nevertheless, we are far from the cliché of the constantly pivoting opportunist, indifferent to anything that does not directly concern him. The Italy of 1928 hardly looks like the one he fought for, in the trenches and in the piazzas, to fulfill the revolution of the "cursed saints."[35] But there's a gulf between his revolt and opposition to the ideals of the regime. If he accepted the end of his official semidissident status, shutting down *La Conquista dello Stato*, which was collapsing in terms of sales and subscriptions anyways, that doesn't mean he had lost all hopes of a comeback. Wounded by Mussolini's indifference and threatened by the last pockets of squadrist resistance, he resolved to find a way back to the center of things.

FIATs for the Soviets!

Some good news finally arrived with the appointment of a new party secretary. In place of Farinacci, whose resignation Il Duce managed to obtain only with great difficulty, arrived the moderate Augusto Turati, who would remain in his post until October 1930.* A journalist of national-liberal extraction, industrious and accommodating, Turati was the prototype of a kind of functionary that Mussolini had come to prefer over hardened militants. Later he would fall into disgrace over the issue of bribes and of habits then considered "against nature," and the dictator would push him aside in favor of even more insignificant successors. His relations with Malaparte at the time were good, reinforced by a common passion for fencing. Turati, too, felt it was necessary to fight the influence of the *fuoriusciti*, above all in France, while avoiding recourse to violence, after the disastrous Bonservizi affair. It was preferable to use what today we would call "soft power," the art of persuasion. If *"900"* had been an excessively elitist and poorly run venture, why not start again with a project aimed at introducing young Italian authors—authentic products of the Fascist revolution—to foreign audiences?

Thus Paris, veritable gateway to educated Europe, regained

---

*Not to be confused, naturally, with the Socialist leader Filippo Turati, who would die in exile in 1932 in Paris, where Malaparte may have had the opportunity to meet him.

importance. In place of the Bontempelli-Frank duo—too compromised—Malaparte put forward a good friend, who was one of the rare figures whose independence and integrity of judgment Mussolini respected. This was Giuseppe Prezzolini, who had continued to reside in the French capital as a functionary of the League of Nations, maintaining a vast network of contacts, going back mostly to the *Voce* period. It was thanks to him that the idea for an Italian book series—published by Bernard Grasset, who had a great passion for politics and current events, and directed by Malaparte, who could count on discreet financial support secured by Turati—took shape. The patronage would be guaranteed by a Committee for International Intellectual Relations, a sort of roving chamber of culture, which was expected to attract prominent figures from around the world—all expenses paid by the Fascist Party—to show the "true" face of Mussolini's Italy.

The first candidate was Benjamin Crémieux, a great Italianist and the author of a preface to *L'Italie contre l'Europe*, the French version of *L'Europa vivente*, yet he withdrew at the last minute. Whereupon the project began rapidly to take on water. The series stalled after the first installment, a short novel by Orio Vergani, *Io, povero negro*, translated by Emmanuel Audisio, one of the first examples in Italy of a "colonial" novel, modeled on English and French precursors. A second title, by Ugo Ojetti, would fail to see the light, to Malaparte's great irritation. Ojetti, a distinguished representative of the prewar generation, who had been one of his mentors, had little in common with the Fascist "new wave"; but he had been editor in chief of the *Corriere della Sera* in 1926–27, and Malaparte cultivated in him a not disinterested friendship. Reading the exchange of letters between Malaparte and Prezzolini, you sense that the real stumbling block was the French publisher's fears that the initiative could seem led and financed by Rome, as indeed it was.[36] Malaparte also considered having *Don Cameleo* translated, and sent Prezzolini an extract titled "Napoleon Disguised as a Lizard," which *La Revue de Paris* was interested in. But in the end he dropped it, in order not to create more problems for himself at home. Ultimately, the only thing left standing for a bit was the committee, which would scrape by in Paris thanks to Prezzolini's interpersonal skills. Nonetheless, Malaparte felt that France was destined, sooner or later, to be back on his agenda.

Meanwhile, he had to find a more stable situation for himself in Italy. All he had gained from his numerous publishing initiatives were several duels and an even greater number of bitter enmities. He looked around, unsure how to proceed, and here, for the second time, Turati came to his aid. Did he do so on Il Duce's orders? It is impossible to say with certainty, but it does not seem improbable. In September 1928, practically overnight, Malaparte became the editor of *Il Mattino* of Naples, the best newspaper in the south, founded in the late nineteenth century by Matilde Serao, one of the grandes dames of Italian letters, and her husband, Edoardo Scarfoglio, a close friend of D'Annunzio. But that glorious period was now well in the past: Malaparte had to cope with a management team paralyzed by interminable disagreements among the staff. He succeeded in bringing order to the newsroom and had the use, finally, after a decade of furnished rooms, of a stately apartment in the Posillipo hills. Above all, though, he cared about remaining close to the capital, to continue following its plots and to ascend to another, more important post as soon as possible. The big occasion was not long in coming: less than six months later, on February 11,

1929, the day of the signing of the Concordat between Italy and the Holy See, one of Mussolini's greatest diplomatic successes, Malaparte became editor in chief of *La Stampa* of Turin.

This newspaper had an entirely different history. Its former owner, the liberal senator Alfredo Frassati, who was close to Giolitti, had been the last bastion of moderate anti-Fascism at the time of the Matteotti murder. Mussolini, who had a score to settle with Frassati, had forced him to cede his capital stock to the minority shareholder, considered closer to the regime: Giovanni Agnelli. Born in 1866, this former cavalry officer of indomitable energy had founded, in 1899, the Fabbrica Italiana Automobili Torino, soon known all over the world by the acronym FIAT. He was then one of the most powerful industrialists in the country, but perhaps not yet the most powerful. He would become so in the Italy of Mussolini, who also had him appointed senator by the king. His adhesion to the regime brought indisputable advantages to him and his company; but the shrewd Agnelli never figured among the businessmen most closely aligned with Fascism, as noted in police reports.[37] Nonetheless, in 1945 he would be put on trial as a collaborator and die of a heart attack prior to the procedure's conclusion. Agnelli was a singular figure, and the claim, real or apocryphal, attributed to his nephew Gianni—"we owe him everything"—can hardly be contested. He was a capitalist in the old style and at the same time a modern captain of industry, a character right out of the novels, immensely popular at the time, of Theodore Dreiser and Sinclair Lewis, with a discipline and an ambition that were almost ascetic; a patriot who wanted to provide rural Italy with a world-class industry, like his peers Pirelli, Feltrinelli, Conti, and Donegani; a brusque, introverted man, attentive to profit and duty, who would later be scarred by the premature death of his two children. Protectionist in Italy, but a supporter of free trade on the global market, Agnelli established a special relationship with the American automobile industry, which remains, after more than a century, part of the operating strategy of the FIAT Chrysler group (now part of the multinational Stellantis).

La Stampa had become, under Frassati's leadership, an authoritative media outlet, on the model of the *Times* of London, but of more limited circulation. After having reached a peak of 300,000 copies during the war, sales had descended to 160,000.[38] It was a sign of the middle classes' bewilderment in the new political environment. The paper also suffered from competition from an enterprising Turinese rival, *La Gazzetta del Popolo*, run by Ermanno Amicucci, a former Socialist who had followed the same path as Mussolini.* *La Stampa*'s new owner hoped to turn it into a popular daily, aligned with the views of the regime; at least, this was the agreement with Turati. The aim was to speak not only to the bourgeoisie but also to the workers of Turin and the rest of northern Italy, who remained strongly politicized. The Communist and Socialist Parties, although outlawed, maintained a core of sympathizers and clandestine militants in the region. Turati and Agnelli knew this and tried to defuse the danger, having realized that police-state repression alone would not suffice. The senator believed in

---

*And he would continue to follow it. During the Salò period, Amicucci would take over the *Corriere della Sera*, to which Il Duce would make regular pseudonymous contributions chronicling the bitter end of his reign, later collected in *Al tempo del bastone e della carota*, a portion of which appeared in English translation as *The Mussolini Memoirs, 1942–1943*, ed. Raymond Klibansky, trans. Frances Lobb (London: Weidenfeld & Nicolson, 1949).

this mission, beyond the fate of the regime, which he considered merely a necessary evil, a more or less unpleasant stage in the evolution of Italian society. His capitalism was tinged with Fordism, evident in his conviction that the company had to engage its employees, the better to control them, not only at work but also in their free time and family life, so as to deliver them from Bolshevik temptation. Nor should we forget the commercial profitability of the operation. At the time, *La Stampa* was only the thirty-ninth most profitable company in the FIAT group, but Agnelli was not a man to invest in a business without being certain of deriving a profit from it. Its first editor in chief, Andrea Torre, had not succeeded in this task. And chance, if that is what it was, had it that the senator met Malaparte in Naples.

We have no details as to how the writer successfully earned the trust of the powerful and suspicious industrialist, perhaps by means of common acquaintances, such as the paper's business manager, Giuseppe Colli, who would later become one of his most intransigent adversaries.[39] If the encounter was truly fortuitous, the choice of Malaparte was not the fruit of chance. Did an order come directly from Palazzo Venezia? The more likely origin was an operation prepared by Turati to put a man he considered trustworthy at the head of the FIAT newspaper. But it is hard to believe he carried it out without the preliminary authorization of Mussolini, who reserved for himself the last word on all important appointments. The fact remains that Agnelli swiftly acquired the consent of Mussolini, who supposedly nonetheless let slip this prophetic remark: "Take him if you want, but don't come whining to me about him later!" The anecdote is unreliable, but the substance real: Agnelli got the go-ahead, but at his own risk and peril. Now, if the author of *Don*

Camaleo had been in disgrace at the time, as he later maintained, it is hard to understand why Mussolini would have authorized the rise of someone who had dared challenge him. In any case, Malaparte did not hesitate to offer the required guarantees. The abundant correspondence with Turati proves that the two met, wrote to each other, or called each other regularly, sometimes even daily, to define the paper's editorial line and to select reliable editors and contributors. His instructions were unquestionably to "Fascistize" the paper.[40] After the war, Malaparte would make out that he had resisted every effort to muzzle *La Stampa*. The opposite is true; but here, too, it is necessary to recognize that, at least in part, he did things his way.

At thirty-one, Malaparte was the youngest editor in chief in the daily's history, and one of the youngest on the national press scene. He had finally achieved a position worthy of himself. He happily left Naples for Turin, after having negotiated a very lucrative contract, and set to work with his customary determination. He wanted to act quickly, to leave an impression on the paper like on everything he touched, turning it into a launchpad for new conquests. His arrival was modeled on the regime's new style, at once "democratic" and authoritarian: he was the first editor in chief to present his program in front of the entire editorial staff, all while leaving his collaborators standing at attention. He was careful to place himself beside the tiny Maccari, in order, according to the gossip, to seem even taller and to enhance his athletic bearing.

Meanwhile a great rival of *La Stampa*, the *Corriere della Sera*, had completed its own "Fascistization." After a few interim editors in chief, among them the venerable Ugo Ojetti, the paper was entrusted to Aldo Borelli, whom we will have numerous occasions to mention, because he was not only one of the rare friends with whom Malaparte never quarreled but above all his main intermediary with Mussolini. *La Stampa*'s new boss had the satisfaction of receiving the customary congratulations even from Fascist personalities who had been more or less openly hostile to him. He knew full well that all this rang false, and he couldn't help himself, in one of his first editorials, from mocking the "free-riding fleas" for whom "there was no place in Mussolini's Italy."[41] The debut was very poorly received: Turati himself was forced to send him a warning. Malaparte understood immediately that the game was not yet won; nonetheless, he made no show of prudence. The tenor of his articles remained roughly the same, insolent and aggressive, across the two years of his editorship; in fact, he redoubled his zeal in denouncing the parasites and profiteers of Fascism. As if that were not enough, he never passed up a chance to enter into conflict with various regime institutions, thus paving the way from the start for his dismissal.

His staffing choices were very personal. Malaparte brought back some old contributors from the Frassati era, such as Gaetano Natale, Giolitti's biographer, and opened the door to young economists of a liberal cast, much attracted by what was happening in the United States. But he also surrounded himself with promising young Fascist journalists, many of whom would later become militant anti-Fascists, without showing him much gratitude after the fall of the regime, from Corrado Alvaro to Elio Vittorini. He recruited, too, a certain Alberto Moravia, who, introduced to him by Bontempelli, had taken his first steps in the columns of *"900"*. Along with the men, the style and graphics of the paper quickly changed: lots of photographs, then rare in the Italian press; shorter headlines, in block capitals, with a strong impact on the public. You could spot here the influence of the American "yellow press" and of big popular foreign dailies like the English *Daily Mail*, led by the pro-Fascist Lord Rothermere. *La Stampa*'s new leader didn't neglect sports, subsidized by the regime, especially soccer, useful (then like today) to promote the docility of the masses. FIAT's team, Juventus, already dominated the scene, to the point that the Italian national team, world champions in 1934 and 1938, is commonly referred to as "Nazio-Juve." Boxing was also extremely popular, with the exploits of Primo Carnera, the "Gentle Giant" from Friuli, who knocked down the American aces Jim Maloney and Jack Sharkey, instilling legitimate pride in millions of Italian hearts. To celebrate his victories, Malaparte had the idea of printing a full-page reproduction of the sole of the champion's shoe: size 55 (US 23).[42]

But his most audacious decision was to ask the creator of *Il Selvaggio*, Mino Maccari, who was going through a rough period, to oversee the paper's culture section. If the adventure of Strapaese ended in defeat for Malaparte, it was a disaster for its true inventor. Maccari, a mere foot soldier in a revolution that never happened, was detested by the more power-hungry "forks" of the regime he had denounced, to the extent that proceedings were opened to expel him from the party. In this case, truly, one cannot accuse Malaparte of opportunism. He felt sincere affection (at the time) for men like Maccari and Longanesi, who, behind their arrogance and boasting, hid values inherited from the provincial Italy of Milziade Baldi. They embodied the more "healthy," spontaneous, nostalgic side of his nature, or that part of it harboring his inner "cursed Tuscan." And it was not enough for Malaparte to hire a hothead. He assigned Maccari, after obtaining preliminary authorization from the party,[43] an investigation on the islands of Ponza and Lipari, two of the best-known and most feared *confino* sites, where opponents of the regime were detained. A provocation? Not entirely. Titled "Un mese a Ponza e a Lipari" (A month on Ponza and Lipari), the investigation is Fascist, even very Fascist, but double edged. Maccari confirmed that the deportees devoted themselves to intense and varied activity; they could play sports, read, write, meet with one another, organize economics, history, and language courses, order books from the Continent, correspond with their families and receive visits from them. But this is precisely where the hidden message lay: the efforts at "reeducation" were entirely inadequate; Maccari denounced a system that was poorly conceived and even more poorly run. The *confinati* (confined men) were for the most part highly cultured figures, sincere patriots whom it would be important to reincorporate into national life; meanwhile they were treated exclusively as a police matter, effectively reinforcing their convictions. What did Il Duce say? Was he aware of this? Furthermore, their living conditions, however preferable to those found in state prisons, were often primitive, and Maccari let it be understood he was aware of some unsavory trafficking. It was the unmistakable sign he had gone too far. Publication of the articles was accordingly judged "inopportune at the present time" by the head of the government press office, Lando Ferretti.[44] Malaparte and Maccari waited for things to die down, letting a few months go by before bringing out the investigation with a great splash, in September 1930. Ferretti's reaction was swift:

> I must again draw your attention to how *La Stampa*, in publishing Mino Maccari's dispatches from "confinement," has taken no account

of the instructions given and the limitations set when the dispatches were previously submitted. It was established that the dispatches would include none of the names of the "confined." What to say, then, of the dispatch published in the current issue 20, which not only cites Silvestri by name but honors him in a prominent subtitle? One really couldn't suggest a better way to give Silvestri the most profitable publicity. All this is serious, dear Malaparte, and was not at all appreciated here.[45]

Matters ended there, at least as far as they concerned Malaparte, who could hardly imagine that, a few years later, he would experience the same treatment. The investigation, moreover, was not without positive consequences: the food and lodging of the *confinati* were improved. The Socialist Carlo Silvestri, cited in the letter, was freed shortly afterward: fifteen years later, during the Republic of Salò, his repeated interventions with Mussolini managed to save numerous anti-Fascists from the firing squad. But Maccari was becoming a cumbersome presence, and, if the editor in chief was still shown some consideration, it was possible to make the life of his culture editor difficult. Malaparte tried to protect him, but there was no way. Maccari fell back into obscurity and poverty through the end of the regime. Returned to Colle Val d'Elsa, he had just enough to feed his family and keep *Il Selvaggio* alive, one way or another. He kept in contact with his former benefactor, to whom he occasionally sent bittersweet letters like this:

> It's been many weeks since I last heard anything from you, nor would I even know where to write to you if I had not run into Margherita [Sarfatti?]. You wrote to me that you were going to send *Il Selvaggio*

something on the new generations and related matters. But I'm sure I won't receive anything. As I'm sure you won't send the hundred lire you promised for your book ad. However, given that I'm completely broke, you could at least reimburse me 120 for the photograph! A flaw in your character is that you offer glimpses of enormous things, and then fail to give a damn. Devil of a Curtino! I'm very curious to see if you'll respond to this letter of mine: I doubt it; and then I'd take it badly, very badly, maybe more than you can imagine. Remember that![46]

These reprimands were not entirely justified, and other letters testify to Maccari's gratitude toward his friend. Still, a residue of bitterness would remain in him, and the same feeling of disappointment can be found in the testimonies of so many other former Malaparte collaborators. Twenty years later, at the writer's death, Maccari would confide to a mutual friend, "I prefer not to talk about Malaparte"; as far as the work was concerned, he suggested one might save, in total, a small anthology of one hundred odd pages.[47] It was the typical reaction provoked by Malaparte in anyone who saw him pass from great warmth, even apparent affection, to sudden coldness. He was never a particularly reliable friend, as we saw in the cases of Gobetti, Aniante, and Frank, and as we'll see even more in the case of Ciano. As soon as someone was no longer useful to him, and especially if they could harm him, he did not hesitate to unload them; and if a turn of fortune rendered them newly useful, he would try to get them back. Coldness of character, the cynicism and opportunism of a petty politician, the contempt for other men typical of the Mussolini-style condottiere? A bit of all this, certainly. But those who felt targeted could also show themselves to be pitiless toward him. The most famous and most cruel judgment came from Longanesi, in a letter to Giovanni Ansaldo, written when Malaparte's corpse was still warm:

> He was not even a great stylist, just a big mannerist, and a proud liar. Sick with narcissism, he lived without loved ones, without passion, always looking in the mirror. A pretend Tuscan, he played at being a lout; instead he was a lansquenet, a Slavonian with secret homosexual tendencies. He loved his *mamma* and *grands hôtels*.[48]

Longanesi could on occasion be as unjust as Malaparte. We see him take up here all the commonplaces we are already well acquainted with: his hidden homosexuality (so well hidden that no biographer has ever found any proof), his German ("lansquenet") and possibly Jewish roots, his "momism"... In so doing, he forgot the essential: because *despite*—or maybe *because of*—his faults as a man, Malaparte became the writer and witness of his time whom we know and who still today attracts the public's attention. It is a secret that few people who lived alongside him succeeded in penetrating.

The life of an editor in chief of a big newspaper was not easy, between the owner, the newsroom, the government, and the party, a hornet's nest of clients and factions, where everyone plotted against everyone else. But Malaparte loved power and did not retreat from obstacles; he was a born fighter and could prove by turns hard and flexible, brutal and compliant, inflexible and submissive. He promoted deserving people into positions of responsibility, eliminated mediocre ones whom others sought to impose on him, and, above all, could be pitiless when it came to punishing or summarily dismissing staff deemed incapable or disloyal. Moreover, he was a hard worker, a conscientious professional, who read the paper from the first line to the last to pick out the smallest typo. Here is a representative example, in the form of a note for the Rome bureau chief, who was then Alfredo Signoretti:

> In the piece on the New Year's reception at the Quirinal, it is reported that the queen's train was held by Duke Cito of the marquesses of Torrecuso, accompanied by the master of ceremonies, the duke of Pragnito, and that among the gentlemen present was also Count Paolo Costa of Carrà e Trinità. Now, Cito of Torrecuso has been dead for four months, the duke of Pagnito died last year, and Trinità has been in the cemetery since last October. This plainly shows that whoever did the Qurininal piece was content to copy last year's. I await a response on this matter. I want to know the name of who did the piece. The man at fault will pay.[49]

This attitude and this language were common coin in the period, not only in Fascist Italy. Malaparte was merely applying the rules of the game, and anyone who still thought of him as an intellectual with his head in the clouds soon had cause to think again. Discipline reigned supreme, without unions or internal committees, at the paper as in the FIAT factories. Initially, Senator Agnelli appeared satisfied; it was his style of command, and sales were up, too. But over time complaints about the authoritarian, at times capricious methods of his editor in chief began to annoy, then to worry him. This was also due to another characteristic of Malaparte's tenure: the space given over to large international investigations. It was not only a journalistic need, but a personal one. For the past dozen or so years, since his return from Warsaw, Malaparte had withdrawn into a more or less provincial, Italo-centric life, and he couldn't wait to set off again, not only to France, which he now knew well, but also on a tour of Europe: Great Britain, Germany, Belgium, all the way to the country that fascinated him most, the Soviet Union. This destination, curiously, did not displease the anti-Communist Agnelli. FIAT had already begun to look with interest to the Soviets, ever since Mussolini had been the first Western politician to recognize the Soviet Union, in 1924, narrowly beating the British Labour government to it. Negotiations got off to a quick start; the opportunities for what today we would call delocalization seemed promising. Even if the phase of openness to capitalism during Lenin's New Economic Policy (NEP) had passed, there remained good possibilities for entering a market of colossal dimensions.

But there was also a more purely political aspect: the myth of the October Revolution was still alive among the Italian proletariat, and it would soon be strengthened by the financial and industrial crisis that slammed Europe after Wall Street's Black Thursday. FIAT, like all domestic enterprises, had to make draconian cuts in salaries and positions. The workers were stirred up; in Turin and other northern cities, the authorities had to intervene to put down attempted uprisings. But in this case as well, police repression did not suffice. It was necessary to adopt countermeasures, to return to soft power. And it was then that Agnelli and his closest associates—a group that Malaparte was never part of—thought of *La Stampa*. The paper supported FIAT's opening to the Soviet Union, but something more was needed: to present an "objective," and thus more critical, vision of living and working conditions in the country, with the goal of convincing readers, especially workers, of the superiority of the Fascist model.[50] Malaparte had carte blanche and couldn't ask for more.

Here we need to make another brief digression. Russia, well

before the October Revolution, had attracted Italian elites, and vice versa. It was not then so distant a country as geography and history might suggest. As early as the first half of the nineteenth century, the great Russian families had replaced the French, English, and Germans in undertaking the Grand Tour, the journey through Italy that was part of the education of a young gentleman, and sometimes imposed as well for reasons of health. Signs of it can be found in nearly all major works of Russian painting and literature of the period. In Rome, near the Pyramid of Cestius, lies the Cimitero Acattolico (Non-Catholic Cemetery), known today as the "English cemetery," where gravestones displaying Cyrillic characters prevailed over all others until the early twentieth century. Numerous dwellings in the capital, later converted into diplomatic residences, still bear the names of their former Russian owners, from Villa Wolkonsky, today the British embassy, to the immense Villa Abamelek, the Russian embassy, which extends over more than sixty-five acres behind the Janiculum Hill. In the ornate, velvet-upholstered rooms of the Antico Caffè Greco, on Via Condotti, lingers the shade of Gogol, who conceived of *Dead Souls* there, and who lived nearby, on Via Capo le Case. The Russian presence can be found from Venice to Sanremo, from Florence to Naples, to the Amalfi coast and on Capri, which still bears traces of the stays of Gorky, Lenin, and Lunacharsky, who also founded a Marxist school, with Bogdanov and Pokrovski, in Bologna. Long before the turning point of 1917, the anarchist Mikhail Bakunin made several attempts to relocate to Italy, in Tuscany, Naples, and Bologna, contesting the terrain with Marx and Mazzini. Anarcho-Bakuninism was still widespread among the places and personalities that populated Malaparte's adolescence. Then came the hour of the Russian muses of socialism, Angelica

FASCISM AND HIGH SOCIETY (1925–1933)

Balabanoff and Anna Kuliscioff, who exerted considerable influence over the formation of a leftist Italian political class, Mussolini included. And after the October Revolution, Italians were among the first, from Gramsci to Togliatti, to Amadeo Bordiga and Ignazio Silone—both later expelled from the PCI—to contribute to the spread of Bolshevik messianism.

Even during Fascism, attitudes toward the Soviet Union were not nearly so negative as one might imagine. If Mussolini persecuted his Communist adversaries internally, in foreign policy terms he sought economic and even political rapprochement with the Soviets, who reciprocated by doing almost nothing to help Italian Communists in Fascist prisons. A systematic analysis of the place of the October Revolution, and of the Soviet Union generally, in the shifting ideology of Mussolini, from beginning to end, would lead to surprising and almost paradoxical conclusions. However variable, emotional, and opportunist he proved to be in his successive political incarnations, however anti-Communist and antimaterialist he publicly declared himself, Il Duce looked toward the Soviet Union with interest, even with a sort of masked attraction. It was not merely, as it would be for Hitler in his pact with Stalin in August 1939, the manifestation of Machiavellism or extreme realpolitik. It was something deeper, which went back to Mussolini's socialist origins: a nonhumanitarian socialism, based on the idea of strength and on the supremacy of the emerging classes over those in decline. The "proletarian and Fascist Italy" he exalted in his speeches—including the fatal one of June 10, 1940, declaring his nation's entry into the war—resonated with him in some intimate way. The Soviet Union had produced a social revolution that did not diverge entirely from the one he himself would have liked to realize in Italy, to liberate the country from the influence of throne, altar, and a limp and faithless bourgeoisie. Wishful thinking? Certainly, but it is undeniable that this tendency would only grow over the years, even if it would never translate into a coherent design.

As Mussolini distanced himself increasingly from the plutocratic democracies, from "selfish" Great Britain and "decadent" France, he would experience a sort of recurrent mental fantasy, in which the young, vital, proletarian nations—Fascist Italy, the Third Reich, and the Soviet Union—were called on to divide the future of the world among themselves, with the addition of Japan, which was imperial, yes, but inspired in him deep awe. As for the United States, if he admired Roosevelt's New Deal, his (very superficial) judgment of it changed according to events. Both the democrat Roosevelt and the dictators Hitler and Stalin were *truly* strong men, and he envied or hated them in turn, knowing he was not (and would never be) on their "level." In 1939–40, moreover, Mussolini would seek to negotiate Italy's own nonaggression pact with the Soviets; well received by Moscow, the proposal would be blocked by the Germans. Subsequently, with one of those brusque changes of course typical of his nature, and without Hitler even having asked him for it, he would hasten in June 1941 to take part in the attack on the Soviet Union. Eventually, however, Mussolini would end up detesting his omnipotent Nazi ally, whereas he would remain fascinated all the way to the end by his Soviet adversary, to the point of declaring, in the last months of his political existence, not without insight, that the Georgian dictator would dominate postwar Europe.[51]

All this helps us understand why Malaparte was not isolated or ostracized, regardless of what he would maintain later, on account of his decision to visit the Soviet Union. *La Stampa* had already accredited a good correspondent in Moscow, Pietro Sessa, who had, in a certain sense, prepared the ground for him. The fact that the newspaper's editor in chief wanted to set out on a journey—because the idea was certainly his—as early as late May 1929, barely three months into his tenure, might have been surprising. But the Soviet Union was very much in fashion, and one could list dozens and dozens of works from the 1920s and 1930s, of every genre and every level, duly authorized by the party, devoted to sounding out every aspect of Soviet life and culture: a percentage equal to, if not exceeding, that concerning every other country combined, including France in the last phase of the Third Republic, Hitler's Germany, and New Deal America.[52] Anti-Bolshevik propaganda was naturally prevalent; nevertheless, the average level of these publications was high, and the Fascist regime financed centers of analysis, often led by Russian émigrés, which furnished accurate and documented information on all aspects of the Soviet reality: from the antireligious campaign to the progress of industrialization, from the establishment of the Gulag (almost unknown in the West at the time) to the role of the Red Army, and even to the purges in its ranks.* That Mussolini, notwithstanding all this impressive material, to which he gave no weight, then chose to follow Hitler in attacking the Soviet Union confirms that the war was a mad decision, in which he bet and lost everything.

---

*I met one of these forgotten specialists, born in imperial Russia to a family of Italian merchants settled in Saint Petersburg, who left the country after the revolution. He showed me copies of reports, worthy of the best "Kremlinology," compiled by him on behalf of Fascist authorities over the course of the 1930s. In 1941–42 he was in Axis-occupied Ukraine, sent to organize radio transmissions of propaganda by the Italian Expeditionary Corps.

The impact of Malaparte's dispatches—the publication of which he cleverly staggered between June 8 and December 20, 1929, thus giving the impression his stay had lasted much more than a month, employing a method he would later repeat habitually—was considerable and well deserved. He published other, very interesting texts on the condition of Soviet intellectuals, in *L'Italia Letteraria*, of which he was no longer the editor, but where he maintained a regular column. His letters of the period do not tell us how he prepared himself for the venture. He surely must have read a great deal prior to departure; his capacity to rapidly assimilate large quantities of material was remarkable. Malaparte lacked the specialized knowledge of a Slavicist or professional historian, or even of a true humanist; his learning, here as in all things, was vast and varied rather than systematic and profound. But his sharp eye and writer's touch proved to be, once again, out of the ordinary. If he never met Stalin, or most of the figures he would cite in *The Kremlin Ball*, it would nevertheless be hard to find, in the long list of Western "pilgrims" to the Soviet Union between the two wars, an observer as perceptive, clear-sighted, unsettling, resistant to cliché.

Collected into a 1930 book titled *Intelligenza di Lenin* (in the sense of "how to understand Lenin"), these articles constituted the overture of a grandiose symphony that would culminate a dozen years later in the major key of *The Volga Rises in Europe*. A well-educated informer (there were plenty) was not fooled, claiming that the book "is the negation of the Fascist Revolution and the overestimation of Lenin's."[53] It was, moreover, starting with his journey to the Soviet Union and not, as has been believed, with his supposed "exile" in France the next year that police surveillance of Malaparte was quietly increased. Of course, this was the kind of love affair that only Malaparte could conceive and experience, made up of conflict and exasperation, of rancor and moody outbursts, never, however, weighed down by indifference or boredom, the great enemies of his life. Like a true lover, he forgave nothing, hid nothing, (almost) never misled, without the blindness that passion often brings with it. He dissected, laid bare, interrogated, and, for once, put himself indirectly on the line. The fabulist Malaparte displayed here a singular acumen in his ability to grasp a fundamental truth of the new Soviet society: the USSR of Lenin and Stalin, exactly like the Holy Russia of the czars, could exist only as a great power, as an empire spread over two continents and a sixth of the globe, or it ran the risk of dissolving. If the Bolsheviks opened up to capitalism in the NEP phase, it was not only out of economic necessity but also because "Bolshevism is the negation of Western freedom, not of European industrial civilization" (IL, 60). The general tone leaves no doubt: he was convinced the Soviet Union was destined to become—or rather, become once more, as the successor state to Russia—one of the great actors on the international stage. His criticisms concerned only apparently secondary points, including the burning issue of intellectual freedom. What follows is a commentary that appeared in a Parisian daily:

> The Italian writer Curzio Malaparte, returned from a stay in Russia, assures us that the government in Moscow holds its writers in high regard: it exempts them from a good deal of oppression but exercises the strictest control over their works. He recounts how a committee tasked with censoring manuscripts suppresses everything that could harm the progress of Bolshevism, and that opposes its principles, its logic. This committee does not hesitate to add chapters or scenes

to a work, or to "suggest" alterations and conclusions. If the author refuses to submit to these arrangements, to these distortions, even, no matter. From the Soviet point of view, the wisest thing is to keep quiet. Because if the writer obeys and displays talent in service of the cause, he will one day be able to enjoy valuable benefits.[54]

Ultimately, *Intelligenza di Lenin* was a successful attempt to grasp the singularity of the Soviet experience, without diminishing or dressing up any part of it. This could please or displease, depending on the case, but it did not place itself at the service of any established ideology and had something to upset everyone. Malaparte introduced the Fascist government and Italian industrialists, without embellishment, to an immense and fearsome interlocutor, from which they could expect both the greatest advantages and the most terrible reactions. He reassured his bourgeois readers in describing the pitiless Bolshevik yoke, all while putting them on guard against the power of contagion that emerged from it. He showed the workers at FIAT and elsewhere that the myth of the Soviet Union was founded on an inescapable historical reality, while simultaneously proving to them that living conditions for the masses were much worse than in the West. Finally, if he refused to openly take a side for or against the validity of the model, he did not hide from the Soviets the sincere attraction he felt for them and for Russia's "immense soul," which announced the feats of the "Great Patriotic War" of 1941–45, waged in the name not of the USSR but of eternal Russia. At the same time, he made them feel how much he still considered them a world apart: "Surely we Russians are Orientals, with all the merits and all the defects common to Asians"—an attaché at the Soviet embassy in Rome ironically affirmed, without for all that managing to hide his own admiration for the Bolshevik experiment—"but to try to understand every word differently than in its usual meaning is too Byzantine, even for a Russian."[55]

And yet this is precisely Malaparte's approach: to never accept doublespeak or ready-made explanations at face value, to always go in search of the proverbial hair in the egg, distrusting current interpretations. Perhaps only a man wary of passions and infatuations yet endowed with an uncommon capacity of vision and perception, always eager to delve beneath appearances and to turn received wisdom on its head, could arrive at a result so rich in contrasts and intuitions.

He was drawn above all to the anthropological evolution of his characters, site of the highs and lows of history; how the work of centuries to create the shape of a cranium or the pleat of a suit can at any moment tip over into its opposite. What certified "Kremlinologist" has better described for us the nascent *nomenklatura*: "And already at the front of the crowd were the Soviet faces, almost German faces, but those from German expressionist films.... A new race was arising in Russia: the Marxist race" (KB, 210)? Malaparte was anything but sated; this first contact was not enough for him. He counted on returning to the Soviet Union to scrutinize all those aspects that had not found their way into his investigation. To keep his hand in, he wrote the preface to the Italian translation of a book by an Austrian sociologist of Romanian origin who had immigrated to the United States, René Fülöp-Miller, in which he denied having been seduced by revolutionary ideas, and counterattacked, underlining how "the surest defense of the bourgeois intelligence against the dangers of Bolshevism ought to consist in understanding the revolutionary phenomena of the modern age. The misunderstanding of such phenomena is the clearest sign of the modern bourgeoisie's decadence."⁵⁶ But his abrupt exit from *La Stampa* meant he would not set foot again on Soviet soil before the new world war. A few years later it would be Corrado Alvaro, another friend from his bohemian years in Rome whom he had recruited for the paper's culture section, who would author a new series of dispatches from the Soviet Union, characterized by the same underlying admiration. Malaparte took offense, and this was one of the reasons the two writers and former friends fell out.* The relationship would only worsen after the war, in the context of polemics about the "precocity" of each's anti-Fascist commitment.

Flaminia

Compared with the Russia trip, Malaparte's other investigations of the period, however skillfully and intelligently executed, failed to make a mark. The reason is simple. On these occasions the objective was chosen by the ownership, or in close consultation with it. And the choice was a means to an end: to demonstrate that the financial crisis coming from the United States affected the French, English, German, or Belgian workers more severely than the Italian ones. Malaparte was ill at ease in this overly narrow role, and he often preferred to leave the writing to his colleagues. He grew bored, as regularly happened to him when he wanted something else, and a

---

*Alvaro would shortly afterward gather the pieces into a book: *I maestri del diluvio: Viaggio nella Russia sovietica* (Milan: Mondadori, 1935). The second, expanded edition, titled *Viaggio in Russia* (Florence: Sansoni, 1943), would appear at the same time as the first edition of *The Volga Rises in Europe*, to the further annoyance of Malaparte.

thousand projects ran through his head. His stay in the Soviet Union gave him the idea for a book he had been toying with for some time, ever since he had witnessed (or not) the Red Army's defeat at the gates of Warsaw. Over the years he had accumulated a wealth of observations and notes for an analysis of—or better, for a lyrical excursion through—the century's revolutions, to pull out their central idea: how to take power by force—always force, only force!—in the contemporary world. And how to preserve it, against everyone and everything, by maneuvering as occasion required the elite against the plebs, one's enemies against one's allies, the audacity of the ruling group against the fear gripping the masses and leading to their destruction... The "cursed saints" of Caporetto, the *arditi* of the Piave, the *udarniks* ("shock workers") of the proletarian vanguard, the ruthless commissars of the people in the back lines: Are they all not perhaps of the same species? How to pinpoint what connects the "intelligence" of Lenin to that of the century's other great revolutionaries—namely, contempt for ideals in the name of efficiency? Does only the attainment of power count, then, while everything else is just window dressing for the naive? Indeed, to establish such power it is necessary to conquer the state:

> During Lenin's years of exile, and up until the eve of his return to Russia, the word *liberty* sounded wrong in his mouth. It was one of those words he pronounced while smiling and narrowing his eyes... His slogan on the eve of the coup d'état carries no hint of hypocrisy: "All power to the Soviets." He was fighting not for liberty, but for the dictatorship of the proletariat. The one who fought for liberty was Kerensky, the Russian people's last defender of liberty, the whole revolution's most ridiculous hero. (IL, 58–59)

Hence an initial conclusion, which might have applied equally well to Lenin or to Mussolini, or soon to Hitler, as it would to so many of their successors, up to the present day: "There is only one way to defend the revolution: to give up liberty, a bourgeois myth" (IL, 101). But is there a method, a universal technique that could apply to a range of different cases, as Machiavelli had prophesied? Malaparte had reached this point in his reflections when, in December 1930, Daniel Halévy arrived in Italy for an investigation into the state of the trade unions. It was an opportunity to reinforce the bonds of friendship formed in Paris, at the time of the ephemeral Committee for International Intellectual Relations. Their meeting was evidently very constructive, as Halévy, back in Paris a few days later, carried Malaparte's project with him. He immediately spoke about it with Bernard Grasset, and the publisher was swift to respond:

Dear Sir,

My friend and colleague Daniel Halévy tells me you are preparing a book on the technique of the coup d'état. I am fascinated by the idea and must promptly ask you to entrust me with the launch of this work. I truly believe I am the person most suited to give it the widest dissemination.

Please be so kind as to give me, as soon as possible, some more precise information about the book and about when the manuscript could be sent to me.

Please accept, Sir, my expression of deepest appreciation,

Bernard Grasset[57]

Daniel Halévy, who would become the architect of Malaparte's first big international success, as well as his most loyal friend and most tireless supporter in France, was a fascinating figure, today unjustly forgotten, perhaps because it is hard to apply any existing label to him, as is almost always the case with free spirits. He was a great intellectual, but above all he was a just man, who passionately sought the truth through his own and others' mistakes. Born in Paris in 1872, he belonged to a republican intelligentsia dynasty: son of Ludovic Halévy, an academic and author of Offenbach's best librettos, grandnephew of Jacques Fromental Halévy, the composer of the opera *La Juive* (*The Jewess*), bound by friendship or family ties to other great families of Republican France (the Breguets, Bizets, Prousts, Berthelots, Blums). He was a restless and curious spirit, always ahead of his time. An ardent patriot, he nonetheless maintained that the Great War had been a disaster for the whole of Europe and took steps to re-create a community of spirits beyond national divisions. He laid out his ideas in books like *La Fin des notables* (*The End of the Notables*), *Décadence de la liberté*, and finally *Courrier d'Europe*, which contains a rather favorable portrait of Mussolini and Fascist Italy, something that was not in fact uncommon among French and English travelers of the period.[58] His collaboration with Bernard Grasset gave birth to an essay series, Les Cahiers Verts, which offers a remarkable panorama of the evolution of the contemporary world. Halévy was attracted by fellow free and restless spirits, and he sought them out among the younger generation, be they named Malraux, Drieu La Rochelle, or indeed Malaparte. After the defeat of 1940 he would be initially moved, along with other progressive intellectuals, by Pétain's call. In 1941 he would publish an essay on "Three Trials: 1871, 1914, 1940," in which one can hear strains of Vichy's "national revolution." He would soon snap out of it, however, and in the dark hours of the war rewrite an impressive biography of Nietzsche, a call to freedom of the spirit in the calamity of the age.[59] Having escaped from anti-Semitic persecution, Halévy would after the war enthusiastically take up again his role as apostle of dialogue between men of opposing ideological and religious faiths. He would die at the age of ninety, in 1962, five years after his Italian friend, whom both he and his wife, Marianne, a woman of equally strong personality, had surrounded with unshakable affection.[60] Thus do we return to a singular aspect of Malaparte's character, as frigid and selfish as you like, but capable of great flights of emotion, when he felt protected by like-minded natures, who could understand and love him, with clarity and indulgence alike.

Malaparte replied to Grasset from Turin on December 22, 1930, sketching out an already rather precise plan for the work, which he counted on finishing by February, "since I think its publication should take place by late April [1931] at the latest." He summarized his career path with his customary embellishments, specifying that "my participation in the Fascist revolution has allowed me to become fully acquainted with Mussolini's tactics." By return mail, on the thirty-first, Grasset hastened to give Malaparte his full approval, assuring him he would "make this work a worldwide success."[61]

The choice of subject, as well as that of a foreign publisher—especially one like Grasset, who, without being situated on the left, had already welcomed numerous works by anti-Fascist authors into his catalog—involved a significant risk. Why, then, did Malaparte run it, at a moment when his professional situation finally seemed satisfactory, after years of uncertainty? At *La Stampa*, he found himself in an ideal position. For the first time in his life he was earning a considerable amount of money, and he would never earn as much again. Agnelli, while keeping him at a distance, had already seated him on some well-remunerated boards of directors.[62] These were what we would today call "fringe benefits," indirect privileges of the job, to which Malaparte was hardly indifferent. He also enjoyed—and this was what counted most in his eyes—a not insignificant amount of power, which allowed him to participate at a distance in the political intrigues woven in the capital without being caught up in any tangles. And, as always in his life, he was pursued by women, even if it is difficult to understand what they meant to him. Consider this curious police report:

> One of his ex-lovers, a Swedish baroness... told us that this classic exploiter of women, when he wanted to have an impassioned scene with a woman to get some money or secrets out of her, would go to the brothel to empty himself completely, so that his exhausted body would not make him show any weakness toward the woman, be it of the senses or the heart.[63]

We are already sufficiently acquainted with Malaparte to know he had no need to preliminarily "empty himself" in a house of prostitution—a place, moreover, of which he had a phobic horror—to remain master of himself. And yet, something was stirring in him ever since he met, shortly after his arrival in Turin, "Flaminia." Behind this pseudonym hides a woman who, while unable to be "like me," had every other advantage: she was beautiful, rich, elegant, and, above all, solidly married, in a social context in which separation and divorce were unthinkable, allowing Malaparte to retain all the freedom of a lover. The few photos that have come down to us portray a slim young blond with a subtle air of seduction. The informers attribute to her an "intimate relationship" with the Crown Prince Umberto; but it was not just any relationship, because she was also part of the Piedmontese aristocracy, the most closed in Italy: a world into which even the senator Agnelli was only begrudgingly admitted, something that did not displease his employee. Malaparte's first biographers did not disclose her identity. I have been able to establish that it was the marchioness Bona Morozzo della Rocca di Bianzé, known to her friends as Bebe, who retained the same charm and beauty to the end of a long life, as a younger relative kindly confirmed to me. She descended from an eminent family of high-ranking officials and military men, always historically close to the Savoyard court, and one of her ancestors was among the lovers of Victor Emmanuel II, father of the country, both literally and figuratively.[64] Her husband, Mario Vittorio Borgogna, marquess of Capriasco, was a rich lawyer, collector, and patron.

"Flaminia" was neither the first nor the last noblewoman to fall into Malaparte's coils. In Rome, the writer had seen a great deal of Roberta (Titti) Masier, also known as "Tampussi," a young "emancipated" woman from a great Venetian family. More than once Malaparte confided that he would have married her, were it not for her father's opposition; but such confessions should be taken with the usual precautions. They nevertheless remained friends, and Titti resigned herself to the role of confidante and counselor—that is, the only lasting relationship with a woman that Malaparte could conceive of. She was also apparently his only former lover to take part in his funeral in Prato.[65] This predilection for blue blood is the source of the rumblings about Malaparte's snobbery. In truth, the former revolutionary syndicalist and bomb thrower of *La Conquista dello Stato* adapted to high society with an ease and a brio that would never desert him; like the correspondence of Henry James or Proust, his own abounds with references to noble titles, whereas those born or raised in that environment omit, at least in private, the appellations, before the name or nickname.[66] Nevertheless, we need not overdramatize what was essentially a matter of revenge against his provincial origins and early years of relative obscurity. The realism of this "cursed Tuscan" would never let him lose his clarity of purpose, not even in the years when he gravitated toward the society life around Galeazzo and Edda Ciano. The real Malaparte is to be found elsewhere.

Besides, for him one woman was not enough, at least for impressing people. Austere Turin was still the capital of Italian cinema—Rome and Cinecittà would overtake it only some years later—and Malaparte showed off in long walks on the avenues and in elegant clubs, with an actress on his arm and a couple of D'Annunzian greyhounds on a leash. He loved to surround his private life with mystery, but his relationship with "Flaminia" must have been known to his intimates, if Maccari did not hesitate to write to him: "It's fortunate you have your woman beside you. She gives meaning to your life."[67] Indeed, "Flaminia" would show the full extent of her dedication at the time of her lover's confinement on Lipari. Here was one more reason, we must conclude, for Malaparte, if this relationship was truly important to him, not to launch himself into a literary venture in which, after having courted disaster with *Don Cameleo*, he risked again, and this time seriously, provoking the rage of Mussolini and the regime. And yet he did it, explaining his actions in these terms in his 1946 statement of defense:

In November 1930, the celebrated writer Daniel Halévy, a reader for the Grasset publishing house, came to Turin to bring me the signed contract and to collect the manuscript of my book. When I left *La Stampa*, in January 1931, the book was ready for typesetting, and, knowing the nature of the book, I decided to relocate to France, so as not to be surprised by its publication in Italy. Hence I sent a letter of resignation to the secretary of the PNF for "reasons concerning my conscience alone" and left for Paris.[68]

Setting aside for the moment any resignation from the party, this declaration contains several more or less intentional factual errors. As we have seen, neither the terms of the contract—which would be signed only on July 29, 1931[69]—nor the manuscript was finalized at that date, and even less was typesetting on the agenda. The first print run was expected to be six thousand copies, plus publicity and author copies. Malaparte secured a royalty rate, considerable for an author almost unknown in France, of 10 percent of the cover price. But the significance of all this was relative. By contrast, the quoted passage's central sentence is plausible, because it was his abrupt and entirely unforeseen firing from the newspaper, at the beginning of January 1931, that swept away his final hesitations. But this reasoning came only after the fact. At the time, the news threw him into a bewildered rage. We do not know the exact cause of his firing, or precisely how the events unfolded. According to a reconstruction by the police:

> People say he received the message from Il Duce accepting his resignation as editor in chief of *La Stampa*, a resignation that Malaparte

had [not] offered. People say it was Senator Agnelli who demanded Malaparte's head, that he had become unbearable.⁷⁰

Mussolini had in fact made a habit of having his cabinet publicly announce his "acceptance" of the resignation of this or that minister, prefect, or other collaborator, without it ever having been offered: thus he presented the man with a fait accompli. But why go after Malaparte? He could not be reproached for a lack of professional success, or a lack of political obedience. Turati, and thus the party, was happy with him: "Well done with *La Stampa*. Best wishes," we read in one of his missives.⁷¹ Moreover, Malaparte regularly sent to Mussolini's personal secretary, through the faithful Signoretti, head of the paper's Roman office, confidential reports addressed exclusively to Il Duce, which have not been recovered, but which probably contained information on FIAT's business, the moods of Turin, the behavior of the workers, and so on. We must not overestimate the importance of such documents: Mussolini was better acquainted than most with Malaparte's tendency to embroider and invent. On the other hand, the dictator, an ex-journalist installed in his preferred role as "editor of the nation," directly or indirectly solicited so many such reports as to be literally overwhelmed. This shows that Malaparte's loyalty toward his leader exceeded his loyalty to his employer, but the latter had no cause for complaint, given that the practice was widespread.

Nonetheless, police reports would prove that it was in fact Mussolini who decided Malaparte's dismissal, whereas everything to date seemed to make it look like the decision was made by Agnelli. And we return to the question: Why? Without fear of going too far astray, we can take various circumstances under consideration: rivalries internal to the paper, in particular involving the business manager Colli; the ongoing fights among Fascist factions that extended to the press; the senator's growing irritation toward this overly independent subordinate; perhaps social and society jealousies as well. We cannot even exclude Malaparte's opposition to measures aimed at rationalizing labor, like the Bedaux or Taylor system applied by Ford, which FIAT wanted to introduce in Europe, and which romantically wounded "my old fondness for the workers."[72] The expression is a bit over the top, but it's true that Malaparte cared little for the militaristic discipline of Turinese industry and could not resist meddling, as always in his life, in matters that did not concern him, going so far as to meet with delegations of workers and acting as interpreter of their demands. There was, after all, something genuine behind these poses: speaking to the workers, Curzio relived the republican rallies of his youth, the poetry readings he used to make to his fellow soldiers in the trenches. It was his Garibaldian heart, the heart of a man of the Fascist Left, that began to beat again, notwithstanding his habituation to the salons and to the dividends from boards of directors.

In any case, Il Duce killed two birds with one stone. On the one hand, he gave Malaparte a new lesson. He appreciated his loyalty, but he hadn't looked favorably on his collaboration with one of the most powerful Italian industrialists; intelligence combined with capital could lead to revolt or dissidence. In this period, Mussolini still had sufficiently quick reflexes to intervene and break up relationships that could, sooner or later, harm him. On the other hand, for the open position atop *La Stampa* he recommended Turati himself, who now needed to leave behind the party secretary role, before he turned it into his own power base. Malaparte's wounded pride was compensated on Agnelli's part by a considerable sum for the era, about which much has been made; in fact neither enormous nor without precedent, it was probably increased after Il Duce's intervention.[73] This fact was behind the rumors concerning not only the writer's venality but also the beginnings of his relationship with Virginia Agnelli. I will try to clarify later why this hypothesis seems improbable. It has also been argued that the industrialist wanted to silence him, to avoid Malaparte spilling about the former's business affairs. The hypothesis is a more credible one, since Agnelli was accustomed to rewarding the discretion of his current and former associates. But it is not clear what secrets Malaparte could have come to know, because, again, he had never been part of the senator's inner circle.

The hypotheses are many, but one thing is certain: Malaparte's postwar claim, according to which "I was an excellent editor in chief from the readers' point of view, but an awful one from the Fascist point of view," does not hold up.[74] In the short term, he could also look toward his future with optimism. Some police informers even pointed to him as a possible successor to Arnaldo Mussolini at the head of Il Duce's own daily, *Il Popolo d'Italia*.[75] And seeing as how the other condition he had stipulated for a friendly separation was not met—a position of equal standing, possibly in the diplomatic service, for which he now had nostalgia—he decided to expatriate for a while, but with a regular passport, *without* breaking with the regime, or with the country. He thought first to go to the United States, "to plot his vengeance."[76] But Paris won out, at least at first, because that is where he decided he bring out *Technique du coup d'État*. Thus were swept away his last doubts about publishing a book he expected, with good reason, to bring him international success.

The Technique of Self-Promotion

Let us turn now to this alleged resignation from the Fascist Party, for which Malaparte, generally quite vague as to dates, for once indicated a very precise one: January 18, 1931; that is, the day after his exit from *La Stampa*.[77] It's a card he played with notable brazenness after the war, especially with French and American interlocutors, trusting probably in the fact that the PNF's archives were destroyed at the end of the conflict, which made it extremely difficult, in his case as in others, to reestablish the truth. One must avoid, again, misconceptions about the benign nature of Italian Fascism: to voluntarily leave the party was an exceptionally serious step, which nobody could afford to take lightheartedly, and which closed the door to any important professional or intellectual activity. Anyone who lost their membership card could expect to go hungry, as his friend Maccari, among so many others, showed. But as so often happens with Malaparte, the tale's point of departure could contain a nugget of truth. It is not impossible that, with his self-regard wounded by Mussolini's silence, and certainly not out of anti-Fascist zeal, he had displayed the *intention* of giving back his card or had led people to believe he had done so, in one of his characteristically impulsive gestures. In line with this behavior, he turned up at a summer ball on Capri showing off his combat ribbons from the Great War, but not the "bug," the Fascist emblem, on his tuxedo jacket.[78] But he quickly settled down and everything went back to normal. He knew that resigning would have nullified his chances of an official position, especially with the title of ambassador, which involved access to state secrets. Malaparte's activity in the period we are preparing to examine, from his arrival in France to his arrest, two and a half years later, proves that he was careful to avoid breaking with the regime. And the first sign of Malaparte's imminent fall into disfavor, perceived by his friend Borelli, was the news that his candidacy had not been accepted by the National Council of Corporations, the new Fascist parliament, in the journalistic-professions category.[79] A candidate... not enrolled in the party? In fact he simply failed to be reelected: a detailed CV for Malaparte, prepared by the Ministry of Popular Culture toward the end of 1941, attests his membership in the National Council of Corporations up through 1933.[80]

It is instead plausible that, at the beginning of the 1930s, Malaparte was distancing himself *conceptually* more and more from a Fascism that had disappointed him and failed, after a decade of daily battles, to allot him the leading role to which he aspired. This initial dissidence was born, therefore, from frustrated ambitions, not from political revolt; and naturally the matter of his *confino* would transform his disappointment into personal trauma. Turati, taking over as editor in chief without the slightest embarrassment, had let him know "as a friend" that he should leave Turin as soon as possible.[81] Too much gossip surrounded his name at this point, and both the paper's owners and its new leadership, determined to turn the page, were annoyed by his proximity. But Malaparte arrived at the Hôtel de la Girelle in Juan-les-Pins, the first stop of his stay in France, only in mid-April 1931, or three and a half months after his dismissal from *La Stampa*. He probably hoped for a sign from Rome. But the master's voice was silent. So he resolved to make the best of a bad situation, and why then not move abroad for a time? Not to America, too far away and where he lacked contacts, but to France, from where he could more easily follow the Italian situation. Before leaving, though, he needed to come to an arrangement with "Flaminia" about the future. And then he had various literary projects in progress: Treves, in Milan, was about to publish his first story collection, *Sodoma e Gomorra*; at the same time, he was working on *Vita di Pizzo-di-Ferro*, to which we'll return later, and finishing his coup d'état book. He had proposed two titles to Halévy: *Europe catilinaire* and *Technique du coup d'État*.[82] Malaparte insisted also on a precaution, which shows how he had no intention of burning his bridges:

> It is understood that the book will appear in French and, potentially, in other languages, but not in Italian. Such a book will be sold in Italy, even in French. One could create a great stir about it, without the Italian press. I'll take care of it.[83]

We find out from a subsequent letter that the manuscript was transmitted on March 18 to Halévy, who suggested some changes, nearly all of them stylistic.[84] The final draft made a few more trips between Paris and Juan-les-Pins, until late April. The text was then sent to be translated by Juliette Bertrand, a colleague of Grasset's focused on Italian authors, who was at the same time (and one supposes, unknown to Malaparte) revising the books by Salvemini and Aniante. She did not have an easy time with Malaparte, who knew French too well to be easily satisfied with the solutions she adopted. It was the first of numerous cases over the years that would pit him against his French and English translators, all accused, sooner or later, of the worst abominations. Halévy had to intervene on several occasions to smooth things over. In July, Malaparte finally reached the capital for the book's launch and dined at the home of Jean Guéhenno, editor of the series Les Écrits, in which *Technique* would appear. Why not in Halévy's Cahiers Verts, as would have seemed more logical? Probably because *Mussolini diplomate*, by the anti-Fascist Salvemini, was already slated to appear there, and the two books would have made uneasy neighbors in the publisher's catalog. As it happened, to Malaparte's great irritation, Mussolini ignored *Technique*'s publication, at least publicly, whereas he "honored" Salvemini with a review, under one of his transparent pseudonyms. Possibly also for this reason, *Mussolini diplomate* was a great publishing success for Grasset, immediately translated in the United States (where Salvemini would soon relocate) and highly regarded in political circles, which only heightened Malaparte's jealousy.

In Paris the writer took lodgings initially at 39 Quai de l'Horloge, on the Île de la Cité, above the Halévys' apartment. Lined with books and paintings, this renovated *chambre de bonne* with a splendid view of the Seine is still owned by the family, as is the rest of the magnificent listed building. But on the eve of his departure from Italy, an important event took place: Il Duce granted him an audience on June 30 at seven p.m. at Palazzo Venezia.[85] What was it about? Malaparte, so apt to vaunt his close relationship with Mussolini, this time displayed rare discretion and was careful not to speak of it when, in 1948, he would present the first Italian edition of *Technique* as the work of a victim of political persecution, or nearly. Had he asked to see him to announce his book's imminent appearance? It seems likely: "Curzio Malaparte, having arrived in Rome, has made a point of telling everyone that the publication of his book on the coup d'état has been delayed, because he wanted the manuscript to be read first by Il Duce, who has approved it," noted an informer.[86] But in a long letter to his friend Borelli—where he clarifies that "I am and remain Fascist," which says it all[87]—we learn that they also discussed his potential

THE TECHNIQUE OF SELF-PROMOTION

return to diplomacy. Ambassador Malaparte: Was it not an old dream of his?[88] But he knew that, in all likelihood, the senior dignitaries of the career, jealous of their prerogatives, would try to oppose him, hence prudence was necessary. Here, too, we should note, Malaparte did not display the least intention of breaking with the regime.

Meanwhile, contrary to both his predictions and his subsequent claims, the Italian press concerned itself with *Technique* immediately and more or less favorably, depending on the case, but without apparent vetoes from on high. He solicited, and received, from Borelli a warm review in the *Corriere della Sera*, and he did not hide his satisfaction.[89] Not all the reactions were so positive, and two freelance journalists would write a sort of anti-*Technique*, to contest its thesis.[90] But this, too, helped to publicize the book, and Malaparte received several offers to publish it in Italy. He waited anxiously, however, for Il Duce's reaction. In a new letter to Borelli, he returned to the meeting in Palazzo Venezia:

> If you see the chief and talk to him about me, you will have my eternal gratitude. All you have to do is remind him of my [his?] promise. When I was with him, I didn't ask him for anything. We were already at the end of our meeting, after an hour of conversation about the general situation, etc., and I still hadn't said a word about my stuff. He was the one who brought up the matter, telling me that he vigorously disapproved of all the dirty tricks I'd been subjected to and that he intended to give me some compensation, moving me into diplomacy.... I wrote to Ferretti: silence across the board. So what, then? What do I have to do?... After the success of my book, the interest in giving me a suitable position is no longer mine alone. I don't mean a newspaper: enough with newspapers. I mean, for

example, the move to diplomacy, at the Ministry's disposal, that is, without a destination. As is clear, I am aiming only for the compensation the chief promised me, without my asking him for it. I am surely not to be deplored for trusting in his word.⁹¹

Behind the verbal contortions, the message is clear. Malaparte counted on the international success of *Technique* to force the chief's hand and convince him to make him an ambassador at large, an itinerant representative of Mussolini's Italy, if he really could not snatch a posting to his taste, especially Warsaw or Moscow. Borelli hastened to go talk to Il Duce, whom, for once, he found in a good mood. After having wryly declared to have read *Technique*, without further comment, Mussolini got to the heart of the matter: "I have nothing against [his entering diplomacy], but Curzio would need to get married," adding that it was a general requirement he wanted to introduce for all officials posted abroad, to make their social life more effective.* Borelli, who knew his friend well and saw in this restriction an insurmountable obstacle, responded with ready wit that Malaparte would prefer a mission without bureaucratic hindrances:

> Il Duce answered me, concluding that he would think about it, that he would do *something* for you, and he immediately made a note about it. He was very cordial in every comment about you, referred

---

*The rule was never rigorously imposed. But the requirement that officials (including military) receive the minister's prior authorization before marrying, already in place before Fascism, was strengthened, especially in the case of foreign wives. It was used, in rare cases, to push out diplomats considered ill suited to the regime. As we shall see later, in the opening to chapter 4, it seemed to touch Malaparte in one specific case.

THE TECHNIQUE OF SELF-PROMOTION

to you affectionately as Curzio (and it's unusual for him to refer to someone by their first name only), and he listened with pleasure as I presented your case. Back in Milan yesterday evening, I saw Arnaldo [Mussolini] and repeated Il Duce's words to him, so he could take an interest in the issue, too. I'm convinced Il Duce's *something* will take the form of *something* that will please you.[92]

Malaparte took the suggestion rather poorly: marriage clearly did not suit him, and what was he to do with "Flaminia"? Borelli sought to reassure him with a new letter, pointing out that "I cannot convey the warmth and affection with which he spoke about you. Even on the marriage issue, he didn't make it a conditio sine qua non for giving you a diplomatic post."[93] Here, then, we find Malaparte faced with the most delicate choice of his career to date. To achieve international success from Paris, he had to distance himself from the regime; but if he wanted to secure the possibility of a new career in Italy, he must not make any false steps. There would have been nothing to reproach him with—such are the calculations people make in all latitudes and in all regimes—if only Malaparte had not wanted retrospectively to date his de facto break with Fascism to his departure for France. He did so in particular in his 1946 statement of defense, which on this point (and plenty others) is a tissue of lies.

Before leaving Turin he found time to bring out a short book with a local publisher, titled *I custodi del disordine* (The upholders of disorder), which, without directly confronting the problem of Fascism, tore into the old groupings of Left and Right of liberal Italy. The thesis once again was that the country's post–World War I salvation could be found only in the nationalization of a revolutionary movement:

FASCISM AND HIGH SOCIETY (1925–1933)

> It is obvious by now that neither the Right nor the Left were aiming to establish a durable order in the country, one that put an end to the uprisings and commotion... From the first years of the Kingdom, Right and Left necessarily favored an unstable political and social equilibrium, which, nullifying the de facto authority of the state, allowed them the greatest freedom of play for their political schemes. (CD, 23, 27)

That Malaparte had at this point begun to nourish serious doubts about the endurance of the regime is probable. Even more probable is that he had understood that Mussolini too had "put on some belly," embalmed by power and servile flattery. That he had confided how poorly he thought of the regime and its oligarchs to his new French friends is certain, based on multiple testimonies. But he *never* wanted to turn his stay in France into exile. Moreover, from Paris he continued to follow Italian affairs and capital intrigues with the same involvement he had during his two years at the helm of *La Stampa*, ready to regain lost ground at the first opportunity. This perhaps explains why, between Italy and France, Malaparte would in this period be the focus of very special attention: at least thirty-four informers from the political police worked in shifts to keep him under surveillance.[94]

Straddling several genres—history, pamphlet, narrative, analysis of mass psychology—*Technique du coup d'État* was a very, maybe overly, ambitious book. If it was never quite *The Prince* of the twentieth century, Malaparte's wager was nevertheless won. The well-chosen title, quick and dry style, sharp phrasing, lucid analysis: everything was made to please in this literary "blitzkrieg," crafted to become the manual of every professional conspirator, even decades

THE TECHNIQUE OF SELF-PROMOTION

later. Malaparte would have been happy to learn that Ernesto "Che" Guevara and his wife read it eagerly in college and then as guerillas, and that the Greek colonels had taken its lessons to heart during preparations for their 1967 coup. Page after page, Malaparte demonstrates how the democracy of the social contract and the Enlightenment, put through the crucible of the Great War, was exposed by specialists in the coup d'état. From Saint Petersburg to Rome, Budapest to Warsaw, Madrid to Berlin, a new class of revolutionaries—cold, clever, and calculating—created, in differing circumstances but with the same determination, a kind of rational model for achieving power. From this Malaparte draws an uncompromising conclusion: "Parliamentary democracies make the mistake of placing too much faith in the triumphs of liberty, while in reality nothing is more fragile than the modern European State" (T1, 165).

If he did not yet know Jünger, whose diary he would begin to read only during the next war, he would deal with concepts similar to those the German writer had introduced in *War as an Inner Experience* (1922) and "Total Mobilization" (1930) and completed precisely in that period in *The Worker* (1932). We do not know whether Malaparte had a notion, direct or indirect, of these works, avid as he was for news of innovations in the fields that interested him. Nevertheless, it is curious to find in his own writings the echo of Jünger's *bürgerliche Scheinherrschaft*, or bourgeois pseudosovereignty; the equivalence between elite soldiers and revolutionaries; and, above all, struggle elevated to a rule of life, against the conservative order and against the illusions of social democracy.[95]

In less than three hundred pages, divided into eight chapters, Malaparte paints a still-timely picture of the path taken by "the new man," "Catilinarian" and the grandchild of Bonaparte, to seize power, after the turmoil of 1914–18. Little does it matter whether he is of the Left, like Trotsky and Stalin, or of the Right, like the Spaniard Primo de Rivera, the Pole Piłsudski, or Mussolini; the authentic revolutionary, faithful to the lesson of the "intelligent" Lenin, knows that ideology counts less than the result. The proof is in the failure of bungled, poorly prepared attempts, be they of the Right, like the 1920 Kapp–Lüttwitz Putsch, against the Weimar Republic, or of the Left, like Béla Kun's Hungarian Soviet Republic, "a lesson to all those who think of revolutionary tactics in terms of politics and not of technique" (T1, 126). Once again it is the elites against the masses, who cannot exist without the leaders who know how to guide the flock: it is the lesson of *Viva Caporetto!*—the true precursor of *Technique*—returning with full force. From one essay to the next, Malaparte would ultimately change rather little, and even after 1945 would not write such very different things, swapping in Stalinist or Maoist communism for the Fascism of times past.

Two personalities stand out in this cohort: Mussolini and Hitler, portrayed at two different stages in their rise. The Italian is the expert revolutionary, who has poured all his energies into creating a new legitimacy, after having smashed the sclerotized liberal state. The German is still a comer, circling his prey, a simple "caricature" of the other man (T1, 232). In repeatedly underlining Mussolini's leftist roots, Malaparte took a gamble. Il Duce did not deny his origins, but he wanted, in that intermediate phase of his foreign policy, to present himself as a great statesman in the service of reconciliation and peace in Europe. It was the image of himself he would offer a little later, in 1932, in his widely circulated conversations with Emil Ludwig, the most famous international correspondent of the

THE TECHNIQUE OF SELF-PROMOTION

Weimar era.* Malaparte—who, we can be sure, would have given a finger to find himself in Ludwig's place—was not entirely in step with this official line. The Mussolini he exalted to French readers is above all the great strategist, who figured out how to plan and carry out the Italian revolution, crowned by the March on Rome. Like Lenin before him, Mussolini thus becomes the necessary man, the indispensable demiurge of national destiny. Hitler, on the contrary, is only a bit player in the story; you notice immediately that Malaparte distrusted him, just as Mussolini did at the time. The author was later reproached for having counted Hitler among the "third-rate dictators" (T1, 228) and for having written that "what the Nazi revolution needs is not an army but a leader" (T1, 230), when various observers and witnesses, in Germany and outside it, had already tried to alert the world to the Nazi threat.

It is not, however, on the basis of these claims that we should measure the prophetic value of the book; its instrumental aim was clearly to cut Hitler down to size with respect to Mussolini. Nonetheless, Hitler had recently made his great leap forward: in the elections of September 1930, the NSDAP passed from 12 to 107 deputies. Malaparte's evident aversion was not, therefore, of a political nature—because he couldn't deny that the German was pursuing a "rational" coup d'état—but psychological. If Mussolini was the masculine figure par excellence, what struck him in the German was his femininity, and worse: the fact of not having become a woman "like me," a

---

*The original German version was confiscated the following year, and Il Duce deemed it better to avoid the circulation of an Italian version. See Emil Ludwig, *Talks with Mussolini: Unusual Conversations*, trans. Eden and Cedar Paul (New York: Little, Brown, 1933).

fully realized, liberated being. The first version of the relevant chapter was in fact to have been titled "A Woman: Hitler," and only after Grasset and Halévy expressed reservations was the title changed to "A Would-Be Dictator: Hitler."* But the message remained the same: Hitler concentrated in himself all the cruelty, brutality, and rancor of a failed woman: "[His] mind, his ambitions, even his will are not in the least virile. He is a weak man who takes shelter in violence, so that he may conceal his lack of energy" (T1, 238).

Malaparte knew that the Latin Mussolini felt a repulsion he would never deny for that "false" German and his troubled sexuality. Malaparte had no difficulty sharing this attitude. He seemed to foresee the fate of Ernst Röhm and other leaders of the SA, most of them homosexual, who would be cut down on the Führer's orders in the Night of the Long Knives, on June 29–30, 1934. He seemed to foresee as well the interpretation Thomas Mann would give of it in an essay a few years later, "Bruder Hitler" (1938): Hitler is a fallen angel, a sexually, morally, and politically unresolved being, who wants to carry out a nationalist revolution to eliminate not everything opposed to him, but everything that is different from him; he is, in short, the anti-*Vaterfigur*, the anti–*padre padrone*. What moves him is not even the struggle for power, but rather the primitive, biological struggle for survival; and to survive, Hitler has to eliminate radically, to root out his adversaries: the democrats, Communists, and Jews. We enter here into a kind of Hobbesian conflict between Bolshevism and Nazism, with the one forced to devour the

---

*The title was restored in the edition that appeared in 1966 in the Cahiers Rouges series, heir to the Cahiers Verts. It is missing from the Italian edition, where the chapters have only numerical titles.

THE TECHNIQUE OF SELF-PROMOTION

other so as not to be devoured, which we will find again, brought to its extreme, in *The Volga Rises in Europe* and in *Kaputt*.

Here is, then, a rough summary of the book, which flew off shelves and had all Paris talking. Malaparte also developed a ruthless promotion technique. He had the Grasset press office circulate an imaginary biography, anticipating what Malraux would do three years later for the launch of *The Human Condition*. One critic emphasized that

> The author... previously took active part in the March on Rome and witnessed the attempted extremist revolution in Warsaw. He is very well informed about the ins and outs of the Bolshevist revolution carried out by Lenin and Trotsky, and about the reasons the latter came to grief against Stalin in 1927.[96]

Another, more discreet, limited himself to claiming the author "had witnessed some [of these facts] and studied the evolution of others."[97] Later, even the young Gaullists of Free France would read "with great interest the [work of an] Italian adventurer who was involved in almost all European revolutions from 1917 on."[98] Halévy and Grasset had not been wrong to bet on the worldwide success of the book, even if talk of "hundreds of articles and hundreds of interviews" was typically Malapartian exaggeration.[99] It was, however, his first work to be rapidly translated into the major languages. A German edition, from Tal in Leipzig, appeared in late 1932, in Renée Adloff's translation, on the eve of the Weimar Republic's collapse, and was banned shortly after the arrival of the Third Reich. Malaparte claimed repeatedly that the work had been burned in the autos-da-fé of books condemned by the Nazis: "in the Leipzig public square," he specified both in his 1946 statement of defense and in the preface to the book's first Italian edition (T2, 11), while elsewhere the place changed. No trace of the title has been found among the lists of works the Nazis sent to the pyre. It is true, though, that this procedure was not uniform and could vary from city to city, from university to university. In the feverish climate of the first months of the *Machtergreifung*, the Nazi seizure of power, it could happen that certain publications, destroyed in Berlin, were saved in Munich or Hamburg, and vice versa. But Malaparte's version accords well with his effort after the war to present himself as a tenacious and declared opponent of Hitler's movement from the beginning, and you can't say that wasn't the case.[100] Hitler, unlike Mussolini, was a lazy and reluctant reader, and he almost certainly never read the book, but he knew its thesis.[101] Some of his followers went so far as to ask if the attack was not inspired by Mussolini, who in fact wondered at the time if he should not try to block the rise of his German rival.[102] Nor did Il Duce's wariness lessen from one day to the next. Only two or three years later did a series of crisis factors, such as the failure of the Anglo-French-Italian Stresa front, the sanctions provoked by the Ethiopian venture, and the Spanish Civil War, pave the way for the fatal Rome-Berlin axis.

The book also elicited denials and takedowns, which did not displease Malaparte: they still made people talk about him. Trotsky did him the honor of attacking him severely, in a speech delivered in Copenhagen on November 7, 1932, on the occasion of the fifteenth anniversary of the October Revolution. The style was convoluted, but he couldn't have given him a greater gift. Here is the essence of the passage in question:

THE TECHNIQUE OF SELF-PROMOTION

> The Italian writer Malaparte, a sort of Fascist theoretician... recently released a book on the technique of the coup d'état. The author naturally dedicates not insignificant pages of his "investigation" to the October Revolution. Unlike Lenin's "strategy," which remains tied to the social and political relations of 1917 Russia, "Trotsky's tactics are not"—in Malaparte's terms—"on the contrary at all tied to the general conditions of the country." This is the main idea of the work! In its pages, the author obliges Lenin and Trotsky to conduct numerous dialogues in which both interlocutors display as little intellectual depth as nature has placed at Malaparte's disposition.... It is difficult to believe such a book has been translated into several languages and taken seriously.... The dialogue between Lenin and Trotsky presented by the Fascist writer is in both its spirit and its form an insipid invention from start to finish.[103]

This stance is understandable. Trotsky, engaged in a battle to the death with Stalin, was afraid of appearing to his supporters as a usurper of Lenin's legacy, rather than his most faithful disciple. He took up this attack again in the new edition of *The History of the Russian Revolution*, adding a mocking aside: "The name of this writer, Malaparte, makes it easy to distinguish him from a certain other specialist in state insurrections called Bonaparte."[104] This did not prevent an informer from claiming that Malaparte had wanted to exalt the figure of Trotsky, "the international Semite."[105] Malaparte would respond, many years after the Russian revolutionary's assassination in Mexico, with an obituary, "Trotsky and the Sibyll," which closed with these harsh words: "In the end, we can say of him what we can say of so many other excellent men of action: he was a failed writer."[106]

FASCISM AND HIGH SOCIETY (1925–1933)

At this point Malaparte was at the center of the French political and literary scene. In Lyon he debated the historical leader of the Radicals, Édouard Herriot, a prominent republican with very little revolutionary about him, but the two men liked each other. In another public event, he was pointedly asked by the journalist Jean-Richard Bloch if he still considered himself a Fascist, causing him some embarrassment. He knew, or at least met, the other main authors in the Grasset "stable," who were the cream of the new French literature: from Mauriac to Bernanos, Maurois to Morand and Giraudoux. Curiously, though, he never approached the writers he more closely resembled: Montherlant, Drieu La Rochelle, and especially Malraux, the closest of them all in terms of theatrical style, storytelling, and obsessions.[107] Many years later, in *Diary of a Foreigner in Paris*, Malaparte would justify this missed connection with a curious anecdote: one day, arriving at the Quai de l'Horloge, he was accosted by a spotty, unruly-haired youth who, stepping out of a taxi, asked him for twenty francs to pay his fare. Afterward, the unknown man entered the building, without even thanking him. A few minutes later, when they saw each other again in Halévy's front room, the young man, who turned out to be Malraux, looked at Malaparte as if he had never seen him before (DFP, 127–28). True? False? It sounds quite like both of them.

Malaparte encountered, up close or from afar, other, older writers he admired, from Jules Romains to André Siegfried and Abel Bonnard;* and he was received in the last great salons of the period. He

---

*After the defeat of 1940, Romains would opt for exile in America and Siegfried for passive resistance. Bonnard would take the side of Vichy and collaboration with Nazi Germany; sentenced to death at war's end, he would seek refuge in Franco's Spain, where he would die in 1968.

THE TECHNIQUE OF SELF-PROMOTION

also made the acquaintance of numerous Anglo-Saxon residents and visitors in Paris, whose friendship proved invaluable. The *Manchester Guardian* correspondent Cecil J. Sprigge facilitated the book's translation for Duckworth, an initiative that saw Malaparte travel to England in January 1933 and begin the series of reports collected, after his death, in *L'inglese in paradiso* (The Englishman in paradise). And then Harold Nicolson, Barbara Harrison, Sylvia Sprigge, and William Bradley, who would become his literary agent in the United States; South American and Chinese writers and artists; Russian, Hungarian, and Austrian émigrés: a bohemian world drunk on books and gossip, watched over by the Comintern, waiting on the next revolution, threatening to boil over. No known romantic adventures, on the other hand, perhaps due to "Flaminia," who at this point lived rather openly at his side, between Paris and Nice, keeping an eye on him, duly surveilled in her turn by police informers, the most reliable of which was a self-described Polish (or Italo-Polish) aristocrat, identified as "R——y."

Malaparte tried, at least initially, to be more discreet in his contacts with the Italians in Paris, having learned from the Bonservizi affair. The French capital hosted, following the escape of influential opposition figures like Carlo Rosselli and Emilio Lussu from Lipari, the greatest concentration of actionists and socialists. Their goals were noble, but their effectiveness was limited; much more was needed to overthrow Mussolini. But OVRA took them seriously and in 1930–31 unleashed an espionage operation in grand style aimed at decapitating the clandestine leadership of Giustizia e Libertà (Justice and Freedom), the main liberal-socialist splinter party. The principal agent sent to France and Switzerland was a Milanese accountant up to his ears in debt, who successfully infiltrated the movement and informed against a considerable number of its members.[108] There is no proof that Malaparte met him. It is possible, on the other hand, that he was aware of the dubious reputation of another writer living in Paris, Dino Segre, known as Pitigrilli, the Turinese author of "sinful" books like *The Chastity Belt* and *Cocaine*, which were wildly successful and, incidentally, far better written than most bestsellers today. Emerging unscathed from the racial laws of 1938, Segre-Pitigrilli continued to collaborate with the Fascist secret police until the fall of the regime; exposed after the war, he fled to Argentina, before coming back to die in Italy, by then forgotten.* Wary of such perilous terrain, Malaparte spent time early on only with figures above the fray, like Pirandello, or outside politics, like Filippo de Pisis and Alberto Savinio, old friends from his time in Rome. He knew he was being watched by the Fascist secret police, probably in connivance with their French counterparts, and he did not want to sabotage his chances when he returned to Italy.

But soon his temperament dragged him toward his usual imprudence. The informers let Rome know he was meeting, at his publisher's or even in public, with moderate-faction *fuoriusciti* like Alberto Cianca and the Socialist Luigi Campolonghi. He met, too, with the escaped historian Carlo Rosselli, who would be assassinated several years later with his brother Nello by assassins of a far-right organization, La Cagoule, in a murky affair involving the French and Italian secret police. It was also reported that figures of the "bourgeois" emigration, like the former prime minister Francesco Saverio Nitti and the republicans Cipriano Facchinetti and Nino

---

*Several of Pitigrilli's novels have been republished in recent years, enjoying success with the public. His name can be found in the lists of OVRA collaborators.

Pitocchi, "have read and commented very favorably on the book."¹⁰⁹ By contrast, his opponents among the more intransigent exiles, like Angelo Tasca, never missed an opportunity to denounce the author of *Technique* as a provocateur and "Fascist writer."¹¹⁰ According to another informer, "today among the [Parisian anti-Fascist] crowd, it is taken for certain that Malaparte was the head of OVRA in France."¹¹¹ This was pure slander, which even today continues to be repeated occasionally. His name does not appear in the lists of OVRA agents made public after Liberation.¹¹² As always on the subject of Malaparte, it was (and is) possible to claim and write everything and its opposite. Confusion reigned, with the help of gossip, fed by the ambiguity of the central character.

Most awkward for him, though, was his relationship with Aniante, whose biography of Mussolini had been very badly received by the dictator, enough to convince the author not to set foot in Italy again. There were rumors that the anecdotes that irritated Mussolini had been added to the book on the initiative, or even by the hand, of Malaparte.¹¹³ Having realized this closeness could hurt him, Malaparte bombarded those in charge at Grasset with letters and messages to distance himself from Aniante's book and to demand they avoid any juxtaposition of it with *Technique du coup d'État*.¹¹⁴ He had been particularly irritated by an advertisement presenting the two works together. At the same time, he begged Borelli to make it known higher up that "the Aniante case is starting to become pathological. I'm telling you all this so that if some malicious person insinuates I launched the book and recommended it, even indirectly, you can deny it in the most categorical fashion."¹¹⁵ And yet, according to an unconfirmed rumor, after the war Malaparte sought to claim part of Aniante's royalties...

FASCISM AND HIGH SOCIETY (1925–1933)

Malaparte continued to send various Italian newspapers dispatches that more or less followed the party line, concerning, for example, the agony of Europe under the Treaty of Versailles, one of Fascist propaganda's major themes.[116] Other, lighter pieces described the last lavish receptions given by the grandes dames of the era, the duchess of Clermont-Tonnerre, the countess de Noailles, or the princess Bibesco, who would remain his faithful friends after the war. But contrary to appearances, Malaparte was never much of a socialite and would never become one, if not out of professional necessity and to get people talking about him. To bustling soirées he preferred intimate dinners, where his conversation could dominate and charm those present. This occurred regularly at the Halévys', where *fuoriusciti* were often invited, if not on the same day; Salvemini, for his part, scornfully refused to meet Malaparte.[117] They were divided by politics, as we have seen, but also by a large pinch of professional jealousy. It seems, however, that one day, due to a mix-up with dates, Malaparte and Salvemini were invited for tea at the same hour; Marianne Halévy, not without difficulty, managed to receive them in two different rooms.

Everything was working out for the best, then? No, because despite his success and growing fame, he continued impatiently to await the reaction of Mussolini, who remained silent. And this prolonged silence was not a good omen. Eventually, Malaparte worried: If he had not written a book against Fascism, if he had placed Mussolini above all the other revolutionaries, including Hitler, had he nevertheless gone too far? Il Duce, who had authorized the book's publication in France, now hesitated to authorize its appearance in Italy. Was it maybe the consequence of certain police reports landing on his desk, which claimed Malaparte had concealed his criticism of the leader behind his attack on Hitler? Or was it because, in international diplomatic circles, many "corporate" eyebrows were raised, reading that Fascism was a milk brother (and brother-in-arms) of Bolshevism?[118] Mussolini might have been broad-minded when it suited him, but he relentlessly intervened as soon as one of his acolytes gave the impression of speaking or acting in his name. He would meditate in the solitude of his immense office, his right fist pressed to his temple, in the pose typical of him in private, hiding his eyeglasses in the drawer whenever the usher Navarra announced a visitor. Or else he would slide his index finger around the too-tight collar of his uniform, intended to make him appear more slender and imposing than he was. We can imagine him smiling as he closely reads many passages, gratified by the talent of that wily Tuscan. The book is audacious, persuasive, yes; almost, he thinks, Mussolinian. But talent can be dangerous, and once again that pain in the neck has gone too far.

Ultimately, thanks to a combination of these factors, *Technique* did not appear in Italy before the fall of the regime. As with other works by Malaparte "before" and "after" Fascism, there was talk of a major reworking from one version to the other. In reality, the only substantive changes concerned the addition of a preface, which contained some undeniable stretching of the facts of his *confino*, and the "promotion" of one of Lenin's supporting cast to a starring role, in the person of the now-unavoidable Stalin. Otherwise, the book's structure underwent only minor changes, as attested by the substantial agreement between the French and Italian editions.[119]

The new assignment continued to be delayed. Malaparte became increasingly agitated, and Borelli, who remained his main channel of communication with the chief, urged him not to lose hope:

Before abandoning yourself to such acute pessimism, have patience, because it's been only a few weeks since I spoke to Il Duce. From what I hear in Rome, some diplomatic assignments should be made on October 28 [anniversary of the March on Rome], so nothing is yet lost.... It wouldn't be a bad thing if you returned to Italy, though, even for a few days, and came to see me: we could go together to see Arnaldo [Mussolini]. As for the rest, it seems that for the moment nothing is moving.[120]

But Il Duce's brother died of a heart attack shortly after, and neither Suckert nor Malaparte was mentioned in the change of diplomatic heads of mission that in fact took place on the date predicted. His displeasure was considerable, all the more so because several of the hires were external, coming mostly from the party ranks, among which he easily could have figured too.

It was hardly a promising sign, and it was perhaps out of an abundance of caution that Malaparte turned down the old proposal from Jean Paulhan, Benjamin Crémieux, and Ramon Fernandez, advanced at the time of the Committee for International Intellectual Relations, to publish a book on Mussolini in Gallimard's Lives of Illustrious Men series. In the same period he also dropped negotiations with English publishers for a similar book. The text was at a quite advanced stage, however, and deserves a brief comment. Malaparte had begun writing it at Juan-les-Pins, in the fall of 1931. He returned to it only after the war, transforming it into a violent and passionate anti-Mussolinian indictment, provisionally titled, in English, "Killing no murder."[121] But here too he stopped himself, without the interruption possibly depending, this time, on a form of prudence. Why did he do so, then? Francesco Perfetti, who was the first to

THE TECHNIQUE OF SELF-PROMOTION

underline the importance of this draft, has offered the most likely explanation, which is once again a psychological one. Mussolini must have remained for him a hope betrayed, despite the war and inglorious end: "Mussolini's gravest error was to persuade Italians he was not a great leader. As long as Italians still believed he was a great leader, they did great things. When they understood he was a little schemer, they abandoned him" (MU, 69). Words with more than a hint of the autobiographical... Now, if in 1931–32 Malaparte had already intuited the end of Fascism, how could he maintain, twenty-five years later, that he regretted this missed opportunity? Hence the decision not to publish anything.

Casting aside his diplomatic aspirations, he decided to remain in France to try to repeat the success of *Technique* with a new work. In an entirely Malapartian paradox, he interrupted his biography of Mussolini to plunge into one of his Soviet precursors. In early 1932, Grasset published *Le Bonhomme Lénine*,* translated, as usual, by Juliette Bertrand. The preface carries the dates "Moscow, 1929–Paris, 1932," but in fact Malaparte reused only a part of the dispatches collected in *Intelligenza di Lenin*.† Here he takes off, rather, from the chapter devoted to Trotsky in *Technique*, to respond to the accusation of not having attributed to Lenin the principal role in the events of October. This time, it is no longer a question of the coup

---

Bonhomme: a familiar and slightly pejorative way to refer to a man, often rendered as "guy," "fellow," "chap," or the like, and in its adjectival form meaning "artless," "simple," or "good-natured."—Trans.

†Still, the French title of what was at least in part a translation of *Intelligenza di Lenin* is very far from the original. I have not determined why Malaparte accepted it. Perhaps promoting the "intelligence" of the first Soviet dictator had become too dangerous?

215

d'état, but of revolution, of sweeping away the old power structures. "Maximilien" Lenin, as he calls him here, was simultaneously Robespierre, Saint-Just, and Napoleon: he was the emancipated petit bourgeois, whose "fanaticism reached the summit of good sense" (LB, 354). Thus the anti-Trotsky became also the anti-Mussolini. Like Il Duce, he is "a modern man, cold, audacious, violent and calculating" (T1, 218); but he is above all "that honest functionary of disorder" (LB, 370). Hence also the man's disconcerting "bonhomie," which is for Malaparte the key to his personality:

> His hatred for Holy Russia, for bourgeois society, for the enemies of the people, is not fierce. The word "destroy" does not have for him what we could call a negative sense. Hatred in him is not a feeling; it's not even an assessment. It's an idea. His hatred is theoretical, abstract, disinterested, even, I would say. He speaks the most appalling words with a smile. (LB, 329)

What makes the case of Lenin unique, what allowed him to overtake his allies and adversaries alike, was an extraordinary interior resource, an acute sense of opportunity: thus he could adapt to circumstances without ever losing sight of his long-range aims, his grand ideological vision. It is the sense of moving in the direction of history, crushing the losers, of passing seamlessly from destruction to reconstruction of the state, of turning the backward proletariat of old czarist Russia into the motor of the greatest modern revolution, with a global impact. Lenin was not an adventurer, or a simple agitator. He knew that what he built would survive him, thanks to objective, rigorously scientific factors, which underlay the class struggle and the dictatorship of the proletariat. What modern dictator

THE TECHNIQUE OF SELF-PROMOTION

could say the same? Although Malaparte was careful to strew the text with references to Lenin's "monstrosity," and to slip in some praise of Mussolini now and then, what he offers us here is the portrait of the perfect revolutionary, one capable of bringing together "technique" and long-term strategy. Lenin died exhausted by the work but left a legacy safe in the hands of Stalin, who could gather it up and perfect it, while the defeated disciple, Trotsky, was deep down only an idealist. History would be the judge.

Today this approach can seem cursory, if compared with the rather more structured analyses of Lenin's development and actions that abound in the "Sovietologist" literature. And yet Malaparte's compelling glimpses strike the contemporary reader who witnessed the unthinkable collapse, without a shot being fired, of the Soviet empire after 1989. But even at the time the book enjoyed an excellent reception that crossed the Alps, to such an extent that some years later, at the beginning of the war, Il Duce authorized the appearance of an Italian edition. At the time Mussolini was thinking about negotiating *his own* pact of nonaggression with the Soviets: publishing Malaparte's book could thus have appeared as a goodwill gesture toward Moscow.[122] Malaparte's publisher, Treves, took advantage of the situation to refloat the idea of publishing an Italian *Technique* as well, which suggests there was still room to realize this project.[123] But in the end nothing happened. Malaparte said he could no longer find the original manuscript of *Le Bonhomme Lénine*; but more likely he was planning to gather all his "Russian" writings into a large single volume, which never saw the light. A retranslation of the French text, prepared in 1950 by Paola Ojetti (daughter of Ugo), was not entirely to his liking, but he soon tired of reworking it. After his death a nearly complete Italian version, with the title *Lenin buonanima* (The dear departed Lenin), was found among the author's papers; it would be published by Vallecchi in 1962.

Success seemed to smile on him, then. Two books, one after the other, had in short order propelled him to the top of the European literary scene. The Corsican industrialist François Coty, owner of *Le Figaro*, whose Fascist sympathies were well known, invited him to speak in the newspaper's lecture series. A cordial relationship was born, and Coty, who knew how to choose the right men, asked him to collaborate in quite eloquent terms:

> Let this thought sink in, however: that the work of a leader that you acknowledge in me is not only French but Latin, and it is as such that I find particular pleasure in ensuring your collaboration.[124]

Malaparte, after having thought about it, decided to walk away, so as not to provoke Il Duce's jealousy. And he did well. And yet, despite his celebrity, his royalties, and the generous compensation from Agnelli, he did not know which way to turn. To prove to Il Duce his zeal as a good subject, he negotiated with Grasset the publication of a large, glossy volume containing a selection of documents from the Exhibition of the Fascist Revolution, held in Rome to celebrate the regime's tenth anniversary. It was a blatantly propagandistic initiative, which the Italian government would have committed to financing, through the purchase of thirty thousand copies. The matter was brought to the attention of Mussolini, who, irritated by all the unseemly horse trading, let it drop.[125] And he continued to ignore Malaparte: no offer, no news, no appointment.

The few friends the writer still had in the vestibules of power no longer seemed able to reassure him. His correspondence with Italy became increasingly slight and anodyne. Had they forgotten him? Did Il Duce mean to make him pay for his success? So Malaparte decided to make another effort, in the spring of 1933, casting a stone into the pond. Its origin was seemingly innocent: some months earlier, hunting for topics that could please Rome, he had told Borelli about the appearance of a French translation of the reflections of Francesco Guicciardini, the great sixteenth-century Florentine diplomat and writer, friend and rival of Machiavelli, introduced by the historian Jacques Bainville.[126] Since both knew that Guicciardini was one of Mussolini's models, and that the Italophile Bainville was one of the few Third Republic intellectuals whom Il Duce appreciated, the idea of a review was immediately taken into consideration. But instead of sending it to the *Corriere*, Malaparte decided to give it to *Les Nouvelles Littéraires*. The piece appeared on March 25, with a provocative title—"Guichardin, moraliste méprisable" (Guicciardini, contemptible moralist)—and the rather naive aim of attracting Mussolini's attention. Nor did the mischievousness stop at the title: also prominent was a long digression on the subject of reasons of state, which transparently alluded to the Fascist dictatorship. Was it a way of announcing that Malaparte was ready to go on the offensive, if Il Duce continued to keep him on pins and needles? The idea was absurd, and the always wise Borelli warned him against childishness that could turn out badly:

> Your article has really displeased everyone. I do not understand why you wrote it, and if I were you, I would write directly to Il Duce or at least to [Alessandro] Chiavolini or [Gaetano] Polverelli [his closest collaborators] to explain yourself. Having said this to you most dispassionately, let me add that you mustn't believe the article will

be the end of the world for you: it was a gaffe, yes, but it won't be long before no one is talking about it anymore.¹²⁷

We don't know if Malaparte followed this excellent advice, but once again Borelli was right about everything. Il Duce, after having read the article with a shrug of his square shoulders, forgot about it.

Malaparte was relieved at this reaction, but also annoyed. Once again, his bluff had been called. The dictator remained walled up in his Olympian detachment: nearly two years had passed since he had promised to do "something" for him, more than six months since their last meeting, which we'll discuss in the following section. Since then, no sign. His heart swollen with bitterness, he turned again to Borelli in a letter from London that was *almost* the announcement of a break:

> There's no place for me in Italy. I will never ask Him for any intervention. He who laughs last laughs best. And don't think I'll be throwing myself into the arms of the anti-Fascist exiles. I live and work for myself. And I won't harness myself to anyone, to them or any others. I don't deal with Fascism now and I won't do so any longer. Mussolini wants Italians to stay on their knees and steal. I have never done, and will never do, either one of these things. It's been ten years, and almost twelve, that I've been merely tolerated within the regime. Very well. Today I am free and walk with my head held high.¹²⁸

Noble intentions...which he never followed up on. Malaparte had hastened to reassure his friend that he would not be "throwing [himself] into the arms of the anti-Fascist exiles," but they would not have welcomed him in any case. Isolation is a poor counselor at times; impatience always is. He did not listen even to the "technical" lesson of Lenin, who had known how to wait in Switzerland until the moment history called on him to act. And so, Malaparte threw himself headlong into the most badly botched of his adventures.

The Jar Returns to the Well...

To understand the political disaster that Malaparte created with his own hands, between Turin, Paris, and Rome, we first need to cite a name that rightfully figures, much more than his own, in the *nomenklatura* of the regime, but also, rather more honorably, in the history of twentieth-century aviation: Italo Balbo. Born in 1896, this early squadrist, a quadrumvir of the March on Rome, the *ras* of Ferrara, can in fact be considered the prototype of the Fascist-style condottiere. And yet he was a modern condottiere, who found unparalleled success in the air force, the regime armed service par excellence, conducting spectacular flights like Rome–Rio de Janeiro, to the point that he came dangerously close to rivaling the popularity of Il Duce. Balbo would give Fascism its greatest international success when, in July–August 1933, he connected Rome to Chicago at the head of a formation of twenty-five Savoia-Marchetti S.55X: two planes would crash into the sea (one on the outward journey, another on the return), killing two "Alanteans," but the rest would achieve their goal. The event would have an enormous impact. The Italian aviators would be rewarded with a parade in New York reserved for national heroes; a street in downtown Chicago still bears the commander's name. At this point Mussolini's jealousy turned to hate, all the more so because Balbo, considering himself untouchable,

FASCISM AND HIGH SOCIETY (1925–1933)

increasingly engaged in unorthodox statements and behavior. Il Duce succeeded in confining him to Libya, as a governor of that colony, where he would initiate notable infrastructure projects, including the coastal highway that would be named, after his death, Via Balbia. He would continue to command attention from his gilded exile but no longer exercise any political influence, criticizing the alliance with the Germans and refusing to apply the racial laws to Libya's significant Jewish community. In June 1940, he would be the only party official to openly oppose the war. Two weeks later, he would mistakenly be shot down by an Italian antiaircraft battery, circumstances that long fueled talk of a secret order from Mussolini, a thesis that today seems to have been debunked.[129] His death would provoke one of the few chivalrous gestures of World War II: an English fighter would drop a note of condolence from the regional commander in chief of the RAF over the Libyan airfield where Balbo was downed.

This, then, was the figure with whom Malaparte had built a seemingly quite solid friendship. Balbo had helped him obtain his first position in the Fascist unions and played a part in finding financing for *La Conquista dello Stato*. He had also protected him after the break with Farinacci, sheltering him on his Ferrara estate, in October 1927, during the crisis at the magazine.[130] Affection? Interest? Perhaps both: Balbo was little inclined to ideology, which simplified things. In 1932 he had nonetheless published a lively account of the March on Rome, *Diario 1922*, from which the then unknown Suckert is conspicuously absent. Malaparte was also connected to the journalist Nello Quilici, Balbo's right-hand man and editor in chief of the *Corriere padano*, his own personal news outlet (all the Fascist leaders had or financed at least one: a boon for the profession).

Under Quilici, a refined intellectual, the paper was open to anticonformists of all stripes, even leftists. After the introduction of the racial legislation, Quilici, in agreement with Balbo, had harbored under pseudonyms various Jewish journalists and writers forced out of their jobs. Quilici accompanied Balbo all the way to the end, and he would die at his side, in the fatal accident of June 28, 1940.

In the period of his editorship of *La Stampa*, Malaparte was in constant contact with Quilici, to provide adequate coverage of Balbo's successes. In March 1931, shortly after his dismissal from the Turinese daily, Malaparte's name figured, alongside that of Enrico Falqui, on the cover of a little book that came out from the extremely official Libreria del Littorio di Roma, with a title in pure Renaissance style: *Vita di Pizzo-di-Ferro detto Italo Balbo* (The life of Iron Goatee, a.k.a. Italo Balbo). A hagiography verging on the ridiculous, its archaic lyricism, modeled on D'Annunzio's *Vita di Cola di Rienzo*, about the fourteenth-century demagogue and self-styled "tribune of the Roman people," is the polar opposite of the cold and lucid analysis of the contemporary *Technique*. It has therefore been asked whether this work, later conveniently forgotten, was really by Malaparte's hand.[131] According to Edda Ronchi Suckert, Malaparte cosigned it at the request of Falqui, but the style, puffed up to the point of bombast, has nothing in common with his.[132] Later, authorship was attributed to the young Vittorini, to whom Malaparte would have, as it were, subcontracted the work.[133] In fact, there is nothing to choose between the suppositions. Malaparte was already a masterful enough writer that he could easily imitate any style. But this is not where the real problem lies: cosigning the book, he took on moral and legal coauthorship, and it is frankly hard to believe he did so simply out of friendship toward Falqui or to allow Vittorini

FASCISM AND HIGH SOCIETY (1925–1933)

to earn a little money. Strictly speaking, it was Il Duce who had cause to complain, because, taking up again *Technique*'s comparison between the strategist Lenin and the technician Trotsky, the authors seemed to imply that without Balbo's technique, Mussolini's strategy would not have been enough to guarantee the conquest of power. The goal of this flattery was easy to understand: fired from the newspaper, pushed to leave Turin, and almost forced to expatriate, Malaparte hoped in this way to revive his old connection to Balbo, to show his adversaries he could still call on powerful friends, ready to intervene in his favor. If we keep in mind that every professional ascent under Fascism was determined by patronage and protection from on high, there is nothing surprising in this behavior, or anything particularly immoral if considered according to the criteria of the period.

The story would have finished there, if Malaparte had not tried to be too clever. In his Parisian solitude, he got the idea that Balbo, insufficiently demonstrative in his displays of gratitude for the book, had abandoned him to his fate, as had so many others. His bitterness grew when, in January 1932, the Italian embassy in Paris did not invite him to a reception in honor of Balbo, who had come to the capital to receive the Aéro-Club de France's highest honor. A venomous correspondence followed with the ambassador, Count Manzoni, a man of the old guard, very rigid, very disinclined to offer justifications. Malaparte then denounced him in the Fascist press as a xenophile and a lover of contemporary art, which in this context was not a compliment and could have had unpleasant consequences for the diplomat. He may have harbored an old grudge against the man, possibly connected to a 1928 telegram to the Ministry of Foreign Affairs in which Manzoni had written: "Suckert, as he is wont to do whenever he comes to Paris, has approached or tried to approach just about everybody, with the clear aim of publicizing above all else himself and his projects."[134] His articles in *L'Italia Letteraria* became more bitter, more mordant. After having carefully avoided doing so in the first instance, he proceeded to make public the names of Italian authors who had come to seek their fortune in Paris (as if he himself were not among their number!), accusing them, more or less openly, of moving in anti-Fascist circles. Even his old mentor Ugo Ojetti paid the price, leading his wife, Fernanda Ojetti, once so motherly toward Malaparte, to stop speaking to him. These acts of petty spite show how Malaparte had quickly lost his initial restraint; they suggest a man with his nerves shot, gnawed at by the uncertainty of the future, keen to try anything to demonstrate his zeal. The choice he had to make was always the same, but this time it was more difficult than ever, because if he had decided to expatriate, he knew, again, that the *fuoriusciti*, spurred on by Salvemini, Tasca, and the Communists, would not have greeted him with open arms. As at so many moments in his life, he risked being caught between two fires. Even for a man like him, seemingly born to be always in the minority, the situation was hardly enviable.

But a hesitant Malaparte would no longer be Malaparte. He finally made a decision, and it was to go on the attack. He returned to Italy for the 1932 summer holidays, August to September, making short stops in Turin and Rome, then heading to Capri with "Flaminia." From there he wrote first to Marianne Halévy: "For the past twelve days I have been in Paradise."[135] Before long, though, he turned to her husband, Daniel, to tell him that the minister of foreign affairs, Dino Grandi, had put the kibosh on his last hopes to enter diplomacy. Soon thereafter, Grandi himself received Il Duce's order to submit his resignation from the ministry and to leave for London as ambassador: he, too, was a troublesome character, of extraordinary personality and intelligence, whom Mussolini wanted to put somewhere he could not overshadow him. Malaparte decided the moment had arrived to request new audiences with both Mussolini and Balbo, on the eve of his return to Paris. A local informer noted that "Malaparte has left Capri for the capital with B. [i.e., 'Flaminia'] to be received tomorrow evening at seven by the head of government."[136] It was the last time they found themselves face to face. Il Duce reassured him; Malaparte did not know he had recently authorized the chief of police to renew his passport, "waiting to see how he behaves."[137] His reception by Balbo, on the other hand, was ice cold—or at least that's how he described it.

It is here that Malaparte, perhaps encouraged by some allusion of Mussolini's against Balbo, commits the irreparable. As chance had it, alas, upon returning to his hotel he found an innocent postcard from Quilici. Malaparte immediately sent back a venomous reply:

> I saw the chief and he received me very well (I can say that it was the first time he received me like that). Balbo received me with a coldness I wasn't expecting. Did he not like *Technique*? What do I care? The truth, dear Quilici, is that Balbo's revolutionary spirit has gone to hell. Italo has gotten fat, [and not] just physically speaking.[138] He would make a good minister for Louis Philippe. And naturally he cannot bear those who keep alive the ready spirit [*spiritaccio*] of the past and the future.[139]

A petulant outburst? A reckless joke? But it could not have escaped him that his correspondent was under surveillance by the political police, seeing as how behind him there was Balbo. OVRA was already at work to discredit Quilici in Mussolini's eyes, presenting him as responsible for "trafficking in favors and criticism of the regime."[140] Malaparte pressed on, citing certain intrigues he was in a position to know well from his time at *La Stampa*: a clear allusion to relations between Balbo and FIAT, about which rumors had circulated for some time. Balbo had discovered the high life, sophisticated women, palaces, fine food—and inside he suffered from it, because, as a true romantic, he was afraid of not always living up to his ideals. His posturing as a soldier of fortune, the product of an exuberant temperament, attracted many malicious comments but fed his popularity.* If he too had "put on some belly," he would later show himself to still be the regime's great rebel, the only one unafraid of the boss. If he was a pleasure seeker, he was not cruel, quite the contrary. But he was a man of action born in struggle: a generous friend, he could become an implacable adversary if someone sought to do him harm. Malaparte created himself a mortal enemy for no reason, precisely when he might have looked to the future with the greatest optimism. Il Duce, having definitively given up on the idea of finding him a diplomatic post, had, however, authorized Borelli to offer him a much-anticipated (and well-compensated) contract with the *Corriere della Sera*. Malaparte's purgatory had—or might have—come to its end.

Taken by surprise, Quilici tried to throw water on the fire, as was

---

*This luxury was exaggerated by police reports and gossip. Balbo's wealth came from his marriage (of love) with a young woman from a noble and well-to-do Friulian family. In Rome, the Balbos lived in a middle-class apartment building for government and military officials (testimony of their son Paolo to the author).

his nature. He kept the letter from his boss and sent Malaparte a dismayed reply, reminding him of everything Balbo had done for him. In closing, he vigorously encouraged him to put such unpleasant talk behind him. Nothing doing. Malaparte multiplied the accusations, writing, for example, to Halévy that "only Italo Balbo, who is openly preparing for the succession [to Mussolini], fails to hide his antipathy for me." From Paris he sent Quilici another, even more violent letter, two dense pages in which he goes beyond assailing Balbo to present himself as a vestal of the revolution and dispenser of advice mixed with threats:

> If you, dear Quilici, really care for Balbo, tell him it's time to pull back, if he doesn't want to find himself in trouble one of these days. I don't believe in his revolutionary spirit. I don't believe in the future of fat men. Even if Balbo were thin, he would need another head and another heart. Do you believe Italians don't know what would happen if Balbo's ambitions were realized? It would be an appalling kind of slavery. Italo has the makings of a provincial tyrant—that is, of a provincial ham actor in love with gold and power. A bad combination.

If the first letter could have been provoked by a spur-of-the-moment impulse, the second was a declaration of war, pure and simple. Malaparte no longer limited himself to formulating heavy-handed innuendos about Balbo's morals; he openly suggested that his erstwhile ally was conspiring against Mussolini. We certainly cannot imagine that his impetuous temperament betrayed him a second time, or that he was so naive as to suspect there would be no consequences. He knew perfectly well that his letters were intercepted by the police and that Quilici was a good man whose first loyalty was to Balbo rather than to him. And yet Quilici twice more invited him to recant, before passing the correspondence to Balbo. It had meanwhile come to Mussolini's attention thanks to the police surveillance.

Why did he do it, then? By all accounts, Malaparte deliberately got himself mixed up in a game that was too big for him.* He had no rancor, no real resentment toward Balbo: it was simply a cynical miscalculation. He had tried to regain Il Duce's favor by betting on the fall of Balbo. Already some years earlier, he had tried to hatch a similar strike against another party official, Bottai, with the aim of increasing his credit with Mussolini. But Bottai had forgiven him with no hard feelings. And so? Maybe he had heard, or thought he had heard, some unflattering words about Balbo from Mussolini's lips, which made him think he ought to make a move.[141] The tactic had worked for him at the time of the Matteotti murder, when he learned how to rapidly align himself first with the hawks, then against the Farinacci-style "ferocious sheep." The rumor was circulating in Rome that after Grandi and Bottai, both recently dismissed, it would be Balbo's turn. Mussolini had already decided to reshuffle his cabinet, in order to discharge his adversary more discreetly. The operation required a bit of time, because it was necessary to keep in mind his popularity, but in the end Balbo had to yield, in November 1933, and accept the position in Libya. His naming as air marshal allayed, on a formal level, his political defeat.

---

*My conclusions here are informed by a conversation conducted one beautiful and cold December day in Rome, around a table at the Circolo degli Esteri (a private club for employees of the Ministry of Foreign Affairs, founded in 1936 by Galeazzo Ciano), between Folco Quilici and Paolo Balbo, who have since childhood continued the close friendship that bound their parents.

FASCISM AND HIGH SOCIETY (1925–1933)

Balbo, meanwhile, was hardly twiddling his thumbs. Back in early January, when he found out about the Malaparte-Quilici correspondence, he rushed to Il Duce, incensed, to denounce his slanderer, accusing him of acting on behalf of his enemy Farinacci, with whom, in fact, the writer had not been in touch for some time. The slope became increasingly slippery; but Malaparte failed to grasp the situation, or maybe he put too much faith in the protection of Il Duce, whom he considered to some extent his instigator. He stayed until late February in London, from where he sent several dispatches to the *Corriere della Sera*, among which stands out a rather penetrating analysis of the saturnine personality of the Prince of Wales, the future Edward VIII, who would be forced to abdicate on account of his relationship with Wallis Simpson and his manifest sympathies for Nazi Germany. Back in Paris, Malaparte was the guest of honor of the International Committee of the Friends of Peace. His society and literary life was ever more brilliant. But he often crossed the Channel to meet Jonathan Cape, the publisher of Lawrence of Arabia and later of Arthur Koestler and Malcolm Lowry. In the English capital he saw opened to him the doors of polite society, where his friend Grandi took center stage.* He liked England and admired its spirit. He did not fail to note the eccentricities of a ruling class who looked on Fascist Italy with a certain sympathy, including Winston Churchill, who languished in a corner, waiting for his time to return. It was a much stronger and more determined society than the one that produced France's Third Republic, now in decline. Malaparte realized that England would fight resolutely when the moment came, to

---

*This was the same Grandi whom Churchill would try in vain to impose on the Americans as minister of foreign affairs in the Badoglio government, after the fall of Fascism.

defend its values and, above all, its interests. It was a message that showed through the lines of those dispatches that we can consider on the whole more lucid and prophetic than reports from the extremely intelligent but cynical Grandi, who deceived Mussolini about the defeatism and decadence of "perfidious Albion."

On June 7, exasperated by Mussolini's slowness, Balbo formally denounced Malaparte at the Special Tribunal for the Defense of the State, for anti-Fascist activities abroad. Il Duce was overtaken by an open action before an institution he himself had created, and which he could not disown. At that point, he did not hesitate to sacrifice the writer to prove to Balbo that he had nothing to reproach himself for. The marshal had returned from his transatlantic flight haloed with glory, and even Mussolini had to submit tactically.[142] The investigation proceeded in great secrecy; as the outcome drew near, Malaparte was summering in Provence, from where he sent the *Corriere* seven "Gallo-Roman" dispatches suggested to him by Borelli. The idea was to underline everything France owed to its Latin heritage, manfully incarnated by Fascism and its leader. Malaparte obeyed with an enthusiasm he believed was much appreciated in Rome, just as the vise was about to close on him. He relaxed at Cap d'Antibes, still without suspecting anything. In early September he announced to Borelli his arrival around the twentieth and arranged to meet him in Milan.[143] Some days later, on the eve of his departure for Italy, he sent a letter to one of his French correspondents, the historian Pierre Bessand-Massenet, which, in light of what awaited, seems singularly prophetic:

> I go to Italy, then, and I return there with great sadness. But I am sure that patriotic considerations, that the rhetoric of false patriots,

won't make me lose sight of the duty of all good Italians: to work on a higher plane than politics, a difficult thing. One needs to remember that Caesar does not offer happiness, only compensation. Happiness must be conquered, must be sought in the secret realms where Caesar does not reign. Friendship, art, goodness: here is what remains, my dear Bessand-Massenet.[144]

Here he is worrying, finally; but too late. Borelli had instead understood how bad things had gotten. He advised him, in a message that prudently he had sent from Switzerland, to not reenter Italy until matters were cleared up.[145] But Malaparte, who spent the first part of his stay in Milan without incident, did not listen to the warnings of his faithful friend. And he was wrong. The evening of his arrival in Rome, on October 7, he was arrested at midnight in his room at the Belsito hotel, on the lovely Via Ludovisi, and transferred to a rather less comfortable cell in Regina Coeli. The jar returns to the well until it breaks.

3. Kremlin and Swastika (1934–1943)

All the silliness we call history is worthless unless it is tastefully adorned.
—Paul-Louis Courier

Oh, What a Lovely Confinement!

Some points in our reconstruction of Malaparte's fall from grace remain obscure, then. But one thing is certain: anti-Fascism, which he invoked after 1943 as the main reason for his arrest, had nothing—or very nearly nothing—to do with it. It is true that police reports designate him a "definite anti-Fascist,"[1] even before the appearance of *Technique*. But his sojourn in Paris by no means represented a break with the regime, and no one knew it better than Mussolini. This is why, unlike how he proceeded in similar cases, Il Duce did not take into account the report the minister of the interior presented him, per usual, the day after Malaparte's arrest. After noting the dates and principal markers of the accused's career, the document drew this conclusion:

> Endowed with unbounded self-love, with limitless ambition, Sukert's [*sic*] political conduct has always been somewhat uncertain.... In reality, Malaparte, as a Fascist, was always ready to attack

Fascism and its officials with harsh criticism, especially when he failed to find support for his ambitious aspirations... On the whole, Malaparte's stay in France, and more specifically the activity he pursued there, even though ably concealed by him, may be characterized as distinctly anti-Fascist and quite harmful.[2]

The very serious accusation of actions contrary to the regime and of conspiracy with the main anti-Fascists abroad could have cost him not his head but life in prison.* The charge collapsed during the investigative phase, almost certainly on Il Duce's orders, and was reduced to the more modest one of offense and slander against a minister. In consequence, it was not the dreaded Special Tribunal for the Defense of the State, to which Balbo had turned, that investigated his case, but a simple provincial commission charged with imposing not prison terms but administrative measures, notably relegation to domestic surveillance. In the end, the dictator had managed the situation with a modicum of Machiavellism. Sacrificing Malaparte to Balbo and, at the same time, stopping the investigation into the Fascist dignitary for allegedly receiving payoffs from Turin sugarcoated the bitter pill he had delivered to the dour marshal.

Naturally, in all his postwar accounts, Malaparte would mention the accusation of militant anti-Fascism as the one that had put him in the stocks, especially given that everyone figuring in the affair,

---

*The death penalty, reestablished in 1926, was applied until 1943, in seventeen cases (which certain historians reduce to seven), of which three concerned attempts on the life of the head of government. In some cases (for the anarchists whom he respected), the dictator appointed pensions to the families of the executed. He had done the same with the families of Matteotti and Amendola (but not Gobetti), which was a matter of some controversy after the war.

from Mussolini to Balbo, from Quilici to the head of the party press office, Marinelli, was no longer around. Malaparte would also pass over in silence the fact of his being expelled from the PNF—of which he was clearly *still* a member—at the moment of his arrest, "for having failed to respect the Fascist oath":[3] a rather ambiguous formulation, but, here too, lighter than the one of having "betrayed" the oath. He would also be expelled, following a dishonorable decision, from the Federation of Garibaldian Volunteers, at this point become a mere instrument in the hands of the party. On this point as well, Borelli's testimony is essential. The *Corriere*'s editor in chief, even in difficult moments, would remain Malaparte's most devoted friend. A great professional and open to the world, he had married Jia Ruskaja, a Russian ballerina in exile, who would open a dance school in Rome, highly regarded to this day (in her turn, Ruskaja was spied on by OVRA). Borelli was able to ensure, in his long time at the helm of the most important Italian daily newspaper, up through July 1943, the discreet collaboration even of moderate anti-Fascists, which often kept them out of the most abject poverty. With respect to foreign policy, the *Corriere*'s style, despite official directives, was generally more sober than the rest of the national press. It is no surprise that Borelli was considered a "liberaloid" in police notices, which regularly pointed to his interventions in favor of Malaparte.[4] As soon as he learned of the arrest, Borelli rushed to Palazzo Venezia. Mussolini, after hurling a sardonic greeting his way—"you've got the wrong address"—furnished him with the key to the matter:

> Do you think we would have let him travel around Italy for two weeks, if he had been a dangerous anti-Fascist? I had to accept his arrest, despite the goodwill I bear him, because I received a formal

request for it from a sitting minister, Italo Balbo, who accuses him of defaming him for nothing less than having taken money from FIAT. For this reason, I absolutely authorize him to go to Balbo and try to talk to him about it.[5]

A lovely bit of Romagnese guile on Il Duce's part! He knew perfectly well that Balbo would have strangled Malaparte with his own hands if given the chance. Borelli opted then to go to the chief of police, the all-powerful and shrewd Arturo Bocchini. Smiling, the latter indicated a huge file on his desk, making it clear there was plenty there with which to arrest Malaparte for his activity in France, but he had received orders from the top not to do it.[6] As Borelli would later recall, the preliminary investigation was dispatched in a few weeks: "Curzio was sentenced to five years of *confino*, not for anti-Fascism, but for having defamed a sitting minister."[7] Clearer than that... After which, Il Duce gave a new ambiguous response to Borelli, who had returned to plead for mercy for his friend:

> We'll see later, but meanwhile Malaparte needs to take a bit of his own medicine. I am not entirely happy with his behavior. Come back next year.[8]

Mussolini was not only magnanimous, as he (sometimes) happened to be with a fallen adversary at his feet. Probably, he was already calculating that the writer, humiliated and having come back to his senses, could still be useful to him, as confirmed by what happened next. Perhaps he also felt somewhat responsible for having encouraged his leap onto the slippery slope of an attack on the regime's most popular man. Il Duce's method, which consisted in making subjects who had become recalcitrant or too independent feel the power of his anger, followed by his forgiveness, was infallible, and he applied it for twenty years, without generally needing to turn to violence, reserving that for determined early adversaries such as Matteotti, Amendola, Gobetti, or Gramsci. *Confino*, which struck even prominent figures in the regime, could lead to further prosecution or, on the contrary, to a measure of clemency, if the person concerned demonstrated good behavior and a will to mend their ways. The treatment inflicted on Malaparte fit perfectly within this tactic. For that matter, everything suggests that his assets, among them the untouched greater part of his compensation from *La Stampa*, had not been confiscated.

What instead arouses skepticism is the version of events given by Malaparte in his 1946 statement of defense. After skating over the "insults to Balbo, written many years earlier," he claims that "the real reason for my arrest and my sentence [was] the anti-Hitler chapter contained in my *Technique du coup d'État*. I later found out that Hitler, come to power in 1933, had asked Mussolini for my arrest."[9] This puerile justification could not have passed muster even in the chaotic atmosphere of the Liberation. In 1933, relations between Mussolini and Hitler were quite tense. Moreover, having just come to power, the Führer had rather more urgent fish to fry. In any case, the book was prohibited under the Third Reich—the question was closed. And Borelli logically deduced from this: If Hitler's hatred had been so intense, why allow Malaparte later to visit Berlin several times and to follow the German troops in the Balkans and Russia, in 1941? And why not, given the opportunity, have him eliminated under the pretext of some accident, seeing as how his undeniable physical courage frequently led him to expose himself on the front line? But as we already know, Malaparte would take every opportunity after the war to paint himself as a victim of political persecution. In an unfinished essay on "Notre Baudelaire" (Our Baudelaire), titled in French but composed in Italian, sometime between 1938 and 1947, he would write that "in 1933 I was arrested in Rome, shut up in the Regina Coeli prison, and after a few months sentenced to five years' internment on Lipari, for the book I had published in Paris two years earlier, *Technique du coup d'État*."[10] In his preface to the first Italian edition, of 1948, he added other fictional details:

> The evidence they had on me were: a copy of *Technique*, in which Mussolini himself had marked the incriminating passages with a red pencil; leaflets from the German Anti-Nazi Democratic Front; a letter I had written months before to a friend, now dead, in which, in the name of all Italian writers, I defended the freedom of art and literature, and I expressed harsh criticism of the behavior of Balbo (I had convinced myself to write the letter following an appeal, sent to me in Paris by Elio Vittorini, for me to return to Italy to publicly take up the defense of literary freedom and of the dignity of Italian writers, the subject of insults and threats from the Fascist press); and finally an article, openly hostile to Mussolini and Hitler, which had appeared in the *Nouvelles Littéraires* of March 1933 with the title "The Immorality of Guicciardini." (T2, 12)

Some nerve! Everything in this paragraph is false: Mussolini's marked-up copy of the book is false, but useful for demonstrating the dictator's resentment of and disappointment in him; false, or at least never communicated to the court, are the anti-Nazi leaflets; false is his interpretation of Quilici's letter, which had nothing to do with the anodyne and *subsequent* letter from Vittorini to the following effect: "And I often wonder why you don't bring back some dismay, that is some order, to the literary matters of Italy, which are going terribly,"[11] but here too useful, because meanwhile Vittorini had become a very influential Communist intellectual. As for the article on Guicciardini, we have seen how that clumsy move had remained without consequences for its author.

What is most depressing in all these versions, and in the others Malaparte would concoct over the years to come, is the subterranean attack on Quilici, more than on Mussolini or Balbo, as if that gallant man, no longer able to defend himself, had been an informer, while in fact he had tried in vain to make him see reason, and had run the risk of hiding from Balbo, for almost three months, the *two* letters from Malaparte. But only one letter, the *less* damaging, was included in the documentary evidence gathered against Malaparte, during his appearance before the provincial commission, on November 14. Can we assume that, in this case as well, Mussolini had intervened to simplify his procedural standing? It seems likely. And it would offer Malaparte, impervious to any notion of gratitude, one more reason to rage against Il Duce, after his fall.

Of course, Malaparte would carefully avoid mentioning all the letters he wrote to those who could have helped him during his detention in Regina Coeli, and later on Lipari, to come up with Fascist credentials of merit. Three days after his arrest, he wrote to Borelli: "I fully trust in the fairness and humanity of the chief, for whom I have always cared and wanted the best."[12] In another letter to his friend, which he obviously knew would be intercepted by the censors, he declared that "prison is a wonderful school" and claimed that he would "soon start a Fascist novel, which I had already spoken about to Treves and to [Telesio] Interlandi."¹³ The former was his usual publisher; the latter, a journalist in Farinacci's orbit who would become, after the 1938 laws, one of the representatives of official anti-Semitism.* Interlandi, we have seen, had already attacked him for the supposed tepidity of his Fascism—for this precise reason he could now become a kind of guarantor. The exiled Malaparte would therefore be delighted to feature among the contributors to Interlandi's weekly, *Quadrivio*, another detail he would subsequently forget. Malaparte turned also to Margherita Sarfatti, Mussolini's former lover and "educator." Their ties went back to the 1920s, when Malaparte contributed to Sarfatti's magazine *Gerarchia*. Later, during his time at the head of *La Stampa*, when Sarfatti would still appear beside Il Duce, he had cleverly named her president of the jury for the paper's literary prize.¹⁴ Now, though, there wasn't much she could do; her influence was on the decline and would shortly, at the introduction of the racial laws, collapse for good. Malaparte solicited letters from France as well, to prove his innocence and show he had never conspired against Fascism during his stay in Paris. The most diplomatic letter bore the signature of Bernard Grasset, when Malaparte had already been sent into *confino*:

> I also hope, trusting in the fairness of your chief, that your stay will be abbreviated. I cannot believe you have been dealt with so harshly,

---

*Interlandi, a gifted and cultivated journalist, had in the 1920s been a champion of the avant-garde. Power-hungry, and probably to repay his debts, in late 1938 he became the official anti-Semite he never privately was, to the point that one of his former Jewish collaborators (whom I met many years later) was dismissed but kept on the payroll of the newspaper *Il Tevere*—just one example of the amount of corruption within the abomination of the Italian racial laws. In the 1980s Leonardo Sciascia tried to partially rehabilitate his name.

when I've always known you as a fervent Italian, and a fervent Fascist.[15]

The international press, especially in France, gave considerable publicity to the affair. *Le Temps*, the great moderate news outlet, emphasized the political aspect:

> As a result of anti-Fascist displays committed abroad, Curzio Erik [*sic*] Suckert has been arrested and is currently in the Regina Coeli prison.[16]

But another French daily, *Le Jour*, came much closer to the truth:

> It is well established, in any case, that Malaparte cannot be considered an anti-Fascist. It seems, too, that he enjoys a certain favor with Il Duce, who had authorized the Italian publication of his *Technique du coup d'État*, which we had first. A Fascist Malaparte was, but an independent Fascist, too passionate and too aware of his own value to blindly take orders.[17]

All this may be understandable in a man struck down out of the blue, who sought to save himself any way he could. The mug shots taken after his arrest, as Guerri has noted, are the only ones of his long career in which he appears shaken up and unkempt: at this point the dandy had one foot in the common grave. Malaparte claimed in letters to his relatives and friends that "this lesson will serve me well." He declared his desire to hole up in a corner of Tuscany, translate Horace, and give no one any reason to talk about him anymore. He said he was ready to apologize to Balbo, enlisting his mother for the purpose (mothers have always been useful in Italy for this kind of intercession). According to a police report, Elvira in fact wrote a dignified letter to Mussolini, who forwarded it to the marshal, "who appeared to understand that if he forgave [Malaparte], H. E. the Head of Government would have nothing against pardoning Sukert [sic]."[18] But the offended party remained unmovable.

Contrary to what he would describe later, Malaparte was treated fairly well: as he wrote to his brother Sandro, he had access to a "paying cell," he could have bedsheets, food, and books delivered, and he did "a lot of calisthenics."[19] But a prison is still a prison, especially if for more than a month one is kept in a state of absolute uncertainty, without outside contact. It really seemed possible he might become, as he quipped in a letter to Borelli, "Fascist Italy's Man in the Iron Mask."[20] When he finally appeared before the commission, on November 13, he pointed out he had never been interrogated. He sought to defend himself, displaying contrition: "I admit my grave mistake and am ready also to admit it directly to H. E. Balbo. My letter to Quilici was a momentary outburst, a thoughtless act, born of a moment of discouragement and exasperation." He also implored the commission to take into account "all the good there is in my past as a soldier and a Fascist."[21] Nothing doing: he was sentenced to five years of *confino* "for sending to Mr. Quilici of the *Corriere Padano* a letter that grievously insulted and defamed the quadrumvir and then air minister H. E. Italo Balbo, whom he accused of absolutely inexistent behaviors and intrigues."[22] This procedure, arbitrary and intimidatory as it may have been, bore nonetheless a semblance of legality: from the moment Malaparte became subject to an administrative sanction, it was unnecessary to proceed to a formal deposition, in the presence of attorneys, or to call witnesses, as in a trial. Evidently, no one was interested in drawing out the story of Balbo's alleged plot. Another small mystery: that his destination would be Lipari does not appear in the minutes, but only in the public statement made some hours later by the state press agency, Stefani. The time it took for Mussolini to make a decision? The island of Lipari, off Sicily's north coast, was far away and hard to get to, but not one of the worst *confino* destinations.

On November 30, after asking in vain to join his brother Ezio in Somalia, where he was working as an agronomist, Malaparte departed for Lipari, accompanied by his mother. He was permitted to make the long journey by train and ship under escort but not in handcuffs—here too he would feel the need to exaggerate, describing in *The Skin* how, as he crossed the marina and passed through the crowd, he was chained like a criminal. Handcuffed or not, the experience would have wrecked anyone. And yet Malaparte seemed to have already made it through the hardest part. Nor was he forgotten by everyone in his misfortune, as he would maintain later; instead he began a voluminous correspondence practically from the moment he arrived on the island. Very quickly, he seemed to breathe again, as testified by one of his first letters to Borelli:

> I was sure I would not create any trouble for you by writing, and that was a great comfort to me. On the other hand, the reasons why I was detained, and why I am here, are not such that they could in any way harm those few I was writing to. Now I am here, calm, and I am organizing my new existence the best I can. I am treated very well by the authorities and, aside from the inevitable limitations of *confino* (at home by seven in the evening, limited space to traverse), my life is normal. The island is beautiful, the climate extremely mild,

the population courteous. In sum, I am well, and little by little I am recovering from the symptoms I suffered in jail, where in the last few days I had a sore throat. My usual ailment.[23]

The reassuring tone was obviously dictated by a concern not to displease those same authorities who read his correspondence. The reference to his "usual ailment," linked to his damaged lungs, makes us understand, retrospectively, that the imprisonment was not in fact without consequences for his premature death, twenty-four years later.

But he hardly sounded like a broken man in a postcard he wrote to Halévy two days later:

Thanks for your postcard and thanks to everyone who signed it. Certainly, the island of Lipari is no Île de la Cité, and the Liparesi are not Parisians. But neither is it Regina Coeli. Little by little, I will forget those two months of isolation in my cell. I suffered a great deal; here I rest in the sun. But what a journey! I intend to work. My splendid isolation will be useful for something, at least. The local people here are very kind. There are only two *confinati*: me and an engineer from Turin: *poca brigata vita beata*. I'll write you a long letter tomorrow. I think of you and Madame with all my faithful heart.[24]

Everything seems to indicate, in fact, that Malaparte was rediscovering his faith in the future. Borelli continued tirelessly to fight for him, but he was no longer alone. Other important figures intervened in his favor, from Bottai and Grandi—two of the rare early comrades who, like Balbo, could still address Il Duce informally, as *tu*—to Carlo Delcroix, president of the Association of Wounded and Disabled

War Veterans, who reminded Mussolini of Malaparte's merits as a soldier and his gas injuries. One day, suddenly, the international press reported the news that the writer's health had weakened and that he was in critical condition. Il Duce, furious, demanded that a team go photograph Malaparte; they captured him stripped to the waist, in perfect health, flexing his biceps like an athlete as he lifted enormous concrete blocks, which were in reality pumice stone.[25] However, medical examinations in Messina and Palermo discovered, or rather confirmed, tuberculosis in both lungs. Malaparte was then granted a war pension, which he would assign to a disabled Prato veteran (evidence of the "humane" side of his nature he so rarely disclosed).

Apart from his health, he approached his stay in a rather serene fashion, convinced that the forced break wouldn't last too long. He liked the local population, who displayed that dignity in poverty that reminded him of the peasants of his childhood and his companions in the Alpine Brigade. In the *Corriere della Sera* he would later publish a series of affectionate articles about the site of his detention, where "the Liparesi conferred on me the title of citizen of the free city of Lipari. And why not the title of free citizen of the city of Lipari?"[26] And of his big heart—something he usually hid because it did not fit his persona—there is yet further proof. Twenty years later, his German translator, on a visit to the island, would write him, "What gave me the most pleasure was the way I heard Malaparte remembered on Lipari, by everyone and especially by the humble and poor."[27]

Nothing was changing yet, but he no longer felt like a pariah. Little by little, his friends began to contact him again, even those who had out of prudence kept their distance at the time of his arrest. His circle of contacts grew larger; he could read, write, and procure a radio for himself. He could not publish, of course, but he could afford to wait. He had already done enough so that his name would not be easily forgotten. Was his *confino* therefore less severe than that of other opponents or victims of the regime? A thorny question. If not the four walls of a prison cell, it was nonetheless a closed universe, subject to permanent surveillance, in unhealthy places and under primitive living conditions. With respect to other testimonies that have come down to us, particularly the two literary masterworks that emerged from a similar experience—*Christ Stopped at Eboli*, by Carlo Levi, and *The Political Prisoner*, by Cesare Pavese—Malaparte seems to have made out better. He himself apparently recalled, a few years later, "in tones of sincerity...the time spent in *confino* on Lipari, where he had lived a year 'of punishment,' yes, but surrounded by every comfort and treated with respect (he was even allowed to keep a lover)."[28] But who can judge such a particular experience, without having experienced it? And what can a man feel, pulled out of his normal life from one day to the next, and deprived of his freedom of movement?

Aside from his mother, who continued tirelessly to shuttle back and forth between the island and the mainland, two important presences would alleviate his solitude. The first was "Flaminia," who did not have the least intention of abandoning him to his fate. Back when Malaparte was forced to leave *La Stampa*, she had done everything to get him the top job at another daily, Bologna's *Il Resto del Carlino*, where her family could call on influential contacts.[29] It was precisely while speaking on the telephone with an editor at this newspaper that she came to know of her lover's arrest, "and she gave the impression of fainting at the news."[30] "Flaminia" soon went on the counterattack. First she turned to her former beau, the heir to the throne, Umberto. "The prince has considered the request, to the great scandal of his family and the court itself, where such an interest is condemned," reads one police report.³¹ Alas, the august personage wielded no real power, since his father and Il Duce were agreed on treating him like the perfect imbecile he was not. Without worrying about conventions or police tailing, "Flaminia" multiplied her interventions in high places, going so far as to personally visit Arturo Bocchini, known throughout Italy for his sensualist tendencies. We lack witnesses for this scene worthy of *Tosca*, fortunately sans dagger; Bocchini would die some years later, peacefully in his bed, following a gargantuan meal. From Regina Coeli to Lipari and beyond, the devotion of "Flaminia" was exceptional, especially if you consider what a scandal could have cost her. And yet, it was precisely then that the relationship entered a crisis, weakened, and faded away. Malaparte was not worthy of such a companion; in any event, their love story was a hopeless one, given the conventions of the time. Later, the writer would recall his beloved in an account of a trip to Paestum, a somewhat cold elegy to a past love.³² Two photos from that trip have often been reproduced, sometimes with "Flaminia" mistaken for Virginia Agnelli.

The other presence was that of Febo, who, if not the first dog in Malaparte's life,* was the one who inspired his never-ending affection, of which he would give a heart-wrenching transposition in *The Skin*. Febo was a stray, but even a stray cannot be a dog like any other in Malaparte's eyes; he made him into the purest exemplar of an almost mythological race, the *cernenghi*, or Stromboli greyhounds, which breed only on the island. He also called him an "Arab sheepdog"

---

*Nor even the first Febo, if this was really the name of the "black poodle with red eyes and long, bushy whiskers" that kept him company in his solitary childhood games ("Angoscia di ragazzo," in S, then in R1, 319).

in a photo sent to Bessand-Massenet, which depicted them on the Lipari house's terrace, along with "Flaminia." Malaparte's love for animals, particularly dogs, went back to his childhood and, despite certain D'Annunzian affectations, was one of the most genuine components of his nature. In the solitude of *confino*, the feeling deepened. Malaparte, as we know, was incapable of deep relationships with men, and even more so with women. The unreserved, uncritical devotion of an animal was the best substitute for an actual human relationship. The chasm between those who love animals, for the power of their instinct, and those who do not love them, in the name of reason, can never be bridged. Malaparte falls into the first group; his love for animals allowed him to display his feelings, without the risk of being unmasked.* His old housekeeper, Maria Montico, told the story of how one day the larder was empty, thanks to a late-arriving check, so she asked Malaparte to go buy something to eat. The writer returned with a nice steak: he offered the first bite to Febo, who appreciated it so much that his owner proceeded to give him all the rest, one bite after another. Malaparte looked tenderly at the dog as it devoured the pieces of meat, without thinking that he would go to bed hungry, as would, naturally, Maria.[33]

Malaparte sought out the presence of animals in all his travels. He admired England's sporting traditions, above all those of the country gentry, while hating the taste (this, too, D'Annunzian) for fox hunts and greyhound races, which incited competition and bloodlust. He would talk about his dismay at not having met dogs

---

*The brilliant film director Fritz Lang, whose personality has many points in common with Malaparte's, went even further. He spent the last years of his life in the company of a stuffed animal, "Peter the Monkey," that he brought with him everywhere, and for which he prepared well-shaken martinis.

or cats in Soviet Russia or Mao's China. He suffered for the animals lost or massacred in all wars, on the scorched streets of Ethiopia as on the Alpine massifs, where the fleeing farmers abandoned unmilked cows and desperately lowing calves. At the end of his life he would be happy when friends offered him a last companion, called Curzio.[34] The company of animals was indispensable to him, while human beings interested him only in the moment of struggle, or in the pursuit of a common goal—be it in the context of war, politics, journalism, travel, shooting a film ... in short, of any occasion calling for the building of something together—as a man entirely sunk into the reality of the present. Malaparte could spend days with the masons building his house on Capri, sharing bread, olives, and onions with them, singing their songs, mourning their dead at sea, and answering to "Curtino." Once the house was finished, he wouldn't have recognized the men if he had encountered them in the town square. This portrait may seem a bit superficial, but it fits him like a glove. Nothing demonstrates it better than his conviction, even if surely in part a pose, to have found in barking with dogs a freer and more spontaneous form of communication than what occurred with human beings.

At the end of February—after only three months, versus the five years he officially had to serve—Malaparte asked Ciano, at the time undersecretary for the press and culture, to intervene with his father-in-law, to whom he had already written himself,[35] to authorize him to publish unsigned articles. At the same time, he confided to other correspondents his hope of being transferred to Tuscany soon. What inspired such boldness? Perhaps Mussolini had discreetly let him know, through his mother or "Flaminia," that he had already made the decision to have him transferred to a more welcoming spot? In any case, he was no longer kept in the dark about current events, since he sent Bessand-Massenet a shrewd analysis of the incidents of February 6 in Paris:*

> Thanks for the letter and thanks for the books (I've sent Malraux a postcard to thank him for the dedication; I'll write him in the next few days),[36] which are the only friends of my solitude.... Montherlant worries too much about establishing his own personal position, his own degree of latitude, in the current disorder. And Malraux is a species of centaur, of which only the head is human. I've read in the papers about the events that have shook Paris. It seems to me, judging from such a distance, that you are on the right track. But there is too much politics in France: everything is transformed into politics, even those killed in the Place de la Concorde.† Everything is immediately parliamentarized, even the antiparliamentary [illegible word—probably "sentiment"] of the youth. A bad disease. I am thinking of a superior, disinterested, truly idealistic humanity, of young people capable of sacrificing themselves with the purity of feeling characteristic of certain gratuitous acts.[37]

---

*Far-right demonstrators, clashing with far-left counterparts on the fringes, attempted to storm the Assembly, resulting in deaths and injuries from clashes with the police. The events of February 6, 1934, are considered one of the most visible manifestations of the crisis of the Third Republic.

†According to the historian Eugen Weber, describing the events of February 6, 1934: "That Tuesday evening and long into the night, as one rioting wave after another broke on the Concorde bridge, as kiosks and overturned buses flared on the square and near it, as the 'Internationale' of participating Communists mingled with the 'Marseillaise,' fifteen people died and fifteen hundred were wounded." *The Hollow Years: France in the 1930s* (New York: W. W. Norton, 1994), 136.—Trans.

Malaparte's language here closely recalls the comments published in the Fascist press at the time on the decadence of French democracy. He sometimes took advantage of his foreign correspondents to toss out hints to the regime, to show he could still be useful. And once again, the chief's magnanimity did not fail. In late June, before the arrival of the great heat and dryness that made life on Lipari so difficult, Malaparte, accompanied by Febo and by Vulcano the canary, was transferred to the island of Ischia, near Naples, which was already a famous spa resort. Later, Malaparte would attribute the dictator's "capitulation" to the fear of an international press campaign, which existed only in his imagination. Nevertheless, the *confino* affair would become the ace up his sleeve that he could bring out over and over, after the war, to testify to his opposition to the regime and to make people forget he was—before, but also *after* his ordeal—one of its most prominent intellectuals.

He would spend four months on Ischia that must not have been too unpleasant, if he considered buying a villa there (perhaps the first version of Casa Come Me?). His health improved, as did his mood. Ciano—who would not have dared do so without his father-in-law's agreement—finally authorized Borelli to obtain another well-compensated contract for Malaparte with the *Corriere della Sera*. He could not yet, however, sign his own name, and so chose the pseudonym Candido: soon, readers all over Italy would know who it was. These articles dealt with a wide variety of topics, beyond politics, depending on his inspiration and what he was reading, ranging from ancient Greece to his love for the Mediterranean, from Aeschylus to Goethe, Dos Passos to the Romanian Panait Istrati. On the French front, he praised Cocteau's play *The Infernal Machine* and Montherlant's novel *The Bachelors*. He would also have liked to review a curious little book he had just received from Halévy, by a certain "Colonel de Gaule" [*sic*], but the *Corriere* told him it was up to the paper's military critic.*

Rumor had it Malaparte would soon be authorized to move even closer to the capital, this time in Tuscany. "Meanwhile, keep working, stay healthy, and trust in the goodness on High, which seems to me has been demonstrated in tangible and precise form," the always conciliatory Borelli exhorted him.[38] His literary activity in this period was intense but unexceptional; spoiled for choice, he seems to have been biding his time, waiting for something better. He wrote some poetry, all intimist and all bad, with the exception of some translations of Emily Dickinson, which were more successful; then some short stories and the scattered pages that would turn into *Fughe in prigione*, published in 1936, and *Sangue* (Blood), which appeared one year later. Here we find Malaparte as storyteller, one generally and wisely keeping his distance from current events, inspired by the verismo of Giovanni Verga and the early Pirandello, with touches of Bontempellian magical realism, without anything to suggest the breakthrough of his major books, aside from his insistence on the scourge of "blood," heralding that of the "plague." It was all in all a modest yield, if we consider the intimate laceration, the sense of guilt that that experience produced in the rather more vulnerable spirit of a Pavese, calling forth pages of decidedly greater

---

*Curiously, among the few foreign contemporary literary works in the private library of de Gaulle in his residence of Colombey-les-Deux-Églises there is a copy of *Kaputt* (information kindly provided to the author by the president of the Fondation Charles de Gaulle, the former minister Hervé Gaymard).

OH, WHAT A LOVELY CONFINEMENT!

substance. Of what Malaparte felt deep down, we find no sign here.*

But he poured the sullen rancor he harbored against the *padre padrone* into *Muss*, overwhelming the first draft of the book, conceived to glorify the tyrant:

> You don't know how much I hated you, Muss. In the interminable, gray, monotonous, squalid days, in the feverish, sleepless, fleabitten nights, in those days, in those weeks, in those months of solitude in the stinking, damp, freezing cell, you don't know how much I hated you... I would hate you and say to myself, "poor Muss." When they entered my cell for the usual body search (they searched us once a month), they stripped me naked, ran their dirty fingers over me, stuck their fingers between my toes, in my ears, in my nose, everywhere... I hated you like a man can hate another man, poor Muss. But when your own cops put their hands on you too... when they hung you by your feet, a wretched corpse, in front of a gas pump, and all your servants came to spit on you, I said only, "poor Muss." (MU, 77–78)

Apart from the dilation of actual time incarcerated, like a new Count of Monte Cristo, in this passage one catches the physical intensity of the relationship binding him to the *padre padrone*, the humiliation of the adult son relegated to the state of a child violated in his intimacy by the omnipotent father. We will see below how Malaparte

---

*But in the preface to the second edition of *Fughe*, from late 1943, his tone changed, with Malaparte claiming that "these are so far the only pages to appear in Italy about imprisonment and *confino* in recent years" (FP, 3). Meanwhile, of course, the regime had fallen.

would once again begin to love Muss, almost physically, when the dictator's end, his reduction to a miserable rag at the hands of his former slaves, would give the son the sense of finally being the *stronger* man. For the moment, though, his principal concern was to leave his ordeal behind as soon as possible. He still hoped to collect his articles concerning England. But their overly laudatory tone was no longer in step with the times: the tension over Ethiopia was poisoning the relations, theretofore good, between Rome and London. Malaparte-Candido adapted as well as he could to the Anglophobic turn in the Italian press;[39] but he gave up on publishing the book, because he would have had to cut or rework the majority of the earlier texts. On the other hand, France did not abandon him: *Les Nouvelles Littéraires*, *La Petite Gironde*, and other newspapers and magazines printed his old and new pieces alike. Halévy and Grasset waited impatiently for his next work. This time, though, prudence prevailed.

October 22, 1934, brought a new concession and a new relocation, even closer to home, as he craved, not to the obscure and peaceful Valdinievole, but to Forte dei Marmi.* Along with its twin Viareggio, it was the most alluring seaside resort on the Tyrrhenian coast, at the center of an enchanting pine grove still steeped with the romance of D'Annunzio and Eleonora Duse. "This is where Shelley was cremated by Byron, following the Ancient Greek rite of incineration," he wrote in excitement to Bessand-Massenet.[40] It was in any case—before the discovery of Monte Argentario, whose

---

*October 22, approaching the anniversary of the 1922 March on Rome, saw the decree of a number of political amnesties in Italy.

development had only just begun—the place where high society vacationed, without the extravagance of Capri or Taormina. Numerous aristocratic, industrial, and financial dynasties had spacious summer homes built there. In the evening, to the muted lamplight, one danced to the rhythm of the (officially banned) blues. The Mussolini family favored the beachfront resorts of Ostia and Riccione, where the dictator's wife, Rachele, did her daily shopping while Il Duce strolled bare chested on the beach (he was a poor swimmer) and sometimes played boccie.* At "Il Forte," on the other hand, habitués drank whisky, gin and tonic, and Negroni and Americano cocktails and smoked strictly English and American cigarettes, which some diplomat or military attaché had brought, scorning domestic or colonial tobacco. The international community was also well represented. Forte dei Marmi was highly sought after by artists and writers of the Belle Epoque, and especially by northern Europeans: Germans, Danes, Swedes, and Swiss. Thomas Mann employed it as a setting, under the fictional name Torre di Venere, for the frame story of *Mario and the Magician* (1929), one of the most transparent premonitions of the age of dictatorships. Even today, under the successive waves of mass tourism, one can admire the remains of various Gothic or Jugendstil villas, softened by the colors and forms of the Mediterranean. Borelli kept asking him for new articles, which little by little approached the current day. Malaparte doubted no longer that the worst was past, and began to devise plans for the future. As he wrote to Marianne Halévy:

---

*Mussolini, distant and impenetrable in Rome, insisted that on their summer holidays he and his family were accessible to "the people," with very limited police scrutiny. All this ended well before the war.

> What worries me now is not my current situation. From a moral and even a social point of view, the situation of a *confinato* is an excellent and very honest, very respectable situation. But afterward? What will I do when I am free? Where to go? Where to settle? *That is the question.* I will never again be completely free. I will settle in the countryside, in Tuscany, close to the sea, or in the Alps, on the Dolomites side, or on the island of Ischia.... It's pointless to think about traveling, about seeing friends again, my little "boat" of the Quai. Not for a few years, at least. A solitary life, in the middle of nature, far from everyone. You know well that I've never loved to live "socially." I am not a social man.[41]

This prophecy was realized only in part. To become a real hermit Malaparte would need freedom, which he still lacked, and which he would continue to lack, like all Italians, till the regime's fall. He spent a somewhat gloomy Christmas beside his sick mother and made a rather surprising confession to the faithful Marianne Halévy, that "*confino* would be easier for me if I too had a child."[42] On June 12, 1935, a year and eight months after his arrest, and a bit more than three years short of the sentence inflicted on him, he was set free "by H. E. the Head of Government's clemency"; given the circumstances, he did not get off too bad, even if later he would naturally claim to have served the *whole* sentence.[43] He then sent, or at least so he claimed, a bold message—never found—to Il Duce to express to him "*la mia gratitudine sconfinata*" (my boundless—literally, "unconfined"—gratitude).[44] He who laughs last laughs best: the chief watched over him, to claim his due.

Galeazzo and Edda

Once down and out, Malaparte would not only return to freedom but also rise to high society. In May, as if in early celebration of the end of his misfortunes, he purchased from a Belgian citizen, a Mr. Baltus or Balthus (no relation to the famous French-Polish painter), the owner's son-in-law and heir, one of the most admired homes along Il Forte's elegant promenade, Villa Hildebrand.[45] The residence took the name of the German sculptor who had built it in 1901, and it was decorated by an even more prominent artist, Arnold Böcklin. The style, quite overblown, was to tell the truth rather un-Malapartian; a few years later, Casa Come Me on Capri would be the opposite, from every point of view. But it was what you might call an excellent calling card, and his eagerness to be accepted again, after the trial he had undergone, influenced or dictated the writer's choice. Another good reason: the price was excellent, to the extent that it was possible to purchase it with his royalties from France and elsewhere, charging the Grasset business manager with delivering the required sum to the owner. This is in any case the improbable version we have from Malaparte,* who was careful not to indicate whether the compensation from Senator Agnelli—which, as previously observed, was in all likelihood *not* confiscated at the time of his fall—was used to finance the purchase, which seems much more likely.[46] In short, it was not the modest country house evoked in the letter to Marianne Halévy, but rather an eminently good springboard from which to resume conquering the world.

---

*It appeared improbable as well to the current business managers of the publishing house, to whom I posed the question, and who could not find any trace of the supposed payment in their archives.

Starting with the beau monde. Because Il Forte rapidly filled up with residents and guests who would set the tone for the summer season. Among them, having by now overtaken all the other, older, and more titled aficionados, the young golden couple of Italian society: Galeazzo and Edda Ciano. Golden and subsequently tragic: in the history of Fascism, often considered abroad even today like an opera buffa, these two stand out as Wagnerian figures. Galeazzo, five years younger than Malaparte, was no longer an obscure reporter dreaming of a future as a playwright in post–World War I Rome (the two plays he wrote at the age of twenty and never dared publish are naive but reveal some talent). Yet he found himself faced with not one but two *padri padroni* who would determine the course of his short life. His flesh-and-blood father was a sailor from Livorno with bushy whiskers and the solid physique of Napoleon's Old Guard, the admiral Costanzo Ciano, whose good marriage and daring displays in the Great War had led to his elevation by the king to the title of count of Cortellazzo and Buccari. An early Fascist, he had at the time of the Matteotti murder been a valuable ally to Mussolini, who had rewarded him with the presidency of a Chamber of Deputies then existing on paper alone. Determined to rise even higher, Costanzo, affectionately called "the jaw" for his appetite for lucre, forced his only son to leave journalism for a diplomatic career and to take a wife who could definitively establish the family in the first rank of the new Italy. His daughter Maria, having married a Piedmontese diplomat, Count Magistrati, found no other way to react to paternal violence than to die in one of the first known cases of anorexia. Galeazzo, who worshipped his father, followed orders, forgetting journalism and the theater, and diligently prepared himself for the diplomatic exam (the one Malaparte had never passed), where he placed twenty-seventh out of the thirty-five admitted: a premonition of the *aurea mediocritas* that should have inspired his life, if he had been wise. He was immediately posted abroad and left for Rio de Janeiro. While on a cruise he met Edda, the eldest child of Benito and Rachele Mussolini.* The meeting was organized by their parents, but the love at first sight was genuine. The nuptials, celebrated with fanfare in 1930, marked one of the rare appearances of a Mussolini very ill at ease in polite society, and was followed by the births of three children, whose initially gilded life would later undergo the trauma of the family drama.

Edda, just twenty, was her father's favorite and strikingly resembled him in her physique and character, if not in her political talent, which she, as a staunch feminist, would have wanted passionately to inherit. "I was the first woman in Italy to drive a car and to wear trousers," she would recall with some exaggeration in her memoirs.[47] Some biographers profess to have found the key to her impulsive nature and difficult relationship with Rachele, advancing the hypothesis that she was actually the daughter of Angelica Balabanoff. An incestuous relationship with her father has also been mooted—as if people's lives were not already sufficiently complicated... Not beautiful but intelligent, seductive, and spoiled—unlike Mussolini's other children, who were brought up in a normal way—Edda early

---

*Or more precisely of Mussolini, then a young teacher and Socialist agitator, and Rachele Guidi, who would marry in a civil ceremony only in 1915, and in a religious ceremony ten years later, to pave the way for the Concordat between Fascist Italy and the Holy See. It is possible that Mussolini had previously married Ida Dalser, with whom he had a secret son, Benito Albino.

on revealed a passionate temperament, characterized by angry outbursts and the refusal of any discipline. Galeazzo, on the contrary, was devoted but fragile, and she was the one who shaped his career and sealed his fate.

After a diplomatic intermezzo in Shanghai, the couple returned to Rome, where the thirty-year-old Galeazzo obtained his first important position, as head of Mussolini's press office, a title elevated two years later to minister of press and propaganda. Nepotism obviously had a part in this promotion, but only a part: Galeazzo showed himself to be a meticulous, industrious, and loyal official. He was able to rapidly gain the trust of the other *padre padrone*, who kept him literally at attention for his entire life. But he was, precisely, merely an official. Without the combined ambition of Costanzo and Edda, and entry into the most powerful family in Italy, he would have remained a good, middle-of-the-road diplomat for the time, esteemed by his colleagues, whom, even after his meteoric rise, he continued to treat kindly, or at least politely. Behind his public postures, modeled on his father-in-law's, Galeazzo loved to work in an informal, modern, American style, rather than in the profession's stuffier traditional manner. As a former chief of staff confided to me, "Galeazzo, as he was known to everyone, had five friends and five sworn enemies, which I couldn't touch. Otherwise, he never interfered with my prerogatives. He respected everyone and everyone respected him." This has been confirmed for me by other witnesses, in a field hardly known for its generosity of judgments.

In October 1935, at the time of the Ethiopian War, Il Duce ordered all Fascist Party officials to take part in operations, including his two eldest sons, Vittorio and Bruno, and his son-in-law: he made the same decision in 1940, at the cost, this time, of Bruno's life.* Galeazzo, a warmonger in politics but personally rather less so, set off in a squadron with the D'Annunzian and squadrist name of *La Disperata*. Going to bomb or machine-gun natives lacking antiaircraft protection, à la *Apocalypse Now*, was neither very desperate, nor particularly honorable, and we will confront the same question later in Malaparte's case. But the Ethiopians were magnificent warriors, supplied with arms and matériel by Swiss, English, and American smugglers, and falling into their hands, following a mechanical failure or a crash landing, was not at all pleasant. Galeazzo released his bombs in bunches as soon as possible and returned to Italy unscathed, breathing a great sigh of relief. Not long after, in July 1936, he received a promotion to minister of foreign affairs, which his father-in-law had held in an acting capacity, after Dino Grandi was sent to London. Edda's insistence had won out over the doubts of Il Duce. Galeazzo remained in the position until Mussolini's last cabinet reshuffle, in February 1943, when he became ambassador to the Holy See.

Historians have generally been severe in their judgments of Galeazzo, regarding him as not having been up to the task, compared with the skillful and shrewd Grandi, but also with a more levelheaded figure such as the foreign affairs undersecretary Giuseppe Bastianini. But Grandi had acted in a still relatively constructive

---

*A pilot officer decorated for his service in Ethiopia and Spain, Bruno died at the age of twenty-three, on August 7, 1941, testing a new airplane prototype. He was a simple, modest young man. His funeral marked the last moment of relative popularity for Il Duce, who dedicated to him one of his two "books of meditations" devoted to family, *Parlo con Bruno*, along with *Colloqui con Arnaldo*, dedicated to his own brother.

climate, as yet unpoisoned by the crises of the second half of the 1930s. Moreover, Grandi and Bastianini came from the trenches and the 1920–21 civil war: they became fully grown men at twenty, for better or worse. Ciano, nonetheless, should be recognized for having opposed with all his might, but too late, the German alliance and the war. Ciano also kept a very detailed and well-written diary, highly appreciated by specialists, but useful reading for anyone interested in the origins of the Second World War. We must ask ourselves, then: Who could have done better, with a similar inheritance and in similar conditions? Only an exceptional personality, and he was not one. He did not lack for good professional qualities: according to the French ambassador in Rome, "The man [was] very different from his reputation, and decidedly better."[48] But the role history reserved for him was beyond his abilities. Galeazzo, having become the unofficial heir apparent to Il Duce, prided himself on his ability to also become his own man and to pursue his own policies. He deluded himself into thinking he could fly with his own wings, until his flight was cut short.

We pick up our story in June 1935, when Malaparte, having learned that Edda and Galeazzo had arrived in Forte dei Marmi and taken lodgings nearby, hurried to them. To underline his condition, he decked himself out in a pair of worn old trousers, with a full beard and bare feet in sandals, and thus attired made his entrance into the Cianos' elegant soirée, proclaiming, "Ladies and gentlemen, here is your convict!" In the general surprise, Edda and Galeazzo burst into laughter and embraced him in front of everyone, after which the new apparel was launched as *the* summer fashion, and the two policemen following the writer were left speechless, not knowing what to do. At least, that's how the legend goes.[49] The seduction operation was unleashed and would not be stopped again.

Malaparte quickly became the idol of a group of revelers flaunting riotous luxury and willfully xenophilic, politically perilous talk. As one observer recalled: "It was the debut of La Capannina and other chic establishments, the height of the carefree 1930s season. My mother found Malaparte extremely unpleasant and a bit of a bore. A good-looking man, of course, but a loudmouth with a little bird's head on an athlete's body. However, all the women went crazy for him."[50] Discredited in the eyes of the common people since before the war, the Ciano "clan" would provoke hatred in the population in the years to come, even beyond their genuine faults. Galeazzo and Edda were consumed by something just as powerful as passion and ambition: snobbery. The former to make people forget his insecurities and a recent and excessively flaunted title, which elicited jokes from the loafers sitting at his table. The latter because, after a childhood of hardships and humiliation, she had not managed to free herself, as her father had done, with a political triumph: "I had always regretted not being a man," she confided at the end of her life.[51] Furthermore, both knew that everything life had given them—and it would give still more, before taking it all back—they owed not to themselves, but to the surnames they bore.

Connected to snobbery was sexual abandon, a sign of distinction in their milieu. In a bigoted and conformist country, where neither the royal family nor the Mussolinis deviated publicly from the established morality, Edda paraded around in a beret straight out of the early film noir *Port of Shadows*, while dancing, smoking, or drinking, at times in shady establishments. It was said she sunbathed nude together with her friends and wagered large sums of money on poker and chemin de fer. Galeazzo did not drink or smoke or gamble. To sunbathing he preferred steam baths, to lose extra pounds.

A handsome but physically lazy young man, he had trouble following the regime's precepts of athleticism, and his shrill voice truly had nothing heroic about it. Both carried on multiple love affairs in a very open *ménage*, even if the rumors about orgies and drugs were untrue. In any event, it was often the police behind such rumors: Fascism was partial to low blows and relied on the underworld. Even Hitler exploited the Latin weakness, attaching to Galeazzo's ample flanks the ravishing Swedish wife of a diplomat of the Reich. But sometimes the Latin weakness prevails over the Teutonic sense of duty. The SS attempted the same operation when Ciano was imprisoned in Verona, in late 1943, pending his trial and execution. They introduced into his cell a fake nurse and real spy, to find out where he had hidden his diary manuscript. But the woman fell in love with him and sought in vain to organize his escape, along with Edda and the marquess Emilio Pucci (later a well-known fashion designer).

Edda attracted men in order to dominate and suffocate them, as her father dominated and would soon suffocate the nation. Galeazzo, less confident and more vain, loved to please, to court and be courted, to talk about and to women, and not only to make love to them. He would rock on his flat feet and puff up his chest, imitating the chief, every time a beauty turned up at the Acquasanta Golf Club, on the outskirts of Rome, which had become something of a branch office of Palazzo Chigi.[52] "It was his downfall," recounted to me one of his former colleagues, who had served in his cabinet. "When he left the office, where he acted like a diligent official, he became a kid again, and all his seriousness disappeared. Regrettably it was there, and in that state of mind, that he hatched his schemes, out loud, under the eyes and ears of the police."

Edda, always happy to display her sarcastic sense of humor, was not impressed by Malaparte's stories: "His conversation charmed the forty-and-up crowd. Curzio was a tireless talker. His favorite topic was prison... He loved to dwell on the sexual obsession that tormented the inmates. 'When the guard slips the key into the lock of the cell door,' he would declaim, 'then does the white and pink specter of the female present itself to the mind of the poor prisoner.'"[53] On the other hand, Galeazzo had always admired Malaparte; the latter represented everything he had tried in vain to become: war hero, major writer, and leading figure in the battles of the first postwar period. Now their roles were reversed, and yet Ciano failed to take advantage. He continued to consider Malaparte, despite the *confino* episode, as his generation's model of excellence. In addition, women liked Malaparte, without his having to make an effort, something that impressed him enormously. Galeazzo, who was not mean but could become so if someone competed with him, was toward Malaparte, from beginning to end, as docile as a young girl in her first love. He was drawn like a magnet to strong characters, while submitting to them: his father, his father-in-law, his wife. Malaparte entered rightfully into this category and, like the other three, sought to manipulate Galeazzo to his own ends. The minister's trusted friends tried in vain to warn him, in more or less veiled terms. Such was the case with the critic, theater writer, and preeminent cycling correspondent of his generation, Orio Vergani, and with Giovanni Ansaldo, another excellent writer, a great bourgeois skeptic, erudite and pliable, who became the editor in chief of the Ciano family's newspaper, *Il Telegrafo*.* Ansaldo suspected, probably

---

*Ansaldo was the author of a manual of good behavior, published under the "Malapartian" pseudonym Willy Farnese: *Il vero signore* (Milan: Longanesi, 1955).

with reason, that Malaparte, whom he nicknamed "the little cardinal di Retz,"⁵⁴ aspired to succeed him at the head of the Livornese daily. After the war, Ansaldo described Malaparte in his diary as a "man morally capable of anything," but also "our profession's biggest figure."⁵⁵ He was referring to journalists rather than to writers; Malaparte would have appreciated the compliment only in part.

Undoubtedly, Malaparte had seen the chance, after Farinacci and Balbo, to attach himself to a third regime dignitary, and precisely to the one with, at the time, the least confident personality and the most promising future. He knew how to reassure him, to flatter him, in terms that, after Ciano's unhappy end, he would rapidly forget.* He wrote to Halévy:

> Galeazzo was truly a brother to me, and I owe him all my gratitude. Thanks to him I was freed after only two years [*sic*]. Thanks to him I am regaining lost time, to quickly recover all the positions I had abandoned in the wake of you know what.⁵⁶

He had written in the same terms from Rome on February 10, 1937, to Ansaldo, knowing the latter would run to show the letter to Ciano: "Here is a man I would give my life for. He has been more than a brother to me. I owe him my freedom, my safety, my recovery, my faith in myself and in others."⁵⁷ Was it all true? There is no doubt "Saint Galeazzo" had intervened in his favor. But it was Il Duce, and he alone, who selected the lesson to inflict on his recalcitrant subject,

---

*Galeazzo, who usually granted favors to "whoever in his life had that nonchalance he had always lacked," was a natural prey for Malaparte, observes Vergani in his book of memories, *Ciano: Una lunga confessione* (Milan: Longanesi, 1970), 114–15.

likewise the august pardon granted him. Malaparte knew this perfectly well. But in displaying his appreciation for the minister, he flattered him, repaying at the same time any gratitude toward the *padre padrone* he had learned to hate. His role at Ciano's side was at least ambiguous. That said, it seems excessive to make Malaparte the Mephistopheles of a man who ran on his own, at a brisk pace, toward his own ruin. And he remained completely outside the decision that would cost Galeazzo his life: the opposition to his father-in-law that, during the Fascist Grand Council session of the night of July 24–25, 1943, precipitated the crisis of the regime. Nor could Malaparte have played the least role in Edda's attempt to save her husband from the mechanism of state interest and to snatch him from the execution that took place one pale dawn in January 1944, at the firing range in Verona's Forte San Procolo. The only real reproach that might be made of him is to have staged—in a remarkable way, from a literary perspective—the fatuousness of Ciano and his world in the chapter "Golf Handicaps" in *Kaputt*, when the latter had just died, having twisted around on the chair to which he was tied, to present his face, rather than his back, to the firing squad. The beautiful gesture may have cost him some additional suffering, because he did not die immediately after the fusillade and required a coup de grâce as he agonized on the ground. It was the best page of his brief life.

Virginia

Let us return to Malaparte's life at Il Forte. He had split up with "Flaminia," after a big farewell scene, on April 4, 1935. Nonetheless, he must have been in an agitated frame of mind, if months later he still complained to Marianne Halévy about having received from his former lover only "a brief letter, which was anyway very cold," in which

> she tells me her behavior is dictated by prudence, by the need to think of the children, etc. Maybe she's right. But couldn't she act differently, speak frankly with me, tell me about her difficulties? Finally, I just sent her a letter in which I asked her to tell me when she plans to come. I hope she replies. I don't even know where she is.... I am ashamed to write you such a stupid letter, but what do you expect? You're the only person in the world I have left, and whom I can trust.[58]

Did he still hope the relationship could be revived? We know from the same letter that the two had spent three days together again in July. But it was no more than a last moment of happiness, because "Flaminia" sent two letters, one after the other, to Marianne Halévy, become the confidante of both of them, to pray that "Malaparte can get back to work in Il Forte, now deserted."[59] It is the language of a woman who has made up her mind, whatever her feelings might be deep down, and who has no intention of retracing her steps.

Malaparte did get back to work, but mostly he prepared himself for new encounters. In Forte dei Marmi he had just seen, or seen again, the princess Jane di San Faustino and her daughter, Virginia Bourbon del Monte, still officially in mourning for the death of her husband, Edoardo Agnelli, a few months earlier. The Bourbon del Montes were an old and once quite powerful family from central Italy, descended from Ariberto, marquess of Tuscany and imperial vicar of Charlemagne, whose lands originally extended over all the upper Tiber Valley and over Etruscan country, to a part of Umbria and Le Marche. In the course of centuries, the family divided into several independent branches, including the Bourbon di Sorbellos, lords of Perugia, and the Bourbon di Pesaros, from which issued in the sixteenth century the great mathematician Guidobaldo (1545–1607) and the cardinal Francesco Maria (1549–1627), protector of Caravaggio.[60] The Ancona branch, the Bourbon del Monte di Santa Marias, less prosperous, had been elevated by Pius IX to the de facto honorific title, in the waning days of the popes' temporal power, of princes of San Faustino for the firstborn male, born from the wedding of the marquess Pietro with a princess of the age-old Roman Massimo dynasty.* In 1919, Giovanni Agnelli, already extremely rich but not yet accepted by all the Savoy and Piedmontese aristocracy, had married his only male son, Edoardo, to Virginia Bourbon del Monte, daughter to Carlo, third prince of San Faustino. It was the great society event of the age, putting an end to the reserve imposed by four years of war.

Virginia was twenty years old at the time, a year younger than Malaparte. Slender, unpredictable, nervous, more elegant than beautiful but with a great physical presence, she had the same tenacious character as her mother, Jane Campbell, an heiress from New Jersey, who, when she was young, would go play the piano or saxophone,

---

*How old? When Napoleon asked Prince Massimo if he really descended from the Roman general Quintus Fabius Maximus, the (alleged) victor over Hannibal, the prince replied: "Majesty, I do not know. It is a story that has circulated in my family for two thousand years." The Massimos played no small diplomatic role in the definitive reconciliation between the Piedmontese "invaders" and the Roman "black" aristocracy, when, in 1935 (after the Concordat, then), a niece of the king, the princess Maria Adelaide di Savoia Genova, married Prince Leone Massimo.

often dressed as a man, in bars in Harlem. Jane was part of a large group of New World heiresses who had around 1890 stormed Rome, London, and Paris in pursuit of titles and dwellings of crumbling splendor to restore, with the same energy their fathers had displayed when they conquered the West and slaughtered the "redskins." Firmly established in Palazzo Barberini, Jane dominated society life in the capital for thirty years, frittering away her entire fortune in the process. Shortly before her death, in 1938, she paid to publish her recollections, in which all of high society of the period appears, including many young actors passing through.* Gary Cooper took a dip in the fountains of the capital, some twenty years before Anita Ekberg, for the admiration of ladies such as the duchess Dorothy Dentice di Frasso, a great friend of Jane.[61] As for Virginia, whom the gossips of respectable Turin had nicknamed "Messalina," she was already ascribed a list of lovers as long as the telephone book (albeit of the period), in which figured not only the aristocracies of blood and of wealth, but also more eccentric choices, according to the avid notes of "Duilio," alias "Baron A. D.," the OVRA agent who would become the main investigator following the secret couple Malaparte-Virginia.[62] Let us not ascribe to such speculations more plausibility than they deserve: sex and drugs were already part of

---

*For better acquaintance with this subject, readers can consult the rather more solid memoirs in two volumes of Giorgio Nelson Page, *L'americano di Roma* and *Il nuovo americano di Roma* (Milan: Longanesi, 1947 and 1949). A nephew of an American ambassador and a close friend of Ciano, the author was one of the major promoters of Fascist propaganda toward the Anglo-Saxon world in the 1930s. After the war, he continued as a frequent contributor of columns in the right-wing press. A colorful personality and inveterate gambler, he wrote many other well-packaged mass-market books, including a novelized life of Gershwin.

the tool kit of the informer who wanted to make his fortune. Virginia had a brother, Ranieri, who was, the story goes, denied a position at FIAT by the senator Agnelli, murmuring in dialect, "If you're a prince, be a prince!" Ranieri married the American surrealist Katherine (Kay) Sage, who later took as her second husband the painter Yves Tanguy, with whom she formed a long and productive artistic union.

Edoardo had died on July 14, 1935, without being able to give the measure of his talent as a captain of industry, during a forced landing of the seaplane piloted by Arturo Ferrarin, one of the pillars of Italian aviation. An investigation was opened to find out if the two had taken off still tipsy, after a night of carousing, but it was quickly dropped for fear of a scandal. The senator had permitted his son, up to that point, only to obey. But in June 1931, Edoardo had gone rogue, narrowly avoiding disaster in a shady stock market deal. Contrary to the commonplace of a Fascism at the service of capital, Il Duce did not hesitate to punish, when necessary, the big shots of industry or finance; the erstwhile socialist even derived a certain pleasure from it. This was the case, for example, with another leading Turinese businessman, Riccardo Gualino, a great pioneer and patron in the fields of cinema, modern art, and design (not to mention a patron of Gobetti), who was sent into *confino* in no time, with most of his properties and assets confiscated.* Unlike the senator, who remained an ex–cavalry officer through and through, whose life was

---

*And the *confino* of the already fifty-two-year-old industrialist and true patriot lasted two years, in more severe conditions than Malaparte's. See his sober account, *Solitudine: L'esperienza del confino durante il regime fascista* (1945; Venice: Marsilio, 1997). After the war he built another financial empire, leaving at his death, in 1964, part of his immense collection to the Palazzo Reale of Turin.

shaped by an iron discipline at every moment, Edoardo, the spoiled heir, was a typical product of the Roaring Twenties. He loved women, cards, and golf, and greatly preferred his Roman bachelor pad, palaces, and hunting trips across Europe to the ordered life of a privileged employee in the austere Piedmontese capital. Everyone acknowledged his considerable charm, which would be passed on to his son Gianni. After a brazen, carefree youth straight out of Fitzgerald, he had brought into the world with Virginia seven children in fifteen years, which was respectable even by the standards of the time and of Fascist demographic policy. The last, Umberto, was only months old at his death. Later, and for a long time in polite society, it was murmured that Gianni hardly resembled his father, while resembling Malaparte a good deal—it was no doubt slander.[63] In his time at *La Stampa*, Malaparte had had numerous occasions to meet the FIAT heir, and later he would boast of having helped him enter the National Council of Corporations, where being known as "daddy's boy" did not make him particularly popular. This claim, too, appears to be unfounded. It is true that Edoardo had not taken part in the Fascist battles of the first postwar period and had enlisted late in the PNF, on January 1, 1926, reflecting in this his father's own lack of political zeal. But at the time of his death he had accumulated a wide range of roles, like that of vice president of the Fascist National Federation of Mechanical and Metallurgy Industries and Turin city councilman, which necessarily made him a regime notable.[64]

A relationship between Malaparte and Virginia would have been very unlikely to begin while Edoardo was still alive, on account above all of the presence of "Flaminia," who, while respecting her lover's freedom, would never have accepted a rival in the same social circles. "Flaminia" declared as much to Malaparte's first biographer, and the determination of such a woman cannot be doubted;[65] particularly as, notwithstanding the discretion of that very closed world, the result would have been a scandal with unpleasant consequences for everyone. Perhaps there was already a flirtation between the two, but unlikely anything more. There is no known trace, anyway, of an intervention by Virginia in favor of the writer, much less her presence on Lipari, contrary to what happened with "Flaminia." Certainly, the haste with which Agnelli wanted to rid himself of his newspaper's editor in chief in early 1931, and the fact that Malaparte was invited by Fascist authorities to leave Turin immediately, raise a few doubts. What did the senator really go complain about to Mussolini? And why did Agnelli demonstrate such generosity to him, providing he disappeared? In the more or less informed circles of the press, a foregone conclusion was drawn, which the vox populi has passed down to the present day.[66] But this is not certain and not even probable; none of the alleged evidence entirely convinces. In the first place, Malaparte was removed from Turin at the behest not only of Agnelli but also of his successor at *La Stampa*, Turati, who did not want this troublesome neighbor. As we have also seen, the settlement received was higher than average, but not exorbitant. All things considered, whether the relationship started before or, more likely, after Edoardo's death matters little. The fact is the senator did not have the least intention of taking such a character into his house, already having to reckon with a rebellious daughter-in-law and to prepare a barely adolescent heir to succeed him. Who could blame him?

Concerning the circumstances of the first encounter, I was able to gather the precious testimony of one of the Agnelli children, Maria Sole, then aged eleven:

It was the summer of 1936. My grandmother, Princess Jane, spotted him one day on the sea promenade of Forte dei Marmi and asked him to approach. She knew who he was, naturally. Everyone was talking about him.... He would spend a lot of time with us. My father had died just a year earlier, and we were still in shock. My mother, who had a very tender and generous nature, could never get along without us, especially in those circumstances. She was too vulnerable.... He would tell us the most amazing stories and take us on long bicycle rides to eat bread and salami in some remote coastal village. It was all very innocent, but for us, given the very rigid education we had received and our ordered life in Turin society, it was an extraordinary novelty.... And then he was an intellectual, something new and exciting—she hadn't come across many.... [My brother Gianni] criticized his affected manner, and Malaparte did shave his chest and arms, which made us laugh. It's also possible Gianni was a bit jealous of our mother. But the determining factor is that, with papa's death, he became the heir. He couldn't go against the senator's wishes.[67]

The old industrialist's hostility was reignited when Virginia began to spend time with the writer, under the obliging gaze of Edda and Galeazzo. Malaparte courted her with consummate professionalism, narrated the agent "Duilio" (who did not conceal a certain worldly admiration), flitting about in a circle of titled beauties, ignoring Virginia, until she fell, lovestruck, at his feet. "T. R. d. M. was in love with her as well. He and Curzio met at Forte dei Marmi, talked about a rivalry and a desperate love. T. made a perfect leap from the Cinquale bridge, which at that point, however, has only half a meter of water."[68] The Cianos had long-standing ties to the Agnellis: right after the war, the senator had offered Costanzo the top job at a navigation company in Genoa, and the admiral had entered the reserves in order to accept the lucrative appointment. Galeazzo had hesitated in the beginning between diplomacy and a well-remunerated position in the FIAT empire. As for Edda, she had a weakness for salacious situations; eccentric characters like Virginia attracted her, being one herself. But it is significant that the names of Il Duce's daughter and son-in-law, too powerful, never appear in the numerous police reports about the affair.

It was the meeting of two unfettered natures, and in it Malaparte saw a new triumph over the misfortune that very nearly did him in. The relationship took shape toward the end of 1935. The police were lying in wait. An informer related how the two lovers stood out for their anti-Fascist alcohol consumption in restaurants, where they refused to drink locally produced cognac and instead ordered the best French brand, amid the regime's campaign against the "unfair sanctions" imposed by the League of Nations.[69] And the money fed the gossip: How did Malaparte, just returned from *confino*, manage to find three hundred thousand lire, the price of Villa Hildebrand? It had been four years since he received the severance from *La Stampa*—maybe Virginia had something to do with it? We are well informed of the couple's increasingly less clandestine movements, thanks to the tailing that the head of FIAT's Rome office, Benedetto Perotti, asked the chief of police to ensure regarding the "well-known lady."[70] Behind this intervention was the senator's right hand, Vittorio Valletta, a small, terse, dictatorial man, who never spoke more than three words in a row in his life, one of the three invariably being "No!"—as union officials of the time, who both hated and admired him, knew all too well. Valletta would lead FIAT with an iron fist until 1966; when he judged the time had come to pass the reins to

Gianni Agnelli, he disappeared behind the wheel of a Cinquecento and no one ever saw him again.* It was Valletta, Malaparte confided, who offered him a blank check, which he haughtily refused, to "leave Virginia in peace." Through the well-informed and competent chief of police Bocchini, Il Duce received daily updates; and perhaps he began to regret pulling him out of *confino* ...

By now Malaparte was as free as the wind, and from Il Forte he went down more and more often to Rome, to lodge at the Hotel de Russie, one of his favorite places. Virginia often took a room there as well, and at least once surprised him with another woman; a dreadful scene followed, to the joy of the informers. The agent "1890," who took the place of "Duilio" in the capital, specifies that Malaparte declared, for anyone there to listen, that he enjoyed the complete trust of Il Duce. He did not hide his projects at table, in the restaurants he began to patronize, between Via Margutta and the Quirinal Gardens. His fellow diners were scandalized by such swagger: "Malaparte is going around claiming that, as soon as he is married, he'll see to it that he becomes the boss of FIAT and takes over *La Stampa* again."[71] If this had really been his goal, an entirely different set of measures would have been called for; a true adven-

---

*Here is an anecdote that would not have displeased Malaparte. Valletta conducted his last great negotiation with the Soviet Union, in 1965–66 (today we know that before doing so he had sought and obtained a green light from the US State Department), to mass-produce FIAT-derived Zhiguli automobiles in the city of Tolyatti (formerly Stavropol, renamed after Palmiro Togliatti). His attitude, always rigid, punctuated by his famous "No!" impressed his Soviet counterparts. One of them, then a gifted young diplomat, whom I met many years later, told me that at the final banquet, after the signing of the painstakingly achieved agreement, he dared to ask a finally radiant Valletta: "Sir, you are a capitalist, and I am a Communist. What is the one value we can share in life?" The old man took him by the elbow and answered: "Why, love, naturally!"

turer would have behaved with the proper caution and greater guile. But Malaparte was like that: he would declare something, and it quickly became true, like the little sailing ship of his childhood. The *other* reality, that of common mortals, held little interest for him, and that only occasionally.

Was he really blinded by love? Good question, which only he could have answered, and maybe not even he. Virginia was hotheaded to the point of incandescence: incapable of calculation, she would expose herself beyond all common sense. If she loved to give of herself, he administered his own person meticulously, avariciously. It was, in any case, his only relationship, except the one with Roberta Masier ten years earlier, that according to him should have resulted in marriage. He confessed to his friend Borelli that "Virginia is a woman of class and I am very fond of her," an expression of affection, but not exactly the height of passion.[72] He called her "Scianflitua."* She, more direct, sent her "Boz" an explicit "I adore you," which, lacking originality, needs no comment.[73] Their complete correspondence has never been found, even as more or less authentic fragments of it surface from time to time.[74] But is it legitimate to presume that it contains grand revelations? Biancamaria Fabbri said their letters demonstrated "infinite love and tenderness."[75] As for the rest? Malaparte, unlike D'Annunzio, was not suited to epistolary romances, of which he quickly tired. Virginia's triumphal ignorance would not have inspired him to make literary or political observations similar to these we find generally in his letters, including those to Jane di

---

*The nickname appears in a short story, "La passeggiata" (The walk), which opens the first edition of *Fughe in prigione* (1936) and describes the transparently autobiographical protagonist's arrest and transfer to Lipari. But the woman who appears at his side here is his mother.

San Faustino, who prided herself on frequenting the Muses. Virginia's princess mother had from the beginning assumed the role of confidante and protector of the secret couple, while diplomatically maintaining contact with the senator: "Deep down Jane is with them and plays two parts in the comedy," according to an informer.[76] We might wonder if, after having favored the relationship, she was not also the one to convince Virginia that things had gone too far.

By this point the passion, or whatever we want to call it, had erupted into the light of day, to the extent that Borelli wrote to him that he had "heard on your account fantastic, exhilarating, and delightful rumors of a romance."[77] Malaparte was also, in a completely new role for him, intent on winning over Virginia's children, whom he had met at Il Forte during the summer of 1936. He concentrated his attention on Gianni, the heir, and the elder sister, Suni (Susanna), "to the point where some ladies wondered if the writer had not by chance become the governess of the Agnelli household," the agent "Duilio" remarked sarcastically. In reality, he knew perfectly well that to strengthen his relationship with a shaken and vulnerable mother, he needed to go through her children. Suni was immediately attracted by this strange character, with whom she remained in contact even after the relationship with her mother ended.* Gianni was more reserved. According to his son-in-law, the writer Alain Elkann:

> He did not talk willingly about Malaparte, but I think he considered him a rather superficial, sly, effeminate character. And yet, when all is said and done, they had certain kinds of duplicity in common,

---

*Forty years later, Susanna Agnelli would describe the period in a memoir, *We Always Wore Sailor Suits* (New York: Viking Press, 1975).

like amusing themselves by offering radically different judgments of the same person, depending on their interlocutor. But I think it was his dynastic loyalty toward his grandfather that weighed in his approach to the whole issue. From the moment his grandfather made a decision in the interest of the family, he would conform at any cost, despite the deep connection he had with his mother.[78]

But initially the children, who adored their mother, seeing her happy, seemed more or less content. The serene family atmosphere allowed the couple to go live under the same roof, and Malaparte boasted to his friends about "our house," the Bosco Parrasio on the Janiculum Hill, a monument of historical and artistic interest, which in 1724 the king of Portugal had given to the Accademia degli Arcadi. The stately villa was rented after Virginia decided to leave the Agnelli residence, on the archaeological walk. It was at this point that the relationship became official. It was at this point, too, as at so many other times in his life, that Malaparte's temperament, exhibitionism, and ostentation betrayed him: enough to make one believe, a psychoanalyst would say, that he did not, deep down, want for things to go as he announced. Because, so close to his goal, he racked up blunders with a rashness unimaginable in a real dowry hunter, leaving his friends, acquaintances, and police informers dumbfounded. But the Malaparte who acted in this whole affair was still the one we know: too eager and unpredictable to be calculating through and through. It was his barefaced, quixotic challenge to the most powerful industrialist in Italy, who had already had the gall to turn him out once before, similar to his challenges to Mussolini, at the time of *Don Camaleo*, or more recently to Balbo. And Don Quixote would lose his Dulcinea.

The wedding was set for October 10, 1936, in Pisa Cathedral, shortly after the minimum period of a year established by law for widowed women who intended to remarry. So claimed, at least, Malaparte, who also said he was ready to convert to Catholicism for the occasion. Was it the truth, or the latest figment of his imagination? The wedding banns have not been found, and Maria Sole Agnelli told me that she, and more than likely the other children too, knew nothing about it.[79] What we do know is that on October 9, 1936, the Ministry of the Interior inquired of Florence's police chief "whether the well-known Suckert Curzio Malaparte was Christian, or Jewish."[80] The date seems to exclude the possibility that the wedding was set for the next day, since the civil and religious announcements should have been published at least fifteen days before the wedding. In any case, the union posed a sufficiently concrete risk to provoke the senator to counterattack, and the project went up in smoke. Malaparte wrote to Borelli:

> I was to be married last Saturday, everything was ready, the announcements sent out, etc., when suddenly the family council gets together, a quarrel breaks out between the senator and Virginia's mother and brother, and so we had to postpone the wedding. But to when? A month? Two months? Poor Virginia, I feel so sorry for her.[81]

So it may have been, but meanwhile, he fumed with rage. The senator not only wanted to force Virginia to give up her inheritance; he also, as Malaparte described to Borelli, demanded to fully exert guardianship rights over her seven children: "Virginia has granted the senator (in complete agreement with me) the guardianship of the children and agreed that they be raised in Turin. But he insists she can only see them twice a month." It was a draconian condition, which no mother could accept lightly, especially when one of the children, her favorite, was ill.[82]

Furthermore, there was no agreement on the financial arrangements, and the legal battle flared. Malaparte went all in and sent the Court of Appeal of Turin a copy of a savage twenty-four-page missive to the senator, in which he asserted his good faith and integrity, affirming in particular to have "met" Virginia only after Edoardo's death. He added a vicious detail, claiming that his exit from *La Stampa* was the result of his refusal to fire some staff members disliked by the ownership: "In my conscience as a Fascist, I was repulsed by the idea of firing five Fascist staffers on the spot, merely because you and your entourage of anti-Fascists wanted it that way." And he concluded: "You are an anachronism in Mussolini's Italy. For many years you could act like the 'master of the ironworks,' but only because the political climate in Italy at the time allowed you to." This attempt to get the senator in trouble with the regime would backfire.[83]

On December 18, the chairman of the Juvenile Court of Turin awarded guardianship of the children to their grandfather, on the grounds that Virginia, "shortly after the death of her husband, entered into a relationship that continues to this day, whose effects can only be gravely detrimental to the children's welfare in material, moral, and educational terms."[84] No adultery, then, but it was still a scorching defeat. Malaparte, however, quickly recovered from this setback. The wedding was postponed for around three years, "with great hopes that at such time the senator will have returned to his Creator," the agent "1890" wrote, with a touch of humor. A few days later he explained that the wedding is, however, the idée fixe of Curzio Malaparte, who hopes by this act to become one of the senator's heirs, to the point that he has convinced the widow to bring a suit against the senator to have all the senator's possessions, and especially the ownership of FIAT, declared the common assets of the senator and the children.[85]

This preposterous plan did not have the least chance of success, as Malaparte would come to realize at his expense. The senator rejoiced, without losing his renowned sangfroid. As a man practiced in studying the reactions of adversaries, he had calculated that three years might be long at his age, but even longer for a woman of inconstant moods like Virginia. He had also foreseen that Malaparte would disappear along with his matrimonial prospects. Who would win the next contest?

Agnelli turned again to Il Duce, become a kind of consultant for high society's relationship issues, and the matter assumed a grotesque aspect. Here was Mussolini, who had previously demanded matrimony for Malaparte, now mobilized to prevent his wedding. The dictator, a man of the people who privately disdained and detested the rich, felt a certain sympathy for that cursed Tuscan challenging the biggest industrialist in the country. He had just granted him a contribution of ten thousand lire that may as well have been an early wedding gift.[86] But what was to be privileged above all was the national interest, and FIAT overtook everything else. In the end, a stratagem was found, involving Malaparte's expulsion from the Fascist Party at the time of his arrest, three years earlier. Of course, it was not essential to be a party member in order to marry an heiress, but the expulsion was a serious administrative measure. It implied a disrepute incompatible with a union that would closely concern a strategic good like the Turin factory, principal supplier to the Ministry of War. Fair enough, Malaparte may have thought: Paris is worth a mass. He needed to overcome the obstacle and rejoin the ranks. Ciano had already intervened on his behalf, but now it was up to the interested party to go all out: "I believe the time has come to officially request and obtain it [the card]. But I want to decide with you what steps I should take, whatever steps seem best to you," he wrote to Borelli.[87] Here he was claiming, then, that the sanction of *confino*, imposed on him "as a disciplinary measure" and *not* for anti-Fascism, in no way adversely affected his integrity as a militant—a version he would forget in 1943, and flip after 1944. Not content, he acted like a melodramatic hero and applied to go as a volunteer to East Africa, in Ethiopia, expecting to be rejected because of the well-known issues with his lungs. The subterfuge did not displease Il Duce, who ordered his minister Dino Alfieri to write to the party's vice secretary, Adelchi Serena, that with "Malaparte having applied to go to East Africa as a volunteer, then not having left for reasons of health, it is appropriate to kindly consider his request to be readmitted to the party."[88] In his turn, Malaparte declared to an emissary of Agnelli, a lawyer by the name of Marghieri, who was unlikely to be moved by such an announcement, that he "would go get himself killed in Spain as an infantry officer."[89]

These good intentions had no follow-through, and the romantic relationship continued on the sly, after a public demonstration of reconciliation between the senator and his daughter-in-law, in the course of a grand reception in Turin. Malaparte left Bosco Parrasio for lodgings nearby, on the ground floor of 5 Via di Villa Pepoli, a private street in the heart of the Aventine Hill, surrounded by gardens and convents. But the two lovers persisted in seeing each other regularly. According to police reports, Virginia "was taken by such a strong passion that no one could keep her from her Malaparte,"⁹⁰ who in turn exhorted her to stand firm with her father-in-law, "whom he here characterized as an odious old man and with other vulgar Tuscan phrases."⁹¹

Mussolini resorted then to another bit of Romagnese cunning, recalling his approach in the Balbo affair. Malaparte had served his sentence, true; but since he was expelled from the party for having slandered Balbo, it fell to the latter to intervene to lift the veto. There was no reason to expect that the marshal was disposed to do so. But was he really ever asked?* Doubts remain, because at the time, Achille Starace, secretary of the PNF, had already decided against it, despite the assurances given to Virginia. Malaparte, following the advice of Borelli, had thrown himself at the feet of Starace.⁹² But in vain: behind Starace was not Balbo, but the all-powerful Duce. The comedy had gone on long enough. The relationship ended between the summer and autumn of 1937, a bit less than two years after its start in Forte dei Marmi. The children would be reunited with their mother, after an intervention by Edda with Il Duce,† and family harmony would seem to have been restored. On April 12, 1938, an anonymous report informed that Virginia had met the marquess F. S. of Genoa, and that this time "the senator

---

*Paolo Balbo does not remember his mother, the marshal's confidante in everything, ever mentioning it, in speaking about the affair.

†Testimony to the author by Edda's niece, Countess Anna Teodorani Fabbri. Virginia would never forget this gesture: in 1946 she sent a million lire to Edda upon the latter's return, destitute, from (anti-Fascist) *confino* on Lipari. Fifty years later, Susanna Agnelli, then minister of foreign affairs, would attend, in a private capacity, the funeral of Edda Ciano Mussolini.

would agree to the marriage."⁹³ But the matter would end there. It would subsequently be the turn of a mysterious English gentleman, a character of equal interest to the police: Could he be an agent of His Britannic Majesty? Malaparte, meanwhile, distanced himself for real. Out of spite, or for the sake of the quip, he would later declare that "the only women worth marrying are very poor women,"⁹⁴ words ill concealing his rancor at losing the match. But the alliance of two *padri padroni*, of such caliber—Il Duce and the senator—was too much even for him. As Maria Sole Agnelli concludes: "Mama may have still seen him for a bit, but we children, never again. She would never have been able to give us up."⁹⁵

The war separated the two lovers for good. In the *Giornale segreto*, only one entry mentions her, and indirectly. Febo had just died on Capri. Malaparte, in Finland, was grief-stricken, seeing over and over, night and day, "the long, pale woman's face" of his dog, which provokes another association:

> And what has always grieved me about Virginia was her incomprehension of animals, her estrangement from animals; she doesn't even know how to pet them or respond to their affection. And she is not even "abstracted," but "distracted." Her femininity is not abstracted but distracted.⁹⁶

And what do we know about what she was thinking? In the absence of rediscovered correspondence, what remains are more or less genuine anecdotes, like the following, from Giovanni Ansaldo. One day in 1942, at the Acquasanta Golf Club, friends of Ciano passed around a photo of Malaparte emerging from a Finnish sauna. The prince Raimondo Lanza, having spotted Virginia seated at another table, decided maliciously to go show it to her. She took the photo with indifference, looked at it "for an appropriate amount of time, neither too long nor too short," and gave it back to him, commenting, "He's aged as well."[97] In this oft-reproduced image, Malaparte hides the essential from the camera behind a birch branch. He honestly looks great, not aged at all, and you can understand how, as a good narcissist, he was happy to have the photo circulated. For that matter, there exists another shot, in the same series, in which Malaparte shifts the branch and appears in all his manly splendor.[98] This version of the anecdote differs slightly from what has come down to us from another witness, and which seems more in line with her character: Virginia brushed the photo with her fingertips, without dignifying it with the least comment.* Nor would she have the time to grow old. After attempting to mediate between the Germans, the Resistance, and the Holy See to avoid the destruction of occupied Rome, she died in a car accident while returning to Forte dei Marmi, on November 21, 1945. It was said she was heading to a last meeting with the writer, maybe even to discuss new marriage plans.[99] No evidence has appeared to support this claim, based probably on "confidences" from the interested party and on the "dedication to a dead woman" of the French edition of *Woman Like Me*, in 1947.[100]

The end of Senator Agnelli was scarcely less dramatic. While he succeeded, with the assistance of Valletta, in saving most of the FIAT plants during the Republic of Salò, avoiding their transfer to Germany, after the war he was accused of collaboration with the Fascist regime, and his companies and assets were temporarily confiscated. He died

---

*As Mario Pansa, chief of protocol for the foreign ministry and a well-known dandy of the period, related it to a colleague, who related it to me in turn.

a sick and broken man at seventy-nine, in December 1945, soon after his acquittal. In the last weeks of his life, he instructed his driver to take him to the main factory's front gate, where he muttered: "I have done all this, and now I am not even allowed to go inside."[101]

The hatred Malaparte would later display toward Il Duce was certainly stoked by his defeat in this venture, all the more so because two or three years later, the inverse occurred. At the heart of the story was Luigi Barzini Jr., a brilliant journalist who also belonged to Ciano's circle, son of Luigi Barzini Sr., who, with the prince Scipione Borghese, had won the inaugural Peking-to-Paris road race, in 1907. Barzini Jr. fell in love with a young Milanese widow named Giannalisa Feltrinelli. Her husband, Carlo, had dominated an imperial and financial empire comparable to the Agnellis', when Il Duce, who found him politically suspect, had him convicted of illegal capital exports, resulting in his death from a heart attack, if not from suicide. But this time Mussolini, feeling responsible for the fate of Giannalisa, agreed to her marriage. Barzini Jr. thus found himself performing the duties of a stepfather and educator of another rebellious adolescent, with whom his relationship was very tense from the off. His name was Giangiacomo Feltrinelli, and he was destined to become one of the most important publishers of the postwar era, before sinking into the mad season of terrorism that was the Years of Lead.[102]

Excellent Prospects

Malaparte was not a man to waste time on broken dreams or love affairs gone wrong. And after the long break imposed by his legal setbacks, he was eager to return to work. In March 1936 he was readmitted to the order of journalists, a practically indispensable condition for once again seeing his own name in print. He burned with the desire to go abroad again, but where? Diplomatic relations with France and England had deteriorated; it would also have been impossible to return to the Soviet Union. On the other hand, there were wars in abundance. He would have liked to accompany, on behalf of the *Corriere della Sera*, the Italian troops who were "pacifying" Ethiopia after the conquest; or else to follow the "volunteers"—roughly eighty thousand men, more than the Francoist troops at the beginning of the conflict—whom Mussolini had sent to fight in Spain. Excellent occasions to prove himself with his pen and to rid himself of the political veto still hanging over him. The plan was cunning, but premature: if he could now sign articles with his own name, it was still too early for a full exoneration, which would have turned a political *confinato*, expelled from the party, into a major official envoy to the battlefronts. Besides, everywhere you looked, writers and journalists were striving to prove their zeal and get ahead, singing the military achievements of the new Italy. Borelli, overwhelmed by the important personal referrals piling up on his desk, could not promise him much. The *Corriere* had recruited a class of excellent correspondents including Guido Piovene, Dino Buzzati, Luigi Barzini Jr., and Virgilio Lilli. *La Stampa* remained out of reach, despite Malaparte's good relationship with Signoretti. As for Ciano, he was too attached to his protégé Ansaldo to make room for Malaparte at *Il Telegrafo*. It was necessary to wait, then, while trying to occupy himself in the best possible way.

And so another idea came to him. If he still had such difficulty being accepted, why not strike out on his own? In the absence of a newspaper, he thought of a magazine in the style of *"900"*, but "very Italian," as required now by the regime's anticosmopolitan campaign.

He was excited by the idea of becoming both editor in chief and publisher again. With time, he was less and less able to tolerate depending on others or submitting to cuts and revisions that even a friend like Borelli had to ask for at times. But how to obtain the necessary authorizations, and where to find the funds? Here his relationship with Ciano again proved indispensable. Malaparte had a very precise idea of what he wanted to create: sumptuous, large-format (25 by 35 centimeters) issues devoted to art and literature, on glossy paper, illustrated with "at least 250" [sic] photographs, drawings, engravings, reproductions of paintings, and so on, organized thematically, so that each issue constituted a monograph, which would allow him also to discuss politics by way of world events. The title? Seeing as how the magazine would offer a whole range of perspectives on contemporary life, it could only be *Prospettive*.

A preliminary remark is due, however politically incorrect it might appear at first glance. Italian culture in the 1930s, even without the contribution of intellectuals gone into exile, was bountiful in every field, and often of high quality, despite the dictatorship. It is a reality that has begun to be confronted abroad, especially in the United States and Germany, maybe more than in Italy. What sense would it make, for example, to talk about cinematic neorealism, if it had not been preceded by the interwar realism of Blasetti, Camerini, and Genina? Painting in these years offered up Sironi, Casorati, Scipione, Balla, de Pisis, Rosai, and Campigli, not to mention the major creative phase of the brothers De Chirico and Savinio. Rationalist architecture, industrial and furniture design, fashion, everything that has somewhat improperly been called Italian "style," was established then, with Piacentini, Brasini, Terragni, Libera, Nervi, and Gio Ponti. In music, Nono, Maderna, and Berio would not be conceivable if Malipiero and Casella, Petrassi and Dallapiccola had not preceded them. In literature, the best-known names are Ungaretti, Montale, and, of course, Moravia. But what about Bontempelli, Bacchelli, Alvaro, Comisso, Cardarelli, Palazzeschi, Papini, or Trilussa? And where were formed the likes of Buzzati, Landolfi, Vittorini, Brancati, Delfini, Piovene, Bilenchi, Bassani, Pavese, or Tobino, if not in that environment? Only when we finally emerge from this *damnatio memoriae* will we return to a more objective vision of this period. And a complete set of the issues of *Prospettive* will be an invaluable tool to help us do so.

Let us now pass to the matter of financing: a legitimate, but thorny, question that has often helped obscure the project's cultural significance. Where did the funds for Malaparte come from? From the Ministry of Popular Culture, which Italians disdainfully called "MinCulPop"? From the Ministry of Foreign Affairs? Did he obtain a particularly favorable loan, never completely repaid, from the order of journalists? The slander that hounded Malaparte until and even after his death—and which he did everything to feed—can for the most part be denied on the basis of documents. A look into MinCulPop's ample dossier on the magazine in the Central Archives of the State shows clearly that *Prospettive* received a monthly payment of five thousand lire in 1937 and of three thousand lire starting from 1938, up until November 1940. After that, despite war restrictions, the contribution returned to five thousand until August 1943, to be definitely suspended after the fall of Mussolini. These deposits—whose receipts were duly signed by Malaparte, or by his efficient editorial assistant, Ms. Pellegrini (no relation to Lino)—were directly authorized by Mussolini. Moreover, Il Duce intervened at least twice—in March and July 1937—to grant a special payment of ten thousand lire. And we will see that money was not all that Malaparte received, then and later, from his cumbersome *padre padrone*.¹⁰³

Can we conclude from this that Malaparte was a war profiteer, a "giant kangaroo," according to the potent term coined by Mussolini in Salò, to indicate the intellectuals abruptly turned anti-Fascist, after having long been paid by the party? The regime could prove extremely generous with public money when it wanted, and it often did. According to one very detailed statistic, established by the US Army's Psychological Warfare Branch after the Americans' arrival in Rome in June 1944, when they had the chance to get their hands on the archives of the Ministry of Popular Culture, concerning the total subsidies granted between 1933 and 1943 to 906 Italian writers, artists, and journalists, Malaparte personally received a total of thirty-five thousand lire over the course of the decade, and was not among those who received regular monthly payments. If the latter point is correct, the sum total seems low, even if, as we have seen, there were not only the payments from MinCulPop but also those derived from other sources, such as Il Duce's personal secretary and the Ministry of Foreign Affairs. We might wonder, then, if this lower indication was not influenced by later dealings between Malaparte and the American intelligence services.¹⁰⁴ The fact remains that Malaparte benefited from Fascism's largesse much less than others heretofore mentioned, such as Sem Benelli (210,500 lire); Ungaretti (144,000); the poet Sibilla Aleramo, former muse of Il Duce (235,000); and even another poet, the "eternally dying" Vincenzo Cardarelli (132,000); or Mussolini's biographer, Yvon de Begnac (124,000). All these cases should be analyzed in detail: if some, like

Ungaretti, had been personal friends of Mussolini since the Great War, and others were simple profiteers, some of the figures on the list received only a few thousand lire and would have gone hungry without those subsidies. It is true that at the same time, the regime would not hesitate to condemn anti-Fascist intellectuals to *confino*, prison, or, again, hunger, preventing them from working.

For the magazines, the American list indicates a total of 256,000 lire for *Prospettive*, which seems right; the sum turns out to be less significant when compared with the subsidies given to modest provincial sheets like *Vedetta Fascista* of Vicenza (946,000 lire) or *Isola* of Sassari (538,000), without mentioning the big national papers. In the same period, and to limit ourselves to France, the regime doled out to an obscure far-right journalist, François Le Grix, roughly two million francs to finance a magazine, *L'ami du peuple*, and turn it into an organ of pro-Italian propaganda, and another 250,000 lire to a small far-right organization, Marcel Bucard's Francist Movement, with the same aim.[105] Here as well, we must not underestimate the importance of the indirect funding that *Prospettive* benefited from, such as the purchase and distribution of a considerable number of copies by diplomatic and consular services. That said, it seems we can now answer the question posed before, that Malaparte was not, strictly speaking, a "giant kangaroo," just as he was neither an agent nor an informer for the regime.

This polemic runs the risk, too, of making us forget the essential: *Prospettive*, despite inevitable ambiguities, represented a window on the world for the young people of Italy, whom the dictatorship had isolated from the great international currents of art and thought. The diversity of topics is reflected in the originality of the monographic format.* Considerable difficulties remained, however, and Malaparte succeeded in publishing only five installments in the first series (1937–38), two of them double issues. It is clear that censors kept a close watch on him, because he certainly did not lack for material. From the first issue, he adapted the well-known Leninist motto, printed in boldface capital letters:

> MUSSOLINI + ELECTRIFICATION = FASCIST REVOLUTION

A clarification followed:

> There are conservative peoples, like the English and the French... stubbornly holding on to outdated formulas and forms of political and social life, and there are peoples like the Italians, the Germans, the Russians, the Americans, undergoing profound political, economic, social, and ethical transformation. Of all the countries in Europe, including Russia, Italy is the one most rapidly and most deeply transforming.[106]

The tone is set. He seems to have returned to the antibourgeois proclamations of *La Conquista dello Stato*, with the homage to the United States of the New Deal and the Soviet Union, the two powers that, as it happens, did not apply the League of Nations sanctions during the Ethiopian crisis. In exchange Malaparte received, he told

---

*The Italian boy (no. 1, July 1937); cinema (no. 2, August 1937); radio (no. 3, September 1937); Il Duce's foreign policy (nos. 4–5, February 1938); the Italians in Spain (nos. 6–7, June 1938).

Borelli, "the chief's encouragement."[107] But his adversaries did not stand down, and the doubts piled up. Malaparte continued to inspire venomous chatter about his vanity and his suspicious enrichment. The magazine was too expensive; after a first moment of curiosity, sales and subscriptions stagnated. Its contents provoked concern as well: some bookstores hesitated to display or sell it, fearing confiscation. Malaparte had to redo his math and reconsider his overconfident resolution to pay contributors more than any other Italian publication. With the material he had left, he still managed to put together three audacious and intelligent issues. He did not give up.

Prospettive swallowed the rest of the compensation from *La Stampa*. In his enthusiasm, he planned to devote issues to the Italian soldier, the Italian landscape, the Italian woman, even—in a last homage to the Counter-Reformation!—to the Italian priest. He discovered, or rediscovered, in himself a genuine passion for being a team leader, an agitator, an organizer, and he believed in the duty of information... in his own way. He loved the editor's life, the meetings that stretched on late into the night, the smoky air of the newsroom, he who should not smoke—and generally pretended to do so—due to the state of his lungs. He loved the sound and the smell of the printing press, the correspondence, and the encouragement and scoldings he gave to his authors, whom he would pester nonstop. He loved to "feel" his audience, to seduce them and irritate them, write headlines as he pleased, choose illustrations and mock them up, provoke arguments, and solicit the public's reaction. *Prospettive* was not *La Stampa*, but it restored all this to him, at the price of inevitable sacrifices and compromises, like the ones Drieu La Rochelle would experience as editor in chief of the *Nouvelle Revue Française*, in occupied Paris, or Aleksandr Tvardovsky, at the head of *Novy Mir*, in the politically thawing Soviet Union of Khrushchev. Malaparte would greatly suffer in the second postwar period from no longer having a vehicle of this sort under his control. When work was over, though, he was still the same: as soon as he slipped on his tailored overcoat from Caraceni, Cucci, or Prandoni—masters of masculine elegance in the period; later he would notice one that was similar but lighter colored, in the photos of Ciano shortly before his execution—and left the office at 41 Largo Sallustiano, he no longer belonged to anyone but himself. On the street, walking his dog, he would fail to recognize a friend, a contributor, a secretary.

After issue 3, publication was suspended. But it was not in his nature to beat a retreat. He turned again to Mussolini, expressed to him for the umpteenth time "his undiminished Fascist devotion," and tried to get a ten-thousand-lire supporter's subscription out of him! Il Duce gave it a pass, but once again did not forget him.[108] Malaparte searched feverishly for a lifeline: wars are fought with the troops available, which at that moment were the "volunteers" in Spain. One of them was a lawyer from Bologna with a name straight out of commedia dell'arte that was nevertheless authentic: Arconovaldo Bonaccorsi became known as "Count Rossi" and, to his admirers, today very rare, "the Lion of San Severa," as well as, to everyone else, "the butcher of the Balearic Islands." From a base on Majorca, his men—the "Dragones de la Muerte"—launched a bloodbath responsible for seven hundred to three thousand deaths, according to various sources, often after unspeakable torture. Unlike the Italian troops, volunteers in name only, these were fanatics recruited from among young delinquents and former squadrists who had *not* "put on some belly." Georges Bernanos gave us an eloquent account of their exploits in one of the best-known books to emerge from the Spanish conflict, *A Diary of My Times*. Ultimately, the Italian military leaders successfully petitioned Mussolini for the recall of Bonaccorsi and the dissolution of the "Dragones." What could have attracted Malaparte to such a figure? We return to his old passion for thuggish types. At this point he had distanced himself from the likes of Tamburini and Dumini, but Bonaccorsi was a close friend, with whom he exchanged emphatic letters, signed "to Bonaccorsi Malaparte from Malaparte Bonaccorsi." He praised his "goodness," "humanity," and "sweetness of soul," and did not forget to ask after his "dear mom," who maybe cooked him a nice bowl of spaghetti alla bolognese to keep him in shape between massacres. The trust between them was such that Bonaccorsi, later transferred to East Africa as consul general of the militia, handed off to Malaparte all the documents related to "the work undertaken in the Balearics," to make sure they reached his residence in Bologna.[109] Their relationship, however, concluded abruptly, from one day to the next, in very Malapartian fashion. Bonaccorsi had in fact become an inconvenient interlocutor, not for his crimes, which he would never answer for, but because he had denounced some corrupt colonial officials.[110]

Self-interest played a role in this unedifying editorial adventure. The Ministry of Foreign Affairs, thanks to Ciano's intervention, had already subsidized a double issue of the magazine entitled "La Sua politica estera" (His foreign policy), a shameless homage to the diplomatic genius of Il Duce, savior of European peace. But for the issue on the war in Spain the figure rose, because the ministry ordered forty thousand copies to distribute free to the soldiers. In return it got an equally shameless glorification of the Italian military contingent, whose contribution did in fact prove indispensable to Franco's triumph. And because Malaparte's taste for striking formulas at times made him lose sight of their meanings, he opened the issue with an editorial brazenly taking up the era's most revolting slogan: "Viva la muerte!"[111] What followed was a very *technical* account by Bonaccorsi of his own exploits. This deplorable and above all stupid text has compounded Malaparte's infamy, almost as much as the Matteotti murder, and it is difficult to find any extenuating circumstances for him.

The biographer, however, must contextualize: Malaparte's pacifist turn would take place only with the Second World War. In that period he still shared with Mussolini the idea that Italians, to exact respect after centuries of foreign domination, had to learn to fight without mercy (this had already been, between the lines, the message of *Viva Caporetto!*). But he did not know that Spain was a site of struggle that international anti-Fascism was about to lose on the military level yet win on the level of propaganda and the battle of ideas. In any event, not even Franco was interested in admitting the decisive role played by his allies. If the caudillo had to treat Hitler with a certain regard, he did not feel the least gratitude to Mussolini, who had granted him too much, too soon, in exchange for nothing, on the basis of vague secret agreements. Consider that without the airlift organized by the Italian air force, Franco would not have been able to disembark his troops from Africa in Spain during the insurrection of July 18, 1936. This sense of frustration pervaded the entire issue of the magazine, the series' worst, behind the rhetoric and formulaic enthusiasm. All in all, the war in Spain would prove to be a resounding failure for the regime. Mussolini would derive no profit from the operation, in terms of either image or substance, and the young representatives of "red Fascism," from Elio Vittorini to Romano Bilenchi, Davide Lajolo to Antonio Delfini, would end up finding more affinity with the republican camp than with the reactionary, clerical crusade of Franco's troops.

The compromises necessary to keep *Prospettive* alive began to take their toll. Malaparte could not fail to see that the latest issues had done little to increase his glory and that the publication's prestige had taken a serious hit. And here was a new obstacle. After having sworn the opposite up until the last moment, the regime introduced the most dishonorable measure in its history, incomprehensible even to a majority of Fascists: the racial legislation, the ground for which had been prepared by a pseudo "Manifesto of Italian Intellectuals in Defense of the Race."[112] It contained a series of discriminatory measures that would combine to fuel an enormous operation of moral degradation, involving blackmail, accommodations, forgeries, and repudiations. The racial laws, sources of anguish and desperation for some, would become for others a lucrative business, fed by corruption and by the more or less compulsory transfers of property. As rumors about Malaparte's origins had circulated for some time, he was invited to clarify matters, and he did so with a letter that, as far as I know, has never been published. Here are the main passages:

> I never thought there might be doubts about my Aryanism. My father is German, of Aryan race, and he is still, after forty-eight years of Italian residence, a German citizen. As a good German, he has never wanted to renounce his nation, his race, his citizenship.*

---

*We will see how, following the war, Malaparte will convert this image of his father, here an excellent, loyal German, into a political deportee.

A description of the family of his Lombard mother follows, along with an account of his war service, to arrive at this conclusion:

> In terms of race, then, I'm all set. Please make all the requests you consider appropriate; I will send you all the information and documents you think necessary. And this to finally prove wrong all those irresponsible people who, out of thoughtlessness, envy, or malice, sowed doubts about my blood.[113]

Today this text can seem inadequate and Pilate-like. And yet it was in line with the flood of self-certifications that flowed in at the time, from all over Italy, and from all sectors of society. Malaparte should be acknowledged, however, as one of the relatively few prominent intellectuals of the time who refused to participate in the sordid promotional campaign for the racial legislation. He also continued to provide a valuable source of support to the magazine's contributors of Jewish or "racially mixed" origin,[114] even if he did exaggerate his merits in this regard at the time of the purge process.[115]

Lawrence of Ethiopia

Following these painful efforts to prove his loyalty, would Malaparte finally be able to leave the country again? And if so, to go where? The war in Spain was drawing to a close and the "volunteers" were about to be repatriated. But Ethiopia, three years after the invasion, was far from pacified. All the party's leading men, as we saw in the case of Ciano, were sent to the front, and all of them had to return with some war decoration, awards that often bordered on the ridiculous, and sometimes surpassed it. Thus Farinacci, come to test himself against the original *ras*, did not hesitate to demand a military disability pension when, fishing with bombs in a lake, he lost his right hand, earning himself the nickname "kingfisher." Writers and journalists were no exception. D'Annunzio, in bad shape, with only one working eye in his devastated mask of a face, stayed home. He had to limit himself to launching from the closed rooms of the Vittoriale, his opulent hillside estate overlooking Lake Garda, the oration "Teneo te, Africa" (I have you, Africa!), the half-blind seer's homage to the new Roman legionnaires, which some took as a bad omen. But Marinetti, who was no longer twenty years old, or even forty, but a full sixty, left in command of a group of "Futurist" Blackshirts, who fought for real, leaving behind a good number of dead on both sides. Malaparte, too, would be called up as a reserve official in April 1937, but he managed to avoid being assigned to the Third Alpine Regiment of Turin.[116]

Glorification of the war in regime propaganda would provoke an inevitable revisionist wave after Fascism's fall. The conventional wisdom today is that the Ethiopian exploit was decided by the air force, by the terror bombing of a defenseless population and the extensive use of gas. It is true the Italians were prepared to use any means necessary to "avenge" the defeats of Dogali and Adua, toward the end of the previous century: names signifying a humiliation etched in the fragile national memory. The conflict lasted seven months, however, until the entry of Marshal Pietro Badoglio into Addis Ababa on May 5, 1936, against a brave and resilient enemy, master of the territory, capable of giving the invaders a tough time. This belated colonial expedition, undertaken in a period when the large English, French, and Dutch empires had already begun to show their cracks, swallowed up the country's economic resources. The League of Nations' vote to sanction Italy helped push the still-hesitant Mussolini into the arms of Hitler. In a public ceremony verging on the pathetic, all the widows and wives of Italy, the queen at their head, offered their wedding bands to the country, "for the redemptive war," in exchange for a little iron ring. But iron was also expensive, and the country produced too little of it. Ethiopia joined Eritrea, Italian Somalia, and Libya in a dream of prosperity for all, in which the soldiers-turned-colonists would build streets, bridges, and towns, give impetus to agriculture and industry, found schools and hospitals, which in most cases still exist today, constituting some of the scant infrastructure of those countries. "Fraternization" occurred so quickly, especially in Ethiopia, Christianized in ancient times, that the regime imposed rules against mixed marriages and sexual relations with the indigenous population.* The Second World War would quickly sweep away such illusions, which nonetheless played no small role in the "mal d'Africa" (longing for Africa) of two generations, to which Malaparte would pay tribute even after the war: "The Italians of Africa are good guys, better than us."[117]

When Malaparte was finally permitted to travel, in early 1939, the UK-financed guerilla war still raged. He should have left two months earlier, and Borelli, an editor of the old school, who made the newspaper office run like a Swiss watch, was growing impatient. He had given him a preliminary contract for fifteen articles, for the not-inconsiderable sum of twenty-five thousand lire. But Borelli

---

*According to Renzo De Felice, the fear of miscegenation influenced Mussolini's decision to adopt the racial legislation, even more than his difficulty vis-à-vis Hitler's Germany. On the other hand, the most famous song of the war was called "Faccetta nera" (Little black face) and carried a "progressive" message: the Italian army was ready to liberate (one imagines how) Ethiopian women from their age-old slavery.

had also gone further, modifying the itineraries of other correspondents from the paper, to make space for him. The tension between Malaparte and Indro Montanelli, another "cursed Tuscan" who would become Italy's most famous journalist in the second postwar period, has often been traced to this, but the dates do not line up. Another dangerous rival was Dino Buzzati, who had not yet published *The Tartar Steppe* but was already appreciated by the public (and the regime). Malaparte had delayed his departure to negotiate, as was by now his custom, other profitable contracts. In Italy he can be considered a precursor of American-style serialization: the possibility of putting out the same article, with another title and a few variations, in various venues, simultaneously or nearly so. His travel plans were, as usual, grandiose: "I will go to Gondar, then to Jimma, Galla and Sidamo, Shewa, Harar, naturally Addis Ababa, etc. On the way back, from Port Said, I intend to make a short trip to Jerusalem."[118] That is, more than 1,800 miles, to be traversed in eighty days, like Verne's Phileas Fogg. And he reassured Borelli, confirming that Il Duce himself had approved the journey and arranged for the Ministry of Popular Culture to provide him with all necessary assistance. He forgot to specify—and he always would—that Mussolini's "support" twice materialized in special contributions of 12,500 lire.[119]

No Phileas Fogg without Passepartout. Did Malaparte, setting out on his journey, know that he would be followed by a police officer? It was the newly appointed vice chief of public safety of Gondar, a certain Mr. Conte, who embarked on the same steamer in Naples on January 19, to go assume his duties in that distant capital. It was a coincidence, or maybe not. Malaparte persuaded himself that this "spy" was charged not only with surveilling him but also with preventing him from fleeing, during the stop at Port Said. The fact remains that Conte produced a report about the trip, which provides us, as it provided his superiors then, with an excellent source of information on the writer's movements. He confirms that he never lost sight of Malaparte, but that the latter knew perfectly well that he was accompanied, since "at the time of boarding he had asked about me; I considered it appropriate, then, to visit him in his cabin." (Not very professional conduct for a supposed spy, but let's set that aside.) During the journey, Malaparte allowed himself a few anti-Fascist quips at table while having lunch with his sister-in-law, of English origin, who was joining her agronomist husband, Ezio, who had been transferred to Bonga (Jimma);[120] the aforementioned Conte; and other passengers. In all other respects, the inspector notes, "my relations with Malaparte have become more friendly than ever; his private life so far could only be judged extremely moral," meaning no contraband, no gambling, no alcohol, no women, no boys. Just one defect: "He suffers from xenophilia." The report ends with the arrival in Gondar, on February 4, and a humorous comment: "As far as rebels go, I did not have the pleasure of seeing a single one."[121]

On this topic we may also call on the valuable testimony of the celebrated gallerist Beatrice Monti von Rezzori:

> I met him in Gondar, in the spring of 1939, during his big reporting trip in Ethiopia. He had stopped for a few weeks in this city where my father was in charge of the Center for Colonial Administration Studies... Their friendship dated back to right after the Great War. My father had been a legionnaire in Fiume with D'Annunzio; Malaparte, who was in Poland, had missed out on that occasion, but they had met each other in the same nationalist circles. Their relations were excellent, very friendly. A born raconteur, he told me

extraordinary stories that I literally drank from his lips, in a voice that was a bit metallic and theatrical.... Curzio accompanied my father and me on long expeditions to visit monasteries way out in the savanna, as far as Lake Tana. One day my father had bought a little jackal from some village boys, his paws tied to a pole. It was a sad sight, and I was happy to have that little jackal, who survived and became very attached to me. He followed me everywhere like a dog, causing much scandal. Curzio enjoyed the spectacle enormously and helped me feed him. Then one day, alas, I didn't find the jackal anymore when I got home. My stepmother had probably gotten rid of it, taking advantage of my absence.[122]

But after Gondar began the more dangerous part of the journey. Malaparte intended to reach Addis Ababa via Gojjam in revolt, more than six hundred miles on the back of a mule, as part of the Ninth Eritrean Battalion, tasked with resupplying isolated outposts. It was the continually obliging "spy" Conte who obtained the necessary authorizations for him. He could have made the journey by plane or reached the capital via a longer and safer itinerary. But where would have been the adventure in that?

He had to catch up with colleagues who had left and returned before him, sending various spectacular proofs of his daring to Borelli and to readers. And there was no shortage of adventure: in the eleven days of the expedition, Malaparte found himself involved in various skirmishes. We know he was courageous, even reckless; but the description, straight out of a western, of his rescue by Conte, promoted for the occasion from "common cop" to "guardian angel to whom, probably, I owe my life," does not sound very convincing. If the faithful bloodhound, "instead of allowing me to pick up a dead man's rifle, had slapped the cuffs on me, I would surely have paid dearly for the rashness of having written *Technique du coup d'État*" (T2, 16). For this endeavor, he would receive a new war cross; but, as we have seen, the flood of commendations was particularly heavy in Ethiopia, at times to ennoble exploits with very little heroic about them. The letters he sent to Italian friends painted a more modest picture of these military ventures:

> At Ghenbevà [Gambela?], on the right bank of the Nile, we had a battle with Fitaurari Desser (a follower of Mengesha). So I took some marvelous photographs. You should know I've been nominated for a distinguished service cross, which the viceroy has already signed off on and sent to Rome. I landed myself in the middle of a mess, shooting bullets and photos, two hundred yards away from the Amhara. A *sciumbasci* [askari sergeant] approached and said to me: "Not be your place here. If you dies, what impression make battalion?" Naturally, I shot a photo of him as well. After an hour of firing, we moved on.[123]

Were they attacked by rebels, then, or were they hunting them down? What was the true balance of forces between attackers and those attacked? And who were the *true* attackers? If the rebels were armed and determined, the mopping up of pockets of resistance proceeded without too much consideration. The operation was entrusted to the colonial troops, especially to the askaris, the unfailingly loyal Eritrean auxiliaries, separated unfortunately from the Ethiopians by an ancient hatred, which would explode in all its horror during the conflict between the two countries in the 1980s and 1990s.

If Malaparte took big risks, then, it is hard to put these endeavors in the same category as those of the Argonne or Bligny. And his description of the captured rebels does not recall the *Sturmtruppen* of General Mudra:

> I happened to read, in a French newspaper, a profile of Abebe Aregai, the infamous bandit of Menz, that would have been the envy of any of Plutarch's heroes. In reality, he's just a bandit like so many others: the only French he knows are a few words picked up in Djibouti brothels, he eats with his hands, is vile and savage like any Shewa lordling, corrupted by liqueurs, by champagne and the chanteuses of the once flourishing nightclubs of Addis Ababa. A cork helmet squashes his face, fat and swollen with sleep. He has a drinker's lips. His eyes, small and rimmed with black, bulge. He seems like a negro from Harlem, dressed like a circus hand.[124]

The portrait is brilliant but with heavy racial, if not racist, undertones—even if these were sunshine and rainbows compared with what the majority of Italian correspondents were writing.

The journey continued until mid-April, without other episodes worthy of note. Borelli assailed him with requests, but Malaparte had dropped off the map after having obtained what he wanted: to regain the audience of a great newspaper. The only hitch was that, despite his warrior spirit, he had not yet been readmitted to the Fascist Party.[125] As chance would have it, Balbo was also in Ethiopia at the time, elephant hunting; if he had encountered Malaparte, he would have gladly changed targets and, unlike Abebe Aregai, one can be sure, he would not have missed. Malaparte then planned to gather his dispatches into a book, whose title he announced—as he often did—before finishing it: *L'Africa non è nera* (Africa is not Black). He would have liked to enrich the book with the lovely snapshots taken during his journey, the start of his far-from-insignificant photographic work. Then, as he did just as often, he stopped and gave up on publishing it. Only a few pages of it would be taken up after his death, in *Benedetti italiani* (Blessed Italians).[126] Rereading them today, these texts provoke a double impression. On one hand, the glorification of the "white" invaders is accompanied by denunciation of the satrapy of the former "Lion of Judah," Haile Selassie, who would be put back on the throne five years later by the English. On the other, Malaparte shows, especially in the passages not published in the newspaper, an authentic respect for the Ethiopians: "There is some secret, mysterious harmony between this people and the nature of its lands, with the landscape, even. This harmony is at the foundation of its civilization, its sense of the heroic and the divine."[127] He goes so far as to call into question whether such a people can ever be entirely colonized, in the process launching a few barbs against France and England:

> The Ethiopians, today, are certainly much more civilized, also in a moral and social sense, than the Gauls were at the time of the Roman conquest, or the English of Kent as described by Caesar, who colored their skin blue and had women in common.[128]

The photos he took were censored as well, because they differed too much from the exoticism of the colonizers' "trophies," with the exception of one or two nudes of young girls, the only ones in his career as an amateur photographer. You could almost read into the work a return to the old idea that history profoundly corrupts mankind, and that the primitive man is necessarily healthier than the civilized one. It is no coincidence that he enriched the text with citations of Saint Augustine, the African thinker who contributed the most to the spiritual refoundation of the West.

No Entry

Back in his own country, Malaparte was impatient to retake control of *Prospettive*. The problems he had to confront were of both a formal and a substantive character: to pair a more modest graphic design with a more convincing approach, sufficient to make people forget about the last two issues of 1938. He also had to confront the new material restrictions affecting paper and ink. First off, he decided to shut down the old, too-costly publishing company. The magazine would appear, from then on, every fifteen days, until the fall of the regime; and it would become a sort of laboratory for future cadres of anti-Fascism—one has only to scan the names of the new contributors.[129]

In place of the luxurious monographic issues of the past, *Prospettive* now appeared in the more modest format of issues containing various texts, essentially but not exclusively literary, laid out in a very striking way. And the price was reduced from ten to three lire. At the level of content, the changes were no less significant. The first issue of the new series—although it maintained the original numbering, with no. 8—signaled the change, starting with the title: "Senso vietato" (No entry). Malaparte would have done better to title it "Double entendre," because the opening editorial is an exemplar of the "honest dissimulation" counseled by Torquato Accetto in the seventeenth century. Behind the ritual glorification of Mussolini emerges the message that "especially in Italy, the origin and constant measure of Western civilization, the concept of power cannot be dissociated from the concept of culture." Hence "the current, tragic times are the most suited to confirming, once again, that a people at war does not defend only its own fields, its houses, its cars, but above all its culture," and so on.[130] The prose is convoluted and scarcely Malapartian, but the denunciation of intellectual life under the dictatorship is transparent enough. In another article Malaparte employed the metaphor of the "landscape seen through a closed window." To further clarify what he meant by this, he published an obituary of Freud—a rare incursion into the psychoanalytic field by the brilliant polymath Mario Praz—at a time when it was forbidden to talk about the inventor of "Jewish" psychoanalysis. He also published a story by Moravia, "La casa nuova" (The new house), a thinly veiled allegory of the calamitous times to come. The date on the cover is October 1939; Italy had declared its nonbelligerency, but Europe was already on fire.

The initial printing of 2,500 copies sold out in a few days. We are far from the inflated numbers of the issues devoted to "His" foreign policy or to Spain. But, considering the worries of the moment, it was a decent result, which spurred him to continue. Even the advertising revenue was good, a sign that, despite the war at the gates, some banks and industries—with the conspicuous exception of FIAT—still managed to find a bit of money for culture. The contents of the other two issues from 1939 would be equally provocative: a satire of the *voi* form of address, introduced officially by the regime in place of *lei*, a third-person form foolishly considered contrary to national traditions. The anticosmopolitan campaign had begun a few years earlier, on the vague instructions of Mussolini and at the zealous instigation of Starace. It was aimed especially at the manners of the middle classes and involved in particular the translation of foreign names (*Onorato* di Balzac, *Guglielmo* Shakespeare, etc.), the adoption of invented Italian terms in place of commonly used foreign words, and the translation of entire titles. Thus a jazz standard very popular at the time, "Saint Louis Blues," became an improbable "La ballata di San Luigi," and in translations of the very popular novels of Edgar Wallace appeared a mysterious Circo di Piccadilly that... performed in the heart of London. All this had sunk to ridiculous depths even before the war, and Starace paid for it with destitution.

An even more burning topic: Malaparte set to work on an issue called "Prigioni gratis" (Free prisons), where, unable to be more explicit in his own home, he assailed the "literary functionaries" of the Soviet Union. If the shoe fits... But someone must have seen that it did, if the print run abruptly rose to four thousand copies, then to five or six thousand, despite persistent difficulties in the supply of paper. In early December 1938, the editorial offices had moved to the most elegant neighborhood in the center of Rome, at 44 Via Gregoriana, behind Piazza di Spagna, where Malaparte also took lodgings. The office was still entrusted to a single assistant, the faithful Ms. Pellegrini, who would become the custodian of the memory of *Prospettive* for all future researchers. But naturally Malaparte did not stop there. For the first and last time in his life, he managed to negotiate simultaneously with the two colossi of Italian publishing. Angelo Rizzoli wanted him to take over the popular magazine *Oggi*, eventually entrusted to Mario Pannunzio and Arrigo Benedetti, while Arnoldo Mondadori offered him work on another weekly, *Tempo*, led by his son Alberto; the latter publisher would bring out, in 1940, his new book, *Woman Like Me*. This slim volume, apparently secondary in his output, can be seen as a form of psychoanalytic self-care and an important key for understanding Malaparte's personality. Rarely has a Narcissus shown himself with fewer precautions and with such self-satisfaction. And yet the tone that might have been irritating, or even excruciating, retains a certain grace, at times even an astonishment, that recalls Baudelaire's *Little Poems in Prose*. This man so closed behind his personality and his multiple masks abandoned himself, for once, in a lyrical outpouring completely missing from his verses, with the exception of the satires of *L'arcitaliano*. In one way or another, Malaparte had always spoken and written of himself alone. But here he did so without deforming reality, without fighting it, by welcoming it, transparently, just as it presented itself to his eyes, accepting it and accepting himself for what he was. Indeed, the book's subtitle could have been "The Happiness of Narcissus," or else, in the idiom of contemporary self-help literature, "The Joy of Accepting Oneself": a moment of happiness never seen again in his work, and maybe in his life.

In order to devote himself to literature and to the construction of his "portrait in stone" on Capri, Malaparte sought a collaborator with whom to share the responsibilities of *Prospettive*. Yet he did not want another Bontempelli to overshadow him. His choice was an old friend, the poet Augusto Mazzetti, a more modest but devoted personality. Twelve issues were published in 1940, the year of Italy's entry into and early setbacks in the war; another twelve appeared in 1941, but many were double issues. The list of authors and texts published smacked increasingly of insurgence. There was no place here, unlike in other Italian magazines, for the names of the Nazi-Fascist cultural *nomenklatura* or of the European "collaborationist" space. Instead we find García Lorca, Hofmannsthal, Rilke, Éluard (translated by Malaparte), Yeats, MacLeish, Eliot,

Rafael Alberti, Machado, J. R. Jimenéz, Pierre Jean Jouve... The German case is the most revealing. The Axis nations actively engaged in a policy of exchanges: expositions, concerts, translations of literary and political works, and so on. Malaparte himself benefited from it, when some of his dispatches were taken up by German publications. One supporter of his work in Germany from the beginning was Gerhard Heller, then in charge of literary censorship in German-occupied Paris, but also curious about Italian things.* After the war, Heller would become Malaparte's principal publisher in Germany, at the head of Stahlberg Verlag, in Karlsruhe, and remain a faithful friend to the end.[131] And yet, the only contemporary German author to turn up in issues of *Prospettive* was the great poet Gottfried Benn, who by then considered himself an internal exile of the Third Reich, after his initial sympathies with the regime had rapidly evaporated. Perhaps the magazine did not represent a chrestomathy of "everything that is forbidden in Europe," as Malaparte would later claim, with his usual modesty.[132] But it did contain authors and texts that were then quite difficult, if not impossible, to find in other publications. The panorama of cultural magazines in the Fascist period, especially the youth ones, was far from gray and uniform.[133] But the regime's autarchy limited their horizons, and it was largely thanks to *Prospettive* if international trends succeeded in making inroads in the stifling atmosphere of Fascist Italy.[134] But such an appraisal was not shared by all young intellectuals of the time.[135]

---

*His memoir, *Un Allemand à Paris, 1940–1944* (Paris: Seuil, 1981), provoked considerable controversy, because in it Heller described how eagerly French intellectuals, on the whole, volunteered to collaborate with the occupiers, even becoming informers.

A good example was the inquiry into surrealism, which Malaparte had launched a few years earlier, and which he returned to now. The point of departure had been a feature article in which he described a (false) conversation in Paris with André Malraux: "And when Malraux told me, not without a hint of irony, that there could be nothing surrealist in Italy, I responded that not only was all the true, authentic, great Italian art surrealist, but that the homeland of surrealism itself was Italy."[136] This pretext had allowed him to exalt a cultural movement that entirely eluded the rhetoric of the regime, that in fact overturned its assumptions. In so proceeding he followed his natural, and not merely programmatic, inclination: Breton's conception of the movement, even if distant from his own, obeyed a similar desire to depart from the real to transfigure it, to violate it, without ever denying it, a sort of "super-realism," which constitutes one of the rare declarations of a Malapartian poetics.[137] The Fascist extremists noticed as much, replying that "surrealism is nothing but Jewish mystification covering a materialism pushed to its wildest consequences, [in] affinity with that other Jewish mystification that is the psychoanalysis promoted by the Jew Sigmund Freud."[138]

Another revealing case was the space in the magazine dedicated to publishing fragments of Joyce's all-but-untranslatable *Finnegans Wake*, in the Italian version by Ettore Settani, a known anti-Fascist, which was approved by the great Irish writer shortly before his death. Joyce was, however, tolerated by the regime, thanks to his anti-English and philo-Italian stances, and the purists of Fascist style had to let it go. But things did not stop there, because, from his refuge in Rapallo, Ezra Pound also wanted to have his say, burying his "caro Malapartissimo" with letters written in an equally incomprehensible Saxon-Provençal-Dantean gibberish. For that matter,

KREMLIN AND SWASTIKA (1934–1943)

Pound's transmissions in "Italian" on Radio Roma represented one of the most surrealist pages of the Fascist decades. No one understood a thing. But since he was a poet known across the world, and an American to boot, who was singing the regime's praises and his hatred of the "usurocracy," he was allowed to rant.

The new series of *Prospettive* was also the occasion for Malaparte to intensify his relationship with an interlocutor who could have become his alter ego, and for a brief period did so: Alberto Moravia. They had gotten to know each other in the fashionable circles of Forte dei Marmi; but he had been aware of the Roman writer ever since the sensational appearance of *The Indifferent Ones*, in 1929. And yet, aside from the talent and the decision to adopt a pseudonym, almost everything divided them. Their origins, to begin with: Alberto Pincherle came from the Jewish Roman intelligentsia through his father, the wealthy architect Carlo Pincherle, and from an ennobled and very Fascist family of Dalmatian origin, the De Marsaniches, through his mother.* Then in matters of health, physique, "force," and character: delicate from birth, affected by bone tuberculosis, obliged to undergo frequent stays in clinics and sanatoriums, the future Moravia early on created his own interior world, without participating in any of the experiences that had formed Malaparte, from boarding school to the war to the struggles of the first postwar period. One of them had a limp; the other was an athlete. One pursued women; the other was pursued by them.

---

*Augusto De Marsanich, Moravia's maternal uncle, a minister and influential personality in the regime and the Republic of Salò, became after the war a leading exponent of the conservative wing of the neofascist Italian Social Movement (MSI).

A decade younger, Moravia belonged to the generation fully integrated into the regime and reacted to the ambient oppression with a protoexistentialist "indifference" that prompted his first novels and stories, which many still consider his best. From there emerges another difference between them. Moravia was a born novelist and would remain so even after the war, when he became a sort of "official" interpreter, with greater or lesser insight, of bourgeois bad conscience and capitalist alienation. Malaparte, on the other hand, has always been the epitome of the "impure" writer, without real imaginative or inventive talent: in his books, even those that can be considered works of fiction, he holds on to reality to incessantly deform it and knead it—taking us back to surrealism. Hence the contrast, for example, on the theme of sexuality, which Moravia put at the center of his works from the start, while in Malaparte it would gain prominence only when it became a metaphor for the contemporary plague in *The Skin*. What is most authentic in Moravia's inspiration comes from the great nineteenth-century literature of psychological introspection and social analysis, from Balzac to Dostoevsky, Flaubert to Conrad and Zola: a strand with which Malaparte, exclusive cultivator of the I, had very little in common. The same difference is noticeable in their styles: Moravia's is quick and dry, almost to the point of banality, whereas Malaparte displays a reverence, at times excessive, for the D'Annunzian well-made page, subject to continual revision.

Were these two very different men made to understand each other? We cannot deny Malaparte's generosity toward his young colleague, whom he had followed since his debut, as we have seen him encourage Vittorini, Landolfi, Falqui, and others. He had opened to Moravia, without knowing him, the doors of *"900"* and *La Stampa* and had encouraged glowing reviews of his first books.* He had also good-naturedly accepted a few caustic observations from the other. For a man like him, always ready to break off a friendship or fight a duel at the slightest criticism, this was no small thing. He made Moravia, first, a regular contributor to *Prospettive*, then, gradually, his right-hand man, beside Giancarlo Vigorelli, in place of the diligent Mazzetti. It was a choice not without risks. Moravia's "decadent" and "morbid" novels had already provoked suspicion and problems with the censors. The situation deteriorated with the racial laws: Moravia had been "exonerated," because he was baptized and the son of a Catholic mother, but his personal situation remained precarious. This convinced him to write a letter to Mussolini, on the eve of his marriage to another gifted novelist, Elsa Morante, in which he promised to change the themes and inspirations of his books. The document is indistinguishable, if somewhat more dignified in tone, from those that many Italian intellectuals sooner or later sent to Il Duce, to solicit his help or goodwill. However, Malaparte, to whom Moravia had first shown the letter, discouraged him from sending it, rendering an excellent service to the subsequent fame of his friend, who could serenely forget it later.[139]

The Pincherles were kept under watch for political reasons, particularly because they were related to Carlo and Nello Rosselli, the

---

*Thus, when René de Ceccatty claims, in his monumental biography *Alberto Moravia* (Paris: Flammarion, 2010), 101, that their fame was "more or less contemporary," in the postwar period—forgetting the earlier international success of *Technique du coup d'État*—it should be clarified that Malaparte was already in the 1930s one of the most prominent Italian intellectuals, from whom the young Moravia sought, and found, support and protection.

intrepid Florentine anti-Fascists cut down, as we saw, in France in 1937 by assassins from a far-right organization, La Cagoule, in cahoots with the French and Italian secret police. (The horrendous crime would inspire Moravia's postwar novel *The Conformist*, which would become the source for Bertolucci's far superior film.) The writer's position worsened with the war, obliging him to resort to a pseudonym, "Pseudo," which, however, a fellow writer of the period recalled, "everyone knew about."[140] And he continued to ensure, alongside Vigorelli, the appearance of *Prospettive*, during Malaparte's absences abroad, until July 1943. And yet, despite this common struggle, the exchanges, discussions, and meetings, their fellowship did not survive the fall of Fascism. When the two men met on Capri after the war, the tension was palpable. As Malaparte wrote to Guglielmo Rulli, for example:

> Moravia is here, on the rocks with his wife, having lost his head. I invited him to lunch, along with some of his English guests. He reciprocated with lunch at Torre Borselli, where he lives, and at the end of lunch he asked me, snickering, if I was sorry Italy had lost the war. I responded naturally that I was deeply saddened Italy had not won. Just imagine what happened: everyone against me, Moravia squawking like an eagle, ditto his wife, his guests as well, and I firmly "my country right or rong" [*sic*]. I didn't back down, and in the end his guests looked at me with sympathy, and him and his wife with contempt.[141]

In an Italy torn apart, recovering its freedom and democracy, Malaparte had become too inconvenient a fellow traveler for his erstwhile colleagues, especially for those who, like Moravia, began to gravitate, with greater success than he did, into the PCI orbit. Moravia initially defended him,[142] then distanced himself, just like Alvaro or Vittorini. Even if formally they respected each other, and from time to time would send each other tokens of their esteem, their paths were destined not to cross again. Malaparte, who in personal relationships was accustomed to playing the part of the leaver, not the left, never forgave him. Among his papers can be found an undated note in which he attacks Moravia's political commitment, an "absolutely false legend of anti-Fascism, of martyrdom, etc.; when he is neither a Fascist nor an anti-Fascist, has never been persecuted, has a passport, can freely circulate abroad, is personally welcome in the circles closest to the upper echelons of political leadership"[143] — claims that he would take up again after 1945, in various letters to foreign correspondents. In private, after having for years called him "Moraviotto," with affectionate and slightly scornful paternalism, he gave him the nickname "Amaro Gambarotta" ("the bitter broken leg"), playing on the name of a liqueur brand well known at the time, which is not exactly the height of elegance. Their disagreements were inevitable on both the personal and the literary level. Both detested, in Malaparte's words, "a certain part of the Roman bourgeoisie, into which flowed after [18]70 a large part of the ghetto."[144] For Moravia, this represented a struggle against his father and against the origins that would pursue him as long as he lived, whereas for Malaparte that world had played only a marginal and episodic role in his work.

But the fundamental reason for their break was something else. After the war, Moravia perfectly reprised the public role Malaparte had played in Italian society until the start of the conflict. Thus their parts flipped after 1945: the author of *Kaputt* found himself increasingly isolated, with flashes of success; the author of *The Woman of*

Rome and *Boredom* became the most recognized and powerful "organic" intellectual in Italian society. Now he was the one who could attract and launch young writers, from the platform of his magazine *Nuovi Argomenti*, following the model of *Prospettive*. He was the one who could cultivate relationships with international movements, speak out about cultural trends, impose himself on the mass media and publishing houses, choose contestation but seduce the bourgeois.* And Moravia constructed, with a PCI that had become hegemonic in intellectual circles, according to the old Gramscian insight put into practice by Togliatti and carried on by his successors, a relationship very similar to that of Malaparte with Fascism.

It is no surprise, then, that Moravia generally refused to meet with Malaparte biographers and scholars. "I asked Moravia about it just once. His reaction made me understand it was better to let the matter drop," affirms the writer Sandro Veronesi.[145] He opened up a bit more in his dialogues with his biographer Alain Elkann, with several inaccuracies, such as the one in which Malaparte is called one of the founders of Fascism in Tuscany. He also told Elkann they had stayed in Paris together in 1934, "at the Port Royal hotel," at a time when Malaparte was in *confino* on Lipari.[146] But the essential is not to be found here; it is in Moravia's judgment of him as a "journalist" and not as a real writer. Elkann draws from this the following conclusion:

---

*A personal but revealing experience, shared by others: I once met Moravia at a dinner in the early 1980s. Based on my accent, way of dressing, and manners, he identified me as a member of the detested bourgeoisie and treated me with ill-concealed disdain. But at the end of the painful evening, when we parted, again ignoring me, he kissed my wife's hand, a gesture no longer in fashion at the time even in conservative circles.

I think Moravia was attracted, in Malaparte's case as in Pasolini's, by a vitality he lacked. They were intellectuals but also men of action, while in his adolescence he had been bedridden. But there's no doubt that at bottom he considered himself a superior writer to him and a true novelist, something Malaparte was not, in his eyes.[147]

Another point of disagreement came in the choice of language as an expression of the writer's authenticity. Moravia explained it this way to a French interviewer, Marc Lambron:

My opinion about writing is very simple: there should be the minimum distance possible between writing and the spoken language of a society. Malaparte wrote in a literary language, somewhere between D'Annunzio and Giovanni Papini; Pavese created a pastiche of the American writers he had translated. There's always a pasticheur aspect to the Italian man of letters, then, a certain need to keep his distance from spoken language.[148]

Moravia made another exception, forty years after the *Prospettive* adventure, and his judgment, showing his old resentments, has been proven wrong, at least on the first point:

Malaparte was too tied to his age and never crossed the midcentury. Maybe today we needn't have too much compassion for such brilliant and cynical individualism. He was intelligent, but not intellectual; that is, he didn't believe in ideas. Naturally he had considerable resources; he had great vitality, and maybe once again he could have found some success. All his life he was looking backward. He wasn't Fascist in the sense of a faith, but of a restorative mentality. The ambitious bourgeois on the attack, just like Julien Sorel or Rastignac. He was a representative of the Fascist illusion. He was caught off guard by the modern world. This judgment of mine was already formed before his death.[149]

It is up to us readers, then, beyond the all-too-human misunderstandings and resentments, to appreciate the quality of the inspiration that brought together two important writers in a difficult time, only to separate them later.

From the Alps to Piraeus

Malaparte did not applaud the arrival of war, this is certain. But did he oppose it? The answer is less simple than it appears. In October 1939, he was kept under observation for fifteen days in Rome's military hospital for a reexamination of his disability. He spent the rest of the year between preparations for *Prospettive* and more or less abortive literary projects, with the exception of *Woman Like Me*. He also hoped to bring out the Italian edition of *Le Bonhomme Lénine*,[150] but the project was interrupted by the war. To Borelli he abruptly announced his intention to go to Albania, which, the preceding April, had been annexed by Italy, in an operation bearing the signature of his friend Ciano. And here some additional explanations are called for.

For the preceding fifteen years or so, Albania had gravitated in the orbit of Italy, which had de facto appointed as president, then placed on the throne, the most astute of the tribal leaders, Ahmed

Zogolli, later Zogu, then Zog I.* Ciano, from the moment he arrived at Foreign Affairs, impatient to free himself from his father-in-law, had turned the Albanese protectorate into his personal fiefdom, nicknamed the "Grand Duchy of Tuscany," as he waited to get rid of Zog at the earliest opportunity. This arrived in March 1939, after the annexation of Bohemia by the Germans and Hitler's entry into Prague. Mussolini, irritated to be faced with a fait accompli and to see the collapse of the Munich Agreement, of which he considered himself author and guarantor, yielded to his son-in-law's pressure, permitting him to occupy Albania as "compensation." Ciano did not have to be told twice. Above all he was keen to prove his attachment to King Victor Emmanuel, delivering to him the gift of another crown, after that of Ethiopia, in the hopes of becoming sooner or later Il Duce's heir, at the head of a coalition of moderate Fascists and monarchists. The Italian landing took place, without encountering practically any resistance, on Good Friday 1939: "The preparations were marked by childish dilettantism," recalled Ciano's caustic cabinet chief. "If the Albanese had possessed a well-trained fire company, they would have tossed us into the Adriatic."[151] The Zog regime was discredited; the great powers had other, more urgent concerns, and the operation ultimately held no interest for the chancelleries.

*The life of Zog (1895–1961) would fill ten novels. Anticipating Gaddafi, he entrusted his personal security to a century of Amazons, to which he added a good dose of mercenaries recruited by a certain Stirling, who boasted of having fought alongside Lawrence of Arabia, and to show it went about dressed as a sheik like him. After the Italian occupation, Zog had to flee, but, in a rather rare instance, in exile managed to become richer than before. The only time things went wrong for him was in London, in the 1950s, when he resold for £800,000 the Mercedes that Hitler had given him for his wedding with the Hungarian countess Geraldine Apponyi—the check he received bounced.

Ciano began to think this modest success could guarantee him another, much larger one: Greece. But since that could entail a conflict with the English, traditional allies of the Greeks, and likely also with the French, it was necessary to wait for the opportune moment. Meanwhile, the conflict on the western front had erupted, and Ciano suddenly became the most determined opponent of the Axis and the war. This conversion has never been completely explained: there was maybe an element of repulsion for Nazi duplicity, of which he now had ample proof, and a reciprocal dislike for his counterpart Ribbentrop; and surely the fear of a world war in which Italy had everything to lose. But there was also a political calculation, for once not shared by his wife. It was said that Edda was then ardently pro-Nazi. It would be more accurate to maintain that she realized, even more than her father, that there were no longer any alternatives to the alliance with Hitler, for better or worse. Moreover, hot-blooded as she was, she wanted France and England to pay for their intransigence and disdain toward Italy during the Ethiopian crisis. Ciano, and in fact Mussolini himself, still hoped for a broad compromise peace, from which all the belligerents would emerge weakened; Italy would thus obtain its share of the spoils—including, perhaps, Greece—without entering the conflict. Sotto voce, he would confide these grandiose projects to his court of aristocrats, military men, diplomats, and party officials, whom he believed, erroneously, to be devoted to him. He saw himself suddenly raised from Il Duce's creature to the great negotiator of a new Concert of Europe. One might indeed be tempted to say of him, "*povero ragazzo*," poor guy, as party hard-liners were wont to do, if it were not an entire country, and not him alone, to pay the price for these foolish ideas.[152]

The illusion did not last long. The invasion of Poland caught

Mussolini by surprise and angered him. Hitler had promised him he would not start a war for another three years at least, or not before the 1942 World's Fair, in the EUR quarter of Rome. And a war delayed may well never happen... At first, Il Duce hesitated to commit himself. What held him back were not humanitarian scruples: everything, in his temperament and in his Hobbesian conception of politics, carried him to war. Nonetheless, even if it had been some time since he had lost touch with the real country, he intuited that the Italian people did not want it, did not "feel" it as they had in 1915, or in 1917 following Caporetto. The army, especially after Ethiopia and Spain, was not ready. For a moment, the diplomat in him seemed to regain the upper hand: he tried to organize a new Munich conference, this time on the fate of Poland, already invaded by the Germans but not yet by the Soviets. When this project failed, Il Duce declared Italy's nonbelligerency, which came to an end nine months later, on June 10, 1940, when Hitler's victorious attack on France swept away his last hesitations. Ciano had revealed as much to the French ambassador in Rome: "If you win some battles, nothing will happen. Otherwise, I can make no guarantees."[153]

Realpolitik taken to the extreme limit of cynicism? Perhaps. But it was, in any case, what Malaparte thought as well; he may no longer have been a Fascist in his heart, but his conversion to pacifism was still to come. The writer had been recalled to arms on June 1, with the rank of captain, joining the Fifth Alpine Regiment near the border crossing at Little Saint Bernard Pass. The assignment pleased him, because the corps was an elite one, and he always loved the company of real soldiers. But he no longer had much desire to fight. He immediately asked to be accredited as a special correspondent for *Tempo*; Alberto Mondadori hustled to obtain the necessary authorization, which arrived on the seventh. As usual, though, Malaparte assured himself of a second contract, with the *Corriere della Sera*, which would publish in installments his account of the battle of the Alps. Must we interpret this choice as a moral refusal of the war? It is certainly what he would claim later. No doubt he was repulsed by the notion of fighting against France, to whose defense he had run in 1914. But his real motivation was that, now forty years old, Malaparte had decided his true role was to testify, not to risk his life: it was time to hang up his rifle in exchange for a pen. Three days later, at six in the evening, from the balcony of Palazzo Venezia, before a crowd ritually cheering but shot through with anxiety, Mussolini pronounced the fatal words: "A declaration of war has been delivered to the ambassadors of Great Britain and France." Malaparte listened to the speech on the radio in his Alpine hut and immediately noted: "These are not the mountains of when I was eighteen, in the other war. Pure, sublime, inspired, innocent, merciful. Today so hard, sharp, hostile."[154] The next day, in the first dispatch he sent from the front to *Prospettive*, he clarified his thoughts in terms announcing his great books to come:

> It is certain that this war will profoundly, irreparably change the world. The transformation effected by the war of 1914–15 will look like a game, compared to the one in preparation. The world, and especially Europe, will be sown with corpses: ideas, feelings, prejudices, philosophies, moral conceptions, traditions. We will return home just in time to attend the most incredible and marvelous funerals. And if we happen to die, struck by some surrealist bullet from Lieutenant Éluard or Captain Breton, we will leave no testament.[155]

Over the next ten days, "nonbelligerence" turned into "nonwar." The Italians did not attack; the French of General Olry's Sixth Army, well equipped, protected by the natural barrier of the Alpine range and a system of fortifications renovated in the 1930s, did not either. The only military operations were symbolic incursions by the Italian air force on Bizerte, and on the Provençal hinterland, as well as the bombardment of the Ligurian coast, between Vado and Genoa, by the French navy. Badoglio, who was not only extremely cautious but also a Francophile and a personal friend of the French commander in chief, Maurice Gamelin, considered it useless to do anything more: the war should have stayed on paper and never been declared. As a good professional, he was perfectly acquainted with the unprepared state of the Italian army: the supreme effort demanded by Il Duce threatened to snap its spine.

But on June 17, Marshal Pétain, called in at the eleventh hour to salvage what he could, sued Hitler for peace. Mussolini, who could not stand inaction, saw his chance to sit at the victors' table slip away. He ordered Badoglio to go on the offensive, despite the unfavorable weather conditions. The result was an absurd four-day battle (June 21–24), begun as the Franco-German armistice was about to be signed. Il Duce obtained merely that it would take effect after the signing of the Italo-French armistice at Villa Incisa outside Rome, or shortly after midnight on June 25. Mussolini counted six hundred dead to obtain his little armistice, twenty times that of the enemy.* At the ceasefire, the penetration into French territory was derisory: from two to five miles deep, with a maximum of nineteen

---

*The final tally was much worse for the Italians, if to the combat losses (642) are added those lost or taken prisoner (616) and the victims of frostbite (2,151). The French had 37 dead, 62 wounded, and 155 prisoners.

at Menton. And only the armistice prevented a French counteroffensive, which would probably have pushed back the attacker well beyond the border.[156]

Malaparte's dispatches on the "war of the Alps," later collected in *Il sole è cieco* (The sun is blind), gave rise to a lively polemic after 1945, when the author added a preface in which he declared his solitary opposition to Fascism and the war. We will discuss this again in due time, but for the moment let us grant that it was one of the most distasteful distortions he ever showed himself capable of. This retrospective and artificial justification detracts from the authenticity of pages that are not at all bellicose, but of a limpid beauty genuinely worthy of an Alpine landscape, where there appears, for the first time with such intensity, the least ostentatious of Malapartian themes: compassion. It comes as no surprise that this sentiment is directed first of all not to men, but to animals, and to the humblest of them: the mule, faithful companion of the Alpine trooper Calusia. Man and animal are tied together in the struggle for survival and thus in a redemptive death, coprotagonists of a "novel" that assumes the style of a Christian parable, because "the mule smells the man, and dies thus in the living smell of the man, dies thus in the warm, living smell of the man" (SC, 187).[157]

Il sole è cieco—whose title was originally to be "Sangue proibito" (Forbidden blood),[158] and later "È in fondo all'uomo" (It is in the depths of man) or "Morte perché" (Why death)[159]—touches us today more on the level of moral interrogation than for its rather dubious value as a historical document. Malaparte, who enriched his account with impressive battlefield snapshots, did not describe a war so much as an initiation into exertion and sacrifice. Here is the site, according to him, of equality among men, an aspiration to beauty and purity that transcends individual destinies. There is no shortage of concessions to aestheticism, especially if we compare these pages with those of another Alpine trooper, Mario Rigoni Stern.[160] But the lyricism of many of the sequences is nonetheless enthralling. The whole thing is dominated by the vision of inaccessible peaks, like in Richard Strauss's *Alpensinfonie*, or in the films of Luis Trenker, the mountaineer and director from Alto Adige, whom Malaparte knew and admired.[161] It is the quintessential form of the ascent, in which man acquires in verticality of spirit what he loses in corporeal substance:

> But up high, on the peaks and on the snowfields, on the immense chain of the Savoy Alps, remote and precise in a sky of pale silk, on that unbroken run of glittering spires and blue glaciers, the clear, still air has its own virgin rawness. (SC, 177)

Malaparte would emerge from that senseless war with another war cross for courage under enemy fire, in his capacity as the regimental commander's liaison officer. The true Alpine trooper's pride he felt for a decoration rather more deserved than the one obtained in Ethiopia strips of all credibility the claim that he would have risked the firing squad for having refused to fight.[162] But most of all he emerged with the conviction that Europe, devastated by a fratricidal war, was rushing to ruin. The situation stabilized on the western front, with the apparent triumph of the Reich's armies and the isolation of Britain in its Churchillian "finest hour." But the fighting raged in East Africa. Mussolini, after the pathetic debut against France, dreamed of conquering Egypt but did not receive the necessary support from Hitler to take Malta, key to the Mediterranean, from where the British intercepted and systematically sank Italian supply ships. This was the moment chosen by Ciano, as if the situation were not already sufficiently tragic, to pull out his old plans for attacking Greece. Occupation, or at least control, of the country would bring an end to the Royal Navy's supremacy in the Aegean and allow Italy to threaten British bases in Egypt, weakening their influence in the Mediterranean theater. Mussolini, short on strategic ideas, finally accepted the plan. Il Duce had a certain sympathy for the Greek prime minister, the general Ioannis Metaxas, who, like the majority of Balkan and southern European dictators, took inspiration from the Fascist model. But Metaxas and the king, George II, were openly pro-British. An agreement was thus impossible, and Albania represented an excellent base from which to bring the venture to a successful conclusion—at least on paper.

The operation was entrusted to a protégé of Ciano's, the general Sebastiano Visconti Prasca, a handsome, athletic man claiming an improbable descent from the dukes of Milan, which did not displease Il Duce, increasingly unimpressed with his paunchy marshals. In addition to being an athlete, Visconti Prasca was an intellectual. A former military attaché in Paris, he had assimilated the theories of Liddell Hart and Colonel de Gaulle, which were, on the contrary, regarded with suspicion by Badoglio. Thus the grumpy, down-to-earth old soldier opposed Visconti Prasca's plan and refused to make the requested elite troops available to him. It was already a bad start. But there was worse: Ciano was convinced by his emissaries that the Greek generals were just waiting for the opportunity to eliminate Metaxas and the royal family, while an Albanese fifth column was ready to rise up in the country. It was at this juncture that the minister decided to send Malaparte to Greece on the most ambiguous of his missions.

His cover consisted once again in a series of dispatches for the *Corriere della Sera*. Aimed at preparing the Italian public for the operation, they would describe the country's backwardness and the anti-Italian intrigues of the innocuous government in Athens. The instructions Malaparte received were clear, as he explained in a letter to Borelli: "Meanwhile I can publish variety items, arts features, even just to justify my peaceful presence down there, seeing as how I'm going in a semi-official capacity." His agreement with Ciano was that, of the articles he published, the "nasty, biting, *Cianesque*" ones would be published in a second phase, once the operation was already underway.[163] Malaparte set off by plane on September 30.

He was charged with another unpleasant mission by an exasperated Ciano: to address the supposed defeatism of Italy's ambassador to Greece, Emanuele Grazzi. In truth Grazzi was a serious and competent civil servant, who deluged Palazzo Chigi with letters and telegrams to repeat two things inspired by simple common sense: the first was that Metaxas enjoyed the unconditional support of the army, on which he based his power; the second, that the English would never permit the occupation of Greece without sending massive reinforcements to defend it. Wasted effort: "Tell Grazzi he can write what he wants, but I'm going to wage war against Greece all the same!" Ciano declared defiantly to Malaparte.[164] Such behavior was typical of someone who, despite his success, was unable to overcome a stubborn inferiority complex in the face of the men who stood up to him, and as far as possible he avoided confronting them directly. Malaparte was thrilled: the ambassador in Athens, like Count Manzoni in Paris before him, was one of the old-school diplomats he regarded as having barred his route to a diplomatic career.

Their first meeting was tempestuous, according to Grazzi's postwar testimony:

> I was unspeakably disgusted by the unprecedented levity with which the minister of foreign affairs, while he wouldn't respond to my letters, official or personal, would talk about waging war on a country as if it were a matter of a hunting party or his own personal affair and entrust with such unusual and delicate messages for the head of a diplomatic mission abroad a writer having no official responsibility and not bound by any obligation to secrecy.[165]

Hence we understand that Grazzi did not look favorably on the meddling by Malaparte, who wanted to meet with everybody. This included the diplomat, poet, and future Nobel laureate George Seferis, who received Malaparte in his office on October 5, 1940:

> Yesterday in the office, a visit from the Italian writer CM. Given the situation, how to even have a conversation with Italians? I nonetheless agreed to meet him. Our exchange is limited to a very superficial conversation. I know nothing about his work. He is a forty-three-year-old man, tall, scrupulously attired, matching necktie and pocket square, alert, who stares at you with searching eyes.
> "I would like to know more about the concerns of young people in Greece," he tells me, and he asks some questions about surrealism.
> "You know," he continues, "France is now finished, and for a number of years. The Germans have swept away all the books that don't suit them; writing by Jewish authors, etc. (I understand that this etc. means everything.)

"It is up to us, then, to ensure the continuation of a movement like surrealism, for example, born under the aegis of the Italians and the Greeks."

I'm surprised at this strange desire for annexation, in line with his country's political bulimia.

"Yes," he says, "but what can I say? Something has to be done: for my part, I haven't stopped publishing my magazine. I told Mussolini that war was war, but that men of letters have to continue their work."

What to answer back to that?...Then we talk about the bombardment of London. He takes on a lyric accent.

"When I learned that my hatter, Lock & Co., was bombed: all of it vanished, it's strange. People would come from every corner of the world to buy their hats at Lock's. It's the end of the world."

What can this immaculately dressed intellectual, who gave me a Fascist salute upon entering my office, who never ceases to overdo it in his efforts to please, possibly have in mind? He doesn't seem to worry about too much.[166]

The writer even managed to be received by Metaxas, who confessed his enthusiasm for *Technique du coup d'État*, or at least that is what its author claimed. Malaparte showed off in fashionable clubs and restaurants, among spies and informers from the world over, talked too much and with everybody, got himself noticed and attracted the attention of the British and possibly the German intelligence services. Had he also been charged with corrupting Greek generals? This accusation, while persistent, has not been proven. But this is not enough to exonerate him. Malaparte made a point later of not collecting in a book the dispatches sent to the *Corriere*, embellished with digressions on Hellenic civilization, the beauty of certain places, and the habits and customs of the population. He did well: the pages are formulaic and sound false. But the articles in the second series, the ones that were to prepare for the attack, are much worse: they give the impression of a rotten, cowardly country, ready to surrender. Metaxas, perhaps the only sincere admirer Mussolini had left in the world (apart from Hitler, whom at this point he would gladly do without), was presented as a satrap driven by a visceral hatred of Italy, which he was about to attack on English orders. Malaparte describes the Greeks as a feeble, ruined people, incapable of defending themselves against any sort of invader. One detects in certain phrases an unpleasant racial aftertaste, heralding the author of *The Skin*.[167] He revealed his intentions to Borelli, without mincing words:

> Every day these idiotic Greeks become bigger drags. I'll come back with a series of articles not *in mente Dei*, but already written, which will make waves. While I'm here I'll stick to generalities, without alluding to specific things. Under the pretext of literature, I'll pave the way meanwhile for the political articles.[168]

When he finally left, on October 26, Grazzi gave a sigh of relief:

> He'd agreed that as soon as the decision was made, the paper would recall him immediately, so that he would have time to join Ciano before operations began, since he had to be at the side of the latter, who wanted to enter Greece with the gangs. Astonished, I asked: "With the gangs?" Malaparte responded to me: "Yes, with the Albanian gangs." I told him then that to attack Greece would take much

more than Albanian gangs; that war was a serious thing and not a children's game; that Greece was very well prepared and very determined to defend itself, from positions that were extremely favorable to defense, which the ministry, through our reports, should know better than anyone.... I implored him, for the love of country, to make use of his closeness to the minister to tell him to think carefully about what he was about to do, and especially to lose the idea of a campaign against Greece that was so amateurish and so absolutely detached from reality. Malaparte appeared shocked by my words and promised me he would do what was in his power to avoid a disaster.[169]

Unfortunately, there is no proof Malaparte tried to stop or slow the course of events. The documents from the Ministry of Foreign Affairs are silent on the matter. Perhaps, giving him the benefit of the doubt, we can suppose he tried to do something; but certainly not to the point of compromising his relations with Ciano by repeating an unpleasant truth to him. At this point, anyway, there was no more time. Mussolini had already come out in favor of the intervention: the decision to invade Greece was made in a series of meetings at Palazzo Venezia between October 13 and 15. The date set was the dawn of the twenty-eighth, the anniversary of the March on Rome. Before the drama came the melodrama: the company of the Opera di Roma was in Athens for a much-anticipated performance of *Madama Butterfly*, in the presence of the royal family, and obviously of Metaxas and Grazzi, who exchanged forced smiles and courtesies. Returning home, the ambassador found an urgent message to decipher. It was the ultimatum to deliver to the Greek prime minister, demanding immediate authorization for the entry of Italian troops into the country; otherwise, hostilities would commence at six in the morning. Grazzi sadly betook himself to Metaxas, who received him in his nightgown, his hands trembling as he took the message. Having finished reading, however, his voice was firm: "No need to wait. The response is όχι! No!" The two solemnly shook hands and parted ways, never to see each other again. Metaxas died of a heart attack a few months later. It was three in the morning: in Greece this date became, quite legitimately, the national holiday known as the "Day of No."

The original, blitzkrieg-style invasion plan had been prepared by Visconti Prasca, but it was modified by Mussolini and Badoglio without his knowledge, turned into an outdated mass maneuver with poor communications and logistics. Furthermore, the transfer of troops into Albania was interrupted in the days preceding the attack, in order not to prematurely alert the Greeks or the Germans, whom Il Duce wanted to present with a fait accompli. The occupation of the island of Corfu, which was supposed to have happened before the start of operations on the mainland, was postponed as well. In the end, only a portion of the troops requested by Visconti Prasca was actually mobilized. Badoglio unloaded the responsibility for this onto the famous Albanian gangs, "who existed only when it came time to present the bill," and who disappeared at the first shot.[170] No fifth column rose up. As in the June attack on France, no consideration had been given to the weather conditions at sea and on land, which were frightful: early snows on the peaks, mudslides down in the valley, storms on the Adriatic. The Greek army retreated in good order before the first Italian assault toward Epirus, then counterattacked, supported from the air by the RAF and on the ground by six British divisions, repelling the Italian offensive well beyond the frontier. The offensive in Greece quickly turned into a fierce defense of Albania. Visconti Prasca was dismissed, Badoglio hastily replaced with a new chief of the Italian General Staff, General Ugo Cavallero, who imposed the classic Italian "catenaccio," in an effort to cut the country's losses. The war lasted another five long months and was resolved only by the Germans' intervention, for which an enraged and embarrassed Mussolini was ultimately forced to ask. Greece was occupied nominally by Italy, but Hitler demanded and obtained control of the main urban centers (Athens, Thessaloniki, Macedonia) and a part of the island of Crete, while Thrace was annexed to Bulgaria. The strategic objective had not been achieved. The operation, which repeated and exacerbated all the military errors committed in the war of the Alps, cost not six hundred lives, but fourteen thousand. Greece was plunged into occupation and a frightening famine. A friend of Malaparte's, the Italo-Greek Alberto Savinio, brother of Giorgio de Chirico, wrote an anguished allegory, "Hunger in Athens": three pages that would merit, alas, a place in *Kaputt*.

The carelessness with which the campaign in Greece was conducted, even after the initial disaster, did not finish there.[171] On January 12, 1941, Malaparte sent Mondadori a letter concerning the contract for *Il sole è cieco*, in which he wrote: "I'll add that early April (it's no secret) will see the start of our offensive on the Greek front—where all our Alpine troopers are concentrated. In April there will accordingly be much discussion of the Alpine troopers, and my book could not choose a better date to appear in the shop window."[172] But this second offensive was absolutely a military secret! A similar indiscretion would have cost Captain Malaparte a referral to a court-martial in any country at war; the gallows in Germany, the Soviet Union, or Japan. Ciano's ambition to march triumphantly on Athens at the head of his marauding gangs had been dispelled; all he could do, as in Ethiopia, was to vent his spleen in bombing the country. Malaparte left for the front again in February and participated in several sorties. Prior to his departure, he had casually revealed to the anti-Fascist writer Leone Traverso that "I'm heading out Tuesday or Wednesday for a destination that will astonish you, as he astonished me this morning, when he called me himself to tell me. I'm going with Ciano on his air raids, as the rear gunner."[173] Greece's antiaircraft defenses were not first-rate, but visibility was poor due to the bad weather, and there was also the risk of running into an RAF fighter. Returned safe and sound to the ground, Malaparte rejoined his brave Alpine troopers, who got themselves decimated along with their mules in maintaining the defensive line in Albanese territory, only for the survivors to be swallowed up, a year later, on the Russian steppes. The new, sober, factual dispatches he would send from Albania were more honest than those sent three months earlier from the Greek capital. But the harm had been done. It was the darkest page in his activity as an official regime correspondent. He had understood this. He would soon forget.

On Eastern Fronts

The war was going badly and about to go worse. In theory, Fascist Italy had already received a good share of the spoils: "a zone of occupation in metropolitan France later extended to Corsica, southern Slovenia, the western and southern part of Croatia, the Dalmatian coast, Montenegro, a large part of Kosovo, western Macedonia and a part of Greece and its islands," according to one prominent French historian.[174] But that was not enough for Mussolini, who yearned to place himself on an equal footing with his German ally, whom he feared, envied, and hated more each day. His ailments, largely of psychosomatic origin, threatened to lay him low.* He hardly ever showed himself in public any longer and would go red with rage, his ulcer the size of a hot-air balloon, at every piece of bad news. As if he wished to hasten his own ruin, he made two mad decisions, which the Führer had not forced on him and to which he was not held by the terms of the alliance. In June 1941 he declared war on the Soviet Union and in December, after Pearl Harbor, on the United States: two suicides, one not being enough.

For the moment, public opinion spared the ailing Duce a bit, while his son-in-law became the most hated man in the country. Edda was almost as unpopular, even if people recognized her courage. During the Greek campaign she worked as a nurse aboard a steamship that was struck by an English submarine, and she swam to safety. Such feats were not the stuff of Galeazzo, who was reproached, however, with errors not solely his own. Malaparte, too, was besmirched by gossip: apart from the payments to *Prospettive*, there was again talk of the concessions he received for the building of his house on Capri. His very sensitive antennae told him the time had come to distance himself from Galeazzo and his "clan," which he no longer needed anyway. Also, his old adversaries could harm him no more: Balbo was dead, Farinacci marginalized, Starace fired, the party hard-liners and purists increasingly discredited and powerless. His first significant gesture was to devote to Ciano and to the

---

*They were lessened at Salò by the diet suggested to him by the German military doctor Zachariae. At the time of his death, at sixty-two years old, an autopsy would prove that Mussolini did not suffer from any serious illness, and certainly not from syphilis, often attributed to him.

other aviator-minister, Alessandro Pavolini, only a brief comment in his dispatches on the bombardments in Greece, which are instead a glorification, à la Jünger or Mishima, of the young, ascetic, and above all anonymous pilot. Six months earlier, such a move would have been unthinkable. The hour for cutting ties had not yet come, but he could begin to think of a different future, without Ciano. And also perhaps, without Mussolini and without Fascism.

On a human level, such brazen opportunism may seem baffling; but in literary terms, Malaparte stood to gain. The mephitic atmosphere of the Ciano "clan," of which he had filled his lungs in recent years, was no good for him, as either a man or a writer. He had tried to become the chronicler of that world condemned by history, mixing Brantôme, Casanova, Proust, and Moravia, but all this was not his natural territory. There are several versions of an unfinished story, modeled on Radiguet's novel *Le Bal du comte d'Orgel*, entitled "Il ballo del conte Pecci-Blunt."* In it one easily recognizes various members of the "clan": Edda and Galeazzo, Jane di San Faustino, Virginia, Filippo Anfuso, and the princess Cyprienne Del Drago, daughter of the former French ambassador to the Holy See, who had married a close collaborator of the minister's,[†] not to mention the beautiful Swede from the Reich's embassy. He would take up the same topic in a comic play set at the Acquasanta Golf Club on July 26, 1943, *Le*

---

*The story has been published in English as "The Ball of Count Pecci-Blunt," the final entry in Malaparte's *Diary of Foreigner in Paris* (New York: New York Review Books, 2020), 229–38.—Trans.

†This grande dame, who honored me with her friendship until her death, in 2010, spoke till the last with great affection of Galeazzo and Edda. But I never heard her mention Malaparte's name. Her sister, the writer Edmonde Charles-Roux (1920–2016), on the other hand, talked profusely about the charm of Malaparte, who was a regular guest of their father.

illustri fregone (The illustrious kitchen maids), its title drawn from Cervantes's *Exemplary Stories*; but he would have the good sense and good taste to leave it in his desk drawer.[175] The play was on the verge of being staged in Rome in 1950, when Malaparte, realizing that the topic was a thorny one and that the characters were still too recognizable, preferred to avoid a scandal as well as more legal troubles, at a time when he had already had his share. And he did well.

These sketches were not only scandalous; they were bad. If we compare them with the chapter entitled "Golf Handicaps" in *Kaputt*, we register the distance traveled in terms of style, of intensity, and, if you like, of the cruelty of psychological analysis. Revenge of the courtier, who regrets having been part of that environment, without taking it seriously? There is something of that there: as we know, Malaparte never loved losers, *vae victis*. And later he never had a compassionate word for the fate of Ciano, sacrificed by his brother-in-law for reasons of state, or for that of Edda, confined in her turn to Lipari after the war.* Could Mussolini have done otherwise? It was not the Germans who forced him to execute the "traitor," whom he would gladly have spared, but the Salò hard-liners, successors to the Blackshirts, among them Pavolini, a former protégé of Galeazzo's. What remained of Fascism—born of political and social violence—languished in incestuous and tribal violence.

After the Verona court's sentence and Ciano's execution, Malaparte

---

*The countess Anna Teodorani Fabbri, who was very close to her aunt Edda Ciano until her death, affirmed that the latter never spoke to her about Malaparte. The ambassador Loredana Luciolli, who used to accompany her, attested nonetheless that shortly after the war Edda betook herself to Malaparte's on Capri to thank him for having had the royalties for the American edition of Galeazzo's diary paid to her. The meeting was very friendly.

crisply noted in his *Giornale segreto*: "The trial must have been an appalling comedy."[176] That's it. He would return to the topic only once, in an article whose questionable taste has often inspired reproach, dedicated to the "ghost of Galeazzo Ciano," whereas it was his still-warm corpse that should have pricked his conscience. It is a surprising piece of writing, which recalls the episode of his alleged meeting with the assassin of Il Duce, in *Muss*, in which Malaparte cites Freud, and well he might, given what the text reveals, not so much about Ciano as about him. He starts from a piece of postwar crime news, to adapt it for his own use. In the village of Antignano, at the gates of Livorno, at the end of the street leading to Ciano's villa, a detachment of soldiers of color was camped. One of them, blind drunk or out of his wits, wandered through the countryside in a sheet, sowing terror among the farmers. Inhabitants and former partisans gathered to hunt him down. But what if it was instead the ghost of Ciano, unable to find peace? The article closes with a few lines revealing much about their relationship of old:

> But how would I have reacted if I had found myself face to face with Galeazzo's ghost? Killing the dead is easy, especially today, and laudable. Ghosts don't appear for no reason. And so in the moonlit mist, which the leaves of the reeds stained timidly green, I spied a white form, a white face, and in that face shone an indescribable gaze, two eyes full of silver tears. It was the specter of Galeazzo. We remained there for some moments, to look at each other, and perhaps we spoke: I don't know what he said to me, I don't know what I said in reply. I remember his voice was a long, sweet lament, which little by little rose in tone, becoming a shrill cry, a hoarse shout, a horrible cackle. Shouting, he raised his arms, turned, and fled. He ran with

large leaps, like a Negro. And I fled as well. I don't know if Ciano's ghost ran away so as not to compromise himself by being seen in my company, or if he ran away so as not to compromise me with him. Human malice is such that no one would have forgiven me for having had relations with Ciano's ghost."[177]

It was this detachment from the facile illusions of Ciano and his world, combined with the need he had always felt for a change of scene, whenever he caught a whiff of something burning, that drove him to ask to leave again for the front. But if he had already understood that Italy, whatever the outcome of the war, would become merely a satellite in the world of tomorrow, Malaparte did not yet believe the Reich had lost. He had sketched out with Borelli a grand itinerary, "along the ports of the Black Sea, leaving from Romania, passing through the ports of Bulgaria and Turkey, and possibly also some Russian ports."[178] After which, as we have seen, he would go follow the bombing of Greece. Only in spring 1941 would he succeed in obtaining accreditation as a correspondent, in the train of the German troops massing in Romania, in the expectation of an attack on the Soviet Union. With that authorization, his alleged anti-Nazi commitment ceases to have any plausibility. We know *Technique du coup d'État* had been banned in Germany, or at least taken off the market, after the ascent of Hitler. But the files of the German police were well organized, and a known Reich opponent would not have obtained the necessary visas. Moreover, the German embassy in Rome had certainly signaled to Berlin that this was a figure who had previously been sent into *confino* and expelled from the Fascist Party. And yet Malaparte easily procured visas and authorizations. As he had already done with Buzzati in Ethiopia, he got Borelli, with the help of Ciano, to give him the place of Virgilio Lilli, assigned by the *Corriere* to cover the *Feldzug*, the German advance in the Balkans.[179] Finally, it is evident that neither the Nazi governor-general of Poland, Hans Frank, nor the many German officers we discover in the pages of *The Volga Rises in Europe* and *Kaputt* would have welcomed at their table a known enemy of Germany.

Malaparte's movements between Italy and the eastern front from the spring of 1941 to the summer of 1943 were subject to so many revisions on his part that it is very difficult to reconstruct the exact itinerary. We will try to do so, comparing archival documentation with the testimony of Lino Pellegrini, his young colleague from the Fascist daily *Il Popolo d'Italia* and the writer's only travel companion, and with other, more recent discoveries.[180] But first we have to ask ourselves: What, at bottom, is the interest for today's reader in knowing whether Malaparte really participated in all the events he describes? Did this type of polemic not perhaps end with its protagonists, while, eighty years later, what matters is the literary result? Are Malraux's *L'Espoir* (*Man's Hope*), or Hemingway's *For Whom the Bell Tolls*, two books often likened to *Kaputt*, perhaps less "true" because those two great storytellers took part in the Spanish Civil War to a much lesser extent than they let people believe? But rarely as in Malaparte's case does knowing the man and his disguises allow one to appreciate the writer's gifts of invention. He gave us not only an incomparable description of that theater of war, the conflict's most horrible and emblematic; he also knew how to re-create the essence of what he did not see but perceived, in a very personal synthesis, combining historical clear-sightedness and a properly "animal" instinct. In so doing, he succeeded in making us participate in what he himself did not participate in.

At the end of March, Malaparte was in Sofia, Bulgaria. The country, allied with the Axis, was tied to the Italian monarchy, because King Boris III, a German prince of Saxe-Coburg-Gotha, had married one of the daughters of Victor Emmanuel III, Giovanna. Malaparte was a guest of the Italian legation led by the minister Massimo Magistrati, loyal brother-in-law of Ciano. In the *Giornale segreto*, he describes the scene in which "the German marshal Liszt [*sic*, for General List] emerges from the royal palace. The crowd, believing it is King Boris in the car, enthusiastically cheers."[181] A rebellious note? The Bulgarians were anti-Communists, but they remained very grateful to Russia, which had in the second half of the nineteenth century helped liberate them from the Turkish yoke. They thus took a dim view of the war in the east and would refuse to take part in it. Boris, a healthy man in the prime of life, would die two years later of a mysterious illness, possibly poisoned by the Nazis.

In Sofia, Malaparte met up with Pellegrini, who would accompany him in the Balkans and Ukraine. They immediately liked each other but Pellegrini enjoyed some advantages: he spoke German fluently, and his paper's credentials gave him freer access to the German armed forces. After the war, Pellegrini, a keen underwater swimmer, motorist, and mountaineer, would become one of the most popular sports reporters in Italy and a precocious environmentalist. Here is what he told me, a few years before his death, in his Milanese apartment, surrounded by his trophies and memorabilia, cheerful and humble till the end of a long and happy life:

> I frankly didn't know his books or hardly anything about him. He never tried to impress me as I'm told he did with others. As a colleague he was excellent in all respects: loyal, precise, always ready to

share information. Each day we would decide together where to go and how to organize our itinerary. We'd exchange impressions, discuss articles and books, but without confiding anything personal. He almost never brought up his family, his influential friends, his experiences. His only quirk was sleeping in the car we had rented in Romania. He was afraid of attacks, while I spent the night in some peasant hut, and nothing ever happened to me. But in the morning he always looked fresh, impeccable in his *Alpini* uniform. I never saw him unshaven or unkempt. He was fastidious, very careful about his stuff, and also a bit stingy. The only time he lost his temper was when he lost his camera, a late-model Contax. After the war our ways parted, and we hardly met again till on his deathbed. But I am grateful for the way he speaks about me in *Kaputt* as a decent human being among so much filth and horror.[182]

Thanks to the good offices of Magistrati, a former minister-counselor in Berlin, and accompanied by Pellegrini, Malaparte managed to be attached to the German columns entering Romania. This was another country formally allied to the Axis, but Hitler had decided to put his hands on its oil wells, which were indispensable for feeding his war machine. Malaparte, perhaps to pay for his trip and to demonstrate his zeal to the Germans, sent the *Corriere* ecstatic dispatches on the Wehrmacht on the march. Here is the epitome of the invincible soldier:

What strikes us, what astounds us in such a formidable army is not the appearance of strength, of its irresistible attacking power; but rather the marvelous attention to detail, the meticulous functioning of every element—down to the smallest, down to the most insignificant—of this enormous, gigantic mass of steel.... The entire column starts shouting: "Heil Hitler! Heil Fleischmann!" It's Fleischmann, the popular German motorcycle champion, divisional courier for the army corps that is marching on Belgrade. He's a lean young man, not very tall, with that gray-blond hair that conceals the years, but makes exhaustion seem sweeter, the severe cut of his jaw and the cold flash of his clear eyes more delicate. Covered in mud up to his ears, he removes a layer with an open hand. His rosy face appears lit up by that particular sweetness that fatigue, effort, and the supreme tension of will spread to the features of champions at the finish line.[183]

After the war, Malaparte would try to forget these texts, and have others do the same. In reality, they do not seem more compromising than what other Italian correspondents wrote and published at the time. But they are the source of another postwar polemic, according to which the writer was well compensated for his articles in German publications, particularly *Signal*, the armed forces' magazine, which appeared in several languages. But to what extent was this the result of a choice of his, rather than the consequence of exchanges between the Axis countries' propaganda offices? Borelli had authorized him to "send a few articles to a few foreign magazines or newspapers," underlining with his pen, however, the first "few."[184] These first dispatches were well received, in Rome as in Berlin. Malaparte boasted that the newspaper increased its sales by fifty thousand copies whenever his byline appeared. What is certain is that his compensation rose to two thousand lire per article, the Milanese paper's highest for a correspondent during wartime; Buzzati, for example, another of the top correspondents of the *Corriere*, received much less, but he could also count on a regular salary from the paper.[185]

Yet Malaparte's greatest satisfaction was of a professional nature: things were moving. Hitler was set on attacking the Soviet Union, ever since the failed visit of the foreign minister Molotov to Berlin in November 1940; but he was careful not to communicate this to Mussolini, and above all to Ciano, whom the Germans no longer trusted. Meanwhile, the Führer had obliged all the Danubian and Balkan states to enter the Tripartite Pact, directed against the Soviet Union, which already bound Germany, Italy, and Japan. One by one, Hungary, Romania, Slovakia, Bulgaria, and Yugoslavia fell into line. Croatia was the last to adhere to the pact, two weeks after the launch of Operation Barbarossa. Hitler had thus established the foundations for a true anti-Bolshevik crusade; but it was not at all certain that he hoped for Italian participation in the attack as well. Yet Il Duce could not accept, after the humiliations already experienced, missing out on the conflict's most important test. He too was attracted by the imagined spoils (grain, oil, steel), but what drew him above all was the mirage of political grandeur. His generals, who saw the abyss opening up before their country, pleaded in vain with him to turn back. Was it not Mussolini himself, fascinated by Soviet power, who had often spoken of the need to come to an understanding with Stalin for dividing up the world? Nothing doing: overwhelmed by fatalism, demonstrating the extent to which his faculties were compromised at less than sixty years old, he bet everything, as in June 1940, on German victory.

What had become of his political skills: intuition, instinct, speed? When Il Duce read a document placed before him—up to several hundred a day, on a wide variety of topics—he would generally mark it with his distinctive "M," in red or blue pencil. This enormous bureaucratic burden, of which he was proud (calling himself the "ox" or "workhorse" of Italy), often had the consequence of paralyzing the nation as it waited for his decisions, a situation that worsened, if possible, during the war. We do not know if Mussolini used his red and blue pencils to underline passages in Malaparte's articles. But it is certain that he avidly read everything, in the Italian press and in the international agencies, that intimately or remotely concerned the German advance and the fate of the countries occupied by the Reich. The increasingly worrying reports that reached him from the Italian military and diplomatic missions described the implementation of a regime of terror, the systematic elimination or deportation of Jews, Gypsies, "inferior" races. In France, after the first actions of the Resistance, the "gentlemanly" occupying regime was already starting to show its true face. Wherever the swastika flew, armed opposition to the Third Reich grew by the day.

But the attitude of the local populations toward Italian troops was generally quite different. In Poland, Italians had helped to evacuate citizens with a semblance of familial or residential ties to the peninsula, and often also those who had none at all. In France, the tiny Italian occupation zone around Menton, where the provisions were also better than in the rest of the country, had become an oasis for Jews and victims of persecution of every stripe in flight from Vichy or the enormous German occupation zone. In Greece, the survival of the famine-stricken countryside often depended on the food distributed by Italian troops, who, vilified in 1940, were now blessed by priests and respected by the partisans of Epirus.* In Berlin there was indignation at this strange "parallel war," and Hitler had

---

*Only in Yugoslavia did antipartisan repression take on particularly brutal aspects.

to personally calm the fury of his acolytes. Mussolini, after having long disapproved of these weaknesses of national temperament, which impeded his transformation of Italians into pitiless Nordic warriors, now spied an advantage here. Under the German boot, the populations of the southern Danube, the Balkans, and Christian Ukraine would naturally turn to the Italians—that is, to him. This would save him from the detestable role of the Führer's southern gauleiter and give him the leeway politically he lacked militarily. Underlying this apparently logical calculation was the certainty of German triumph, fed by the rumors circulating about Hitler's "secret weapons."

The occupation of Yugoslavia provided further confirmation. King Alexander I had been killed in 1934 in Marseille, along with the French minister of foreign affairs Louis Barthou, by Croatian extremists, the Ustaše, financed by Rome and Berlin. His son Peter was too young to ascend to the throne, and the regency council was headed by Alexander's cousin, Prince Paul, who had continued the authoritarian but pro-Western line of the late sovereign. Nevertheless, under German pressure, Paul eventually joined the Tripartite Pact, in late March 1941. After which, an attempted coup d'état by the military, supported by British intelligence, provoked the intervention of the Wehrmacht, on April 6, and the bombardment of Belgrade. It was the so-called Operation 25, entrusted to the general Wilhelm List, mentioned earlier, which led to the conquest of Yugoslavia and Greece, joined by the Italian Second Army's offensive on the Dalmatian coast. At the time Malaparte found himself in Bucharest, at the Athénée Palace hotel, which inspired in him a remembrance of the Europe of "wagons-lits," dear to the bards of the last great European season straddling the Great War, from Stefan Zweig to Paul Morand, Valery Larbaud to the count Harry Kessler. But compared with them, Malaparte once again stands out for his detachment and lack of nostalgia:

> To see how this class is disappearing, to see what progress is being made in the Europe of 1941 by the slow and now rapid decline of the class called liberal (and it was a race, a blood, not only a social class), you needn't go to Paris, or Madrid, or Geneva. You need to come here.[186]

Borelli then tried to send him among the Croatian Ustaše, but without success. Malaparte had already launched himself on Belgrade, where he claims to have entered with the German troops, while "no other Italian or foreign journalist, and no German, had so far been able to set foot there."[187] Did it really happen like that? Let's look at the dates. The Germans occupied the Yugoslavian capital on the night between April 12 and 13. Malaparte's first dispatch, with a dateline of the seventeenth, was transmitted on the nineteenth, from Timișoara, in Romania, to which he had returned from Belgrade along with the Italian consul, before leaving for Bucharest and his dear Athénée Palace by the twenty-third at the latest... The fact remains that they are some of his best pieces to date, a true prelude, in terms of style and atmosphere, to *The Volga Rises in Europe* and *Kaputt*. Whether he is describing the gangs of looters who sneaked into the ruins, or "the desk thrown onto the tram tracks by an explosion, [in which] there was the register of the war council's confidential expenses"; evoking a street corner in the historic center, or "that Turkish patisserie, famous throughout the Balkans for its aphrodisiac sweets, [of which] there remains nothing but a jumble of charred debris," he seems as if he had spent years in

Belgrade, and not days or hours. Even allowing for an inevitable measure of fabulation, this is great journalism, in which the particular illuminates the whole and a predilection for the unusual and the grotesque does not hurt the story's realism. The photographs accompanying his pieces have this strength as well, so much so that, as with those of Africa, it was not possible to publish them.[188]

Yugoslavia was reduced to a puppet state, under German control. Croatia, fiercely anti-Serb, obtained its independence, under the reign of a prince of the House of Savoy, Aimone d'Aosta, Duke of Spoleto, who was careful not to go there to be crowned King Tomislav II. The real power was in the hands of the Ustaše *Poglavnik*, Ante Pavelić, one of those responsible for the assassination of King Alexander, a terrorist who had long been financed and protected by the Italians, but who was passing quickly into the service of the Germans. Malaparte was constantly on the move, and his abrupt displacements become increasingly hard to follow. Here is his itinerary in early May: Budapest, Zagreb, Novi Sad, along the Danube–Sava river route carrying grain and oil, which the German sappers and bridge builders were restoring after the previous month's bombardments. He took advantage of it to deliver a lecture, on May 12, at the Italian Cultural Institute in the Croatian capital, Zagreb: "New State, New Literature." The title can seem puzzling today; regrettably, the text has not come to light. Probably, as he often did, he spoke off the cuff, on the basis of notes. Malaparte was present in Monfalcone on the twentieth for the meeting between Il Duce and Pavelić, whose "face lit up with an extraordinarily intense and pure smile" at the sight of Mussolini.[189] If we think about the description of this sinister character who would appear in *Kaputt*, we can measure the degree of doubling achievable by the journalist

Malaparte. To take a break from current politics, he translated for *Prospettive* a long poem by Pierre Jean Jouve inspired by Tasso, *Le Combat de Tancrède et Clorinde* (*The Combat of Tancredi and Clorinda*).* As in his versions of Emily Dickinson and of Paul Éluard, Malaparte shows himself a better translator than poet. But this truce in the lap of the Muses is brief. In a June 20 message to the newspaper sent from the Athénée Palace in Bucharest, become his headquarters between missions, he affirms that "the Russian thing is imminent." The borders were about to close.

On June 23, a new message: "I'm leaving and will return tomorrow evening, to call in another piece."[190] As a matter of fact, he sent a series of dispatches from Moldavia, on the Russian frontier that the German and Romanian troops had just crossed, in which he describes the first deaths and the first prisoners of the Red Army to fall into German hands. It was a short trip, inversely proportional to the quantity of material he drew from it. When Borelli ordered him to specify his exact itinerary, he had to confess, peevishly: "The locations recalled in the article I'm transmitting this evening by telephone are included in the territory already announced as occupied in the [military] bulletin. I remained at the front for four days. I returned this evening dead tired. Since I went with the correspondent for *Il Popolo d'Italia*, we agreed the articles should appear on the same day."[191] This means he had to wait a week before joining the German troops on the march, around July 3–4.† At this point he gives his coordinates in Iași, then written in the French manner

---

*To be precise, Jouve was inspired to write the poem after hearing the madrigal that Monteverdi had based on canto XII of *Gerusalemme liberata* (*Jerusalem Delivered*).

†Which matches up with Pellegrini's recollections and testimony to the author.

as Jassy, a Romanian city eleven miles from the Prut River, which marked the border with the Soviet Union. He would stay there for approximately ten days. But he would not be present for the pogrom against the city's Jews,[192] which would kill roughly twelve thousand people, described in one of the most striking episodes of *Kaputt*.[193] He was drawn toward a new goal: Bessarabia and Ukraine. Still flanked by Pellegrini, he entered the region on July 18,[194] aboard an old Ford V8, behind a motorized column of the Wehrmacht, part of the Eleventh Army, under the command of the general Eugen von Schobert, who would fall two months later in combat. And he continued to date his dispatches from Ukraine for a month, whereas his service notes show that no later than the seventh he was back in Bucharest, from where, on the twelfth, he left again for Italy.[195] The Ford gave up the ghost; he and his companion returned to base, less triumphantly, on a German truck. Which doesn't mean that, as usual, Malaparte had not demonstrated courage. As Pellegrini recounts:

> Once, steps away from us, a German battalion opened fire, which I wasn't expecting; instinctively, I bent down; Malaparte remained upright, then rebuked me. In Jassy, under the Soviet bombardments, I remained awake; he managed to sleep.[196]

So far, we are dealing simply with some liberties taken in terms of dates, which does not prevent us from appreciating the content of his always-fascinating articles. But the best was yet to come. In his 1946 statement of defense, he claims to have been arrested by the Gestapo in the village of Pestchanka in Ukraine, "accused of propaganda in favor of the enemy," expelled and delivered to the

Italian police. (The Germans, on this occasion, could not confiscate the partial manuscript of *Kaputt*, because a Romanian—or Ukrainian, or Russian—peasant had sewn it into the lining of his fur coat.)* Why, then, is there no official record of his arrest? Because "my arrest by the Germans was kept secret, as a matter of prestige involving the Fascist government and the Italian high command,"[197] he would claim at the time of the purge. Convenient! Back in Rome, according to Malaparte, he was sent before a disciplinary commission presided over by the new minister of popular culture, Pavolini, forbidden any journalistic activity for four months, and sent again into *confino*... in his unfinished house on Capri, until early January 1942.[198]

Does this reconstruction hold up? Not so much. In Berlin, certain indirect compliments by Malaparte about the Red Army undoubtedly raised some bushy Teutonic eyebrows. Pavolini sent a confidential note to Il Duce to draw his attention to the fact that Malaparte's dispatches were not "always on pitch" and contained "claims that contrasted with the German war bulletins."[199] But as usual, Mussolini let it be, and the arrest in Ukraine was pure invention, whereas the alleged disciplinary proceeding in Rome was in all likelihood an angry outburst by Pavolini without consequences. Aside from the testimony of his companion Pellegrini, which is categorical here as well, †we must refer to the dates. The last dispatch

---

*To add credibility to this story—which was greeted by the ninety-five-year-old but perfectly lucid Pellegrini with healthy laughter when I mentioned it—he even invented the name of the peasant, Roman Suchena.

†"Starting with the commander von Schobert, a very decent man, all the German officers gave us their full cooperation. Their radio transmitted our dispatches without any prior restraint," Pellegrini repeated to me when I made him aware of the documents concerning this episode.

was published the same day as his return: expelled, punished, or simply "back on leave," as he wrote candidly to the supplier of a shipment of wood.[200] But Borelli flew off the handle because he thought he was still in Ukraine, from where he continued to date his dispatches, and not on Capri! It was at this point that MinCulPop officials intervened, probably on Pavolini's initiative, to prohibit the newspaper from publishing other "pseudo-dispatches" from a Malaparte no longer in situ. It was not censorship of contents, then, but a measure of ethical obligation, limited in any case, seeing as how the *Corriere* was left free to publish other articles and features by Malaparte, provided they did not make reference to a war of which he was no longer an eyewitness.[201]

At the end of the summer, the allegedly *confinato* Malaparte left Capri without the least obstacle, to go to Rome. He immediately took back from Moravia the reins of *Prospettive*—which was *also* a journalistic activity—and stayed long enough to wrap up two or three (excellent) double issues. The considerable correspondence with contributors to the magazine attests that he spent the fall in his office, even as he announced his imminent return to Russia. I found an unpublished text from June 1942 in which he meticulously reconstructs his movements at the front, but he is careful not to mention his supposed arrest by the Germans and the so-called disciplinary proceeding opened against him at the Ministry.[202] And so? The key to the affair is revealed in a letter to his brother Sandro:

> I have no desire to return to Russia, it's too cold, and then it doesn't seem like things are moving quickly. In fact, yesterday the German communiqué declared that, with the arrival of winter, operations for the siege of Moscow will be postponed until the right season. So

I won't be able to enter Moscow; and the aim of my trip is precisely to describe the fall of Moscow. I phoned Borelli, begging him to reconsider, and Borelli has to give me an answer this evening. Which may also be that the *Corriere* authorizes me to postpone the trip until the season is right.[203]

Here, then, is the real reason behind Malaparte's return to Italy. After spending six months in the Balkans and Ukraine, he simply wanted a rest break to look after his two babies: the almost finished Capri house and the magazine, without forgetting his dog Febo, about whom he continued anxiously to ask for news. This is when, probably, he began to write *Kaputt*, bringing some order to the notes he had brought back—sewn into a coat or not—from his trip, waiting for the right moment to leave again, to make his entry into Moscow.

On December 11, Borelli sent him a new contract and ordered him to return to Russia at the end of the year, adding, to avoid any confusion: "It is understood that the articles must be written not from Berlin or Warsaw but from the Moscow front; otherwise they would not have the character that justifies the exceptional nature of the terms we've set for you."[204] This proves, by the way, that there was no German objection to the trip at the time; otherwise the editor in chief of the newspaper would have learned about it from the Ministry of Popular Culture, since every correspondent had to request the necessary visas for abroad through ministry officials. Thus Malaparte obtained, without the least difficulty, the renewal of his passport for Croatia, Hungary, Romania, and ... Germany.[205] A singular kindness to a sworn enemy of the Reich, unless, naturally, the Gestapo was hoping Malaparte would lead them straight to Stalin's lair! But the letter is of interest for another reason: by the terms of the generous agreement, Malaparte earned not only two thousand lire for every article published, but also a thousand lire "for every article that cannot be published for reasons independent of you." Borelli knew in advance, then, that certain dispatches from his correspondent on the eastern front risked being cut by not just German but also Italian censors. It is odd that Malaparte, always ready to invoke his anti-Fascist merits after the war, did not recall this circumstance that showed he was already suspected of some pro-Soviet sentiment. Odd, but in line with his character.

In any event, he finally set off on January 6, after having signed the usual second contract, this time for articles accompanied by photographs, for *Tempo*. His goal was no longer Moscow; he had decided to follow the siege—and fall—of Leningrad, from the Finnish border. As he explained in a new letter to Sandro:

> I believe and hope I will not stop long in Smolensk, where things are rather uncertain, and I don't really want to risk my skin with the frightful cold and hardships in such a place. So, after Smolensk, I will go to Sweden, and from there to Finland, to go up Finland as far as Petsamo, beyond the Arctic polar circle, to see and describe the war in the polar night. It's an enormous, difficult trip, with atrocious hardships. It seems to me I should finish up in two months, also because one can't hold out too long up there. By the end of March I plan already to be on my way back.[206]

Was Borelli aware of this revised itinerary? As usual, he ranted and raved but surrendered in the end, pleading with his most capricious correspondent "not to get any crazy ideas about changing sectors."[207] But such commands were of little use with Malaparte. His working method, by now well established, consisted in relatively brief stays followed by long periods of elaboration or "digestion." Can he be criticized for it on a professional level? The proof is in the pudding, as they say, and Malaparte's had never been as good. His power of assimilation was such that in the end it hardly mattered whether he remained on site for months, weeks, or simply a few days. Exhibit A: he was among the first to understand that Moscow would not fall.

As the expert "chameleon" that he was, Malaparte managed to slip beneath all the masks: attesting to this was his *Giornale segreto*, which he had kept erratically for years, but in 1942–43 it became less schematic. He announced as much upon his arrival in Berlin, the first stop in his journey, on January 10–11, 1942: "After a long time I've started writing again, each evening, in my 'journal.' An old custom of writers of civilized times, which should not be lost."[208] He sounds like Captain Jünger in his Parisian hotel room, or in his bunker on the eastern front... But whereas Jünger observes, savors, patiently dissects down to the least detail, Malaparte excels once again in the art of composition. In clashing tones, with continually new images, he manipulates a flow of life (and death) wherein each element—a soldier's helmet, a horse's mane, the leaves of a dwarf birch—tellingly reflects the whole and is reflected in it. The comparison that comes immediately to mind is with Goya's Black Paintings, or Géricault's *The Raft of the Medusa*. But there are also literary equivalents to the great fresco of *The Volga Rises in Europe*, starting with the novel by Boris Pilnyak about Soviet industrialization, *The Volga Flows into the Caspian Sea*, unpublished in Italy until after the war, but discovered by Malaparte in French translation in Paris, in

1931.* Initially, he had thought of a more direct title, à la Eisenstein, "La Guerra e lo sciopero," which would be forbidden by the Fascist censors, but which he would preserve for the first part of the work (a title rendered as "War and the Strike Weapon" in David Moore's translation). The double issue of *Prospettive* (40–41) entitled "Guerra e sciopero" (War and strike), with its blood-red cover and "military dispatches" from D'Annunzio, Apollinaire, Guynemer, Barbusse, and Carco, would appear only in December 1951. Did that constitute, with eight or nine years of distance, the complete text, as it was written then? Doubts remain. In any case, the final title of the book, clearly inspired by Pilnyak's, announced the immense spoils the war would bring to the Soviet Union, transforming it into a genuine European superpower.

Malaparte was welcomed in Berlin by an old acquaintance, the former undersecretary of state for propaganda Dino Alfieri, now the colorless ambassador of an Italy fatally hitched to the German train. Alfieri had taken the place of Bernardo Attolico, who had fought strenuously alongside Ciano to keep the country out of the conflict, to the point of infuriating Hitler. In the German capital, Malaparte saw a number of people, among them Arnoldo Mondadori, whom he accompanied on his business meetings with German publishing houses, like the highly official Deutscher Verlag. But on January 22 he was already in Kraków, then in Warsaw, then in Zakopane. This tour of occupied, brutalized Poland, reduced administratively to a Nazi "Generalgouvernement," ended on February 10,

---

*Except by accident, he never cited it. Conversely, in a dispatch from the Leningrad front, he mentions Pilnyak's first novel, about the Russian Revolution, *The Naked Year*, which he probably knew in its 1926 French translation.

with his return to Berlin, still in the company of his Nazi "guardian angel," a certain Stockmann, or Stöckmann, or Stokman (the casualness with which Malaparte took down names is well known), no doubt a tougher character than the good inspector Conte was in Ethiopia. From Poland, Malaparte sent the *Corriere* dispatches that would be published with a slight delay, the last one on February 22. He never included them in their complete form in his books, because they are very ambiguous. At first glance they give the impression of glorifying German efforts to restore the dignity of the Polish people and, especially, of the Polish worker, which is rather bewildering if one thinks of the terror gripping that unfortunate country under German control.[209] On the political level, Malaparte took up an idea that Mussolini had presented to Hitler as early as January 1940: the need to reconstruct an embryonic Polish state to oppose the Russians (but between the lines, also to contain the Reich). This time the Germans were on alert and reacted. These claims worried the bureaucrats in the Ministry of Popular Culture, who could not figure out anything better than to ask the opinion of the press advisor of the German embassy in Rome.[210] Meanwhile, the Italian high command heard from the German military authorities that

> Malaparte is currently held up under the pretext that no decisive events are expected [at the front]. In reality, [he is an] unwelcome element, because he has maintained in his writings an attitude contrary to National Socialism and, among other things, praised the efficiency and organization of the Russian army in his earlier articles.[211]

His journey east was abruptly interrupted. From Poland, Malaparte was sent back to Berlin in mid-February 1942, still flanked by his guardian angel. Thus he did not manage to push as far as the Russian "Nebenland," the Soviet territories occupied by the Germans. But everything unfolded in the proper manner: Malaparte was still treated as a major correspondent from an allied country and a favored guest of the Reich. With evident relief, the Ministry of Popular Culture could respond to the high command that "the matter can be considered moot, since he has already proceeded north"; that is, to Finland.[212] But another diplomatic incident erupted a month later, when Berlin became aware of the last article in his Polish series, chronicling the evening at the residence of Governor-General Frank, whose publication had been deferred to March 22. Here too we can wonder if it was not Mussolini himself, to whom all the thorniest texts had been submitted in advance, who had decided in favor of publication. The article is striking, because truly *everything* is said between the lines. On the surface it is an exaltation of this brownshirted condottiero; but Malaparte's pen has already, imperceptibly, traced the demonic features of the character we will discover again in *Kaputt*:

> A delicate, strong face, illuminated by an intelligence and a sensibility that bring out the rueful fold of his lips and the play of his heavy, lively eyelids. It is not perhaps what one would call a Gothic visage, but rather an Italian Renaissance face, maybe Florentine, maybe Venetian. There is Gothic in him as well, and it is in the color of his forehead, in that long face of his, in that rueful expression of his mouth. He spoke to me in a low voice in perfect Italian, with a kind of abandon. And he rested from the day of intense work.[213]

That's not all. He adds that Frank's "is not a policy of force but of balance, very intelligent, absolutely modern in character," relying on the "proletariat, and more on the working class than on the peasant masses," and not on the old feudal classes, because "the future of the Polish people" belongs to the proletariat; an example that could be pursued, on a much larger scale, in the "future organization of the Russian territories, of this other 'Nebenland'"! It is here truly that the Nazis, and Frank above all, feeling themselves unmasked, understood that Malaparte could hurt them. The new lords of the thousand-year Reich did not have the least desire to bring socialism to their inferior-race slaves. Their reaction this time was swift and direct: the Reich's Ministry of Foreign Affairs complained to the Italian authorities about "a vision too close to the Polish point of view."[214] They also demanded that the writer offer Frank a formal apology, of which, however, no trace has been found. It is truly remarkable that Malaparte never later laid claim to this lack of confidence in him on the part of the Nazis, instead fussing over implausible persecutions by Hitler himself, which evidently was more flattering to his ego. In any case, the incident represented only a relative inconvenience for him, since at the time Malaparte was already in Finland, following his alternative itinerary, from which to cover operations for the capture of Leningrad. When, some months later, two other Italian correspondents, Lamberti Sorrentino and Alberto Mondadori from *Tempo*, managed to travel to Warsaw in his place, it would be too late.[215] Malaparte had once again preempted everyone.

Finnish Interlude

Finland was not only the strategic observatory he had chosen for himself but a land seemingly made expressly to seduce Malaparte. The majestic indifference of nature was the best answer, in his eyes, to the follies of history. The snow, the forests, and the lakes of Finland reminded him of the Alpine glaciers, and at the same time of the marine grottoes of Capri; that is, the two places he loved most in the world. But it was not only Finland's landscape that attracted him; he also admired its men and institutions. Upon his arrival in Helsinki, on February 21, 1942, meeting the press and the Ministry of Foreign Affairs officials there to welcome him, he publicly praised this "free Protestant country," dusting off his paternal religion for the occasion. And the Finns, too, seem to have all in all preserved quite a positive memory of this "Baron Munchausen in the land of the white ogres."[216]

A month after his arrival, though, he was struck by the greatest sorrow in his life, at least as he described it in a letter to Guglielmo Rulli:

> When I left, Febo was not feeling well, but nothing suggested anything so violent and sudden. Febo started to do poorly when I started traveling, to stay away for three, four, or five months. Perhaps I deceive myself, but I believe Febo died because of my leaving. This is also what Eolo, Febo's brother, did. And so I feel tremendous remorse, the first time in my life I feel myself under such a deep and sorrowful emotional responsibility. For me Febo was the dearest of brothers, friends, lovers. There has never been anyone in my life, no one, who had or has a place like Febo's.... Do you know I'm afraid to return to Capri? To arrive and no longer find him there, to know he's out there, in the water in the cold. Alas, and yet what more did I ask for? I asked for so little! Febo was enough for me.[217]

The hyperbole of these lines may surprise, even irritate. And Malaparte certainly never wrote anything similar about any human being, much less about a woman. Let the reader draw what consequences they see fit. In any event, he survived the shock. In Finland, Malaparte discovered the sauna and the pleasure of rolling naked in the snow: there was nothing better, for a narcissist like him, than to expose himself in a context from which sex is strictly excluded. Nevertheless, a few ailments, a few signs of his age, did show. On September 2, 1942, he was operated on at the Eira Clinic in Helsinki for a long-neglected appendicitis. And there, Indro Montanelli—another character whose claims ought to be taken with more than a grain of salt—declared archly to have seen him "stretched out on his bed in a bathing suit and in a pose somewhere between Madame Récamier and a weary gladiator, under a cascade of flowers and telegrams."[218]

As soon as he recovered, he went for a few days of rest in Stockholm, another capital that he liked and that would inspire the first pages of *Kaputt*, maybe the only ones in the whole book distinguished by an atmosphere of peace and serenity.[219] He had no intention, however, of burying himself in the far north: his letters and the *Giornale segreto* indicate he was in Rome and on Capri at least from early May 1942 to mid-February 1943 (except for a return to Finland from late July to late September) and from April to June 1943, with another brief, few-weeks Finnish stay. The *Corriere* resigned itself in this period to putting out his dispatches, dated from that front. Which shows how little effect Borelli's threats and various official warnings had on him. In total he would spend approximately five months in Finland, rather than the two years he declares in *Kaputt*.[220] And his stays were carefully monitored by Finnish military intelligence, which checked his correspondence and recorded his telephone conversations, particularly with the editor in chief of the *Corriere*.[221]

This gave rise to a few mishaps, because Malaparte, forced to disclose his collaboration with *Signal* on the form he filled out on arrival, quickly gained a reputation as pro-German. Now, if it is true the Finns were allies of convenience of the Germans, it was also true they distrusted Hitler's invasion plans, fearing that sooner or later such plans could be turned against them. Thus Malaparte had his first request to travel to Karelia refused outright. In the end it was granted: in his account, following an intervention by Marshal Mannerheim, whom he had met in Warsaw twenty years earlier; more likely and more modestly, thanks to the official charged with guiding and surveilling him, Captain Jaakko Leppo, who would later state he found his Italian interlocutor pleasant and ... innocuous.

In Helsinki, at the Hotel Torni, Malaparte met up again with Pellegrini, who had preceded him there and was now briefly joined by his wife, Elena, a beautiful young actress who would later become his trusted companion in their sports and nature reportages throughout the world:

> Our rooms were on different floors, one over the other, him in 213, my wife and I in 313. We would part ways right after dinner. He went to bed early. He was very reserved. Sober, almost ascetic: he ate in moderation, and just about the only time he smoked or drank was for show, when he was being photographed. He could also be a bit of an old maid. Once he got mad because my wife and I got a little excited and made too much noise. I had to apologize the next morning. He said to me, "Every time you go with a woman is one day less in your life." I never saw him courting a woman; he was gallant sometimes with my wife, but nothing more.[222]

All Europe had admired the resistance of the Finnish David against the Soviet Goliath in the "Winter War" of 1939–40. The conflict ended with Finland's defeat, formalized by the Moscow Peace Treaty of March 1940, but it represented a great moral victory for the rights of peoples over totalitarianism and the spirit of conquest. A year and a half later, the Finns, riding the wave of German victories, went on the attack in the "Continuation War" (1941–44), which saw them initially reconquer the region of Karelia-Ladoga. Malaparte wrote enthusiastically to his Italian friends that "before me, no one had ever obtained permission for that front. I spent several days exactly ten miles away from the Winter Palace [of Leningrad]."[223] Among the *sissi*, the intrepid skiers of the Finnish White Army, who continually harassed the Red Army divisions, he rediscovered the brotherhood of the Alpine troops.

But the Russians held on, and Malaparte, always impatient, began to doubt he would be there for the city's capture: "I haven't sent so much as a line to the *Corriere*, so far," he wrote to Rulli, "but there's nothing to say, waiting for Leningrad to fall. And I'm fed up with waiting. All the more so since, if it doesn't fall, they're liable to blame me. And I don't want the responsibility."[224] So he changed his itinerary. The *Giornale segreto* indicates that Malaparte arrived in Rovaniemi, the capital of Lapponia, a little over six miles south of the polar circle, and pushed on as far as Inari, where the Germans had constructed a forward line of defense. From there he would send other magnificent dispatches, on "modern warfare transposed to the reindeer age." Had he really managed to arrive at the far northern front, as far as Petsamo and the "frozen sea" controlled by the Bavarian *Gebirgsjäger* of General Eduard Dietl, the hero of Narvik, and to the Murmansk sector, commanded by another of the best leaders of mountain troops, General Georg Ritter von Hengl? The testimony of Pellegrini, who firmly denied it,* has been confirmed by Finnish researchers.²²⁵ At the end of 1944, the Red Army would, at the cost of extremely heavy losses, successfully occupy the Petsamo region, which would be definitively annexed to Russia with the Paris Peace Treaty of February 1947.

What Malaparte, like every war correspondent, had reason to complain about was the censorship. Previously, his dispatches from Ethiopia, and even the encomiastic ones from Greece, were often subject to cuts. He protested each time, but since his articles were generally transmitted via radio by the legation or by the closest Italian consulate, or else by the Wehrmacht's flying transceivers, the text landed in the hands of the censor even before it reached the newspaper, where in any case the editor in chief and the section chief were subjected to draconian laws. But after the start of operations in the east, the situation worsened, so that at times the articles' content and meaning were distorted. The most serious case, and the one that would have damaged him the most, was that of a dispatch published by the *Corriere* on July 5, 1941, about the Russian attack on the small Romanian city mentioned earlier, titled "In Jassy, martorizzata dal tradimento ebraico" (In Jassy, tormented by the Jewish betrayal).²²⁶ The reaction of the interested party, already conscious perhaps that this hateful title would haunt him for a long time, was furious but in vain, as described in a memorandum from the Bucharest bureau to Borelli:

---

*"He let readers believe he had reached the front line on the Lapponia front, whereas he had stopped at Rovaniemi. I was there and still have the photographs to prove it" (testimony of Lino Pellegrini to the author). According to a written statement given to him by General Hengl, Pellegrini was indeed the only Italian correspondent present in that sector of operations.

Malaparte says he has ascertained that his article on an episode in Jassy was cruelly edited down and that the title conflicts with the content. Indeed it does not correspond with either factual reality or the spirit of the article, much less with Malaparte's professional honesty. He adds that it is pointless to have a special correspondent at the front if then one publishes information from Berlin affirming the opposite of what he affirms.[227]

Malaparte nevertheless sought to turn the situation to his advantage after the war, declaring in his preface to the 1951 Aria d'Italia edition of *The Volga Rises in Europe* that his dispatches had been censored, cut down, and modified without his knowledge, and that only now had he succeeded finally in establishing the complete text. Which is not very plausible, but two fortuitous circumstances had come to his assistance. A first Allied bombardment pulverized most of the *Corriere* archives, and the original dispatches from Malaparte and the newspaper's other correspondents from various war fronts disappeared in the blaze. A second bombardment struck the warehouse of the publisher Bompiani, in February 1943, destroying all copies of the book's first edition, already printed but not yet distributed. Bompiani had preserved a copy of the proofs and promised Malaparte a reprinting, which, however, due to events connected to July 25 and then to the German occupation, appeared only in late 1943. It is still possible to find on the antiquarian book market a few, highly priced copies of this second edition, which had been immediately impounded by the police of Salò. It is worth clarifying that this measure was not provoked—contrary to what Malaparte would later claim—by the work's pro-Soviet and anti-Fascist content, but solely by the fact that Malaparte was wanted by the Italian Social

Republic as a supporter of the "Kingdom of the South," as we will see in the next chapter.[228]

To analyze this book, which occupies a central place in his oeuvre, we thus find before us not two versions, as in the case of *Don Camaleo* or *Il sole è cieco*, but indeed three: the original articles, the 1943 edition—which was the basis for the first translations, including into French, in 1948—and the definitive edition of 1951. But since the texts sent by Malaparte to the *Corriere* are no longer available, we can compare only the versions published by the paper—after the interventions of the censors—with those the writer presented as original. For the French edition he wrote an important preface— *not* included in the Italian edition of 1951—in which he forcefully asserted that the Soviet Union was for all practical purposes the continuation of imperial Russia, and thus an integral part of Europe and of the postwar rebirth of the old continent. Indeed, the preface was titled, in a very allusive way, "Why the Volga Is a European River and Why the Seine, the Thames, and the Tiber (along with the Potomac) Are Its Tributaries." The text expands on the point to considerations we can call prophetic, in the incipient Cold War climate:

> We must remember this truth, on the eve of the great struggle that could end with the collapse of Soviet Russia. Because many people abandon themselves to the very simplistic prejudice that the war against Soviet Russia, yesterday's and tomorrow's, is simply Europe's struggle against Asia, against Asiatic ideologies. It is against European ideologies that Germany fought yesterday in its war against the USSR; it is against European ideologies that America will fight tomorrow, in its inevitable war against the other Europe.[229]

The variations from one edition to the other have by now been carefully established.[230] Any specialist, if not any reader, can judge whether the content changes in any essential way. The modifications are on the whole quite subtle. After extensive practice in self-censorship under the dictatorship, Malaparte had become a master in the art of cutting or adding a sentence, or sometimes even just a word, in such a way, however, as to change the meaning of what he meant to express. Such doctoring was disagreeable but understandable, then, and various Italian writers and journalists who emerged from Fascism and the war did worse to try to soothe their consciences (not to mention the French intellectuals judged to have collaborated with the Germans in 1940–44). But above all it was useless, seeing as how the leap in vision and inspiration between these dispatches and the earlier ones is striking. In Ethiopia, in the Alps, and in Greece, Malaparte had not yet developed a conception of war as biblical scourge, such as would swallow up in its path both victors and the defeated, men and animals, nature and technology. Only the titanic dimension of the conflict on the eastern front succeeded in unleashing the complete range of his writerly sensibility: the cruelty, the compassion, the disgust, the indolence, the terror, the rage, all the way to the irruption of the sublime and to Christological redemption. This turn, which announced the literary revolution of *Kaputt* and *The Skin*, is much more powerful and convincing than any subsequent reconsideration.[231]

Of course, Malaparte was still the same; history had only a superficial hold over him, and in the next chapter we will see the limits of his commitment. But he opened the May 15, 1942, issue of *Prospettive* with an article from the Leningrad front that would have considerable resonance, starting with the title: "Sangue operaio"

(Workers' blood). It is among his most equivocal texts, capable of prompting the most diverse, even opposing interpretations. The conclusion, above all, is ambiguous, and it is no surprise that Malaparte later dropped it. As in *Viva Caporetto!*, it is not easy to determine for whom the writer's heart really beats. Does he have it in for Stalin, who sacrifices without batting an eye the managers and workers alike defending Leningrad? Or does he not, rather, express a deep, subterranean admiration for the courage and dedication of those worker soldiers who, in sacrificing themselves, rediscover the Russian national tradition, above and beyond Communist values? And does not the sacrifice, the gift of oneself, rather represent the resurgence of a Christian element?*

We find the same questions at the center of a theatrical sketch included in *Volga*, "The Siege of Leningrad," which can be seen as an allegorical premonition of *The Forbidden Christ*. The action takes place in the German-besieged city, shrouded in bitter cold and hunger. A stranger, dressed in worn workers' overalls, enters a hovel whose occupants, weak from starvation, are by now prey to hallucinations. The man, who says he is called Ivan Dobre, or John the Good, silently pulls out a piece of bread from his jacket and offers it to each of those present. But their eyes do not see anything but a stone stained with blood, and with the last of their strength they try to attract the attention of passing soldiers, to get them to arrest

---

*Notwithstanding these ambiguities, President Napolitano testified to me that the "Sangue operaio" issue was greeted in his circle of young intellectuals and university students as a sign that the tide of the war was turning. At one of our many meetings, during the writing of this book and after, he made the exquisite gesture of offering me the copy of "Sangue operaio" he had cherished since then.

this provocateur or spy. The stranger responds sweetly, his gaze brimming with the infinite forgiveness of the Savior on the cross, that "all of you are dying of hunger because you do not believe in bread." Then everyone falls to their knees before Jesus, come back down to earth to bring to humanity the bread of communion, promise of eternal life.[232]

A young French critic, having emerged from the ranks of the Resistance, rightly wondered when the book appeared in France, in 1948:

> Is this proletarian moral of the Russian army truly European? And if one pushed the demonstration all the way, would we not have to conclude that the victory of such an army could only ever depend on its fanaticism, on the more or less perfect fanaticism of its spirit?[233]

The superiority of the Soviet system emerges clearly in these pages, maybe the most audacious that Malaparte ever published during Fascism, albeit a Fascism militarily in decline and entering its death throes. But they are entirely consistent with his impressions from his first trip to Russia, in 1929. Malaparte sees in the Communist war machine an example of absolute, fanatical devotion to the cause that has nothing in common with the Western socialist tradition, or even with Italian and German fascisms; and this is precisely what reawakens his old hostility toward cowardly bourgeois pacifism. Once again, he was seduced by strength, health, and the historical and natural necessity of this successful "organism." The same theme was taken up by Henry Miller, whom Malaparte probably did not meet in Paris in the 1930s, but whose work and reputation he admired.

FINNISH INTERLUDE

In an unpublished 1948 letter, Miller goes beyond offering compliments to display a singular affinity with his Italian colleague:

> I am now in the midst of your book [the French edition of *Volga*] and find it difficult to put down. I know of no correspondent writing in the English language (of war) who has anything like your poetic approach.... The writer always triumphs over the thinker or the theorist. Your pages testify to your profound interest in humanity, despite the almost "theological" interest in mores, politics, technic, etc. Reading you on the Russian campaign, I have the feeling of being back in ancient times; you have really caught the underlying significance of these world wars which have only begun.[234]

A fundamental question tormented Malaparte, faced with the enormous clash between the two great totalitarianisms of the twentieth century: Which of the two would devour the other? At this point, he no longer harbored doubts: he bet on the Russians, because they were inspired by a double faith, in the past and in the future, which pushed the Soviets to retrace the Volga toward the heart of Europe, toward Hitler's Reich. This highly prophetic last point would nonetheless be cut from the published book.* Regardless, upon the publication of *Volga* in Italy, in 1943, the text would be taken as a sign by young intellectuals and college students, who saw in the resistance of Leningrad, and soon of Stalingrad, the real turning point of the war. One of them noted in his diary at the time:

---

*Contrary to his claim, in the preface to the French edition of *Volga*, according to which "I have reestablished here the complete text."

KREMLIN AND SWASTIKA (1934–1943)

People talk a lot about the dispatches sent by Malaparte from the Russian front to the *Corriere della Sera*. In content and tone they are in sharp contrast with everything being published in the other daily papers: shot through with open political and human sympathy not only for the people of the Union but also for the power of the Soviets and for the soldiers of the Red Army. There are plenty who would like to send Malaparte back to jail or to *confino* for defeatism and treason.[235]

This vision would be clarified in the drafts of *The Kremlin Ball*, a later work that it would nonetheless be good to introduce at this point, on account of its thematic affinity. It would be the third stage of Malaparte's reflection on the Soviet "mystery," the core of which dates to his Parisian stay of 1947–49, when he swung once again toward anticommunism. Unhappy with the result, he would continue to rework the manuscript until his death; he also counted on updating it with the developments of de-Stalinization during his last trip to the Soviet Union, en route to China, in October 1956,[236] but he ran out of time. If behind *Volga* we can recognize the influence of the militant reportage of Babel or Pilnyak,* the undeniable point of reference for the allegorical tendencies of *The Kremlin Ball* was now Bulgakov, whom Malaparte declared to have met during his stay in Moscow in May–June 1929. This is unlikely, because the great Soviet writer, already isolated and persecuted, was then preparing

---

*But not Vasily Grossman, as it has sometimes been said, whose major works, however, came later. If anything, it would be interesting to know if the author of *Life and Fate* had not managed to obtain in the immediate postwar period, possibly through his friend Ehrenburg, the French editions of Malaparte's books.

to send Stalin the famous letter in which he vainly pleaded to leave the USSR. But so what? Malaparte's exceptional talent for assimilation allowed him to "Bulgakovize" at will. Here is an example, which seems straight out of *The Master and Margarita*: "The Moscow spring was entering through the windows with the dulcet, tepid violence of a pregnant woman" (KB, 40). Bulgakov's satire helped him understand that "Marxist society in the USSR is already in decline" (KB, 5). Is there a contradiction, then, between this and the great popular momentum that stopped Hitler's invasion? No, because

> the people were expecting something different from the communists, a solemn and spectacular return of the old Russia, but an old Russia represented by new men, Marxists, communists, revolutionaries, and not that thing similar to communism presenting itself as Nazism. (KB, 47)

Stalin's great victory over European decadence, then, would be to transform the fight against the invader into the "great patriotic war": to reposition Marxism at the center of Russian history, to make it the fulcrum of the regime, and from there to set out to conquer the exhausted and torn old continent. Malaparte was among the very first to understand what nearly all the English and American war correspondents and the great Sovietologists of the time did not: the frontiers of the postwar Soviet Union would extend as far as the Red Army had reached, penetrating into the heart of Europe toward Berlin. But would that be enough to make *Homo sovieticus* the accredited representative of the contemporary age? How would he manage to divide the planet with *Homo americanus*? If Malaparte decided not to finish the book, it was perhaps because he, like everyone else, was not clear on the developments of the Cold War and of de-Stalinization. He would have had to wait for 1989 and the fall of the Berlin Wall to write this last page.

In early June 1943, Malaparte returned to Finland for the last time. As usual, he stopped first in Berlin, by now hammered by Allied bombardment. He spent only two or three days there, but they were enough for him to meet up again with some "official" friends, like Arno Breker, Hitler's favorite sculptor. He proceeded to Stockholm, where in a theater he saw a Soviet propaganda film on the Battle of Stalingrad culminating in the scene, "very beautiful and true," of the surrender of Field Marshal Friedrich Paulus.[237] Did he understand then that the game was surely up for the Germans? As for the Fascist regime, Malaparte knew perfectly well that it was reduced to a Potemkin village, whose cardboard facade masked, for a little longer, emptiness and ruins; but everyone, including him, still pretended to believe in it. From the Swedish capital he wrote to Borelli:

> I agreed as well with Polverelli [the new minister of popular culture] on the tone of the political articles: to show Italian public opinion that it's not just Italy that is threatened by grave dangers, but many other European nations as well. So we don't seem like the only ones who are screwed.[238]

How to interpret these final insinuations? Less than twenty days before the Allied landing in Sicily, and just a month before the fall of Fascism, there were rumors of a possible Italian exit from the war. Mussolini himself was thinking about it; in recent months he had received urgent messages from the Hungarian and Romanian governments to negotiate a separate peace. Even various German diplomats and military men looked to Mussolini as the only man in a position to make Hitler understand the need to put an end to the conflict. The martial tone of Malaparte's letter should not overly surprise us, however: even in happy and protected Stockholm, spies and informers were about. Malaparte would declare later that in Stockholm he had approached Prince Eugene, brother of King Gustav V, a collector and patron whom he had (maybe) already met the previous fall, during his first stay in the capital. The goal was to pave the way for Italy's transition to a Swedish-type neutrality, with the intervention of the crown, traditionally a friend to the Bel Paese. On this occasion he "boasted of having had contacts with the English Embassy for negotiations concerning the disappearance of Mussolini and of having been persecuted by the Gestapo."[239] The kernel of truth here is, once again, his ingratitude to Mussolini: because it was Il Duce who had authorized the mission in Finland and Sweden and had him receive ten thousand crowns out of the state's anemic currency reserves.[240] It was the last page in the long story of their relationship, the last sign of the *padre padrone*'s benevolence that Malaparte would naturally forget the day after his fall. And yet, during the eighteen months of the Republic of Salò, Mussolini would attack by name, or have them attacked by his collaborators, numerous regime turncoats and profiteers, the "giant kangaroos." He would never, as far as I have been able to determine, mention Malaparte, either in public or in private.

In reality, the writer was unaware of the events being orchestrated in Rome. At the meeting of the Grand Council of Fascism during the night of July 24–25, Mussolini lost a no-confidence vote, throwing the regime into crisis. The real initiative passed into the hands of Victor Emmanuel III. The sovereign, formally outside the deliberations of the Grand Council, sanctioned the coup d'état, forcing the resignation of Il Duce, whom he would have rather unregally arrested at the conclusion of the session. In his place he named Marshal Badoglio, who hastened to declare that "the war continues," something that neither the Italian people nor the Germans believed, and he began to sound out the Allies to see how to emerge from the conflict. Malaparte, like nearly everyone, was caught by surprise by the speed of events. He had expected to return to Italy in mid-August for the summer holidays. But as soon as news of the coup spread to Stockholm, he understood it was better to bring up his departure and he managed to catch the first plane bound for Rome, with a stopover in Berlin.

He spent the evening of July 27 in the German capital with other Italian journalists, who competed in raging against the regime they had diligently served up until three days earlier, as one eyewitness ironically observed.[241] In this overwrought atmosphere, Malaparte solicited accounts of how the Germans reacted to the news of Mussolini's fall. In *The Skin* he would write of that night in Berlin that two officials of the Italian embassy had been invited to a cheerful little party at the house of a high-society friend. Suddenly, the radio announced the arrest of Mussolini, and immediately two of the young women present slipped off their evening gowns to put on ... uniforms of the Wehrmacht and to rush back to barracks. This scene, which recalls the Visconti film *The Damned*, had been liberally "Malapartized" for narrative ends. Things had gone more innocently: the little party was not in fact a transvestite orgy. Simply, an officer, the fiancé of one of the young women, dead drunk, had been partially dressed as a woman as a joke by his women friends; but when he realized the gravity of the situation, he decided to return to his command post. In the 1950s, one of the two now-former diplomats, meeting Malaparte by chance in the street, asked him why he had changed the scene: "He listened carefully, with that face of the slightly spoiled child. And then: 'Get out of here, it's much more beautiful the way I wrote it.'"[242] Can you blame him?

Malaparte left the next day at dawn for Rome. What would he find there waiting for him?

4. Chronicles of the Plague (1944–1946)

But pity is superfluous wherever sentence is pronounced by History.
—Czesław Miłosz, *The Captive Mind*

"It's of No Importance Whether What Malaparte Relates Is True or False"

In this chapter we will confront Malaparte's three great books dedicated to the "plague" of war.[1] We know he wanted to use this term for the second of them, as attested also in its opening: "Naples was in the throes of the 'plague.'" But the success of Camus's novel compelled him reluctantly to abandon it: the title would be preserved for a single chapter.[2] The first two installments of the trilogy, *Kaputt* (1944) and *The Skin* (1949), are far better known than the third, *Mamma marcia*. They were read and discussed everywhere, until the Iron Curtain fell: in Czechoslovakia, for example, *Kaputt* appeared before the Communist coup d'état of February 1948, whereas the translation of *The Skin* was subsequently blocked by the new regime. Thus Malaparte rapidly earned the reputation, which endures to this day, as the first interpreter of the worst cataclysm the old continent had known since the Middle Ages. And it was no coincidence: the Second World War, with its procession of atrocities, was *the* ideal theme for his pen and the background he needed to reveal himself in his full maturity as a writer. He had always associated with, sought out, and courted the tragic sense of history, but only now could he really grasp it. Malaparte, moving more than ever between reality and imagination, life and legend, here displays a striking degree of adherence to the atmosphere of the age. And this vision has not been belied by the immense quantity of testimonies, documents, and materials to have appeared since.

Naturally, the leopard cannot change its spots. And so Malaparte fudged the dates, to make it look as if he had finished *Kaputt* before the Allied landing in Sicily (July 9–10, 1943) and the fall of Mussolini (July 25), in order to present himself to readers as a militant anti-Fascist. The chaos of the period favored about-faces even more flagrant than his own, and Malaparte's case was certainly not an isolated one. The events of July 25 caught him by surprise, as we saw, and he rushed to Rome to see things more clearly. Here he learned that the Badoglio government had had Il Duce arrested and disbanded the PNF, even while hastening to declare that "the war continues," to avoid German reprisals. But the settling of scores had begun. Malaparte was attacked by the new dignitaries, who generally had profited from twenty years of Fascist largesse much more than he had, starting with Badoglio himself. We can understand his irritation, even if he immediately boasted: "Just think that I was in Stockholm, and I came to Italy out of pure civic duty. Some nice reception I got."[3] Malaparte was arrested on August 2, not "for having publicly wished the Italians would rebel against the Germans,"[4] as he claimed, but with the rather less honorable charge of engaging in profiteering during the regime. And so he was shut up again in the Regina Coeli prison, in anguish and uncertainty, exactly like ten years earlier. He was freed after a few days and authorized to travel to Capri, thanks to the intervention of Guglielmo Rulli, who had been named foreign press chief in the new government. According to the latter's son:

> My father turned to the lieutenant colonel Giuseppe [Giovanni] Frignani of the Carabinieri, with whom he had frequent contact at work. Frignani "loaned" my father a Carabinieri officer uniform, and together they showed up at Regina Coeli with a fake transfer order. The thing worked, and Malaparte came out and could leave Rome.[5]

On August 9, the Italian high command informed the Ministry of Popular Culture, where Polverelli had been replaced by the ambassador Carlo Galli, that "in view of the situation in which he has found himself, it has been resolved that the reserve captain Curzio Malaparte cease to serve as a war correspondent."[6] It was a decision without practical consequences, because Malaparte did not have the least intention of leaving again for abroad, especially to countries still occupied by the Axis, from which his colleagues sought to be repatriated as soon as possible. He relocated to Capri and barraged Ms. Pellegrini with messages from there. Rulli had led him to understand that *Prospettive* could be authorized by the new government, as it was not. He absolutely wanted to open the new issue with his editorial on "conscientious objection," in which he reclaimed the legacy of Gobetti, which had abruptly become timely again: "It must be printed as soon as possible, immediately, possibly by compelling the typesetters to work through the night," he wrote to his faithful secretary, adding with unconscious irony: "Our way of being anti-Fascist must appear clearly, albeit with a certain style." He also asked for news of Moravia, who, "I think, wrote something in tune with the moment, and courageous, which is to say, less ambiguous than his usual stuff."[7] Silence, on the other hand, concerning his other, more compromised associates. In short, he didn't want to pass up an opportunity to get back in with the right crowd.

"Obbiezione di coscienza"—which is Malaparte's only piece of writing from "the forty-five days of Badoglio"[8]—is an ambiguous text, more clever than convincing, of which he composed two distinct drafts.[9] It opens with a claim for the leading role played by *Prospettive* in permitting "the formation in Italian youth too of an actual moral conscience...which had seemed the prerogative of solely protestant and liberal countries, accustomed and fortified by long centuries in the exercise of freedom." Naturally, Malaparte was careful to recall the best of the magazine—like the inquiry into surrealism—and to forget the rest. And he arrived at the conclusion that, despite Mussolini's "persecution" (which existed only in his imagination), the magazine had more than any other fought to maintain the independence of Italian literature in the years of the dictatorship, under the only guise possible, of "objection." All things considered, it was a lost opportunity, even if the article remained unpublished, due to the ban on the magazine. With more humility and clarity, Malaparte could have laid claim to the undoubted merits of *Prospettive*, within the limits imposed by the censors and the political climate of the time; whereas its refashioning into some sort of ideal successor to Gobetti's *Rivoluzione Liberale* was easily contradicted by the facts. It was the first demonstration of Malaparte's incapacity, across the post-Fascist period, to engage in true self-criticism, with the result of rendering his position even more difficult and uncomfortable than it already was.

Meanwhile, the war continued in earnest, and despite the secret negotiations begun with the Badoglio government, the Anglo-Americans were increasing the pressure to make Italy the first Axis country to surrender. From Capri, Malaparte described the situation at length to his friend Rulli back in Rome:

> The second evening after my arrival, five English warships came to place themselves in front of Galli, that is, right under the nose of [Punta del] Massullo, and for half an hour they bombarded Castellammare, striking the arsenal multiple times. Deaths, injuries, destruction, etc. The bulletin didn't say a word about it! We saw large naval projectiles, tracers, cutting through the sky between Sant'Agata and the top of Agerola. Our own, silent. Only after the English had left, battery 305, behind Massa, fired off three shots, probably to announce the end of the thing. I won't tell you what happened in town! The people here offer up a truly ignoble spectacle. Two steps from Naples, which resists so courageously. Just think that I managed to obtain ten days of truce in the bombardments. If they hadn't arrested me, I might have been able to be useful. But now they can all go to hell.[10]

What follows are remarks of notable literary ferocity, worthy of chronicles of the plague:

> Think that in the [Naples] cemetery the bodies are broken, wrecked, unrecognizable, bodies with three arms, four legs, two heads, bodies

without arms, or with only one leg, or without a head, put back together in a hurry, and you go find where is the head of this one, and the arm of this other one, and it ends up there are always some extra arms, extra legs, extra heads, which the corpse carriers stick on this one or that one.... The soldiers, instead of digging in the shelters full of bodies, are "rented" en bloc to private citizens, especially to shopkeepers, to clear out the rubble and recover what can be salvaged: in front of B's store, covered by a building that collapsed, some thirty soldiers are working under the guidance of the owner, who hopes to save his fake antiques... Yesterday, around two hundred American planes came to bomb the shoulders of Naples and of Salerno. And at a certain point, two Anglo-Saxon fighters came down in front of the Grotta Bianca, skimming the water, and slipping by my house, machine-gunned one of our escort boats. The population, to take refuge, not knowing what to do anymore, dressed up as birds and clambered up into the trees, where they are chirping in Caprese.[11]

The thin ice on which the king and Badoglio were treading broke just a month later, at the armistice with the Allies, signed on September 3, 1943, and announced by the Allies on the eighth, contrary to what had been agreed with the Italians. The crown's vain hope of getting the country out of the war without pushing it into a new conflict tragically vanished. September 8 has remained in the Italian collective imagination, even more than Caporetto, as the mother of all national disasters, and one can draw a parallel with what happened in France in June 1940, with the defeat, exodus, and division of the country. The king and Badoglio abruptly left Rome, which was quickly occupied by the Germans, to establish the Kingdom of the South, under Anglo-American control, with its provisional seat first in Brindisi, then in Salerno. The legitimate government's return to Rome would be possible only nine months later, when the Allies entered the capital, on June 4, 1944. Meanwhile, a rather reluctant Mussolini, who had been interned first in Ponza, then in Sardinia, and finally on the Gran Sasso massif, in Abruzzo, was liberated by a command of SS paratroopers and installed at the head of the Republic of Salò, under German control. Italy was thus cut in two. In the south the front was static, because the Allies were concentrating on preparations for the Normandy landing; the central and northern parts of the peninsula, meanwhile, would become the theater of a bloody civil war lasting sixteen months, until the definitive liberation of the country, on April 25, 1945, and the surrender of the German troops stationed in Italy, on May 2.[12]

Malaparte worried immediately about what posture to take with the new victors and decided that the best defense was attack. But not in the capital, which was about to be abandoned by the legitimate government: "I'm not coming to Rome, out of fear of being locked up there," he wrote to Rulli, and one can't blame him.[13] The south was in the hands of the Allies, and thus it was there he had to make his play. As early as October 8, 1943, he sent them a note, in which he emphasized his anti-Fascist activity starting in 1931, when "I publicly and resoundingly distanced myself from the PNF."[14] A clever formulation: better to abstain for now from boasting about any pretended "resignation" from the Party, not knowing whether it would emerge from the paperwork now in Allied hands that he was expelled in 1933. Among his other inventions, Malaparte claimed to have been stopped by the police and sent to Forte dei Marmi as a precautionary measure during Hitler's visit to Italy in May 1938 (was it feared he could make an attempt on the Führer's life?), and returned to his alleged arrest by the Gestapo, in Ukraine, in August 1941.[15] Meanwhile, he strengthened his relationships with the anti-Fascists taking refuge on Capri, like Benedetto Croce and Alberto Cianca, once Giovanni Amendola's right-hand man.

Malaparte turned first to the English, in the hope that his prewar contacts in London literary and society circles could be useful to him. Adrian Gallegos, a young Anglo-Spanish painter, raised in Roman high society, now an officer in the SOE, the British military intelligence service, left a vivid account of his encounters with the writer:

> During my stay in Capri I often lunched with three Italian friends. One was Curzio Malaparte, the author and journalist, and the others were Alberto Tarchiani, who subsequently became Ambassador to Washington, and Emilio Cianca, who became a Cabinet Minister....
> [Malaparte] had managed to find his way to Capri, where he had a house close to the Faraglioni, as hideous outside as it was lovely inside.
> The four of us could not have been more unlike each other. Malaparte, the internationally known author of *Kaputt* [which in reality had not yet appeared], had had a chequered career and had become famous through his great ability, intelligence and determination to rise to the top. He was in early middle age and had a businesslike face surmounted by closely cropped greying hair....
> ... I had been thinking of ways and means of starting a partisan movement in the Sorrento peninsula, recruiting and arming a few volunteers as a start, then perhaps capturing more arms from the enemy so as to arm yet more men and infiltrate them into Naples and beyond....

Malaparte was enthusiastic.

"I know how we could make a start right away," he said. "We could use the arms of the Fascist militia."

"Are they still armed?" [Badoglio had officially disarmed the militia the day after July 25.]

"Yes, with carbines, forty of them. Not much, but they would do as a start."

"They would come in very useful. And do you think we could find volunteers easily?"

"Lots of them," said he eagerly, "but I insist that I be allowed to join too and I'll show you how many I can recruit."[16]

These café conspiracies would later push him to claim to have been one of the five(?) officers who rebuilt the Italian army in the south. The truth is a bit less heroic. The English rejected the services of Malaparte.[17] Another well-known representative of the Capri community, the Swedish physician and writer Axel Munthe, author of the edifying *Story of San Michele*, had warned them: "Malaparte is one of the most arrant knaves around, even for an Italian."[18] It was now the Americans' turn.

On November 22, according to the *Giornale segreto*, three US military policemen and a carabiniere arrived at Casa Come Me to arrest him. Malaparte was immediately transferred to the Naples prison, where he would remain in isolation until the thirtieth, in a "horrible, extremely damp" cell, with scarcely any food.[19] Unsurprisingly, he welcomed with relief his first interrogation by the colonel Henry H. Cumming, to whom he would dedicate *The Skin*. The *Giornale segreto* does not provide details, but everything must have gone well, since the writer's detainment was quickly turned into house arrest, and he began to cooperate with the Public Safety Division of the Allied Military Government. The Americans, unlike their British colleagues, seemed to want to give him credit. Some providential help came from an old friend, the journalist Percy Winner, who had spent many years in Italy before the war as an Associated Press correspondent. Winner formally testified that Malaparte "has been known to me intimately in France and Italy for the last 19 years. By giving valuable data through me to the American authorities, his anti-Fascism has been established, which I can testify under oath. This was especially so during [the] period 1939 to late summer 1941. WILLIAM PHILLIPS, then American Ambassador in Rome[,] can attest to the great importance of military and political data given by MALAPARTE through me to the Embassy."[20] Was this real espionage, or did Winner exaggerate to help a friend in difficulty? During the conflict, Winner had risen through the ranks of the American secret services to become deputy commander of the Psychological Warfare Branch: the same propaganda and information service for which Malaparte was now apparently working. The writer resolutely denied having played this double game, but only some years later, when he no longer needed American protection.

Shortly after the war, Winner published a short novel, *Dario*, for which Malaparte was the clear model, and their relations quickly cooled. You can understand why. *Dario* is well written, well documented, and quite malicious. Malaparte commands the scene from beginning to end, with his charisma, eloquence, and cynicism leading him to take advantage of anyone and everyone, without hesitation. It is the portrait of a great carnivore and a little man. His last name, Duvolti (*due volti*, or "two faces"), symbolically heralded his transformation from regime propagandist to editor of the official PCI newspaper *L'Unità*, under the pseudonym Volto (an abbreviation for *voltafaccia*, or "about-face"). Endowed with great magnetism, he exploits the women who pursue him and the friends who believe in him. He loves only Mussolini, up to the moment he finally repudiates him, and his dog Ferro, which, however—and it is a cutting psychological feature—does not reciprocate and distrusts him. Without being exactly a spy, he passes on to Vincitore ("Winner") useful information on the course of events: for instance, he considers Italy's entry into the war inevitable, contrary to the opinion prevailing among the diplomatic community in the capital.[21] Following publication, Malaparte's denial was not long in coming: "However criminal the Fascist war was, I would never have dreamed of raising a single finger to help the Allied armies win and destroy my country. And I disdain with all my heart those Italians who, under the pretext of politics, betrayed their own country, their own soldiers, giving military information to the Allied armies," he wrote indignantly, in a letter to the editor of *The New York Herald Tribune*.[22]

There remains the no less controversial question of his military enrollment. Malaparte, a reserve officer, was called up by both Italian states, technically enemies, of the north and of the south. With respect to the Italian Social Republic, the question was quickly resolved, because, having refused to show up, he was automatically declared a deserter and "Badoglist." It was the writer's final break with the "last Fascism," destined to become postwar neo-Fascism through its main formation, the Italian Social Movement, founded by survivors of Salò. For the rest of his postwar life, Malaparte would be stalked by the hate and contempt, duly reciprocated, of the neo-Fascists.[23] On the other hand, he had no intention of going to fight with the troops of the Kingdom of the South; so he put forward the excuse of health problems (cystitis and hepatic colic) to avoid the call-up.[24] After a new order to return to service, on September 21, 1944, he managed to be recruited as a liaison officer with the American high command, in the intelligence division. Subsequently he passed under the orders of the Peninsular Base Section, in Livorno. It was then, in May 1946, that he wrote for *Tempo* an article on the plague of war in its immediate aftermath, "Quanto costa una donna a Livorno?" (How much does a woman cost in Livorno?), which is a sort of preview of *The Skin*.

Malaparte never offered himself up as a volunteer, then, even if he would later claim as much.[25] Here again, we need not consider this a form of cowardice: Malaparte never had the makings of a shirker. It is true he refused to fight until such time as the Allies authorized a modest Italian military contribution to the liberation of the peninsula, so as not to leave all credit for it to the Resistance, in which Communist groups predominated. His attitude can be explained, then, as disgust at civil war, the most ignoble of wars, as he recalled in an open letter to the English commander of the Mediterranean sector, Marshal Harold Alexander, guilty of insulting, in his view, the honor of Italian soldiers from both sides:

> The rebellion against the shameful manner of the armistice was immediate and general, in the army as in the country; because it was rebellion among those who went to fight in the north, and it was rebellion, substantially of the same origin and the same nature, that drove many of us to fight alongside the Allies. Not, following the

spirit of the armistice, as mercenaries, but as free men ... If the war was lost, it was not for this that our national honor was defeated, humiliated, and corrupted.[26]

These are the essential facts to keep in mind for the reconstruction of Malaparte's itinerary, more winding than ever. First, he took up again and revised the text of *Kaputt*, *after* the fall of the regime, bringing it to completion in the spring of 1944, and not in September 1943, as he later maintained. This allowed him to get a more precise idea of the political situation and above all of the balance of power, which in the south now inclined toward the Allies.[27] However, in comments concerning the dates of appearance of his works, in Italy and especially in France, he generally indicated the year 1943, with the addition "shortly after the landing of the Allies [in Sicily]" for the first edition of *Kaputt*. It was a primacy to which he was very attached: "In late 1943, I published *Kaputt*, which was the first book published in Europe during the Liberation," he wrote in one of his countless autobiographies.[28] Only toward the end of his life, or after his death, would the date of this first edition, published in an improvised fashion by a small Neapolitan publisher-bookseller of great sophistication, Gaspare Casella, be corrected to October 1944.[29] Is this point important? Yes, if we are to believe Lino Pellegrini, according to whom the first version of *Kaputt* was decidedly anti-English and bore the ironic title "God Shave the King," which would in the final version be reserved for the episode concerning the encounter with the governor-general of Warsaw, Hans Frank.[30] But how could a shrewd man like Malaparte bet still, in 1942–43, on an Axis victory? We know from other testimonies that he was inclined to think the opposite. As early as the previous year, three months before Hitler's attack on the Soviet Union, Ansaldo noted in his diary: "Long chat with Malaparte, who considers the war lost and implores me—in the name of his pretend friendship—to free myself from radio commitments."[31] And yet the doubt remained, and it was connected to the reputation as a Nazi collaborator he had acquired among certain young intellectuals now on the left.[32] Hence the need to give new luster to his old, newly precious anti-Fascist credentials, starting, obviously, with the purported "five years" spent in prison (K, 274). The operation was unsuccessful and had a direct consequence in Malaparte's decision to move to Paris, "after fourteen years of exile in Italy" (DFP, 5), as we will see in the next chapter.[33]

Kaputt represented, from every angle, a turning point in Malaparte's work. The title itself is a clever invention that, like its author's pseudonym, resonates in all languages, with the same lugubrious connotations. Malaparte had never gotten so close to history without believing in it, or at least without believing it had a meaning or instructional value for leaders, individuals, and peoples, destined to fall again and again into the same errors and lunacies. He remained faithful to himself: there is no trace of indignation, and even less of social engagement or metaphysical concern, in what he tells. One could also say a good deal about the compassion and emotion he displays. A Malaparte who suddenly became Camusian, Silonian, or Bernanosian would no longer be the one we know, without becoming necessarily better: a sermonizing or contrite tone is reserved precisely for the least successful pages.[34] What strikes us instead is the observer's detachment, since Malaparte never had a better chance to be on the front line of events, without participating directly. One can again establish a parallel with Jünger, who, a highly decorated fighter in the other war, in this one became the cool and disenchanted observer of his 1939–45 diary.[35]

Indeed, Malaparte had never been less politically or socially engaged than in this apocalyptic trilogy, confining himself to the role of memoirist and interlocutor in encounters that were often imaginary, but which all had some basis in truth. He generally leaves the leading role to his companions, like the Italian journalists and diplomats Pellegrini, Sartori, Casertano, Mameli, or Soro, as in the attempt to save the Jews from the pogrom of Jassy. Only rarely does he take the side of the victims. Of course, he remains in the spotlight, and it is always thanks to him that the action starts up again, from one chapter to the next. But whatever he does or says—his complaints, his stubbornness, his fits of shame, and his copious tears—no longer concerns us. He suddenly becomes a straight man or sidekick, in the tradition of charlatans or variety show presenters, who leave the quip or retort to the leading man, be it a Nazi governor or an American general, a Fascist minister or a Croatian dictator. Such a move is possible only on the basis of an admission of impotence, a loss of virility. The role is similar to that of Drieu La Rochelle in his most melancholy novel, *The Man on Horseback* (1943), a role the Frenchman would continue to play in the meanders of the occupation, withdrawing more and more from the reality around him.

The difference is that in the Italian there is no slide toward suicide; he is always ready to get back on his feet at the earliest opportunity. Malaparte also anticipated the idle dreamer characters of the postwar, like the antihero of *La Dolce Vita*, who seek in vain to touch, to grasp the life being made and unmade before their eyes. In the chapter "Golf Handicaps," he describes Roman society on the eve of the crisis of the regime, with full names and nicknames, more or less as we would find them twenty years later in Fellini's film. His refusal to denounce or be indignant prompted accusations of indifference, not to say complacency. But it would, precisely, be to ask him to be a different man, or worse: it would mean overlooking how his behavior consists in miring himself in the war, calmly wallowing in it, traversing the length and breadth of it, *without* engaging in it himself and *without* taking a position, because he wants exclusively to recount it. Why weigh down this catalog of infamies with rhetorical hymns to virtue? His task was to make us share that hallucinatory atmosphere, communicating to the reader the tactile, auditory, olfactory, and sensory—but *not* sensuous—impression of a world in decomposition.

Reality can be altered—who knew it better than he!—but one must respect and preserve the *sense* of what it points to: in this approach, Malaparte is perhaps without equal. It is here his gift for superimposing the imaginary on the real appears to most striking effect. Seen from this perspective, *Kaputt* and *The Skin*—the case of *Mamma marcia*, incomplete and posthumous, is a bit different—are actually reliable documents, contrary to what has often been said. To call the books "novels," then, is inaccurate. Yet it doesn't seem incorrect to characterize them as "reportage," even if of an uncommon level, insofar as they could have been, in their respective times, *The Jewish War*, by one Flavius Josephus, or *A Journal of the Plague Year*, by Defoe, known to have inspired Camus. Malaparte was certainly not the only great contemporary chronicler of the modern plague. Other memorable works of the period devoted to the end of European Europe include the visionary anticipation of Witkiewicz in the tryptic *Farewell to Autumn*, *Insatiability*, and

Narcotics; the trilogy *Stalingrad, Moscow,* and *Berlin,* by Theodor Plievier; and Céline's saga of escape through Germany in flames.*

But what dominates in Malaparte is the breadth of vision, the power of the brushstroke, the richness of tones. He passes directly from a salon to a bivouac, a golf club to a crumbling ghetto, a castle to a torture room, a starving city to a forest paralyzed by intense cold, making us understand it is always the *same* Europe, the *same* humanity on parade before us. Wherever he penetrates, into the most luxurious environments and the most sordid recesses, he is perfectly at ease, or at least appears so, as a man of the world plunged into the heart of the horror, flaunting that poise and style he never abandoned. And in so doing (or *not* doing), he managed to peel back a layer of European civilization, almost as if, pulling on a lock of hair, he could yank out the entire cranium, as in an allegory by Goya. Malaparte could arrive at this result by placing not only his qualities but also his defects at the service of literature. He carefully avoided choosing between intuition and reproduction: he wanted to be a chronicler in the sense that the truth is always *intentional* in what he writes, even if it assumes absurd or delirious forms. The story is fictional only where the author passes over to the other side of the mirror, to show us that what is true is not only what we can see. It is the opposite, for example, of *Naples '44*, by Norman Lewis, an honest testimony by a British officer who limits himself to relating

---

*Another frequent comparison in recent years has concerned Vasily Grossman's chronicle-novels *Life and Fate* (1960) and *Everything Flows* (1972). Notwithstanding the powerful impact of these works, Malaparte's approach seems to possess a much wider perspective.

what he *sees*.* And even what Lewis sees has a selective value, corresponding to his puritan education, sense of duty, and scrupulous precision: he observes, selects, and cuts. Malaparte instead offers us the totality. He does not take anyone's side, never forgets his role as an observer and often as a voyeur, in a Proustian sense: to be there as if by chance, to creep up on events, to eavesdrop on conversations or meetings, which become tesserae in his rich narrative mosaic.

Arriving at his full maturity around the age of forty-five, Malaparte could finally devote himself to a topic that seemed cut out for him. So aware was he of this fit that he treated it with a great deal of respect (more clearly in *Kaputt* than in *The Skin*), in order not to spoil its exemplary value, to fall into unintentional parody, into the "monotony of horror."[36] Far from setting out to shock the reader with hideous but facile effects, he measures out his ingredients carefully, making considerably more discreet use of them than it may appear, and it is here especially that he shows himself to be a masterly narrator, in full possession of his materials and methods. The plague becomes more, then, than a metaphor of war and defeat, a sort of dark reabsorption of the sensible world. His taste for the horrid, or rather for horrid beauty, passes over Baudelaire, Dostoevsky, and Lautréamont to rediscover the world of the Tuscan tales of Sacchetti and Boccaccio: full of humors and vital fluids but slimmed down, spare and matter-of-fact. It is a world captured in fine, realistic detail,

---

*To cite two other titles, today almost forgotten: *The Gallery* (1947), by the American John Horne Burns, which takes its title from the Galleria Umberto, destroyed by Allied bombing, and *Eclipse* (1946), by the British war correspondent Alan Moorehead. The Italian bibliography is vast and generally very critical toward *The Skin*; see Eduardo Capuano, *Una giornata a Napoli, 28 settembre–1° ottobre 1943: Quello che non vide Malaparte* (Naples: Gallina, 1994).

without preconceived judgments, in which farce goes hand in hand with tragedy, and sorrow is almost never taken as such but rather turned to mockery and derision.

The two books are too well known to require summarizing here. If it is difficult to do so without risking parody, it seems nigh-on impossible to transpose them to the stage or screen.* Suffice it to recall that *Kaputt* is a sort of journey to the end of the night through central Europe, from Romania to Poland, from Yugoslavia to Germany, as far as Ukraine and Russia, reaching up to Sweden and Finland, with a final return to Italy, to Rome and Naples, the point of departure for the next volume. An itinerary punctuated by a succession of "disasters of war," in which one passes continually from reality to allegory and vice versa, without anything being either entirely true or entirely false. He reveals as much himself, with a slightly too insistent wink, in the page of *The Skin* where the French officer Pierre Lyautey asks him what truth there is in *Kaputt*, and the American colonel Jack Hamilton answers for him: "It's of no importance whether what Malaparte relates is true or false. That isn't the question. The question is whether or not his work is art" (S, 283). Malaparte paints a world shaken to its foundations, in which it has become nearly impossible to distinguish true from false. And this world is essentially the one we live in today, eighty years later, characterized by an unending series of massacres and the ceaseless

---

*It is the case with the film version of *The Skin*, by Liliana Cavani and her American screenwriter, Robert Katz, which, despite the best intentions and some excellent cinematography, concentrates inevitably on the book's external aspects. The story revolves around an unconvinced and hardly Malapartian Mastroianni, who distractedly surveys the surrounding decadence with the disenchanted gaze that made him famous in *La Dolce Vita*.

intellectual tendency toward lies and bad faith. *Kaputt* glides like a bird of prey over all of Europe at war; in *The Skin* Malaparte undertakes a shorter journey, moving up the Italian peninsula with the American "liberators," from Naples to Rome to Tuscany, aside from a digression to the Ukrainian steppes for the "Black Wind" episode, possibly taken from a draft of his previous book. Finally, in *Mamma marcia*, the narration becomes highly irregular, with frequent back-and-forths in time and space. Still elusive and aloof but less haughty, here he shows us how his conscience reacts to the shattering of a civilization's values. And perhaps, from the shoals of the cult of the "I" there might emerge a message, or at least a universalizable tension.

In Which Is Told the Story of a Chamber Pot and a Cigar

Is it better to show or to hide the horror, in order to better condemn it? Or else to interiorize it, make it one's inspiration and accomplice, with the aim of finding there our own unconfessed fantasies, realized by others? It is the wager of the twentieth-century intellectual confronted with the agony of Europe, "this wounded animal," as Churchill would call it, in a rare metaphysical departure from his fighter's temperament. Are we in a better position to understand such horror today? It is doubtful. If born of human imperfection, the absolute can become a diabolical temptation, which purifies souls on the gallows. Starting in the 1930s, Malaparte had understood that the hierarchical, pyramidal mental structures of Soviet communism and National Socialism were based on the ecclesiastical model. The single party in each case was modeled on the Universal Church, with salvation or damnation offered via class or race, and an infallible guide at its head. Did the single-party congresses not perhaps resemble church councils? And could not the same be said for the apparatuses of mobilization and propaganda, but also for those of repression and destruction, in the hands of functionaries bound to obey unto death, *perinde ac cadaver*, ready to face, if necessary, excommunication and the stake?[37]

This analysis can seem banal: the dogmatic and clerical aspects of totalitarianism and its hunt for heretics have become commonplaces. At the time, though, such an analysis was (relatively) new. We know Malaparte was endowed with a powerful capacity for assimilation, to the detriment of analytic rigor. It is not so much the eye, the faculty of observation, that prevailed in him, as it is the capacity to turn his gaze inward, a little like the piercing eyelashes of his childhood god Auramada. If the revolution devours its children, barbarity for him was no less the product of a civilization preparing to devour its fathers.

Looking back on all the tragedies of the last century, one is struck by the ambivalent role of intellectuals. They were often the ones to give the signal for revolt against oppression; but equally often they laid the groundwork for the fanaticization of spirits, the moral chaos, the absolute absence of good faith or, at least, of common sense. Malaparte, who felt little love for intellectuals before the war, had absolutely no intention of exonerating them of errors committed in its course. The intellectuals he puts in play are generally insignificant, if not depraved, figures, apart from some witnesses of the good and beautiful Europe of yesteryear, like Axel Munthe and few others. The sole exception is perhaps Spain's minister to Finland, Count Agustín de Foxá, marquess of Armendáriz, to whom Malaparte attributes the role of Virgil in *Kaputt*, although "in a certain sense, he is my antithesis."[38] A diplomat, but also a journalist and writer of talent, lately rediscovered, Foxá (1903–59) was a high-class misfit. A convinced nationalist, he was among the authors of the hymn to the Falange "Cara al sol" (Facing the sun) and was the movement's representative in Fascist Italy. Aligned with Franco but not with much enthusiasm, after the war he devoted himself above all to his passion for literature, theater, and journalism. He was the author, in particular, of a good historical novel covering the period from the fall of the monarchy to the civil war, translated into Italian, possibly through Malaparte's intervention.[39] Far from being, "like all good Spaniards...cruel and funereal" (K 186), Foxá was a great gentleman, cheerful and sociable—characteristics perhaps insufficiently Malapartian for the role assigned to him in the book.*

Auschwitz and the Gulag were born, as with every inquisition, from a poorly maintained library, where corrupt knowledge emits the intoxicating odor of corpses. Totalitarian extermination is first of all a *cultural* operation. Intellectuals, transformed into sorcerers' apprentices, contributed to the preparation of a work that camp builders and prison guards would not have been capable of carrying out without their involvement and zeal. Unmasked, they hide the tools of their trade behind their back, invoking professional honor and the desire to fulfill a mission. Adolf Eichmann, at the end of the trial against him in Jerusalem, did not rail against his death sentence, but asked that it be postponed so he could write "his" truth. It was not just a defense trick. The idea that it is the book that saves and

---

*I owe this testimony to the ambassador Ludovico Incisa di Camerana, who knew Foxá well. According to Pellegrini, who saw him again after the war, Foxá does not seem to have appreciated his portrait in *Kaputt*, and he did not say a single word to him about Malaparte, who had recently died.

preserves the memory of the chosen people thanks to the devotion of the scribes, the conviction that the Just One will not die as long as his memory remains: Eichmann drew these from the Talmud, which he had thoroughly studied, to better know his adversary before seeking to annihilate him, without actually feeling any visceral aversion to him. Can someone be programmed for destruction to such an extent, without being possessed by hate?[40]

Malaparte could declare all he wanted his loathing of voyeurism, his refusal to passively scrutinize men, without intervening, as they descend through all the stages of abjection. It's what he would do in his chronicles of the plague, which have more than merely descriptive value. There has been too much talk of the scandal and the excesses of these pages, of their Grand Guignol aspect. In this way, one remains on the surface. Deeper down, we find an inverted eschatology of the human condition, evoking the angel softly, implacably transformed into Lucifer. He finds this sweetness, cloying and cruel, in the smile and the hands, sometimes in the blushes and the timidity, of the assassins who confide in him. Malaparte is much more attracted to this than to violence; the sweetness accentuates the insignificance of the guilty, the opacity of their nature. In the "Naked Men" episode of *Kaputt*, the author finds himself face to face, in the elevator of a Rovaniemi hotel, with the omnipotent "Reichsführer-SS" Heinrich Himmler. The man in charge of the Final Solution, the superior of all the Eichmanns and bureaucrats of the crime, was also a perverted intellectual, in search of the Holy Grail and the origins of the Aryan race, for which he went seeking as far as Tibet and the Andes. Shortly after, Malaparte sees him again, naked in the establishment's sauna, surrounded by colleagues, naked as well, who whip him vigorously with birch twigs. This nudity—

sexually neutral, corporeally nonexistent, out of sync with respect to the wretched being it shields without revealing—announces the symbolic dissolution of the Nazi dignitary in the water and steam: "In a twinkling of an eye only a pool of perspiration on the floor would be left of him" (K, 339). Himmler disappears into the absence of form and identity, drowns in the indistinct, and disperses into the inhuman. It is the opposite of the "healthy" nudity among men that the writer celebrates in the sauna ritual, where one also finds Malaparte at his most puckish.[41]

Only a woman, with her fleshy substance, can transform this search for nothing into an aspiration to life, but only on the condition that this woman resembles *him*. We have seen how Malaparte gave us a preview of this portrait in *Woman Like Me*, and it is the model that he himself would like to be, if history with its ignominies did not exist:

> I would like [for her to] appear to me like a gentle force of nature, righteous and incorruptible; an element of the grace, force and purity that are in the air, in the light, in the plants, in the stones and in the landscape. (W, 2)

No one is certain of being saved, in the judgment of history: as soon as it enters the scene, it destroys every certainty in its path. Malaparte loved nature, especially flowers, almost as much as animals; now this Garden of Eden was threatened by filth. The terms he proceeded to use to describe nature are similar to those in the previous quotation, but they are cast in a negative or privative light:

> The silence was horrible. The light was dead, the smell of the grass, the color of the leaves, of the stones, of the clouds that drifted

through the gray sky—everything was dead, everything was plunged into a vast, empty, frozen silence. (S, 164)

In *One Thousand and One Nights*, Scheherazade survives the royal fury, interrupting the story only when the vendetta is finally turned into a love song. The life instinct, rekindled by feminine guile, forces the wife-destroying sultan to return to the maternal womb, to choose what perpetuates itself rather than what cancels itself. "I've just read your *Kaputt*," wrote Marianne Halévy to Malaparte on November 23, 1947: "I thought, if I may say so, of *One Thousand and One Nights*!"[42] What extraordinary intuition there is in this juxtaposition! Only those who stand athwart circumstances and, seated on the highest branch of the tree, fearlessly contemplate the hand that saws it can aspire to be prophets. This is the case with a young Turinese chemist deported to Auschwitz, Primo Levi, who was unlike Malaparte in every way, except for an extraordinary capacity for premonition. His first gesture, which he would manage to confess entirely only at the end of his life, was to unconsciously conceal evil so that it does not exist, so that it loses its magical paralyzing power, so that it takes on the structure of the bad dreams that leave us at dawn. The same incredulity prevailed among Italian Jews, who just the day before had seemed indistinguishable from their compatriots: in the sealed boxcars began their systematic dehumanization. They were good, educated citizens, prosperous and respected; among them were the staff and residents of the Jewish Home for the Aged of Venice; they had yet to accept their pariah status.[43] In Levi's *The Drowned and the Saved*, we see how this "bourgeois" reaction becomes much more than a sudden burst of dignity: with the help of a few nails and a blanket, they managed to divide off a part of the boxcar, transforming it into a makeshift latrine. A chamber pot, which a foresighted mother had managed to bring with her for her own suckling infant, passes from one to another of the fifty occupants, protecting them, in part, from "a trauma for which our civilization leaves us unprepared, a deep wound inflicted on human dignity, an obscene and ominous attack, but also the sign of a deliberate, gratuitous malice."[44] This common object, which we usually hide from view, becomes suddenly more precious than the money that could ransom them, than the weapon that could defend them, than the prayer book that could console them. Because it proves that "we are not yet beasts, not as long as we try to resist,"[45] according to Dante's admonition that "you were not made to live your lives as brutes, / but to be followers of worth and knowledge," which would echo in a famous page of *If This Is a Man*.

This chamber pot is a bulwark turned instrument of resistance, of surrealist subversion against abominable reality. Even more than suicide, it shows how a conscious being can fully reconcile strength of mind with control of body, to assert himself as he is, in his singularity and totality. Hiding our bodily functions from others' eyes is not only a modesty reflex. It is the last sliver of autonomy available to a being in constriction, or in the hands of others: in a hospital, nursing home, prison, barracks, and so forth. What does it matter if this sliver is torn away from him by force? Consensus is not in play; his spirit remains free. But if it is lost *voluntarily*, his spirit plummets definitively into the castaways' camp; his vulnerability is revealed not only to his torturers or his companions in misfortune but also to himself. He has lost everything; he can only wait passively, like Gregor Samsa, for a relative or a neighbor, not necessarily an enemy, to squash him like an insect, almost out of pity. Deprived since birth of his goddess mother, the bastard Genet is reduced to the condition of garbage: "He is not the product of a woman; he is her excrement."[46] In *Salò, or The 120 Days of Sodom*, his most reactionary film, and thus his least subversive, Pasolini goes even further in his demonstration. He stages a series of ever-more-degrading tests, inspired in part by Dante's infernal circuit but devoid of any possibility of redemption. The atonement via blood, sex, and fecal material has the aim of showing that a human being can become an object, passing through the stages of brute, then of beast, and finally of inert matter, rejected by the "healthy" organism. His reification becomes total then, in the name of the "excretion of guilt," to once again cite Sartre. In the language of the concentration camps, such a person was called *ein Stück*, "a piece"; whether alive or already a corpse matters little, as they are already *kaputt*, broken, shattered. For the executioner, this loss of the victim's human consistency is much more reassuring than any physical disappearance:

> For they have a terrible strength, the dead, and they might burst their irons, smash their coffins, and break out and bite and tear the faces of all and sundry, relations and friends. The police ought to bury them with handcuffs on their wrists and, having nailed up the coffins securely, lower them into very deep, specially dug holes, and then tread down the earth above the grave, to prevent those bastards from coming out and biting people. Ah, sleep in peace, you bastards! (S, 72)

The resurrection of the dead is the nightmare of anyone who has ever wanted to annihilate their adversary, to reduce them to *nihil*.

Levi's chamber pot becomes a cigar in Malaparte, in an episode of *Kaputt* that one would be tempted to describe as "marvelous," if it were not dominated by terror. But it is the marvelous of Chagall, a painter whom Malaparte loved and evoked often, perhaps because he was so different from him. Everywhere around him in the shtetls of Ukraine and Poland, Chagall found a naive art, both erotic and religious, that promised an ascension to heaven, a return to true life, the engaged couple's flight on the back of a donkey, through the window that becomes a crescent moon, "a Jewish Chagall sky, crowded with Jewish angels, with Jewish clouds, with Jewish horses and dogs dangling in their flight over the town" (K, 138). And yet we are in the antechamber of the *anus mundi*: the Warsaw Ghetto that Malaparte has gone to visit, in counterpoint to the lavish soirée awaiting him in the royal palace, now the residence of the Nazi governor-general Frank. The visit, often called into doubt, did happen and was registered without comment in the *Giornale segreto*, on January 25, 1942. The only difference with respect to the book and to the novelization of Malaparte's dialogue with Frank is the fact that the visit happened after, and not before, the reception hosted by the governor-general.[47] The *Giornale segreto* indicates that, after the visit, there was also a breakfast at the Belvedere Palace with the champion boxer Max Schmeling and with "those from yesterday evening" (among them Frank?). And here it should be clarified that, as a general rule, the German authorities had tried to impede similar inspections on the part of correspondents from neutral countries accredited in Berlin, like the American William Shirer. Even among journalists from the Axis countries, there were relatively few who wanted to, or could, take a close look at such an abomination.[48] Malaparte evidently had no hesitations. It was not only the special correspondent's intuition, or even the curiosity of a man attracted to the macabre in all its expressions everywhere. It was the concern of a writer before the cornerstone of his edifice. It is easy to believe he would have willingly gone to "visit" Auschwitz, whose existence he already suspected. In the absence of a concentration camp, he opted for what was closest. Such an attitude may scandalize, but it is right to recognize the adherence to reality of his "imaginary" description, confirmed by the testimonies of rare survivors, like the memoirs of Marcel Reich-Ranicki, an eminent German literary critic of Polish descent, who found himself trapped in Warsaw and used as an interpreter in the Jewish administration of the ghetto.

During his visit to the "forbidden city," Malaparte encounters two girls fighting over a raw potato. One manages to make off with her meager prize; the other remains on the spot, her "eyes full of hunger, modesty, and shame," and suddenly smiles. Confused, as he rarely is, Malaparte would like to offer her money, but the girl refuses with great dignity and moves away, continuing to smile. The author's embarrassment grows; he searches his pockets for something that could establish a bond, however tenuous, between them. He finds nothing else but a cigar; he runs after her, reaches her, and offers it to her. Let us read closely the following passage, where there is not a wasted word:

> The girl gazed uncertainly at me, blushed, took the cigar, and I understood that she was only accepting it to please me. She said nothing, not even thanks; she walked away slowly without turning, holding the cigar in her hand, bringing it close to her face from time to time to inhale its scent, as if I had given her a flower. (K, 98)

This cigar, fictional or not, is a marvelous invention, in the Chagall sense. It would have sufficed to substitute it with a rose, a handkerchief, or a piece of bread, and the pathetic effect would have weakened the literary quality of the page; the scene would have lost its power of attraction-repulsion. The cigar—and this being Malaparte, it could only have been a luxurious Havana, just received from a German officer—is an even more incongruous apparition than Levi's chamber pot. Nonetheless, it would not be enough to move us, without the girl's reaction. Astonished—and what could still astonish a being laid so low by disaster?—she doesn't thank him. She could do it for a handout of money or food, which implies pity in the donor; but not for a personal object, which implies guilt.* She does not turn around even to grant the unknown man a last smile, her attention captured by a fantastic object, which, since she cannot eat it, she sniffs, in anticipation of the Chagallian heaven awaiting her, because "Jewish children have wings" (K, 103). There is an undertone here of coquetry, of mischief amid the horror, in which a lesser writer would have slipped into moralism or cheap indignation. But never as here do we see Malaparte abdicate his role of actor, so insisted on at the time of the other war, and confine himself to that of spectator. It is not uncommon to interpret this cigar as the penis he relinquishes symbolically, refusing to take on the manly role par excellence, that of protecting a weaker being. What has become of strength, once so ardently praised? The opposite happens to the girl in the ghetto, who shows herself here to be as subversive and rebellious a character as the uprisers would later be. If this

---

*In a popular Neapolitan tale, a beggar sits on the steps of a church. Indifferent to the passersby who fail to give him money, he insults those who do.

unknown girl no longer has the ability to organize a line of defense, like the bourgeois of Primo Levi, she still has the instinct. She refuses brutalization, dehumanization, reification. She survives.

Music and Gallows

With Hans Frank, the brownshirted new "king of Poland," Malaparte takes us into the assassins' lair. But the good husband, good father of five, good Catholic from Franconia, former scholarship recipient at the University of Rome, passionate about the Renaissance, polyglot, a jurist educated prior to the Third Reich (he was born in 1900), interlocutor and protector of figures like Heidegger and Carl Schmitt (as president of the Academy for German Law, founded by the regime), Frank is a cultivated assassin, with a freshly shaved face (hence the play on words in "God Shave the King") and delicate white hands, on which his guest searches in vain for traces of blood. These hands have done something worse than kill, at least for the moment. They have played, prior to the guests' arrival, Beethoven, Brahms, and Schumann, as well as—something incongruous for a Nazi dignitary—Frédéric Chopin, promoted to honorary German, in homage to the genius loci.[49] This preference of his did not prevent the Nazis from blowing up the monument dedicated to the Romantic composer in the center of Warsaw, or from prohibiting the public performance of all musical works relevant to Polish national feeling, starting with Chopin's.[50] They were right, from their point of view, because "those notes of the 'Prelude,' so pure and light, floated in the warm air like propaganda leaflets dropped from a plane. On each note was printed 'Long live Poland!' in large crimson letters" (K, 153). And it was no accident that Gottfried

Benn, the great poet of internal exile under the Third Reich, wrote then two very beautiful poems titled "Chopin" and "Finis Poloniae." A noble soul, forced to bend to the demands of realpolitik, Frank plays for himself alone, then, in a cell of the Belvedere Palace, ideally dressed in a monk's habit, far from the eyes of his adoring wife and his courtiers, who dare not disturb him. They know the extent to which their leader is a superior man. Such depends not only on the power of life and death he has over his subjects but also on this artistic demand opposed to the directives he himself must promulgate, with great regret.*

Frank is a man who confronts suffering bravely and takes on the weight of great responsibilities. His encounter with Malaparte takes place during a gala luncheon, conducted in the language of conversation par excellence, French, which is also the language of the Marquis de Sade, a figure that would not have been out of place in this assembly. Frank's Italian, while sketchy, was nevertheless better than Malaparte's nonexistent German. We will highlight as we go the precision of the details, such as the description, among the guests, of the cryptic manager of the Jewish workforce with the "abbot-like face" (K, 78): audiences came across him again, more or less the same, forty years later, interviewed in the famous documentary

---

*The French writer Lucien Rebatet, a refined music critic and rabid anti-Semite, declared himself open, in the same period, to certain concessions: "For my part, I would not see any harm if a great musical virtuoso from the ghetto were authorized to come play for the Aryans for their pleasure, like the exotic slaves in ancient Rome." But wait: "If this should turn out to be the pretext for an encroachment, however minimal, of this horrible species on us, I myself would shatter the records of Chopin and Mozart, performed by the marvelous Horowitz and Menuhin." See *Les Décombres* (Paris: Denoël, 1942), 569. This passage—along with many others—was omitted from the postwar reprinting.

Shoah, by Claude Lanzmann. In front of Frank and his accomplices, Malaparte had never before seemed so aware of his hereditary Germanness, however hard he tried to push it away. Wherever he is revealing the phobic structures of persecution, the solitude of executioners, their biblical terror before victims, Malaparte is perfectly at ease. He discovers that

> the disease from which they suffer is mysterious. They are afraid above all of the weak, of the defenseless, of the sick, of women and of children. They are afraid of the aged. Their fear has always aroused a profound pity in me. (K, 12)

It is on account of this fear that Primo Levi, Hannah Arendt, and Bruno Bettelheim talked about executioners' need to disperse the ashes of their victims: a ritual act to conceal the traces of their crimes, almost as if to make it so that, symbolically, they never happened.

At the governor-general's table, Malaparte offers us a hunting trophy in the sauce of the hour—quite heavy, featuring a goose roasted in its own fat—and provokes the scandalized laughter of his interlocutors, evoking the womanliness of the Führer, an old theme from *Technique du coup d'État*. However, he avoids responding directly to the tricky question that the Catholic Frank poses to the Protestant Malaparte, and that is whether Christ as well was a woman. There is nonetheless something troubling in this chapter of unmatched virtuosity. No sooner does it touch on the properly musical sphere than a misunderstanding sets in, because Frank *feels* the music much more than his interlocutor. Malaparte, so gifted in terms of his social, literary, and visual imagination, is unable in this matter to say or feel anything but banalities. The chameleon who becomes an aristocrat among the aristocrats, a diplomat among the diplomats, a soldier among the soldiers, a worker among the workers, is manifestly in difficulty here. Conversely, music lives in Frank, to the extent that all his massacres are musical, abstract, harmonious massacres. And he is offended because his audience of Polish and Jewish subjects do not applaud him, do not inundate him with gratitude. Music and gallows become an inseparable pair. It is this envelope of *Kultur* that allows him to conceal and justify his exclusively criminal behavior. But, unlike the brutes under his command, he maintains an intimate fear of sin, derived from his Catholic, pre-Nazi education.

In the period when Malaparte was writing, two major postwar events had yet to occur but were already in the air. Firstly, the Nuremberg trials, at which Frank would accept his fate and end up on the gallows, contrite and repentant, but still convinced of his own innocence and of the exceptional purity of his own soul.[51] Secondly, the publication of *Doctor Faustus*, written several thousand miles away by Thomas Mann, who, in his Californian exile, had already anticipated everything. Frank's sadness is that of the inconsolable artist, of the musician "tripped up" by the march of history, like the composer Adrian Leverkühn in the novel. In the scene in which Leverkühn concludes his devil's bargain, Mann describes masterfully how the devil insinuates himself into "superior" consciousnesses, pretending to deliver them from the transience of the common man:

> This is precisely the secret delight and security of hell, that it cannot be denounced, that it lies hidden from language.... No, it is bootless to speak of it, for it lies apart from and outside of language, which has nothing to do with it, has no relation to it.... And now I shall

tell you that precisely minds of your sort constitute the population of hell.⁵²

The condition sealed by the pact to permanently give up love—"Your life shall be cold"⁵³—finds its natural expression in music. It corresponds to the art and ambition of Leverkühn; it represents, in Mann's eyes, both the greatest accomplishment and the greatest temptation of the German spirit, as he had predicted with the rise of National Socialism, in the essay "The Sorrows and Grandeur of Richard Wagner." Nothing could stem the sadness of Frank, because it isolates him in his misunderstood vocation, separates him from those who ought to love him, at the same time depriving him of accomplices. This is what inspires the Christian compassion in some of his victims, for whom Frank and his gang are truly "those *pauvres gens*," as the Princess Radziwill says (K, 76, 83), who export not a superior *Kultur* but a neobarbarous form of destruction and subjugation. The failure of National Socialism is first of all the failure of its *Kultur*, of which Frank is an exemplary master. In vain he dreams of inviting the great conductors Furtwängler and Karajan to undertake with him the reeducation of that ungrateful public. (Neither of them "visited" occupied Poland.) Only the Jews can give him some satisfaction.

Reich-Ranicki devotes a long section of his memoirs to describing the ghetto prisoners' superhuman efforts to not give up classical music—officially forbidden them, even more than it was other Poles, as the "Aryan" and "German" art par excellence. The ghetto literally resounded with music, from dawn to dusk. In addition to various choirs and chamber groups, it was possible to constitute a nearly complete symphony orchestra, under the direction of a first-rate conductor, Simon Pullman, later killed at Treblinka, flanked by another three respected professionals (Marian Neuteikh, Adam Furmanski, and Israel Hamerman). The Warsaw Ghetto orchestra gave some forty concerts between late 1940 and April 1942, when its activities were prohibited by the German authorities, three months before the ghetto's liquidation.[54] All the musicians, without exception, were deported and died in the camps. But before that happened, Frank had even tolerated—such was his disinterested love for the music—their execution of pieces officially forbidden to Jews. One day, recounts Reich-Ranicki, during the performance of a Mozart symphony, two or three uniformed officers showed up. They listened in silence until the end, applauded, and left, showing their approval.[55] This little-known page is perhaps one of the noblest of the Jewish people's resistance to the Shoah. It's hard to believe Frank failed to understand this. But who will speak of the executioners' immense sadness at not measuring up to their victims?

The Italian is on the defensive. He is annoyed by Frank's swooning, seeing in it a manifestation of that cruel sentimentalism he is constantly noting in the Germans (to denounce, as we have seen, is not in his nature). Malaparte does not understand that Frank, a believer walled into his sense of guilt, looks to music as a way to escape his own fears, equating music with prayer. He would likewise understand nothing about the fate of Leverkühn or his Faustian pact. Nowhere in his work, so rich in artistic and cultural references, do we find a noteworthy observation concerning music, old or new. If Malaparte happens to mention Debussy or Stravinsky, Milhaud or Shostakovich, Honegger or Hindemith, it is in an essentially anecdotal mode, because like him they are part of a twentieth-century who's who, such that, citing them, he is citing himself; praising them, he praises himself; they are "like me." It is music, more than any other aspect, that reveals the parvenu side of Malaparte, the point at which his Germanness, so deeply rooted, abandons him. Resistant to any metaphysical interrogation, Malaparte can perceive music only in its immediate, external dimension. If he appreciates the result, he is ignorant of the path to it. Again, he describes Frank's passion for music but does not "feel" it. He knows it is a symptom of the Faustian sickness of the absolute, and that the Nazis are sad because the world does not love their music; or rather, because they know it is not *their* music, it does not belong to them, to the point that they would insist on having it performed, the better to appropriate it, by *their* victims being led to the gallows in the death camps.[56] But he does not succeed in revealing

> the complexity of his character—a peculiar mixture of cruel intelligence, refinement, vulgarity, brutal cynicism and polished sensitiveness. There had to be a deep zone of darkness within him that I was still unable to explore... an inaccessible hell from which dull fleeting glows flashed unexpectedly. (K, 149)

Malaparte, lest we forget, is a sane, healthy man, with the instinct and reactions of a sane man, sharpened by Tuscan realism. He knows perfectly well the master of the house is a dangerous and intelligent psychopath, and not a bureaucrat drunk on power or a common criminal. But he doesn't know *why* the other man has arrived at such extremes, or what he really thinks. Where does the charm of the tale Frank tells himself really lie? It is the fable of the gallant knight of art, who has had to plunge, against his will, into the abysses of history, because men are neither so good nor so inspired as to nourish themselves on his musical offerings alone. The scene in which, at the end of the dinner, the guests go to the gate of the forbidden city to shoot at the "mice," the Jewish children who try to escape through holes dug under the wall, in order to look for food in the city, is one of the rare passages in *Kaputt* in which Malaparte has recourse to simple description of the horror, being unable to interpret it, or no longer interested in doing so. It is a grand finale, a bass drum strike, where the monstrosity obviates any need for psychological analysis. Frank, who picks up a soldier's rifle and takes aim, sheds all psychological depth and sinks to the level of a mere assassin. He loses his form, his facade of *Kultur*, his attempts at justification and musical abstraction. Vanished is his identity, or what he put up as such, as someone able to consider himself different from those surrounding him, superior not only to his victims but also to his accomplices.[57]

We can obviously argue that the real Frank is the one who "betrays" himself in that moment and puts his banal, ignoble nature on full display. But then the entire structure Malaparte has erected to ennoble this figure, to grant him a share of dissatisfaction, to make him an interlocutor and not simply the object of the devil's wiles, no longer holds up. It melts like the makeup that drips down the face of Aschenbach in *Death in Venice*, revealing him to himself and to others, a wretched victim of a project of amorous fabulation, a puppet of flesh rather than poetry, in pursuit of the adolescent Tazio. Mann chooses to make him die in that moment, because his hero, revealed in his wretchedness, can move someone to pity, but he loses all exemplary force. As for Leverkühn, his Nietzschean madness, by novel's end, is a vain attempt to renege on the frigidity called for in the pact, and therefore not to respect its provisions: "A total chilling of your life and of your relations to humans lies in the nature of things—indeed it already lies in your nature."⁵⁸

Frank exits the scene to become a subject of analysis for criminal psychology. He no longer interests us as readers; his supposed "complexity" crumbles before our eyes; he becomes just one more of the trilogy's many nightmarish apparitions, like the Croatian dictator Ante Pavelić, who uncovers, with "that tired good-natured smile," an Adriatic oyster basket containing "forty pounds of human eyes" from his Serb enemies (K, 278). A plausible episode, alas; and yet invented out of whole cloth.⁵⁹ One reads it with a shiver of grim anticipation, thinking about the massacres in the former Yugoslavia after 1989, or in Chechnya. But the description offers an entirely external idea of the character's excess, of his cruelty, devoid of aesthetic trappings. The same thing goes for the other butchers who fill these pages without ever rising to the literary dignity of their victims. And even the victims rarely rise to the level of animals, which are more than ever the fellow travelers, the real brothers in arms, the only consolers of Malaparte.

On the Side of the Goose

Milan Kundera, rereading *Kaputt*, evoked the notion of "delirious beauty," the "poetry of the improbable" of the surrealists.⁶⁰ Yet Malaparte is above all an adept of magical realism: a realism as meticulous as Kafka's, in which "the insect" Gregor Samsa anticipates the zoological and anthropomorphic universe revealed here. Malaparte divides this universe into noble animals (horses, birds, reindeer) and ignoble ones (mice, flies, other insects): all of them are for him denaturalized, torn from their harmonious relationship with creation.

Dogs constitute, it must be said, a pack of their own: we know the extent to which the writer identified with them. This makes their fate even more painful, and they hearken back to the archetype of Febo, his faithful companion on Lipari, his greatest friend and possibly the love of his life. The suffering of animals is a distinct phenomenon, with its own characteristics, with respect to the suffering of human beings or of disfigured nature; and it is the only kind capable of inspiring an authentically religious feeling in Malaparte. Machines, too, suffer and agonize in *Kaputt*, as previously in *Volga*. Consider the Futurist evocation of the Soviet armored car, a "rotting machine... iron carrion, overturned in the mud" (K, 37). Thus the animal kingdom opens itself to the pity that men no longer have the right to inspire or invoke: "that fearful Christian pity that beasts have. It occurred to me that beasts were Christ... They have the look of Christ, the look of a beast" (K, 333). Pity alone offers an escape from the steamroller of history, inverting the formula from Miłosz cited as an epigraph for this chapter. Animals are the most innocent victims of the madness of men; and every time men are described as victims, they are "animalized," becoming related to the sacrificial lamb. This concept would be taken up by Malaparte in an unfinished essay, "Les Métamorphoses" (The metamorphoses), in 1945:

> There is nothing in the world more contemptible than man, this perverted animal, this animal degraded by reason. In the eyes of man there is an innocent, pure animal, who looks at you with its long pure look, full of pity and contempt. "The assassin is always a man," a German soldier in Russia told me in August 1941, "his victim always

an animal. An assassinated man becomes once again a hunted, frightened animal. This is why an assassinated man arouses pity. Because he is not a man but an animal."[61]

Kaputt and *The Skin* contain two spectacular evocations of victors' banquets, where the food served is a sacrificial animal, a miraculous food, the body of Christ who remits the world's sins. The first scene takes us back once more to the luncheon given by the "king of Poland," where the goose, served on a silver plate, is "executed" by an SS firing squad before being roasted on a spit. Frank repeats this ritual execution, followed by his tablemates:

> "Fire!" shouted Frank in his turn, and the laughter grew in volume; they fixed their eyes on the goose, cocking their heads on their right shoulders and closing their left eyes, as if they really were taking aim. Then I laughed too, while a crawling sensation of shame overcame me little by little. I felt a sort of hurt shame. I felt on the side of the goose. (K, 75)

We have already encountered this impotent shame of Malaparte's, expressed in similar terms in the episode of the girl and the cigar. Frank's rifle shot here explicitly announces the one the governor-general is preparing to fire, after dinner, against the "mice" trying to flee the ghetto. What we are witnessing, then, is a trial run of the crime that will be perpetuated shortly on the most defenseless subjects of Nazi atrocities, children. It is this crime against humanity-animality that pushes Malaparte to side with the victims, with an ardor unusual for him.

We will find the same attitude in *The Skin*, during the banquet given by General Cork (an evident stand-in for General Clark).* The American commander is certainly not a professional exterminator like his Nazi counterpart, but he embodies the moral responsibility of the victor, his lack of innocence before history—a responsibility he shares with the vanquished, who proved unable to defend his homeland, family, or property. At table, the food preferences of the fellow diners differ. Malaparte offers a bravura description of the fried Spam, boiled corn, and canned milk of the Yankee military canteen, served by Neapolitan waiters in livery, who disdain their uncouth new masters. And now arrives the evening's main course: "Siren mayonnaise," garnished with coral, taken from the city aquarium. The fish is evidently mythological, and the amused onlookers expect some sort of magic trick. But laid out on the silver platter (the same platter evoked in *Kaputt*) appears the boiled corpse of a little girl. Cries of horror ring out from the virtuous tablemates, among them a feminist bluestocking, which is one of the best caricatures to ever emerge from Malaparte's pen. The puritanism of this Mrs. Flat is the complement of Mrs. Frank's fanaticism: two women on the verge of a nervous breakdown, representing everything that

---

*Mark Wayne Clark (1896–1984), commander of the American Fifth Army, was the primary person responsible for Allied operations during the 1943–44 campaign, which earned him the hostility of his British counterparts Montgomery and Alexander and in general of English military historians. Clark was popular among the Italians, even as he made some debatable decisions, such as the bombardment without any strategic utility of the Abbey of Monte Cassino and the triumphal entrance into Rome (June 4, 1944). The Eternal City was thus the first capital liberated by the Allies; but it was a minor objective, compared with the destruction of the German troops in Italy, who were able to retreat north, behind the Gothic Line, which held for another ten months.

ON THE SIDE OF THE GOOSE

Malaparte fears and refuses in the woman who is not "like me."* He then has a good time responding that "in Europe a fish doesn't have to look like a fish" (S, 226). What Malaparte really means is the opposite: the more the victims are innocent, like the little girl, the more they resemble animals, the only innocents by definition, the only ones who suffer a punishment without its origin in the atonement of a sin but in a pure, gratuitous, Christological sacrifice. Is the fish not the symbol of the savior for the Christians of the catacombs? The theme of the inaccessible innocence of the siren has attracted other major authors of the twentieth century, from Tanizaki to Tomasi di Lampedusa. The siren is similar to the goose, as the little dead girl in Naples resembles the dying girl in the Warsaw Ghetto. Men should nourish themselves on this meat, on this manna, if they truly want to free their souls from evil. We are already in the realm of atonement, heralding *The Forbidden Christ*.

General Cork's banquet is one of the most famous episodes in *The Skin* and one that contributed to Malaparte's fame as a writer, or even as a man, of hazy sexuality, with shades of pedophilia and necrophilia.[62] We shall return to this aspect. But if one really wants to find a moment, perhaps the only moment, in the chronicles of the plague where his narcissistic libido shows through, one must return to the book's preceding episode, "The Black Wind." Here Malaparte follows up a scene of crucifixion on the Ukrainian steppes in 1941 with the (equally imaginary) account of the disappearance

---

*Cavani, to introduce some flirtation between Mrs. Flat and Malaparte in her film version, had to make this character younger and radically different. Needless to say, this little romantic idyll, just like the one between the protagonist and a lady of the Neapolitan aristocracy, played by Claudia Cardinale, is not only foreign to the book but antithetical to Malaparte's vision.

of Febo in the narrow streets of Pisa. Malaparte's anguish does not spring from his abandonment by a lover, because it is unthinkable that Febo has left him on purpose, but from the impenetrable hostility of the surrounding world. Wicked men have taken away and possibly killed the dog, without anyone intervening to prevent it. After searching in vain at the municipal pound, he finds Febo in a veterinary clinic, where he is subjected, along with other strays, to atrocious vivisection experiments: "In him I saw Christ crucified, I saw Christ looking at me with eyes that were full of a wonderful tenderness.... Febo kissed my hand, and not a moan escaped him" (S, 171). The doctor yields to the writer's pleas and prepares to give the poor beast a compassionate injection. But in that moment Malaparte marvels at the unreal silence reigning in the clinic, where the other tortured dogs remain silent like Febo. The doctor explains that "before we operate on them ... we cut their vocal cords" (S, 172).

Rarely has Malaparte allowed us to penetrate with greater clarity into the most hidden sectors of his psyche. It seems undeniable that into Febo's fate he has transposed his own sadomasochistic nightmares, the obsession with violence and blood, and at the same time the fascination all that holds for him, and which he carries inside from the other war. According to his secretary, Hitler demanded that his female German shepherd, the faithful Blondi, was always immaculately clean. He could not touch or pet her if she was muddy or if she gave off the least smell, because a soiled animal is like a human being: its abstract innocence is lost. It was on Blondi that the dictator ritually tested the poison with which he would kill himself, in case a hand tremor prevented him using a pistol.[63] Malaparte, who detested every ideological abstraction, would like to lick the dying Febo's nose, to feel his jerky breath on him, "like me." I believe it is one of the rare love passages written by Malaparte, and by far the most beautiful.⁶⁴

An author occasionally projects onto a character in agony the image of the being most dear to them. It is to a certain extent a way to bring about a form of survival through this exorcism. The symbolizing form of the sacrifice prevents reality from surreptitiously appearing, from punishing the victim who has already atoned through a literary childbirth. In *Doctor Faustus*, Mann lent the features of his beloved grandson to the character of Nepomuk, "Echo," the child who, in sacrificing himself, wants to help Adrian Leverkühn escape the chill surrounding him. But the devil will snatch him away from the composer, plunging Leverkühn back into the solitude sealed by the infernal pact. Malaparte's exorcism translates into an active gesture vis-à-vis Febo, as opposed to the role of passive spectator he normally assumes in the plague chronicles. One can see here an effort to galvanize sorrow, suppressing its most evident manifestation, a cry or sob, replaced by a caress and the hand that Febo kisses for the last time.

The choice of vivisection, too, among all possible tortures, is revealing.* The idea of man reduced to the state of guinea pig for the sake of science, of racial selection, of eugenics, and so on, was a key theme of the debates over progress around the turn of the twentieth century, which took on a newly sinister aspect in wartime. Malaparte was aware of this, to the point of railing at multiple points in *Mamma marcia* against "modern civilization, [which] is in a hurry to make corpses disappear. One day it will be in a hurry to make the

---

*The young protagonists of Pasolini's *Ragazzi di vita* (*Boys Alive*) will prefer to kill cats with stones or by drowning.

sick disappear, or the useless" (MM, 229–30). If elsewhere he claims that "I've always dreamed that one day it might be given to me to be killed like a dog" (S, 316), it is once again to accuse the being of history of assassinating the being of nature. It is a crime now devoid of national or ideological identity, on the left as on the right, whether concerned with SS members who practice pulling out the eyes of cats, Soviet soldiers who send out dogs with explosives strapped to their backs against the tanks of the Wehrmacht, or German officers who fish for salmon by tossing grenades into the lake.

It is no accident, then, if between human and animal, Malaparte introduces another "character," the fetus, which he encountered for the first time as a child while paging through his father's illustrated books by German scientists of the Romantic period, such as the influential work of Karl Ernst von Baer, a precursor of modern embryology, on animal evolution which anticipated Darwin's theories. Malaparte did not have a scientific education, but it is likely that these themes had captivated him via his favorite uncle, whose name he bore, Kurt Suckert, a bizarre character and reader at the University of Göttingen, who as a good Saxon loved to go bask in the Tuscan sun. Toward the end of *The Skin*, Malaparte describes his own arrival in newly liberated Rome, where he is hosted by a gynecologist friend. In the latter's apartment-laboratory he discovers a great quantity of jars containing fetuses of various dimensions and in various states. They assume the role of the chorus in Greek tragedy, like the tortured dogs surrounding Febo in the Pisa clinic.*

---

*Malaparte perhaps had in mind one of the greatest texts by Leopardi, "Dialogue between Frederick Ruysch and His Mummies," in *The Moral Essays (Operette Morali)*, trans. Patrick Creagh (New York: Columbia University Press, 1983).

Without being able to claim the innocence of beasts, the fetus is not yet contaminated by the original sin of men. It is an organism in an intermediary state, a subproduct of evolution, which the narrator elevates to the dignity of interlocutor. Can we read into this a quasi Célinian condemnation of abortion? Difficult to say: Malaparte never distinguished himself in the demographic battle of the Fascist period, when it was an official theme of the regime, or after the war. A hint of sexophobia, however, weighs on the spell emanating from these pages. In an exemplary way, the fetus embodies the moral of the book, the fate of man brought back to his incomplete physiological nature, to be a denier devoid of true substance, a corpse "of a monstrous species: corpses which have never been born and have never died" (S, 328–29). He is capable of stirring and expressing himself, seeing as how Malaparte grants him the floor, but not of giving sense and direction to his terrestrial adventure. He is a fallen angel, a wrinkly little monster, almost demonic, whom life has not accepted and has shoved back into the gaseous fluctuations of a jar. He is, however, less repugnant than "a man or a nation in the hour of triumph" (S, 333).

Suddenly, one of these wretched creatures separates itself from the chorus and complains to the author about not having provoked the crowd's pity, when "they cut my throat, they hanged me by the feet from a hook, they covered me with spittle" (S, 334). It is in fact the corpse of Mussolini, the dead Duce, the toad and chameleon of yesteryear, now reduced to the state of a fetus. Malaparte claims to have seen him a few days earlier, in Piazzale Loreto, in Milan, hung by his feet beside the corpses of Clara Petacci and his last followers, in the same place where, in August 1944, fifteen partisans had been executed by Fascist militiamen and left lying on the asphalt as a warning. How indeed could Malaparte have missed such a spectacle, at least in his imagination? It almost seems, to read him, that the crowd had waited for his arrival before performing. Photos of the ignoble spectacle spread rapidly around the world, and as far as we know, even Hitler managed in time to see them in his bunker in the Reich Chancellery, some hours before his suicide, repeating his order that both his and Eva Braun's bodies be burned. In this emblem of fratricidal hate, in this explosion of collective madness, commentators have also seen an instance of mass amorous neurosis.

In a televised interview near the end of her life, Edda Ciano Mussolini recalled in striking language what was for her the Italians' last expression of love toward their *padre padrone*, whose body they were in some way devouring in order to continue carrying him inside them. It is, anyway, the final demonstration of what Malaparte never stopped proclaiming over the course of his chronicles of the plague, wherever he was, under whatever sky: "Everything that man gives to man is a foul thing" (S, 334). Here we can finally acknowledge in him a good dose of sincerity: the conclusion corresponds to his idea of history as the permanent source of unhappiness, as an element dissolving the vital instinct man draws from beast, and which he has betrayed out of a desire to elevate himself to the status of supreme judge of his own actions.

Skin and Mud

A follow-up to *Kaputt*? Quite a challenge. Malaparte had initially worked on a more stripped-down, intimist project, inspired by the almost mythological nudity of nature on Capri, "Un delitto cristiano"

(A Christian crime), of which various drafts survive.⁶⁵ But it was the choral dimension, the fresco both real and surreal, that attracted him now. And this was what his new French publisher, Guy Tosi, was also claiming loudly:

> We have too much regard for your talent not to gladly receive any manuscript from you. We therefore await God Is an Assassin [maybe "Un delitto cristiano"] with hope that *The Plague* will not be far behind. There is no denying the public is waiting for the continuation of *Kaputt*; we have announced and promised it too many times for there not to be some slight disappointment when we have to announce that the publication of *The Plague* has been pushed back.⁶⁶

And Malaparte, after working on some suggestive fragments, titled "Gli ultimi giorni di Capri" (The last days of Capri) and "I giorni della grande peste" (The days of the great plague),⁶⁷ finally yields:

> The topic of [*The Skin*] will be not Europe at war but postwar Europe. It will be a less cruel book than *Kaputt*, even as cruelty is not excluded, but more enjoyable, in the sense that it will be horrible and cheerful at the same time. I would be happy to have this new book appear in France first, even before Italy. Now that Fascism is no longer there to impose on us an intellectual nationalism as futile as it is stupid, I would like to accentuate the international character of my literary work.⁶⁸

The Skin is the only book by Malaparte dominated by a collective hero: the Neapolitan people in their wretchedness and grandeur.

We know Malaparte did not love losers, but he wanted to show us here that, in the moral confusion of the war and postwar, there was no victor without blemish or fear. There is no liberator in which a bit of the occupier does not hide, no liberation without a settling of accounts: audacious claims giving this book a contrarian, bitter, and pessimistic dimension relative to the atmosphere of euphoria, of often cowardly relief, that seemed to prevail then in people's minds. This is the main reason why *The Skin*'s reception immediately brought to the surface a dichotomy persisting to this day: abroad, readers have generally greeted it as a credible portrait of a city that became a metaphor for the defeat of every political and moral value; in Italy, where the book was greeted with more succès de scandale than critical acclaim, it still tends to be reproached for being, as one recent assessment has it, "a serenely anti-Resistance novel, intentionally written to talk less about Fascists than about the 'gray zone' of non-Partisans."[69] And the novel is still often viewed today as the embodiment of Malaparte's moral and political indifference.

From beginning to end, the book's dominant tone is a bitter one, recalling the moral of *Mother Courage and Her Children*. "Die Welt stirbt aus," the world dies, the cook exclaims in Brecht's play, while the Thirty Years' War devastates central Europe. And in the final scene, the farmer adds: "It's high time you got away yourself. There are wolves around and, what's worse, marauders."[70] In a newspaper article of 1946, Malaparte suggests how the Neapolitans have become the new "cursed saints":

> Among the many reasons the Allies judge us harshly is this: that in processions, demonstrations, ceremonies, or political congresses, we yell everything except "Viva l'Italia!" How many times must it be

repeated that the Allies, in this tragic Europe of more or less defeated nations, think better of peoples who have preserved love of and pride in their own names, as opposed to peoples ashamed of having a homeland?[71]

This identification with history's losers was, however, as aesthetic and provisional as his identification with the workers of Prato in his adolescence, or with the vanquished of Caporetto. Once again Malaparte was incessantly seeing himself in one or the other of several mirrors, without any one dominating. "I prefer the defeated, but I wouldn't know how to adapt to their condition," he would later say in an interview, and for once we can believe him.[72] But, even without knowing the United States, he had perfectly understood that for the Americans, heirs of the Puritan fathers, there was a direct relationship between moral sin and political-military defeat. And it is with this conviction that they disembark on the old, too-old continent:

> I like the Americans because they are good and sincere Christians, because they believe Christ is always on the side of those who are in the right; because they believe that it is a sin to be in the wrong, that it is immoral to be in the wrong; because they believe that they alone are honorable men, and that all the nations of Europe are more or less dishonest; because they believe that a conquered nation is a nation of criminals, that defeat is a moral stigma, an expression of divine justice. (S, 15)

There is also a good dose of Fascism, understood as a taste for force, in Malaparte's infatuation with the United States, of whom he claimed, well before 1945, that it would become the "European" power par excellence of the second half of the twentieth century (and beyond), without which Europe would be nothing, and with which it would no longer be anything special. This is the sense of *The Skin*'s dedication to "all the brave, good and honorable American soldiers...who died in vain in the cause of European freedom," where the accent falls on "in vain." Behind the ritual tribute to the Yanks, Malaparte offers himself up as a mediator between the two sides of the Atlantic and wears the victor's uniform, presuming to speak in the name of the defeated. A servile attitude? Less so than one might think. The United States boasts of being the great democracy of free and equal men—perhaps a bit less free for the Black GIs, who in the narrow Naples streets pursue the white flesh still forbidden them at home—and they show, guns (and atomic bombs) blazing, that they were, and will be, the strongest.

From Naples to the bombardment of Kosovo, to two wars in Iraq and beyond, this concept of "exporting democracy" does not seem to have changed much. In Malaparte's eyes, the Americans are happy, their consciences clear, because they are on the right side of history, which they naively relate to nature: theirs is an innocent history, the opposite of real history. The liberators expected, then, to be loved; whereas the German invaders spread fear through cruelty, because they could not be loved. The former had now taken the place of the latter; but was there not the danger that, when all is said and done, one victor is as good as another, as claimed from the very first pages of the book? From the Neapolitan perspective, too ancient and too skeptical to be truly "liberatable,"[73] all liberators are also conquerors. The Americans remained foreigners, if certainly less bloody and more accommodating than the Germans, who had been chased away during the "Four Days of Naples"; the insurrection

SKIN AND MUD

that set the city ablaze on September 17–20, 1943, concluding with the departure of the German garrison, is often considered the first act of "popular" resistance in Italy. In reality, it is debatable whether these events can be attributed to any organic political agenda. The population rebelled above all because of hunger. The Germans had already decided to evacuate Naples and offered only modest resistance, which did not prevent them from destroying a large portion of the city's archives, of incalculable historical value, in retaliation.

The Americans were also soldiers from outside, who never really managed to conquer the hearts, and not just the bodies, of the defeated-liberated, in a city that was one of the three largest and richest capitals in Europe when the United States was still little-known Indian territory. The only possible dialogue was based on trade and the black market, on fraud and grift: be it in money, in kind, or in matériel, like the Sherman tank taken apart by a gang of street kids. Malaparte bet on the two tables at once, to gain sympathies both in Europe and across the Atlantic, where *The Skin* would not be published until 1952, in a heavily edited version, preceded by its scandalous reputation. He presents himself to American readers as someone wholly won over to the values of liberal democracy, ready to praise the honesty, generosity, and purity of the victors. All this is embodied in the new Virgil at his side, who is no longer a disenchanted representative of the Old World like the count Foxá, but the good, loyal colonel Henry H. Cumming, alias Jack Hamilton, passionate lover of ancient literature. Henry-Jack is destined to die at the end of the book, first of all because heroes cannot survive the scourge of history, just like Camus's Tarrou in *The Plague*; and then because Malaparte has an instinctive but already confident understanding of the American public, and he knows that such a fine death, enlivened by a noble dedication, will open many doors for him.* But to the very end, the character maintains the typical American ability to look at everything, including the horror, as if it were *the first time*. If Malaparte happens to criticize the US soldiers, he is careful to emphasize the innate morality of their action, their disinterested vision of liberty and equality among men, inscribed in their constitution and their customs, or their compassion and solicitude toward the suffering population.† Again, it is not (only) opportunism. He genuinely salutes the Americans as the victors of today and above all of tomorrow, the liquidators of a bankrupt Europe. In the draft of an essay from September 1947 one reads:

> We cannot overlook what Europe is, what we are. There is only disgust in ourselves, in what we are; in what suffering for too long has done to us, which surpasses the pride we have in ourselves, in Europe.[74]

This situation is reflected in the fate of the city's monuments. The Palazzo Reale, the residence since the seventeenth century of so many luckless sovereigns, among them Joachim Murat, miraculously survived the bombs to be transformed into camp kitchens, showers, and latrines with the arrival of the Fifth Army (S, 81). A beautiful

---

*Cavani goes even further to ensure a good reception for her film in American cinemas, introducing a love story (and that makes three!) between the GI and a young mother, who will in this way be saved from the street. In reality, there were a certain number of marriages between Neapolitan women and American soldiers or officers (all white, since those of color were not authorized to marry white women).

†In the 1960s, Roberto Rossellini would shoot the "Napoli 1943" episode of an anthology film, *Mid-Century Loves*, which, behind a thin love story, is an homage, almost a kind of restitution, to the suffering of the Neapolitans.

exhibition of photographs organized in 2004 in the rooms of the Palazzo showed that it suffered more damage *after* the liberation of Naples than before.

May we conclude, then, that Malaparte exaggerates, that he sees all the wounds and miseries of Naples without admitting a crumb of its grandeur? He has long been reproached for having overlooked in his gloomy tableau the signs of recovery that, notwithstanding everything, were already perceptible then, such as the reopening, applauded by the whole population, of the Teatro di San Carlo, on May 16, 1944. *The Skin* provoked a wave of indignation, even in those who declared virtuously to have never read it. Malaparte had taken this into account, but he did not foresee just how much the scandal would contribute to the book's success. A furious controversy followed, occupying the front pages for months, and Malaparte was even "morally banned" from Naples by a city council vote. It was an unhoped-for publicity occasion, into which he jumped two-footed, sending a flood of open letters to the city's mayor and to other leading Neapolitan personalities (of which a small minority took up his defense), to protest that his book

> is not a defense but an exaltation of the Neapolitan people, of their Christian pity, of their spirit of sacrifice, of their marvelous dignity in misery, in hunger, in the anguish of sorrow and of universal corruption (and by universal I mean it was an ill common to all of Europe).[75]

In vain he declared that "I love Naples more than any other city in the world"; the climate had deteriorated too much.[76] In reality, what Malaparte was deliberately destroying was the traditional picturesque image of Naples as the city of "annema e core" (soul and heart), conveyed around the world through postcards and folk songs. Naples now takes the place of Jassy and Bessarabia, of Warsaw and Ukraine, in his description of the disasters of war, which remain fundamentally the same, in the east as in the west, in the south as in the north. To claim he exalted the Neapolitan people is certainly excessive. But he was not dishonoring them; he was simply making them a living example of Europe consumed by the plague. His reconciliation with the public had to wait until October 1955, under the auspices of a new mayor, Achille Lauro, a former Fascist Party member purged in 1945, who became the strongman of the city a few years later. Unlike his fellow citizens, Lauro never hid his admiration for *The Skin*, a book in which he would have deserved to appear.[77]

If the attitude of the Naples authorities brought Malaparte a good return in notoriety, the book's placement on the Index Librorum Prohibitorum by the Holy Office, announced with great prominence in the *Osservatore Romano* of June 17, 1950,[78] was greeted with greater embarrassment by its author, and especially by its publisher. Indeed, this was a provision that every good Catholic had to take seriously, and it might also lead to unfortunate consequences on a material level. Placement on the index might have helped *The Skin*'s circulation in progressive circles, but it deprived the book of a Catholic and conservative audience that, despite everything, had remained faithful to him. Malaparte was then fully committed to the fight against clerical influence in postwar Italy and he thought, perhaps rightly, that beyond the fate of the novel in question this was an attempt to intimidate and silence him. As was his wont, he immediately went on the counterattack. He denounced the rising tide of obscurantism in a declaration concluding with the following words: "Today the Church hinders the lay world's efforts to achieve the very liberty outside of which there is no liberty at all, not even for the Church."[79] Not content with that, he even wrote an open letter to the pope in which he declared: "I am not, alas, a believer. I consider myself a Christian, but outside both the Church and every other Christian denomination."[80] He received the support of some prominent figures, who were not necessarily on his side. But all was in vain, and the condemnation was not withdrawn: "Christianity is not safe in the work of Curzio Malaparte!" thundered the influential magazine of the Jesuits.[81] But the Vatican continued to pay particular attention to him, as would be demonstrated a few years later in its much more open attitude to *The Forbidden Christ*. We will see what effect all this would have on the church's effort to recuperate Malaparte on the eve of his death. And today the view of the church toward the novel is much more nuanced, as a prominent Jesuit author explained:

> You have to go back to the spirit of those times. It was not easy then to accept the desperate picture of humanity depicted in Malaparte's novel, which really is quite severe. But today we can read it in a different way and understand the dimension of soul-searching it contains.[82]

Broadly speaking, in *The Skin* Malaparte had grasped and represented the moral climate of the city, more than the facts in themselves. Naples thus became the symbol of a fallen homeland, a central theme of the soliloquies later gathered in *Mamma marcia*. This homeland was, after all, neither Italy nor Europe, but the notion of Western civilization, as it had managed to survive until the war, after all the shocks of the first half of the twentieth century, because it had not fallen to the lot of the Italians alone to turn their backs on the enemy: that experience had been shared by all—by the British, the Americans, the Germans, the Russians, the French, the Yugoslavs—by all, victors and vanquished. There was not an army in the world which in that splendid war had not, on some fine day, had the pleasure of throwing its arms and its flags in the mud. (S, 57)

The Neapolitans thus become the Europeans, the Westerners par excellence, in this regard exactly like the Jews threatened with extermination in the east, because—be it a matter of persecution, occupation, or liberation—their only aim was to survive. Let's take the amply debated passage in which Malaparte depicts some "horrible toothless women, gaunt-faced, wizened and plastered with rouge" (S, 119): a description that reveals, once again, his repugnance for the woman who is not a "gentle force of nature, righteous and incorruptible," who is not "like me." They are trafficking children with the *goumiers*, Moroccan soldiers, "with their dark, scintillating eyes and their long, powerful fingers" (S, 122).* After which, Malaparte launches into a defense of the Neapolitans—who have never forgiven him for having generalized this repugnant practice, which concerned only isolated and quickly reported cases—and concludes

---

*Was it any different elsewhere, particularly in liberated France? The writer and journalist Jean Galtier-Boissière recorded the following, after leaving dinner at the house of some friends one night in Château-Thierry: "A neighbor's little daughter is friends with three black soldiers. The mother explains all the advantages of this triple relationship, the chocolate, the coffee, the soap. The doctor asks her whether she fears the possible consequences...'Nothing to fear [is] the response of the happy mom; the little one is only thirteen years old: she hasn't menstruated yet." See *Mon journal depuis la libération* (Paris: La Jeune Parque, 1945), 308, entry of July 31, 1945.

that, to survive, it is better to sell one's own children than to eat them. This highly Malapartian mix of cynicism and pity barely conceals the taste for force, reduced here to a simple biological level. What he reproached the Neapolitans for, as with the Jews of the pogrom or the fleeing Fascists, as in the past with the deserters of Caporetto, is simply their complicity with defeat, their subjection to misfortune, the harmlessness of their complaints. Be they Garibaldians in the Argonne forests, Alpine troopers on San Bernardo, bare-handed Soviet partisans against German tanks, Israeli volunteers in the 1948 war of independence, he would have truly respected them, and he would have—at least for a little bit—identified with them.

Another scourge comes to the fore, previously unknown (or at least never so explicit) in his work: sex, seen not as joy of the senses rediscovered after the horror of war, but rather as a form of violent, humiliating possession, as degrading for the possessor as for the possessed; the only true means of communication and exchange in the conquered-liberated city.* A facile and less demanding subject, compared with the "high" vision of evil expressed in *Kaputt*? One may find it so, but not in the way he treats it. His correspondence

---

*Capable of laughing, or at least of smiling, at misfortune, the Neapolitan people consoled themselves with the songs in which, so many clichés notwithstanding, there can be found a great part of their vitality and expressive force. The most celebrated of those inspired by the events of 1943–45 is "Tammurriata nera," by Edoardo Nicolardi and E. A. Mario (author in 1918 of the famous patriotic song "La leggenda del Piave"), which tells the story of a girl, "looked upon" with great sympathy by the American soldiers, and from one of these innocent exchanges of looks is born "a little Ciro or Peppe" who is "black, black, black." A small masterpiece of humor and delicacy, it entered the repertoire of all Neapolitan performers, closer to De Sica than to Malaparte.

from the period attests to how Malaparte hesitated before venturing onto dangerous ground that could bring him advantages in the eyes of the general public but also harm him. In the end, his choice was probably motivated by a desire to add a new string to his bow, as well as by the impossibility of limiting himself to portraying such a sordid reality without adding his own personal fantasies. The degradation of instincts is, along with sorrow and death, the fruit of all military occupations, and it certainly was not invented by Malaparte. Much has been written about the persistent obsession of these pages, of the pansexualism Malaparte gives voice to through his characters. But it seems to me he proves himself here to be the writer we have known since the beginning. The absence of emotional participation, denial of the pleasure principle, and refusal of physical action—one sees him fondling a "wig," never a woman—ensure that, in every circumstance, he refuses to take part in the spectacle surrounding him. Rarely has sexual material been treated with such cerebral detachment amid the profusion of olfactory, auditory, and tactile sensations on every page. A comparison could be made with Shostakovich's long-banned grand opera *Lady Macbeth of Mtsensk* (1934), pervaded by the same exhausted and frustrated eroticism. Malaparte would ultimately confess as much in *Mamma marcia*, with its very stark, almost dogmatic, opposition between sex and liberty.

If it is impossible to speak of the "animalization" of human behavior, given the noble content Malaparte assigns to the term, one might introduce the concept of "passivization." Malaparte's passive narcissism is reflected in the spectacle of a city that lies down without any emotional involvement before the rutting occupiers. The violation of "white" flesh—because every sexual act in *The Skin* participates in rape—is entrusted to characters who are not only anonymous, indiscernible, like the soldiers in Goya's execution squad, but essentially nonwhite, not to say nonhuman: Blacks, or rather "negroes" and Moroccan "goumiers," with a Brueghelian accompaniment of dwarves, hunchbacks, and cripples, performing the same role as the chorus of fetuses. A racist and Fascist reflex grips the writer here, harking back to an ancestral fear in Mediterranean populations of the Moorish invasions and raids of centuries past. With this difference: that the Black soldiers, depicted in *The Skin* as quite peaceful by nature (unless they are drinking), had enjoyed a certain measure of sympathy from the common people.* By contrast, the indigenous Moroccan troops sowed terror among civilians—men, women, and children—in their advance on Rome, which risked becoming a real *kaputt mundi*, and not just in a play on words. Pius XII entreated the Allied commanders to prohibit their access to the Eternal City. Moravia's novel *Two Women*, brought to the screen in 1960 by Vittorio De Sica (with a heartrending Sophia Loren, in one of her best roles), transforms rape into a metaphor, more than a consequence, of the war. The "rain of fire" that falls on the outskirts of the city, after the eruption of Vesuvius, had actually spared Naples. The volcano's last eruption to date, on March 18, 1944, partially destroyed outlying municipalities such as Massa di Somma and San Sebastiano, which had to be evacuated, but it did not reach the city, which was

---

*Corrado Alvaro noted, in an undated page from 1945: "A negro lives with an extremely poor Neapolitan girl. He's about to be sent back to America. The girl begs him to take her with him. He answers that he cannot, constantly shaking his head. She doesn't know, but he's certainly thinking back to the condition of negroes, and to the danger he would expose himself and her to, bringing a white wife back to his southern town, he who in the poor girl's eyes appears to be the rich and powerful victor." *Quasi una vita* (Milan: Bompiani, 1959), 391.

also protected from dispersed ashes by contrary winds, a fact Malaparte concedes (S, 260), perhaps reluctantly. But the eruption, actual or pretend as the case may be, is presented under the aspect, enticing for any person of letters, of the biblical curse that strikes Sodom and Gomorrah.[83] *The Skin* faithfully follows here the language of Genesis. It was not only "the populace" who saw "in the wrath of Vesuvius the anger of the Virgin, of the Saints, of the Gods of the Christian Olympus, who had become incensed at the sins, the corruption and the viciousness of men" (S, 262). It was Malaparte who set himself up for once as judge, with the intention of metaphorically rooting out sin and sinners. The French Communist writer and inveterate agnostic Roger Vailland was perhaps the only one to point out then what seems to us rather obvious today: "Your final apocalypse, from the eruption of Vesuvius to the dialogue with the fetuses, is fundamentally Christian."[84]

Nowhere does this judgment appear less up for debate than in the book's two central chapters. There Malaparte describes the customs of the homosexual community that, from all over Europe and, it could be said, from all over the world, has rushed to huddle in the recesses of the city and turn it into the world capital of sexual inversion. This is incontestably the point where the writer's sexophobic prejudice transforms into explicit homophobia, his racism against nonwhites into discrimination against nonheterosexuals. This has led some critics to claim that homosexuality in Malaparte plays the same phantasmal role as the Jew in Céline. One can certainly see the persistence of a "hostile diagnosis." This did not prevent him from counting several homosexuals as friends, such as the painters Rosai and de Pisis and the author's most gifted disciple, Carlo Coccioli, of whom more will be said in the next chapter. Biancamaria Fabbri nostalgically recalls the merry evenings spent with the most famous gay couple of intellectual Paris, Cocteau and Jean Marais, on a barge on the Seine, with a Malaparte who had never seemed so at ease. Of course, he was steeped in a culture that under Fascism was officially natalist and antidecadent, hence homophobic.* It's enough to recall a novel like *The Gold-Rimmed Spectacles*, by Giorgio Bassani, or a film like *A Special Day*, by Ettore Scola; and Malaparte, too, had thought to ingratiate himself with Mussolini by playing up the manliness of Il Duce against the femininity of the Führer at the time of *Technique*. But nobody had gone so far as to describe, as in the episode of the "son of Adam" (without Eve) of *The Skin*, the mock birth of a homosexual: a sequence of collective hysteria, almost a pre-Christian rite, for which Malaparte drew inspiration from the condemnation of sterility that struck the tribe of Sodom, along with his own intimate horror of procreation.

Nor does he stop there. The focus of his reasoning is not literary but, for once, truly ideological. He holds up and denounces the "gods of an Olympus that was situated outside nature, but not outside history" (S, 87). In other words, homosexuals belong to history just like other men. And they cannot aspire to the innocence of animals. It is not even possible in their case to invoke the passivity of the girls who sell themselves to the Black soldiers, because their choice is not dictated by hunger, fraud, or vice. Malaparte created a portrait not of a common invert, which interested him as little as

---

*However, in authors like Giovanni Comisso or Sandro Penna, homosexuality merged with Fascist vitalism.

a common heterosexual did, but of a precise nature: that of the decadent aesthete, who by war's end had become the "Marxist pederast."* This was, in his eyes, one of the evident products of the war, the best demonstration of the irreparable decline of the West. In the character of Jeanlouis, the Apollonian scion of a great Lombard family, he depicted the representative of an International ruled by snobbery, luxury, and sensuality, and at the same time the committed intellectual and pedagogue who wanted to pacify the world through sexual liberation—a bit like if Luchino Visconti had met André Gide's Corydon.† If Jeanlouis inclines left, spurred by his desire to protect the weak and the humble, provided they are young and beautiful, Malaparte finds no trace of a democratic sensibility in him, but rather a "narcissism that had been perverted into masochism" (i.e., the opposite of *his* narcissism). This is precisely what drives the vast tribe of deviants toward "the new proletarian folklore" (S, 125).

Malaparte rarely took female homosexuality into consideration. In his archives one finds an unusual unpublished fragment, in which he describes an evening spent in Amsterdam in the company of two lesbians, who have sex almost in front of him. Apart from the voyeuristic element, the text is interesting above all at the end, when one of the two women bursts into tears, thinking of the child she conceived one day "out of anger, to humiliate myself, out of con-

---

*In both Italian and French, the word for "pederast" has often been used as a synonym for "homosexual," as a pejorative but not necessarily with pedophiliac connotations. In this book I have accordingly also rendered *pederasta* and *pédéraste* as "queer" and even simply "gay," depending on context—Trans.

†Some have mentioned, without offering any proof, the name of Visconti as a possible real-world source for the character of Jeanlouis.

tempt. Maternity was my vendetta. That little girl reminds me of the most painful period of my life." It is a perfect analogy with the mock-birth sequence in *The Skin*: we are presented with the same symbolism of "a cold, immobile, ecstatic obscenity."[85] As he would explain at length in *Mamma marcia*, Malaparte did not limit himself to considering the relationship between Fascism and male and female homosexuality (Rossellini would allude to this with the evocation of drug-addicted, pro-Nazi lesbians in *Rome, Open City*), on which there is today a vast and questionable literature, mixing psychoanalysis and history.[86] For him, the anthropomorphic vitality of inversion—the Olympian god who closely follows the movements of history without ever finding the place that nature assigned to him—pushes his supporters toward a new model: the radiant future of the Communist revolution. Malaparte, who was at the time already on the outs with the PCI and its intellectuals, was one of the first, with the Arthur Koestler of *The Yogi and the Commissar* (1945) and the George Orwell of *1984* (1949), to debunk the idea, very widespread in the wake of the Liberation, that a triumphant communism would have abolished the chains of bourgeois morality; that it would have led to the emancipation of sexual minorities, to the end of the economic exploitation of sexuality, and so on: in short, May '68 antedated to the moment Stalin set his sights on conquering a devastated and guilt-ridden old continent. The knowledge Malaparte retained of the Soviet world of the 1920s and 1930s, and of the repression that was raging then against the freedom of bodies and not just of ideas, drove him to warn the youth of Europe:

> It has been observed that the behavior of homosexuals in the face of Nazi and Fascist tyranny presents some particularly strange

aspects. Many homosexual intellectuals are communists, or they act like communists. Should not the sexual reaction to tyranny also come into play with regard to communism, which is itself a form of tyranny? (MM, 321)

In *The Skin*, however, Malaparte is still in the preliminary stage of this reasoning. The amalgam of communism and homosexuality circulating before his eyes on the streets of Naples appeared to him as the latest false flag, emblem of the alleged humanist renewal on display at war's end. To the dematerialization of history (suddenly rendered light, innocent, Edenic, similar to nature) fervently preached by Jeanlouis—"Europe will be a continent of free men, that's what Europe will be" (S, 121)—Malaparte relentlessly opposed the idea of moral and physical corruption:

> And I laughed to myself... as I imagined Jeanlouis and all the young "heroes" like him sitting in the midst of the other little slaves in the *piazzetta* of the Cappella Vecchia, propped up against that wall of flesh as it gradually dissolved in the fading light, and little by little was swallowed up in the night like a piece of rotten flesh. (S, 125)*

The scene is set for the appearance of these chronicles' final scourge: the rot. But first we need to return to the writer's personal situation, between *Kaputt* and *The Skin*.

---

*The passage from living "flesh" to dead and rotten "flesh" is a constant in Malaparte; but sometimes the two overlap. Consider, for instance, the encounter with "Mussolini's assassin," with his face like a "piece of meat."

No Such Thing as Bad Publicity

At this point Malaparte struggled to navigate with the current, as he had previously known how to do so well. If his first concern at the fall of Fascism was to obtain protection from the Anglo-Americans, the second was directed at not forgetting the other victors, the Soviets, whom he had known for a long time. Hence the choice, in 1944–45, when he felt most threatened, to move closer to the Communists, from whom he could expect the most trouble after the Liberation. Betting on both options still seemed possible, when the final sprint against the Third Reich cemented the unnatural alliance between capitalism and Bolshevism. At the time, Stalin also enjoyed tremendous popularity in the United States, where "Uncle Joe" was celebrated in Broadway theaters and Hollywood movies. We might recall *Mission to Moscow* (1943), allegedly commissioned by Roosevelt himself, directed by Michael Curtiz after *Casablanca*, in which Stalin smiles peaceably at the US ambassador; *Song of Russia* (1944), by Gregory Ratoff, with Robert Taylor; and *Days of Glory* (1944), by the French-American Jacques Tourneur, with the newcomer Gregory Peck in the improbable role of a Soviet partisan. All these films would disappear from screens after the start of the Cold War and McCarthyism.

Malaparte could on the whole be pleased with everything he had written about the Georgian dictator, starting in the 1930s. Even the anathema Trotsky had pronounced against the writer could prove useful. But there was a hitch: to regain Moscow, he now needed to pass through the PCI militants just emerging from underground, many of whom had old scores to settle with him. He preferred to invest in the idealism of youth, and so we find him courting a group of Neapolitan university students close to the party, among them

CHRONICLES OF THE PLAGUE (1944–1946)

Giorgio Napolitano,[87] later a very distinguished president of the Italian Republic, who kindly shared with me his recollections:

> I met him in January 1944, on Capri, where part of my family had been evacuated. We had just published the first (and only) issue of a magazine called *Latitudine*, close to the Communists but independent, dealing with topics like hermeticism, surrealism, and American literature, and including quotations from heretical authors like Gide and Malraux. I had the idea of giving a copy to Malaparte. He was generous with his praise and encouraged us to continue. Unfortunately, our magazine was poorly received by the leaders of the Neapolitan federation of the PCI, which meant the end of it and increased my reservations about the party. I decided then to distance myself and went and got my first work experience, with a branch of the American Red Cross. This gave me the chance to see Malaparte often, almost daily, until around the fall of 1944, when our paths diverged. As soon as I got off work, I would join him at the Hotel Quisisana, which was his meeting place. From there we would set off on foot to his house at Capo Massullo. Conversation with him was incredible, it could make your head spin. I was not yet nineteen, but I still realized he was telling tales. Yet he had an outstanding capacity for seduction, and remarkable charm. He talked about everything: the people he had met, his travels, his ideas about art and the future of the world. It was almost like a performance of *Kaputt* playing out before my eyes.

Asked about Malaparte's relationship with both the Communist Party and the American intelligence services in this period, Napolitano offered:

I'd say he was almost an avowed Communist. Just imagine, he confided to me he was ready to open up a school of Leninism in his own house! His meeting with Togliatti was very friendly. Malaparte told me how very impressed he was by him. After that he was authorized to become a correspondent for *L'Unità*, the Communist daily, on the Florence front, provided he adopted a pseudonym. At the same time, Malaparte tried to set up an expeditionary force to fight the Germans. The enrollments were collected in a café. I signed up too. Of course, nothing ever came of it. After the liberation of Rome, some influential party leaders had denounced Malaparte's Fascist baggage. The issue quickly took on such proportions that Togliatti, regretfully, was no longer in a position to defend him.[88]

Malaparte always denied having applied for membership in the PCI at this time, and no related documentation has been found.[89] The fact is he did not have time for it. He never denied, however, having approached the former no. 2 of the Communist International and party secretary, Palmiro Togliatti, who had landed in Naples, returning from exile in the Soviet Union, in March 1944, at which point he was immediately appointed minister in the national-unity government of the Kingdom of the South. It was the legalistic and antirevolutionary "Salerno Turn," so called after the city in which the government had relocated en route to Rome. The credit has long been attributed to the perspicacity of Togliatti, who merely deftly applied the instructions of Stalin. Moscow's man was the bearer of a much more moderate policy line than that of the domestic Communist party, which had been hardened by the partisan war in the north. Togliatti was in search of figures who could support this line, all the better if they were compromised with the old regime, as it made them more controllable. Malaparte was at the top of his (possibly Moscow-approved) list. And so on Easter Sunday 1944, just two weeks after his return from exile, Togliatti made a pilgrimage to Casa Come Me on Capri. Legend has it that, upon entering the living room, he recognized a Matisse "from twenty-five feet away," the only politician, alongside the former Fascist Party official Bottai, whom Malaparte considered capable of such a feat. This helped establish a bond of complicity between them.[90]

It was then that the leader of the PCI, following an old Stalinist procedure, asked for and received an autobiographical confession of some thirty pages, in which Malaparte asserted his attachment to "my working-class origins and solidarity with the material and moral interests of the working class to which my family belongs" (which, of course, it did not) and denied any "authentic" participation in Fascism. In exchange for this tissue of lies, written all the same with his usual brio, which would be published only the day after his death, Malaparte counted on a good and proper whitewash. The pro-Soviet articles such as "Sangue operaio" and the translations of Éluard, Alberti, Lorca, and so on in *Prospettive* did the rest. Togliatti, in order to capture this coveted prey for his menagerie of repentant intellectuals, was ready to grant the pardon for which Malaparte was pretending to beg. The former explained the case to one of his slightly perplexed colleagues in terms that could not be clearer: "Don't pay too much attention to compromises with Fascism, if they happened, 'anyways, they all were [compromised],' and if we wanted to be purists, more than half of Italians would have to be put into concentration camps. Focus on personal qualities and the services they could offer to the party."[91] And to Beatrice Monti, rediscovered on Capri, Malaparte couldn't resist one of his vicious quips, even one ultimately at his own expense: "Doesn't it bother you to be seen with a bad sort like me? Now it's Togliatti who's feeding me."⁹²

That said, the two men were made to understand each other, and not only out of self-interest. The secretary of the PCI was much closer to Malaparte than to his French counterpart Maurice Thorez, a man of genuinely working-class origins. Distinguished, bespectacled, slightly plump, from a family of Piedmontese teachers and white-collar workers, brother of an eminent mathematician, capable of casually citing Thomas Aquinas and Alexandre Dumas, Togliatti was, like Malaparte, cold-natured to the point of minerality, more similar to a headmaster than to a political agitator, indifferent to human relationships, shaped by twenty years of survival in the ranks of the Comintern, a dissembler by vocation and not only by Bolshevik discipline. After having faithfully served Stalin, even in the massacres of anarchists in Spain, he nurtured the ambition of making history not as an apparatchik stained with the blood of the purges, but as the leader of a truly national Communist party. In this way he intended to emerge from the overwhelming shadow of Gramsci, still venerated by the party's base. Malaparte had enough good sense at that stage to understand that making room for the PCI in the government was the only way to avoid a new civil war, after the one already being waged against the Fascists of Salò. As he observed in the *Giornale segreto*, "Moscow doesn't want a communist state in Western Europe, if not as a member of the USSR. Otherwise, they prefer a popular-front government."⁹³ It was in fact as part of a renewed Popular Front that the PCI appeared in the decisive elections of 1948, which it would nevertheless lose resoundingly.

But things did not go as the two men hoped. Togliatti may indeed have had a mandate from the all-powerful Stalin; but the majority of the party apparatus could not accept Malaparte's about-face with a light heart. Thanks to Togliatti, he was able to go "fight" against the Germans and Fascists in Florence, whence he sent fiery dispatches to *L'Unità* under the very Tuscan pseudonym of Gianni Strozzi, a humanist and politician of the sixteenth century, going so far as to describe in impassioned terms the death of "*our* dear comrade Potente" (emphasis mine), a well-known Communist partisan. There were four articles in all published between the eleventh and the twenty-third of August 1944, after which, his identity revealed, the series had to be interrupted, following protests by militants.[94] Malaparte has long been accused of also taking part in the smear campaign against the philosopher Giovanni Gentile, assassinated on April 15, 1944, in Florence, to put an end to his attempts at national reconciliation. I have not found any trace of his involvement in this sad episode, whereas Togliatti politically endorsed the attack.[95] Malaparte's contributions to the Communist press organ were also noticed by the intelligence services in Salò, inspiring the Italian Social Republic's minister of popular culture, Fernando Mezzasoma, who would follow Il Duce all the way to Piazzale Loreto, to make the following dismissive note in pen: "Eminent profiteer was inserted into the list of the giant kangaroos, for having received a salary of five thousand lire a month from MinCulPop until July 25."[96] Which proves that neither the Fascists nor the Communists wanted him on their side. And they had good reason.

Togliatti, reluctantly, had to yield. Malaparte was expelled from the paper on the spot and turned away from the party he had not managed in time to join. The success of *Kaputt* was not enough to protect him. On March 22, 1945, he was arrested again, on Capri, by the order of the high commissioner for the confiscation of the profits of Fascism, this time with the charge of "having organized and conducted Fascist action squads in Florence and Prato under the orders of the former militia consul, Tamburini."[97] Liberation quickly turned into purges, but Malaparte could count, once again, on the crucial support of Togliatti. It is in large part owing to the PCI secretary general's deposition in his favor that he was absolved on May 6, 1947, during the trial in the Rome Court of Assizes, of the charge of having enriched himself with the profits of the regime.[98] Two months later, on July 9, 1947, it would be the Florence High Court that dropped, by request of the prosecutor general, the other charge, concerning his participation in squadrist expeditions. But Togliatti's help, however discreet, was not accepted by everyone on the left, as documented by the indignant reactions to Malaparte's exoneration, reported by the Interior Ministry's information services.

The PCI had always claimed, as the French Communist Party did, to have constituted the dominant force of the partisan movement. In reality, if the Communist formations acted with courage, determination, and an undeniable spirit of personal sacrifice, at times they also exploited the situation to preemptively eliminate future postwar political rivals. Perhaps the best-known case was the massacre in Porzûs, in eastern Friuli, where a group of "white" partisans (liberal, socialist, and Christian democratic) belonging to the Osoppo Brigade were wiped out by Communist partisans fighting alongside the Yugoslav troops of Tito. Among the victims was the brother of Pier Paolo Pasolini, who would be obsessed all his life by this tragedy. After the war, Malaparte acted as a spokesperson for the Osoppo Brigade survivors, to "openly promote the trial of the partisan war."[99] Almost eighty years later, the controversy around those grievous events has not died down. Togliatti was aware that a Communist insurrection, like the one devastating Greece at the time, would have concluded in a bloody defeat and eliminated the PCI from the postwar political scene. He succeeded, not without difficulty, in extinguishing the insurrectionist flames, with the support of Stalin, who shared this analysis. But the legal purge, and especially the illegal one, created hundreds of victims between 1945 and 1947; in certain areas, especially in the Tuscan-Emilian Apennines and the Po Valley (the so-called triangle of death), it dragged on till 1949.* It may seem implausible, but the first books and films in Giovannino Guareschi's Don Camillo series, describing this reality with manifest good humor and a rosy outlook, did a great deal to ease the tension and avoid the worst. The end of this extension of the civil war was decided when the base of the PCI understood that the Communists, after the start of the Cold War and the anchorage of Italy in the Western camp, had no chance of instigating an insurrectional movement. Togliatti had it right, and the PCI could enter a slow journey within institutions, bringing it, thirty years later, to "Eurocommunism."

In such conditions, a Malaparte very worried about his own fate, his own dogs, and his own property—"for me uncertainty is fear," he confessed to his friend Prezzolini[100]—made the only decision that could save him, to move again toward anti-Communist circles.

---

*The number of death sentences handed down by regular courts at Liberation was 259, of which 91 were carried out. The number of prison sentences was six thousand, of which the vast majority were served in full. As a percentage of the population, the legal purge was one of the lowest in Europe. The illegal purge, naturally, was something else. See the detailed account of Hans Woller, *Die Abrechnung mit dem Faschismus in Italien 1943 bis 1948* (Munich: R. Oldenbourg Verlag, 1996).

But here as well, no one was exactly waiting to welcome him with open arms. Many were indignant about the way he had forgotten his past benefactors, in particular Galeazzo Ciano; not to mention the Salò "nostalgics," who came out of hiding and threatened to settle scores with him. His old colleagues were not much warmer. For instance, right after *Kaputt* appeared, the Florentine writer Giovanni Papini, who shared a French translator with Malaparte, Juliette Bertrand, referred in his diary to "an atrocious book (*Kaputt*) by a German-Italian, Kurt Suckert (who has taken the name Curzio Malaparte)."[101] Now, Papini knew perfectly well who Malaparte was, having first met him at the time of *La Voce*, thirty years earlier. The former had been even more Fascist than the latter, glorified by the regime and an admirer of German *Kultur*, even after 1933. But he wanted to attest in this way, for posterity, the contempt in which he held a man whose ideological nonchalance seemed even greater than his own. And the derogatory epithet for Malaparte, "German," as with "Jewish" in the past, spread through leftist and rightist circles alike.

Malaparte then decided it would be good to look abroad again, as he had always done in moments of tension at home. In France, where Halévy and Grasset were also going through a difficult period, he found an enthusiastic new mentor in the figure of Guy Tosi, a refined literary critic of Italian origin, then editorial director at Denoël. Tosi had become an enthusiast of his work during the war and wanted to present it to the public as following on from "Hemingway, Malraux, Saint-Exupéry, Cendrars, Koestler, and a few others." Naturally, given the times, Tosi took great care to highlight everything in Malaparte's biography that showed his anti-Fascism and attachment to France, while adding in one suggestive comment, "[even] if it isn't true."[102] But the road remained steep. If the influential right-wing critic Kléber Haedens lavished praise on *Kaputt*, "an extraordinary book, its pages dripping with blood,"[103] others, better informed about the author, like the no less influential left-wing critic Maurice Nadeau, expressed some reservations:

> A singular character, who does not inspire sympathy as much as curiosity.... He was not, however, the out-and-out opponent of Mussolini's regime, but at most its enfant terrible, and now that the beautiful edifice is in ruins, Malaparte's bad conscience has driven him to a nihilism that has all too many reasons to seduce us.[104]

The other reviews had a similar tone. Pierre Descaves floated the parallel, which would become common, with Céline, specifying that "in this anomalous book, Bardamu's style has been revised by D'Annunzio."[105] René Tavernier drew a comparison with the shock of *The Outlaws*, by Ernst von Salomon, after the Great War: "Here we have an Italian voice, illuminated by a prestigious past but wounded, embittered by a defeat in which all illusions of political grandeur have foundered for good."[106] Finally, Robert Kemp found even more distant and sophisticated reference points: "After the Dantesque, after Goya, here comes Swift or Hogarth."[107]

American critics attended less to the properly literary aspects of Malaparte's work and launched a veritable campaign against the writer's "shameful past."[108] The American correspondents in Italy had read up on the author of *Kaputt*, collecting information about him that, in some cases, went beyond his actual responsibilities. Standing out among the more critical voices were the musicologist Howard Taubman, biographer of Toscanini, and Vincent Sheehan, drinking companion of Hemingway and author of a fine book on interwar Europe.[109] Prezzolini, well acquainted with the moralism of the Americans, had cautioned Malaparte, who as usual had ignored the warning. He was convinced that the name of the translator, Cesare Foligno, an anti-Fascist persecuted at the time of the racial laws, would be enough to clear him through customs. His disappointment at this campaign was enormous, then, and he reacted by accusing his by-now ex-friend Percy Winner of having been the source of these "calumnies." As he wrote—in English—to his American publisher:

> What *The New York Times* pretends from me? That I should kill Mussolini? No, thank! I am not a criminal. . . .
>
> Let me know by cable, please, if you judge that I could help you by sending a letter to *Time*, to *New York Times* etc. with the purpose to reestablish the truth. But, do you think it is absolutely necessary to reestablish the truth? Personally, I dont' [*sic*] care whether some American journalists think I am a fascist or an antifascist. The question is, whether their opinion can trouble or not the success of KAPUTT.[110]

Of course it could "trouble" it! "Selling 15,000 copies is not bad," commented Prezzolini, "but without the critics' campaign you would have sold 200,000."[111] Prezzolini was exaggerating slightly, but this time Malaparte took him very seriously. What is more, he was furious because Italian literature had come back into fashion in America. Not only noted anti-Fascists like Ignazio Silone and Carlo Levi, but also authors only slightly less compromised than he was, from Moravia to Alvaro to Vittorini, were welcomed with open arms. This offensive drove him to even more flagrant falsifications and to attack Mussolini as if he really were about to kill him a second time. Every criticism or request for clarification was treated as a form of lèse-majesté, and his thin-skinned sensibilities made him incautious. He defended himself in ever-clumsier ways, lashing out blindly, to the point of ridiculousness, and beyond: "I am the only Italian writer who suffered long years of prison and *confino* (the Fascists arrested me and put me in prison eleven [*sic*] times for my literary work)."[112] He would have done better to admit his real but relatively limited responsibility and lay claim to his true and incontestable merits. Deep down, he was convinced he could achieve a succès de scandale, and he was not wrong. Thanks to the controversy, sales went through the roof, even if they failed to reach the "300,000 in a few weeks in New York alone" he boasted of with his correspondents.[113] He had, it must be said, assimilated a golden rule of the new media strategy from America: there's no such thing as bad publicity.

The controversy retraversed the ocean and spread across Europe: to Germany, Belgium, and once again France. Malaparte was confronted with a well-prepared accuser in the form of Janine Bouissounouse, a prolific author of historical biographies, married and transplanted to Rome, who was very plugged into the political and cultural life of the peninsula. After a thorough investigation, she launched her attack in a long article, featuring the first fairly accurate reconstruction of the *confino* affair:

> A simple settling of accounts among accomplices. He had called some high-ranking Blackshirted official an idiot. The latter enjoyed the chief's favor at the time, and he made him pay dearly for his

insolence. That's it. The taking of a position, the moral dilemma, the break with the party, the anti-Fascism: he organized all this later. Since you've read *Kaputt*, you can surmise his powers of orchestration. The truth, with him, is always a molecule buried inside an enormous cocoon of lies that he amuses himself with unraveling and in which he himself becomes tangled.[114]

Malaparte answered with a painful series of corrections leading nowhere: Bouissounouse was right about (almost) everything. This fight prefigured the even more painful *querelle* with Francis Ambrière, two years later, which we'll discuss in the next chapter. In the end, all he won from the opposing party was a bit of scornful sympathy: "But yes, Malaparte, you are an adventurer, of an interesting and rare species, and this is why, everything notwithstanding, it is difficult to be angry with you, one hesitates to judge you."[115]

Why did he do it? A question of temperament, once again. And then, not to reply to so many precise accusations would have been like admitting their validity. But he did it poorly and got bogged down; at times he seems to have lost his head and betrayed signs of a persecution complex:

> In revenge for the publication of *Kaputt*, the Germans deported my father, age 80, completely destroyed my family home in Forte dei Marmi, and "accidentally" killed my only nephew, Giorgio Ronchi, age 13.[116]

Apart from the fact that the Germans, scant months before the end of the Third Reich, had rather more urgent problems to attend to than the publication of *Kaputt*, Erwin Suckert was never deported or threatened with a death sentence,* and he would die at the ripe age of ninety-one, a few months before his son. As for Villa Hildebrand (not, strictly speaking, a family home), it had been damaged, like so many other houses on the Tuscan coast, but it had not been destroyed, if the writer could already return there for stays as early as 1946. Finally, if it is correct that the adolescent Giorgio Ronchi died on August 26, 1944, there is not the least indication that retaliation or a vendetta against his uncle was involved.†

After France and the United States, it was Germany's turn to offer *Kaputt* a stormy reception, when it was published there in 1951. The climate was already hardly favorable. Malaparte had visited the divided and ruined country as early as the spring of 1946, with the authorization, or more likely at the request, of the Allied Psychological Warfare Branch,[117] venturing as far as the camps for German prisoners of war in Belgium and France. He had drawn from the

---

*Nor does his granddaughter have any memory of such a thing (testimony to the author of Laura Ronchi Abbozzo).

†"What killed my little brother was definitely not a stray bullet during the Battle of Florence, which took place in a location distinct from us; we were in Arcetri. As far as I know, it was a projectile fired from a cannon located on the slopes of Monte Morello, on the estate called 'il Borro' (which incidentally we owned). It was our farmer who told us that on that day (August 26, 1944) and at that hour (early afternoon, I think) the Germans decided to abandon a cannon behind their house, but first they shot all their grenades (is that what cannon projectiles are called?) at the city. So in a certain sense it was a 'stray bullet' that struck my little brother; he was definitely not a military target" (written testimony of Laura Ronchi Abbozzo to the author). (Arcetri is in the hills south of the city center; Monte Morello to the northwest of Florence—Trans.) See also the charter of the Giorgio Ronchi Foundation (http://ronchi.isti.cnr.it/), which has over the years developed a notable program of publications and cultural exchanges in the biological and medical fields.

visit a series of very accusatory (and well-compensated) articles, published in the daily newspaper *Il Tempo* between June 16 and August 11, 1946, with the title "Germania nuda" (Germany naked), which stirred protest even from anti-Nazi associations in Germany.[118] *Il Tempo*, not to be confused with the weekly magazine *Tempo*, had just been founded in Rome by an enterprising film producer and businessman, Renato Angiolillo, who would turn it into one of the most influential anti-Communist and pro-US press organs of the postwar era. Malaparte became close friends with Angiolillo, and we will see the latter's important role at the time of the writer's hospitalization following his return from China. Malaparte had also planned to travel to Nuremberg, to recount the execution of the Nazi leaders at the trial's end, but to his great disappointment the newspaper recalled him, as it appeared no journalists would be allowed to attend.[119]

Gerhard Heller and Hellmut Ludwig, Malaparte's publisher and translator, respectively, had been very impressed with *Kaputt*, but they knew the book would cause an uproar. The Federal Republic of Germany, established less than two years earlier, had begun to take its first steps on the international scene following the exhortation of its chancellor, Konrad Adenauer, to set aside a history still too heavy to take on. *Kaputt* risked reopening wounds still not fully healed. Heller, mentioned earlier for his role in occupied Paris, was the first to realize as much. But he had admired Malaparte since his stays in prewar Italy as a student and was determined to spread the writer's books in the new Germany. He limited himself to inserting a very prudent preface, accompanied by a letter from Malaparte to German readers, in which, with his customary nonchalance, the writer listed his anti-Hitler credentials, denying absolutely to have written "ein deutschfeindliches Buch," a book hostile to the Germans.[120] A wasted effort, to judge by the violence of the reaction.

The writer Friedrich Sieburg had opened the dance, at the release of the French edition of *Kaputt*, in an article with the sententious title "A Writer Must Serve the Truth"; Malaparte had reacted immediately, pointing out that "Sieburg was a Nazi, as was his right; whereas I have always been anti-Nazi."[121] Which was not entirely correct: Sieburg was an old conservative, very cunning and sufficiently opportunistic to have lived with the Third Reich, like so many others, without overly compromising himself, before returning to his position as an editorialist in the Federal Republic as its economic miracle began to gain momentum. His campaign, which reprised all the arguments against Malaparte of the American and French press, was nonetheless effective. A veterans' association provocatively invited Malaparte to give his royalties to soldiers of the Wehrmacht who died in battle.[122] More significantly, the diplomat Gustav Braun von Stumm filed a lawsuit in a Karlsruhe court claiming he had been defamed by the version given by Malaparte, in *Kaputt*, of the suicide of his wife, Maria Giuseppina Antinori of Florence, during the war.[123] Another suit was filed by a judge of the Berlin appeals court, who felt called out in the "Siegfried and the Salmon" episode.[124]

These affairs cost Malaparte dearly. He had to pay considerable statutory damages, and above all, to watch as one German film coproduction after another went up in smoke in the years that followed. He then tried to counterattack, denouncing the dangers of an alleged revival of German militarism in a new series of dispatches in May–June 1952. In the most brilliant of them he recounts his visit to Hitler's refuge in the Bavarian Alps, "damaged by bombardments, but even more by the American soldiers' souvenir craze."[125] An interminable polemic pitted him against the son of Erwin Rommel, concerning the order allegedly given by the field marshal at El Alamein to abandon the Italian soldiers in the desert.[126] Another of his bêtes noires was the scarce regard that Wehrmacht generals, whose memoirs were starting to appear, had for the Italian army; in this he found confirmation of the revanchism that continued to dominate German public opinion. He also quarreled, naturally, with the intellectuals, denouncing their "nationalist, provincial philistinism."[127] The following year, he returned to the theme of German unity, to conclude that "the central problem of contemporary Europe is called Germany."[128] He pursued the theme in a dozen articles published in *Tempo* between July and September 1953, on the most diverse topics, including a fine portrait of Heidegger, quickly denazified and teaching again at Freiburg University. His tone was often so aggressive that the Federal Republic's ambassador in Rome had to publicly respond to his claims.[129] The paradox is that, despite such polemics, Malaparte returned regularly and always with pleasure to Germany, especially to Baden-Baden, in the footsteps of Dostoevsky, and to the Black Forest, often in the company of the faithful Heller. Which goes to show that his German Romantic soul—and, who knows, perhaps nostalgia for his origins—continued to hold a certain attraction for him.

Must we deduce that Malaparte was obsessed by the possibility of a reappearance of Hitlerism and militarism? It is highly doubtful. He was too attentive an observer not to realize that the nostalgic, neo-Nazi resurgences were insignificant. Perhaps the *Schuldfrage*, the question of collective guilt, had not yet been resolved for all Germans, and it would not be for many more years; but the division of the country in the context of the Cold War was enough to make any possible return to the past unlikely. Only the Communist press of the German Democratic Republic, aligned with Moscow, continued to repeat this complaint, for propaganda reasons. What motivated Malaparte's attacks was ultimately something entirely different, more personal in origin: the childhood memory of when "the German [had] woken up." Germany was still and always the failed father, waiting to rediscover that "mamma marcia" that was now in his eyes Italy and, with her, Europe.

In Praise of Rottenness

Malaparte's first notes on "rottenness," much of which would flow into the drafting of *Mamma marcia*, date to this period, the first half of the 1950s. Taken up and abandoned several times, *Mamma marcia* is apparently only one of the countless literary, journalistic, and cinematographic projects for which the writer drew inspiration from the passage from hot war to cold war. He had on several occasions announced its finalization and imminent appearance; it was the text he was supposed to bring as a gift to his French friends on the occasion of his return to Paris; but it never came to anything. In the meantime, he had written and published a good deal and applied himself in the theater and cinema, not to mention his interventions in politics. After the fraught reception of *The Skin*, his main worry was to finish his great fresco on the disasters of war and now the postwar. But with *Volga*, *Kaputt*, and *The Skin*, a cycle closed and imposed a renewal of contents. Above all, it was clear that Malaparte's visionary style could not be adapted to a properly narrative frame. His final efforts proved it: an unfinished novella,

Il compagno di viaggio (The fellow traveler), somewhat successful but limited in scope, that relates the touching story of a soldier who wants to bring home his officer's casket;* and a rather disappointing political novel, *Storia di domani* (Story of tomorrow). In comparison, *Mamma marcia* is, or rather would have been, by far the most important work of the last phase of his creative life, even as it is clear Malaparte failed to find a balance between his intentions and the result. This was probably why he interrupted its writing numerous times. In a certain sense, he had become a victim of his own success, and he was too demanding a perfectionist to be content, as so many others were, with continuing to recycle the same material. His case recalls that of Malraux during the Second World War, after the big successes of *The Human Condition* and *Man's Hope*. One could for that matter find a parallel between *Mamma marcia* and *The Walnut Trees of Altenburg*, another work pushing the novel to the limits of an "antinovel," outside any notion of school or genre, and also destined to remain unfinished.

What is striking at first sight is the coherence of the book in its formal incoherence and the heterogeneity of its materials. Enrico Falqui, his long-standing collaborator, as loyal as he was ill-treated, who edited the first edition of *Mamma marcia* two years after the author's death, reconstructed a text that was incomplete but organized according to quite a precise plan, all things considered. Malaparte talked with him about it constantly in the Rome clinic where he was slowly passing away. Thus it would be unjust to renew

---

*Malaparte, who as we know had no problem drawing "inspiration" from others' books, may have been acquainted with the draft of a story of the same title by his friend (or by now ex-friend?) Alberto Savinio, later collected in *Tutta la vita* (Milan: Bompiani, 1953), 95–106.

the accusation against Falqui of having betrayed the intentions of a writer who was anxious to consign this text to posterity. *Mamma marcia* was to have delivered him from a certain inclination to facileness and compromise that had emerged in his work, starting with *The Skin*. We can distinguish in the book three parts of roughly equal length. The first is centered on the dialogue-confession of the writer, returned to his home country, with his mother, who is close to death. The second comprises three short stories—two set in Saint-Germain-des-Près, the other among a group of partisans in Norway—and two poems. The third part, finally, consists of two essays, "Lettera alla gioventù d'Europa" (Letter to the youth of Europe) and "Sesso e libertà" (Sex and liberty), in which the author has used various passages from earlier articles, speeches, and interviews.[130] A fragmentary work, then, but with a strong internal coherence, in which Malaparte gives up the epic perspective, the lyrical impulse, the lush upholstery to which he had accustomed the reader, to take up again in a sparer, at times more intimist, style his favorite theme: the dissolution of modern man, his self-destruction that nothing seems able to stem, in him or around him. The "rottenness" thus becomes the same sort of obsessive, repetitive, symbolic stylistic feature as "kaputt-death" or "skin-plague" in the preceding volumes of the trilogy.

To this day, the critical attitude toward *Mamma marcia* acknowledges that it contains noteworthy pages but considers the work too eclectic and disjointed to figure among Malaparte's masterpieces. Hence the sorry fate of the book, which even in Italy has been out of print for many years. It is to be hoped that this judgment is destined to change, when a critical edition of the text finally becomes available. Even so, there would already seem to be ample evidence of an uncommon virtuosity, embracing all literary genres in the service of an inspiration that rarely proved so lucid. Never had he shouted his rejection of history with so much Célinian, Bernanosian, or Pasolinian fury—for once with genuine commitment—or greeted, at the same time, the face of the man who suffers with such Christian fraternity. It is in this spirit that he completes his "uterine journey" (MM, 17), the return to the mother, who is at the same time the beginning and the end of every living being, and whose death heralds that of the son. The relationship is natural, animal, prehistoric, the only one that for Malaparte can be opposed to the servitude and violence of the human condition:

> The mother who dies is like a dog that dies. What binds a man to his mother is an animal mystery: it is the secret, magic, deep life of the animal world. A man is not born of a single woman, but of all women together, of the entire female world, of the entire animal world. (MM, 57–58)

Elvira Perelli Suckert died at the beginning of 1950. Her son had previewed this agony in a text of the 1930s, "La mamma in clinica," collected in *Fughe in prigione*, reflecting the ambivalence of his feelings. Their relations, we have said, were not always easy. Nonetheless, he wrote on January 16 to Tamburi: "I am despondent, deeply shaken by my mother's death. That white-haired old woman who seemed to take up so little space on this earth, now that she is dead, I realize she filled the world. And so I am alone, for the first time truly alone."[131] Only after the disappearance of Febo had he confessed his solitude so openly. Whether it was just a coincidence or a psychosomatic shock, a few days later he in turn was admitted to a specialist clinic in Florence, for an inflammation of the nerve centers and a case of "bronchitis that has caused me to suffer tremendously for the past twelve days," as he explained to Marianne Halévy, adding:

> [My mother] had prepared packets with the name of each of her children. For me she left a packet containing the Garibaldian red shirt I had worn in the '14 war, which she had devoutly saved without telling me. She had died like that, saying to me: I knew that you would be there.[132]

But Malaparte was still Malaparte, and he soon got back on his feet to take his place at center stage, always concerned about keeping up appearances. His mother had withdrawn; his adversaries were still there. And yet in *Mamma marcia* his invectives, censored in the first edition of the book, had a new emphasis. He now seemed obsessed with the idea of identifying with the disinherited, those victims of history he had never had much love for. This vision of palaces and banks where the powerful lurk, seen as the new Sodom and Gomorrah, verges on demagogy. But his tone, too, had changed, at least in part; a new note resounds here: humility. Malaparte still wanted to astound and seduce his fellow men; but he sought also to console them, to protect them from the plague bacterium that would not disappear, that insinuates itself into the path of generations. Thus we find, to the end, his need to fight everything that reduces man to the level of fetus or guinea pig, swallows him up like a dirty bandage tossed in a bucket, grinds him up like garbage, turns him into the lowest kind of thing.

Once again he lashed out at the *padre padrone*. In a fragment of *Muss* that is organically part of *Mamma marcia*, Malaparte had tried to take his leave once and for all of the figure of Mussolini, probably without succeeding. To do so, he targets the initially triumphant, then disgraced, physical shell of the dictator—that is, his rotting corpse. After returning once more to the mockery of Piazzale Loreto, he proceeds to an imaginary visit to the Milan morgue:

> I bent over to look him in the eyes.... "Poor Muss," I said to him, with the same voice as my mother. I was shaking so badly that I leaned with both hands on the cold marble table.... What did it matter to me if he had been wrong, if he had committed cruel and stupid errors, if he had led Italy to ruin?... In the room of the morgue there was a strange, cold silence, smooth and cold. A silence made of the smooth and cold skin of a corpse.... There was nothing alive in that room, nothing, not even the buzz of a fly. Not even the terrible fly around the naked foot of Nastasya Filippovna, in the shadowed alcove, in front of Rogozhin and the Idiot. Nothing alive, nothing at all warm. Only then did I realize that the corpse was naked. I felt myself blush.... I had never seen a naked corpse. To date I had seen thousands and thousands of my fellow soldiers dead, on the battlefields of the Col di Lana, of the Grappa, of the Piave, of Bligny, of the Chemin des Dames, of Ukraine.... But I had never seen a naked corpse. I felt myself blush. It seemed to me a lack of respect for the dead man, an insult. I slowly raised my hand. Mussolini stared at me with that serene, patient gaze of his, a gaze without anger, a bit sad, of that same sadness that is in the eyes of dead men and animals, of dead men, dogs, and horses. I slowly raised my hand and brought it near his face. I knew I would have extinguished forever that wonderful gaze, I would have blinded forever those eyes that were so serene, so noble. I knew that my act was one of pity, not

of fear. I wasn't afraid of his gaze. But I would have given my life not to have to carry out that final gesture, not to have to blind him, not to have to blind each of us, every Italian. Slowly I brought my hand closer to his face, seeking out his eyelids, pressing with two fingertips. He seemed to resist.... I pressed, I almost tore the damp eyelids from below the eye socket, slowly I closed his eyes, extinguishing forever that good and serene gaze of his. And suddenly, darkness invaded the room. (MU, 90–92)*

This scene recalls and strikingly completes the scene we cited in the second chapter: his false pursuit of Mussolini's alleged assassin. Here Malaparte displays, along with the entire catalog of his repugnances, starting with his blushing at nudity, the impossibility of his liberation from that man he loved and hated so much. Even in his final fall, Mussolini preserves his power, shows himself to be *stronger than him*, and truly becomes the corpse "like me." But this humility does not last long, and Malaparte soon returns to being the victim, and never the accomplice, of the motherland's degradation, of her inability to generate a line of strong, noble, and just men. The woman "like me," emerging from the war, has lost that gift of self ensuring the ancestral virginity of the world, its innocence before history. Here Malaparte puts himself in the position of the Virgin's son, of Christ born from an undefiled woman, a bit like how Pasolini

---

*Even in the pathos of this page, Malaparte cannot help turning matters to his own ends, adding: "I hadn't seen him up close since 1932, or spoken to him. And I blushed at that stupid pride of mine that had always kept me from asking to see him, to speak to him, after I had got out of prison." In fact he had tried to see him again on several occasions. As for Il Duce's financial contributions, he not only accepted but also solicited them.

would have his mother play the role of Maria at the foot of the cross in *The Gospel According to Saint Matthew*. We need not see in this recourse to maternal *pietas*, I think, a symptom of enduring Italian *mammismo*. Malaparte did not share the incestuous fixation with his mother that has characterized certain homosexuals, Pasolini among them. What Malaparte was pursuing in his praise of the woman-mother as giver and guarantor of life was once again the ideal of strength in sacrifice and adversity, the "virile" ideal of woman, as he had previously evoked it in the stories and portraits (or self-portraits) of *Woman Like Me*, *Sangue*, and *Sodoma e Gomorra*.

Conversely, the feminization of man deeply repulsed him. This is what prevented him from proclaiming with Drieu La Rochelle: "If I don't have children, what is the difference between me and a queer?"[133] These two components—faith in maternity, rejection of paternity—reappear, paired and for once harmonized, in a war memory. Malaparte, arriving in Formia with the American troops, comes to the aid of a pregnant woman, horribly disemboweled in the course of a bombardment. He uses a knife to cut the umbilical cord and ties it with a shoelace to save the baby, whom he carries in his arms to a Red Cross truck (MM, 59–61). In *The Skin* we witnessed the mock birth of a homosexual; here we witness the attempt to give life to a baby on the part of a false father, in place of a dead mother. But the child, however, is alive; it is *not* fake. Whence the new polemic against homosexuals, who refuse to defer to the natural function reserved to women, that of ensuring the perpetuation of the species, and take refuge in the sterility of vice, antechamber of death. The preacherly tone in which he addresses the "youth of Europe" was likely intended to give the impression that he disdains every prejudice. But the peroration on "sex and liberty" concludes by opposing the former to the latter and gives rises to one of the most atrocious sentences, behind the apparent mercy, in all his vast repertoire: "Homosexuals have always inspired deep pity in me. They seem like women condemned to death" (MM, 295).

It is a classic example of the language of substitution, like the "pity" inspired in him by the Nazi leaders' fear. Because here it is Malaparte who is confessing his fear of dying by confessing his sterility, gnawed by the cancer of unhappy narcissism. In reality, he does not urge abstinence or the control of sexual impulses on young people, as he pretends, but invests them with his own phobias. His inability to love others, or at least to pity them, which his mother reproached him for, derives from his inability to accept their weakness, their powerlessness: they must die from the cancer they do not want to eradicate. The pessimism of *Kaputt* and *The Skin* could find justification in the abominations of war, hunger, foreign domination. But now Malaparte takes the view that at this point all of "Europe is nothing but a family of assassins, panderers, and cowards" (MM, 91), where it is impossible to distinguish between oppressors and oppressed, liberators and liberated or, as Primo Levi would say, the drowned and the saved. Intellectuals like Aragon, Éluard, and the Soviet writer Alexander Fadeyev,* who "sang of liberty in a world full of concentration camps, of livid Siberias, of silent, frightened crowds," or who, like Sartre, "the favorite of the Germans from 1940 to 1944, sang of liberty in the dusty mirrors of the Café de Flore" (MM, 152), figure prominently in this indictment. In his eyes they

---

*A hard-line Stalinist, chairman of the Union of Soviet Writers, and tormentor of Akhmatova, Zoshchenko, and Pasternak, but a good storyteller himself and at least consistent in his errors, Fadeyev was the only prominent intellectual to shoot himself in the head after his leader's crimes were revealed.

became mere cogs of conformism, imposture, and terror, exploiters of the revolutionary illusions of Marxism.

Kaputt and *The Skin* compiled an inventory of evils; the ambition of *Mamma marcia* was to offer a logical demonstration of the same: namely, that Europe's decadence was an eminently cultural phenomenon. *Kaputt* was "a cruel book," as its preface claims, because cruelty had become the Hobbesian condition of Europe and Europeans. In *Mamma marcia*, Malaparte wanted to go further, to prove that the war had not taught men anything or produced any spiritual renovation. Culture, which Europeans considered their almost exclusive patrimony before the Great War, was the great victim of the second global conflict; but what resurfaced after 1945 was for the most part naught but disguise and imposture. It was not by virtue of their millennial civilization that Europeans survived Fascist subversion, but thanks to the combined forces of the Americans and the Soviets, who would proceed to divide up the old continent. The corpse smell of this Europe is worse than what emanated from the smoking ruins of the conflict, because it represents the decay of postwar ideals. Confronted with this new threat of dissolution, Europeans can only lie to themselves and return to the path that led them to disaster:

> It is the incredible hour of the vanquished. The tragic and ridiculous thing about the French situation is that the France of the Resistance and Liberation reconstructed precisely the same state that was defeated in the war of 1939–1945. The Germany of 1945 brought back to power the same political class as the Weimar Republic. And in Italy the political class in power is the same one that Mussolini so easily battered and dispersed in 1922. (MM, 248–49)

It was not entirely true, naturally. But thinking about the partycratic skirmishes of the French Fourth Republic, or how Germany and Italy wiped the slate clean after the long night of dictatorship, it was not entirely false, either. We need to understand, then, that if there is equality of beings in the face of death, salvation calls for "only that type of victory that interests us, and which can interest a civilized, wise, intelligent man; it must be a conquest of a moral nature. In fact, I will even say that there are no 'victories' in any war" (MM, 250–51). This is the moment when Malaparte, leaving behind the role of witness and straight man, stands as a prophet of a new humanism, as Dante's Virgil yields his place to the Virgin before the gates of Paradise. He tries to explain it to his dear old friend Jack, his dear, pure, American friend, reappearing before him as if by some enchantment, in the delirium of his illness. Jack still believes that the Old World can be purified and saved by the redeeming blood of the Yankees. And yet he also ends up surrendering to the evidence: "In fifty years, America too will be a country like Europe, a country without freedom and without justice, in the hands of the cops and the judges and those who command them" (MM, 86).* History and the bitter taste of victory will have corrupted the innocence.

Abruptly, the vision gives way to one of the most vertiginous sequences in all of Malaparte. As in Borges's Aleph, to which all things tend and all things return, Malaparte gives us one of his rare ecstasies, outside any rational control. Rottenness becomes the positive sign of existential renewal, a bit like the revolt of the "cursed saints" of *Viva Caporetto!* And yet it comes in one of the book's most

---

*These words are put into Jack's mouth. An underpinning of prudence in Malaparte's invective?

IN PRAISE OF ROTTENNESS

nauseating passages, the memory of an episode of the Great War in the woods of Reims, where Lieutenant Suckert's company has to hold an area of the front during an attack by German storm troopers. Onto the battlefield, like improbable magi, come three prostitutes who have lost their way amid the fighting. Surprised by the bombardment, these three poor mothers without Courage hide in a shell crater. Under the strain, in fear, they cannot resist the urge to void their bowels. The soldiers come to observe the indecent spectacle, and their laughter turns into murderous hatred:

> "You're here, now stay here," cried the soldiers, laughing. "You've come, eh? You've come to make love, eh! And now you'll die like all of us. You want to go home, eh? We want to go home too! But we gotta die here." (MM, 117)

Fortunately the soldiers lower their weapons and forgo firing on the three wretched women huddled in the pit. But they begin, one after the other and then all together, to urinate on them, "like madmen, with that madness that suddenly overtakes men when they know they have to die" (MM, 118–19). In place of rifles, their members, which they shake out till the last drop, are the symbol of what wants, despite everything, to live.* These soldiers led to the slaughter, who do not even have the strength or the chance to desert, as in *Viva Caporetto!*, express their anger with the only means left to them: their corporeal reality. They do so, as others vomit up their ration

---

*Thus Corrado Alvaro observed, at the moment of Italy's declaration of war on June 10, 1940: "In Rome the strongest impression is of a fermenting vitality. Young men, on a whim, urinating in the middle of the most fashionable streets plunged into darkness, and walking with their member out" (*Quasi una vita*, 241–42).

of food or alcohol, going on the assault against enemy trenches, staining the barbed wire with their own blood and their own filth. If they had not been driven mad, if they could calm down and reflect, they would understand those wretched women are as exploited as they are. The only thing they did wrong was to have come to bring the fighters a last semblance of pleasure in exchange for a bit of money. But they did it *voluntarily*, thus passing, unawares, over to the side of the exploiters, of all those—ministers, generals, bankers—on whom the soldiers would like to fire, or at least urinate. If the soldiers are programmed for death, in a moment of anarchic revolt they manage to manifest their refusal to be immersed in their own muck, to be reduced to the status of *ein Stück*, "a piece." It is the opposite of the moribund secretion of the victims of Pasolini's *Salò*, or of the guilty secretion in Genet, condemned to mess up forever for having messed up once. Their brandished sex becomes a chamber pot or a cigar: they want to live. They piss in order not "to be pissed," as they kill in order not to be killed. Accordingly, the rottenness, the garbage, the refuse launched against the others becomes the weapon of redemption. A follower of socialist realism would have bowed to the solidarity of the exploited binding the soldiers to the prostitutes. Brecht, thanks to his old anarchic chromosomes, successfully avoided this politically correct trap, while Pasolini very nearly fell into it with his melodramatic evocation of his own *Mamma marcia*: the humiliated and betrayed prostitute of *Mamma Roma*. Malaparte reverses the approach. They are all equally guilty and innocent, but what distinguishes them from the amorphous mass is not a simple primitive will to survive. It is a concretion of being, a hard nucleus nothing could crush, a little fire at which Narcissus can warm his numb fingers, in a world that is no longer "like me."

5. From Paris to Mao
(1947–1957)

I am a cold old animal who cares only for a few beings.
—Lou-Andreas Salomé to Sigmund Freud, February 15, 1925

Paris Is No Longer Worth a Mass

MALAPARTE'S SECOND LONG STAY in Paris—his third, if we consider his intermittent political mission between 1923 and 1925—lasted almost two and half years, from June 1947 to the end of 1949, and concluded, all things considered, in disappointment, if not exactly in failure. One commentator has referred in this regard, very generously, to his "conflicted attraction for France."[1] Malaparte knew his choice of France would bring a change of setting more than of climate; but he did not imagine to what extent the climate would affect the setting. In Italy he had managed to weather the storm of the purge without too much damage and ultimately been acquitted of the political and administrative charges, with the intervention, very likely, of Togliatti. But the repeated arrests had worn him down, and the personal attacks that continued to rain down on him more or less everywhere, from Right and Left, persuaded him to pursue a change of air as soon as possible. The frantic rush to obtain backdated titles of anti-Fascist merit, set off at Liberation in the Italian (and European) intellectual community, found in him, on account of his personal history and his temperament, an easy scapegoat.[2] He felt threatened by the "fascism of anti-Fascism,"[3] and this fact finally overcame his last remaining doubts. But he remained as ever a stranger to discretion, polemic still running through his blood. "Resistancism" became then one of his favorite targets. He immediately challenged the returning anti-Fascist emigrants' moral and cultural authority to give him lessons, "since there were no writers among [them], in the artistic sense, just polemicists of little value,"[4] which was unfair if one considers Silone, Salvemini, Borgese, and numerous others. His quarrel was similar to that of the "internal emigrant" Gottfried Benn with the anti-Nazi writers returned to Europe, like Klaus Mann, son of Thomas, who killed himself shortly after, in despair at no longer finding a place for himself in his erstwhile homeland.

Once again, then, Paris became the destination: in 1931, as a challenge to the Fascists; in 1947, as a reaction to the "false" anti-Fascists; but always in the name of freedom—his own, naturally. This is what he claimed, at least, but what the stays truly had in common was something else. His trip north in 1947, like the one in 1931, was not, strictly speaking, a matter of exile. This new separation, in his intentions, was once again only provisional in nature: Malaparte was standing by in expectation of a prominent role in post-Fascist Italy. The Republic had just been proclaimed on June 2, 1946, after a contested referendum, which gave it a strong majority nationally (12.7 million votes against 10.7); but suffrage in favor of the monarchy had prevailed in southern Italy. Umberto II, after some hesitation, commendably chose (real) exile, so as not to further divide the nation. Malaparte paid homage to him in a fine piece, "Saluto repubblicano all'ultimo Re d'Italia" (A republican salute to the last king of Italy).⁵ But the future of the country, called to confront enormous problems of every kind, remained uncertain, against the background of a now-inevitable Cold War. In the spring of 1947, the Communists were expelled from the government, in Rome as in Paris, and the political contest was radicalized. Malaparte did not wait for the result of the elections that, in April 1948, on the heels of the Communist seizure of power in Czechoslovakia, would award a clear victory to the coalition led by the Christian Democrats of Alcide De Gasperi. The possibility—theoretical anyway, given the international balance of power—that Italy could fall into the Soviet camp was definitively averted. If Malaparte preferred to follow developments from Paris, the result of the vote affirmed his conviction that he would soon be able to reenter Italy and find a position worthy of him there.

He demonstrated his choice of sides in a series of explicitly anti-Communist articles of the period, published in *La Gazette de Lausanne* under the general title "L'Italie sans masque" (Italy unmasked):

> In the north of Italy, in 1945, during the days of Liberation, the massacre was appalling. The newspapers spoke of 300,000 victims. The government neither denied nor confirmed this figure. This enormous and stupid bloodletting, which cost the life, alas, of many innocents, was perhaps necessary, from the moment it became inevitable. I would have preferred it to be simply more useful for something.... This massacre not only left the taste of easy blood in the mouth of too many people; its first consequence was this wave of more or less political assassinations, which covered the streets of Italy with blood for two years.... What happened in Italy after the Liberation? This:

the anti-Fascist government was tripartite. There were, then, three Mussolinis in the place of one. And I'm not counting the hundreds of little Mussolinis who make up the majority of anti-Fascist parties. The old Fascist threat: "You are an anti-Fascist!" was replaced by the new anti-Fascist threat: "You are a Fascist!" Out of fear of being accused of Fascism, people acted as they did in the times of Mussolini: they applauded in public and did "resistance" in private.[6]

He returned to the attack on the eve of the elections:

The protagonists in this fight are, on one side, a fluid mass of frightened voters... on the other, the Communist Party, flanked by the CGT, which relies on a workers' militia (the former Red Partisans) armed and led by former Italian communist emigrants, officers in the Soviet Army, come from Moscow. It's not necessary for this army to occupy the streets to exert negative pressure on the minds of voters. Its mere existence (which for the past three years has recalled to Italian memories unspeakable violence, horrible crimes, all left unpunished) suffices to shake the faith of the country.... Because Italy is not communist. The Italian people do not want revolution. They want to work, to live in peace. The fate of Western Europe depends on the result of the next elections in Italy.[7]

This in terms of the political battle. But also on a personal level, Malaparte never wanted to cut off relations with his own country, of which he had an almost carnal need in order to nourish his polemical style, his sarcasm, his indignation—his inspiration, in short. As cosmopolitan as Malaparte was, and notwithstanding his incendiary declaration against his ungrateful country, he had no desire to exile himself for real, and maybe forever, unlike the intellectuals who roamed across Europe, from east to west, anxiously awaiting a visa for the United States, Canada, or Australia. Nor did he wish to be mistaken for an Eliade, a Cioran, or any of the thousand others who fought through countless obstacles to survive, not knowing anything of Paris beyond squalid hotel rooms and soup kitchens. Once again, his model was D'Annunzio, who in 1910 had moved in grand style first to Paris, then to Arcachon, on the southwest coast (fleeing not a purge but his creditors); and he had returned to native soil in 1915, acclaimed by delirious crowds as an apostle of the union between Latin sisters against the Teutonic peril: footsteps Malaparte was most willing to follow in, should the occasion present itself again.[8] From 1946 on, his warnings about the dangers of German rearmament were aimed above all at the French public, among whom this fear remained exceedingly strong. Hence, for three good reasons, Paris was reaffirmed as the ideal destination for a few months or a few years, but not more: first of all thanks to the proximity that would allow him to follow daily events in Italy and to return there as soon as the climate changed; secondly because he was confident of having preserved in France, despite the war, a following of admirers and readers, which would grow with the works in progress; finally, Paris appeared to be quickly becoming again the center of the art and life of free Europe, and Malaparte could never accept remaining far from the limelight for too long.

These predictions were right, except for one essential point: Malaparte soon discovered that all sorts of rumors and unfavorable—at times completely absurd—details about him were already circulating, often thanks to the zeal of compatriots whose anti-Fascism had fractionally preceded his own. Despite his best efforts, then, he had not managed to achieve a miraculous conversion, such as that of his friend Rossellini, who accompanied him to France on June 30, 1947.* The great director had recently completed two of the most iconic films of anti-Fascism, *Rome, Open City* (1945) and *Paisan* (1946), after having completed, a few years earlier, two of the most beautiful films on the regime at war, *The White Ship* (1941) and *A Pilot Returns* (1942), born of a collaboration with Vittorio Mussolini, the oldest son of Il Duce, possibly an even more radical Fascist than his father.† It is better to avoid cheap moralizing and floods of rhetoric, of the kind common in the immediate postwar period and still found echoing today, in the face of these and so many other instances of transformism: Fascism lasted more than twenty years, shaping two generations of Italians, and the cinema, like journalism, had been one of its essential propaganda tools.⁹ What would have happened to the French after twenty years of occupation and Vichy? For his part, Malaparte, who evidently failed to learn the lesson of the debate with Mme. Bouissounouse, succeeded only in making things worse, from the moment he arrived. If he had been cleverer or better advised, or above all humbler, he could have made an act of contrition, true or false, as had so many others, and invoked the tough conditions of the dictatorship to present himself as a repen-

---

*A highly controversial author in France, Morvan Lebesque, who during the German occupation was one of the leaders of the Breton independence movement, described a conversation with Malaparte, Rossellini, and some French intellectuals that took place at the time: "When Malaparte recounts something, he [Rossellini] leans over to one of us: 'Don't believe it, I beg you.'" See "Malaparte et le sens de l'humour," *Horizon*, March 1948.

†A similar case, in Japan, is that of Akira Kurosawa, who, for his 1946 protest film *No Regrets for Our Youth*, adapted the contents of his earlier work of wartime propaganda, *The Most Beautiful* (1944).

tant or involuntary Fascist, obliged to equivocate in order to survive. But he was neither clever, nor contrite; he was Malaparte, in short. And he did exactly the opposite.

No sooner was he installed in his first Parisian lodging, a sublet room at 56 rue Galilée, than he started giving interviews stuffed with lies old and new, such as the one in *Combat* on July 4, in which he declared that "the Fascists imprisoned me on Lipari and I remained there for five years," adding that Hitler, upon ascending to power, had "sentenced [him] in absentia"... perhaps to be decapitated with an ax, according to Nazi custom?[10] In a country like France, which made the secularity of the state a republican dogma, he ably reclaimed his well-buried Protestantism to give the art historian Marcel Brion an imaginative new version of his supposed resignation from the PNF: "In 1931, following the Lateran Treaty, which put non-Catholics in an unacceptable situation, I loudly left the Fascist Party."[11] Here he really outdid himself!

The police were interested in him as well. Already during his stays in Paris in the 1920s and 1930s, the French intelligence services had followed him closely, in the belief that he played "a very wide-ranging and high-level role."[12] A new file on him was established by the prefecture in 1947–49, when Malaparte applied for a residency permit. Apart from a few inevitable inaccuracies, the report by the famous Cinquième Bureau was very well done. There one can read, notably, that "in August 1935 he was pardoned by a decision of Mussolini and seems to have returned into the good graces of the Fascist regime." Nonetheless, his credentials as a decorated veteran of Bligny and the fact that "in private his behavior is irreproachable" ensured that the permit was granted, then reviewed without problems. The only difficulty arose toward the end of his stay, in April 1949, when his name was linked to the publisher Louis Nagel, alias Lajos Nemès, a Hungarian settled in Paris, who notably had brought out *Existentialism Is a Humanism*, by Sartre, before being unmasked as an alleged Soviet agent. The matter passed without consequences, but all of Malaparte's trips to France after that, even the most anodyne, were duly recorded, up until his death. The situation becomes paradoxical: having left Italy disgusted by the atmosphere of the purge, in France Malaparte encounters a diffident and often hostile attitude, one in which everyone claims to have a monopoly on virtue and where "they look on me as an enemy. They believe they themselves invented the Resistance, that it's a French idea, like the Revolution of 1789" (DFP, 202). Which leads him to conclude, exasperated: "I am more and more convinced that I prefer real collaborators to fake resistants" (DFP, 131).

What is more, when Malaparte arrived in Paris, anti-Italian prejudice was at its peak. The national fiber of France was more sensitive than ever, and defeated Italy became a sort of outlet for venting about the prohibitions and crimes of the Occupation. The wound from Mussolini's woeful, absurd attack on France, on June 10, 1940, the so-called stab in the back,* of which nary a mention was made

---

*The expression, recalling the *Dolchstosslegende*—the myth about the German defeat of November 1918, that it was caused by a collapse on the home front under Communist and pacifist pressure—appears doubly inappropriate. First of all, there was no betrayal: Fascist Italy was allied with Nazi Germany, not with France. This consideration is intended not for the purposes of moral absolution but to situate the facts in their historical context. Secondly, there was no surprise: at least since Italy's declaration of "nonbelligerence" in 1939, but in reality starting even earlier, the government in Paris had harbored few doubts that Mussolini was going to enter the war in due course. This explains why the Alpine frontier had been reinforced by the French beginning in the 1930s, which allowed for its effective defense at the time of the Italian attack.

during the Vichy regime, when Italy was being counted on to moderate the Germans, was revived at the Liberation. Emotion, as is too often the case, counted more than historical truth, and the thirty dead soldiers on the French side in what was, effectively, four days of war against Italy weighed more heavily than the 1,200 dead of Mers El Kébir, caused by the preemptive, undeclared attack by fellow Allied power the United Kingdom against the French fleet, which was about to fall into German hands. Also forgotten was the protection Jews found in the Italian occupation zone, from 1940 to 1943, and the absence or clemency of measures taken there against political opponents. The wave of indignation also served concrete political interests. The Treaty of Paris with defeated Italy, signed on February 10, 1947, had in the end allowed it to keep Val d'Aosta, whose annexation had been considered by de Gaulle, but took away Briga, Tenda, and Mont Cenis. The new eastern borders spared only Trieste, placed under Anglo-American control until 1954. Finally, Italy had lost its fleet and its colonies. Thus the Fascist war ended in national disaster, and Italy's "cobelligerence" with the Allies from 1943 to 1945 brought none of the promised advantages, becoming for Malaparte, as for the majority of his compatriots, the source of great bitterness. He avoided taking part in the controversy between supporters and opponents of signing the Treaty of Paris. But later he spoke out against the Memorandum of Understanding of London, which ratified, in October 1954, the transfer of Trieste to Italy, in exchange for the annexation of the majority of the surrounding area of Istria and Dalmatia, largely ethnically Italian, to Tito's Yugoslavia. In these reactions, which are consistently opposed to those of the Communists, one can glimpse his continuing attachment to the values of irredentism and the Great War.[13]

More immediately, though, Malaparte knew his eyewitness account of fighting on the Alpine front, *Il sole è cieco*, could become awkward. He hastened to bring out a new edition in Italy, with relatively minor modifications.[14] But that seemed insufficient to him, and so he had the terrible idea of adding a "compulsory statement," in which, as in the preface to *The Skin*, he puts his credentials as an anti-Fascist dissident, generously backdated, on full display. As if that were not enough, he declares to have lived with shame "the sad, sad days of the stupid, vile, wicked, treacherous attack against defeated and humiliated France" (SC, 40–41), alleges to have been the "only" intellectual to have opposed the conflict, and concludes with a claim that the articles had been censored. These inventions brought him no advantage whatsoever. Tosi told him he was sending page proofs of the translation;[15] but publication would be postponed, probably for reasons of timeliness, and in the end the book would appear in France only in 1958, shortly after the author's death.

The accusation of being a more or less undeclared former Fascist was coupled with other attacks on his bad faith: "I don't hold it against Malaparte that he was a Fascist," wrote Francis Ambrière, soon to become his sworn enemy.[16] "He was perfectly within his rights to glorify Mussolini; my unease begins when, with the tyrant dead, his former disciple insults, defames, and repudiates him." Hard to say he was wrong. But the basic problem was that Malaparte, while presenting himself as a writer of the future, embodied perhaps more than anyone, whether right or wrong, a certain European past that young people above all were hurrying to erase in order to regain confidence in life. It was the time of new fashions and trends, from neorealism to existentialism, from personalism to humanism, which Malaparte had sniffed out or anticipated and even contributed to publicizing in Italy through *Prospettive*. But at this point they were being carried on by other thinkers, while he had come to look like the relic of a bygone era. A ringmaster of the salons of yesteryear, he proved unable, despite his flair and flexibility, to transform himself into a habitué of the cafés, *caves*, and nightspots, which generally opened after he had already gone to bed with a raw steak across his cheek, if a sufficiently fresh one could be found at the butcher's. This disorientation and risk of losing contact with the public were essential in his decision to play the sex-and-violence card in his new book, on which his anxious hopes for a comeback rested: "*The Skin* will come out in a few days, and the brawling will start up again, I think. I don't care. If the book is killed in France, it will be reborn elsewhere, in England, in Italy, in America. But I'll suffer from it anyway. Because Paris is Paris," he wrote to the publisher Roland Laudenbach, in terms expressing both the impatience of the newcomer and the ambivalence of his feelings about France.[17]

The novel had already appeared in installments in the magazine *Carrefour*, in 1947–48. But it was its appearance in book form the following year, championed by Tosi and by Jean Voilier (whose real name was Jeanne Loviton), a much-debated figure who took over the publishing house after the mysterious death of Robert Denoël,* that gave the work an international springboard, even before the

---

*The publisher of Céline and Rebatet, Denoël had exposed himself a good deal during the Occupation. Still, no partisan organization ever claimed responsibility for his death. Voilier was accused by those close to the publisher, who had just changed his will in her favor, of instigating the murder, but without proof. Friends of Voilier assure me there was an interesting, and even romantic, correspondence between her and Malaparte, which apparently went missing after her death, in 1996. But the legend of the femme fatale (she had previously been linked to Valéry) clings to her to this day.

Italian edition. His American publisher, Dutton, which had just brought out the translation of *Kaputt*,* immediately got in touch to ask him for the rights to *The Skin*, pursued by English and German publishers.[18] Franco's censors even authorized the book's translation into Spanish, evidently with the aim of displaying the disasters of a conflict that the caudillo was proud to have kept his people out of; at the same time, Franco forbade publication of *The Hive* (1951), Camilo José Cela's masterpiece, which is very similar to *The Skin* in its description of the misery and moral corruption of Madrid after the civil war. It was a great satisfaction for Malaparte, and yet, true to himself, he took advantage of it to accuse Dutton of having deceived him about the size of his royalties.[19] Thus he found himself again at the center of the scene and could consider himself partially avenged for the "long persecution" he suffered in Italy. Critics' reactions were generally even more favorable than for *Kaputt*. Max-Pol Fouchet wrote, in *Carrefour*, that "Malaparte's evil genies are his genius. And in this respect he is a genius." According to Kléber Haedens of *Samedi Soir*, "Being in Naples, he describes for us the eruption of Vesuvius. But he is wrong to speak of the famous volcano as if it were a stranger. Because *he* is Vesuvius." Finally, Paul Lévy called Malaparte, in *Aux Écoutes*, "the herald of martyred, defeated Europe, a herald both noble and desperate, whose song will remain unforgettable." The citations could continue.[20]

He wrote triumphantly to a friend: "Everyone recognizes that I am still the greatest," which shows his fear of no longer being so. D'Annunzio and Pirandello continued to crush him from beyond

---

*With the probable mediation of the European correspondent of *The New York Herald Tribune*, Richard A. Watts Jr., according to Paul Shapiro, "Bury the Dead," in *Fourth International*, May 1948.

the grave, and his former disciple Moravia was successfully exhibiting the credentials of racial and political persecution. But in his heart he was well aware of having told some whoppers in creating his new literary package. As he wrote, for example, to Tamburi:

> My book's success is really huge. It even makes me laugh sometimes. Because, in contrast to what many believe, I am neither a vain person nor an *emballé*. I know the (current) limits of my work, I know very well that I could do better, and I will do better, and I am perfectly aware that *Kaputt* is much better. So then, why so much fuss over *The Skin*, which is not worth a fingernail of *Kaputt*? For me, there is a mystery underneath: and you'll see that at the first opportunity, they will fiercely avenge themselves for having been obliged to applaud now.[21]

Objectively, such a severe judgment is very rare from him and may surprise us. *Kaputt* and *The Skin* have shared the favor of readers the world over for roughly eighty years. And yet it is hard to deny that the first chronicle of the plague retains a sweep, a truth, and a force that, in the second, too often yield to mannerism and repetition. This success represented, in any event, just a brief respite.

Much of the Parisian intelligentsia continued to treat him coldly. Malaparte failed to make any contact with "the lieutenant" Éluard or "the captain" Breton, as he had christened them in *Prospettive* in 1940, even though he had done more than anyone else to introduce them to Italy. Their aesthetic choices, and not just their political ones, had become irreconcilable. Malaparte's opposition to socialist realism, for example, now appears prophetic and well founded; but it could only be considered heretical in the atmosphere of the time:

I've just read the latest novel by Aragon, *Les Communistes*. Undeniably, this novel is more evidence of the decadence of the bourgeois "realist" novel than a work of the new communist art. In the second and third centuries, Christian art, inspired by the new Christian conception of art, did not exist. Those Christian artists did nothing but copy the models of Roman artistic decadence. There is no difference between the portrait of a Roman merchant painted or sculpted by a pagan artist and a portrait of a merchant painted or sculpted by a Christian artist. There is no difference between a bad bourgeois novel of 1949 and the communist novel of Louis Aragon.[22]

The existentialist clan, with whom he had sought to come to terms, refused all his overtures.[23] At that point all he could do was vent his spleen in the vicious pages of *Mamma marcia*. History will decide if the works of Malaparte age more or less well than the novels and plays (for the philosophy, the discussion is different) of Sartre, Beauvoir, and their disciples. Here, too, Malaparte could complain of anti-Italian prejudice to explain his growing isolation. Arthur Koestler experienced the same rejection after breaking with Sartre, who reproached him for his anticommunism, and ended up choosing England, where intellectuals had (and have) less political influence—and is that such a bad thing?—but often bigger print runs and direct access to an audience across the Atlantic. Koestler bid farewell to Paris with a caustic essay on "The French 'Flu," the title a pun combining "influence" and "influenza," in which he panned the false promoters of progress, à la Sartre, and the poets turned party functionaries, such as Éluard and Aragon.[24] This may be why Koestler, considered a major thinker in postwar liberal culture, was for a long time marginalized in France, just like Orwell or Raymond Aron. But Malaparte did not wish to cross the Channel and he did not yet feel ready to cross the Atlantic. His *Diary of a Foreigner in Paris* shows he continued to wonder about the cosmopolitan, internationalist, almost militarized "Marxist race," whose development had not been foreseen by either Christian morality or Darwin, and which seemed on the brink of taking over the entire West. And he was surprised by the extent of the phenomenon in a country like France, in which the art of living and the Cartesian spirit should have ensured a greater resistance to degenerating influences.*

The Two Straw Hats of Italy

From the furnished room on rue Galilée he moved to a more comfortable apartment, at 209 boulevard Pereire, near a Baldi, probably his milk brother, Giacomo, who had been living in France for some time. But he preferred to reside, as he often did, just outside the city, and left Paris for the Château des Alouettes in Herblay (now Herblay-sur-Seine), in the northwest suburbs. His publishers Tosi, Laudenbach, and Charles Orengo of Éditions du Rocher of Monaco displayed angelic patience, but he was always quick to call them "poor neurasthenics" or "incompetents" at the first sign of any dispute. He had broken with Juliette Bertrand, now a "militant communist,"[25]

---

*The writer Paul Guth, recipient of some of Malaparte's confidences at the time, recorded in his book *Quarante contre un*, vol. 2 (Paris: Denoël, 1951): "He describes for me this new Marxist race spread across the world, in the street, the factories, the movie theaters, the stadiums, the subway, hatless, disdainful of adornment and grooming, hard, arid, gripped by the conspiracy of economic crisis, collective life, sport, propaganda, and war" (256–57).

but fortunately he found another enthusiastic and competent translator in the person of a Monacan diplomat, René Novella, future ambassador of the Principality to Rome.[26] Their epistolary exchanges allow us to understand the writer's way of working. Malaparte has often been described as capricious and changeable, whereas, like a great professional, he was capable of long discussions about a word, an expression, or a turn of phrase in French and also in English, even as his acquaintance with the latter language was more limited. The faithful Halévys loaned him their villa in Jouy-en-Josas for long periods. It was here their granddaughter, Claude Nabokoff Joxe, remembers meeting him:

> He was more fascinating than friendly, rather curt with the little girl I was then. Among the family, the attitude was ambivalent. My grandparents adored him, while my mother distrusted him and criticized his political U-turns. He was always frozen in a pose. It could be said that he wore a mask and that he was always afraid the mask might fall.[27]

He was once again welcomed into high-society homes, at the Bibescos' and the Vilmorins', adulated by famous actresses like Véra Korène and Yvonne Printemps, always brilliant and eloquent when he felt supported and indulged, but with a growing tendency to remain aloof. Marginalized by the most modish intellectual circles, he was inevitably drawn again to the world he had frequented before the war: diplomats, socialites, illustrious expats, and politicians who had missed the boat, such as Paul Reynaud or Gaston Bergery. Who else was left of his generation anyway? Drieu La Rochelle had committed suicide, Morand was in Switzerland, Giraudoux was dead.

He avoided Malraux, whom he had only ever run into in the 1930s, as we saw. He met Mauriac and his wife once or twice, and they covered him with reproaches. He did not seek out Montherlant, remote and compromised by his collaborationism. With Camus, "one of the French writers I admire the most," he came close to blows in a nightspot. In contrast, Céline, still imprisoned in Denmark, received from Malaparte a part of the royalties from *The Skin*, converted into crowns: a not inconsiderable sum, and an even more courageous gesture, given he had never met this sulfurous character, pilloried at the time by public opinion. Céline responded with a letter to Guy Tosi, to which was attached another, for Malaparte.[28] But since the latter had never been found, it was argued that Céline refused the help.[29] On the other hand, Malaparte claimed that the money was accepted, but that he had never received the least expression of gratitude.[30] Who was right? Malaparte's archives contain a handwritten response in Céline's characteristic style; the date and contents prove it is precisely the response entrusted to Tosi:

> Dear Malaparte, I am deeply moved by your beautiful gesture, so warm, so fraternal! To refuse would be pitiless! But I have arranged with Tosi [illegible] for this providential sum to be placed at your disposal in Paris in another way... *Kaputt* is on everyone's lips here. I mean the lips of the members of the reading elite, rather timid as a rule, but for Denmark it is a triumph. Thank you again, fraternally, till soon, I hope! Give my love to Camus, my colonel! L. F. Céline.[31]

Fortunately others, no less distinguished, were there to testify to their esteem: Cendrars, Cocteau, and other independent spirits. Right after reading *Kaputt*, Cendrars wrote to Tosi: "Tell him from

me that the book is a masterpiece and that I wish him all the best."³²
This was music to Malaparte's ears; he admired the writer and had
an instinctive liking for the man, whose life, along different paths,
was as adventurous as his own. Contact was soon established, and
Cendrars redoubled his praise:

> I read *Kaputt*. It is brilliant and revolting... I believe as you do that
> civilization is doomed. Precisely for this reason we must say what
> we have in our hearts. Others would speak of the stomach. [I extend
> to you] My friendly hand, Blaise Cendrars.³³

Shortly afterward, upon the publication of *Bourlinguer*, one of his
most beautiful books, devoted to his journeys around the world,
Cendrars would dedicate the chapter on Naples to "the brilliant
and revolting Malaparte, author of *Kaputt*," in the same tone of
fraternal complicity. In the absence of the young existentialists, who
scorned him, Malaparte connected with the young "hussars,"
Romantics and Stendhalians, orphans of a chivalric tradition that
was also a bit his. Michel Déon lived abroad at that period and
regretted the missed contact between them;³⁴ but there was Roger
Nimier, whose impertinence he appreciated, and who called him
"dear Maestro" and invited him to dinner with Orson Welles.³⁵ He
connected especially with two twentysomethings: Gwenn-Aël Bolloré, future businessman and passionate sailor, who had followed
de Gaulle to London at seventeen but would later oppose the general
at the time of the Algerian War; the other, already mentioned, was
Roland Laudenbach, whose uncle was Pierre Fresnay, star of screen
and stage, unforgettable in two of the most important French films
of all time, Renoir's *Grand Illusion* (1937) and Clouzot's *The Raven*

(1943).* Together, Bolloré and Laudenbach had just launched a publishing house, whose aristocratic name—La Table Ronde—seemed made for Malaparte, and where he felt immediately at home. Stimulated by the enthusiasm of these young people, he became convinced that he could become a recognized intermediary between the two Latin sisters. He particularly wanted to explain to the French that Italy is "the most complex country in Western Europe" (DC, 94), which the French had never grasped in all its multiplicity:

> To love a country, you need to know it. France does not know Italy. By this I don't mean that France does or does not love Italy. But it is certain that the French do not know Italy. It is very difficult to know this country: a strange country, a singular, secret people. What it does, even if it does it exactly like others do, is completely different, has something that is its own, that belongs to its nature, to the character of its history, of its destiny. I hope to have created a useful work that provides for a better knowledge of the two peoples, to prepare what I hope is part of the fate of our common (common up to a certain point) history.[36]

Beyond *The Skin* and the theater, of which we will speak soon, Malaparte wrote and published ceaselessly. First the translation of *Don Camaleo*, which he would have liked to have presented on the cover as "the book that nearly killed Mussolini," or as "the best gunshot of the twentieth century," and which the publisher had the good sense (and the good taste) to avoid.[37] But he was not prevented

---

*Malaparte's original contact with the Fresnay family dated back to the writer's stays in France in the 1920s (testimony of François Laudenbach to the author). Another connection was their mutual friendship with Gerhard Heller.

from using the title "A Gunshot" for at least the preface to the French edition, which opened with an awful bit of bluster: "*Don Camaleo* is the book, now famous in Italy, that nearly killed Mussolini." It was followed by translations of *Volga* and *Woman Like Me*, well received by both the public and critics. Finally came a brilliant pamphlet for use by the French, *Deux chapeaux de paille d'Italie* (1948; The two straw hats of Italy), and a work of light entertainment, *Coppi e Bartali*. To launch all these projects, Malaparte counted on the collaboration of Orfeo Tamburi, the painter he had helped and hosted in Rome in the *Prospettive* period, and whom he had now convinced to follow him to France. Tamburi created not only the illustrations for these books but some powerful covers, including the one for *Kaputt*. However, the relationship was the source of profound frustration on the part of Tamburi, who, unlike Malaparte, decided to relocate to Paris permanently. Legitimately convinced that he could become a new Filippo de Pisis, based on the elegance and delicacy of his drawing, Tamburi found himself for the rest of his life, until his death in 1994, stuck in the role of the humble genre master, obliged by gallerists and dealers to reproduce Métro scenes and urban landscapes ad infinitum, commissions well remunerated but, he believed, beneath his talent. Hence, perhaps, the acrimony, mixed with affection and gratitude, toward his benefactor.

A through line in these texts of unequal importance could be called the "dioscuricism" of Italian identity, as it emerged from the war. *Coppi e Bartali* grew out of a commission by a French sports magazine—Malaparte published an Italian version in the weekly *Tempo*—and sketched out a lively double portrait of the two postwar Italies through the two rival cycling champions. If the Tuscan champion Gino Bartali is the man of the earth, hard, concrete, trustworthy (and devoutly Catholic), the legendary Fausto Coppi, known as "il campionissimo," is the man of the air, inspired, nervous, temperamental, and secular. (Malaparte almost seemed to foresee that he was destined to die young, like those loved by the gods; in fact he was struck down by malaria, after a safari in Africa, at the age of forty.) *Deux chapeaux de paille d'Italie*—whose title played on a then-celebrated farce by the nineteenth-century playwright Eugène Labiche, *The Italian Straw Hat* (1851)—expressed another, and much greater ambivalence. The pamphlet, which drew on articles Malaparte had published in the French and Swiss press, was ready to print at the end of 1947; but he added some pages to it in the wake of the April 1948 elections, to support the thesis that, with the Communist threat averted, it was now necessary to guard against the clerical one. In the words of an observer of the period, "the author welcomes the defeat of the Communist Party, but still fears the Catholic dictatorship of De Gasperi."[38] Malaparte never published a complete Italian version of the work, probably because he wanted to return to it with greater detachment. Transferred to the political plane, the antinomy tended to dissolve. Malaparte seemed to have already a clear intuition—not at all obvious at the time—of the future "historic compromise" between Christian Democrats and the PCI to dominate Italy's weak postwar democracy:

> Pitting one against the other (since all of Italian politics consists in the struggle between the Catholic party and the Communist Party), De Gasperi and Togliatti have many features in common. Meanwhile they belong, the one and the other, to a church: the church of Rome and the church of Moscow. They are two clerics, not two laymen. I believe that they hate each other, but that deep down they respect

and esteem each other. Their own struggle, like every struggle, is a succession of moves and gestures that at times have the air of death grips, at other times of embraces, of friendly impulses. I wouldn't be surprised if I was told they secretly kiss on the lips: Is it possible to know who of the two is Judas, and who is Christ? Maybe they take turns. (DC, 107)[39]

In the same period he also produced a great number of articles, interviews, addresses, and declarations in which, in an often sharp tone, only apparently lighthearted, he mocked the national defects of the French and the Italians, the two peoples he knew best, distributing pills of wisdom, at times still pertinent, to each. Ultimately, if many of his peers snubbed and rejected him, Malaparte could certainly not complain about a lack of interest among publishers and the public. And yet already there seems to have emerged in him that block that would keep him from any major publication for the rest of his life. Among the numerous projects that would not be realized were an essay promised to La Table Ronde, "L'Europe aux anciens parapets" (The Europe of the old parapets),[40] and above all the *Diary of a Foreigner in Paris*, for Denoël, with Tamburi's illustrations, a much richer text than the *Giornale segreto* and nearly completed. Is it possible to speak of a form of intimate self-censorship in an author who made impertinence and provocation his emblem? Had the "chameleon" begun to slow down? Another revealing case is that of *The Kremlin Ball*, one of Malaparte's major incomplete texts, which Gaston Gallimard himself was interested in. A preliminary contract was drawn up in July 1948; but, despite repeated requests from the publisher, nothing happened. A semblance of an explanation appears in a letter from Gallimard, which seems written to cheer him up: "I truly don't believe it would be reckless to bring it out." Had Malaparte suddenly become prudent, at the height of the Cold War? It hardly seems likely: the explanation resides, rather, in the growing dissatisfaction that gnawed at him, in the writer's block that made him also give up another project, to which Gallimard showed himself willing to transfer the contract for *The Kremlin Ball*; namely, *Mamma marcia*.[41]

He read and reread with unfailing admiration the memoirists of the seventeenth century and Chateaubriand, his model in all things, but with the feeling that this golden age of French civilization would never return. He willingly sojourned at Royaumont Abbey, for the preceding thirty years a meeting place for writers and thinkers, "an extraordinary place to work."[42] He spent several weeks in Switzerland, perhaps thinking of moving there, like other writers unable to rediscover their place in their homeland, from Thomas Mann to Erich Maria Remarque. He amused himself by perfecting the canine language he had "learned" in Lipari, on multiple occasions being surprised and reprimanded by police or hostelers, especially at night, as he barked at guard mastiffs or stray dogs, who responded eagerly. For that matter, he loved the nightlife, in his own way:

> I work at night and in the country. I cannot live in the city; I have never lived in a city. When people say I live in Rome, no, I live on Via Appia, well away; when people say I live in Paris, no, I live in Jouy-en-Josas, a hundred yards from Léon Blum, in the middle of the woods. At night I work, from time to time I get up from my desk, I take a walk in the woods, a mile or two in the rain, in the fog, et cetera. I go back in and work until dawn. At dawn, I go to sleep.[43]

He sent postcards to the being he held most dear, to the new "Febo Malaparte, Capri";[44] but he preferred not to return to the island, where the summer of 1949 was sweltering, "without a drop of water." He decided then to go back to Forte dei Marmi, where he was enormously disappointed at the first signs of mass tourism, finding the place so different from the one he knew in the 1930s. He complained about it with one of his most patient correspondents, Marianne Halévy:

> Forte has become a petit bourgeois beach, packed with people: horrible, hoarse-voiced Milanese and the whole gilded mob of war profiteers. The women, even those from the Milanese nobility, are decked out in a ridiculous manner. It's the provinces and bad taste in all their nationalist horror.... I don't feel at ease here. And, above all, the noise. Frightening. Hundreds of thousands of motorcycles. Everyone running and shouting. Italy is China, motorized.[45]

He left Forte in September, driving back through northern Italy toward France. From Milan, where he spent a few days to follow the publication of *The Skin* in Italy, he wrote a revealing letter, addressed this time to Daniel Halévy:

> PCI's official newspaper, *L'Unità*, published a very long article in response to my piece, full of insults and impotent rage. The danger was that they might speak approvingly of my anticlerical epigrams. In Florence last Sunday I attended an enormous communist celebration: 500,000 people marched, dressed in red, under swarms of red flags.... Togliatti spoke; his speech was flat and stupid. Mussolini, too, spoke terribly, when he spoke to Florentines. He was

intimidated by so many intelligent stones, by so many ironic statues. Togliatti had the air, certainly, of being less intelligent than his listeners. And he knew it.[46]

But his return to France would be short lived. The polemics with Ambrière, the hostility of engagé intellectuals, and the scorn of the existentialist circles all left their mark. His frenetic activity was not enough to secure him the role of cultural ferryman he vainly sought: it was the confirmation of a failure. He grew impatient and bored, succumbing to a growing melancholy, until he decided to pack his bags again and recross the Alps south, not as a poet in a D'Annunzian helmet, but as a combatant deeply wounded by the same France for which he had declared his great love at every turn. Here, too, we find the reason he held back from publishing that bitter *Diary*, so revealing of his states of mind, whose title shows how he considered himself, despite everything, a "foreigner" in Paris—the opposite of the version he spread in Italy, to make his compatriots believe it was nostalgia that brought him home, when everyone in the French capital was encouraging him to stay… But did he *truly* love France? It is rare for any relationship to remain the same over the length of its existence. We can imagine how much that was the case for Malaparte, so impervious to passion: if there was ever any love affair, it occurred in his earliest youth, when Marianne, under threat, bestowed graces upon her gallant defenders, and the wide-eyed adolescent Curzio discovered the beautiful landscape of Champagne, while his flamethrower destroyed its contours:

> Among the crowds are many men between forty and fifty, soldiers from the other war, the type of Frenchmen I like best. It's still the

France of 1914 that obsesses me, this generation of soldiers, of victors, of *poilus* that is my own. Their faces are completely different from those of the men of younger generations, those born between the two wars....

Almost all the men who were twenty or twenty-five years old in 1914 have mustaches, short unkempt hair, low foreheads, pale eyes in dark faces, dull skin.... It's a harder race of men, who dress more simply, remaining faithful to the heavy-soled shoe, the tight-ankled velveteens, the peaked cap, the narrow tie over a shirt of coarse cloth.

Each mustache droops at either side of the mouth, a mouth stained by smudges of lipstick, by the Pernods and absinthes of old, by the ever-present Caporal stub at the corner of the lips. (DFP, 30–31)

Next comes a long aside, in which he describes the inhabitants of the working-class districts of La Villette, Saint-Denis, Pantin, Buttes-Chaumont, and Villejuif as the repository of the "ancient race of Frenchmen, of Frenchmen of France," the only one still resisting, more and more feebly, the invasion of the new man—formless, indeterminate (also sexually)—who has invaded Europe, echoing the writer's anthropological attention to the new "Marxist race" from the long-ago trip to the Soviet Union. But there are also unpleasant echoes of the "grands vignerons gaulois aux longues bacchantes" (great, long-whiskered Gallic vintners) dear to the old Right of Barrès, Maurras, and Rebatet. Also visible in this nostalgic evocation, outside history, is the same "old Bolshevik" element that we saw Malaparte glorify at regular intervals since the Great War, against bourgeois pettiness and, now, the spineless bards of the postwar. There is, too, an echo of the battle of Strapaese against the first signs of globalization between the wars, lending these pages a certain pungent topicality. And, together with all this, he expresses once again his old predilection for another victim of the times:

> imagination, grace, and that passionate madness of the eighteenth century. Madness that is cold, pale (if it can have a color), lean, blue and white, dry and polished smooth like a cuttlefish bone; that is the secret spirit animating the entire mechanism of French civilization. A civilization that is at this point the most fragile in the world, because it is nothing but a memory, regret, long habit. It is no longer love but the memory of love, etc., no longer hate but, etc. (DFP, 83)

These two old, not at all incompatible Frances, with their very distinctive physical and moral traits, pitilessly disappear. In the amorphous one that rises in their place, he realizes he is irreparably a "foreigner," even if he writes and speaks the language perfectly, and even if he were to spend the rest of his life there. Already at the time of "I morti di Bligny giocano a carte," we have seen, his psychological attitude was tinged with resentment. It is true that at the moment of Mussolini's fatal slide toward the axis with Hitler, Malaparte remained *quite* pro-French and *rather* anti-German. But we are too well acquainted with his contempt for losers to see in this anything more than a sentimental reflex, and he was careful not to take the semipublic position of a dying D'Annunzio or of a Marinetti against the alliance with the Third Reich. At the outbreak of the new war, if an event pained him, it was much more the invasion of Poland in September 1939 than the collapse of France in May–June 1940, whatever he may have claimed later.*

Ultimately Malaparte, too, would embody that typically Italo-French syndrome, in which the unconcern on one side is met with jealousy on the other, and the Italians often respond to what they consider the arrogance of their "cousins" with apparent self-derision, too often taken literally. Hence the failure of Malaparte's attempts to make Paris understand that recent Italian history was rather more tragic than a sort of belated Stendhalian vulgate. Faced with his Parisian colleagues and the Parisian public of 1947–49, so haughty and confident of their rightness, Malaparte had the classic reaction of the scorned lover and rediscovered his inner *arcitaliano* that, in many respects, he had never lost:

> Now I'm beginning to think I cannot accept this in France, on the part of the French, in a country I fought for, whereas my accusers did not fight for this same France.... I think I'll spend a few months in England, before embarking for the United States.[47]

In the end, it would be the health of his dog that provided him a pretext to return to Italy, without losing face or giving the impression he was running away from a France that had closed its doors to him. A tragicomic version comes down to us in a family letter sent by Françoise Joxe Halévy, daughter of Daniel and Marianne:

---

*Malaparte's love for Poland went back, as we saw, to his "diplomatic" mission to Warsaw in 1919, apart from his paternal family's distant Polish origins. And the Poles reciprocated: the first edition of *Kaputt*, authorized by the Communist regime in 1963, sold out in a few days, and the book went for high prices on the black market. A Polish intellectual, still officially Communist, spoke to me several years ago, in impassioned terms, about the book as a great homage to the sufferings and the spirit of resistance of his people.

> The event of the day in the house is that Malaparte has left for Italy... because his dog is sick! If he put him in a nursing home, that would cost 40 to 50 francs a day, and it's more economical for him to take him to Milan, to some friends who will take care of him!!! We laughed ourselves sick when he told us this. "You have two children? You have never spent eight days like the ones I spent with this animal!" He made him chicken and rice, spaghetti, veal skewers, poultices...[48]

Fortunately, his relations with French intellectuals did not stop there. Malaparte, despite the disappointments, continued to favor ties with his transalpine colleagues. Capri, above all, remained a privileged site of visits and encounters. He regularly received Raymond Guérin, a solitary and ill-tempered talent, whose work has yet to receive, so many years after his death, the recognition it deserves. Casa Come Me allowed him to forge friendships on the left as well. One example was Roger Vailland, a Communist, yes, but above all a kind of libertine from the seventeenth century lost in the twentieth, who was his guest on Capri in the summer, and then in the fall, of 1950. Vailland expressed his gratitude to him for having been able "to write entirely under your roof my little book on Vatican politics.... I am even more grateful to you in that the hospitality you offered me was not without risk for you."[49] Malaparte continued to read, write, and think in French to the very end of his life, even as he increasingly applied himself to English, which he saw emerging as the new lingua franca of the contemporary world and of Western literature at large. But the lover's slight, which he was much more accustomed to provoking than submitting to, prevailed in the end. The result was that this France that was slipping away from him became more indispensable than ever. It was once again to his dear friend Marianne Halévy that he opened his heart, to the extent the expression can apply to Malaparte. Behind the eternal persecution complex, one glimpses a wounded sincerity:

> I miss France very much. But you have certainly surmised that the maliciousness, the vile slander, and the cowardly acts that I did not deserve and with which I have been overwhelmed in France have made me suffer atrociously.... In order not to be driven (in reaction) to hate France, which I love and have always loved, I have decided to keep my distance for a while.... I will return, naturally, when I have finished my new book, in 1953.[50]

Theater

The Paris years revealed another, more debated, side of Malaparte's talent: the theater, from which, he declared, the Fascist censors had kept him away during the regime.[51] In reality, politics had little to do with it. He had never stopped thinking about the theater, accumulating drafts and fragments over the course of the years. But he had undergone the trauma of all his generation, caught between the magniloquence of D'Annunzian tragedy and Pirandellian subtlety. We saw how Malaparte tried his hand at theater in the early 1920s, becoming close to the avant-garde and the Futurists, but these efforts went nowhere. In 1928 he wrote a play for Tatiana Pavlova, one of the first great prima donnas of the period, titled *La coscienza dei morti* (The conscience of the dead). The police prohibited its performance on the eve of opening night at Rome's Teatro Valle, even though the play had "no political character."[52] A decade later he tried again, with *Monsieur Candide o Candido in famiglia* (Mr. Candide, or Candide with his family), this time on a contemporary subject: boredom in a crumbling bourgeois family, reflecting the decadence of an entire family, almost as a response to Moravia's *Indifferenti*, which had deeply impressed him at the time.[53]

Malaparte's renewed interest in the stage was probably influenced by the success of the "theater of situations" of Sartre and Camus, as well as by the hope of winning a new audience, especially among the young. In addition, the challenge of introducing himself as a French-language author excited his vanity and should have, according to his intentions, consolidated his fame as a multifaceted, cosmopolitan author. He set to work with his usual doggedness and churned out in a few months, one after the other, *Du côté de chez Proust* and *Das Kapital*. Dragging in two of the greatest icons of modernity, Proust and Marx, was a measure of his ambitions; that this would pique the public's curiosity was the only thing he was right about. Because his theatrical adventure concluded with two fiascoes—all the more striking if you think that Malaparte had at his disposal prestigious venues and excellent performers, among them Yvonne Printemps and his friend Pierre Fresnay.* And yet

---

*The premiere of *Du côté de chez Proust* took place at the Théâtre de la Michodière on November 22, 1948, directed by Pierre Fresnay, with set design by Jacques Damiot, clothing by Lanvin, and starring Yvonne Printemps, Pierre Fresnay, and Jacques Sernas (who, thirty years later, would play the part of General Guillaume in the film version of *The Skin*). *Das Kapital* would be staged at the Théâtre de Paris on January 29, 1949, directed by Pierre Dux, with set design and costumes by Jean-Denis Malclès, and starring—in the principal roles—Pierre Dux, Renée Devillers, and Alain Cuny. See the testimony of Orfeo Tamburi, "Yvonne, Malaparte e Fresnay," in *Ciel de Paris / Cielo di Parigi* (Rome: PAN, 1983), 197–98.

things seemed to get off to a good start, such that *Das Kapital* was contested by two companies and the great Michel Simon hesitated for a long time before turning down the leading part, perhaps for political reasons.⁵⁴ The negative critical response has changed little since then, and the only play to have obtained a certain consideration is a third one, *Anche le donne hanno perso la guerra*, which Malaparte wrote upon his return to Italy. But none of these works has entered firmly into the contemporary repertory.*

Must we share this lack of appreciation? Yes and no. Malaparte was far too theatrical himself to successfully hide behind his characters and be content to make them act in his place. Nor did he know the tricks of the trade, in terms of timing, say, or how to make a line land. Hence, in a reading at least, the gap between authorial intentions and results catches the eye. If we recall that the revolution of Beckett, Ionesco, Pinter, and Adamov was right around the corner, we can see how far Malaparte, once ahead of his times, had fallen behind with respect to his contemporaries. That said, each of these efforts deserves a bit more attention.

Du côté de chez Proust is presented as an "impromptu in one act," and it stages, in an hour and a half of performance, only a piece of the immense edifice of the *Recherche*. Malaparte was not interested (thankfully!) in reproducing the entire Proustian fresco, so much as showing its social determinism, which becomes a parody of the bourgeois order. In the *Diary* he recounts how, during an evening in the company of the theater director and actor Jean Vilar and the painter Léon Gischia, he publicly declared himself a Marxist,

---

*A new version of *Anche le donne hanno perduto la guerra* was staged by the Yvan Baudouin–Lesly Bunton company, in Brussels, in the 1993–94 season. It has never again been performed in Italy, as far as I can determine.

because "there is a somber beauty in Marxism that fascinates me" (DFP, 125). He might have used the quip as an epigraph for this work, which is indeed basically a Marxist remake, ably constructed around three characters: the aesthete Saint-Loup, the courtesan Rachel known as "Quand du Seigneur," and Proust himself. They represent the three estates of French and European society on the eve of the 1914 war: the aristocracy, steeped in decadence; the proletariat, forced to sell its labor or body to survive, but whose inner energy is entirely devoted to uplifting the oppressed; and the bourgeois, party to all the enthusiasms and illusions but destined ultimately to remain outside the game being played by conservatives and revolutionaries. On stage, Proust's asthma expresses this refusal to fight for life. Malaparte attributes to the author of the *Recherche* his own conception of the inevitable decline of societies, if, exactly as happens with men, they no longer have the strength or courage to face up to the adversities of history. It's the common thread connecting his inspiration to *L'Italia barbara*, by way of the chronicles of the plague:

> I'm haunted by the question of why and how societies decay, if they rot on their own, or under pressure from an external force, the work of a social push against which they have no other defense but to decay.... Because here lies the key to the enigma. Here lies the entire meaning of my activity as a writer. (DP, 91–92)

The bourgeois has burned his bridges with the revolutionary proletariat, without being accepted as an equal by the aristocracy. He passes from one to the other, without ever choosing. This is why Malaparte picked an author like Proust, to whom he was not particularly similar, but whose clear, pitiless vision he admired, even in the masochistic admiration he professes for the *côté de Guermantes*, "this noble, cruel, disinterested race... in which can be traced, like the curve of falling water in the design for a hydraulic machine by Leonardo da Vinci, the curve of the decadence of an entire society" (DP, 15). There is no doubt a Malapartian madeleine in this approach. He may have always detested the bourgeois and their values: in reality he knew very well that he too was bourgeois, and that the proletarians and aristocrats he frequented so often never truly considered him one of them. We know he turned his back on his family and social environment as far back as his flight for the front in 1914, without ever being fully reconciled with his origins. He could not prevent them sticking to his skin: there was objectively something in him of the parvenu and the Proustian snob, but also of the Sartrian renegade. (Noteworthy in this regard is the wink at *Dirty Hands*, the play by Sartre that had just triumphed on the Parisian scene, as Malaparte records, with a trace of envy, in his *Diary* [DFP, 126].) Perhaps no one more than he grasped the grotesque aspect of the funeral procession in the *Recherche*, the theatrical genius of that "lisping, chatty old queer" shut up in his cork bedroom.[55] But the play ends feebly, without a genuine denouement: an elegant curtain raiser on a secret that never arrives. In fact, this was the opinion of some eminent Proustians, whom *Le Figaro* had the idea to interview as they exited the premiere.[56] Stung, Malaparte offered his own version of events in an unpublished page, in which he paints himself as the victim of a homosexual cabal:

> The reaction came after, at the exits, when the fresh air of the autumn night awakened the Proust worshippers from the dream, or the nightmare, in which I had held them for a whole hour. Christian

Bérard seemed shattered; he walked beside Fath, followed a few steps behind by Christian Dior. Bébé lifted his arms to the heavens, crying in a broken voice: "What has he done to our idol? What has he done to Marcel Proust?" Fath, supported by a young blond man, murmured: "It's a desecration, an abominable desecration!"... "You are the most detested man in Paris tonight," said Yvonne Printemps to me in her dressing room, merry and laughing, looking at me obliquely in the mirror. In the hatred of the sexual inverts for those who profane their secret world there is something resembling a kind of regret. The homosexuality that had its idol in a Proust is no longer equal to the times, it's antiquated, it's a conservative, right-wing homosexuality. Many have observed that the conservative, right-wing intellectuals had in great numbers been collaborators with the Germans.[57]

With *Das Kapital* the scenario changes, but not the theme. This more robust work, with its classic three-act structure, allows us to better understand what Malaparte intended when he opposed the "Marxist race" to bourgeois humanism. The play was written in one go, in May 1948, at the home of Roland Laudenbach, on rue François Millet.[58] After the chamber music of the Proustian intermezzo comes a dense choral composition for some twenty characters; Malaparte personally worked with his actors at length.[59] We are in London, in the Marx family's wretched lodging, the day after Louis Napoleon Bonaparte's coup d'état in Paris, on December 2, 1851. The three protagonists are Marx; his wife, Jenny; and his assistant, Godson. An Englishman from a good family, Godson is fascinated by the German exile's struggle for universal justice but increasingly perplexed by the inhumanity of this vengeful obsession. In the course of the dialogue, interrupted by the chorus (English policemen, wives and children of French émigrés, etc.), Marx and Godson appear as two incarnations of Judeo-Christian morality. On one side, the biblical implacability that Marx transposes into a materialist theory of history, from which God is banished, along with the *non-*revolutionary man, who must be exterminated. On the other, Christian pity, which in Godson appears as a refusal to purify man with redemptive violence. Here we see almost a presentiment of the conflict brewing between Sartre-Marx and Camus-Godson. What fascinated Malaparte was the impossibility of reconciling virtue with forgiveness; and it is ultimately to Jenny, the woman "like me," whom he entrusts the solution to this dilemma. Jenny is in fact the aristocratic sister of a Prussian minister, who got herself kicked out of the paternal house and broke with her class to follow the messiah of the proletariat. She has already lost a baby, whom she could not breastfeed, and risks losing another, the little Mush, a sacrificial victim similar to Alyosha in *The Brothers Karamazov*. Jenny has thus already "lost her woman's war," which consists in preserving the species amid the calamities provoked by the folly of men. But she has not yet renounced the true power, love, which her husband neglects:

> You don't know what a woman is, Karl. A woman is not the image of herself, or that of her children, or of courage, will, or man's pride. She is only the image of the ailments of man. She takes upon herself everything that in man is weakness, fear, doubt, desperation. She liberates man from everything preventing him from being strong, courageous, alone. I've taken upon myself everything your shoulders

are too weak to bear.... The time has passed when I could still hate you, Karl. It was the time when you didn't yet need me, or your children.... The strength of man is the tears and the suffering of being loved. (DK, 331–32)

Jenny's abnegation is not enough to move Marx, or even to raise the slightest doubt in him. The death of his children rekindles his hatred of the capitalist world, which is in his eyes the real oppressor of the innocent and the weak. If capital knows no pity, why should he, who wants to destroy it? Moreover, he is possessed by the abstract fanaticism of the intellectual. At the beginning of the play we see him coldly inspect ten-year-old girls battered by their work in a mine as if they were material evidence in a trial against the bourgeois order, while Jenny and Godson seek simply to console the little ones, giving them their last scraps of food. At the death of Mush, Godson can no longer hold back and, horrified, finally finds the strength to separate himself from his master:

> The law of the revolution is to throw the corpses into the trash! So that they don't come to testify, one day, that the revolution got it wrong, that they died pointlessly, by mistake...for who knows what? And so then, into the sewer, into the garbage, these bothersome witnesses! (DK, 326)

Das Kapital is in my opinion the most ambitious, most successful, and most modern play that Malaparte ever wrote. If you consider the topicality of terrorism and ideological fundamentalism, you recognize the arguments of Godson and above all of Marx, rehashed by their disciples of today. But at the time Malaparte was daring to question the received truths about the sanctity of the revolutionary struggle. By what right does this Italian, an ex-Fascist and maybe also a spy and a provocateur, permit himself to mock the great myths of the liberation of peoples and to describe in such a way the apostle of class struggle? *L'Humanité* dedicated a banner headline to him: "To the door, Signor Malaparte!" The reception of the Parisian public, which had been lukewarm but not hostile to the Proustian intermezzo, was violent in the case of *Das Kapital*. In the testimony of Daniel Halévy:

> The public's hostility was incredible. I recall only one who maintained some sangfroid, and he demonstrated it in his article, that was Thierry Maulnier.* All forces were leading to disaster. Bernard Grasset, who accompanied me to the third performance, said to me, "If the play were Sartre's, it would be performed a thousand times!"[60]

Only a few other faithful friends came to his aid: "You have created an *unusual* great play," Laudenbach wrote to him. "I was ashamed of the French and their stupidity, and I detested these nasal grandes dames and the little journalist twits. Furthermore, French society doesn't love to be mocked, or for Louis Napoleon to be mocked. They don't love jokes: they are serious people."[61] Gaston Bergery chose, in his own image, a tone of worldly badinage:

---

*Indeed, his was one of the rare levelheaded articles on the play, in *La Bataille*, February 5, 1949. Another unprejudiced review was that of the Christian existentialist philosopher Gabriel Marcel, in *Les Nouvelles Littéraires*, February 3, 1949. Malaparte also received friendly notes from the academic Jacques de Lacretelle and the prince Bibesco.

The stage-level box was perfect, with its back area for sheltering in secrecy. Annabella, Bettina's friend, was pleasant, as was her Romanoff (true or false?). Over the armrest, I chatted with Jacqueline. I glimpsed, from behind, the entire House of French Thought, previously of Culture: Aragon–Chateaubriand and Elsa Triolet–Queen Victoria.[62]

Other acquaintances, thinking to do him a favor, offered to review the text for him. Malaparte resented it. His French, often flowery and overly precious, does not maintain the extraordinary plasticity of his Italian; but it is generally precise (despite the spelling mistakes and barbarisms that pepper his manuscripts) and leaves few doubts about his intentions. The remarks, largely justified, with which he overwhelmed his translators, going down to the smallest detail, confirm his mastery of the language and perpetual dissatisfaction. Style, then, had little to do with the negative reaction; the truth was, this was an opportunity finally to get rid of him, to oblige him to flee. And yet the most corrosive attack came not from the extreme Left but from the critic of *Opéra* magazine, Francis Ambrière, winner of the Prix Goncourt in 1940 (awarded in 1946) for *The Long Holiday*, a good novel recounting his experiences as a prisoner of war. Ambrière, who, let us remember, had already warned his compatriots about Malaparte's arrival in Paris, did not limit himself to slamming the play; he added a defamatory touch, comparing the audience who left the performance early to the column of refugees in the exodus of 1940, "machine-gunned by Malaparte's old friends."[63] Trotted out again for the occasion was the "stab in the back," with an additional false note, because that machine-gunning, notwithstanding would-be testimonies (even recent ones), has never been verified.*

Malaparte threw himself headlong into the debate with his usual vehemence, without imagining his interlocutor had come well prepared: the play had been only a pretext for going on the attack, plain and simple. Here we had an encore, in short, of *l'affaire* Bouissounouse—and it is worth asking if she furnished him with the necessary documentation—but this time without any sense of humor or feminine grace. What is more, Ambrière transferred his polemic to the widely read columns of *Il Figaro*, a bien-pensant daily that, during Coty's ownership, as we saw in chapter 2, had been rather favorable to Malaparte. Ambrière called him out in no uncertain terms as a "morbid knave who loves the shadows," defying him to disavow the anti-French poems of *L'arcitaliano*.[64] Not satisfied, immediately afterward he published a translation of one of the collection's most explicit compositions, "La ballata dei francesi e delle dame di Francia" ("Ballad of the French and of the ladies of France"), which proves that the attack was premeditated. He struck another blow with a personal memory, difficult to prove but with an obvious impact on his audience:

---

*Independent of humanitarian considerations—the Italian air force certainly bombed civilian targets during the Ethiopian War and, probably, during the Spanish Civil War and the invasion of Greece—the problem was of a technical and strategic nature. The Italian air force's sorties over French territory had never gone beyond Provence and had involved only military installations, as shown in onboard documentation. The rest of the damage was provoked by panic. As a distinguished military historian has written, the thousands of French who swore to have recognized the tricolor cockades of Italian airplanes on the exodus routes did not know that in 1940 the cockades had been substituted by the fasces (Giorgio Rochat, "La campagne italienne de juin 1940 dans les Alpes occidentales," in "France-Italie," monographic issue of the *Revue Historique des Armées*, first quarter 2008, 77–84).

THEATER

There were five million of us, Belgians and French, living in a prison camp near Kraków.... Who knows if Malaparte was the Italian I saw once, leaving Wawel Castle at the side of Governor-General Frank and in conversation with him? My Polish friends were telling me news about their country, the German abuses, the ignominy of Frank, surrounded by his dignitaries' wives, all of them worked up, amusing himself after drinking by blowing up Jewish children's skulls with explosive bullets.[65]

Ambrière recognized this added nothing to *Kaputt*, except to make its author look less like an eyewitness and more like an accomplice. When Malaparte tried to paint him as an Italophobe, he replied dryly that "I love Italians who do not resemble you."

The situation worsened to the point that Malaparte challenged him to a duel, banking on both the scandal and his well-known reputation as a swordsman. But Ambrière, against all expectations, accepted. It broke down only when the witnesses were unable to meet at the established time, without reconciliation and amid reciprocal accusations of cowardice.* There was also some unpleasant French-on-French aftermath, with the risk of another duel, because Halévy intervened

---

*Many legends have been spun about this tragicomic affair, including Tamburi's version in *Malaparte come me*. But the incontrovertible testimony of the Italian diplomat Onofrio Solari Bozzi, who as a young amateur fencer living in Paris was called on as a training partner, attests to the athletic rigor with which Malaparte prepared himself: "I was surprised by his agility, by how aggressive his attacks were, by the quick precision of his gestures in the most unexpected lunges. I remember that twice he made the sword jump from my hand and that, in one attack, he used the weapon like a whip." Solari Bozzi's account of the duel that wasn't has been published as an appendix in the French and Italian editions of this biography.

with his usual generosity to defend his friend from the "collective beating," recalling his old merits as a fighter for France. Ambrière, in difficulty, lost his temper and called him a "visibly ill-informed old man." The polemic spread to the Italian press, not least because Malaparte had not hesitated to accuse the writer Guido Piovene, whom he then considered his great rival in Paris, and the gallerist Gualtieri di San Lazzaro of taking part in the "plot" against him.[66] This rather sad episode brought Malaparte's long dueling career to a close; it also put an end to his ambitions as a playwright on the Parisian scene.

He held on in the capital for a few months more, but his decision to leave was certainly influenced by that bitter campaign and the two plays' lack of success. His last effort in this field, *Anche le donne hanno perso la guerra*, was staged by the author at the Venice International Theatre Festival, on August 10, 1954. But his inspiration was the same, and we can consider it the final part of a trilogy. The text is in Italian, with some preparatory fragments still in French, from the period 1947–49 ("Les Amazones," "Les Femmes de Sienne," "Les Femmes aussi ont 'gagné' la guerre"), which address more or less the same theme, in different historical contexts, such as Siena in 1530, besieged by the Spanish of Charles V.[67] The most original of these sketches, however, is the first, which takes place roughly half a century after the death of Hitler, in the Europe that the Americans liberated but then abandoned, as in 1918, to close themselves off in a new isolationism. The Amazons decide to conquer the continent then, to "do with our men, after their victory, what the Americans did with our women after the last war," the author explains in a page accompanying the text.[68] The beginning is intriguing, but the draft ends there.

Back in Italy, Malaparte worked on a three-act "burlesque" of the same title, in late 1951: the action unfolds in a residential quarter of contemporary Rome. It is a species of vaudeville, with echoes of Oscar Wilde and German expressionism, in which we witness the "conversion" of a young professional executive into a high-end prostitute, courted by, among others, his father-in-law, a retired general. It is a failed attempt at bawdy music hall, foreshadowing *Sexophone*, and Malaparte did well to keep it in a drawer. This Albert who becomes Albertina, probably in homage to Proust, represents that confusion of the sexes that Malaparte attributes, as we know, to the crisis of bourgeois identity.[69] "Homosexuality"—he would write in a first version of the incomplete essay on "sex and liberty," from 1951–52—"is for many a refuge against the obligation to take on an unwelcome responsibility, to accept a dogma, to bend their back. It's a form of freedom, and of heresy, that makes up for slavery in other fields."[70] The director Guido Salvini, to whom he had sent the script, made him understand it would have been impossible to stage: "It has been established by the censors that gays and lesbians must not act as such on the stage."[71] After an intense exchange of letters, Malaparte landed on a completely different subject, even as he maintained a title that seemed to him effective.

The final version of the play bears the dateline Baden-Baden, July 1953–Forte dei Marmi, March 1954, and carries us back to a precise historical framework. The action unfolds in Vienna[72] at the end of the war, and thus at the beginning of the Soviet occupation, in a ruined apartment in the upscale part of the city, inhabited by a group of women trying to survive, far from their dead or imprisoned men. They are forced to take turns prostituting themselves with the soldiers of the Red Army in order not to be deported. The victors want to destroy them in body and soul, to the point of reserving their services for the troops, not even for the officials. The class war must pass through the liquidation of the last vestiges of bourgeois dignity. Hence the political commissar who comes to requisition the apartment, to turn it into a brothel, displays a certain regard solely for the housekeeper: "You are a woman of the people, Frau [sic] Lena. It's not poor wretches like you that we're interested in humiliating" (DOP, 177). Among the other women erupts the whole range of passions, from the lowest—competition, rage, greed—to the noblest, like the attempt to protect the weakest of them all, an intellectually disabled girl. And we arrive at the rediscovery of humanity, when Enrica, widow of an official who died at the front, finds herself before a young Ukrainian who treats her with unexpected respect. But it is precisely that respect that compels her to pull back, because she fears falling in love and so betraying her husband's memory. The desperate soldier kills himself, but the commissar officially denies the act:

> Many men get out of the war with a sense of guilt. Andriy was one of these. If he had not killed himself, he would have ended up much worse. We don't know what to do with men like him.... A society of free men cannot be built of such beings. (DOP, 189)

The women return to their unhappy life, but they are sustained by the task of witnessing: "Because each of us is guilty of what the others suffer" (DOP, 185), Enrica concludes.* It is the moral of Jenny

---

*The Italian version, brought out by Cappelli and Aria d'Italia in 1954 and republished in a special Malaparte-themed issue of the magazine *Sipario*, in August–September 1998, differs at some points from the French version, translated by Halévy and published after Malaparte's death. Missing is the final scene of the return and capture of Enrica's husband, for whom she sacrifices herself.

Marx, adapted to the new situation. Thus ends the play and thus ended Malaparte's theatrical career, even if other projects would continue to attract him to the end: be it a simple synopsis in French for a three-act play on "Les joyeux compères de Yalta" (The merry fellows of Yalta), or a nearly complete work like "L'altra coscienza" (The other consciousness).[73] Today *Anche le donne hanno perso la guerra* appears dated and full of (often naive) incongruities in its language and psychological characterizations. Its homage to woman, victim of male egotism, paragon of virtue in adversity, is too insistent and recalls the icons of the same socialist realism Malaparte was fighting on the ideological level. But the subject is interesting, and a good director could have drawn a worthwhile performance out of it. Staged in the wake of the Soviet Bloc's first major crisis—the East German uprising of 1953, which had struck him deeply—the play's content was profoundly anti-Communist, like Malaparte's articles of the period. The "Marxist race" continued to fascinate him, but the Soviet Union had lost nearly all its appeal in his eyes, and Malaparte was already ready to turn toward new experiences, like China. The play even obtained a critical success, confirmed when it was revived in Milan at the end of the year, and then toured through Italy, with the excellent Santuccio-Brignone company.[74] The ever-adept Borelli had approached Giancarlo Pajetta, at the time in charge of the PCI's propaganda department, to ensure that "the play be judged without partisan passion, on the artistic and moral level." But its reception by the Communist press was highly negative and returned to calling out the "umpteenth and most blatant proof of the boundless vanity and chameleonic snobbism that Gramsci already identified as Malaparte's essential features."[75]

The atmosphere of the Venetian premiere was depicted in a lovely

FROM PARIS TO MAO (1947–1957)

page of Orio Vergani's diary, which takes stock of his friend's multiple incarnations:

> Fascist mobilization around Malaparte for his play at La Fenice. Count Cini; the former ambassador to Berlin, Alfieri; and his old boss at the *Corriere*, Borelli, captain the propaganda machine. It's his first premiere in Italy, after the two Parisian experiences: luxury intellectualism. Here he is in his box, looking slightly heavier and yet as if reinvigorated by maturity, impeccable in his suit, ready with anecdotes and with a bit of gray in his parted hair—and a past full of adventures, contradictions, controversies, ingenuousness, shrewdness, world triumphs and leaps into the darkness, virtues and faults that at times landed him safely on shore and at other times instead drove him out into the high seas.... At the end of the performance, he twice comes out onto the stage. When the whistling starts, he cracks a smirk; but he says nothing and disappears. Marinetti in his old age was more courageous. Unfortunately, Curzio remains the same. The previous evening, he complained about the hostility of a well-known Roman critic, married to a woman we all knew over thirty years ago. He attributes the critic's hostility to an old grudge over the woman: "Unfortunately we couldn't all screw her." This cynicism explains the emotional inconsistency of his drama.[76]

It is a telling portrait and a judgment that we can on the whole still share.

Cinema

Meanwhile, Malaparte had launched into a new adventure: cinema. *The Forbidden Christ*, his only successful foray into the field, shot in the summer of 1950, is a good, at points even very good, film, rediscovered today after long neglect. The title and some sketches on the subject had already figured in Malaparte's papers, but the idea of turning them into a movie probably came from his collaboration with an old Florentine friend, Roberto Maltini. A former president of the Fascist university students' association and passionate about cinema, Maltini had after the Ethiopia conquest received the commission to set up the East Africa Film Industries; later he successfully participated in various productions at Cinecittà, including the regime's Hollywood-style spectacular *Scipio Africanus: The Defeat of Hannibal*. After the war, he caught up with Malaparte again, newly returned from France, and together they worked in Siena on the script for the film, although it was not Maltini's new company that later produced it.[77]

Announced during production with a clever publicity campaign, which also exploited the sad story of Jane Sweigard, on which more later, the work was favorably received the following year at the Cannes and Berlin film festivals. At Cannes, the competition was fierce: De Sica won the grand prize for *Miracle in Milan*, jointly with an unknown Swedish film, and Buñuel the best director award for *The Young and the Damned*. Malaparte, disappointed, did not pass up the opportunity to complain that "they went to great lengths to introduce me to the public as a collaborationist" and that "my mistake was to think I was at home in France." He accused the Italian delegation of "passing off De Sica as a hero of the Resistance (which is false, no offense to De Sica), and [the director Pietro] Germi and

FROM PARIS TO MAO (1947–1957)

Malaparte as Salò Republicans (which is false, not to exalt Germi or Malaparte)."[78] In Berlin, it was the first edition of the festival, and the Golden Bear was given to *Justice Is Done*, by André Cayatte, but *The Forbidden Christ* won a special prize for its leading actors, Raf Vallone and Elena Varzi.

One may deem *The Forbidden Christ* a redundant work, as American critics did when the film came out in the United States, under the absurd title *Strange Deception*.[79] From the very first sequences, though, one is struck by the refined editing sensibility at work, in the geometric planes of Tuscany as seen from a helicopter and in ensemble movements like the sequence of the crucifixion ritual, a phenomenon that would soon fortunately disappear from the anthropological heritage of Central Italy. "The locations will be those of lean Italy, the Italy of Giotto, Masaccio, Piero della Francesca," he explained in a letter. "The peasants' costumes must be real, but with a few alterations of a pictorial nature."[80] Malaparte gave proof as well of a very assured instinct for cinematography. His interest in the "seventh art" went back to the 1930s, and his visual sensibility was sharpened by his experiences as a war photographer. The set design was entrusted to the faithful Orfeo Tamburi.[81] But who was really in charge of the shooting? As usual, Malaparte wanted to show he was everywhere, and he had himself immortalized in the launch campaign as glued to the movie camera, like Malraux during the Spanish Civil War at the controls of a plane he had never piloted. In reality, the work owes much to its director of photography, the Italo-Hungarian Gábor Pogány, and to some promising young assistants, among them Antonello Falqui, son of the cosigner of *Vita di Pizzo-di-Ferro*. Ditto for the music. In the credits,

Malaparte is named as the composer, his latest vanity, chronologically speaking. His musical knowledge was virtually nonexistent: "I don't know a single note, I know nothing about harmony," he would confide in private.[82] But at the presentation of his film in Paris, he did not hesitate to declare in inspired tones: "Yes, I composed the music for my film myself, out of an inner necessity."[83] He lied less with his compatriots, who knew him better. Hence in the credits of the American version one finds "music by C. M."; but in those of the Italian version a more modest "commento musicale di C. M." (musical accompaniment by C. M.). He limited himself, then, to selecting or improvising folk tunes for the soundtrack written by a professional, the maestro Ugo Giacomozzi, while declaring, according to the occasion, that he was inspired by a war chant of the Polish uhlans, by the odes of Finnish explorers, and finally by a song "I had expressly dedicated to them [the Finnish explorers], entitled 'La Careliana.'"[84] Let us move on...

That said, the movie is undeniably Malapartian, down to the last yard of film, favored by a stellar Franco-Italian cast. For the leading role, Malaparte had initially thought of Fresnay. But, faced with the latter's hesitations, the choice fell on Raf Vallone, an actor of multiple talents, former partisan, former professional soccer player for Torino, former journalist for *L'Unità*, at the time one of the rising stars of the PCI, here in his best role of a distinguished career. Beside him was another faithful Malapartian actor, Alain Cuny, as well as Gino Cervi (Peppone in the Don Camillo movies but also excellent in dramatic roles), and Philippe Lemaire, the first husband of Juliette Gréco. In a very male film, devoted to the brotherhood and hatred between men, the beautiful faces of a few females, sacrificed to a tale that leaves them rather little space, stand out: Rina Morelli, Elena Varzi, who later married Vallone, and a sweet and elegant (even excessively so, for the part) seventeen-year-old debutant, Anna Maria Ferrero, whom Malaparte treated with special consideration during the filming.*

The Forbidden Christ was born as a literary sketch, but the idea of turning it into a sequel to *The Skin* was quickly abandoned, notwithstanding the preliminary contracts signed in 1947 with Bompiani in Italy and Denoël in France. The flourishing neorealist cinema of Rossellini, De Sica, De Santis, and company proved much more tempting to Malaparte, because he had been able to observe its impact on a public disoriented by five years of war and suffering. Critics, too, were on the lookout for the new. And yet his style was to a great extent the opposite of a neorealist aesthetic. He had offered his reasoning on the matter in a letter to Fresnay, when he still hoped to involve him in the project:

> I wanted my film not to be a news item, or a "fictionalized history," or a more or less mundane "adventure," or a neorealist chronicle..., [but] a film that is popular without being banal; and that it pose a question that is not specifically Italian, French, or English, but common to all men today, from whatever country. The problem of justice, of love, of personal and collective responsibility.[85]

---

*In Paris I was unable to meet Anna Maria Ferrero, who had married the French actor Jean Sorel, on account of her illness (she died in 2018), to ask about her memory of that experience. It is well known that she inflamed the jealousy of Biancamaria Fabbri and Jane Sweigard, both of whom wanted the part. Sorel, who met her later but became her great confidant, told me that Malaparte had chosen her simply because he considered her perfect for the part and was not aware of any romance between them.

The language here is very ecumenical and was repeatedly employed in interviews and declarations; nonetheless, it should not be taken too literally. His choices were dictated by practical considerations as well: *The Skin*'s placement on the Index was a heavy penalty, and Malaparte wanted to recover the Catholic audience, not only in Italy and Europe but also in Latin America, where the film's theme and setting could ensure him a large following. He obtained the favorable opinion of the ecclesiastical commission for cinematography, a first step in his reconciliation with the Church, although some parishes advised against the film, and for a long time it was excluded from Catholic film programming.

In the film, Bruno returns from prison in the Soviet Union to his hometown in the Sienese countryside shortly after the war's end. It should be noted that at the time virtually the only Italian prisoners of war to be repatriated were those who had declared themselves Communists, or at any rate in favor of the USSR. The majority of the tens of thousands of soldiers interned in Soviet camps had to wait until 1954, in some cases even later. Hence, for an Italian viewer of the time, Bruno appeared to be a Communist, all the more so as he was identified with Raf Vallone, whose political sympathies were well known. Malaparte denied it, writing again to Fresnay: "There is no political subtext in the fact that these two ex-prisoners return from Russia. It was necessary for them to come back today; and it is only today that prisoners are coming back from Russia."* But the explanation is not entirely credible: nothing prevented him from having Bruno return from an English detention camp in India or

---

*Malaparte's reference to *two* ex-prisoners is obscure; perhaps it reflects an earlier draft in which Bruno returned with a friend.

Kenya, or from an American one, as his brother Ezio did, having been captured in Somalia.[86] This wink to the Left would not prevent the critic and French Communist Party member Georges Sadoul from referring to *The Forbidden Christ* as Malaparte's "neo-Fascist film" in the title of a piece in *Les Lettres Françaises*. In Italy, during the film's first showing in the Communist-majority city of Perugia, the audience was showered with anti-Malaparte flyers as the director illustrated the film's content.[87] It was another, less biased French critic, however, who saw the author's intentions most clearly:

> The man who assumed the responsibility for giving birth to *Kaputt* and *The Skin* is sufficiently acquainted with the weight of souls to make *The Forbidden Christ* with his own hands.... In the procession scene, which has already entered the anthology of cinema, the Devil, generally represented by a character with horns on his forehead, with the head of a bull or a goat, is incarnated here by a young worker in overalls, with the name of one of the biggest industries of Northern Italy on his chest. The spirit of evil, the dark force that gets placed on the Index, is the proletariat, the downtrodden masses.[88]

What happened in Bruno's village during the German occupation? What usually happens in all occupations (and collaborations), which the inhabitants hasten to forget once peace returns. But Bruno stubbornly refuses, thinking only of avenging his brother Giulio, a partisan tortured and shot in 1944, after being denounced by an informer—the sad fate of many in civil wars, in which hate, resentments, and local interests are overlaid. Who betrayed Giulio? Who is the Judas hiding among his old playmates, in the café on the square, in the carnival booths, in all the gathering places for this small community that is striving to recover the old life rhythms of before, as if nothing had happened? Sullen, Bruno ignores his friends' warm welcome and refuses to follow his parents down the path of forgiving and forgetting. He behaves the same way with his fiancée, who confesses to having given herself to Giulio the day before his arrest. He roams the village streets at night. The church is closed. A stall owner hangs up a picture of Stalin but conceals Mussolini's in a cabinet. The butcher has put a cow's head in his shopwindow: the clotted blood around the animal's neck is "something horrible, something dirty," an image of innocence sullied by men and by their mad descent into the plague of history. In another sequence, the butcher slaughters a cow with a nail gun, fired at point-blank range. The publicity poster for the film even reproduces a Tamburi drawing of a knight with the head of a cow. These two sequences could have figured, substituting the cow for a donkey, in *Au hasard Balthazar* (1966), Robert Bresson's masterpiece. But they recall above all the magnificent evocation of the mules in *Il sole è cieco*, where those innocent animals silently bear the "weight" of men's guilt, like "that mule with its broken back, splayed across the path, and the pistol he fires in its ear, and the wild red eyes that stared at him, and the disappointment, the love, the desperation in those slanting red eyes" (SC, 168–69). In a fragment from the same period, one reads:

> The decadence of civilization has begun when men are detached from beasts, when they have forgotten the function of beasts in nature and in human life. When they have deluded themselves that Christ's sacrifice was final and sufficed to render beasts useless as intermediaries and sacrificial victims. When they believed that the Divine Lamb had redeemed and saved them forever.[89]

FROM PARIS TO MAO (1947–1957)

This glorification of blood corresponds to Malaparte's double approach: forgiveness and revenge, the two poles impossible to reconcile. We find these two opposing movements in Bruno's attitude toward his mother. She had been unable to prevent Giulio's death, unable to protect her son, in this way becoming complicit in the disorder of human passions, against the higher order of procreation. The blood of violence and death stands against the blood of origin and life, the blood spilled to kill against the blood offered in birth. Bruno, who runs to embrace his mother upon his return home, pushes her away when the woman inadvertently reveals to him the name of the childhood friend who has betrayed Giulio. The mechanism of aggression-sanction is the story's constant, unfolding before the viewer's eyes and imparting a dramatic tension, the sense of the inevitable that goes back to the nineteenth-century Italian tradition of verismo and, further still, to the ancient Greek tragedians so admired by Malaparte. Hence, perhaps, the static aspect of the composition, with slow takes of faces, hands, and torsos that communicate the sense of fatality looming over men: an approach that would be found again in Pasolini's first films, from *Accattone* to *The Gospel According to Saint Matthew*. If the gods are implacable, what of Christ? Hidden, speechless, "forbidden" to men blinded by greed and ignorance, he remains the measure of all things, the world's savior, born and crucified for us. How can we, then, reconcile hope in man and the acceptance of the inexorable fate oppressing him? How can we accept, exclaims Bruno, that "not even freedom has managed to make the rest of us free men"?

This is what is at stake in the conflict between two keepers of the faith who contend for Bruno's tormented soul: the hermit and Father Antonio. The former represents the intransigent, accusing, rigorist side of faith, the paladin par excellence of aggression-sanction. He is the one who, in the Goyaesque procession sequence, harangues the crowd and invites sinners to imitate the fate of Christ's death on the cross. The latter, Father Antonio, is an old artisan in the odor of sanctity, who embodies the force and humility of forgiveness. But Malaparte is not Bresson—he remains skeptical. His innate realism drives him to distrust sanctity. One perceives in Father Antonio an element of exaltation, that of the prophets and healers who still traveled the countryside in those years. When, in a spirit of sacrifice, Father Antonio accuses himself of betraying Giulio, Bruno, overwhelmed with rage, plants a knife in his heart, and this new absurd crime resolves nothing. Blood does not wash away blood; "even tears are not enough to wash it away." Bruno will later spare the true culprit but, as he flees toward the mountains, continues to cry out his rejection of a justice paid for with the blood of innocents. Christ remains forbidden, at the film's end as at its beginning, because he "demands the love that entails sacrifice, and not sacrifice separated from love."[90]

The pace of the story is sometimes slow, and the dialogue often suffers from overemphasis, as in the theater; but one cannot deny the authenticity of a work that unites the primitivism of the theme to the modernity of the message. The story of the soldier who returns home to discover the betrayal carried out behind his back is not only eternal, from Homer's *Odyssey* to Iraq and Afghanistan in recent times; it is exemplary of the human condition, where it is impossible to separate radically and once and for all the victim from the oppressor, to prevent the oppressor from surviving in their victim's thirst for revenge. Malaparte does not arrive at the end of his demonstration, does not push himself so far as to wholly believe in the positive message he wants to communicate. His inner torment is not a sham: in evil he is at his ease, while rebelling; in goodness he listens but rejects any concession, any comfort.

From Berlin he had described in frantic terms to Marianne Halévy the enthusiasm of the audience: "People were crying, on their feet applauding, and I could hardly hold back tears.... I was dragged to the Grunewald at night, to an open-air movie theater (25,000 viewers!)."[91] But evidently the producers were not of the same opinion. And so ended his cinematic adventure. Malaparte spent the final years of his life chasing financing that always disappeared at the last minute. Like Pasolini, he had the means and potential to create an important cinematic work alongside his more properly literary work, even if in terms of film, it seems, "he loved only westerns, they relaxed him."[92] Among the four or five projects that fell through were an Italo-German coproduction, *Feuchtes Feuer* (Damp fire); a film about the figure of Mary Magdalene, *La carne umana* (Human flesh); and a science-fiction story, *Il grande Ming* (The great Ming).[93] The most important was probably *Lotta con l'angelo* (Wrestling with the angel) (1952), inspired by news items, centered again on guilt and grace, of which there remains a quite detailed first draft.[94] The title, even setting aside the numerous painters who took inspiration from this biblical theme, from Rembrandt to Delacroix, closely recalls two books Malaparte could not have failed to know: *Combat avec l'ange*, Giraudoux's novel about the end of Aristide Briand, brought out in 1934 by Grasset, their common publisher; and especially *La Lutte avec l'Ange*, the title of the first version of *The Walnut Trees of Altenburg*, by Malraux, published in Lausanne in 1943 and pulled from circulation shortly afterward. These quasi homonymies, so frequent in his work (*Il Volga*, *La peste*, "Killing no murder," etc.), were not the source for him of any particular embarrassment. But, a few days before shooting was to start in Pisa, the title was modified, without explanation, to *L'angelo perduto* (The lost angel).

The protagonist had already been chosen, a twenty-year-old woman of good family and modest talent, Biancamaria (or Bianca Maria) Fabbri, who became the writer's companion of two or three years. The financing seemed secure for once, and the expectations of critics and public augured well. But something was missing. Inspiration? The fact is that Malaparte bid farewell to the company, took up his special correspondent role again, and disappeared with his manuscripts and his dogs. "This chapter, too, has closed. Bianca Maria didn't understand how lucky she was. I'm sorry, though, for the tearful end of Bianca Maria. Because you understand, those who start out as extras, will always be extras."[95] Abandoned by her Pygmalion, the young woman soon abandoned the movies, after two final efforts of debatable significance: *Il più comico spettacolo del mondo* (*Funniest Show on Earth*) and *Il paese dei campanelli* (*Town of Bells*). Fifty years later, she emerged from silence with a slender but noteworthy memoir, which no commercial publisher wanted and was thus self-published. It is the only true portrait of the writer as seen by one of his women, and it deserves to be known for this reason alone. But it is also and above all a moving testimony. Biancamaria recounts without false modesty the story of a fragile, anxious girl like so many others, from the Milanese upper-middle class, neglected by a distant father, and who had the misfortune of falling madly in love with a Narcissus on the decline. "She was beautiful, kind, childlike, never acting like a diva or an intellectual," confided a distant relative, the countess Anna Teodorani Fabbri.[96] Malaparte showed himself to be unbearable, vain, cruel, and shamelessly chauvinist. He took her with him everywhere, on visits to Picasso, Matisse, Chagall, or Vlaminck, to see Cocteau on the barge of Jean Marais, and so on; but he never missed a chance to humiliate her in public, to make her feel clumsy, uneducated, nonexistent. Inevitably, he told her that "without me you will never be anything, you could only become a whore," after which he fell to his knees, sobbing and begging for her forgiveness. In private he was even worse, refusing to have a child with her, in revolting terms—"If you get pregnant, it's the fruit seller's. I've had the mumps"—and in fact she did but lost the baby. Most of the time he refused to sleep next to her, but then would make love "marvelously," as a kind of reward, after she had shown enthusiasm for the pages he had just read to her in the middle of the night, after which he would go to sleep in a separate room, be it on Capri, in Forte, or in a hotel. And he was naturally jealous: if she wore too skimpy a bikini, she might earn a few slaps. How could she bear it, then? Out of masochism? It does not appear so. In her kindness, in her simplicity, Biancamaria would ultimately understand the need to distance herself from him, one fine day toward the end of 1952, "with a telephone token in my pocket and a suitcase in my hand," to better find him again, in her memory:

> I would like what I've written about Malaparte the man, about his fragility, about his sensitivity, to be read by young people and for it to encourage them to read and reread him in order to understand him. I'm not fit to judge the writer, just the man. He was authentic, clean.[97]

She died a few years ago, forgotten by everyone.

"But I Loved You, Damned!"

If women counted little in Malaparte's life, he counted a great deal in the life of a certain number of them. For some it was a poisoned chalice, and in at least one case the poison proved lethal.

The idea of a Malaparte draped in women à la Drieu La Rochelle is exaggerated (as it was for Drieu, for that matter). But this was so merely because he never gave them the chance to distract him from his projects, from the strict organization of a life centered on his work and his destiny, perpetually intertwined. It was said of Enzo Ferrari that he preferred his cars to their drivers; Malaparte certainly preferred books to women. Take his duels: the list varies from twelve to twenty and often involved prominent political and literary figures; but not a single one is known to have been provoked by the beautiful eyes of a woman. His political misfortunes, starting with the most serious, in 1933–34 and 1943–44, have nothing to do with rivalries over women. At times he made use of them to advance his career or his position, maybe even his finances, or to try to get out of prison; but he never thought that committed him to any emotional reciprocation or entailed any form of loving gratitude.

Here ends any resemblance to Drieu, a temperament vulnerable to the point of masochism, capable of seeking the protection of his mother-sister-lover with the same attitude that brought him to push away any form of emotional stability. Drieu wanted to be consoled in order not to be saved, the better to stay walled into his detestable self. Malaparte's narcissistic libido was acquainted with misfortune and at times courted it, but he rejected any drift into self-destruction and remained solidly anchored in the principle of self-preservation, which was the motor of his life. In the face of any attempt to unsettle him by means of emotion or feminine seduction, Malaparte closed up like an anti-Orpheus, like a clam or hedgehog. Numerous candidates for this inevitable defeat, from "Flaminia" to Virginia, distanced themselves from him when they finally understood that neither their eccentricities nor their devotion could melt his heart. But others refused to accept this reality, and in the end they paid dearly. This attitude, which for Malaparte came naturally, was reinforced with time.

Physically, he had not yet changed, or very little; the heaviness of middle age had yet to catch up with him. Tamburi made a lovely portrait of him in November 1948, in Paris, which displays the same perfect profile he had at thirty, and he was now fifty. A journalist described him this way:

> The man was imposing, without being strong. His well-oiled black hair imparted a manly aura to his childlike features. He had a prominent forehead and bright eyes, but with a certain roundness, due perhaps to a Slavic origin, that at times gave his face the expression of a big baby.[98]

And the writer and filmmaker Roger Boussinot, who met him in the same period on Capri:

> He has stayed young, although next year he will celebrate his fiftieth. His cheeks are round and childlike; his eyes, whose sweetness is accentuated by the presence of lower lashes as full and long as those on top, are such that few women can resist.[99]

He pointed proudly to his weight of 163 pounds, in ideal proportion, according to dieticians, with his height of six feet. And yet in the space of a few years, toward 1950, his body began to soften, to yield, almost from one day to the next. Here he is, then,

> with his gray handkerchief, his too-short jacket whose three buttons are undone and that squeezes him a bit, because the cinema and big print runs have nourished him well, and with the face of an emperor sick of spaghetti, who now wants to go ring the bells of a new destiny for Curzio Malaparte.[100]

Inwardly, he became the cold old animal he had basically always wanted to be. His *Diary* contains no trace of romance, not even the much-talked-about one with Jean Voilier, the vestal virgin of French publishing. And yet there was no shortage of opportunities in newly carefree postwar Paris. On the other hand, there were also plenty of chances for voyeurism, as when, in the course of an evening with some Brazilian friends of Véra Korène's, he asks to admire their unshaved underarms, as was fashionable in the period, where, under the black tuft, peeks out "something rosy, deep, and moist" that makes him blush (DFP, 129). The reader who knows Malaparte understands this was unlikely to have involved any erotic or fetishistic interest, but rather that, as a professional, he wanted to verify a passage of *The Skin* he was writing... Many women were associated with his name up until almost the very end; but, precisely, only with his name, or with the real thing? These included a French lady he met on Capri, Anne H., who helped him revise his texts and letters in French and English, nicknamed Loula in the *Giornale segreto*; gentlewomen of polite society, like M. I.; a very young Chilean beauty, Rebequita, whom he met during his travels in South America in 1952–53; actresses like Biancamaria Fabbri, Silvana Mangano, Egle

Monti,* and Silvana Pampanini; young girls in flower of the Roman, Neapolitan, or Venetian aristocracy, often the daughters or the nieces of the ones he had frequented before the war; a Florentine journalist, Oriana Fallaci, who would become famous for her very aggressive style of interview (before it was fashionable) and, later, for her anti-Islamic ravings, who displayed Malaparte's narcissism, but not necessarily the talent; and yet others, without counting the "old" ones, like the ever-faithful and selfless Roberta Masier.

Muses, lovers, comforters, girlfriends, confidantes, mere escorts, or frauds—who can say? Even during simple gatherings, especially in the case of cultured girls of good family, he loved to put his charms to the test, with mixed results. Marie-José de Corbigny, who would become Roland Laudenbach's sister-in-law, remembers meeting Malaparte two or three times at her parents' house, in Brittany, where he would disembark with Gerhard Heller from the sailboat of Gwenn-Aël Bolloré: "seductive, courteous, a great talker, very anti-Communist, he got along immediately with my father who was, like him, a veteran of the Great War."[101] Conversely, Diane de Margerie, who came across him at one of the literary events at Royaumont Abbey, found him odious in his makeup and decried how he busied himself with checking off a list of his conquests.[102] In the same period, Anne de Lacretelle saw him roll up to an after-party at her parents' on the arm of Jean Voilier, "who displayed him like her official lover. He was well-dressed, in a striped pale-gray suit that attracted attention, his thrown-back hair very black and possibly dyed. Not at all friendly."[103]

*Egle Monti later became a journalist and, until the very end, sent Malaparte a great quantity of often amusing letters, abounding in gossip, of which he was very fond.

But regarding the important things he maintained a hermetic reserve, which served to feed interest in his figure and agreed with his nature as an old dog who withdraws to gnaw on his bone far from the crowd. Even the young writers he advised, protected, and encouraged, with a generosity he never showed to his contemporaries or potential competitors, knew about and respected this discretion. I was unable to interview Malaparte's last "pupil," the Venetian journalist Nantas Salvalaggio, who died in 2009; but the essential part of his testimony had already been gathered by Guerri. Another of the young writers Malaparte assisted in this period, on another level entirely, was Carlo Coccioli, born in Livorno and transplanted to Paris, who left behind in Italian, French, and Spanish (he spent the last part of his life in Mexico, where he died in 2003) a tormented, uneven, and profound oeuvre, in which Malaparte's influence is often recognizable. They had their disagreements, such as when Malaparte's preface to one of the young writer's novels, *La difficile speranza* (The difficult hope), was not published due to a delay in the text's transmission, something that sent him into a rage.[104] The "exuberant, nervous, electric" Coccioli, for his part, according to René Novella, blamed Malaparte for starving his guests on Capri."[105] But their relations remained friendly to the end.

Did Malaparte give so little of himself because he thought he still had an important work to complete? It is a romantic hypothesis, which seems only partially true. A meticulous administrator of his days and nights, like so many confirmed bachelors, he was more obsessed than ever with not squandering his energies, as he had confided to Pellegrini in Finland, and to so many others later. Irene Brin, alias Countess Clara, one of the sharpest observers of manners in the period, recounted mischievously how a friend of hers, a witty and beautiful actress, would sigh, "I would have loved him so much, if at the right moment he had not always started declaiming Russian poetry."[106] And yet, despite his unslackening personal discipline, the 1950s, the last years of his life, seemed dominated by uncertainty and fumbling. Never had he accumulated so many ephemeral, aborted, or decidedly bungled projects.

The Cimitero Acattolico (Non-Catholic Cemetery) in Rome, mentioned in chapter 2, the final resting place of Keats and Shelley, is also known as the Cimitero degli Inglesi (English cemetery), even though His Britannic Majesty's subjects are in the minority there with respect to the total of other communities represented: Russians, Scandinavians, Americans, Eastern Europeans, Italian Protestants, Orthodox Christians, Jews, or those belonging to other religions, including Muslims, Animists, and Confucians. It is one of the capital's most picturesque sites, an international enclave at the foot of the Aventine, which since the mid-eighteenth century has received the remains of the mighty and the humble lovers of Rome and Italy, come here to die from all over the world; a heterogenous and cosmopolitan club of travelers, aristocrats, diplomats, political exiles, archaeologists, great invalids in search of sun, great divas and opera singers in search of a composition, and great courtesans in search of protection. The cemetery is adjacent—behind the three hundred pines and cypresses screening it from that section of the Aurelian Walls—to the pyramid of Cestius, a "folly" of the first century BC, where that eminent *civis romanus*, infatuated with the Egyptian fashion that was all the rage, had himself buried in a Malapartian manner with his beloved dog.

One Sunday morning, under a low sky more typical of London

than Rome, I am greeted at the cemetery entrance by its director, a polite, efficient lady, of the type more easily imaginable at the head of an exclusive girls' boarding school or a very fussy hotel, in Devonshire or Cornwall. She is flanked by an American with the air of an old hippy, sweet and shabby, which suddenly reminds me that here also lies Gregory Corso, among the most gifted representatives of the Beat generation. It has been twenty years since my last visit to these parts; in the meantime computers have appeared. But a search for "Sweigard, Jane" in the recently digitized registry produces zero results, under her own name or in the various country-of-origin categories: United States, United Kingdom, Australia, and the entire Commonwealth are passed through the sieve. The director takes the time to consult the analog registry for 1950, but she finds nothing there either. We have the idea of searching the computer using only the first name: up come pages and pages of Janes, Jeans, and Joans. We must arm ourselves with patience and tenacity: Would these fine Anglo-Saxon virtues come to the aid of this Latin biographer's passion? And here, finally, appears the mention of a Zweigart, Phyllis Jeane, known as Jane, born in Oakland on February 26, 1921; died—with no indication of place—on July 21, 1950. Yes, it is her.

The tomb is a humble thing, a simple granite stele, with her name, dates of birth and death, and the indication "Native of California." On the other hand, it is very well maintained, under a bed of freshly cut greenery. Nothing else. I ask if anyone, an individual or a foundation, provides for the maintenance, but such information is private and would have to be the subject of an official request. Ultimately, what does it matter? Are there at least frequent visits? "You are the first since I've been here," the lady replies, in a tone that makes me

FROM PARIS TO MAO (1947–1957)

think she has been there for a rather long time. I take my leave, thanking her with all the cheer compatible with the nature of the place. At the exit, the angelic old hippy asks me whether, by chance, I would like to also have a look at the final resting place of Belinda Lee, the voluptuous English actress for whom, in roughly the same period, an Orsini prince risked excommunication by Pius XII. Thanks, but fortunately for her, she never ran into Malaparte.*

Jane Sweigard—thus had she simplified her name—disembarking in Italy to try to pursue a career at Cinecittà, was a big, strapping girl, more athletic than attractive, based on the few images that have come down to us. It is not known exactly how she reached Capri and stole into Malaparte's private life.[107] Certainly, from the moment of her arrival, she showed clear signs of incoherence. She was penniless, and the carabinieri contacted the US consulate in Rome to have her repatriated. And then, for reasons that have never been clarified, Malaparte intervened to host her at Casa Come Me, taking charge of all her expenses. Their bond, if we can call it that, lasted a couple of months in total, from May to July 1950, but that was a very long time, if you consider what it is to deal with an unbalanced person. Jane, or Jana, as he preferred to call her, nevertheless took on a sufficiently public role that he introduced her to friends as his companion of the moment. What could have led an expert like him to fall in love with someone mentally unstable? But was he really in love? The doubt is more than legitimate: he probably fancied that

---

*In 1960 Belinda Lee, periwinkle eyes in a ceramic face on a statuesque body, had a part, alongside Enrico Maria Salerno and an exceptional Gino Cervi in the role of the Fascist Party official Sciagura, in possibly the finest film of the Italian civil war: *It Happened in '43*, by Florestano Vancini, loosely based on a story by Giorgio Bassani and with a screenplay by Pasolini.

"BUT I LOVED YOU, DAMNED!"

Jane, from a good WASP family, could pave the way for him overseas. And in one way or another he made her believe he would give her a role in his film—shooting on *The Forbidden Christ* was about to begin—and that then she would share his life.*

What followed, predictably enough, was sad and banal: having finally grasped the situation, Malaparte slipped away to Rome, where Jane followed him, without, however, managing to see him. Now it was her turn to disappear, after having left him a note at his hotel ending with the words, "But I loved you, damned!" Malaparte later had a gold bracelet with this inscription made for himself, and we can wonder at the poor taste of the thing.[108] The official account is that, afraid of being stopped by the police again and repatriated, the young woman rushed to Ostia, where she swallowed a strong dose of barbiturates and flung herself into the waves. Fished out by some beachgoers, she was taken to a hospital and died without regaining consciousness. Malaparte pushed himself as far as the threshold of her room but did not have the courage to enter; he remained outside the door, sobbing and crying that he would have married her had she managed to survive.† But destiny wanted nothing to do with Malaparte the good husband and family man. The press ran with

---

*In a juicy novel by Salvalaggio, *Piumino di cipria* (Milan: Rizzoli-BUR, 2002), Malaparte appears in the double aspect of the great Malasorte ("misfortune"), on the verge of leaving for China, and of another writer, Bardi (= Baldi?), who, half an hour after meeting the protagonist, offers to marry her, publish her novel, introduce her to Gide, have her do a film with Carné, etc.

†He would behave similarly some years later, when his brother Sandro died at the hospital in Prato. After quickly embracing him, he would run away: "I came from far away, arrived in Prato at night, entered the hospital, walked the deserted corridors, pushed open the door: my brother was lying there white and motionless on the bed" (S, 8).

the story, and Malaparte no less so. To a French weekly, he gave a painful, teary story in which once again he takes center stage, and she becomes a sort of "corpse like me":

> For three days she struggled against death, in a coma. At one point I thought she was regaining consciousness. I had run a piece of ice over her lips: she moaned, I called to her, embraced her, she lifted up her right arm, seeking me in the air, and two days later, she was dead.... I had bought her a tombstone. I paid Barclay's [*sic*] Bank for it. I gave her a funeral; I filled the chapel with flowers as if she had friends. Her tomb was very close to Keats's and Shelley's [untrue!] at the foot of a cypress. Her body belongs to me now, because the tomb is mine. Poor Jana is mine forever, she is finally at peace. I want my friends in France, too, to know that she died for something pure.[109]

What conclusion can we draw from this sad affair? Nothing, if not that one romantic fiasco was worth another, namely Pavese's suicide, twenty days later, with in the middle another American actress, Constance Dowling. The affair also had a lamentable aftermath, because in an interview Malaparte denounced "the ignoble people" of Capri, namely the fashionable society he had never really loved or frequented, which had mocked his brief relationship with Jane. It was an old quarrel among residents that thus returned to the surface, accompanied by new attacks against Casa Come Me, judged to have marred the island's beauty. Malaparte's declarations were taken up by the national press, as if they constituted an attack on the whole population of Capri. He ran the risk not only of a moral ban, like what happened in Naples, but of a nighttime raid by a group of drunk revelers. The whole thing ended with a trial some months later, in which Malaparte, in absentia, was ordered to pay legal fees. He did not set foot again on the island for five years, when tempers had finally cooled.[110]

According to one of the most stubborn anecdotes of his black legend, Malaparte, after the grandiose funeral he wanted for Jane, allegedly murmured through tears to a friend come to console him: "In the end, it's excellent publicity for the film."* If not true, it was very well invented. Malapartians and anti-Malapartians alike may turn it to their advantage.

From Music Hall to the Long March

Malaparte's activity in the last phase of his life was still frenetic, but it was for the first time also marked by dispersion, at times by incoherence, even. If the issue was not, in a man who had always displayed an ascetic vocation for concentration and writing even through life's tempests, a slackening of internal discipline, was it a lack of inspiration? The real, more mundane problem was that the walls of disinterest and silence had risen around him, despite the global success of *Kaputt* and *The Skin*, as if he still had to pay a price for it: if we cared to split hairs, we might distinguish between what, in the seven or eight years he had left to live after his return from Paris, he *wanted*

---

*Three years later, however, he would write to Carla Rulli from Santiago: "I was very fond of a poor girl, and she killed herself, and still no one knows why" (letter of January 9, 1953, in Rulli Archive). Now, apart from the fact that he knew very well why Jane killed herself, we are acquainted with Malaparte's tendency toward a certain sentimentality in his letters to sympathetic female correspondents.

and what he *was able* to accomplish. If he was counting on more time, by now he knew he did not have an unlimited supply. Malaparte did not fear a challenge. He still wanted to tame the public—unlike his dogs, which he respected too much to train—and he was more obsessed than ever by his debt to posterity. Why not, then, devote himself to finishing one or two truly important projects, like *Mamma marcia*, the *Diary*, or *The Kremlin Ball*? Why not immerse himself in the contemplation of art and the spirit, if he no longer believed in men and their vain intrigues?

Here, too, there was no contradiction with his past or his innermost nature. If he had always put books before all else, if he had feared not being a truly great writer—and he knew he was not on the level of a D'Annunzio or a Pirandello—literature had never been his life's exclusive aim. For him writing meant immersing himself in the current of events to draw out a universal message, even at the cost of moving from history into anecdote: his lively, flexible, exuberant temperament could adapt to both, disdaining them at the same time. Thus we return to confusions about the commitment of Malaparte, who, as a true narcissist, always preferred appearance to existence. For him the mirror had the same value, if not a greater one, as ink on paper. But as an unhappy, saturnine narcissist, he sensed this would never be able to satisfy the part of him that sought the world in order to refuse it, who courted notoriety so that he might spurn it, who wanted to be admired by women he did not desire and by men he little respected. Simply put, the current would not flow between life and him *outside the fight*, outside existence conceived as a daily battle. He could not have swapped it out for the sensual fever of D'Annunzio, the funereal eroticism of Pasolini, the emotional and ideological volatility of Drieu, the imaginary museum of Malraux, the political masochism of Aragon, the brilliant farces of his friend Cocteau, the colleague whom he perhaps felt closest to in this last phase of life, with whom he exchanged letters of conspiratorial tenderness. Here is Cocteau:

> It is impossible for me to leave your wonderful city [Rome] without telling you of my deep gratitude for your kindness [*gentillesse*] (in the exact sense of the term). I have spoken from my heart about you on the radio in Palermo and to the *Giornale di Sicilia*. But these things of the heart are poorly expressed in words. The great chain between certain souls is the sole consolation in an uncultured world intent on destroying itself.[III]

Just like Cocteau, this eternal funambulist, Malaparte needed to embellish life, to disguise it, to create causes only to abandon them as soon as they stopped exciting him, to militate for a faction, until going over to the other side, as an exceptionally gifted and curious child quickly tires of completing assignments that are too easy, or of spending recess playing with inept schoolmates. And as he began to lose it, he continued to admire the eternal youth of his older colleague: "I don't see any wrinkles in his pale and gray mask, but something silvery, gossamer, quivering, as if he had just passed through a forest and emerged with impalpable spiderwebs on his face" (DFP, 83).

In addition to these lyrical flights, we must take into account the eternal realism of his character, which had never encumbered itself with too many scruples in the management of everyday life. Malaparte was always the best—and worst—advocate for himself, with a deftness that recalls the cloth merchants of Prato, the *cenciaioli*, who starting in the Middles Ages invaded the whole world, a bit like the Chinese of today, or like the bankers of Florence and Genoa, inventors of modern finance. He knew how to sell and to sell himself, and never tired of controversies and crusades. "Now break out... some lovely theory on the modern painter's need to *enter* physically into the dimensions of cinema, which is the art of modern perspective, etc.," he advised Tamburi around the time of *The Forbidden Christ*.[112] He understood that the public loved surprise, that good books alone no longer assured an author a prominent position or any social influence. Hence his enthusiasm for the United States, the key country of the future, which he was impatient to discover, even as a thousand commitments, the state of his health, and perhaps a certain fear of not arriving in top form for his date with the New York intelligentsia would make him repeatedly postpone the trip, which in the end did not happen.

Meanwhile, he sought and multiplied contacts with major American authors: Henry Miller, Dos Passos, Steinbeck, Faulkner; but curiously not with Hemingway, the most "Italian" among them, a regular visitor to Venice and Cortina, whom he seems to have never particularly liked. Malaparte had the most important American quality, he was a fighter, but it was written that the much-anticipated meeting would never take place. As a consolation prize, he showed off in front of news cameras on the terrace of Casa Come Me in a full cyclist's outfit. He loudly declared, emulating the Italian champions Coppi and Bartali, his intention to undertake a cycling tour of America, "because, if there's one thing in the world that deserves to be have been invented by a Latin, it is precisely the bicycle" (CB, 12); at the same time he needed to inveigh against the mechanization imposed by American power.[113] Memories of when his father terrorized pedestrians on his Phaenomen velocipede? In reality, as he confided to Borelli, it had been a sports-bar joke, which was picked up by the press the world over: "And so now I'll have to do it for real! America is not a country of cyclists and I risk getting stuck in Colorado or Kansas with a pair of flat tires. I'll sell the exclusive and recover my expenses. Look at the mess I've got myself into!"[114] The "cicloraid" stayed at the center of society gossip for all of fall 1955, and Malaparte regularly added new ingredients to keep the public's attention: a famous masseuse arrived to look after his muscles; the best doctors were at work day and night to fine-tune a diet meticulously calculated down to the last calorie; two hundred California beauties would pedal alongside him as far as Hollywood, where he would offer a precious flask of the water of Capri, infused with herbs he had personally chosen, to a then-single Grace Kelly, and one of the island's extremely rare blue lizards, captured with his own hands, to Marilyn Monroe.[115]

The important thing was not that he believed in it, but—once again—that it got people talking about him. He asked Moravia, with whom he had maintained a love-hate relationship, to join him in a relaunch of *Prospettive*. But the project collapsed after the appearance of a single double issue, in January 1952, without the letter-manifesto Malaparte had planned to send to his former coeditor:

> If *Prospettive* returns to light today, it is not because freedom has returned to Italy, but because freedom is newly endangered, by means of the same spirit that had suppressed it in those years. And I speak above all, dear Moravia, of intellectual freedom, especially in terms of literature, besieged and oppressed and corrupted by the same Fascist laws that today, in the hands of the priests, reveal themselves

to be more insidious and oppressive than before.... The pretext of communism does not suffice to justify the establishment of a dictatorship of priests, and it is neither honest nor possible to accept the dictatorship of priests under the pretext of a possible dictatorship of the proletariat.[116]

One may note the discreet approach to the PCI that Malaparte allowed to show through in these words, but the result was disappointing. Moravia, already well established on the left, avoided committing to his erstwhile fellow traveler and readied himself to take over editorship of a new literary magazine steeped in Marxism, *Nuovi Argomenti*, from which, predictably, Malaparte would be excluded.

And so he set off again. There was nothing like travel and foreign correspondence for lifting spirits and leaving behind quotidian troubles. In late November 1952 he flew to South America, on the invitation of the Chilean government, to represent Italy at the Santiago World Congress of the Press and Literature. He was feted alongside Neruda, Camilo José Cela, and Ehrenburg. The great Chilean writer Jorge Edwards, then at the beginning of his career, preserved a rather vibrant memory of their first meeting:

> He was friendly, imposing, a handsome man, dressed in a way you didn't see yet in these parts: olive green suit and deerskin shoes. A great talker and a great charmer, he would speak, softly and in French, sentences like this: "All cities have a prevailing scent: in Buenos Aires it's gasoline, here it's bougainvillea."* A pretty girl, whom

---

*There is no evidence Malaparte reached Buenos Aires in the course of the trip.

I knew a little, because she was the niece of the writer José Donoso, approached, and I made introductions. I still wonder if I did the right thing...[117]

The young woman was called Rebequita Yáñez: eighteen years old, tiny in stature, with the face of an angel, sensuous lips, a fiery personality. Malaparte conquered her on the spot, or was it the other way around? Certainly, from the testimony of the many friends Rebequita later freely confided in, it was a sexually "torrid" relationship. Rebequita would remain at his side for two or three years. Together, they arrived at the frontier with Argentina and traveled through Uruguay, from Montevideo to Punta del Este, a landscape that thrilled him, with its endless beaches, luxury establishments, and sweet, exotic, and patient women. Rebequita also found a rival in the person of Susana Soca, a diplomat's daughter, young and from a good family but of modest means, for whom Malaparte had tender words when writing to an Italian friend, but quickly left to her fate.[118]

He mapped out an expedition following the traces of the Inca civilization, then returned to Santiago, where he expected to stay for an entire year, taken up with countless projects, among them a film called *Camas calientes* (Warm beds), on the wretched life of Chilean miners,[119] and another on Robinson Crusoe, which would instead be made two years later by Luis Buñuel. He consoled himself by dominating the salons and social gatherings, inventing the most bizarre stories when they proved useful, or simply when he felt like it. One evening in Montevideo a journalist asked him about the origin of the pink jersey worn by the leader in the Giro d'Italia bicycle race. Malaparte explained that the organizers had wanted red, but Mussolini was against it, out of anti-Communism. This impressed his listeners much more than if he'd simply admitted that pink was the color of the pages of the newspaper *La Gazzetta dello Sport*, which had launched the competition in 1909.[120] In his articles he addressed the most varied topics, from his warm encounter with Pablo Neruda—a great poet but at the time still a hardcore Stalinist—to the fortunes of Peronism, which Malaparte, sharing the opinion of Borges, saw hovering like a fascist threat over all of Latin America.[121] Was it on this occasion, observing the sufferings of the great disinherited masses of the *campesinos*, that his tentative return toward communism received further impetus? Better not to allow ourselves to be fooled by these noble intentions: his preoccupation remained more aesthetic than ideological. When, upon his return to Italy, he was asked what in Chile had struck him most, he did not hesitate to "Malapartize" at will:

> Marvelous artisans there make packets composed of the bones of domestic animals. This produces a mosaic with the brilliance and polish of ivory. I sought to introduce this fashion to Italy, but our workers were unable to acquire the necessary "knack" for adjusting the bones.[122]

After four months, itching to return to Europe, he departed for Italy, with Rebequita at his side. Besides, his dachshund Pucci had taken ill and died during his absence, as had happened to Febo when he was in Finland. The era of salons was coming to an end, and he knew it; but he believed more than ever in his own charisma and gifts as a communicator, and he exploited them at every opportunity. What would he have done, or dreamed of doing, in the period of television's dominance, and then in that of the internet and social media?

For the moment, he was excited by the radio and defended it as a public utility with arguments that can sound quite contemporary:

> For goodness' sake, no changes, that's all we need. We'd be in trouble if the radio were free; it would fall into the hands of the industrial trusts, and then who would save us from Processed-Cheese Radio? If, for example, a dairy became the owner, they would broadcast propaganda for their products all day. Cheese, cheese, cheese. I feel like I can hear it now. But then I'd prefer to go into exile.[123]

This attack on cultural commercialism did not stop him from becoming the creator, like D'Annunzio, of advertising slogans, or from accepting invitations to speak on any subject whatsoever. In an oil company magazine, he called for the creation of a motorsport academy on Capri, despite his well-publicized love for nature and solitude. In Naples, certain of whose hideous sexual mores he had once described, he crowned "the most beautiful girl in the city," during an evening at the Teatro Mediterraneo, on September 24, 1955, which represented a sort of public reconciliation with the city. He considered being part of the jury for Miss Italy or presenting the Sanremo Music Festival, and as a warmup, he attended the Versilia beauty contest and tryouts for Miss Tempo-Universe, not to mention the Carnival of Viareggio. He boasted of having introduced waterskiing and the soccer lottery Totocalcio to Italy, which was completely false. He gave his patronage to the associations of veterans of the two world wars, who in his eyes deserved the nation's gratitude and respect. We also find him deeply involved, in the mid-1950s, in the political agenda of the World War II field marshal Giovanni Messe, a rugged and honest soldier of a Gaullist temperament, with whom he had been on excellent terms during the war, who meant to turn war veterans into an anti-Communist pressure group. Relations between Malaparte and the marshal went sour before long—how could it have been otherwise?—in a dispute over who would be the real leader of the movement, which soon went down into the stormy waters of the Cold War.[124] He continued to find disappointment in politics, despite repeated attempts. When he agreed to become the Italian Republican Party (PRI) candidate for Prato in the May 1956 municipal elections, his fellow citizens took sweet pleasure in handing him a stinging defeat. The party, however, nearly doubled its electoral tally, going from 514 to 861 votes, while remaining in last place in the city. The regional secretary warmly thanked Malaparte for participating, which did nothing to prevent the latest, inevitable quarrel.[125]

But he always started over, as if nothing had happened, with the wind at his back. And he never passed up a chance to be photographed in the most unusual poses. In Florence one day, he was chatting with an old friend, a fruit seller and part-time boxing referee; when the latter had to step away, Malaparte took his place and began to serve customers. As if by chance, a photographer from the local paper passed by and captured the writer wrapping up a kilo of oranges, after having expertly recommended the juiciest among them.[126] And he obviously always topped the list of Italy's most elegant men, alongside Luchino Visconti, Arturo Benedetti Michelangeli, and Gianni Agnelli, without, according to one commentator, "the excesses I attribute to the queer invasion. Bourgeois civilization is going to pieces due to the tendency to emasculate everything."[127] Here was his prescription:

The jacket was single-breasted, with three buttons. But from the lapels to the calculated distances between the three buttonholes, from the position of the breast pocket to the two plackets, from the fitted waist to the width of the sleeve, that jacket was different from the hundred thousand single-breasted three-button jackets we are used to seeing. And the vicuna of the pants was soft like pure cashmere but fell straight down over the shoes; its gray hue did not clash with the blue of the jacket, almost as if there were blue in the vicuna. The shirt was of the finest "matte" cotton, while the light-wool tie was without reflections. The socks were cashmere, as light as silk. Well-proportioned V-neck sweater, showing just the right amount of the top of the tie. Single-sole shoes, of excellent craftsmanship, with slightly broad and flat tips, as they should be with such a suit. Comfortable shoes. Malaparte hates moccasins. Merely to follow an American vice, the redskins' footwear has been made fashionable, even over here. If I had asked Malaparte to remove his jacket and sweater, I would have seen that he uses neither suspenders nor a belt. If he ever celebrates his hundredth birthday, as he has just cheerfully celebrated his fifty-sixth... he will have the same solid, well-made physique.[128]

But since this is Malaparte, how could there be consensus? The malicious ridiculed his old-fashioned style, mocked his slicked-back (and dyed), 1930s-style hair, his pompous gait and affectations, duded up like the *milord* in the Édith Piaf song, or a hotel porter from times gone by.

His increasing homophobia manifested itself in terms that would today be considered beyond the pale. He criticized the tendency of contemporary theatrical productions to "emasculate"—a theme decidedly dear to him—the voice and the acting. In October 1955 he caused an uproar, after an article in which he attacked RAI, Italy's public broadcasting company, over the criteria for choosing its announcers and correspondents: "Enthusiasts of 'special friendships' are entrusted with tasks sharply at odds with their delicate and precious nature."[129] The episode would have a farcical conclusion, because the journalists who set out on a "punitive expedition" to Capri ended up reconciling with their accuser over a meal.[130] Not even then, though, would Malaparte pass up a chance to underline in a new article that "we were seated around that table from four in the afternoon to eight in the evening, peering at the couples of beautiful young women, in large part French, English, and American, with dull eyes and sharp voices, crowding the café terrace. Strange feminine fauna one meets these days in Capri! September is the month for *mignons*, October for female couples."[131] He hated the idea that after the war magical spots like Capri, Ischia, and Taormina had become oases for Anglo-American irregulars and homosexuals: W. H. Auden, Gore Vidal, Tennessee Williams, and so on. He wrote to Raymond Guérin with an invitation to visit him on the island, "far from the filth of Rome and Naples," but he shut himself up more and more in the splendid isolation of Punta del Massullo, renamed (by him) Punta Malaparte. The writer Félicien Marceau, married to the Italian actress Bianca Della Corte and a Capri stalwart for many years, recalls a Malaparte who was conspicuous above all by his absence:

> The Capriote fauna quickly came together again in the aftermath of the war. It was still the same mix of revelers, aristocrats, and failures of every stripe, who formed a strictly separate group with respect to

the local population. I still see the former Hungarian prime minister Kállay, fleeing the Soviet occupation of his country, awaiting a visa for the United States, or the beguiling Venetian countess Adriana Ivancich, Hemingway's last great love, who afterward would take her own life, and so many others. With Malaparte, the people didn't know what attitude to take. We knew he had run the gamut with Fascism, and everyone gossiped about the support and favors that had allowed him to build the incredible Casa Come Me, right at the water's edge. People met him on the street sometimes, tall, dark, in the style of a certain type of handsome Italian man of the period, like Pippo Infuso, Ciano's former chief of staff. But all things considered, he was little seen in island society life. I do not believe I ever encountered him at any of the important soirées, at the home of the princess of Sirignano or the duchess of Bagnoli, or of some American heiress. I never went up to his house and I only spoke to him once, when we happened to run into each other at the port. He asked me what I was writing, and I revealed the title of a short essay I was working on then: "Casanova, or the anti–Don Juan." That's it. A few days later I was in Rome, in the same suite as Margherita Sarfatti at the Hotel Ambasciatori. Ecstatic, she told me Malaparte had just suggested to her the title for one of her articles, a perfect title: "Casanova, or the anti–Don Juan"![132]

And Beatrice Monti von Rezzori:

> I do not remember having met Malaparte on Capri in that period [during the war], but maybe a bit later, toward 1945 or 1946, by chance, in the little square. He was walking his dog, as usual. I was eighteen years old, and I noticed that people were turning as I passed and smiling at me, something I didn't mind at all, after a very austere

life during the war. There were parties everywhere, the great Caprese diaspora was returning to the island. We all had a mad desire to have fun after those years of privation. Malaparte did not participate in all that; one hardly ever saw him. Perhaps he preferred it that way. There were Munthe's sons, the Cerios, the princes of Sirignano, the Fersen heirs, Paolo Gaetani, Mona Williams von Bismarck, Norman Douglas, and all the Italian intelligentsia with Moravia, Elsa Morante, et cetera. Curzio kept to himself, attending to his persona. I've always had the impression that he was a loner, one look at his house and you understand. Thirty years later, when I accompanied my friend Bruce Chatwin there for his article for *Vanity Fair*, he had the same impression.[133]

Nonetheless, maybe to overcome isolation, he was more anxious than ever to write and to participate, to be present. He contributed to all the newspapers, to any forum that would have him. In the absence of a magazine to edit, as in the era of *La Conquista dello Stato* or of *Prospettive*, he sought and found a space all his own, commenting on current events in the column he wrote from 1953 to his death, in *Tempo*, a Milan-based weekly magazine, successor to the one published by Alberto Mondadori under Fascism, not to be confused, as noted earlier, with the similarly named daily, to which he had contributed since its founding. The column was called Battibecco, a vernacular and very Tuscan term that might be translated as "squabble" or "contestation."* It was also the title he wanted to give all his poetry, among which figured the verse ballads of the

---

*A first edition of the articles appeared during his lifetime (Milan: Garzanti, 1955). The definitive edition was later collected by Falqui (BA2).

last period, which returned to the satirical style of *L'arcitaliano*. In the column he lambasted the great and less great of this world, and while amusing his audience delivered some hard lessons on the art of savoir vivre. There were nearly four hundred installments, some hardly longer than an epigram, pungent and biting. They ranged from a portrait of Churchill—"whose importance in the conduct of the war was enormous, but the war was won by Stalin and Roosevelt, not by him"[134]—to a meditation on the Parthenon, from a publicity campaign to modernize Prato's municipal hospital to an homage to the Italian soldiers of the Foreign Legion, killed while defending Dien Bien Phu in the First Indochina War. But he also addressed speed limits on national highways, the pensions of parliament members, an "anti-kissing" ordinance from the Turin police, and the controversial love life of Fausto Coppi, who, while still married, moved in with his lover, the mysterious "woman in white" who had all Italy dreaming. Malaparte also envied the nickname an announcer had applied to Coppi during a memorable stage of the 1949 Giro d'Italia, and which had become part of sporting legend: *un uomo solo al comando*, "a man on his own in the lead"; whereas he was more and more on his own, but less and less in the lead. Perhaps for this reason, his preferences would later swing to Coppi's great French rival, Louison Bobet.

Malaparte was perfectly at ease in the role of ham or musketeer: he settled accounts, disclosed the deeds and misdeeds of his friends and enemies without embarrassment or shame, cultivated his own notoriety, handled an abundance of readers' letters, and could even believe he was performing a kind of pedagogy and aid to the people, writing about everyone and everything. Under the title "Write to Me and You Will Have Justice," he spoke out against delays in the payment of war pensions and bureaucratic mishaps or judicial complications that readers alerted him to, and he publicly called on ministers and administrators to respond.[135] And too bad, or all the better, if the solons of government or academia took umbrage at this: his amusement doubled. Often the tone is so withering as to recall, thirty years later, the fearsome editorialist of "Pages of the Sibyl." All that would have been truly comforting in the oppressive and bigoted climate of Italy then, if Malaparte had not become the champion of a form of *qualunquismo*, not out of sympathy for Guglielmo Giannini's short-lived political movement, but out of innate skepticism. This vigilante's conscience led him to constantly set, not without a good pinch of demagogy, the "wretched," poor, and rejected, whose improbable defender he became, against the oppressive state, the bureaucracy, the church, the dominant morality, and so forth. The force and brilliance of the style often gets the better of the arguments' merits, and the desire to judge often precedes the need to understand. Age had not dimmed his ardor; on the contrary, he liked nothing better than to take a contrarian view, and the weekly's editor would often have to calm him down or refuse his articles for fear of legal consequences.[136] Malaparte thundered, insulted, sneered, cried out in indignation or compassion. Did he really succeed in addressing flagrant injustices? Perhaps so; on the other hand, he contributed to maintaining an excess of excitement in public life and a mistrust of institutions, everlasting features of Italian society.

The Battibecco pages have been referred to as instances of painful patriotism. Yes and no: Malaparte was certainly patriotic, even chauvinist; he loved to insult his country and fellow citizens, provided he was the only one authorized to do so, and his country was, from the first day of his life to the last, Italy, only Italy, of which he had a carnal, absolute need. His relationship with the peninsula recalls those peasants from his childhood who cursed God Almighty for the bad harvest but rained blows on their children if they failed to make the sign of the cross before a meal (who knows how many times he would have seen this at the Baldis' house). Besides, what would he have done without his audience, without a country where quarrels between population and government were (and are) the order of the day? Can we imagine a Danish or Dutch Malaparte? Like Pasolini, who would succeed him in the column, initially under the same title, he excelled at denouncing the scourges, delays, and hypocrisies of Italian society and of the West in general. But he struggled to propose solutions, and fundamentally he was uninterested in doing so, because if there were solutions, what role would he play? There was in Pasolini, however, a laceration that would not be closed by any false accommodation, even in the injustice of his most extreme theses: he was a wounded being, who wounded to survive. Nothing similar could be said of Malaparte, who was always domineering, without the least tolerance for those who did not share his point of view, and entirely incapable of self-criticism. According to a writer of the next generation, Sandro Veronesi, who made an insightful (and courageous) juxtaposition of the two: "They were two 'indefensibles.' Malaparte was indefensible by the Right and Fascism just as Pasolini was indefensible by the Left. They were two free spirits, who had an irreducibly individualistic and, especially Pasolini, artistic orientation. And in their difference, they would also resemble each other, to my mind—and sometimes their thoughts resembled each other."[137]

Malaparte gave the impression of never having taken himself so seriously as he did in that last period, and it is worth wondering if, at this point, his narcissism was not joined by an element of paranoia: "The great success of Battibecco is not due to my writer's art, but to the fact that the Italian people are hungry for truth, and to my habit of speaking clearly and freely telling the truth at a time when lying is obligatory."[138] Armed with a whip, he flogged the bad guys and drove the moneylenders from the temple but spared his carefully powdered cheeks. Let it be noted, furthermore, in view of his ostensible conversion at the last, that one constant of these texts is their anticlericalism, the denunciation of Vatican interference in affairs of state, as he proclaimed in the open letter to Moravia. We find traces here of the verbal violence that characterized his first literary outings, in line with pre-Concordat Fascism.* More than ever, Malaparte seemed to hate how forgetful Italy was of the past, on its way toward a moralistic clericalism.

His real comedown arrived with the discovery of the variety show, or rather with the conviction it had to be renewed, modernized, given an American tone. The Italian musical, revue, or vaudeville certainly cannot boast the history of Broadway or Viennese operetta. But it has a respectable tradition, with some political and social opposition during Fascism, and it still had a good following among the pre-TV public of the 1950s, especially in the provinces and in resort towns, which generally had a summer season. It was a lucrative

---

*For example: "The smell of dead flowers hung over [Saint Peter's] Basilica, and it was certainly the Holy Father [Pius XI] who was giving off that smell of rotten petals and overripe flesh" (DONC, 331). But according to Father Castelli, a strenuous defender of the inner religiosity of Malaparte, "These aspects are dated and belong to that particular political and social moment.... Let's consider [instead] 'La commedia di Santo Natale' (The comedy of Holy Christmas), in which he denounces the commercialization of the great religious holiday" (testimony to the author).

circuit, and many actors, stage designers, and directors got their start there, not disdaining to return between one film and another: Fellini paid tribute to it in nearly all his films, especially in one of the last, *Ginger and Fred*. It caught Malaparte's imagination, and in May 1955 he threw himself into the production of *Sexophone*. This dismal pun heralded disaster, after two other titles had been discarded, *Senso vietato* ("wrong way" or "one-way street") and *Battibecco*.[139] He took on not only the text, direction, and stage design, assisted as always by Tamburi, but also the role of impresario. Here is how a French daily gave its readers the news:

> Indeed, Malaparte thought the features of his wit would advantageously replace the dancers in panties and ostrich feathers. Onstage there would be only six "Bluebell girls" and two black dancers surrounding the *enfant terrible* of Italian letters.[140]

The plans were grandiose, the idea being to take the show across the Atlantic, after a run-in tour in Italy to raise the necessary funds. In this activity, which all his friends advised him against, Malaparte rediscovered the ardor of his twenty-year-old self; he loved being the star and everything that came with it. He personally chose the dancers and musicians and gave himself, of course, the lion's share of the time onstage, where, made up and smiling like the master of ceremonies in the film *Cabaret*, he led audiences through a bungled satire of national prudery, at a time when the Vatican was still dictating sexual behavior in Italy, via the Christian Democrats.* Onstage

---

*Italian political parties, including not just the Christian Democrats but also the Communists, conformed to these dictates until 1968 and in some respects even later, until the referendum on divorce in 1974.

"he was a leading man who played his part perfectly, but with the anxiety and fear of forgetting his lines," observed Biancamaria Fabbri.[141] In one number, appalled audiences see an ambassador running after a lost bra. Another, "the dance of the three sexes," in which Malaparte expressed his increasingly spiteful homophobia, becomes "the dance of the three twerps," with a not exactly unforgettable chorus: "L'Italia è libera / Dio la conservi / Siam tutti servi / In libertà" (Italy is free / God preserve her / We are all servants / At liberty).[142] Let us stop there and draw a veil over the rest. One critic came up with a rather predictable formula, "*Kaputt* per Sexophone," and that just about says it all.[143] The pathetic misadventure ended in the Tuscan spa town of Montecatini, where the novice impresario had to confront the anger of a hotelier with little love for the Muses, who refused to extend credit to the company. This lackluster finale made him understand he needed to do an about-face. But the affair would result in heavy financial losses, aside from the blow to his prestige.

Friends and biographers have wondered what drove Malaparte to these errors and, frankly, this buffoonery. Beyond the exhibitionism at his core and the craving for popularity, was it perhaps a need for money? It would be the simplest explanation, but it is not entirely convincing. He had always been careful in his spending and still had a good income, thanks to his journalism and royalties. But the era in which he had earned a good deal of money was over. His two properties in Forte and Capri, his divo's wardrobe, and the quality of life he did not wish to give up, for reasons of prestige, cost him dear. At this point he thought he might have to turn Villa Hildebrand into a restaurant or a hotel, or else sell it. As the good (if not always loving) son he was, he was looking out for his now elderly parents. After his mother's death, it was Erwin, increasingly short-tempered and senile, who caused him the most problems; he would continue past the age of ninety to make life impossible for those close to him. Malaparte went so far as to confide to close friends like Borelli that he was "penniless," even if such claims must be taken with the usual grain of salt.[144] On the poorly asphalted postwar streets he drove the cars of a Hollywood producer: a Plymouth, then a zabaglione-colored Oldsmobile Rocket 88 convertible.[145] But curiously, he was never seen behind the wheel of a Ferrari, red like a Garibaldian's shirt, which was one of the most visible symbols of the Italian "miracle."* His passion for powerful cars nearly cost him his life in Chile, in late November 1952, when the Cadillac carrying him from Valparaiso to Santiago went off the road on a curve. He had always liked to flaunt the addresses of elegant spots he now struggled to afford. René Novella mentions visits to Capri when Malaparte, "completely out of money, could only offer us salad from the garden and some squid caught that morning."[146] Biancamaria Fabbri recalls that the grocer and the butcher "were fed up with extending credit to Malaparte."[147] According to his old frenemy Giovanni Ansaldo, now at the head of Naples' *Il Mattino* newspaper, "His little society trick is clear: he stays free at [his publisher's], and comes down to spend his days at the Excelsior, where he'll eat an olive, or not."[148] In Forte dei Marmi, where he now rarely returned, he was almost never seen in the fashionable spots, among the remnants of the interwar beau monde; instead he would sit at a café table with his dog, or in a movie theater in the afternoon, shut up in increasingly distant solitude. In Rome he had left his apartment

---

*Today, Ferraris come in all colors. At least the prancing horse of Francesco Baracca is still there.

on Via Gregoriana for hotels: the luxurious Hassler, overlooking the Spanish Steps; the solid Ambasciatori, on Via Veneto; or the more discreet American Hotel, in the bourgeois (and rather un-Malapartian) Parioli neighborhood. But often he limited himself to merely meeting people in these spots, while he was generally the guest of Renato Angiolillo, the owner-publisher of *Il Tempo*, in his sumptuous residence on the Via Appia. Angiolillo was probably his best friend and patron in this last part of his life. What drew them together? I asked Gianni Letta, Angiolillo's closest collaborator before succeeding him at the head of the newspaper:

> First of all, the same experiences: Angiolillo was also subject to *confino* during Fascism, then to a certain form of anti-Fascist vindictiveness at Liberation. And then they shared the same taste for freedom, for anticonformism, also for a certain aestheticism. Angiolillo, a big horse breeder, had given his purebreds names taken from the language of journalism: one was called Elzeviro, another Editoriale, and so on. Finally, the cinema: before jumping into production, Angiolillo had written screenplays, including one of the first films made by De Sica, *A Garibaldian in the Convent* (1942), which is a small masterpiece. He and De Sica would also make generally disastrous excursions to the Casino de Monte-Carlo, but Malaparte never joined them. He had at his disposal an old, refitted stable on the grounds of the property, where he could work in peace, with total freedom.[149]

He dined, when he could, in fashionable restaurants, where he was sure to be recognized, and sometimes finished the evening in local nightspots, patrolled by the first, ravenous paparazzi of the postwar era. It was the price to pay to get noticed, because he hated the noise and the crowds, and the smoke bothered his damaged lungs. It was, in short, the circuit dear to the Rome of Cinecittà, which would soon become the compulsory itinerary of *la dolce vita*: a cliché that Malaparte would not have put up with, because Via *Vittorio Veneto*—the full name of the famous avenue—remained for him tied to memories of his youthful soldiering. He surrounded himself with starlets, here too as a tribute to his role as a Pygmalion; but the break with Rebequita returned him to solitude forever: "He was jealous to the point of shutting her up in her room and hiding her shoes. One day she decided she had had enough. She fled, jumping out of a window and running barefoot to the Chilean Consulate in Rome, and had herself repatriated."[150]

The more likely explanation for the dispersal of his energies is nonetheless psychological. Malaparte was not only a loner but someone who fought to put off the moment of truth. This frenzy hid a growing fear of literary sterility. His traditionally difficult relations with publishers worsened with age: ever more spiteful, cantankerous, and moody, he continually accused them of promising better conditions and better print runs to unworthy authors. "I have it in for all Italian publishers, who bear a great deal of the responsibility for the cowardice and dull conformism of Italian literature," he wrote to Enrico Vallecchi, guilty of not wanting to reprint *Kaputt*.[151] He ranted and lashed out at everyone, with full names and personal accusations, verging on slander and defamation, especially against colleagues and rivals on the up. As in the newspapers and magazines, he always wanted to dominate the scene and have the last word on everything. After a final conflict with Valentino Bompiani,[152] he decided it was time to become his own publisher, in collaboration with a friend. This was Daria Lapauze Guarnati, a Venetian lady of French origin whom he had met before the war, when she had launched, along with the architect Gio Ponti, the wonderful avant-garde magazine *Aria d'Italia*, first expression of the great Italian school of design.[153] In this matter we can turn to the valuable testimony of Beatrice Monti von Rezzori:

> Daria Guarnati had fallen under his spell and had transformed *Aria d'Italia* into a publishing house to bring out his books. Malaparte had quarreled with everybody, he asked for absurd advances, demanded that some authors be dropped from the list, and so on. She was a very strange lady, her face covered by a thick layer of white powder, as in a kabuki performance, her head covered in fire-red curls. In his paranoia, Curzio had convinced himself that Guarnati, who had opened La Galleria del Sole in Milan, was investing in it the royalties she wasn't paying him. In short, he asked me to meet her and, if possible, to visit her at home. That way I would have the chance to let him know what was happening there and to do a job he thought would be interesting for me. Yes, at the beginning I had fun. After two years I also became a business partner of Daria's, and subsequently the sole owner of the gallery. Malaparte didn't understand much about contemporary art...[154]

Aria d'Italia's first publications were new editions of *Kaputt* and *The Skin*. Malaparte considered putting out a chronological series of his complete (revised) works. But the dedication of this slightly eccentric lady, who shared with him a love of dogs, failed to alleviate his persecution complex. Off the bat he sent her a draft contract with a rather bizarre clause:

You waive the right to raise any objection regarding the appropriateness of publishing my works in terms of their political, social, moral, or religious content. Your refusal to publish any of my works at all will entail the immediate termination of this contract, except for the settlement of what is due [me].[155]

The partnership went ahead for a few years, but this did not prevent him from persecuting the poor publisher with his complaints: "I am very worried about the inexplicable delay caused by your slowness, your prevarications, your incredible and unnecessary complications," he wrote her shortly after.[156] Outside the old books to reprint, though, he constantly postponed the appearance of the novels he had been announcing for years under different titles: *Un delitto cristiano*, *Una tragedia italiana*, *Il ballo del conte Pecci-Blunt*, *La lotta con l'angelo*, and so on, not to mention *The Kremlin Ball*. For each of these projects he had over the course of years drafted fragments of varying, and often notable, length, but the whole eluded him. It was the sense of composition, of an overall architecture, that seemed to have abandoned the writer.

If a major work was beyond him, then, he consoled himself with *Those Cursed Tuscans*, a short, cheerfully malevolent treatise in which Malaparte lambasted his adversaries of yesterday, today, and tomorrow, displaying a tart and pungent imagination. Even here there was nothing new: the oldest texts come from toward the end of his so-called *confino*, in Forte dei Marmi, and the book's original dedication, obviously removed, was a cheerful ribbing of Galeazzo Ciano, a fellow Tuscan. The book had already been typeset by Vallecchi under a different title, *Viaggio in inferno* (Journey to hell), when Malaparte blocked its publication in December 1943. A decade later he returned to the book and brought it out with the same Florentine publisher, and its success allowed him to recoup at least some of what he had lost in the *Sexophone* disaster. As it happened, this was also the last work he published in his lifetime, on the eve of his trip to the Soviet Union and China.

The problem with *Those Cursed Tuscans*, which was also the last work by Malaparte to be broadly distributed internationally, is its penchant for chauvinist lines like "[Tuscans] have a way of kneeling which is rather more a way of standing up with their legs bent" (CT, 44), for stale jokes and genre sketches, that is unbearable at times and, what is worse, rings false. It was the return in force of the provincial identity, in large part imaginary, that the young Curzio had tailored for himself, a bit like how as a child he had invented for himself a treasure island or pirates' cove behind the sofa or in a corner of the yard. It is no coincidence that Longanesi, after their quarrel, called him a "fake Tuscan" (that is, a hypocrite). During his life, Malaparte regularly yielded to the temptation to take refuge in a "Tuscanism," a "Prato-ism," that had little to do with his guiding principles, his cosmopolitanism, his inexhaustible curiosity about the world. It was an outlet for his antihistoricism, his skepticism, his refusal to believe in the march of progress, his contempt for the fate of Europe.[157] The book's best moments display the delightful accents of a distinctly Italian *prosa d'arte* tradition, but they are short lived:

> Seated on the ground in the middle of the ragpickers I would delight my fancy endlessly by picking through the heaps of refuse, out of which came an endless stream of incredible and marvelous things: sea shells, fragments of colored glass, droplets of amber, little pearls

from rivers in India, stones of every color—green, purple, blue and yellow—all of them seeming infinitely precious, though the most precious of all was the Indian stone that the ragpickers called "moonstone" and was indeed as pale and shimmering as the sliver of a new moon.... Sometimes certain strange and dry little creatures came tumbling out of the rags, some resembling tiny sea horses, others in the mummified form of lizards and toads, and still others in foetal form with their heads crushed flat. (CT, 98)

But this virtuosity stumbles against a ground of thought that is truly reactionary, in the sense that the values of childhood fantasy, transposed without filter into an adult sensibility, establish a mythic image opposed to reality. The equivocal nature of Strapaese storms back and pushes Malaparte to oppose Pratesi to Florentines, Tuscans to Italians, Italians to Europeans: "The only defect of the Tuscans is that of not being all from Prato," "a dead Tuscan is worth more than all other living Italians put together," "Tuscans are the bad conscience of Italy," "It would be an even greater blessing if, in Italy, there were more Tuscans and fewer Italians" (CT, 83, 236, 214, 19), and so on. Thus he contributed to perpetuating clichés on their way to extinction, when the real question of the moment was represented by the tumultuous social transformation produced by the "economic miracle" and by mass media. This is why younger writers like Calvino, Volponi, and Sciascia—to which one might add Moravia, who, closer to Malaparte in terms of age and experience, became in that moment the high priest of alienation—are more trustworthy interpreters of a changing Italy, whereas he would have liked to freeze it in one last nostalgic family portrait. Here, too, we can compare him to Pasolini, who, pursued by a lost-paradise complex, opposed nature to history, and primitive, supposedly authentic, man to the one alienated and reified by modern civilization. Malaparte would not go so far, not even as a provocation, because his temperament was too realist, too sunny: he was a fighter and a factionist, but not a man flayed alive like the Friulian poet (nor was he really a poet). Malaparte may have possessed a sense of tragedy, but he also had an extraordinary capacity to recharge himself through anger, insult, or mockery. Just compare Malaparte's final homage here to Sacchetti, Boccaccio, and Aretino, so close to him in terms of their acrid bonhomie, cynicism, and indifference to passion, with the substantial failure of a film like *The Decameron* (1971), in which Pasolini is unable to transmit the joy of living that animates Boccaccio's characters, even when they are victims of someone cleverer than them.

Taken as high-quality entertainment, *Those Cursed Tuscans* still has plenty of pleasures to offer readers: the Pazzi conspiracy of 1478; Charles VIII's visit to Prato, when the inhabitants "all turned around against the wall and took a pee" (CT, 110); the last Habsburg archduke's departure from Florence, in 1859. Malaparte excels here at bringing to life in just a few strokes a world of craftspeople, innkeepers, priests, chicken thieves, mercenaries, women of easy virtue, and so on. He preserves the sense of concision, of the killer formulation, of the unforeseen comparison. He is amusing, touching, swift. He stays—and keeps the reader—interested. It is another example of the mistake many outside Italy have fallen into, taking Malaparte at face value, wrapped in his black legend, considering him an emulator of Cellini, Casanova, Cagliostro, and naturally the Marquis de Sade, or giving him the aura of a guru, whenever he gave free rein to his whims and imagination.

The mistake was repeated with *Benedetti italiani*, the apocryphal title of a posthumous collection the faithful Falqui did not wish to be credited as editor of, because it brought together texts that had not been revised for publication, of disparate origins and content. As far back as the 1930s, Malaparte had flirted with the idea of a book about his compatriots, but he lacked the methodical spirit and preparation to take it on. After the war, he outlined fifteen chapters, each a sketch of the typical man or woman of the various regions of the peninsula. To this material, modest in terms of both quantity and quality, the publisher added a group of articles from the period 1936–37, some successful—the evocation of Piero della Francesca's sequence of frescoes *The Legend of the True Cross*, or the story of a colonist ship leaving for Abyssinia, drawn from the aborted project "L'Africa non è nera"—others less so, but all with only a vague relationship to the topic. If the book preserves the quality of quickness and intelligence of *Those Cursed Tuscans*, it also highlights the lack of perspective when, passing from anecdote to theory, Malaparte falls into banal generalizations. Thus he returns to the defeat of 1943–45 and the "Italians' inability to translate their material ills into moral suffering and, more precisely, their own history. We have no religious sense, which is to say, or rather to repeat, that we are unable to translate the problems in our lives into moral suffering" (BI, 143). All things he had said much better elsewhere, such as in the dialogue with the dying mother in *Mamma marcia*. But most of the time he mixed erudition and wordplay, juggled jokes and memory fragments. The result, always enjoyable at the level of the writing, doesn't hold up when the author insists on offering an image of the national character. We are very, very far from the splendid radio program *Viaggio in Italia* (Journey to Italy), later collected in a book, by his rival Guido Piovene, or from the brilliant panorama

The Italians that his friend—but also a competitor from the time of the Virginia–Giannalisa Feltrinelli affair—Luigi Barzini would write expressly for the American audience in the early 1960s.*

Aside from *Those Cursed Tuscans*, however, his last projects were focused not on literature, but on cinema. And they were also his last disappointments. Borelli had just been named president of a production company, CINES, which seemed prepared to invest significant capital in quality films. Had the moment finally arrived for the awaited follow-up to *The Forbidden Christ*? A preliminary contract, signed in Rome on January 20, 1956, would have assigned to CINES and another company, Imperial Film, the rights to a script adapted by Malaparte from an unfinished novella, *Compagno di viaggio*.[158] The idea was, obviously, to then create a film from it. But notwithstanding many good intentions, the project never took off. Malaparte declared himself ready to sell his "tea service [made by] Faberger [*sic*] of Petersburg, the great jeweler and silversmith of the Court of the Czar, in gold and platinum."[159] But in the end he had to resign himself to the inevitable. The screen wanted nothing more to do with him.

"This Suburb of Prato Called Peking..."[160]

If Malaparte's real business no longer lay at his desk or behind a movie camera, it would nevertheless involve a work of art, albeit one of an unusual genre: the staging in three acts of his spectacular

---

*Barzini would try again with *The Europeans* (New York: Simon & Schuster, 1983), with a less sure touch and less success.

death. The project, at once hyperrealist and completely surrealist, could never be replicated, due to the disappearance of its director and protagonist in the last scene, a masterpiece and testament to a life, the apogee of a vocation without legacy.

To explain the genesis of this last adventure, we need to pass through politics again. We left Malaparte very anti-Communist but fascinated by a sort of Christian communism at the time of *Das Kapital* and *The Forbidden Christ*. Upon his return from Paris, he had inevitably reconnected with moderate circles, among whom he still counted the majority of his friends and readers. The publications he contributed to could certainly not be identified as leftist. But that does not mean he should be classified as a man of the Right, in the sense the term had in the 1950s. Politically, he had no affinity with neo-Fascist, monarchist, or "nostalgic" groups. For him they were ghosts of the past; for them he was just a renegade and an opportunist. As for the Catholic world, where he still had admirers, the anticlerical barbs of *Battibecco* and the risqué satire of *Sexophone* had reopened the old wounds from when *The Skin* was placed on the Index. If the Communists treated him harshly, bien-pensants thought he had become the devil incarnate. Attacks were flying in from all sides. Nonetheless, thanks to his popularity, personal history, and talent, Malaparte continued to inspire the interest and even the covetousness of the Vatican hierarchy and the leaders of the Christian Democrats, the party that had enjoyed an absolute majority since 1948, something that will allow us to understand subsequent events.

He was not necessarily the enemy of all, then. And Malaparte knew the attacks coming at him from one side would provoke interest in the other, in a game of communicating vessels. But the Italian political situation was more fluid now, in the mid-1950s, than in the immediate aftermath of the 1948 elections. In the PCI, besides Togliatti, who had never forgotten him, various young intellectuals, already a bit tired of the rhetoric of the Resistance, would have liked to drop the edict of proscription that loomed over him. And so, in the summer of 1956, in the wake of the quarrel between Malaparte and the Italian Republican Party after his defeat in the Prato municipal elections, *L'Unità* suddenly started to give flowers to the "greatest Tuscan writer," a "man of high moral stature," and so on. On the other side of the barricade, in the ranks of the Right, one immediately wondered if this was not the announcement of Malaparte's conversion to communism.[161]

It was, rather, the clearest sign of a rapprochement, after a series of preliminary contacts, entrusted to two Togliatti protégés. The first was the former partisan Davide Lajolo, author of an autobiographical novel, *Il "voltagabbana"* (The "turncoat"), in which he recounted, with uncommon honesty, his path from the Fascist Left to the Resistance and communism, as well as a biography of his friend Pavese.[162] Lajolo had already drawn attention for a favorable review of *Sexophone* (but perhaps that is no merit).[163] Beside him was the thirty-year-old Maria Antonietta Macciocchi, a flamboyant Neapolitan feminist and philosopher, freshly named editor in chief of the party weekly *Vie Nuove*. Malaparte welcomed the courtship, delighted to be able to play the two off each other and thus raise the bids. Later, Lajolo would draw the following conclusion:

> Malaparte was an absolutely contradictory man, with enormous defects and great virtues. He had managed to make a virtue out of even his hypocrisy, courage out of the cowardice in each of us.

I fought him and I cared for him ... an inimitable journalist even in his crowing, his inventiveness, his imagination, a corrosive writer, a man apart, above all a defender of his own side [*parte*], that of Malaparte.[164]

But it was especially Macciocchi who conducted the seduction campaign with brio. Malaparte's archives contain some revelatory letters she wrote to him in the period, and the idea of the trip to China probably came from her. To pique his interest, she flooded him with books, articles, and documents, without ever forgetting to flatter his vanity: "I would still like to speak with you about the trip, and then, I confess, I would like to hear you tell another perfect story, like the one about the Chinese porcelain."[165] And again: "I read *Those Cursed Tuscans*: your prose is so bold and so clean. What a happy, cheerful book, worthy of a young man, has been written by the great, acclaimed writer you have been for some time."[166] Such compliments counted for a man whose certainties had been worn down by so many trials. And yet, here too it seems unjust, or at least ungenerous, to accuse him of double-dealing. Malaparte lived by his pen; all he did was adapt himself, with his legendary nonchalance but without disavowing himself, to the situation at hand. And then, he had to earn a living like everyone else, without an agent or secretary, and that was not always easy. Of course, he was famous, his work translated half the world over. But the big publishing houses, radio, and the nascent television industry, which gave work to many talented writers, repeatedly closed their doors to him. The magazines he had given life to no longer existed. The major northern papers ignored him. None of the postwar literary prizes, large or small, had crowned him. After *The Skin* had been nominated, apparently without his knowledge, for the 1950 Strega Prize, won by Pavese for *The Beautiful Summer*, he solemnly declared he would never again participate in a literary competition.[167] In another declaration he clarified: "I am delighted the prize went to Cesare Pavese and I am even more delighted to declare that, if I had received the prize, I would have refused it."[168] Possibly...

Malaparte counted many more adversaries and detractors than friends and supporters; in thirty years of battles, of rises and falls, he had accumulated so many grudges, envies, and hatreds that he needed to defend himself with every means available. Besides, is the situation today so different, in Italy, France, and elsewhere? How many intellectuals do we see readily accept well-remunerated positions (which were never offered to Malaparte) in governments, organizations, institutions, or the media that are on occasion in conflict with their private ethics?* Why not recognize that Malaparte, who was faithful to himself as few others have been, did exactly the same thing, knowing how to adapt to interlocutors and circumstances? And he was not satisfied to fly blind. His epistolary polemic with a Neapolitan friend, Guglielmo Peirce, who in the same period was taking the opposite path, from Left to Right, showed that Malaparte had foreseen the gradual evolution of the Western Communist parties toward more moderate positions, following the inapplicability of the Marxist formula to the class struggle in the more developed capitalist countries.

---

*As an example of this double standard, I could quote many intellectuals of my own generation who claim that Berlusconi the politician was a threat to democracy, all the while consenting to have their films financed and their books published by his media empire, considering this to be "a completely different issue."

Matters moved swiftly and then, after a series of reciprocal displays of goodwill, came the turning point: Malaparte was invited by the secretary of the Union of Soviet Writers, the very official and mediocre Boris Polevoy, to travel to Moscow for Italian Cinema Week. One excuse is as good as another: Togliatti patiently did what it took to get the new masters of the Kremlin to open the doors of the Soviet Union to a writer who was famous but inconvenient from every point of view. First act: the departure. Malaparte flew from Rome to Moscow, via Stockholm, on October 12, 1956. He did not know he was already ill, and this would be his last trip, even as he complained of pains in his armpit and chest, which often made it excruciating for him to lift his suitcase or typewriter. He had just returned exhausted from a "writers' cruise" organized by the Greek government, featuring spectacular productions of his favorite tragedies, *Electra* and *Antigone*; it was a packed program, which he did not want to miss, in order to seal his reconciliation with a country he had last visited in 1940, in quite other circumstances. In a photo taken on the Acropolis, between Carlo Levi and the Greco-Hollywood actress Katina Paxinou, he appears bloated and waxy. But, incredibly for a hypochondriac, he did not undergo any kind of checkup before leaving again. At least his mood was better than his health. Indeed, he brought with him two excellent contracts, negotiated separately, as usual: one with *Tempo*, the other with *Vie Nuove*. A double affiliation, with Right and Left, that did not seem to bother him at all. The following year, Macciocchi would succeed in sending another intellectual disliked by the party apparatus, Pier Paolo Pasolini, as the correspondent for *Vie Nuove* at the World Festival of Youth and Students in Moscow.

Malaparte stopped in Moscow for only a few days. He had little interest in the film festival and made only a brief appearance in the theater, seeing as they were showing Fellini's *La strada*, but not *The Forbidden Christ*.[169] He took the opportunity to wander around the places he had seen twenty-five years earlier—and this time he seems to have seen nothing. His first dispatches regurgitated all the old Western pilgrims' clichés he had mocked before the war: no prostitution or criminality, clean and well-run cities, a carefree, well-nourished population, passionate about culture, and so on. One struggles to recognize in these lackluster pages the mark of one of the most lucid and intuitive connoisseurs of the Soviet world. And yet perhaps the worst thing lies not in what he said, but in what he did not: a few vague references to the "grave errors" of Stalin, so recently denounced by Khrushchev; nothing on the events in Budapest, where popular revolt seemed to have triumphed, before being crushed by Soviet repression. But it is a price he paid without batting an eye, because something much more spectacular awaited him. He was in a hurry to reach the second act: the invitation, this time coming from the Chinese government, to travel to Peking via the trans-Siberian air route. This, too, involved a barely concealed pretext. He was asked to participate in the commemoration of the writer Lu Xun, who had died in 1936, precursor of the proletarian revolution. We may doubt Malaparte's interest in this eminent colleague, of whom he had probably not read a single line. But he did not show it: on the contrary, he advised his Spanish publisher, José Janès, to bring out a translation of the Chinese writer's masterpiece, *The True Story of Ah Q*. He was dying to see this still-mysterious country, the true aim of his journey. He was infatuated from afar with Chinese communism, which he opposed to the bureaucratic fossilization of Soviet totalitarianism. "Chinese civilization is the only one that can really give new force to socialism," he allegedly declared to Macciocchi before leaving.[170]

Who had obtained this invitation for him? Once again, it is difficult not to think of the hidden diplomacy of Togliatti, and of his authority as the former second-in-command of the Communist International. Malaparte's correspondence with Macciocchi reveals that the itinerary "Stalingrad, Samarkand, Ulan Bator, and then Peking" had been established from the beginning according to the writer's wishes.[171] The PCI secretary expressed many reservations about the de-Stalinization process—too fast and too public, in his eyes—set in motion by Khrushchev at the Twentieth Party Congress, in February 1956, and he was worried about the cracks that could open up at the frontiers of the empire, undermining its unity. But it was above all Mao's China that was giving serious signs of indiscipline. After refusing to follow Moscow down the road of normalization with revisionist Yugoslavia, it protected Enver Hoxha's Albania, the only satellite to have openly opposed the denunciation of the cult of Stalin. In addition, Mao was preparing to launch the Great Leap Forward, a plan for radical industrialization whose effects would be disastrous, but which would allow him to challenge Soviet leadership on the political, economic, and ideological level.

All of this went well beyond the frame of Malaparte's visit, but it provided the backdrop. That a major bourgeois author could write that the Soviet Union and China were marching together for the progress of humanity and the triumph of socialism could not fail to produce a certain impression on his (equally bourgeois) audience. The invitation did not seem to have taken him by surprise, and indeed a Chinese embassy official had been present for his arrival at the Moscow airport. After stops in Novosibirsk and Irkutsk, he landed in Peking in early November, then moved on to the Great Wall and the Xinjiang region. It was love at first sight. "I do nothing but wander around, looking, smelling, writing, happy and crazy, and above all enchanted," he confided to Borelli.[172] Rarely in Malaparte does one find pages so tender—the word does not seem uncalled for—as those he dedicated to the countryside, the art, the architecture, and above all the daily life of the Chinese people, who persevered in their long march through history, despite foreign invasions and fratricidal strife. A tenderness that lingers on the spirit of sacrifice, the kindness, and the smiling dignity of everyone he met, especially the humblest among them: once again, his aesthetic and moral taste for the "old Bolsheviks" and the first Christians returns. What happened to the vitriolic and irreverent streak of the cursed Tuscan?

After a few weeks, though, the drama arrives. On November 11 he noted on a sheet of paper, "I have a bit of a fever this morning."[173] A grim premonition. The state of Malaparte's health worsened; he had to interrupt his trip and cease sending dispatches. Soon it was necessary to transfer him to the hospital in Hankow (Wuhan), in the southeastern region of Hubei, 750 miles from the capital. The first diagnosis referred to pleurisy, but closer examinations indicated the presence of a primary carcinoma in the lungs. He sent Borelli an anxious but firm telegram, in which the absence of punctuation seems to amplify the dramatic tenor:

> Serious complication arisen diagnosis bone tuberculosis fourth rib affected letter follows [I] continue to fight with great courage.[174]

His courage was indeed remarkable, but we know this was a quality he never lacked. He understood very early that his life was in danger and wrote to Macciocchi and Borelli that he wanted to return to die at home.¹⁷⁵ The anonymous provincial Chinese doctors had been right, and now the problem, from being strictly health-related, became political. Since Italy and the People's Republic did not have diplomatic relations, the Italian Ministry of Foreign Affairs followed the status of the writer's health through the Swiss legation. The news rapidly went around the world, as his very tiring return flight from Peking was being arranged. Two doctors arrived with all haste from Italy on the request of the Chinese authorities, who had no desire to see a famous foreign intellectual die on their soil. One of the two was a family member, Giuliano Abbozzo, who had married one of the writer's nieces; the other was the brother of Pietro Ingrao, Togliatti's heir apparent. They had to travel to Switzerland to obtain emergency visas, arranged by a Florentine industrialist.¹⁷⁶ Agonizing weeks passed. Malaparte failed to recover; he suffered, and the least effort exhausted him.

The case was closely followed by the Italian government; the Christian Democrat leaders, Amintore Fanfani and Fernando Tambroni, hoped that Malaparte would return as soon as he was in the condition to make the trip. We see the emergence, then, of the competition the writer had intuited, and possibly hoped for, between the "two straw hats of Italy" over the illustrious patient. The government was ready to send to China at the state's expense the doctor Cesare Frugoni, one of the luminaries of Italian surgery, but Malaparte tapped the brakes:

> I warmly thank you Tambroni Frugoni all friends stop But considering situation mind calmer I want to wait to decide for clinical examination and consultation results main Peking hospital where I will be transferred tomorrow stop So hold off on Frugoni departure

and await my further communication stop Please to avoid unpleasant misunderstandings follow my objectively and resolutely considered decisions.¹⁷⁷

A few days later, Malaparte dictated a long letter for Angiolillo, "a little furtively, with the complicity, that is, of the nurses, who are all very nice. The doctors have prohibited me from writing; in a half hour I can't even write a postcard." It is such a catalog of grievances and recriminations against false friends, traitors, and jealous slanderers, half of them hiding out with impunity in the editorial offices of the newspaper owned by... his correspondent, that reading it leads one to surmise that Malaparte was better, finally back as we knew him. But then comes the serious news:

> For the past two months I have only gotten worse. The pleural liquid is still the same, various complications have arisen, and one yesterday, in my side: if, as the doctors think, it's bone tuberculosis, it means it's spreading; if, as I fear, it's a tumor, it means it's spreading lymphatically. I am resisting and fighting with all my strength, but sometimes I feel like the sickness is stronger than I am, and I need great courage not to let myself be overwhelmed. I'm not afraid to die: I suffer thinking that I no longer have time to reestablish the truth against the slanders I've been persecuted with all my life.¹⁷⁸

The drama fused the idyll with that land of intense delight. His photos from China are practically the only ones he ever took in color—technically, but also symbolically—and the only ones that exude an air of peace and serenity. This is the sensation he wanted to pass on even in his final trial:

Here, given the criminal American blockade, they do not have the possibility of producing the most modern medicines. I am perfectly looked after, treated with tender concern by everyone, including the other sufferers, and the Russian patients in this hospital, all specialized workers, and engineers working to build the bridge over the Yangtze. They come to visit me, bring me flowers and candy, phone me to see how I'm doing. On Christmas Eve evening they surprised me with a Christmas dinner in my honor, with European-style foods, with all the doctors of the hospital around the table, and representatives from the Hankow writers. These Chinese who recall the existence of Christmas and celebrate it to please me are truly kind. I was moved like you can't imagine.[179]

But after the idyll comes the realism of the cursed Tuscan, and the tone suddenly becomes rather less lyrical:

Just a little while ago they phoned from Peking, insisting I be transported to one of that city's hospitals. And it seems like the doctors here are very disposed to see me go. Which seems to me a bad sign, and I have the impression they want to dump me so as to avoid responsibility. My fear now is that they want to open me up and saw away at the affected ribs. You know how these things go: you know when the cutting starts, you don't know when it ends.[180]

The sickness progressed inexorably: he was now losing almost ten pounds a week; his cough kept him from sleeping; lymphatic ganglia appeared in his right armpit and pressed on the breast area. But in the new hospital he continued to be treated with such care that, after having resisted the transfer to Peking, he refused on several occasions to return to Italy. Hence his highly controversial decision, a few months later, to give Casa Come Me, as a token of gratitude, to the People's Republic, to make it a place for Chinese intellectuals and artists to stay and meet.[181] He recounted to his last confidant that, despite his well-known distaste for being touched by anyone, he had abandoned himself without the least resistance to the nurses who looked after him and ably employed acupuncture to alleviate his pain.[182] Obviously, even in the midst of his suffering, he was performing in his own way, as described by Dr. Abbozzo:

> Malaparte was looked after with a kind of care and devotion that European hospitals are little accustomed to. His room was very pretty and overflowed with flowers and gifts: precious, like a sixteenth-century wooden Buddha sculpture, or humble, like small plaster masks from the Peking Opera. In my opinion, Malaparte was not unaware of the nature of the sickness consuming him bit by bit; he simply pretended to believe what he heard from the doctors, in whom, moreover, he displayed a deep and sincere trust. And when, abetted by an uncommon gift for languages, he happened to improvise a few words in Chinese, he responded to the compliments paid him: "Yes, I speak Chinese fairly well but, alas, with a strong tuberculous accent."[183]

But a much more important document is the three-page letter he sent to Maria Antonietta Macciocchi, a text that allows us to understand the extent to which his stay in China had become a political matter. Here is the central passage:

> For some time there has been in play in my illness a propaganda campaign against the People's Republic of China, of which you must

have had some echo even in Italy. The center is Hong Kong. It is said that I am dying because in the People's Republic there are no hospitals, there are no doctors, they've all been killed, there is no medicine, etc. The slander campaign has turned into a series of attempts to take me out of China, to have me treated in American or Western hospitals, etc. Two days ago the agent* for France Presse phoned me from Peking, saying he had been charged by the Hong Kong Bank to place himself at my disposal to transport me to a Hong Kong hospital, or to an American hospital in Formosa [Taiwan]. I told him in no uncertain terms that I am excellently looked after in China, that Chinese hospitals are fully equipped, the Chinese doctors excellent, and that I want nothing to do with the English and the Americans, much less with the partisans of Chiang Kai-shek in Hong Kong or elsewhere: even though I am a free man, not committed to any party, my friends are on this side and not on the other. I've had all this communicated to the office of President Mao and of Prime Minister Zhou Enlai. I admire the People's Republic. I feel I'm in a just, free, good, healthy country here, and I want to avoid any act that could harm Mao's China. It's when I saw the *callampas* of South America, and the horrors of American colonialism in Central America, that I decided to make my own way.... I've also received lots of telegrams from Europe, from China, and the Party Central Committees of Vietnam and North Korea have telegraphed me. They are all very happy about my conduct and my letters, my declarations, my refusal to leave China for a hospital of the enemies of China.[184]

---

*It is a Lacanian sign of his persecution complex that the correspondent for Agence France-Press became in his account an enemy "agent."

Do these expressions of indignation sound right? Not exactly. They may remind us of something we have encountered before: the letters from Lipari, in which he lavished compliments on his jailers. Maybe in this way he hoped to secure the sympathy of the Italian and international Left, at the same time keeping up his usual relations with the pro-American Right of Angiolillo or Tambroni? It would merely be his latest sleight of hand. Even struck down by sickness, aware that death was not far off, he plowed straight ahead, always upping the ante, as he had done all his life. Nonetheless, one has the impression that China had captivated him to an unprecedented extent, enough to make him lose his keen and dispassionate sense of reality. The arrogance he displayed with Macciocchi, proclaiming that "I've seen things that no one else has seen before," shows how far we are from the clear-sighted observer who could decipher the interwar Soviet Union with such subtlety. What happened to his ability to go beyond appearances? Of course, he had too little time before his hospitalization to discover the reality of China, and it would be unfair to reproach him for not having understood what was really happening in the country. But there is a considerable distance between this and perceiving nothing, absolutely nothing about the grotesque dictatorship that was preparing to sacrifice millions of human lives on the altar of the Great Leap Forward. His gratitude for the dedication of his saviors did the rest.

The dispatches from Malaparte's last trip, along with some other related texts and notes, were assembled anonymously and published by Vallecchi after the death of the writer, under the title *Io, in Russia e in Cina* (1958). One cannot escape a sensation of deep unease reading, in particular, the final passage, which he may have been inclined to omit from the book version:

> Those who have experienced China up close are better able than any others to calmly and objectively evaluate the sorrowful events occurring in Europe in recent months. I too suffered when reading the news from Budapest in the papers, but this suffering was never accompanied by doubt. The great and positive Chinese experience absolves any errors, because it is the manifest and undeniable proof that the sum of positive facts, in the movement of progress, is always greater than the sum of the errors. (RC, 343–44)

Malaparte had not had recourse to such doublespeak since Fascism and the war. With one difference: back then he certainly knew he was lying, but he considered himself obliged to do so. In China, it was not opportunism but egocentrism that made him confuse the care he received with the glories of the regime. Malaparte revealed himself to be suddenly incapable of *seeing*—the same man whose entire body of work, one could say, rested on a virtually unparalleled quality of observation. Was it a reflection of his illness? This seems so only in part: from his very first dispatches, the tone is the same, and there are painful concessions to the regime, such as his praise for the supposed freedom of religion granted to the Catholic minority. Likewise, his interview with Mao is as bleak a document as the more famous meeting, nine years later, between the Chinese dictator and Malraux. Malaparte claims to have been received in a private audience, on the leader's initiative. This is doubtful, but it hardly matters. Obviously, Mao told him how much he admired his books: "*Technique du coup d'État* has been my favorite book for the past twenty-five years." But wait, where have we heard this before? Mao promised him to release persecuted missionaries and to grant freedom of religion to the Chinese.[185] Is that all? And was Malaparte really so ingenuous? Did he honestly share the abysmal degree of ignorance and infatuation of the Western "Maoists"? Here he rattles off a string of sycophantic compliments, worthy of the dreariest totalitarian hagiography:

> I was fascinated by his gaze, which is firm, serene, sweet, profoundly good. All foreign visitors agree on the outlines of a portrait of him in which firmness is complemented by goodness. If his prodigious life as a man of action, as a revolutionary, is the mirror of his courage, of his spirit of sacrifice, of his iron will, his face is the mirror of his good, generous soul. One shudders to think what the Chinese Revolution might have been if at its head there had been a fanatic, a butcher, a lucid, abstract, pitiless theorist. But what amazes and moves all the Chinese Revolution's foreign observers is its lack of factionalism and fanaticism, it spirit of conciliation, its profound sense of equilibrium and humanity. (RC, 121–22)

End of citation, and let us out of pity forget the rest. What happened to the great portraitist of Lenin, Mussolini, and the Governor-General Frank?

Malaparte's stay in Peking's central hospital lasted roughly a month, until early March 1957, when the Chinese authorities finally decided to allow his repatriation. A new, equally exhausting flight, in a specially equipped Soviet plane, took off for Rome, via Prague and Milan. Was it really, as he led people to believe, the private turbojet of Khrushchev and Marshal Bulganin, which had just dropped them off for an official visit to India, at the time the only Soviet plane that was perfectly pressurized? Unfortunately, I was unable to conduct research in the archives of the air ministry of the former Soviet Union;

but anyway, if it serves the legend of Malaparte...[186] A poignant photo of his arrival at Rome's Ciampino Airport on March 11 shows him on Angiolillo's arm, surrounded by a crowd of admirers, his face covered by a gauze mask, but still impeccable in a double-breasted raincoat with a fur collar. He had had the time to carefully prepare himself for the final act. One correspondent wrote, entranced: "Here we have a writer welcomed like a stadium hero."[187] And he still takes center stage as he bids farewell to his readers in the last Battibecco:

> It was a crowd almost entirely unknown to me. But it was a crowd of friends, and in that cry—Malaparte! Malaparte!—I heard the echo of those distant voices that, in my hospital rooms in Chungking, Hankow, and Peking, would whisper in my ear: Get better, Malaparte. Come back to us soon. Take heart.[188]

"To My Dear and Most Devoted Friend...Gianni Schicchi!"

How do Italian writers die? Well, in general. In the manner that corresponds to them best, in any case. Luigi Pirandello passed away on December 10, 1936, at 8:55 a.m., as he worked on the third act of the most revolutionary of his theatrical allegories, *The Mountain Giants*, so revolutionary it is still not understood today (assuming the author himself ever understood it). Averse to the unexpected and detesting all improvisation, he left meticulous instructions. He refused a religious funeral and the tribute of a nation and asked that his anonymous remains, naked under a shroud of coarse cloth, without candles or a procession or music, be taken away at dawn by the cart that collects the corpses of the poor. He did not, however, succeed in getting his ashes scattered to the winds of Sicily. They would instead be buried at the foot of a solitary pine on his property, in the district of Agrigento fittingly called Chaos.[189]

Gabriele D'Annunzio was struck down by a cerebral hemorrhage on March 1, 1938, at eight o'clock in the evening, in the Vittoriale degli Italiani. Wearing the uniform of an honorary brigadier general of the air force, at his feet an urn containing earth from Fiume mixed with ashes from that "martyr city," he received the legionnaires' tributes in the wing known as Schifamondo, after the disgust for the world he felt so strongly when far from the Muses, especially scantily clad ones, and so be it if at the end of his life they were mercenaries or poor girls from the countryside, to whom he ascribed Greek names and divine attributes. The state funeral was celebrated two days later. In the official photographs, behind Il Duce—barely managing to conceal his relief at finally being liberated from that cumbersome partner—one could recognize D'Annunzio himself in a double-breasted suit, following his casket. It was his oldest son, Mario, who had the misfortune of being the spitting image of the father who had always tormented him.

Filippo Tommaso Marinetti died of a heart attack at the Hotel Excelsior in Bellagio, on Lake Como, on December 2, 1944. He had just finished his last composition, *Quarto d'ora di poesia della X Mas* (Quarter-hour of poetry of the 10th MAS), an ode to the Italian soldiers engaged on the eastern front against Tito's partisans. His death ensured he would not be assassinated by the Resistance or subjected to a humiliating trial following Liberation. The funeral ceremony took place on December 5, in Milan's Piazza San Sepolcro, where the Fascist movement had been officially born, twenty-five years earlier. It was the farewell of the last true believers, before a

Mussolini stiffly at attention, in a uniform that was too big, wan and corpse-like himself.

Cesare Pavese swallowed sixteen sleeping pills in his room at the Hotel Roma in Turin, at dawn on August 27, 1950. The success of *The Beautiful Summer* served only to reinforce in him the idea that it would be his last book and his last summer. He returned to die in that city that resembled him: gloomy, taciturn, and distant, crushed by the heat. The staff respected his instructions, kept journalists and the curious away so he would not be disturbed. Beside his twin bed—narrow, uncomfortable, also resembling him—would be found a scribbled note, in which he asked that there be no gossip around his death. Which is usually the best way to provoke it.

Pier Paolo Pasolini announced at nineteen that he wanted to be pierced, crucified for love. He would continue this search throughout his life, which was an interminable eulogy for a "best of youth" that was never truly his. He would meet his exterminating angel—or were there more than one? Does it matter in the end?—in a sordid corner of Ostia beach. This noble, torn, often unjust man left a body of work that is inexhaustible and repetitive, as insistent as his appetite for death. The Western intelligentsia, having come to know of his disappearance, did not disappoint. They screamed of conspiracy and political assassination, declared themselves a committee of inquiry, wielded incendiary formulas (being unable to wield the ax) against the bourgeois society that had killed him. Pasolini was dead. The ridiculous, on the other hand, does not kill.

Malaparte is not out of place in this gallery. He spent the first few days after his return from China in Angiolillo's villa, where an infirmary had been set up to dispense primary care. But it was only a reprieve before his transfer to the Sanatrix clinic, where he would occupy room 32, which quickly became legendary. He immediately established two conditions: to be the sole demiurge of his end and to have a scribe at his disposal capable of giving an hour-by-hour account, receiving his confidences. A paradox? We know his repugnance at physical decay, at terminal illness, which had kept him from visiting his dying brother Sandro, his friend Filippo de Pisis, or his unconscious lover Jane. He might as well transform his agony into a last demonstration of his courage, bravura, and strength: values of an entire life, to which he chose to pay tribute till the last. Moreover, he had already described his end:

> "Cancer of the stomach," murmured the doctor. "Nothing to be done." And that "nothing to be done" sounded in Paolo's ears like a lethal diagnosis of himself, of his condition, of his entire life.... Already, the summer was warming the leaves of that white tree softly rustling in his breast. ("Giugno malato," in S, 170–76; RI, 233–37)

A sado-voyeuristic spectacle of 120 days and 120 nights would unfold around him. No one wanted to miss the occasion, one personality drew out another, and all the political, cultural, and social *nomenklatura* duly filed in, as if everyone were sure that Malaparte —who still had good periods, as do many sick people—was doomed, and they had to take away a souvenir: a look, a nod, a quip. One went to visit Malaparte for a coffee break or at happy hour, before lunch or dinner, before heading out to the movies or a cocktail party, before heading to the newspaper office or the radio station. And he gladly participated in this ceremony, as long as his strength held out. The clinic staff, entirely devoted to him, could not refuse him anything; the crowds of visitors exhausted him, to the great exasperation of clinicians and family members. But some of those who did not go, out of discretion or owing to an impediment, came to regret it. Here is Beatrice Monti von Rezzori again: "I don't know why, maybe I was abroad at the time. Then I was obviously sorry about it. Later I spent a few days at a friend's in Rome, in an apartment on Via Gregoriana, and something struck me. There was a strangely familiar atmosphere, I couldn't figure out why, and then suddenly I knew. It was the same apartment where he had lived in the thirties, in the period of *Prospettive*, which he had kept until his death."[190]

Every day the mail brought a voluminous correspondence, containing every sort of advice for a miraculous recovery, and obviously poems, stories, and the like, which the dying man was asked to kindly read and above all to get published. But there were also best wishes from ex-soldiers and ex-Garibaldians—one of whom sent him his war cross—and prisoners and retirees. Two girls, Albertina and Silvia, wrote to him almost every day from boarding school. Malaparte responded, or had others respond, until his strength ran out, as if this were the mail from readers of Battibecco. Among the messages was one from the mayor of Capri, on behalf of city authorities and the population: Malaparte had finally reconciled with "his" island, even if God only knows what new controversies would have arisen had he survived. His French friends did not forget him. The Halévys wrote (it was Marianne who physically did so, because Daniel had lost his sight) that they hoped to see him again soon. Laudenbach did the same. Cendrars said he was sure "the sickness can be beaten, I've just come through it."[191] The doctor Camus, Céline's friend, who tried but failed to see him one day, when the patient was too ill to receive him, expressed his belief that "you will emerge victorious from this new fight. You are accustomed to winning."¹⁹² But Malaparte confided to the journalist Jean Neuvecelle that "my body is a battlefield."¹⁹³

Great luminaries took turns at his bedside and debated which course of treatment to follow. But there was no hope. The diagnosis by the doctors in Hankow, with their rudimentary equipment, had been right. Malaparte would continue to invoke his love for China and the Chinese until the very end. The journalist Igor Man later recounted how, during his visit to room 32, Malaparte had asked him, "Do you know how you say *death* in Chinese? You say it with a sudden sound, a gentle, spontaneous whisper. *Death*, in Chinese, has the same sound as the number four [*quattro*]. This: ssss. It's the sign of the four extremities, the four seas."¹⁹⁴ The cancer, aggravated by the gas lesions from the Great War, ate away at his lungs. Only his dogs, to his greater dismay, were not allowed in to keep him company. From the "Stromboli greyhounds," Febo I and II, he had moved on, as we know, to dachshunds. Pucci had passed away in the lap of Biancamaria Fabbri, when Malaparte was traveling in Chile; of Pucci's son, Cecco, we know nothing; Zita, which Malaparte had presented to Biancamaria, would die of a sudden ulcer in Milan, a few hours after him.¹⁹⁵ Not even Curzio, his last canine friend and namesake, would be able to join him in the clinic. The door to room 32 was now guarded day and night by a police officer, on the order of the minister of the interior, Tambroni, whose career would be scuttled three years later, when he was forced to resign as prime minister over having accepted the votes of a neo-Fascist party. For the moment, though, he seemed like the new man of Italian politics, and Malaparte liked him.

But he continued to search stubbornly for the "scribe" to whom he could dictate his truth for posterity. After casting aside some more well-known names, he chose a journalist from the Roman paper *Il Tempo*, Franco Vegliani, who thus became his first, and for a long time only, biographer. They hardly knew each other, but Malaparte had sensed in the young man a candor and quality of attention, devoid of prejudices or servility, that pleased him.[196] The choice could not have turned out better. Vegliani, born in Trieste in 1915, marked by war and deportation, would become a fine writer of little success, rediscovered after his death thanks to the efforts of Giorgio Bassani and Claudio Magris.[197] This representative of another generation and another environment was not closely involved in the most controversial episodes of the Malapartian epic. The result was a lovely four-handed book, in which the younger man seeks to free himself from the cumbersome tutelage of the older. One place Vegliani did not exaggerate was in his descriptions of Malaparte's courage at the end. His Neapolitan friend Guglielmo Peirce confirmed it a year after the writer's disappearance, adding a hint of arsenic:

> Malaparte already seemed like a skeleton under the covers. His hair, once black and shiny, had become gray and at the temples even white. The same Malaparte who was always so neat, clean, and coiffed now had unkempt hair, straight and raised at the back of his head, and was unshaven. A grimace of pain altered his face. He complained constantly and from moment to moment would change his position in bed like someone who cannot find rest: he lifted off the covers, pulled them to him, cast them off again. He stretched out and bent his legs.... He had an outburst of old affection. He said: "Ah, if instead of [going] to China, I had gone to your place in Posillipo, none of this would have happened to me!" He asked to get up and

go sit in the armchair beside the bed. He was wounded in his pride.... Wheezing, he had an overcoat thrown over his shoulders, put a pair of slippers on his (white, skeletal) feet, and lowered himself into the armchair, moaning with pain. And then came something unexpected. He began, in an increasingly high voice, to utter strange phrases: "Do you understand? Tell him! He has to die first, and then me!" Then suddenly he said the name: Montanelli. It was really embarrassing; I would have liked to sink into the ground. Malaparte, making that absurd, mad, wicked curse, looked terrible, frightening, almost like a madman.[198]

He trotted out the same joke of questionable taste to anyone who assured him he would pull through: "No, I will die... but half an hour after you!" Perhaps it was a form of peasant exorcism. In any event, Vegliani's access to his last days was not exclusive. A week before he died, Malaparte dictated his final message to *Paris Match*. And here, as in the interview he gave after Jane's suicide, his shamelessness reached the height of grandiosity. Had he not perhaps said to Guérin, "The modern world is ashamed of death. And therein lies our damnation"?[199] And so Narcissus gazed one last time into the pool, in search of his own image:

> In his disease-ridden body, the hands alone had preserved a certain vitality, a form of exuberance, even. Bony, translucent, they traced arabesques over immaculate sheets. When someone pays him a visit, Malaparte is vain enough not to appear cut off from the world. He likes to talk about the fashionable restaurants in Rome. He describes them as if he had gone the day before. He discusses the menus. Then suddenly his voice goes hoarse, his face darkens. And gravely, weigh-

ing every word, as if he wished to address everyone alive, he says: "One thing I'm sure of, one thing my agony has taught me, is that in death there are two of us. Two to die. To die one beside the other."

This perfect double, this reflection in the water, is none other than his final incarnation: the corpse "like me," the only one yet to be accounted for. At his request, the journalist added the following all-caps postscript:

> THE DOCTORS HAVE SO MANY PATIENTS;
> I HAVE ONLY ONE: MYSELF, MALAPARTE.[200]

The moment had come for the great chameleon to decide on a final profession of faith. Was he ready to do it for real? Aside from the extreme Right and the Gobettian and actionist radicals, all parties wanted to elicit an adherence from him that would not be susceptible to a repudiation from beyond the grave. Even the marquess Falcone Lucifero, minister of the royal house, brought him a message of good wishes from the ex-king Umberto II, in exile in Portugal, that touched him. But he continued not to forgive the republicans for his crushing defeat in Prato.[201] Nevertheless, when the party sent him an honorary membership card, he responded with an emotional letter in which, behind a hint of repentance for his conduct during the Fascist period, he expressed the true meaning of his libertarian ideology:

> I received the PRI membership card as a symbolic act reaffirming my old faithfulness to Mazzinian ideals and renewing that brotherly bond between me and you that nothing has yet broken nor could ever in the future break. I have already clarified the reasons for which

some time ago I decided not to join any party. If it were not the PRI, I would surely have rejected the card. But since it's the PRI, of which I was a member for all the years of my youth, and since it's you, dear friends, with whom I shared the anxieties and hopes of our generation, I have accepted the card as a symbolic gift that, while leaving my political freedom of action intact, creates an ideal bridge between my maturity and my boyhood, between our Italy of yesterday and our Italy of today and tomorrow. My sickness, this cruel sickness, prevents me from being with you, from telling you aloud what I am trying to express in this letter: when and if my recovery comes, my first embrace will be for you, in my beloved Prato, among those I count as my dearest friends in the world.[202]

But the real battle at his bedside was fought between the two major formations of the Italian political scene. The Christian Democrats and the Communist Party mobilized their respective leaders, Fanfani and Togliatti, to lay siege to room 32. As one contemporary account described it:

For the past two months, a secret battle between the reds and the whites has raged. Togliatti's visits are followed by Fanfani's, Lajolo's visits bring Father Rotondi's in their wake, Secchia's visits are preceded by Tambroni's. Every day the two armies are enriched by new and more important personages. And the few true friends, those who do not ask to enter room 32, follow from without the dramatic phases of the patient's last human adventure. If the "white" faction leans on the naked terror of the unknown (the terror provoked by a famous priest who will one day reveal to him the gravity of his sickness), the "red" faction bets on more concrete elements: the trip to China made at their party's expense, the villa to be left to the artists of Mao Zedong, and a certain statement of defense that, in 1946, at a time when Togliatti and "32" were adversaries, was at the center of a polemic in the press.[203]

These two dominant figures of the Italian political landscape never acted without calculation. Fanfani, a fervent, flexible, and astute Catholic, was another "cursed Tuscan," from Arezzo. He was personally fond of Malaparte but, most of all, he did not want to leave the impecunious dying writer at the mercy of the Communists. Thus Malaparte received a prize from the Presidency of the Council of Ministers worth the sum, substantial for the time, of 1.5 million lire. But day after day the expenses unrelentingly rose: "Curzio's agony was heartbreaking," noted an old friend from Berlin, the journalist and diplomat Cristiano Ridomi. "He didn't have the money to pay for his stay. He struggled because he couldn't transform his death, too, into a splendid adventure, as he had in every phase of his existence."[204] In the end it would be Angiolillo who paid the clinic bill (and never spoke of it).[205]

Togliatti, for his part, had entered the final season of his long political career, preparing to distance himself, cautiously, from Soviet totalitarianism, in his "Yalta Testament" (1964). As a man well aware of the value of confessions, sincere or extorted, he had carefully preserved, in his safe, Malaparte's 1944 "autobiography," along with the request to join the party that the writer had submitted to him in exchange for his political rehabilitation. He still planned on pulling it out at the right time. He sent him a first letter to test the waters; then, on April 12, took action. Malaparte received a PCI membership card personally signed by Togliatti, accompanied by a message expressing "deep fraternity, affection, and admiration," truly unusual language for the cold and composed leader.[206] And yet Malaparte did not react: he did not offer thanks or even confirm receipt. In his response to his republican friends he had pledged to refuse any other party affiliation. But the motive, or calculation, was probably another. Indeed, rumors flew of his imminent religious conversion: a spectacular gesture, especially at a historical juncture in which the Communist leader was still officially under excommunication.

The Vatican hierarchy did not regard Malaparte as being on par with a Bolshevik atheist, but he was still, officially, a Protestant. Only a few years earlier he had claimed as much in a letter to an influential American pastor:

> I am Protestant (Lutheran) as you may know, and I have never failed, in all my literary works, to express very clearly my aversion to Papism and clericalism, and to their influence on civic life in Italy.[207]

No need to emphasize the instrumental character of such declarations, made to appease audiences across the Atlantic. In any event, while all his brothers and sisters had become Catholics long before, Malaparte had never taken the plunge. Had the time come for him as well? His old friend Lino Pellegrini, who recalled an openly anticlerical Malaparte in Ukraine, was surprised to find him surrounded by devotional images:

> He lay beside an image of the Madonna, and there were other sacred images as well. He said, "I have a tubercular tumor, feel here..." He took my hand and placed it on his chest, where there rose a ball of cancer big as an orange: "See what I'm reduced to..." He pushed

aside the covers, rolled up his pajama pants, showed me his legs, skeletal, covered with cancer nodules.... When I said, to give him courage, "I saw the photos of your arrival at Ciampino. You stood upright on your own; that means you'll get through this," he replied: "It was Jesus who kept me on my feet."[208]

He would have liked to talk about the matter directly with the pope, but that was expecting a bit much, even for someone like him. However, Pius XII did design to receive the writer's sister Maria, accepting from her hands a small Chinese doll, given to Malaparte by pupils of the Hankow sisters, and sending in return his apostolic blessing. According to his other sister, Edda, Malaparte expressed his intention then to write a book about Christ, if he left the clinic alive.[209] The idea was not half bad: *The Story of Christ* (1921), fruit of his erstwhile friend Papini's conversion, had enjoyed worldwide success, after all. The first religious man who knocked on his door (or perhaps entered without knocking) was an imposing Belgian Dominican and Passionist, Father Félix Morlion, who told him without mincing words: "Think of repenting and atoning—there is still time!" After which, a tearful Malaparte would beg his brother Ezio to send the undiplomatic holy man away. The pope himself, upon learning of the manner of this approach, evidently murmured, shaking his head: "Malaparte is not a man to be taken with fear. He's a soul to be saved!"[210] The pontiff, who had a memory like a steel trap, had probably not forgotten the open letter that Malaparte had sent him after *The Skin* was placed on the Index, in which the writer proclaimed himself a Christian of no denomination.

It was then that two prominent confessors, both Jesuits (Malaparte's preferred order since his time at the Collegio Cicognini), prepared separately to spring into action, not without a touch of pastoral rivalry. Father Felice Maria Cappello was an eminent canonist of the Gregorian University, who confessed a long procession of worshippers every Sunday in the magnificent Church of Saint Ignatius of Loyola and also performed chaplain duties at the Sanatrix clinic. He was said to be close to His Holiness, possibly even his secret confessor. Father Virginio Rotondi was the young, suave, and enterprising protégé of another well-known Jesuit, Father Riccardo Lombardi, the latter nicknamed "God's microphone" for his eloquence on the radio (he is credited, in particular, with one of the most effective slogans of the 1948 election: "In the privacy of the voting booth God can see you, Stalin cannot!"). Father Cappello never spoke publicly about Malaparte's conversion,* whereas Father Rotondi talked extensively to a journalist about his long mission as a savior of souls, among them those of a former prime minister and of Renato Guttuso, the PCI's official painter, not to mention the spiritual comfort given to Pasolini, Anna Magnani, Sophia Loren, and other figures from the worlds of art and entertainment.[211] His intervention was evidently requested directly by Angiolillo, because "Malaparte couldn't be left to die in the hands of the Communists."

Was the owner of *Il Tempo* acting in league with Fanfani and Tambroni? Very likely so.† Thanks to Angiolillo, Father Rotondi had access to a room next to the writer's, from where he could monitor the comings and goings of visitors, practically without leaving

---

*However, he confided to his biographer that Malaparte was lucid and conscious at the moment of his conversion; see Domenico Mondrone, SJ, *Padre Cappello* (Rome: Edizioni Pro Sanctitate, 1972).

†Gianni Letta also told me that, in 1973, he brought Father Rotondi to the bedside of the dying Angiolillo, at the latter's request.

his bedside. Malaparte, who had allegedly already been secretly baptized by Father Cappello on June 8, the eve of his fifty-ninth birthday, also allegedly called Father Rotondi a month later, on Sunday, July 7, to make a new act of contrition to repent of all his acts against the Church. On this occasion he would have repudiated the publication of *The Skin*, accepting the Holy Office's condemnation.[212] If that was the case, no trace of such a resolution remains: *The Skin* continued to be, along with *Kaputt*, the author's most translated and sold book. After which Father Rotondi gave him communion and confirmed him, a duty generally reserved for bishops, thanks to a personal dispensation from the pope. Not long after, at an unspecified date, Malaparte, with his last ounce of strength, allegedly tore up his brand-new PCI membership card in front of him.* Why, then, was this card rediscovered thirty years later in the family archives by Guerri, according to whom Malaparte must have hidden it under his mattress, later handing it over to his brother Ezio, to avoid it being removed by... some well-intentioned person?[213] Rulli and Borelli, who took turns tending the door to room 32, had to intervene at least once to keep the Jesuit away, when their friend was too tired to receive him.[214] One may well wonder if Father Rotondi's imagination did not at times rival Malaparte's own. He described, for example, how during a visit to room 32 he encountered Pietro Secchia, a Stalinist hard-liner and avowed adversary of Togliatti.

---

*Malaparte also received the visit of the bishop of Prato, Pietro Fiordelli, with whom he had had some frank exchanges of views in the past, and who would officiate his funeral in Prato Cathedral. In the testimony published in the *L'ultimo viaggio di Malaparte*, Msgr. Fiordelli offered a slightly different version of events, in which the writer received the baptism, communion, and confirmation from Father Cappello, assisted by Father Rotondi.

FROM PARIS TO MAO (1947–1957)

They then had a private talk in a window recess, at the end of which a repentant Secchia burst into tears. Why, then, did he continue to embody, with undeniable consistency, the uncompromising anticlerical revolutionary soul of the PCI until his death in 1973?

This conversion, clearly, comes shrouded in a halo of Malapartian ambiguity. In any case, the writer did not give the majority of his visitors the impression of having attained the inner peace that prepares every good Christian to confront eternal life. Throughout the last phase he was greatly weakened, and Father Rotondi, no doubt out of missionary zeal, tended to show up when the other man was faring worse. The duel of room 32 was Malaparte's final masterpiece: as always, for him the real pleasure lay in the seduction and the surprise much more than in the result. Even so, in it we also find a last touch of his Tuscan realism. Let us take a step back: in Florence in 1954, in his frenzy to multiply his own activities, Malaparte had staged a memorable version of *La fanciulla del West*, directed by Dimitri Mitropoulos, with sets designed by Ardengo Soffici and featuring Eleanor Steber and Mario Del Monaco. Aficionados are well acquainted with the live recording of this performance, which for the first time restored Puccini's unpopular American opera to its rightful place as an uneven but first-rate work. Critics and eyewitnesses agreed that Malaparte, despite his lack of musical taste, knew how to expertly guide the action onstage.* The success of the evening led him to come up with other projects, all of them unrealized: Wagner's *Götterdämmerung*, Mussorgsky's *Boris Godunov*, and Gershwin's *An American in Paris*, which if nothing else shows the eclecticism of his tastes.[215]

---

*Something he did not fail to underline himself, with legitimate satisfaction, in the Battibecco installment devoted to Mitropoulos (BA, 196–98).

And yet it was another Puccini title that Malaparte's last act irresistibly brings to mind: *Gianni Schicchi*, a work that can be likened to Verdi's *Falstaff* and Strauss's *Rosenkavalier*, a great composer's ironic farewell to the passions of this earth, based on canto XXX of Dante's *Inferno*. We are in early fourteenth-century Florence. Relatives of a rich, recently deceased merchant, Buoso Donati, prepare to divide up his assets, each trying to make sure that no one else receives the biggest share. At the reading of the will, however, they discover that he has left all his property to the monks of a nearby monastery ("Who would have ever thought / When Buoso his last journey would be taking / We would be crying and sobbing without faking!").[216] They then turn to Gianni Schicchi, a "new man" they disdain but who is well known for his imagination and audacity. Schicchi, after stalling a bit, quickly devises a plan: he will take Buoso's place in bed, play the part of the dying man, and dictate a new will and testament to a hastily summoned notary. Everything comes off as planned, but at the moment of modifying his will, the false Buoso declares to the notary that he intends to leave everything he has to "his dear, devoted friend... Gianni Schicchi!" The parents, enraged and confused, cannot react, out of fear of being denounced as accomplices. Gianni Schicchi can finally offer his daughter a large dowry, allowing her to marry the young man she loves. This extremely Malapartian story, in Puccini's splendid score, manages to interweave the glorification of the common people's strength with the horror of bourgeois cowardice and a taste for bitter yet smiling—and, in its own way, noble—mockery. Any resemblance to what happened around the occupant of room 32 is purely intentional.

Last days of lucidity, last visits allowed, last sallies: the dying Malaparte was always Malaparte. Onofrio Solari Bozzi was struck by "his diaphanous arms and hands, so different from the ones that held the saber," but also by how "his deep black eyes lit up" when he learned that his erstwhile fencing partner had held on to the swords and masks.[217] To Giorgio Napolitano, entering the room, he exclaimed: "What an impression Togliatti made on me! He looks like an old sage."[218] And finally, Lino Pellegrini:

> I was on my way to the Belgian Congo for one of my reporting trips. The plane, having departed from Milan, made a layover in Rome, and I took advantage of it to go see him in the clinic. I had been warned that he wasn't doing well, and indeed I found him gray in the face, just skin and bones, eaten away by the cancer. He was suffering, and I didn't know how to lift his spirits. "It's here," he told me, touching his chest, "it's here inside, from the other war." The telephone rang, and it was Angiolillo, from *Il Tempo*: "I'm here with Pellegrini. He's come all the way from the Congo just to see me!"[219]

The final phase of his death throes was particularly painful, in the sweltering dog days of the Roman summer. Morphine and oxygen no longer gave him any relief. He suffered as never before. Consumed as he was from the inside out, his face nonetheless remained of marble, spared destruction by the sickness. Semiconscious, he invoked not his mother, as many dying men do, but his brother Sandro: the eldest, the favorite, the most handsome, dead for six years now, also from lung cancer. Early in the afternoon of July 19, having regained consciousness, he ordered Maria to go buy a sheet of bond paper, the kind used for official documents. She had to write that "Curzio Malaparte is not dead!" and he would have duly signed it. But he did not have time to perform this final conjurer's trick.

"TO MY DEAR AND MOST DEVOTED FRIEND"

The curtain dropped a bit before four o'clock p.m. The whole family had already gathered: his two sisters, Maria and Edda; his other brother, Ezio; and Claudia, Sandro's widow; along with the scribe Vegliani. Now his close friends hastened to him: Rulli, Borelli, Mazzetti, Angiolillo. Father Rotondi, who had been outside the clinic on another urgent call, returned just in time to take his hand and collect his act of faith, which incidentally he was the only one to hear. One last cry, and Malaparte collapsed on his pillow.

Photographers and the curious thronged the waiting room. Togliatti, always well informed, beat Fanfani to the room by a hair. But Sister Carmelita was on guard. Providence had done things properly, because she too was a cursed Tuscan, from near Prato no less, the last in a series of devoted and generally mistreated attendants. She had taken care of him for the preceding four months, skipping meals, and it is with her that he had his last *battibecchi*, squabbling to the very end: "Malaparte, you must rest... No, I don't want to... Malaparte, you're acting like an idiot... And you, you're a witch!" and so on. Utterly devoted, she barred the way to everyone. Malaparte had never tolerated, for his entire life, anyone watching him dress: the man was public; the bare body, private.[220] Father Rotondi ran to triumphantly announce to the radio the miraculous conversion, news that was promptly broadcast.[221] The church's position has not changed in the many decades since, according to the recent testimony of a fellow priest:

> Father Rotondi spoke to me several times about the action he had undertaken with great patience and great tenacity, together with Father Cappello and the sisters of the Sanatrix clinic, to bring about the conversion. Initially Malaparte had some mistrust, and let's not

forget that he was literally surrounded by emissaries from the Communist Party. Then things gradually improved. Some years ago, I listened to a cassette on which Father Rotondi had recorded some of his dialogues in the clinic with the writer on spiritual themes. Malaparte's voice was very clear, even if already weak; there were no doubts about the strength of his approach to the faith. The matter of the tearing up of the membership card? I wouldn't give any importance to such things. Of course, in those years, communism was the church's most dangerous enemy. But everyone knows that Malaparte, even weakened by the sickness, remained lucid until the end. He knew perfectly well what he was doing. What's important is that he died as a Christian, in the arms of a priest.[222]

The Communists were greatly embarrassed: they began immediately to talk about coercion of the will of a dying man. In the PCI's magazine, *Rinascita*, the unflappable Togliatti published Malaparte's 1944 "autobiography," accompanied by an article brimming with praise. The battle to claim the legacy of the recently deceased continued in Parliament, in the press, and in the streets, by means of documents, declarations, and revelations—and swiftly degenerated into farce. The international press saluted "the final dispatch from the deathbed of possibly the best-known and most notorious man of letters in the world."[223] Gianni Schicchi had foreseen it all. Friends and adversaries were confused, all equally fooled: here is his true legacy. Alone in not being fooled was posterity, which would preserve the image of him as a great writer and as a man, despite everything, who was superior to his legend. But even he could not imagine, perhaps, just how modern this image was, and how it would outlive him.

"TO MY DEAR AND MOST DEVOTED FRIEND"

On the occasion of the centenary of Malaparte's birth, in 1998, Italy dedicated a stamp to him that connected, with an insight rather rare in official commemorations, the beginning and the end of his saga. In the foreground is a portrait of the suffering face of the occupant of room 32; in the background appear the barbed wire, trenches, and bloody fray of the Great War. The synthesis is audacious but correct. He had begun his adult life in combat, and in eternal combat he finished it. Where he had done, and given, his best.

Conclusion
Capri, or The Bird That Swallowed Its Cage

THE CAST CHOSEN by Jean-Luc Godard for his 1963 film adaptation of Moravia's *Contempt* was surprising, even by his usual standards. Michel Piccoli and Brigitte Bardot, the couple in crisis, were joined by a B western villain, Jack Palance, in the role of the Hollywood producer, and, as his secretary, an Italian starlet, Giorgia Moll, known up to that point for television ads for toothpaste and corn ointment. And then, naturally, there was Fritz Lang playing Fritz Lang: the director of *Metropolis*, *M*, and fifty or so more films made on both sides of the Atlantic, of which many are masterpieces and none are forgettable. While I personally find much of the existentialist dialogue between Bardot and Piccoli painfully outdated (like Moravia's novel), Moll and Palance (who was allegedly always drunk during the filming) are superb. And when we see Lang direct a schlocky version of the *Odyssey* on the peeling rooftop terrace of Casa Come Me, or recite Dante and Hölderlin with all the resonances of Mitteleuropa, we feel ourselves suddenly transported to an elsewhere called, simply, art.*

---

*Today it is known that these scenes were shot by Lang himself. And you can tell.

CONCLUSION

"Today more than ever I feel like a bird that has swallowed its own cage...": Hölderlin himself would not have disavowed the metaphor coined by Malaparte in his preface to the second edition of *Fughe in prigione* to describe his state of mind when he conceived this "sad, hard, and severe" house in his image. Its origin doubtless lay in the shock of his arrest, when he was pulled from a hotel bed and thrown into a Regina Coeli cell; in choosing his own prison, he turned trauma into therapy. But his reflection expanded to the destiny that awaits man when he accepts the loss of his own inner freedom. Bruce Chatwin wrote that Casa Come Me "was intended to satisfy his 'melancholic yearning for space' and at the same time to reproduce, on his own grandiose terms, the conditions of his exile on Lipari."[1] Agreed—except for the melancholy, which Malaparte generally reserved for his (almost always awful) poetry. But Chatwin seems wrong when he goes on to talk about "Tiberius's refuge" and introduces the misleading notion of "self-love among the ruins." Once again, Malaparte is classed with the backward-looking aesthetes, with whom he shared very little. No, Narcissus did not come here in search of a last moment of happiness before the evening tide. It was not here that he wanted to take revenge for the banality of his origins or defend himself against the degrading march of progress. These walls do not give off bitterness or spleen; there is no more room here for the throes of decadence than for the awaiting of death. Everything is squared off, neat and clean, visible, without anything soft or uncertain; everything is uncomfortable, of a discomfort made to last. The man who conceived it was one who controlled body and mind; he found a place that resembles him, and no one can possess it in his place. Ten new owners might inhabit these walls and carve their names here: it will never become a "house like someone else."

CONCLUSION

There is no doubt it was conceived, realized, and furnished down to the smallest details according to Malaparte's wishes. Any advice, suggestions, or proposals he received in the course of the work were subordinated to this design. Hence his contentious relationship with the Rationalist architect Adalberto Libera, to whom many disciples and historians of architecture still attribute the building. What we know is that Malaparte treated building companies, foremen, and craftspeople the same way he did his translators, bombarding them with criticisms and observations, meddling in everything, wanting always to win the point and nearly always succeeding.[2] He put the house on the same level as his books, making it a genuine self-portrait in stone; and it is clear he could not share ownership with others. His difficulties with the Capri locals, the memory of which has been passed down to this day, were born of rumors about the privileges he must have enjoyed to buy the land and to build such an unusual home there. The reality is perhaps simpler, even if the interested party sought as usual to muddy the waters a bit.

In 1945, when the investigation into his alleged war profiteering was opened, Malaparte declared he had in January 1937 bought from two area farmers "a rocky, trackless, difficult-to-access piece of land, roughly two miles from any built-up area, in the locality of Matromania, for the price of eight thousand lire." He subsequently obtained, "without any political pressure from high or low," the required permits from the Capri building commission and the Naples fine arts commission. After some months, "I began the construction of my house, economizing, without the costly assistance of architects and engineers, with the collaboration only of the foreman Adolfo Amitrano of Capri." The price agreed on was 130,000 lire, paid over six years, which corresponded to the time necessary

CONCLUSION

for construction.³ To address this, he asked for an initial loan of nine thousand lire from the journalists' provident institution,⁴ and later another, for a hundred thousand lire, from the Banca Commerciale of Milan. During his travels, the work was followed by the inflexible Ms. Pellegrini, editorial assistant at *Prospettive*, who arranged regular payments to Amitrano and his subcontractors.⁵ Pellegrini was also the one, awaiting the return of Malaparte from the eastern front, to request and no doubt obtain a postponement of the petition for a review of the assessment of the land and the house, introduced in the Court of Naples by the journalists' provident institution, which in May 1941 was still owed 7,500 lire.⁶ Nothing seems to have come of it, probably owing to the war. But in January 1945, sensing the coming storm, Malaparte hastened to ask for a measure of clemency from the land registry of Sorrento, which reassessed the plot of land from fifteen to fifty thousand lire.⁷ He pointed to other sources of income he was able to draw on: dispatches from Ethiopia and Finland, author's royalties, benefits from his service as an officer, and a hundred-thousand-lire loan (likely the one from the Banca Commerciale), with Villa Hildebrand used as collateral for the total construction cost, which now came to three hundred thousand lire.⁸ The sum was considerable, more than double the original estimate; however, it was not beyond Malaparte's means, and everything seems to indicate he could have coped with the operation without appealing to Ciano or others for help.⁹ Consider in this regard the detailed testimony of the son of the ambassador Rulli:

> Starting in the early thirties, my parents owned a small apartment near the *piazzetta*, the main square of the town of Capri. I think they were the ones to introduce Capri to Malaparte, who wanted to

CONCLUSION

break away from Forte dei Marmi, after his relationship with Virginia Agnelli ended. My father was poised to acquire a plot of land in Anacapri, and I think it was Malaparte who found and fell in love with the land of Capo Massullo, close to the Natural Arch, proposing that he and my father buy it together. There was one big problem with the plot, however: the building permit. So it was available for very little money. My father told me they had already obtained the assent of the mayor of Capri, but they could not "expose" him too much. Another influential Neapolitan friend had a letter written that was "agreed on" by the [Monuments and Fine Arts] Department of Naples. In the building permit for our house, there is in fact cited a letter no. 5736 of December 1, 1938, from the Department of Medieval and Modern Art of Campania. The letter represented the keystone for overcoming all difficulties. The famous legends about how permission to build was obtained by figures like Ciano or Bottai were false, and actually put into circulation for a purpose. Malaparte purchased the plot that was then divided in two: Rulli (Pizzorulli) the upper part and Malaparte the lower part (the Roccione), with my father having the right to spit on the head of Malaparte—a fact my father would recount with great gusto, even in the former's presence. The two houses (ours and Malaparte's) were built by the Amitranos—a small Caprese company—composed of *mastro* Adolfo (the father) and Ciro and Ciccillo (the sons). Nardino (Ferdinando Verde) became the watchman of both houses. Our houses were connected by a long staircase, and in the summer we would use the access to the sea and the cove below Malaparte's house. Money and the costs of the Capri house were a problem common to them both. It's clear from their letters, too, that financial matters were a constant worry for Malaparte until the royalties for certain books began to

CONCLUSION

come in. My father explained that one of the reasons Malaparte had to ditch the architect and turn to the Amitranos as well was that they had proposed more reasonable solutions, both financially and technically. They made so many and such changes to Libera's design (with regard, especially, to the cistern and the channeling of water) as to make it almost a different design. It was a point my father insisted on a great deal.[10]

Born from his lone inspiration and built with his own strength, Casa Come Me was often referred to as "Casa Matta," in the sense not of a madhouse or of the architectural "follies" fashionable in the nineteenth century, but of a casemate (*casamatta*) or military bunker, a replica of those forts and shelters carved out of the rock or flush with the ground that proliferated across Europe in the Great War: their wretched occupants really did go mad, subjected helplessly to enemy fire. Therefore, it really cannot be called a "villa," as many publications and tourist guides still do. Its owner disdainfully rejected a term evoking rest and relaxation, pleasure grounds and retirement homes. It was nothing at all like Villa Hildebrand, since transformed into a hotel after a few changes in ownership.[11] In his later years, to get publicity or, more likely, out of a need for money, he thought about transforming the Forte house into a nightspot, with the then-obligatory Cuban or Brazilian band, restaurant, and dance floor paved in marble from the yacht of the former king Farouk of Egypt. He would talk for hours with his milk brother Jacques Baldi about the food menu and staff uniforms. Such depravity would have been inconceivable here on Capri, where time and space meet to the point of making man almost superfluous. "I believe there is no place like on this couch against the wall where you can

CONCLUSION

experience the vertigo of omnipotence: provided you stay here without moving and with the necessary humility, having before you, beyond the window glass, the spectacle of the sky, the rocks, and the sea, as if nothing else existed in the world," Alessia Rositani Suckert tells me. With her husband, Niccolò, she has fought for years and with all her might, which is fortunately considerable, to save this vessel from decay and abandonment, in the name of family pride and for the love of beauty. For many years, Casa Come Me remained under judicial receivership, effectively unsupervised, humiliated by neglect and vandalism. The house was sacked on several occasions, and from time to time stolen correspondence, manuscripts, and photographic albums show up, authentic or forged as the case may be, in antiquarian sales.

Does the house express a will to power, then? Let us say, rather, a will to strength, to return to the guiding idea of his existence. We climb to the celebrated roof terrace, sliced by a cement sail, to contemplate the horizon and take a few photos, being careful—especially me, here for the first time—to watch where we place our feet. There is no parapet; a misstep would be fatal and deprive readers of the pleasure, if indeed that is what it is, of reading this biography. Then we head back down. The time has come to enter the cockpit of the house, the immense living room, "something extraordinary, never before seen, fifty feet by twenty-six . . . I repeat, fifty by twenty-six!" he enthused to friends.[12] Indeed, its dimensions seem modeled on the Sala del Mappamondo in Palazzo Venezia in Rome, designed in 1466 for Cardinal Barbo, future pope Paul II, stripped a few centuries later of its furnishings by Mussolini, who left behind only a desk and two armchairs, for the rare visitors permitted to sit down in front of him. As we have abundantly seen, Malaparte would have liked to stride those cold marble floors more often than he was permitted by the distance imposed on him by the *padre padrone*. In the end he decided to create a substitute, brighter and less prisonlike than Il Duce's office but based on the same principle: a command post inspired by a monastic unsociability worthy of Le Corbusier. Not for nothing, the few pieces of furniture are well spaced out and seem bolted to the floor like on a ship. One is struck by the lack of a center. Mussolini and his German imitator Goebbels wanted to impress interlocutors and subjects, forcing them into a long walk across the room to meet the boss. Malaparte rarely received visitors and impressed primarily through subtraction. Here there is no desk and just two small couches, not even a chair, for which he must have harbored an aversion, because one can hardly be found in the entire house (with an exception that we will come to at the end) or the garden, though they may have disappeared in the meantime. One must sit on a couch, a counter, or a bed, all of them difficult or impossible to move. Or on the ground, then.

Design objects and the carpets brought back from Finland are no longer here. There is almost nothing on the walls, except for a few works of quality: the Dufy recognized from afar by Togliatti, the portrait by Campigli, and the bas-relief by Pericle Fazzini, which the artist considered his masterpiece, have all miraculously been saved; gone, on the other hand, are the collection of watercolors by Marie Laurencin, along with the paintings by Savinio (the presence of a Matisse has never been confirmed).[13] "It's a clear sign that the seating is uncomfortable, tables are rare, and mirrors are banished. It's not the dwelling of a voluptuary, a dilettante, an Ashurbanipal," observed his friend Guérin.[14] It is the least one could say. But it was not so rare in those times. Malaparte shared this dedication to discomfort with many in the generation of the trenches and the one that succeeded it, of those who turned twenty between the wars. A prominent place is given to the fireplace, indispensable for protecting against the cold and humidity, in winter and at times in spring and fall, because naturally the house was not heated. And winter was his favorite season to spend on the island. Photos of the time show a small collection of Abyssinian masks and vases, now also gone,[15] along with a fresco supposedly detached from the palace of Ras Imru. I now understand Alessia's words better. It was enough for him to hole up in a corner to feel lulled by the waves, especially when the sea was rough and the foam crests reached the roof and the lower floor had to be evacuated, something that can still happen today. And yet Malaparte did not have the instincts of a sailor: he never owned a boat and instead relied on a local fisherman for his rare outings. A good but not extraordinary swimmer, he would take a rapid dip in the sea, then dry off on his feet and be on his way. Besides, there was no place on these sharp rocks for sunbathing; no solarium, no lounge chairs, not even the space to lay a towel: nothing at all. But that nothing contains real incantatory force, a gathering of energy. It was thought up and systematized by a mind that brought together the cult of order, a rejection of history, metaphysical nakedness, and indifference to others. It is on these characteristics that Malaparte built not merely a house but an entire life. The depths or the heights, the sea or mountain peaks, the waves or glaciers represent, in this perspective, more or less the same thing, in the same way *Il sole è cieco* could be the diary of a naval expedition, and not of the war of the Alps.

The dining room, one floor down, is instead a replica of a Tyrolese

CONCLUSION

or Bavarian *Stube*, complete with a big ceramic stove, slightly incongruous in these Mediterranean surroundings. It can accommodate six, at the most eight, people, if they agree to squeeze in, corresponding to the number of guests the house can welcome. From the dining room, a narrow corridor leads to four monastic cells, spartanly furnished (a cot, a wardrobe, a nineteenth-century print or two), and two small bathrooms. An only slightly more comfortable room, at the top of the stairs, was reserved for his mother while she still lived.

Five of us sat down at the table in an ambience that could not have been more inviting. My fellow diners were two architects, the Finn Markku Komonen and the Mexican Maya Segarra Lagunes, and the pianist Minna Pöllänen, wife to Markku and former student of Wilhelm Kempff, whom she used to visit in his equally austere and sunny refuge in Positano: "He also had a Malapartian side: if in the middle of a Bach partita or a Beethoven sonata he forgot a phrase, he would invent it then and there, and no one would notice." A reliable Romanian couple, Lucian and Maria, look after the house, especially the spacious, well-equipped kitchen, resupplied with provisions arriving on the water taxi. Finally, there is Luna, a small, mischievous dog, still timid because of the poor treatment suffered before she ended up here, who cautiously accepts our pets and prefers to poke around in a corner of the garden, where Malaparte had erected a small canine cemetery. Had she sensed something? Animals have their reasons of which reason knows nothing.

For the past fifteen years, Alessia has organized summer architecture workshops here in partnership with the Catholic University of America, in Washington, DC.* Photos document the stays of

---

*This was the case as of June 2010, when my visit took place.

CONCLUSION

these young people, come from every corner of the world to discover the magic of the place and work there for a few weeks in an atmosphere of concentration and fun, between swims and field trips. The house is not hostile to visitors who respect it: it can become a source of inspiration for others without losing its soul. The misanthrope Malaparte would not have scorned this legacy. "You sense a desire here to return to the purity and simplicity of the island's traditional dwellings, contaminated by the eclecticism of the nineteenth century: something archaic and modern at the same time," observes Markku.[16] "His letters from Helsinki attest to the importance he attributed to the meeting of light and material," I say in my turn. "He was exhilarated by the immaculate white of Finnish nature; it reminded him of this sea. For him it was always a question of reintegrating man into the nature from which history has separated him."

Casa Come Me, from an architectural and above all an ideological point of view, has had to reckon with a cumbersome rival, its counterpoint in every way: the Vittoriale degli Italiani, on Lake Garda, a formerly German property adapted in the early 1920s by D'Annunzio and a young architect, Gian Carlo Maroni, and then constantly retouched, enlarged, renovated, and never completed, with a succession of other constructions and memorabilia in the park, including an amphitheater, a mausoleum, and the bow section of a military cruiser.[17] Be it a testament to the power of symbols or a simple coincidence, Malaparte began construction on the eve of the death of his loved and hated precursor, whom in his own way he imitated all his life. Light against shadow, the uncontaminated expanse of a living room supporting alone the entire structure of the place, against the medievalizing fugue of little rooms overloaded with gloomy bric-a-brac. Everything is haunted by *l'oscena vecchiezza*,

CONCLUSION

"obscene old age," for the man by the lake; everything is lament for the strength that wanes, the lifeblood that dries up, the body that yields, the brain that leaks fluid into a puddle where worms come to wade: all the images of magnificent decay, of vile splendor, that punctuate his last texts.

It is no surprise that Malaparte, like the Mussolini of Palazzo Venezia before him, sought to liberate himself from the inescapable model of D'Annunzio, to show that he was not looking back, but indeed toward the future. And yet it is possible to choose both; only for bigots are their visions incompatible. And so the Vittoriale and the anti-Vittoriale have confronted each other from the two ends of the peninsula for the better part of a century, like separated brothers greeting each other, standing on the other's ruins.

"Wenn bei Capri die rote Sonne im Meer versinkt," sings Lola, the eponymous protagonist, heartbreaking and tormented, of Fassbinder's 1981 film. This isn't Hölderlin or D'Annunzio, to be sure, but it gets the idea across. The sun reddening on the horizon is a staple of the papier-mâché Capri that Malaparte reviled. Fortunately, a scenic trail, less than two miles long but steep enough to deter the lazy, connects Punta Tragara to Punta del Massullo, between the Grotta Bianca and the Grotta Meravigliosa, which frame the house like two translucent wings, green-blue in the depths, flecked with gold and coral at the surface. When in full-on night we retrace the path by the feeble light of our mobile phones, after a hearty and well-lubricated dinner, I realize, stumbling repeatedly in the brambles, that the hike is better appreciated on an empty stomach. An anecdote still making the rounds features the amiable writer and bon

CONCLUSION

vivant Edwin Cerio, for many years the island's mayor: having learned that the owner of Casa Come Me had given a new name to Punta del Massullo, Punta Malaparte, he hailed him loudly one day in the main square: "Good day, Mr. Massullo!" And yet the nickname was not wrong, if taken in the sense of his allegiance to the place. Malaparte really wanted to be one with this land, with these rocks. If he chose to be buried elsewhere, it is perhaps because the blustering heights of Spazzavento offered an even more radically naked eternal resting place.

But how did he spend his time on Capri, in the course of regular annual stays every year from 1937 until his death, with a single, long interruption in the early 1950s, after the death of Jane Sweigard? Contrary to expectations, his name appears only infrequently in chronicles of the island's social and cultural heyday; and even when he is there, he cannot be seen. Malaparte, who offered so much of himself to the camera, was rarely photographed on Capri outside the protection offered by the rampart of Casa Come Me.* He would pass through in a hurry, or with studied indifference, the most celebrated and crowded places, like the *piazzetta*, followed by Febo or preceded by Pucci. When he sat at a café table or beneath the arbor of a (then) modest trattoria, he could be alone, or lead the conversation, depending on the circumstances, without completely revealing

---

*Inside he was more available, at least when he wanted to be. After a lecture in Paris, I was approached by two elderly ladies who, in a lovely gesture, presented me with a pair of photographs taken at Casa Come Me in the summer of 1948. The women were part of a group of French tourists who, unaware of who owned the house, had the temerity to ring the doorbell, charmed by the place's beauty. They were introduced by the housekeeper and warmly received by Malaparte, who had himself photographed with them, baring a shaved chest, dressed only in a pair of Tyrolean shorts, smiling and in fine form.

himself. The most famous image shows him naked to the waist, flanked by two young masons, a vaguely Pasolinian trio, which nonetheless, if one looks more closely, reveals a certain military bearing. He was still and always the leader at the head of the Garibaldians, the askaris, the *Alpini*, ensuring they dug the foundations of his house as one digs a trench. The isolation was probably not always of his choosing or to his taste, and at times must have weighed on him. It flattered his keen sense of superiority, but we need not exaggerate his hermit's vocation. He had thick skin, but the rejections, noninvitations, and society squabbles must have upset him, as they would anyone, sooner or later. If he had wanted to disappear for real, he could have gone and buried himself anywhere else and never resurfaced. Too easy. Malaparte was neither Salinger nor Howard Hughes. He wished to be heard and understood without appearing, to be conspicuously absent. This reverse form of exhibitionism requires steady nerves, discipline, and a good sense of timing. If he could not match the descendants of Tiberius, princes of Capri society, in terms of wealth, bloodline, or fame, he may as well subvert the rules of the game to his advantage. It was a risky wager, but one he ultimately won. The Krupps pass away, monarchs disappear into exile, femmes fatales succumb to Alzheimer's. Malaparte remains.

In none of his notebooks or letters have I found the merest hint of annoyance, boredom, disappointment, or impatience associated with his stays here. He was not upset by the monotony of long pre-television hours in the company of only an inkstand, a housekeeper, and a dog, without even the Bach and Mozart records that delighted T. E. Lawrence, returned from Arabia, in his hut on Pole Hill. On the contrary. Even for those who claim—incorrectly, in my humble

CONCLUSION

opinion—to be well acquainted with this man's existence, his typical day will remain a mystery. What was he up to, here as in Villa Hildebrand, in Rome, on the French Riviera, in the Black Forest, in the thousand hotel rooms of his life, once the last guest, the last woman left? His enormous capacity for work, at least in the good years, the hours dedicated to grooming and physical fitness, and his care of animals do not suffice to provide a plausible response, especially since he did not require much sleep. And so he took refuge in himself, to gnaw on his bone. His life was not long; but even counting all the adventures, real or imagined, that he claimed, one is struck by the gap between the concentrated character of these events (some months in Russia, Ethiopia, the Balkans, or in Finland; a couple of years on average for his love affairs) and everything he was able to draw from them. The secret, in large part, is shut up in these walls. And there it remains.

At the far end of the living room, a simple wooden door leads to a utility room, and immediately after that to two doors side by side. On the right, Malaparte's bedroom and bathroom; on the left, two similarly sized rooms, where I will spend the night, which had in their time hosted the writer's various female companions. These areas are more spacious than those on the ground floor, but just as austere. The sole luxury in Malaparte's room is a double bed, the only one in the house, which one nonetheless hesitates to call *conjugal*. He shared with the "divine" Gabriele and Il Duce an unpleasant macho taste for inflicting long waits on his current favorite, for leaving her hanging on a summons that came late, or not at all. Biancamaria Fabbri's account differs little, on this point, from the letters of D'Annunzio's last favorite, Luisa Baccara, or the diary of

CONCLUSION

Mussolini's lover Clara Petacci. I enter the bathroom adorned with green porphyry, take out my toothbrush and gaze around me, extend a toe to touch the chilly floor of the Pompeian-style shower-bath, set almost flush with the ground. Returning to the bedroom, I lie down and try to get comfortable, to immerse myself in the sensations that the vestals admitted to his presence must have experienced. I close my eyes: alas, nothing. The erotic echo of the place seems rather faint, and I blame the excellent dinner and my lack of sensitivity for the fact that I fall asleep like a log.

The next day, before I leave, Alessia shows me into Malaparte's study, which one enters from his bedroom. We find ourselves at the house's farthest point, a bit like the prow of a ship aimed at the open water. Low bookcases or drawers run along three of the four walls, like in Hemingway's Finca Vigía, in Havana. They contain the remnants of his library: a few hundred books and magazine issues, often bearing the customary inscriptions of colleagues; I recognize the signatures of some future bitter enemies. Many of the books are covered with marginal notes and underlinings, the paper yellowed, the spines broken: these are the treasures not of a bibliophile but of a reader who took books seriously. I fish out an essay in Cyrillic script on the October Revolution; a little further on, my eye is caught by a bloodred cover of a famous issue of *Prospettive*... Another stubborn legend—the last we will evoke here—has it that he wrote facing the wall, so as not to be distracted by the surrounding beauty. The truth is the opposite: there is a carve-out in the continuous surface of the furniture, directly below the window, revealing a lower level with space for a large notebook or portable typewriter, and before it the reassuring presence of a dear, solid old chair, where

CONCLUSION

he too must have sooner or later sat down to write, like anyone else. I hesitate, even if no one is watching; Alessia must have understood, for she has left me alone. And then, no, I do not sit down.

Punta del Massullo / Punta Malaparte
June 2010

Notes

ACKNOWLEDGMENTS AND A NOTE ON TEXTS AND SOURCES

1. *Malaparte*: vols. 1 (1905–26); 2 (1927–31); 3 (1932–36); 4 (1937–39); 5 (1940–41); 6 (1942–45); 7 (1946–47); 8 (1948–49); 9 (1950–51); 10 (1952–54); 11 (1955); 12 (1956–57). Citations to these volumes are made in the notes with the title *Malaparte* followed by the volume in question, a colon, and the relevant page or pages.
2. "He wrote his books and plays in French directly, without translators" (Biancamaria Fabbri, *Schiava di Malaparte* [Rome: Edicoop, 1980], 57). "He tells me he's writing, in French, his *Journal d'un étranger à Paris*" (Giovanni Ansaldo, *Anni freddi: Diari 1946–1950* [Bologna: Il Mulino, 2003], 322, entry of August 17, 1949).

INTRODUCTION

1. "Quaranta minuti alla televisione: Tiro incrociato su Malaparte," June 1953, in *Malaparte*, 10:368–70.
2. Letter to Roland Laudenbach dated January 5, 1948, in *Malaparte*, 8:14–15 (original in French).
3. Interview (with a Belgian publication?), October 1949, in *Malaparte*, 8:588.
4. Preface to Malaparte, *Les femmes aussi ont perdu la guerre*, trans. Daniel Halévy (Geneva-Paris: La Palatine, 1958), 7.

5. Giordano Bruno Guerri, *L'arcitaliano: Vita di Curzio Malaparte* (1980; Milan: Bompiani, 2008).
6. Quoted in the illustrated volume *Malaparte: Una proposta*, published by the "Amici di Capri" (Rome: De Luca, 1982), 34.
7. See, e.g., Raymond Guérin, *Du côté de chez Malaparte* (1950; Bordeaux: Finitude, 2003); Walter Murch, "Malaparte's 'Partisans, 1944,'" *Zoetrope: All-Story* 2, no. 3 (Fall 1998); Karl Lagerfeld, *Casa Malaparte* (Göttingen: Steidl, 1998); Bruce Chatwin, "Among the Ruins," in *Anatomy of Restlessness: Selected Writings 1969–1989*, ed. Jan Borm and Matthew Graves (New York: Penguin Books, 1997); Maike Albath, "Die Seele war nicht mehr zu retten," *Frankfurter Rundschau*, July 3, 2006, and "Der Politjonglier," *SWR2*, March 20, 2008; Dominique Fernandez, preface to *Kaputt*, by Curzio Malaparte, trans. Juliette Bertrand (Paris: Denoël, 2006); Bruno Tessarech, *Pour Malaparte* (Paris: Buchet-Chastel, 2007); Milan Kundera, "*The Skin*: Malaparte's Arch-Novel," in *Encounter*, trans. Linda Asher (New York: HarperCollins, 2010); Jean-Pierre Martin, *Éloge de l'apostat: Essai sur la vita nova* (Paris: Seuil, 2010), 35–36; Olivier Rolin, *Bric et broc* (Lagrasse: Verdier, 2011); Frédéric Beigbeder, *Premier bilan après l'Apocalypse* (Paris: Grasset, 2011). The *Encyclopedia Britannica*, usually well researched, passes over the confinement on Lipari, to claim that "during the 1940s Malaparte repudiated fascism and was expelled from the party" (*Encyclopedia Britannica Online*, July 15, 2022, s.v. "Curzio Malaparte," https://www.britannica.com/biography/Curzio-Malaparte).
8. GS, dated October 12, 1943, in *Malaparte*, 6:452.
9. Francis Ambrière, "Das Kapital au Théâtre de Paris," *Opéra*, February 2, 1949.
10. Max Favalelli, "Sur les bords de l'Arno, Max étudie avec Malaparte la technique du coup de ... fourchette" (1953), in *Malaparte*, 10:336. Coming out of the far-right press, Favalelli successfully reinvented himself in the postwar period as a food critic and crossword maker.
11. See the exhibitions *Malaparte fotografo: Un reporter dentro il ventre del mondo*, on the occasion of his centenary, Prato 1998, and *Malaparte: Arcitaliano nel mondo*, Fondazione Biblioteca di via Senato, Milan 2010.
12. Malaparte to Howard B. Bishop, April 15, 1947, in *Malaparte*, 7:558–59.
13. Testimony of Alessia Rositani Suckert, who recovered one such large bill.

14. Thomas Mann, *Death in Venice*, trans. David Luke (New York: Bantam Dell, 1988), 337. The barber says this to Gustav von Aschenbach, after having convinced him to wear makeup. But the next sentence—"Now the signore can fall in love as soon as he pleases"—is the opposite of what Malaparte desired, which was for everyone to fall in love with him. Malaparte's sister Edda wrote that, upon his return from World War II, his doctors gave him a yellowish powder for the protection of his face and the veins of his neck. His mother mixed in a little face powder, "otherwise he looked like a corpse" (see *Malaparte*, 6:634).

15. Thus, to judge by certain "testimonies," it seems that Malaparte could not see a terrace without being seized by the irresistible impulse to strip naked and sunbathe. But as Biancamaria Fabbri, who was well placed to know, points out: "I don't remember, in three years of living together, ever having seen him walk around naked; he was very reserved, both for himself and for others" (*Schiava di Malaparte*, 81).

16. Umberto Saba, "Ritratto di Malaparte," in Saba, *Epigrafe: Ultime prose* (Milan: Il Saggiatore, 1959), 101.

Chapter 1

1. Interview with Edda Ronchi Suckert, in *Malaparte*, 3:675.
2. Franco Vegliani, *Malaparte* (Milan: Guarnati, 1957), 46.
3. Herbert Van Leisen, "A Parigi con Malaparte," in *Malaparte*, 6:665.
4. Unpublished fragment, in *Malaparte*, 8:447–49 (my emphasis).
5. *A Sem Benelli di Curt [sic] Suckert, allievo tredicenne della IV ginnasio del Regio Collegio Cicognini* (Prato: Tipografia Succ. Vestri, n.d. [May 1912]).
6. Interview of Laura Ronchi Abbozzo by the author.
7. As kindly confirmed to the author by Pastors Jürg Kleemann and Christian Holz. But a great part of the archives of the community was destroyed during the war, then by the flood of Florence in 1966.
8. In the description of Biancamaria Fabbri, who met him late in his life. *Schiava di Malaparte*, 65.
9. Claim made in an interrogation conducted by American intelligence services in Florence, September 14, 1944, by the former editor of the *Corriere della Sera* during the Badoglio period, Bruno Fallaci (uncle to Oriana). Carbon copy, in Italian, with the initials "P.W.B.," D Secret,

found in the file labeled "Malaparte Curzio," in ACS, Min. Cult. Pop., Cabinet, 2nd deposit, folder 8 (henceforth "Fallaci interrogation"). We will have multiple occasions to return to this document, which, notwithstanding inaccuracies and its hostile tone, contains useful information.

10. Bruce Chatwin, "Self-Love among the Ruins," *Vanity Fair*, April 1984, 104; then as "Among the Ruins," in *Anatomy of Restlessness*, 163.
11. Oliver Matuschek, *Stefan Zweig: Drei Leben, eine Biographie* (Frankfurt: Fischer, 2006), 20–22. Translated by Allan Blunden as *Three Lives: A Biography of Stefan Zweig* (London: Pushkin Press, 2011).
12. Alain Sarrabayrouse, "Le terroir et le sang," introduction to Malaparte, *Sang et autres nouvelles*, trans. René Novella (Paris: Éditions du Rocher & Garnier Flammarion, 1989), 7–27.
13. Alfredo Signoretti, *"La Stampa" in camicia nera* (Rome: Volpe, 1970), 110.
14. Vegliani, *Malaparte*, 49.
15. See *Malaparte*, 1:53.
16. Jean-Paul Sartre, *The Family Idiot: Gustave Flaubert, 1821–1857*, trans. Carol Cosman (Chicago: University of Chicago Press, 1981), 2:44.
17. Orfeo Tamburi, *Malaparte come me* (Milan: Editoriale Nuova, 1980), 52–53.
18. Guérin, *Du côté de chez Malaparte*, 52.
19. Fabbri, *Schiava di Malaparte*, 99.
20. Curzio Malaparte, "La bicicletta," *Corriere della Sera*, January 29, 1938, reprinted in *Malaparte*, 6:317–20. Troubetzkoy (1866–1938), too, had been fingered by gossips as a lover of Elvira Perelli and father to Curzio or to one or other of his brothers.
21. Enrico Roda, "Venti domande a Malaparte" (1947), in *Malaparte*, 7:675.
22. Thus did Malaparte describe her to Guérin, *Du côté de chez Malaparte*, 56.
23. Ansaldo, *Anni freddi*, 81, dated September 2, 1946.
24. Robert J. Stoller, *Perversion: The Erotic Form of Hatred* (New York: Pantheon Books, 1975), 149. "The ubiquitous fear that one's sense of maleness and masculinity are in danger and that one must build into character structure ever-vigilant defenses against succumbing to the pull of merging again with mother, I shall call symbiosis anxiety" (ibid).
25. Tamburi, *Malaparte come me*, 26.
26. Fabbri, *Schiava di Malaparte*, 66.
27. Originally "Carattere dei Romani," *Corriere della Sera*, April 16, 1937.

28. See Guerri, *L'arcitaliano*, 86.
29. Malaparte, "L'amore e la morte a Capri," *Epoca*, August 9, 1952, in *Malaparte*, 10:162–64.
30. Dominique Fernandez, "Drieu et Pavese," in *L'échec de Pavese* (Paris: Grasset, 1967), 205–16.
31. Malaparte, "Due razze," *Tempo*, November 17, 1955, in *Malaparte*, 11:646.
32. "Il cimitero delle donne" (fragment), in *Malaparte*, 11:669–71. Related to this is the episode of the corpses stripped by a group of peasants and Gypsies after the Jassy massacre, in *Kaputt*: "I never would have thought that it would be so difficult to take a slip off a dead girl" (K, 176).
33. Letter to Roland Laudenbach, Capri, April 16, 1950, in *Malaparte*, 9:188–89 (original in French).
34. See Fernand Braudel, ed., *Prato: Storia di una città* (Florence: Le Monnier, 1986), 4:374.
35. Radio interview, July 2, 1952, in *Malaparte*, 10:145–49.
36. Curzio wrote an ode for the wedding of Giorgi's daughter with a certain Aristide d'Amico, December 31, 1913. A copy lacking any information about the printer is held in AM.
37. Senator Guido Bisori, speech quoted in *L'ultimo viaggio di Malaparte*, ed. Giuseppe Billi (Prato: Edizioni Libreria Cattolica, 1998), 73–74.
38. Maurice Vaussard, *De Petrarque a Mussolini: Evolution du sentiment nationaliste italien* (Paris: Armand Colin, 1967), 207.
39. Camillo Antona-Traversi, *La guerra vista da Parigi, 1914–1915* (Campobasso: Casa Editrice Colitti, 1917), 159–60.
40. Quoted in a post of May 30, 2006, "Les Chemises Rouges 1914-1918 à Bligny," signed PG, on the website of the association Les Garibaldiens, https://www.wmaker.net/lesgaribaldiens/Les-Chemises-Rouges-1914-1918-a-BLIGNY_a3.html.
41. Interview given (to a Belgian newspaper?) in October 1949, in *Malaparte*, 8:587–90 (original in French).
42. Guerri, *L'arcitaliano*, 26.
43. *Malaparte*, 1:84.
44. See a biographical fragment from 1954, in *Malaparte*, 1:73–75.
45. *Malaparte*, 1:73 (original in French). He superimposes here, in a very Malapartian foreshortening, his experience as a Garibaldian volunteer and that of his time as a combatant returned beyond the Alps in 1918, in

order to claim "to have spilled my blood for France in 1914." See also Paolo Giacomel, *Tu col cannone, io col fucile: Alessandro Suckert e Curzio Malaparte nella Grande guerra* (Udine: Gaspari Editore, 2003).

46. Quoted in Luigi Martellini, chronology in Malaparte, *Opere scelte* (Milan: Mondadori, 1997), lxxxi.

47. For an overview, see Mario Isnenghi, "La Grande guerra," in *Le guerre degli italiani: Parole, immagini, ricordi, 1848–1945*, ed. Isnenghi (Milan: Mondadori, 1989). More recent is Mark Thompson, *The White War: Life and Death on the Italian Front, 1915–1919* (New York: Basic Books, 2009): well written but sketchily documented and often superficial in its judgments.

48. "Malaparte contro Cadorna," *Cronache*, July 26, 1954, in *Malaparte*, 10:761–63.

49. Vegliani, *Malaparte*, 59–60.

50. Letter of August 17, 1915, in *Malaparte*, 1:88–89.

51. See *Malaparte*, 1:85, 179. More noteworthy would be his later collaboration with a "newspaper of the trenches" put out by Giuseppe Ungaretti in Paris. See François Livi, "*Sempre Avanti*... (1918–1919): Malaparte soldato e scrittore sul fronte francese," in the proceedings of the international conference *La bourse des idées du monde: Malaparte e la Francia*, Prato-Florence, November 2007, ed. Martina Grassi (Florence: Olschki, 2008).

52. Two notable comparative studies are Eric J. Leed, *No Man's Land: Combat and Identity in World War I* (Cambridge: Cambridge University Press, 1979), and especially George L. Mosse, *Masses and Man: Nationalist and Fascist Perceptions of Reality* (1980; Detroit: Wayne State University Press, 1987).

53. *Nota a "I morti di Bligny giocano a carte"*, in AR, 202–11. This text of January 1937 is tainted by a note of Francophobe spite. In the same period, Fascist propaganda had publicly encouraged a core of veterans and family members to ask for the remains of Bligny combatants to be transferred to Italy. The Francophobe note would return in new remembrances by Malaparte of the episode, in 1938 and 1939, in contrast with an earlier version, published in *La Stampa*, July 14, 1929, still inspired by Italo-French brotherhood in arms (in *Malaparte*, 2:368–75). Interesting historical clarifications can be found in Alain Segal, *Poésie inspirée par les combats de Bligny en 1918, ou Curzio Malaparte entre Bligny et Reims*, Travaux de l'Académie nationale de Reims, 2006.

54. Testimony to the author of Onofrio Solari Bozzi, who also had the kindness to give me copies of some photographs taken during the trip. The most striking shows a smiling and relaxed Malaparte sitting at the table of a little countryside *auberge* near Bligny.
55. Mario Caracciolo, *Le truppe italiane in Francia: Il II Corpo d'armata, le T.A.I.F* (Milan: Mondadori, 1929).
56. This second edition bears the colophon Varsovie [*sic*], Edizioni di Oceanica. See Matteo Noja, "Una bibliografia di Malaparte," part 1, in *Mensile della Biblioteca di via Senato* 2, no. 4 (2010): 20–23.
57. In ME; cf. *Malaparte*, 1:280.
58. Henri Barbusse, *Under Fire: The Story of a Squad*, trans. Fitzwater Wray (New York: E. P. Dutton, 1917), 292.
59. Letter from Paris dated May 4, 1919, in *Vita and Harold: The Letters of Vita Sackville-West and Harold Nicolson, 1910–1962* (London: Weidenfeld & Nicolson, 1992), 83. The Englishman would become a friend of Malaparte, who cites him on multiple occasions in his works. See also Harold Nicolson, *Diaries and Letters, 1930–1964*, ed. Stanley Olson (New York: Collier Macmillan, 1980).
60. Thus Michel Ostenc, in *Intellectuels italiens et fascisme, 1915–1929* (Paris: Payot, 1983), could argue that "Malaparte's rebellion is at once conservative and anti-bourgeois, Catholic and anticlerical, reactionary and revolutionary, in a way not unrelated to Fascist manipulations. It lends itself to opposing interpretations" (123).
61. Jünger's *In Stahlgewittern* (1920) was first translated into English in 1929, by Basil Creighton. In the introduction to his 2003 retranslation, Michael Hofmann heavily criticizes his predecessor's version. For additional context, see Modris Eksteins, *Rites of Spring: The Great War and the Birth of the Modern Age* (London: Bantam Press, 1989).
62. André Malraux, *Les Noyers de l'Altenburg* (Paris: Gallimard, 1948), 271.
63. See Renato Barilli, "'Viva Caporetto!' come opera archetipo," in *Curzio Malaparte, il narratore, il politologo, il cittadino di Prato e dell'Europa*, conference proceedings (Prato, June 1988), ed. Barilli e Vittoria Baroncelli (Naples: CUEN, 2000), 2:19–39.
64. According to Oriana Fallaci in a profile of Malaparte in *L'Europeo*, May 2, 1954, in *Malaparte*, 10:674–76.

NOTES TO CHAPTER 1

65. Particularly in the statement of defense (ME) he wrote in 1946, for the trial concerned with war profiteering; see *Malaparte*, 1:203–4. Always careful not to be exposed, though, he wrote, "For not having requested the prescribed authorization, the Ministry of Foreign Affairs relieved me of my duties," and not "dismissed me from the diplomatic service." Elsewhere he would characterize himself, more accurately, as an "officer attached to our Royal Legation (in Warsaw)" (*Malaparte*, 2:185).
66. I am grateful to Federica Onelli at the Archive of the Ministry of Foreign Affairs for her research into the documentation of the legation to Warsaw (MAE-D. G. re personnel, ser. 8, vol. 2, "Varsavia"). Malaparte's very legible signature is "Curt Erich Suckert," with the initial *C*, used by him during and after the war as the first Italianization of his name in an official context.
67. Vegliani, *Malaparte*, 84.
68. *Malaparte*, 1:183.
69. *Malaparte*, 1:189–93. Actually, Barbusse's movement was already strongly oriented toward communism and the dogmas of "popular literature."
70. "Taci, Canzone Rossa, / e attendi; è l'ora / della riscossa." "Alla Brigata Cacciatori delle Alpi," in AR2, 195.
71. See also Maurizio Serra, *Marinetti: Retrato de un revolucionario* (Madrid: Fórcola Ediciones, 2020).
72. Mussolini, speech in Rome of February 1, 1938, reproduced in the *Dizionario mussoliniano* (Milan: Hoepli, 1940), 201.
73. I refer to the vast debate provoked by Claudio Pavone's *Una guerra civile: Saggio storico sulla moralità della Resistenza* (Turin: Bollati Boringhieri, 1994); translated by Peter Levy as *Civil War: A History of the Italian Resistance*, ed. Stanislao Pugliese (New York: Verso, 2013).
74. Testimony of Edda Ronchi Suckert, in *Malaparte*, 1:278–80. On Fascist syndicalism and "labor Fascism," see the numerous interventions by Malaparte in the period 1922–23, collected in *Malaparte*, vol. 1, and the seminal study of A. James Gregor, *Italian Fascism and Developmental Dictatorship* (Princeton, NJ: Princeton University Press, 1980).
75. In particular between Guerri, who affirms it (*L'arcitaliano*, 43–45), and Edda Ronchi Suckert, who firmly denies it (see *Malaparte*, 1:219–26).
76. Kurt E. Suckert, "La Marcia su Roma: Grandezza e decadenza degli eroi," *La Nazione*, October 31, 1922, in *Malaparte*, 1:303–5.

77. Information extracted from the report of October 8, 1933, of the Ministry of the Interior for Guido Leto, head of OVRA, in ACS, Min. Int., Div. Affari Riservati, political police division, category 1 personnel files, folder 96/A, "Suckert Kurzio" [sic] file.
78. See also Luisa Mangoni, *L'interventismo della cultura: Intellettuali e riviste del fascismo* (Bari: Laterza, 1974), chap. 1, and the more recent work of Giovanni Belardelli, *Il ventennio degli intellettuali: Cultura, politica, ideologia dell'Italia fascista* (Bari: Laterza, 2005).
79. See the editorial "Nuove strade e nuovi compiti dell'integralismo fascista," in issue 25-26-27, July 5, 1925, in *Malaparte*, 1:579–82. See also *Alla conquista dello Stato: Antologia della stampa fascista dal 1919 al 1925*, ed. Stenio Solinas (Rome: Volpe, 1978).
80. The file preserved in ACS, Min. Int., 1.82/3.2.15, *La Conquista dello Stato 1925–1926*, is incomplete and does not allow us to draw solid conclusions.
81. For the thank-you letters Vittorini sent to him in 1927, see *Malaparte*, 2:37, 54, 149, etc. They were published for the first time by Claudio Quarantotto, as an appendix to his article "Il fascista Vittorini," in *Il Borghese*, July 1972. See also Cesare De Michelis, "Il giovane Vittorini," in *Moderno antimoderno* (Turin: Aragno, 2010), 231–61.
82. See *Malaparte*, 1:679.
83. The standard reference is Mauro Canali, *Il delitto Matteotti: Affarismo e politica nel primo governo Mussolini* (Bologna: Il Mulino, 1997). I thank the author for the additional information he provided me.
84. Unpublished letter, dated Livorno, December 31, 1945, in Rulli Archive.
85. See Didier Musiedlak, "Charles Maurras et l'Italie: Histoire d'une passion contrariée," in *Charles Maurras et l'étranger*, ed. Olivier Dard and Michel Grunewald (Paris-Berne: P. Lang, 2009); Musiedlak, "L'Italie fasciste de Georges Valois," in *Georges Valois*, ed. Olivier Dard and Michel Grunewald (Paris-Berne: P. Lang, 2010). Valois would break with Maurras's movement shortly after, due precisely to its excessively conservative stamp.
86. See *Malaparte*, 1:326. The Parisian anti-Fascists have generally maintained that Malaparte was tied to the Fascist secret service through at least 1928–29. In this capacity, they allege, he organized Dumini's clandestine

departure from Paris; see Franco Fucci, *Le polizie di Mussolini: La repressione dell'antifascismo nel Ventennio* (Milan: Mursia, 1985), 17, 25–26.

87. In his detailed reconstruction of the Suckert deposition, Mauro Canali, in *Il delitto Matteotti* (445–55), observes that the time at which the writer indicated this meeting happened (between 8:00 and 9:00 p.m.) was surely false, because Dumini's Ceka returned to Rome between 10:30 and 10:45. It's a detail that should have sufficed for the investigators to cast doubt on the truthfulness of his testimony.

88. According to Canali (*Il delitto Matteotti*, 381), there were several meetings in Paris between Suckert, Dumini, and Bonservizi.

89. Amerigo Dumini, *Diciassette colpi* (Milan: Longanesi, 1967), 68. The writing of the book has generally been attributed to Longanesi and the journalist Indro Montanelli, two former friends who, after having broken with Malaparte, never passed up an occasion to damage him.

90. Ibid., 268.

91. According to the first postwar publication on the subject: Achille Saitta, *Dal terrorismo alla dittatura: Storia della Ceka fascista* (Rome: G.E.T. Edizioni Polilibraria, 1945), 296–98.

92. See Alexander J. de Grand, "Curzio Malaparte: The Illusion of the Fascist Revolution," *Journal of Contemporary History* 7, no. 1/2 (1972): 73–89.

93. ME, in *Malaparte*, 7:312.

94. See, again, Guerri's damning take in *L'arcitaliano*, 80, and, contra, upholding his innocence, the dossier assembled by Edda Ronchi Suckert, in *Malaparte*, 1:899–921. But Canali's reconstruction leaves no doubt as to the essential role he played throughout the affair.

95. ME, in *Malaparte*, 7:312.

96. Court of Rome summons of February 9, 1947, in *Malaparte*, 8:515.

97. Canali, *Il delitto Matteotti*, 601. Without mentioning Togliatti's embarrassment, after he had worked hard to rehabilitate Malaparte, in the face of opposition by the leadership and the base of the Communist Party (see also chap. 4).

Chapter 2

1. Henry Miller, *The Rosy Crucifixion: Plexus* (New York: Grove Press, 1965), 313. After World War II, preparing for the repeatedly postponed trip to

NOTES TO CHAPTER 2

the United States, Malaparte was cheered by the chance to meet Miller there.

2. After some administrative and police-related problems at the time of his imprisonment, his name was definitively altered in Prato's population register only in June 1937; see *Malaparte*, 4:89–90. An earlier decree had gone missing. For the change to be made in the lists of the authors and publishers union, he had to wait another two years (ibid., 680–81).

3. *I Malaparte ed i Bonaparte nel 1° centenario di un Bonaparte-Malaparte: Operetta* (Turin: Felice Borri, 1869). I found a rare copy of the book in the rich Jesuit library in Villa Malta, in Rome.

4. For example, an anonymous report of February 16, 1932 (and thus well before the anti-Semitic laws), described him as "the Masonic Jew Kurt Schuchert" [*sic*], in ACS, Min. Int., "Suckert Curzio" file. The legend continues to circulate. A well-known literary critic, with good knowledge of Malaparte, said to me recently: "He was surely Jewish."

5. Letter dated Rome, September 14, 1938, addressed to the minister of popular culture, Alfieri, or to his chief of staff, Luciano. In chap. 3 we will return to this revealing document, which can be found in ACS, Min. Cult. Pop., Reports 1922–1944, folder 7, n. 65, "Malaparte Curzio—*Prospettive 1935–1943*" file.

6. Document displayed in the exhibition *Malaparte: Arcitaliano nel mondo*, curated by Matteo Noja and Laura Mariani Conti (Milan: Edizioni della Biblioteca di via Senato, 2010).

7. "Fallaci interrogation."

8. Letter to Leo Longanesi, January 4, 1926, in *Malaparte*, 1:776.

9. Malaparte, "È morto Curzio" (1955), in BA1, 379.

10. According to Angelo d'Orsi, *L'Italia delle idee: Il pensiero politico in un secolo e mezzo di storia* (Milan: Bruno Mondadori, 2011), 187ff.

11. See *Malaparte*, 1:261–64.

12. See ME, in *Malaparte*, 1:281–84.

13. Giorgio Spini, *Italia di Mussolini e protestanti* (Turin: Claudiana, 2007). An ideological battle wore on to the end, however, between the movement's more secular wing, represented by Gentile, and what could be described as its caesaropapist wing, associated with another great historian, Gioacchino Volpe.

14. But even twenty-five years later, he would declare himself a nonpracticing

NOTES TO CHAPTER 2

Protestant, "and above all anticlerical" (Guérin, *Du côté de chez Malaparte*, 43).

15. Letter from Gobetti of August 14, 1925, in *Malaparte*, 1:593–94. The reference to "artist" (*artista*) pertained above all to another work by Malaparte, a philosophical tale à la Voltaire entitled "Viaggio agli Inferi," whose writing he had interrupted to finish *Italia barbara*, but which he had promised to Gobetti. The manuscript was confiscated by the police during a search of Gobetti's home. The complete text was reconstituted and published in *Malaparte*, 1:684–751, followed by the beginning of a novel from the same period, *L'ultimo fauno* (ibid., 1:752–66).

16. Malaparte, "Gobetti tornerà in Italia," *Tempo*, February 16, 1956, in *Malaparte*, 12:400.

17. I restrict myself to referring to Emilio Gentile, *Le origini dell'ideologia fascista (1918–1925)* (Bologna: Il Mulino, 2001), translated by Robert L. Miller as *The Origins of Fascist Ideology, 1918–1925* (New York: Enigma Books, 2005); and to the reissue of Renzo De Felice, *Il fascismo: Le interpretazioni dei contemporanei e degli storici* (1970; Bari: Laterza, 2008).

18. In the book he wrote after enlisting in the French Foreign Legion, in 1944, and published five years later, upon his return to Italy, titled *Vent'anni e un giorno*, rev. ed. (Milan: Rizzoli, 2008), with a preface by Giordano Bruno Guerri.

19. See the mission statement of *"900"* in *Malaparte*, 1:827–29; see also "La polemica intorno a *'900'*: Un vivace commento delle *Nouvelles Littéraires* e una nuova intervista con Massimo Bontempelli," in *Malaparte*, 1:834–37. For an overview, see Mangoni, *L'interventismo della cultura*, chap. 2.

20. See *Malaparte*, 2:113.

21. Nino Frank, *Mémoire brisée*, vol. 2, *Le bruit parmi le vent* (Paris: Calmann-Lévy, 1968), 224.

22. *Malaparte*, 10:402. Bontempelli's nephew and literary executor, the ambassador Alvise Memmo, confirmed for me that the esteem and friendship were reciprocal until the end. A decade older than Malaparte, Bontempelli would outlive him by three years.

23. ACS, Min. Int., "Suckert Curzio" file. The file, which stops in December 1933, shortly after Malaparte's arrest, is surely incomplete, as indeed are the majority of the approximately two thousand files delivered to ACS after the war. The letter "A" follows the file's reference number, implying

that it was delivered, like a hundred or so files relating to "sensitive" figures, much later than the great majority of the others. Mauro Canali, who examined the material before I did, notes that the file in question here was the first of two about Suckert, the second having never been delivered, or gone missing.

24. See *Malaparte*, 2:103, 2:105–7. According to a report sent from Paris on December 1, 1927, most likely from the same informer who had referred to Malaparte's search for a publisher, "nothing led one to expect the dispute with Frank" (ACS, Min. Int., "Suckert Curzio" file). In a manner typical for him, Malaparte accused Frank of being "maliciously hostile" to him (letter to Prezzolini dated Turin, June 27, 1929, in *Malaparte*, 2:347–48). Frank's memoirs are rather reticent on the topic of the "Germano-Tuscan who still signed his name Kurt Suckert" (see *Mémoire brisée*, 1:29–35). But as he would write in a preface to *Malaparte come me*, by Tamburi, "For so many years, I tried to hate him. But I didn't succeed at it, and I didn't understand why; with the passing of time, I also came to feel a certain compassion for the 'soldier of misfortune' and that scourged life of his, beneath the mask of optimism."

25. *Malaparte*, 2:30.

26. Numerous examples can be found in *Malaparte*, 2:233–35, 757–59, 861–63; 3:37–42, 455–61; and again, after the war, in 10:532–33, etc.

27. Antonio Aniante, *Mussolini*, trans. J. Bertrand (Paris: Grasset, 1932), 65, 70, 128. See also the reconstruction by Emmanuel Mattiato, "Cardarelli, Aniante, Malaparte et 'il mito della sorella latina' (1924–1934): La France (mal) vue d'Italie," in *La France et l'Italie au miroir: Échanges humains et culturels, XVe–XXe siècles* (Éditions de Savoie, 2012).

28. C. E. Suckert, "Ritratto storico di Mussolini," *La Nazione*, June 19, 1923 (Malaparte's emphasis).

29. Curzio Suckert, "Lettera aperta all'On. Mussolini," *La Conquista dello Stato*, October 31, 1925, ibid., 627–29. Aurélie Manzano, in a doctoral thesis supervised by François Livi ("Dans le bouillonnement de la création: Le monde mis en scène par Curzio Malaparte," Paris-Sorbonne University, December 2011), observes that the reference to "integral Fascism" no longer appeared in the subtitle of *La Conquista dello Stato* starting on January 1, 1926 (p. 29)—coinciding, then, with the constitutional step from Fascism-as-movement to Fascism-as-regime.

NOTES TO CHAPTER 2

30. Curzio Malaparte, "L'Arcimussolini," *La Conquista dello Stato*, January 15, 1927, in *Malaparte*, 2:18–19. In the same style, see also "Necessità di una rivoluzione," *L'Italia Letteraria*, Fogli della Sibilla, April 3, 1927, ibid., 54–55.
31. Yvon de Begnac, *Taccuini mussoliniani*, ed. Francesco Perfetti (Bologna: Il Mulino, 1990), 353, 362, 439–40. The authenticity of the notebooks is beyond doubt, the style embellished with typically Mussolinian images. Nevertheless, the volume's editor urges caution when reading these notes, most of them undated, which Mussolini did not reread or revise.
32. Giuseppe Bottai, *Diario 1944–1948*, ed. Giordano Bruno Guerri (Milan: Rizzoli, 1977), 602.
33. See Guerri, *L'arcitaliano*, 92–95 and, contra, *Malaparte*, 1:774–75 and *Malaparte*, 2:11, 141.
34. See "Rivoluzione antipolitica," *La Conquista dello Stato*, May 15, 1928, and "La rivoluzione sono io," ibid., April 15, 1927; "Giacobini dell'anno sesto," *Il Mattino*, October 12–13, 1928, in *Malaparte*, 2:169–70, 58–59, 229–30.
35. Testimony of Edda Ronchi Suckert, in *Malaparte*, 1:244.
36. See *Malaparte*, 2:172, 202, 215, 268–69.
37. ACS, Min. Int., Political Police Division, personnel files, 1927–44, folder 12, n. 776, "Agnelli Senatore."
38. See Nicola Tranfaglia, Paolo Murialdi, and Massimo Legnani, *La stampa italiana nell'età fascista* (Bari: Laterza, 1980), 98–99.
39. See *Malaparte*, 2:74. An energetic man with anti-Fascist views, Colli (father of the philosopher Giorgio Colli, coeditor of the first complete edition of the works of Friedrich Nietzsche) would become, after the war, the managing director of the *Corriere della Sera*. In this capacity, he would successfully oppose the rehiring of Malaparte as a contributor to the Milanese daily; see Glauco Licata, *Storia del "Corriere della Sera"* (Milan: Rizzoli, 1976), 327–29.
40. See the testimony of Alfredo Signoretti, a collaborator and, later, successor of Malaparte (1932–43), after Turati's brief stint in the role (1931–32), in *"La Stampa" in camicia nera*, 40.
41. Malaparte, "L'Italia e le mosche," *La Stampa*, March 3, 1929, in *Malaparte*, 2:308–10.
42. Signoretti, *"La Stampa" in camicia nera*, 133.
43. See *Malaparte*, 2:414–15.

44. Lando Ferretti to Malaparte, Rome, January 20, 1930, in *Malaparte*, 2:480.
45. Ferretti to Malaparte, Rome, September 28, 1930, in *Malaparte*, 2:649–50, 710.
46. Maccari to Malaparte, September 18, 1931, in *Malaparte*, 2:801–2.
47. Orio Vergani, *Misure del tempo: Diario* (Milan: Baldini & Castoldi, 2003), 486.
48. Letter of July 23, 1957, quoted in Guerri, *L'arcitaliano*, 86. At the time Ansaldo wrote a column in the weekly *Il Borghese* called Dictionary of the Illustrious and Wretched Italians that got as far as the letter *M*, later collected in a single volume. But he preferred to avoid drafting, or publishing, the planned entry on Malaparte.
49. In *Malaparte*, 2:710–11.
50. For all these aspects, see the well-documented official biography, by Valerio Castronovo, *Giovanni Agnelli, la Fiat dal 1899 al 1945* (Turin: UTET, 1977), esp. chap. 5.
51. According to confidences reported by his chief of staff in Salò, Giovanni Dolfin, and confirmed by other testimonies. See Dolfin, *Con Mussolini nella tragedia* (Milan: Garzanti, 1949), 137, 235–38.
52. Among them all, I limit myself to citing the admirable *Diario caucasico* (Milan: R. Ricciardi, 1975), by Paolo Vita-Finzi, who at the time of the experiences narrated therein was a young Italian consul in Georgia.
53. Reader's report, Naples, September 4, 1930, in ACS, Min. Int., "Suckert Curzio" file.
54. *L'Intransigeant*, August 13, 1929, reprinted in *Malaparte*, 2:388–89.
55. V. Kournossow to Malaparte, letter of December 17, 1929, in *Malaparte*, 2:426–27.
56. Malaparte, "L'Europa davanti allo specchio," preface to *Il volto del bolscevismo*, by René Fülöp-Miller, trans. Giacomo Prampolini (Milan: Bompiani, 1930); original ed., *The Mind and Face of Bolshevism* (London: Putnam's, 1927).
57. Grasset to Malaparte, Paris, December 8, 1930, in *Malaparte*, 2:684.
58. Daniel Halévy, *Courrier d'Europe* (Paris: Grasset, 1933), 269–304. Curiously, in the panorama of Italian letters that closes the book, Malaparte goes unmentioned. An in-depth study of the trips to Fascist Italy undertaken by French journalists and intellectuals in the 1920s and 1930s can be found in a doctoral thesis by Christophe Poupault, "À l'ombre des

Faisceaux: Les voyages français dans l'Italie des Chemises noires (1922–1943)" (Paris Nanterre University; Sapienza University of Rome, 2011).
59. The first edition was translated, by J. M. Hone, as *The Life of Friedrich Nietzsche* (London: T. Fisher Unwin, 1911).
60. As described to me by Marianne Halévy's granddaughter, Claude Nabokoff Joxe.
61. In *Malaparte*, 2:694–95, 697.
62. At least this seems to be indicated by the summons with attached agenda sent to Malaparte and personally signed by Agnelli from the board of directors for the Turin–Milan expressway. Note no. 795, of September 12, 1929, in AM, n. 053/185, "Agnelli Giovanni" correspondence.
63. Note dated Rome, October 11, 1933, in ACS, Min. Int., "Suckert Curzio" file.
64. The Morozzo della Rocca family was kept under surveillance due to its close relationship to the crown, as numerous police advisories attested, in ACS, Min. Int., Political Police Division, 1927–1944 personnel files, folder no. 872.
65. Vegliani, *Malaparte*, 69.
66. See, for example, a letter to Guglielmo Rulli from Capri, of October 15, 1946: "I've had guests: Count C. and daughter, the duke of M. with his new bride on their honeymoon," and so on, in Rulli Archive.
67. Letter dated Colle Val d'Elsa, November 11, 1931, in *Malaparte*, 2:837–38.
68. ME, in *Malaparte*, 2:769–70.
69. The text can be found in *Malaparte*, 2:769–70; however, a search of the archives of the publishing house has not turned up the original.
70. Report dated Rome, May 15, 1931, in ACS, Min. Int., "Suckert Curzio" file.
71. Turati to Malaparte, Rome, January 13, IX (1931), in AM, Turati correspondence.
72. ME, in *Malaparte*, 7:329–30. This is followed by a melodramatic tale of a worker who kills himself after being fired on the spot.
73. In the atmosphere of the Liberation, when tales were told of a million lire or more, Malaparte declared that it came to 550,000 lire (*Malaparte*, 6:755), a sum he lowered to 200,000 lire two years later (letter to Lewis A. Coser, June 5, 1947, in *Malaparte*, 7:622–24). It was, in terms of purchasing power, the equivalent of a few million euro, and far from what

one could expect from the "compensation prescribed by the national contract for journalists" (ME, in *Malaparte*, 7:330). But precedents do exist, even from the period. Agnelli had built a reputation for generosity by purchasing the discretion of former associates: Malaparte's predecessor, Andrea Torre, had been dismissed in 1929 with a payment of 923,000 lire (see Tranfaglia, Murialdi, and Legnani, *La stampa italiana*, 99). According to a police note of October 13, 1933, the payment had been raised from two hundred thousand to three hundred thousand lire (ACS, Min. Int., "Suckert Curzio" file). This sum seems lower than reality.

74. ME, in *Malaparte*, 7:330.
75. These reports are also found in ACS, Min. Int., "Suckert Curzio" file. Francesco Perfetti considers them groundless (preface to MU).
76. Police note dated Rome, May 15, 1931, in ACS, Min. Int., "Suckert Curzio" file.
77. See *Malaparte*, 6:698 and vol. 7, part 2, for the complete text of ME and related documents.
78. Informer's report of August 24, 1932, which does not, however, mention any potential resignation from the party, in ACS, Min. Int., "Suckert Curzio" file. In a short story by Vitaliano Brancati, "Il vecchio con gli stivali," the protagonist, a municipal employee, returning home late one evening, spits and urinates on the party emblem. Afterward, satisfied with his anti-Fascist gesture, he carefully washes it and the next morning heads off to the office, with the emblem in his buttonhole.
79. Borelli would write an important preface to his correspondence with the writer, reproduced in *Malaparte*, 3:148–58 (hereafter "Borelli preface"). The correspondence with Borelli extended up to the eve of Malaparte's death and is the richest of those preserved in AM: roughly five hundred letters and around a hundred telegrams. Together they constitute, above all for the years 1930–43, an irreplaceable document for following the writer's evolution.
80. ACS, Min. Cult. Pop., Cabinet, 2nd deposit, folder 8, "Malaparte." Obviously, this document does not allude to any alleged resignation from the party.
81. Letter of February 13, 1931, in *Malaparte*, 2:731. The version preserved in AM is not the original but, as in most cases, the one typed up by Edda Ronchi Suckert.

NOTES TO CHAPTER 2

82. Letters from Turin, February 7 and March 23, 1931, in *Malaparte*, 2:731–32, 755.
83. Letter from Turin, March 10, 1931, in *Malaparte*, 2:747 (original in French).
84. Letter of March 18, 1931, in *Malaparte*, 2:749–50.
85. Message from the spokesman for the head of government (i.e., Mussolini), Lando Ferretti, to Malaparte of June 29, 1931, in *Malaparte*, 2:767.
86. Report from Rome, August 20, 1931, in ACS, Min. Int., "Suckert Curzio" file.
87. This affirmation was replaced by an ellipsis in the typed version of the letter preserved in AM.
88. Letter from Juan-les-Pins, dated August 18, 1931, in *Malaparte*, 2:779–81.
89. Gino Veneroni, "Tecnica del colpo di Stato: La rivoluzione 'invisibile,'" *Corriere della Sera*, September 22, 1931.
90. Giuseppe Musacchia and Edoardo Pirani, *Il colpo di stato non è rivoluzione!* (Rome: Luzzatti, 1932).
91. Letter dated Juan-les-Pins, September 2, 1931, in *Malaparte*, 2:793–94.
92. Letter dated Milan, September 17, 1931, in AM, Borelli correspondence; emphasis in original.
93. Letter from Milan, October 2, 1931, in AM, Borelli correspondence.
94. According to Giuseppe Pardini in his introduction to an anastatic reprint of the issues of *Prospettive* from 1939 to 1943 (Florence: Casa Malaparte, Franco Cesati, and Vallecchi Editore, 2006), 1–2.
95. See Maurizio Serra, "Jünger, decadente mancato," in *Al di là della decadenza: La rivolta dei moderni contro l'idea della fine* (Bologna: Il Mulino, 1994).
96. Camille Mauclair, "Un livre avertisseur," *L'Éclaireur du soir*, August 13, 1931.
97. "Technique du coup d'État par C. Malaparte," *Matin-Dimanche*, August 1931.
98. Kenneth Pendar, "Le dilemme France-Etats-Unis," reproduced in *Malaparte*, 2:792.
99. ME, in *Malaparte*, 2:721.
100. See also Malaparte 3:235. For the most complete analysis of the Nazi autos-da-fé, see Volker Weidermann, *Das Buch der verbrannten Bücher*

(Cologne: Kiepenheur & Witsch, 2008), which contains the official list of works sentenced to the pyre (246–53). The foreign authors on the list were few, apart from the Soviets, and included no Italians and just one Frenchman, Henri Barbusse.

101. In the record of a conversation with a contemporary collaborator: "Do you know the doctrine of the *coup d'état*? Study it. Then you will know our task." Hermann Rauschning, *Hitler Speaks: A Series of Political Conversations with Adolf Hitler on His Real Aims* (London: Thornton Butterworth, 1939), 19.
102. Note dated Rome, August 28, 1931, in ACS, Min. Int., "Suckert Curzio" file.
103. The complete French text is available at https://www.marxists.org/francais/trotsky/oeuvres/1932/11/321125.htm.
104. Leon Trotsky, *The History of the Russian Revolution*, trans. Max Eastman (1932; Chicago: Haymarket Books, 2008), 3:833.
105. Note of October 11, 1933, in ACS, Min. Int., "Suckert Curzio" file.
106. Published posthumously in *Tempo*, December 12, 1957, in *Malaparte*, 2:852–56.
107. Morand would refer to "Malraux, our Malaparte" in an entry dated October 21, 1972, of his *Journal Inutile* (Paris: Gallimard, 2001), 1:811.
108. See Paolo Alatri, *L'antifascismo italiano* (Milan: Feltrinelli, 1961), 2:199–217.
109. Report from Paris of October 22, 1931, and July 22, 1932, in ACS, Min. Int., "Suckert Curzio" file.
110. A. Rossi [Angelo Tasca], *The Rise of Italian Fascism, 1918–1922*, trans. Peter and Dorothy Wait (New York: H. Fertig, 1966), 345. The book appeared under the pseudonym A. Rossi in 1938 with Gallimard in France and Methuen in England, arousing considerable interest. Tasca, one of the founders of the PCI, had already broken with Stalinism and was preparing to denounce the Molotov-Ribbentrop Pact, the following year, in an even blunter essay.
111. Note from Paris, September 25, 1931, in ACS, Min. Int., "Suckert Curzio" file, which continued thus: "And it would have been noted that he appeared in Paris with the lawyer B.'s wife, [presumed to be] his lover."
112. As Canali confirmed for me.
113. Vergani, *Misure del tempo*, 477.

114. See, in particular, the letter dated Reims, December 31, 1932, of André Sabatier, which seeks to reassure him, in AM, Sabatier correspondence.
115. Letter from Paris, December 20, 1932, in AM, Borelli correspondence. See also Pardini, introduction to *Prospettive 1939–1943*, 2n8.
116. Curzio Malaparte, "Analisi cinica dell'Europa," *L'Italia Letteraria*, January 3, 1932, in *Malaparte*, 3:11–14.
117. Nevertheless, Perfetti states, in his preface to MU, that in Paris Malaparte met Salvemini alongside the republican journalist Camillo Puglionisi.
118. Report from Rome, August 20, 1931, in ACS, Min. Int., "Suckert Curzio" file.
119. I therefore share the opinion of Perfetti in his preface to the reprint of the book (Milan: Oscar Mondadori, 1992). In general terms, we can agree as well on the essentially formal nature of the redistribution of the eight original chapters into sixteen in the Italian edition. On the other hand, we cannot agree with Malaparte when he wrote to Bompiani on May 11, 1948 (*Malaparte*, 8:312), about wanting to reinsert into the Italian edition passages that he had had to omit or modify upon the request of Grasset. There is nothing to see here, with the exception of a few stylistic changes and the already cited modification of the title of the Hitler chapter.
120. Letter from Milan, November 19, 1931, in *Malaparte*, 2:844–45.
121. The existing fragments of the 1931–32 draft, completed but not finalized in 1955, can be found in *Malaparte*, 10:544–55 and 11:677–712. The nonsensical title was probably inspired by the 1944 Henry Miller pamphlet "Murder the Murderer." In an unpublished letter of June 28, 1948, Miller offered to send Malaparte a copy of the pamphlet.
122. Request by Malaparte of December 11, 1939, and letter by the minister Pavolini to Malaparte of the 14th, in ACS, Min. Cult. Pop., Reports 1922–1944, "Malaparte Curzio" file.
123. Letter of January 19, 1933, addressed to Malaparte, who found himself in London at the time, in AM, Ansaldo correspondence.
124. Letter of December 20, 1932, in AM, Coty correspondence.
125. Letter from Malaparte to the minister Alfieri, head of the exhibition, of October 2, 1932, and reply of the latter, of October 4, 1932, in AM, Alfieri correspondence.
126. Letter from Paris dated December 20, 1932, in AM, Borelli correspondence.

127. Letter of April 6, 1933, in AM, Borelli correspondence. In his letter, Borelli mistakenly refers to *L'Ère Nouvelle* instead of *Les Nouvelles Littéraires*.
128. Letter of May 12, 1933, in AM, Borelli correspondence.
129. See Claudio G. Segrè, *Italo Balbo: A Fascist Life* (Berkeley: University of California Press, 1987), 275.
130. In 1944 Bruno Fallaci claimed, clearly inaccurately, that Balbo had helped Suckert become secretary of the Fascist unions of Florence ("Fallaci interrogation"). According to Pardini, at the time of the Matteotti murder he had also assumed the duties of political secretary to Balbo.
131. See Giordano Bruno Guerri, *Italo Balbo* (Milan: Mondadori, 1998), 138–40.
132. See *Malaparte*, 2:739; Martellini, chronology in Malaparte, *Opere scelte*, xcii.
133. See Guerri in his further account of the Balbo-Malaparte break, in *Italo Balbo*, 279–81, and Gianni Grana, "Malaparte, la critica, il pregiudizio: Configurazioni e rettifiche," in *Malaparte scrittore d'Europa*, 161–78. According to Francesco De Nicola, *Introduzione a Vittorini* (Bari: Laterza, 1993), 22–24, in this way the writer repaid his "moral debt" to Malaparte, who had helped him early in his career.
134. Telegram from the Royal Embassy of Italy in Paris no. 2127 of January 9, 1928, passed along to the Ministry of the Interior, in ACS, Min. Int., "Suckert Curzio" file.
135. Postcard of August 1, 1932, in Joxe-Halévy Archives (original in French). The letter to Daniel Halévy referred to in the next sentence, undated, is doubtless from a few days later.
136. Note from Naples, September 13, 1932, in ACS, Min. Int., "Suckert Curzio" file.
137. Handwritten note, probably from the chief of police, Bocchini, dated August 29, 1932, in ACS, Min. Int., "Suckert Curzio" file.
138. The text published by Edda Ronchi Suckert reads here: "dico solo fisicamente" (just physically speaking). But the typewritten version—which, according to a note by Edda, was inaccurately copied from the original by the historian Duilio Susmel (the Lettera 22 typewriter characters are the same, however, as those appearing in other Malaparte letters of the same period)—says: "e non solo fisicamente" (and not just physically), which is clearly rather more explicit. AM, Quilici correspondence.

139. Letter dated October 3, 1932, in *Malaparte*, 3:76. For the other correspondence cited below in this section, see, in *Malaparte*, vol. 3 (pages in parentheses): Malaparte to Halévy, October 29 (82); Quilici to Malaparte, November 1 (89–90); Malaparte to Quilici, December 12 (108–9); telegrams from Quilici to Malaparte of December 25, 1932, and January 21, 1933 (123).
140. A "category 1" file on Quilici exists (ACS, Min. Int., series A, folder 75, "Quilici Nello"), but it does not contain any reference to the case.
141. This thesis is shared by Signoretti, *"La Stampa" in camicia nera*, 109–16, and by Guerri, who was the first to unearth the Malaparte-Quilici correspondence at ACS, in his reconstruction of the episode, *L'arcitaliano*, 138–61.
142. According to a police report of October 15, 1933, "It is said that Il Duce wanted to tread carefully, but that Balbo dug in his heels, hence the arrest," in ACS, Min. Int., "Suckert Curzio" file. This thesis seems very probable to me.
143. Letter from Cap d'Antibes, Garoupe Beach, September 2, 1933, in AM, Borelli correspondence.
144. Letter from Cap d'Antibes, Garoupe Beach, September 9, 1933, in AM, Bessand-Massenet correspondence (original in French).
145. Borelli preface, in *Malaparte*, 3:151.

Chapter 3

1. Report of February 16, 1930, published by Francesco Perfetti in the previously cited reprint of T2. A new report of September 8, 1931, after the publication of *Technique*, drawn up by an anonymous infiltrator of "intellectual circles," would emphasize the author's "criminal plan" and "nefarious ideas."
2. Report of the Ministry of the Interior for Guido Leto, head of OVRA, Rome, October 8, 1933, in ACS, Min. Int., "Suckert Curzio" file. The report was supplemented by a series of suspect or heretical citations drawn from Malaparte's works.
3. The double news item—"Curzio Suckert arrested and expelled from the party"—appeared in a public statement from the PNF press office, October 10, 1933.

4. ACS, Min. Int., Political Police Division, folder 167, "Borelli Aldo" file; see the report of December 6, 1933. See also Gaetano Afeltra, *"Corriere" primo amore: Storia e mito di un grande giornale* (Milan: Bompiani, 1984), 202–9.
5. Borelli preface, in *Malaparte*, 3:153.
6. Ibid., 3:154.
7. Ibid., 3:155.
8. Ibid.
9. *Malaparte*, 3:159. The same claim, with some additional flourishes, shows up two years later in his preface to the book's Italian edition: "Not content to have burned my book, Hitler asked Mussolini for my head, and he got it" (T2, 11).
10. "Notre Baudelaire ovvero La Patrie parisienne," in *Malaparte*, 3:354.
11. Letter from Vittorini of January 12, 1933, or three months after the first letter to Quilici and a month after the second, in *Malaparte*, 3:163.
12. Letter to Borelli of October 10, 1933, in *Malaparte*, 3:301.
13. Letter to Borelli of October 20, 1933, in *Malaparte*, 3:309–10.
14. See Françoise Liffran, *Margherita Sarfatti: L'égérie du Duce* (Paris: Seuil, 2009), 344, 535.
15. Letter from Paris, December 27, 1933, Italian translation in *Malaparte*, 3:334–35. A similar letter, from Grasset's business partner, Louis Brun, reached him the day after his arrest.
16. "Arrestation de M. Curzio Malaparte," *Le Temps*, October 10, 1933.
17. "Curzio Malaparte aux îles Lipari," *Le Jour*, November 16, 1933.
18. Police note of December 2, 1933, in ACS, Min. Int., "Suckert Curzio" file. The letter from Elvira Suckert, née Perelli, was registered with no. 211339 in ACS, personal secretary to Il Duce. But Malaparte would deny it was ever sent (MU, 88).
19. Letter to his brother Sandro of October 31, 1933, in *Malaparte*, 3:313.
20. Letter to Borelli of November 10, 1933, in *Malaparte*, 3:314–15.
21. Letter to the commission of November 14, 1933, in *Malaparte*, 3:316–17. Here too, obviously, Malaparte makes no reference to his supposed resignation from the party.
22. Text of the writ in *Malaparte*, 3:315–16. Note, again, the reference to *a* letter, rather than to two letters.

23. Letter dated Lipari, December 11, 1933, in AM, Borelli correspondence. That Malaparte believed he could not cause harm to his correspondents by writing to them confirms he was not considered a political prisoner.
24. *Malaparte*, 3:330–31 (original in French). Marianne Halévy would write him words of encouragement on January 14, 1934, and also later, in Italian, to avoid lengthy delays with the censors. The Île de la Cité is where the Halévys' house is located in Paris. *Poca brigata vita beata* = "few people, happy life" (Italian proverb).
25. I am grateful to Fernando Mazzetti for telling me this anecdote.
26. Letter to Pierre Bessand-Massenet, from Forte dei Marmi, December 2, 1934 (original in French).
27. Letter from H. Ludwig, from Munich, August 25, 1953, in *Malaparte*, 10:431–32.
28. The quotation is from the travel diary of the inspector Conte, in *Malaparte*, 4:489, to which we will return later. In his confidences to this police official, assigned to surveil him during his trip to Ethiopia, Malaparte provided a conciliatory account of his *confino* period, quite different from what he would recount after the war.
29. Police report dated Rome, October 12, 1933, in ACS, Min. Int., "Suckert Curzio" file, which mentions the steps taken by Count Morozzo della Rocca, the father of "Flaminia," vis-à-vis those with connections to *La Stampa*—another indication that the relationship between the writer and Virginia Agnelli had not yet begun at that date; otherwise, it would have been fanciful to hope for an intervention from the senator.
30. Ibid.
31. Ibid.
32. Malaparte, "Temporale a Pesto," *Corriere della Sera*, May 27, 1936, in *Malaparte*, 3:707–10.
33. Vegliani, *Malaparte*, 111. In December 1939, after a driver had run over a dog and then beaten it to death in a Roman street, Malaparte launched a press campaign calling for him to receive an "exemplary punishment."
34. Malaparte, "Il cane Curzio," *Tempo*, August 2, 1956, in *Malaparte*, 12:513–14.
35. This request, or entreaty, has not been found.
36. To my knowledge, neither the postcard nor the letter has been found.

37. Letter from Lipari, March 1, 1934, in AM, Bessand-Massenet correspondence.
38. Letter from Milan, September 6, 1934, in AM, Borelli correspondence.
39. The change is noticeable starting with "Finestra sugli inglesi," *Corriere della sera*, October 26, 1934, in *Malaparte*, 3:521–23; then "Le belle maniere inglesi," *Corriere della sera*, January 15, 1935, in *Malaparte*, 3:574–77.
40. Letter dated Forte dei Marmi, December 2, 1934, in AM, Bessand-Massenet correspondence (original in French).
41. Letter of November 29, 1934, in *Malaparte*, 3:547–48 (original in French, with the exception of the italicized sentence, which is in the language of Shakespeare).
42. Letter dated Forte dei Marmi, December 29, 1934, in Joxe-Halévy archives. This wished-for paternity was probably a *captatio benevolentiae*, at a time when the Halévys' beloved daughter had just given birth. We will find the same one, some years later, in his letters to Carla Rulli, the wife of his lifelong friend Guglielmo Rulli.
43. The prevarication was facilitated by bureaucratic confusion: a year and a half later, February 7, 1937, perhaps in the wake of the Virginia Agnelli affair, the Ministry of the Interior's chief of staff wrote to police headquarters to order that "Malaparte (Suckert), *confinato* in Forte dei Marmi, not move from that location and not draw attention to himself with his conduct." The police replied that such measures could not be applied, seeing as the person concerned "has been released from *confino* by H. E. the Head of Government's clemency" (*Malaparte*, 4:25). But in certain cases—as in the preface to the Italian edition of *Don Camaleo*—Malaparte would not hesitate to extend his time in "prison and *confino*" up to 1938.
44. Thus he confided to the inspector Conte, in *Malaparte*, 4:489, as well as to other interlocutors. With his punning message Malaparte likely intended to flatter Il Duce, although the latter's sense of humor was notoriously lacking.
45. Baltus remained on friendly terms with Malaparte. After Sylvia Hildebrand, he married Adrienne Revelard, a literary critic at Radio Belgique, where she would present *Kaputt* to listeners (see *Malaparte*, 7:189–91).
46. *Malaparte*, 3:625–26.
47. Edda Ciano, *My Truth*, as told to Albert Zarca, trans. Eileen Finletter

(New York: William Morrow, 1977), 38—a source to be consulted with caution.

48. André François-Poncet, *Au Palais Farnèse: Souvenirs d'une Ambassade à Rome, 1938–1940* (1961; Paris: Tempus Perrin, 2013), 113. The latest biography to appear is Michel Ostenc's justly subtitled *Ciano: Un conservateur entre Hitler et Mussolini* (Paris: Éditions du Rocher, 2007). The standard reference remains Giordano Bruno Guerri, *Galeazzo Ciano* (Milan: Bompiani, 1979).

49. Vegliani, *Malaparte*, 100–101. Orio Vergani offers a slightly different version—"I was the one who picked him up one night in Il Forte and brought him to the Hotel Royal to thank Ciano, who had had him freed" (*Misure del tempo*, 478)—without any mention of the fanciful apparel. Since this comes from a trustworthy witness, I tend to believe his version, which in any case does not exclude the possibility that such a scene occurred at a later time.

50. Testimony to the author by the ambassador Alvise Memmo.

51. E. Ciano, *My Truth*, 112.

52. From 1922 to 1961, Palazzo Chigi was the official residence of the minister of foreign affairs.—Trans.

53. Quoted in Duilio Susmel, *Vita sbagliata di Galeazzo Ciano* (Milan: Palazzi, 1962), 103.

54. Giovanni Ansaldo, *Il giornalista di Ciano: Diari 1935–1943* (Bologna: Il Mulino, 2000), 131, entry dated March 2, 1937.

55. Ansaldo, *Anni freddi*, 81, entry dated September 2, 1946, and 274, entry dated January 27, 1949.

56. Letter dated Forte dei Marmi, May 23, 1936, in *Malaparte*, 3:705 (original in French).

57. Ansaldo, *Il giornalista di Ciano*, 132.

58. Letter to Marianne Halévy, dated Villa Hildebrand, October 9, 1935, in Joxe-Halévy Archives (original in French).

59. Letters from "Flaminia" to Marianne Halévy, dated respectively Pontecchio, October 9, and Turin, November 22, 1935, in Joxe-Halévy Archives.

60. I thank Ruggero Ranieri di Sorbello for providing these facts.

61. Testimony to the author by the ambassador Alvise Memmo, who had learned it from his father, the cavalry colonel Giorgio Memmo. The story of these heiresses of the New World, during the war and the German occupation of the capital, in 1943–44, still awaits its Saint-Simon. An

elegant obituary of Dorothy di Frasso, which mentions the episode involving Gary Cooper, can be found in Laurenzi, *Due anni a Roma*, 20–22.

62. I refer to the thirteen-page report on "Mario [*sic*] Suckert aka C.M. and Virginia Agnelli," dated Milan, April 15, 1936, in ACS, Min. Int., Political Police Division, folder 12, no. 784, Virginia Agnelli file. The report contains other errors, like attributing to Malaparte a past as a D'Annunzian legionnaire in Fiume. "Duilio" operated mainly in Forte dei Marmi and other resort towns. In Rome, the couple were followed by the agent E.A., codename "1890." Mauro Canali has explained to me that, according to the strict system in use by the political police, the agents did not know each other, especially when they worked on the same figures, and the information they collected was carefully verified.

63. The previously cited report by "Duilio" assigned paternity instead to Count A. of Turin. Such malicious gossip seems even more ridiculous once he adds that none of Edoardo Agnelli's children should be attributed to their legal father. When, as delicately as I could, I put the issue to Maria Sole Agnelli, she replied with a patrician smile, "Ridiculous, but you know, it's inevitable that certain families provoke similar stories. We are used to it" (testimony to the author).

64. ACS, Min. Int., Political Police Division, folder 12, no. 779, "Agnelli Comm. Avv. Edoardo."

65. Vegliani, *Malaparte*, 104–6.

66. "His relationship with Virginia Agnelli was born in Turin and Malaparte went away only in exchange for a large sum" ("Fallaci interrogation"). Likewise: "The senator had Malaparte dismissed with a generous payout, with the agreement there was no more talk of marriage. A part of his payout was used to purchase the villa in Forte dei Marmi" (Vergani, *Misure del tempo*, 477). Fidia Gambetti, a leading young intellectual of the day, noted in his diary: "Mussolini sends [Turati] to assume the editorship of *La Stampa*, where meanwhile Malaparte had had time and means to get himself into a world of trouble with Agnelli *and family*" (*Gli anni che scottano: Il primo lungo viaggio dentro il fascismo* [Milan: Mursia, 1967], 121; my emphasis). The senator's official biographer limited himself to a cryptic reference to Malaparte's destitution, as explained by reasons of a private nature (Castronovo, *Giovanni Agnelli*, 491). Finally, according to the authors of a history of the Fascist press, basing themselves on a message from the prefect of Turin

to Il Duce, Agnelli was ready to pay Malaparte the amount he demanded to put an end to the relationship between his daughter-in-law and the writer (Tranfaglia, Murialdi, and Legnani, *La stampa italiana*, 120–21).
67. Testimony to the author.
68. Vergani, *Misure del tempo*, 477. The initials of a wealthy ennobled Turinese industrialist are well known, at least in certain circles.
69. This report, dated Bologna, November 21, 1935, came to the knowledge of Malaparte, who inserted it among the exculpatory evidence, in the appendices, of ME, in *Malaparte*, 7:351.
70. Various messages from Perotti to Bocchini are preserved in ACS, Min. Int., "Agnelli Virginia" file.
71. Note dated Rome, December 11, 1935, in ACS, Min. Int., "Agnelli Virginia" file.
72. Letter dated Rome, October 2, 1936, in *Malaparte*, 3:728–29.
73. In place of "Boz," some hasty interpreters wished to read "Bog," after "Bogart." But the American actor was practically unknown in Italy at the time, and Malaparte would never have taken anyone as a model anyway. What's more, it would not have escaped the English-speaking Virginia and Jane that "bog" is an informal British term for "toilet." A photographic reproduction of this letter, dated December 24, 1936, appears in ACS, Min. Int., "Agnelli Virginia" file. Maria Sole Agnelli confirms: "She called him *Boz*," finding *Curzio* "too metallic" (testimony to the author).
74. The only letter attributed to Virginia held in AM, dated Coronado, California, June 7, 1940, entirely typewritten in perfect English, except the handwritten signature, "Scianflitua," is a fake, or refers to another correspondent.
75. The correspondence with Virginia was kept in a wardrobe in Capri, along with the correspondence with Senator Agnelli and with "Flaminia" (*Schiava di Malaparte*, 75–76). These documents, as with other manuscripts and documents, were stolen or went missing in the years when Casa Come Me remained uninhabited.
76. Probably "1890," December 19, 1936, ACS, Min. Int., "Agnelli Virginia" file. *Malaparte*, vol. 4, contains many (rather bad) poems dedicated to a "Jane," which would seem to be the princess of San Faustino.
77. Letter dated Milan, June 3, 1936, in AM, Borelli correspondence.
78. Testimony to the author.

79. Testimony to the author.
80. *Malaparte*, 3:729.
81. Letter dated Forte dei Marmi, October 15 [1936], in AM, Borelli correspondence.
82. See the documentation and letters collected in *Malaparte*, vol. 3, part 5, in particular the letters to Borelli of October 25 (p. 675) and 30 (pp. 732–33).
83. I was able to consult a copy of this document, dated Rome, November 30, 1936—attached to a transmittal letter of December 4 to the First Chair of the Court of Appeal of Turin, Ricci—and containing other elements of notable interest, thanks to the generosity of Claudio Quarantotto.
84. A copy of the judgment (no. 224) appears in ACS, Min. Int., "Agnelli Virginia" file.
85. Reports of December 19 and 24, 1936, in ACS, Min. Int., "Agnelli Virginia" file.
86. Note of June 17, 1936, by the minister Alfieri to the chief of police Bocchini, in ACS, Min. Cult. Pop., Reports 1922–1944, folder 7/65, "Malaparte—*Prospettive*" file.
87. Handwritten letter from Rome, Hotel de Russie, October 29, 1936, in AM, Borelli correspondence.
88. Note of June 17, 1936, from Alfieri to Serena, in ACS, Min. Cult. Pop., "Malaparte Curzio" file.
89. Note of December 29, 1936, in ACS, Min. Int., "Agnelli Virginia" file.
90. Note of June 14, 1937, in ACS, Min. Int., "Agnelli Virginia" file.
91. Note of February 20, 1937, in ACS, Min. Int., "Agnelli Virginia" file.
92. Letter from Borelli, dated Milan, October 30, 1936, in AM, Borelli correspondence.
93. In ACS, Min. Int., "Agnelli Virginia" file.
94. Enrico Roda, "20 domande a Curzio Malaparte," in *Malaparte*, 7:672–76. This did not stop him from claiming the opposite, writing to Carla Rulli, about a Chilean flirtation of his: "I don't say she is poor to emphasize a defect of hers. I say it because I cannot 'think' of a woman, worry about what she lacks, and her material life. For me it would constitute, if not slavery, a limit, a break. And I must be free to be able to write what I want" (letter from Santiago of January 9, 1953, in Rulli Archive).

95. Testimony to the author.
96. GS, in *Malaparte*, 6:279.
97. Letter from Ansaldo to Malaparte of December 9, 1946, in *Malaparte*, 7:231–32, in which he asks his permission to include the anecdote, without proper names, in the book he is writing. This was *Il vero signore*, 247–48, where Ansaldo mentions "a very well-known writer, now famous around the world," and "a lady bearing one of the greatest names of Italian industry, who had had with the writer with the birch branch in his hand relations known to all." The original text of the letter, held in AM, shows that Ansaldo really wanted to pay homage to Virginia's self-control. In any event, Malaparte did not give him satisfaction: "He finds a way to tell me he had not read the anecdote concerning him in *Il vero signore*" (*Anni freddi*, 321, dated August 17, 1949).
98. Presented for the first time in the exhibition *Malaparte: Arcitaliano nel mondo*.
99. See Guérin, *Du côté de chez Malaparte*, 53; Tamburi, *Malaparte come me*, 30. Maria Sole Agnelli would not offer any comment to me on the likelihood of this story. A cutout from the newspaper *Quadrante* of December 22, 1945, with information about Virginia's death, is preserved in the writer's archives; see *Malaparte*, 6:719.
100. "The woman to whom the book is dedicated died tragically, in November 1945, almost before the eyes of the author," Malaparte declared to one of his translators, the Monegasque diplomat René Novella, in a long letter of April 15, 1947 (*Mi scriveva Malaparte 1946–1956*, 2nd ed. [Pistoia: Gli Ori, 2010–11], 26–29). Perhaps for this reason, Biancamaria Fabbri claimed that "his love for Virginia lasted nine years" (*Schiava di Malaparte*, 99).
101. Testimonies of Maria Sole Agnelli and her son, Bernardino di Campello, to the author.
102. His son, Carlo Feltrinelli, described this painful story in *Senior Service* (Milan: Feltrinelli, 2001). Luigi Barzini Jr., more skillful than Malaparte at passing from Fascism to anti-Fascism, sent his colleague a very favorable letter in February 1946, during the purge process (see *Malaparte*, 7:379–80).
103. ACS, Min. Cult. Pop., Reports 1922–1944, folder 27/65, "Malaparte—Prospettive 1935–1943" file, and ACS, Min. Cult. Pop., Cabinet, 2nd

NOTES TO CHAPTER 3

deposit, "Fascicoli intestati a Personalità e Testate giornalistiche," folder 8. These payments were entered under heading 23 of the ministry's budget, but sometimes ascribed to the Directorate-General for Tourism or the Ministry of the Interior. Guerri (*L'arcitaliano*, 179) had previously heard from the publisher Gherardo Casini, at the time director general of the Italian press, that Malaparte had received a monthly payment of five thousand lire for the magazine. By way of comparison, a popular song of the era told the story of a young man who wanted to marry, "If I could have a thousand lire a month..." A senior official earned between fifteen hundred and two thousand lire.

104. ACS, Min. Cult. Pop., Reports 1922–1944, folder 5, *A Complete List of All Subsidies Given to Italian Newspapermen, Artists and Writers 1933–1943* established by the PWB (Psychological Warfare Branch), published as an appendix to Giovanni Sedita, *Gli intellettuali di Mussolini: La cultura finanziata dal fascismo* (Florence: Le Lettere, 2010), 187–244.

105. Sedita, *Gli intellettuali di Mussolini*, 142–43. Bucard, Doriot, Déat, and other exponents of French Fascism were also subsidized by the Ministry of Foreign Affairs.

106. Reproduced in *Malaparte*, 4:118–19.

107. Letter to Borelli of July 7, 1937, in *Malaparte*, 4:96.

108. See Pardini, introduction to *Prospettive 1939–1943*, 5n19.

109. Letter of April 4, 1938, in AM. We do not know what became of this material, of clear importance for understanding the origins of the Fascist aggression against republican Spain.

110. Letter to Bonaccorsi of January 29, 1938, in *Malaparte*, 4:316. AM contains many letters that testify to their brotherly relationship, while it lasted.

111. Malaparte had thought of using the title "Viva la morte!" for a novel set in the Prato countryside, announced for 1938 by the publisher Vallecchi. The few remaining fragments (see *Malaparte*, 4:239–305) suggest an early version of *The Forbidden Christ*.

112. See, most recently, Giorgio Israel, *Il fascismo e la razza: La scienza italiana e le politiche razziali del regime* (Bologna: Il Mulino, 2010). But the essential reference remains Renzo De Felice, *Storia degli ebrei italiani sotto il fascismo* (1961; Turin: Einaudi, 2005).

113. Letter from Malaparte, on *Prospettive* letterhead, of September 14, 1938. It is unclear whether the typewritten copy held in ACS, Min. Cult. Pop.,

Reports 1922–1944, "Malaparte—*Prospettive*" file, was addressed to the minister Alfieri or to his chief of staff. In any case, it was forwarded to Il Duce, who initialed it without comment.

114. Umberto Saba gave Malaparte credit for this much (*Ritratto di Malaparte*, 98–99), but also specified that Malaparte had first advised him to get baptized and that, faced with his refusal, "Curzio looked at me like an adult [looks at] a child lacking life experience."

115. Malaparte would claim that "in 1938 and 1939 I did my best to help Jews persecuted by Fascism, and for this reason was threatened with another deportation to Lipari. Despite this threat, I was able to save many Jews, among them the writers Alberto Moravia, Umberto Saba, Giacomo De Benedetti, Alberto Chimichi, etc." (see *Malaparte*, 7:117). To my knowledge, no evidence of the alleged threat of redeportation to Lipari has been found.

116. See his application for a review of the case, addressed to the military district of Lucca, in *Malaparte*, 4:63.

117. Curzio Malaparte, "Un fratello, molti fratelli," *Tempo*, July 15, 1954, in *Malaparte*, 10:747–48. It is possible that in this evaluation Malaparte was also influenced by his brother Ezio's long stay there.

118. Letter to Borelli of November 16, 1938, in *Malaparte*, 4:462.

119. Note from the minister Alfieri to the chief of police Bocchini of November 30, 1938; note from the chief of staff Luciano to the new minister Pavolini of May 5, in ACS, Min. Cult. Pop., Reports 1922–1944, "Malaparte—*Prospettive*" file.

120. It was Bonaccorsi, then vice commander of the forces in Addis Ababa, who had helped him have Ezio transferred to Ethiopia; see his thank-you letter dated Rome, April 19, 1939, in AM.

121. See *Malaparte*, 4:488–94. The report was added to Malaparte's 1946 statement of defense.

122. Testimony to the author. At this point, I asked her: "You were very young, very good-looking, and still are. Did he court you?" "Never."

123. Letter to G. Rulli from Addis Ababa, March 11, 1939, in Rulli Archive.

124. Curzio Malaparte, "L'assalto al bastione dei briganti," in *Corriere della Sera*, October 28, 1939, in *Malaparte*, 4:629–30.

125. The issue would emerge anew at the time of his war correspondence in

Greece and Albania, but there again without follow-through. See the request for "sensitive information" of December 16, 1940, addressed to the vice secretary of the PNF, Gaetani, to the chief of police, Senise, "about the reasons behind Curzio Malaparte's assignment to *confino*, with the aim of evaluating the appropriateness of his readmission to the Party," in *Malaparte*, 5:437.

126. These dispatches were eventually collected in VE.
127. *Malaparte*, 4:530.
128. *Malaparte*, 4:556.
129. See Pardini, introduction to *Prospettive 1939–1943*; see also Anna Nozzoli, "Appunti per una storia di 'Prospettive,'" in *Curzio Malaparte, il narratore, il politologo, il cittadino di Prato e dell'Europa*, 211–21.
130. *Malaparte*, 4:621–22.
131. Numerous letters from him can be found in *Malaparte*, vol. 8.
132. Letter to Prezzolini of April 24, 1946, in *Malaparte*, 7:35.
133. See the excellent anthology *Le riviste giovanili del periodo fascista*, ed. Alberto Folin and Mario Quaranta (Treviso: Canova, 1977).
134. See Maurizio Serra, *L'esteta armato: Il poeta-condottiero nell'Europa degli anni Trenta* (1990; Lavis [TN]: La Finestra, 2015).
135. Such was the case, for example, of Ruggero Zangrandi, in *Il lungo viaggio attraverso il fascismo: Contributo alla storia di una generazione* (1948; Milan: Feltrinelli, 1962), 398, in which he denounced "the muddle of *Prospettive*, a magazine founded by Malaparte in '37, in the wake and in the tradition of the old *Selvaggio* of Maccari[?] and, hence, without prejudice and with generally quite distinguished, nonconformist contributors. But with fundamentally ambiguous results in the end, just as the figure of the editor in chief was always ambiguous." Zangrandi and Fidia Gambetti are the best examples of gifted and honest young intellectuals who passed from "red Fascism" in the 1930s to communism during the war, and then to political disillusionment in the postwar era (to the point that Zangrandi committed suicide in 1970).
136. "Il surrealismo e l'Italia," *Corriere della Sera*, October 12, 1937, see *Malaparte*, 4:232–35.
137. For the influence of surrealism, and in particular of Lautréamont, on the writer, see Gianni Grana, *Malaparte* (Florence: La Nuova Italia, 1968), 53–55.

138. "Una tipica manifestazione giudaica," *Vent'anni*, March 2, 1940, in *Malaparte*, 5:82–83.
139. Draft letter from Moravia to Il Duce of March 7, 1941, published by Giuseppe Pardini in an appendix to "Malaparte, Moravia e 'Prospettive,'" *Nuova storia contemporanea*, no. 1 (January–February 1999): 128.
140. Gambetti, *Gli anni che scottano*, 396.
141. Letter from Capri, October 15, 1946, in Rulli Archive (phrase in quotation marks in English in the original).
142. See his letter to the Florence prosecutor general, included in the appendices to ME, where he underlines in particular that "during the anti-Semitic campaign, Malaparte demonstrated courage in his defense of Jewish writers and journalists and managed to get some exonerated" (in *Malaparte*, 7:374–76).
143. See *Malaparte*, 4:478–80.
144. *Malaparte*, 4:478–80. This reference to the "ghetto," possibly surprising in a non-antisemite like Malaparte, shows up more than once. He would say, for example, clearly alluding to Moravia, to his companion Biancamaria Fabbri: "You can't trust crippled Jews with sweaty hands" (*Schiava di Malaparte*, 35). Such expressions, it should be clarified, are very rare in his writing and clearly dictated by resentment.
145. Testimony to the author.
146. Alain Elkann, *Life of Moravia*, trans. William Weaver (Hanover, NH: Steerforth Italia, 2000), 131; see also de Ceccatty, *Alberto Moravia*, 134. I have found no trace of this stay in Malaparte's papers.
147. Testimony to the author.
148. Interview published in *Le Point*, April 1989, and testimony of Lambron to the author.
149. See the interview with Michele Bonuomo that opens *Malaparte: Una proposta*, in which Moravia nonetheless recognizes his debt to Malaparte for his first journalistic contributions.
150. Letter to Borelli of March 1, 1940, in *Malaparte*, 5:79–80.
151. Filippo Anfuso, *Da Palazzo Venezia al Lago di Garda (1936–1945)*, 2nd ed. (Bologna: Cappelli, 1957), 97. Appearing first in French translation, in 1949, Anfuso's is the most important and best-written testimony of the last phase of Fascist foreign policy, alongside Ciano's diary.

152. A fairly accurate biography in English is by Ray Moseley, *Mussolini's Shadow: The Double Life of Count Galeazzo Ciano* (New Haven, CT: Yale University Press, 1999).
153. François-Poncet, *A Palazzo Farnese*, 132.
154. *Malaparte*, 5:212–13.
155. Curzio Malaparte, "Lana caprina," *Prospettive*, June 15, 1940, in *Malaparte*, 5:217–18.
156. See the well-documented reconstruction by Frédéric Le Moal and Max Schiavon, *Juin 1940: La guerre des Alpes; Enjeux et stratégies* (Paris: Economica, 2010).
157. An earlier tribute to a dead mule, on the Saasit road, can be found in an unpublished passage of Malaparte's dispatches from Ethiopia (see *Malaparte*, 5:606–8), followed by this observation: "It is strange that men, whatever color they may be, do not cause me sorrow." It was probably the unorthodox reference to "color" that prevented publication.
158. A draft of "Sangue proibito" can be found in *Malaparte*, 5:519–42.
159. Letters to Mondadori, dated Capri, December 9, 1942, and February 12, 1943, respectively, in *Malaparte*, 6:202, 321–22.
160. See the first part of *Quota Albania* (Turin: Einaudi, 1971), dedicated to the French campaign. His most popular book, about the Russian campaign, is his 1953 account *The Sergeant in the Snow*, trans. Archibald Colquhoun (Evanston, IL: Marlboro Press / Northwestern, 1998).
161. Also relevant is the influence of mythological themes and of his beloved Greek tragedians, which Emmanuel Mattiato has highlighted in his "Curzio Malaparte et le chant de sphinx," in *Fictions de l'Histoire: Écritures et représentations de l'Histoire dans la littérature et les arts*, ed. Michael Kohlhauer (Chambéry: Université de Savoie, 2011), 175–202.
162. Letter to Sandro of July 8, 1940, in *Malaparte*, 4:254 and 4:517.
163. Letter to Borelli of September 26, 1940, in *Malaparte*, 5:322. This plan was preliminarily submitted to Mussolini by Pavolini, in a note of October 23, 1940, in which it says that "Malaparte has been sent to Greece at the request of the Ministry of Foreign Affairs.... The articles of a political character will be published only after his return"—that is, after the start of military operations. In ACS, Min. Cult. Pop., Reports 1922–1944, "Malaparte Curzio—*Prospettive*" file.

NOTES TO CHAPTER 3

164. See *Malaparte*, 5:322.
165. Emanuele Grazzi, *Il principio della fine (l'impresa di Grecia)* (Rome: Edizioni Faro, 1945), 225–26.
166. Giorgos Seferis, *Journées, 1925–1944*, trans. Gilles Ortlieb (Paris: Le Bruit du Temps, 2021), 455–56. The Greek edition of the diary comprises nine volumes; the cited French title corresponds to the first four; as yet no English translation of the relevant volume has appeared.—Trans.
167. The first article would be published in the *Corriere* the day of the invasion, October 28, with the allusive title "Il Pascià del King George" ("King George's pasha"; see *Malaparte*, 5:359–63); the others in the days following.
168. Letter from Athens, October 11, 1940, in AM, Borelli correspondence.
169. Emanuele Grazzi, *Il principio della fine*, 228–29.
170. Anfuso, *Da Palazzo Venezia al Lago di Garda*, 97.
171. The best account was written by another Italian journalist who fought there as an officer, Mario Cervi, *The Hollow Legions: Mussolini's Blunder in Greece, 1940–1941*, trans. Eric Mosbacher (New York: Doubleday, 1971).
172. In *Malaparte*, 5:485.
173. Letter to Leone Traverso, dated Rome, January 24, 1941, in *Malaparte*, 5:493.
174. Musiedlak, *Mussolini*, 404.
175. A nearly complete version appears in *Malaparte*, 7:399–483.
176. GS, dated January 11, 1944, in *Malaparte*, 6:469.
177. Curzio Malaparte, "Era un fatto vero: Il fantasma di Galeazzo Ciano in fondo alla via della Gorgona," *Tempo*, June 1945, in *Malaparte*, 6:657–61.
178. Letter to Borelli, dated Milan, December 10, 1940, in AM, Borelli correspondence. Also discussed was the idea of a report, never realized, from the Republic of Ireland, which was officially neutral, but whose sympathies inclined toward the Axis, out of anti-English rivalry.
179. For the most detailed reconstruction of the role of the Milanese daily in coverage of the war, see the doctoral thesis of Emmanuel Mattiato, "Les écrivains-journalistes du 'Corriere della Sera' durant la Seconde guerre mondiale: Curzio Malaparte, Dino Buzzati, Orio Vergani, Virgilio Lilli et Indro Montanelli," 3 vols., with numerous unpublished items, Paris Nanterre University, 2004.

180. In particular, those of Mauro Canali, "Curzio Malaparte e i servizi segreti americani," *Nuova Storia Contemporanea* 13, no. 4 (July–August 2009): 13–22. Following that, the journalist Fabio Fattore re-interviewed Pellegrini, but his account, which contains useful details above all about the Romanian episode, does not modify the overall picture: "Curzio Malaparte, corrispondente di guerra," *Nuova Storia Contemporanea* 14, no. 3 (May–June 2010): 93–114. See also, finally, Enzo R. Laforgia, *Malaparte scrittore di guerra* (Florence: Vallecchi, 2011).
181. GS, in *Malaparte*, 5:563.
182. Testimony to the author.
183. "Il motociclista Fleischmann," in *Malaparte*, 5:593–94. This passage contradicts the claim, in the author's preface to the French edition of *The Volga Rises in Europe*, according to which "I described the German soldiers without hate or sympathy, with absolute objectivity" (original in French).
184. Letter of December 11, 1941, in AM, Borelli correspondence.
185. Afeltra, *"Corriere" primo amore*, 141.
186. Curzio Malaparte, "La sera di Bucarest," in *Malaparte*, 5:576–77. This is where he gained the (unjust) reputation of having followed the war "from the hotels of Bucharest" ("Fallaci interrogation").
187. Curzio Malaparte, "Coi primi italiani a Belgrado," *Corriere della Sera*, April 20, 1941, in *Malaparte*, 5:602–7.
188. Curzio Malaparte, "Risveglio di Belgrado," *Corriere della Sera*, April 22, 1941; "Un faentino fra i primi entrati nella città di Belgrado," *Corriere Padano*, April 23, 1941; "Belgrado dopo la resa," *Corriere della Sera*, April 23, 1941; "L'ora che segnò la sorte di Belgrado," *Corriere della Sera*, April 27, 1941, in *Malaparte*, 5:608–24.
189. Curzio Malaparte, "Dov'è nata la nuova Croazia: Lo storico incontro di Monfalcone," *Corriere della Sera*, May 20, 1941, in *Malaparte*, 5:654–57.
190. In *Malaparte*, 5:659.
191. Note for Borelli, dated Jassy, July 8, 1941, transmitted by the Royal Consulate of Italy, in AM, Borelli correspondence.
192. On this brutal tragedy, see the definitive research of Radu Ioanid, *The Holocaust in Romania: The Destruction of Jews and Gypsies under the Antonescu Regime, 1940–1944*, trans. Marc J. Masurovsky (Chicago: Ivan R. Dee, 2000), chap. 3.
193. Pellegrini's testimony is categorical; see "Le guerre di Malaparte," *Storia*

illustrata, no. 192 (1973): 58. Malaparte was, however, the first to denounce this atrocity in 1944. In 2008 he received a fictionalized tribute in the film *Gruber's Journey*, by the Romanian director Radu Gabrea, in which one sees a Malaparte who, in search of a Jewish doctor, discovers traces of the pogrom. The sole incongruous aspect of the film is that we see him roaming around in the uniform of a captain of the Wehrmacht, whereas Malaparte, during his time on the eastern front, had always and only worn the uniform of an *Alpini* officer.

194. I deduce the date from a July 17 service note from the *Corriere della Sera*'s Bucharest office to the newspaper's editor: "Malaparte and Pellegrini of *Il Popolo d'Italia*" will probably leave tomorrow," in AM, Borelli correspondence.
195. Malaparte's activities and dispatches from Bucharest and Jassy were carefully monitored by the Royal Embassy of Romania in Rome; see dispatch no. 4463 of June 23, 1941, from the ambassador Grigorcea and attached press review. Malaparte is mentioned in the embassy's daily press reviews until July 11, which corresponds to his return to Italy.
196. Pellegrini, "Le guerre di Malaparte," 60.
197. See *Malaparte*, 7:291.
198. See *Malaparte*, 5:482–83, 495, 713–14.
199. Note of August 10, 1941, in ACS, Min. Cult. Pop., Reports 1922–1944, "Malaparte—*Prospettive*" file.
200. Letter dated Rome, September 15, 1941, in *Malaparte*, 5:720.
201. See Canali, "Curzio Malaparte e i servizi segreti americani," 15, which reproduces the two documents discovered in the archives of the Ministry of Popular Culture and of the Milanese daily.
202. This is a three-page typed memo, signed by Malaparte, dated Rome, June 18, 1942, sent to the Ministry of War in order to obtain payment of his benefits, where he claims to have been attached to the Wehrmacht in Russia and in Ukraine through mid-December 1941, which is false. The Ministry of War's personnel department sent a note (no. 08395/b) on August 4 to the Ministry of Popular Culture for further details. I have not turned up subsequent traces of this correspondence (ACS, Min. Cult. Pop., Cabinet, 2nd deposit, folder 8, no. 4, "Malaparte Curzio" file).
203. Letter dated Rome, December 9, 1941, in *Malaparte*, 5:738–39.

204. Canali kindly supplied me with a copy of the original letter, drawn from the *Corriere della Sera* archives, which corresponds to the text published in *Malaparte*, 5:739–40.
205. Phonogram of the chief of police, Ministry of the Interior, to the commissioner of Rome, and copied to the Ministry of Foreign Affairs and the Ministry of Popular Culture, in *Malaparte*, 5:745–46.
206. Letter dated Berlin, January 15, 1942, in *Malaparte*, 6:13.
207. Letter dated Milan, April 2, 1942, in *Malaparte*, 6:65.
208. In *Malaparte*, 6:228.
209. *Malaparte*, vol. 6, contains five of these dispatches: "Inverno in Polonia" (17–21), "Amazzoni e operai nelle strade di Cracovia" (23–26), "Sorge il Nebenland in Polonia" (47–51), "Fine del romanticismo politico" (56–60), "Anche Kant è un soldato alle soglie del mondo slavo" (61–65), whereas the writer claims to have sent only three. I haven't been able to establish if he also sent one about his visit to the Warsaw Ghetto (see also chap. 4).
210. Note from the prefect Luciano to the adviser Hans Mollier of February 13, 1942, in ACS, Min. Cult. Pop., Reports 1922–1944, folder 7/65, "Malaparte—*Prospettive*" file.
211. Letter of January 23, 1942, from Colonel Delio Vecchi, head of the high command's Office of the Press and Propaganda, to D. G. Casini of the Ministry of Popular Culture, in ACS, Min. Cult. Pop., Cabinet, 2nd deposit, folder 8, n. 4, "Malaparte Curzio" file.
212. Casini to Vecchi, February 16, 1942, ibid.
213. "Sorge il Nebenland in Polonia," 49–50.
214. Communiqué of the Italian Embassy in Berlin of June 23, 1942, in ACS, Min. Cult. Pop., Reports 1922–1944, "Malaparte—*Prospettive*" file, and letter from the Ministry of Popular Culture to Malaparte of July 3, 1942, in *Malaparte*, 6:150–51.
215. Sorrentino would collect his dispatches after the war, adapting their tone, in *Isba e steppa* (Milan: Mondadori, 1947). But without repeating the success of *Kaputt*.
216. See Eero Saarenheimo, "Münchhausen juopuneiden karhujen maassa," *Alkoholipolitiikka* (1967): 254–55; idem, "Kaputt di Malaparte letto da un finlandese," *Settentrione*, no. 17 (2005): 6–8. I am grateful to Markku Komonen for alerting me to these texts.

NOTES TO CHAPTER 3

217. Letter dated Helsinki, Hotel Torni, March 25, 1942, in Rulli Archive.
218. Montanelli, introduction to Tamburi, *Malaparte come me*, 6.
219. See also Torbjörn Elensky, "Den förlorade generationens provokative Dandy" [The provocative dandy of the lost generation], *Svenska Dagbladet*, November 24, 1996, and idem, "En person som kallas 'jag': Curzio Malaparte överlever historien" [A person called "me": Curzio Malaparte outlives history], *Res Publica* 39, no. 1 (1998).
220. Jonne Ahvonen, in the article "Malaparte in Finlandia: Quando e dove?," *Settentrione* 17 (2005): 9–18, arrives at exactly the same conclusion, based on a meticulous calculation not of the writer's absences from but of his visits to Finland.
221. See "Ritratto della Finlandia" (unpublished), in *Malaparte*, 6:86–90.
222. Testimony to the author.
223. Letter to G. Rulli, dated Helsinki, Hotel Torni, March 25, 1942, in Rulli Archive.
224. Letter to G. Rulli, dated Helsinki, August 24, 1942, in Rulli Archive.
225. See Ahvonen, "Malaparte in Finlandia," 12–13.
226. Cf. *Malaparte*, 5:481. It was on the basis of this article that after the war Ruggero Zangrandi would denounce Malaparte's alleged anti-Semitism (see chap. 4).
227. Memorandum by Costa, Bucharest office, to the editor in chief of the *Corriere della Sera*, dated July 17, 1941, 12:10 a.m., in AM, Borelli correspondence.
228. Letters from Bompiani to Malaparte of February 16 and March 20, 1943, in *Malaparte*, 6:323 and 328.
229. Malaparte, *La Volga naît en Europe*, 9.
230. See, in particular, *Malaparte*, 9:816–24.
231. I refer readers to the third part of the previously cited thesis by Emmanuel Mattiato, appropriately titled "L'énigme Malaparte: Une poétique du reportage de guerre," 330–440.
232. *Malaparte*, 6:190–92. In the same vein is another theatrical fragment, from August 1954, inspired by the Russo-Finnish war of 1940, "La mano dell'uomo," in *Malaparte*, 11:35–50.
233. Max-Pol Fouchet, "L'ouvrier et le militaire," *Carrefour*, June 30, 1948.
234. Unpublished letter from Miller to Malaparte, dated Big Sur, California, June 28, 1948.

235. Gambetti, *Gli anni che scottano*, 384.
236. Letter to Philippe Rossignol, of the publisher Denoël, dated Capri, September 8, 1956, in which he informs him that "the book is almost ready," in *Malaparte*, 12:609–10.
237. GS, in *Malaparte*, 6:384–85. Malaparte wrote, erroneously, like nearly everyone even today, "von Paulus." The noble predicate was an invention of Soviet propaganda, after the field marshal's capitulation, to increase the status of the defeat, as a typical representative of the Prussian military caste (and Paulus was not this either).
238. Letter dated Stockholm, June 25, 1943, in *Malaparte*, 6:387.
239. See "Fallaci interrogation."
240. Authorization by Il Duce of May 15, 1943, and payment order of May 31, signed by the Minister for Exchanges and Currencies Bonomi, in ACS, Min. Cult. Pop., Reports 1922–44, "Malaparte—*Prospettive*" file.
241. Leonardo Simoni (Michele Lanza), *Berlino, Ambasciata d'Italia 1939–1943* (Rome: Migliaresi, 1946), dated July 27, 1943. Lanza is the other protagonist, alongside Ridomi, of the pseudo-orgy described in *The Skin*.
242. Cristiano Ridomi, *La fine dell'Ambasciata a Berlino 1940–1943* (Milan: Longanesi, 1972), 120–24. Here the author also points out that German radio announced Mussolini's resignation ("for health reasons") with a twenty-four-hour delay. In a novel, *Avventura '43* (Milan: Longanesi, 1966), which Ridomi had previously drawn from his Berlin memories, Malaparte shows up in the guise of Marzio, a journalist in the uniform of an *Alpini* captain, "with a fountain pen in his hat" (128). The protagonist, Alexandra, says of him: "He would be a handsome man, too, if he didn't have that fish mouth and those knobbly knees" (132).

Chapter 4

1. Giuseppe Pardini, *Malaparte: Biografia politica* (Milan: Luni, 1998), 295, was the first to propose this classification.
2. "I am writing The Plague and I will infect everyone," he wrote from Capri on November 28, 1946, to the publisher Valentino Bompiani (in *Malaparte*, 7:221). After *La peste* (The plague), he thought about *La pelle umana* (The human skin) (see the letter to G. Rulli from Capri, October 15, 1946, in Rulli Archive) before deciding on *La pelle*; see "Malaparte, Napoléon de

la littérature, dispute La Peste à Albert Camus," in *Malaparte*, 7:589–93 (unpublished text, in the third person, probably by Malaparte himself). Finally, in an undated interview from 1949, he declared caustically: "The definitive title is *The Skin*. Because I too, you can be sure, care about mine" (in *Malaparte*, 8:519–20).

3. Letter to G. Rulli from Capri, August 20, 1943, in Rulli Archive.
4. "Lettre à mes camarades français de 1914–18," which opens the French edition of *The Skin*, 13. See also the beginning of chap. 18 of *Kaputt*, "The Blood," 408–10, in which Malaparte talks about leaving prison in Rome, on August 7, as if he had been shut up there by the Fascists.
5. Testimony of Daniele Rulli to the author. Malaparte also asked for help from another diplomat friend, Luca Pietromarchi, then head of the Armistice and Peace Cabinet at Palazzo Chigi. The latter intervened successfully with Carmine Senise, newly reinstalled as the national police chief. Testimony of his son, Antonello Pietromarchi, to the author.
6. Note 1396/s.q., in ACS, Min. Cult. Pop., "Malaparte Curzio" file.
7. The two letters are both dated Capri, September 3, 1943, in *Malaparte*, 6:438–42.
8. Pardini, "Malaparte, Moravia e 'Prospettive,'" 109.
9. The first, sent to Ms. Pellegrini on September 3, was published as an appendix to ibid., 113–25. The second is included in *Malaparte*, 6:680–90.
10. Letter from Capri of August 20, 1943, in Rulli Archive. This long text (six typewritten pages) contains numerous additions by hand, evidently the fruit of a rereading, which is rather rare in Malaparte's correspondence.
11. Ibid. and letter of August 21, 1943, sent with the preceding one.
12. See Ennio Di Nolfo and Maurizio Serra, *La gabbia infranta: Gli Alleati e l'Italia 1943–1945* (Bari: Laterza, 2009).
13. Letter from Capri of September 5, 1943. In the same letter, Malaparte asks his friend if the Badoglio government has abolished "the laws on the prohibition against marrying foreigners, [otherwise] how am I gonna get married?" Nothing has come to light about these marriage plans. At the time, Malaparte was spending time with the Frenchwoman Anne H., who was already married, though.
14. "Nota per le Autorità politiche anglo-americane di Capri," in *Malaparte*, 6:447–49.

15. In his 1946 statement of defense he would write that "at every announcement of a visit by some important foreign political figure, I suffered the fate of all former *confinati* and those on a warning: I was stopped and let go some time later" (ME, in *Malaparte*, 7:282, 288). I have not found the least evidence of this.
16. Adrian Gallegos, *From Capri into Oblivion* (London: Hodder & Stoughton, 1959), 18–20. Malaparte's "greying" hair must have been due to a dye shortage. It would become jet black again in subsequent descriptions.
17. See Peter Sebastian, *I servizi segreti speciali britannici e l'Italia (1940–1945)* (Rome: Bonacci, 1986), and Mireno Berrettini, *La Gran Bretagna e l'antifascismo italiano* (Florence: Le Lettere, 2010). Sebastian kindly confirmed for me the lack of any trace in English archives of a relationship between Malaparte and the SOE.
18. Bengt Jangfeldt, *Axel Munthe: The Road to San Michele* (New York: Tauris, 2008), 339n. I am grateful to the author for the supplemental information he kindly provided me about relations between the two writers, quite different from the image *Kaputt* would offer.
19. See *Malaparte*, 6:454.
20. ACS, ACC, box 46, reel 177C, folder 1617, quoted in Canali, "Curzio Malaparte e i servizi segreti americani," 20. The Malaparte-Winner correspondence would have been photographed by the police. See also *Malaparte*, 5:206.
21. Percy Winner, *Dario, 1925–1945: A Fictitious Reminiscence* (New York: Harcourt & Brace, 1947). I was able to consult this nearly unfindable text thanks to the kindness of Mauro Canali, who is preparing an Italian edition.
22. *Malaparte*, 7:580. Malaparte was reacting to a review of *Dario* in the *Herald Tribune* of March 30, 1947, which presented Winner's novel as "a case history in political opportunism" (*Malaparte*, 7:548).
23. There nonetheless figures among his papers a letter, undated but probably from late 1951, addressed to the editor of an unspecified newspaper, in which he reacts to the controversy over *Kaputt* in Germany: "It is probable that it was the intention of Marshal [Albert] Kesselring [commander in chief of the German forces in Italy and the Mediterranean] to raze all of Italy to the ground; and he certainly would have done so, if the Italians, without distinction of party, Salò Republicans, Partisans, soldiers of the Italian Liberation Corps, and Allies had not prevented him" (in *Malaparte*,

9:809). If the letter had been sent at the time, something we have not been able to establish, this claim would have created a scandal, whereas today it is a (relative) commonplace in the historiographical debate.

24. Letter to Ms. Pellegrini of September 3, 1944, in *Malaparte*, 6:441.

25. See his message to the Naples chief of police of January 1, 1945, at the time of the investigation into his alleged war profiteering, in which he specifies that he was mobilized "not at my request," in *Malaparte*, 6:515, 653. And yet in an autobiographical fragment from 1944—probably a draft of his 1946 statement of defense—one can read: "In the days following the armistice of September 8, 1943, I was with the Allies straightaway, as a liaison officer with the American high command, from the landing at Salerno until the complete liberation of Italy" (*Malaparte*, 7:118). In a November 1, 1952, letter to the head of *Time* magazine's Rome bureau, he would claim that "it was I... who wrote and sent to the Ministery [*sic*] of War of the Badoglio Government in Bari [*sic*, for Brindisi] a plan for the organization of a regular Army of Liberation which would fight with the Allies against the Germans" (*Malaparte*, 10:183; original in English).

26. Curzio Malaparte, "Al carissimo generale Alexander," *Il Tempo*, June 15, 1950, in *Malaparte*, 9:255–58.

27. Guerri, *L'arcitaliano*, 205–13. The *Giornale segreto* indicates the author's progress on various chapters: thus "The Mice of Jassy," begun on March 27, was finished on April 2, 1944 (see *Malaparte*, 6:485, 487).

28. "Portrait de l'auteur par lui-même," in *Malaparte*, 8:125–27 (original in French).

29. Cf. the edition edited by Martellini, in Malaparte, *Opere scelte*, 1531–47.

30. Pellegrini, who had alluded to the possibility of a first, somehow pro-German draft of *Kaputt* in previous interviews, was unequivocal with me: "In Helsinki, he showed me the manuscript of the book, entitled 'God Shave the King.' The content was different, even contrary [to that of the final book], decidedly anti-British. He explained the title to me this way: 'You see, God can't save the Brits, he has to confine himself to giving them a shave.'" The title appears just once, without comment, in a note of the GS, dated Oulu in Finland, August 11, 1942 (see *Malaparte*, 6:265).

31. Ansaldo, *Il giornalista di Ciano*, 295, dated March 21, 1941. The conversation took place in a Bari hotel, where both were part of Ciano's retinue.

Ansaldo had reluctantly agreed to present propaganda programs on the radio, to try to combat the influence of the BBC's programs in Italian, which already had a large following.

32. An accusation taken up in particular by Zangrandi, in *Il lungo viaggio attraverso il fascismo*, 421, 425, in which he recalls Malaparte's reputation as pro-German and his articles regarding "the social danger represented by the Jews" in the East. I have clarified in the preceding chapter that these articles had undergone interpolations by the censors, about which the author complained in vain. Zangrandi's book paved the way for a copious literature of memoirs by so-called red Fascists, all generally highly critical of Malaparte.

33. DFP, 5, dated June 30, 1947.

34. This opinion is shared by, among others, Gianni Grana, "Malaparte, écrivain d'Europe," *Chroniques Italiennes*, no. 44 (1995), and William Hope, *Curzio Malaparte: The Narrative Contract Strained* (Market Harborough: Troubadour, 2000).

35. See Ernst Jünger, *A German Officer in Occupied Paris: The War Journals 1941–1945*, trans. Thomas S. Hansen and Abby J. Hansen (New York: Columbia University Press, 2019).

36. Thus Dominique Fernandez, in his preface to the reprint of the French edition of *Kaputt* (Paris: Denoël, 2006).

37. This is the central question pervading my book of dialogues and reminiscences with the great Jewish Hungarian-French intellectual François Fejtö (1909–2008). See Fejtö and Serra, *Le Passager du siècle: Guerres, Révolutions, Europes* (Paris: Hachette, 1999).

38. GS, dated August 15, 1942, in *Malaparte*, 6:268–69. And he adds, with rare warmth: "I am extremely sorry he's leaving. I've grown fond of his intelligence, his spirit, his goodness, and, in a certain sense, his frankness." The references to Foxá in Finland are numerous in the *Giornale segreto*, among them sketches of speeches delivered by (or attributed to) his Spanish friend in *Kaputt*. But after the war, the tone would change in his regard as well: "As good a speaker as he is, he's just as bad a writer. No offense to de Foxa [*sic*], but I tell his stories better than he does" (DFP, 86).

39. *Madrid da Corte a Ceka*, trans. Carlo Boselli (Milan: Garzanti, 1942). In Spain, the book was republished in 2006 by Ciudadela de Los Libros

(Madrid). On the "bittersweet friendship" between Malaparte and the Spanish diplomat, see the documented observations of his biographer, Luis Sagrera, *Agustín de Foxá: Una aproximación a su vida y su obra* (Burgos: Editorial Dossoles, 2009), 58–62.

40. This is the question famously put by Hannah Arendt in *Eichmann in Jerusalem: A Report on the Banality of Evil* (1963; London: Penguin Modern Classics, 2022).

41. He organized a memorable joke with the Romanian press attaché, Titu Mihailescu, and their Finnish escort, Captain Leppo, at Foxá's expense. The Spaniard underwent the steam baths for the sake of diplomatic courtesy, but refused to roll around in the snow, at the end of the session. Malaparte had the alarm sounded, after a fake Soviet attack. Everyone rushed outside in the altogether, including Foxá, to general hilarity (see Pellegrini, "Le guerre di Malaparte," 62).

42. In *Malaparte*, 7:721.

43. On this point, see the acute reflections and testimony of Cesare Musatti, "Considerazioni psicologiche sul comportamento degli ebrei italiani di fronte alla legislazione razziale," in *Mia sorella gemella la psicanalisi* (Pordenone: Studio Tesi, 1991), 116–29.

44. Primo Levi, *The Drowned and the Saved*, trans. Michael F. Moore, in *The Complete Works of Primo Levi*, ed. Ann Goldstein (New York: Liveright, 2015), 3:2490–91.

45. Ibid., 3:2491.

46. Jean-Paul Sartre, *Saint Genet comédien et martyr* (Paris: Gallimard, 1952), 15.

47. As we saw in chap. 3, Malaparte was escorted by two German officials and by a certain Valcini, a local Italian journalist; see *Malaparte*, 6:232.

48. Shirer, for his part, noted that, starting on November 19, 1939, or just two months after the invasion of Poland, Frank implemented a policy of extermination of the Polish Jews packed into the Warsaw Ghetto (*Berlin Diary: The Journal of a Foreign Correspondent, 1934–1945* [New York: Knopf, 1943], 201–2). Malaparte would cite precisely this text—"read, for example, *Berlin Diary*, where he describes his meetings with Nazi leaders"—in a reply of November 15 to the *Partisan Review* editor William Barrett, who had accused him of consorting with Nazi dignitaries during the war (*Malaparte*, 10:195). It is not clear, though, whether such a letter was sent.

49. To the American psychiatrist of the Nuremberg prison, impressed by his high cultural level, Frank repeated his preference for Chopin over Wagner. See Douglas M. Kelley, *22 Cells in Nuremberg* (London: Allen, 1947), 145–51. This confirms the plausibility of Malaparte's account.
50. See *The Author of Himself: The Life of Marcel Reich-Ranicki*, trans. Ewald Osers (Princeton, NJ: Princeton University Press, 2001), 155.
51. "It was evident that Frank considered himself a great tragic figure, a representative of God who had sold his soul but was about to recover it at the cost of his life. This sentiment permitted him to also regain the attitude of superiority and domination he had always tried to achieve. In reality, he was about to use the certainty of his own imminent death as a crutch to support his own Ego," notes Kelley, *22 Cells in Nuremberg*, 150. According to other witnesses, including my dear friend Anthony Freire Marreco (1915–2006), then a junior member of the British prosecutor's team at Nuremberg, Frank was a "lost man," avoided by other defendants who (like Speer and the military men) still hoped to save their lives.
52. Thomas Mann, *Doctor Faustus: The Life of the German Composer Adrian Leverkühn as Told by a Friend*, trans. John E. Woods (New York: Knopf, 1997), 260, 261, 263.
53. Ibid., 264.
54. Shirli Gilbert, *Music in the Holocaust: Confronting Life in the Nazi Ghettos and Camps* (Oxford: Oxford University Press, 2005), 43.
55. Reich-Ranicki, *The Author of Himself*, 158.
56. Compare, in Spielberg's *Schindler's List*, the sequence in which some young SS soldiers, while liquidating the Kraków Ghetto, interrupt the massacre to gather around one of their number, who is playing the piano in one of the ransacked houses, and discuss whether the piece is by Bach or by Mozart. Some survivors reported that certain guards were moved even to tears during the Sunday concerts by their victims at Auschwitz, and also played with them. This rehumanization ceased the moment the music stopped (Gilbert, *Music in the Holocaust*, 188–89). Here too one returns, paradoxically, to *One Thousand and One Nights*.
57. In "Portrait de l'auteur par lui-même," Malaparte adds: "A certain episode of my visit to Frank merits a clarification. When Frank raises the rifle and aims at the child, I don't give him the time to shoot. I lower his arm and say to him: 'Don't do this. If you do this, I will tell it all in the *Corriere*

della Sera, and you'll have big problems. The Italian people don't like for children to be killed.' Frank stared at me. 'What tender hearts you Italians have!' he said and gave the rifle back to the soldier" (*Malaparte*, 8:126; original in French). This "clarification," fortunately omitted from the book, is worse than a boast: it's bad literature.

58. Mann, *Doctor Faustus*, 264.
59. The episode was contradicted by a friend and colleague of Malaparte's, who covered the Balkans and knew Pavelić well, Giuseppe Solari Bozzi, in *Storie di altri: Dal taccuino di un giornalista* (Soveria Mannelli (CZ): Rubbettino, 2009), 97–98. Anfuso, too, who had dealings with Pavelić, describes him as "a classic of Balkan terrorism, [who] encircles himself with time bombs. He has the eyes of an agitator; otherwise, he can pass unobserved; he speaks an excellent Tuscan" (Anfuso, *Da Palazzo Venezia al Lago di Garda*, 157–58).
60. Kundera, *Encounter*, 171.
61. In *Malaparte*, 6:733 (original in French).
62. A preview of this can be found in an article of March 21, 1940, in the *Corriere della Sera*, "Il corpo di Napoli," in *Malaparte*, 5:105–7.
63. Traudl Junge, *Until the Final Hour: Hitler's Last Secretary*, ed. Melissa Muller, trans. Anthea Bell (New York: Arcade, 2004).
64. In reality, as we have seen, Febo became ill and died in January 1942, when Malaparte was somewhere between Berlin and Helsinki: "After Regina Coeli, the greatest sorrow of my life," GS, in *Malaparte*, 6:236.
65. In particular in *Malaparte*, 6:524–605, 621–28, where the title "Il Cristo proibito" also appears.
66. Letter from Guy Tosi, dated Paris, May 20, 1947, in *Malaparte*, 7:603–4.
67. See *Malaparte*, 7:605–20.
68. Letter to Guy Tosi, undated (September 1947?), in *Malaparte*, 7:704–5.
69. See d'Orsi, *L'Italia delle idee*, 308.
70. Bertolt Brecht, *Mother Courage and Her Children*, trans. John Willett (New York: Penguin Books, 2007), 82.
71. Curzio Malaparte, "Viva l'Italia," *Il Tempo*, May 19, 1946, in *Malaparte*, 6:61–62.
72. "20 domande a Curzio Malaparte," *Tempo*, July 20, 1955, in *Malaparte*, 11:464.

73. Olivier Remaud, "Littérature et mythologie dans 'La pelle' de Malaparte," *Chroniques Italiennes*, no. 44 (1995): 2.
74. "L'Europe aux anciens parapets," in *Malaparte*, 7:695 (original in French).
75. "Lettera aperta al sindaco di Napoli," February 19, 1950, in *Malaparte*, 9:83–85. The writer also appealed to the Italian Council of State about the legitimacy of the city council resolution (9:185–88).
76. See also the attack of the philosopher Edmondo Cione against "the impostor Curzio": *Napoli e Malaparte* (Naples: Pellerano e Del Gaudio, [1950]).
77. See "Napoli, i Napoletani e Malaparte pentito," *Roma*, October 17, 1955, in *Malaparte*, 11:601–4. Cavani seems to have been inspired by him in her film for the invented character of the smuggler.
78. "Decretum Proscriptio Libri," *Osservatore Romano*, June 17, 1950.
79. "Una dichiarazione di Malaparte," *Tempo*, June 17, 1950.
80. Letter to the pope in *Malaparte*, 9:259–68.
81. Ernesto Valentini, SJ, "In merito ad una recente condanna all'Indice," *La Civiltà Cattolica*, no. 2401, July 1950, 26–36.
82. Testimony of Father Ferdinando Castelli to the author.
83. In this case as well, Malaparte had written an earlier version before the war, in an article in *Tempo* of February 8, 1940, "Al cratere del Vesuvio in automobile," in *Malaparte*, 5:57.
84. Letter sent on August 18, 1950, during Vailland's stay on Capri, to Malaparte during the filming of *The Forbidden Christ*, in *Malaparte*, 9:312.
85. "Donne pederaste," in *Malaparte*, 9:606–9.
86. For an example at once brilliant and characteristic of the limits of this interpretation, see Susan Sontag, "Fascinating Fascism," in *Under the Sign of Saturn* (New York: Farrar, Straus & Giroux, 1980). Alice Kaplan, in *The Collaborator: The Trial and Execution of Robert Brasillach* (Chicago: University of Chicago Press, 1999), highlights the homophobic overtones of the sentence pronounced against the collaborationist writer.
87. "At 11 Giorgio Napolitano came down with [his magazine] 'Latitudine.' An intelligent young man," he noted in GS, February 27, 1944, on the occasion of their first meeting (see *Malaparte*, 6:477).
88. Testimony to the author.
89. Pardini, *Malaparte: Biografia politica*, 312. The controversy flared up again in January 1949, at the time of Malaparte's clash with the PCI, after the

publication of his short anti-Communist novel *Storia di domani*. In an address in Bologna, Togliatti claimed to possess a party-membership application from the writer along with his "autobiography" (about which more later). Malaparte reacted by sending a denial from Paris to *L'Unità* regarding the first point, but he glossed over the second, saying that "these autobiographical pages do not contain anything I have not already said and repeated for many years." Togliatti let it slide, and the matter concluded with a new letter from the writer, this time to *Il Tempo*, in which he recognized the fair play of the PCI secretary (*Malaparte*, 8:330–31, 357). And the exchange of winks between the two continued...

90. "Quaranta minuti alla televisione con Malaparte," June 1953, in *Malaparte*, 10:370. In "Due cappelli di paglia d'Italia," Malaparte would increase the distance to a hundred feet and substitute the Matisse (which probably existed only in his imagination) with a Dufy: "A communist leader who recognizes a Dufy a hundred feet away is certainly one of those monsters who frighten the bourgeois. I was fascinated" (DC, 104).

91. Italo de Feo, *Diario politico 1943–1948* (Milan: Rusconi, 1973), 133–34, entry dated July 15, 1944. De Feo was then one of Togliatti's secretaries. He broke with the PCI in 1948.

92. Testimony to the author.

93. GS, entry dated March 3, 1944, in which Malaparte recounts his conversation with a correspondent for the *London Sunday Times*, O. H. Brandon, in *Malaparte*, 6:486.

94. The articles are reproduced in *Malaparte*, 6:502–14.

95. See Francesco Perfetti, *Assassinio di un filosofo: Anatomia di un omicidio politico* (Florence: Le Lettere, 2004), as well as Alberto Indelicato, Giuseppe Are, and Hervé A. Cavallera, "Sull'assassinio di Giovanni Gentile," *Nuova Storia Contemporanea* 9, no. 1 (January–February 2005): 151–60.

96. I found this comment on a page in ACS, Min. Cult. Pop., Cabinet, folder 49, "Malaparte Curzio" file.

97. ACS, Min. Int., DGPS, Direzione Servizi Informativi Speciali (SIS), Sez. II, 1944–49, folder 158, "Malaparte Curzio" file. The file contains press cuttings and an exchange of letters between the Interior Ministry cabinet and the Naples prefect Selvaggi about the circumstances of the arrest of Malaparte, who had been immediately released after the notification of the open case against him.

98. The acquittal verdict was confirmed on December 20, 1947, by the Florence Court of Appeals; see *Malaparte*, 7:386–96. Togliatti had been deposed on November 19, 1946.
99. In *Malaparte*, 12:466–68.
100. Letter of April 27, 1946, in *Malaparte*, 7:36–38.
101. Giovanni Papini, *Diario* (Florence: Vallecchi, 1962), 267.
102. Guy Tosi, "Curzio Malaparte et 'Kaputt,'" *Parigi*, April 19, 1946. Tosi (1910–2000) would later become director of the French Institute of Florence. I am very grateful to him for his encouragement and advice for my research.
103. "Himmler tout nu fouetté par ses soldats," *Paris Matin*, June 28, 1946.
104. "'Kaputt' de Malaparte," *Combat*, July 17, 1946.
105. "'Kaputt' par Malaparte," *Tel Quel*, August 20, 1946.
106. "La voix de Malaparte," *Carrefour*, August 29, 1946.
107. "Une épopée de Malaparte," *Les Nouvelles Littéraires*, September 26, 1946.
108. See Howard Taubman, "Diary of an Ex-Fascist Journalist," *Stars and Stripes*, November 3, 1946; Orville Prescott, review of *Kaputt*, *New York Times*, November 5, 1946; "Dubious Chronicle," *Time*, November 11, 1946; Robert Pick, "History as a Nude with Lessons," *Saturday Review of Literature*, November 16, 1946; and the fiercest of all, Vincent Sheehan, "Out of Fascism on the Evil Side," *New York Herald Tribune*, November 17, 1946.
109. *Between the Thunder and the Sun* (London: Macmillan, 1944). Sheehan, after settling on Lake Maggiore, would write popular biographies of Luisa Sanfelice, Verdi, and others, and some now-forgotten novels.
110. Letter to Nicholas Wreden, vice president of E. P. Dutton & Co., Capri, November 28, 1946, in *Malaparte*, 7:223.
111. Letter from Columbia University, December 31, 1946, in *Malaparte*, 7:238–39.
112. Letter to Robert Pick of the *Saturday Review of Literature* (New York), of April 19, 1947, in *Malaparte*, 7:564.
113. See *Malaparte*, 7:507.
114. "Que pensez-vous de Kaputt?," *Les Nouvelles Littéraires*, January 16, 1947.
115. Letter from Janine Bouissounouse, dated Rome, February 15, 1947, in *Malaparte*, 7:516–17. He would rather less elegantly call her a "species of camel," writing to Tosi about the matter (see *Malaparte*, 7:584).
116. Malaparte, "Portrait de l'auteur," 126 (original in French).

117. See *Malaparte*, 7:207.
118. Ibid., 87.
119. Letter of May 13 (where it is specified he would be paid fifteen thousand lire for each article) and of September 30, 1946, in AM, Angiolillo correspondence. The prohibition applied to all *Italian* journalists; at Nuremberg there were certainly Allied ones, including John Dos Passos, who later readapted his dispatches into one of his best late novels, *The Great Days* (1958).
120. Malaparte, "Brief an die deutschen Leser e Ein Wort an den nachdenklichen Leser," in *Kaputt*, trans. Hellmut Ludwig (Karlsruhe: Stahlberg Verlag, 1951).
121. See Friedrich Sieburg, "Ein Schriftsteller muß die Wahrheit dienen," *Gegenwart*, March 15, 1949, and the letter from Malaparte to Hellmut Ludwig, dated Paris, April 30, 1949, in *Malaparte*, 8:501–2.
122. *Malaparte*, 9:785.
123. See *Malaparte*, 10:360–67.
124. See *Malaparte*, 10:733–34.
125. "Viaggio in Germania," in *Malaparte*, 10:122–24.
126. See *Malaparte*, 10:85, 97–98, etc.
127. "La paura nelle stilografiche: Gli scrittori e gli artisti tedeschi hanno timore di far udire la propria voce," *Epoca*, June 7, 1952, in *Malaparte*, 10:128–31.
128. "Esplorazione della Germania d'oggi: 'Gli orrori della guerra,'" in *Malaparte*, 10:497.
129. Which provoked a new response from Malaparte: "Rispondo all'ambasciatore von Brentano," *Tempo*, August 9, 1956, in *Malaparte*, 12:530.
130. *Malaparte*, 10:217–21, contains the list of fragments omitted by Falqui.
131. Original in Grossin Archive, reproduced in *Malaparte*, 9:25. This letter is not included in Tamburi, *Malaparte come me*.
132. Undated letter, but probably of January 1950, dictated to Dr. Camus (see chap. 5), in Joxe-Halévy Archives (original in French).
133. "Journal d'un délicat," in *Histoires déplaisantes* (Paris: Gallimard, 1991), 51. See also Maurizio Serra, *Les Frères séparés: Drieu La Rochelle, Aragon et Malraux face à l'Histoire* (Paris: La Table Ronde, 2008), chap. 4.

Chapter 5

1. This is the title of the article by Alain Sarrabayrouse in *Chroniques Italiennes*, no. 44 (1995). See also the proceedings of the international conference *La bourse des idées du monde: Malaparte e la Francia*, and the contribution of Jean-Claude Thiriet, "Paris la haine," in *Curzio Malaparte, il narratore, il politologo*, 1:315–25.
2. See the reflections of Cesare De Michelis, "Il conformismo degli intellettuali," in *Moderno antimoderno*, 45–69.
3. See Francesco Perfetti, "Curzio Malaparte 1947–1949: Contro il fascismo dell'antifascismo," *Nuova Storia Contemporanea* 6, no. 3 (May–June 2002): 79–92.
4. Fragment [1953?], in *Malaparte*, 10:353–56.
5. The publication date (if there was any) is not indicated; see *Malaparte*, 7:270–73.
6. Curzio Malaparte, "L'Italie sans masque," *La Gazette de Lausanne*, January 24, 1948, and "Les nouveaux messieurs," *La Gazette de Lausanne*, January 28, 1948. These articles and those that followed (including a portrait of Togliatti) were collected in DC.
7. Malaparte, "L'Italie subira-t-elle le sort de la Tchécoslovaquie?," *Carrefour*, March 18, 1948 (original in French).
8. Guy Tosi, *D'Annunzio en France au début de la Grande Guerre* (Florence: Sansoni, 1968).
9. See Jean A. Gili, *L'Italie de Mussolini et son cinéma* (Paris: H. Veyrier, 1981).
10. Dominique Arban, "'Je ne comprends rien à ce qui m'arrive,' nous dit Malaparte," in *Malaparte*, 7:658–59. In the interview, he also boasts of having "saved" numerous Jewish intellectuals, including the wife of De Chirico, Umberto Saba, etc., intervening with Ciano.
11. Letter to Marcel Brion dated Chamonix, February 8, 1948, in response to a harsh attack by Brion, "Pour un traité de l'imposture Suckert-Malaparte," in his report on *Une semaine dans le Monde*, January 30, 1948. The two texts appear in *Malaparte*, 8:43–44 and 49–53.
12. I was able to consult this twenty-nine-page file, cataloged as M6, Police Headquarters, Criminal Investigation Department, Fifth Service, AC: 176.084, thanks to the kindness of Prof. Didier Musiedlak and Dr. Nicolas Patin.

NOTES TO CHAPTER 5

13. In October 1954 he would publish a series of touching remembrances of the Great War in *Tempo*; see also "Anche i nostri morti guardavano Trieste," in *Malaparte*, 10:842–60.
14. Guerri, *L'arcitaliano*, 192–94.
15. Letter dated Paris, February 6, 1947, in *Malaparte*, 7:511–12.
16. "Monsieur Caméléon," *Le Figaro*, February 5, 1949.
17. Letter dated Forte dei Marmi, September 14, 1949, in *Malaparte*, 8:561–62 (original in French).
18. See the account of Georg Dietz, "Der letzte Mensch," in *Die Zeit*, August 3, 2006.
19. Letter to Prezzolini, dated Capri, May 30, 1950, in *Malaparte*, 9:241–43.
20. See "Ce que la critique internationale pense de 'La Peau,'" in *Malaparte*, 8:659–65.
21. Letter dated Capri, February 27, 1950, in *Malaparte*, 9:110–11, reproduced in Tamburi, *Malaparte come me*, 156–57. Shortly before, in the same terms, he had written to Rulli: "But if your critical judgment about my book is fundamentally right, your secondary assessments are belied by events. *The Skin* has been a much bigger seller than *Kaputt*" (letter from Paris of December 13, 1949, in Rulli Archive).
22. Undated fragment (1949–50), in *Malaparte*, 9:409–11.
23. Nevertheless, Sartre apparently asked Janine Bouissounouse for an article on *Kaputt*—perhaps for his magazine *Les Temps Modernes*?—according to what she herself wrote to Malaparte, on February 15, 1947; cf. *Malaparte*, 7:516–17.
24. Arthur Koestler, "The French 'Flu," in *The Yogi and the Commissar and Other Essays* (London: J. Cape, 1945).
25. Letter to Tosi of May 7, 1947, in *Malaparte*, 7:583–84.
26. Novella (1922–2018), in addition to producing the delightful *Mi scriveva Malaparte*, wrote about Malaparte at length in his interesting memoirs, *Du rocher aux sept collines* (Monaco: Éditions Gérard Comman, 1992), 130–50. Following on our correspondence, in 2013 he kindly arranged to present my book in Monaco.
27. Testimony to the author.
28. Louis-Ferdinand Céline, *Lettres* (Paris: La Pléiade, 2010), ed. Henri Godard and Jean-Paul Louis, letter 47-100 (November 20, 1947), 977. I thank

my friends Frédéric Vitoux and François Gibault for their clarifying assistance on the topic.
29. See the note corresponding to the preceding letter, ibid., 1843.
30. Orfeo Tamburi, "Le 'corone' di Malaparte," in *Incontri* (Bari: Adriatica Editrice, 1965), 51–52.
31. Letter dated Copenhagen, November 19, 1947, in AM. Céline refers to the doctor Clément Camus, a friend and intermediary, whom Malaparte would host on several occasions on Capri. Raymond Guérin described him as "the indefatigable and spry Doctor Camus, an eloquent erotologist and subtle analyst of social mores," in *Du côté de chez Malaparte*, 59.
32. Letter dated Paris, December 18, 1947, in *Malaparte*, 7:726–27.
33. Letter dated Aix-en-Provence, February 11, 1947, in which Cendrars sends his regrets for not being able to travel to Capri, where Malaparte had invited him.
34. Testimony to the author.
35. Letter dated Tuesday (probably early February 1949).
36. Malaparte, "L'Italie sans masque," article 8, "France et Italie."
37. Letter to Roland Laudenbach, dated Chamonix, April 20, 1948, in *Malaparte*, 8:99–100.
38. "Malaparte: 'Il ne faut pas mettre de culottes aux statues,'" *France-Dimanche*, August 29, 1948.
39. We do not know Togliatti's reaction. But "De Gasperi wrote me a lovely letter" (letter to G. Rulli from Paris, October 15, 1949, in Rulli Archive).
40. A long fragment can be found in *Malaparte*, 7:686–97.
41. Letters from Gallimard of July 12, 1948, of September 21, 1949, and of January 12, 1950, and letter from Dionys Mascolo, director of the publishing house, of June 11, 1951, in AM, "Corrispondenza con diversi editori."
42. Letter to Roland Laudenbach of August 19, 1947, in *Malaparte*, 8:682 (original in French).
43. Interview (with a Belgian publication?), October 1949, in *Malaparte*, 8:587–90 (original in French).
44. Orfeo Tamburi, "Mercoledì, 19 luglio 1961," in *Incontri*, 83–87. This is Febo II. Recall that Febo I died when Malaparte was in Finland.
45. Letter from Forte dei Marmi, August 27, 1949, in Joxe-Halévy Archives (original in French).

46. Letter from Milan, September 29, 1949, in Joxe-Halévy Archives (original in French).
47. Letter to Roland Laudenbach, dated Forte dei Marmi, September 15, 1949, in *Malaparte*, 8:562–64 (original in French).
48. Letter of December 5 (1949), in Joxe-Halévy Archives (original in French). The dog in question was not Febo II, but probably the dachshund Pucci, who appears in various photos of the Parisian period.
49. Letter from Vailland, dated Capri, August 14, 1950, in *Malaparte*, 10:307 (original in French).
50. Letter dated Forte dei Marmi, April 8, 1952, in *Malaparte*, 10:79–80 (original in French). Cf. his article "Io voglio bene alla Francia," *Epoca*, April 26, 1952, in *Malaparte*, 10:87–90.
51. See Myriam Tanant, "L'Italie interdite: Malaparte et le théâtre," *Chroniques Italiennes*, no. 44 (1995): 1.
52. See *Malaparte*, 2:139, 202. The text was not published and has not been found.
53. The play's first act and drafts of the second and third can be found in *Malaparte*, 4:700–753.
54. See the documentation in *Malaparte*, vol. 8, part 1.
55. "Très vieux pédéraste blèse et babillard": According to D'Annunzio in an autograph note found among his papers at the Vittoriale, quoted by Nicola Francesco Cimmino in *Poesia e poetica in Gabriele d'Annunzio* (Florence: Centro internazionale del libro, 1959), 99.
56. "Curzio Malaparte a-t-il trahi Marcel Proust?," *Le Figaro*, November 24, 1948. The most flattering judgment came from the prince Bibesco, a surviving friend of Proust, who, however, was also a friend of Malaparte's: "It is an extraordinary synthesis of what Proust was and what he did. Shame that it's just a single act; we could have used five." The others were scandalized: "The work itself seems adapted from the Russian ... It includes Marxist sentiments that Proust knew nothing about in 1905" (Elizabeth de Gramont); "Malaparte could not offer a likeness of Proust, because the author of *Kaputt*'s sensibility is truly sadistic, and Germanic in style" (Christian Mégret); "He has betrayed the figure of Proust, turning him into a spaghetti show, which proves he doesn't know French cuisine" (M. Waterman), etc.
57. "Frammento di 'Sessofono,'" in *Malaparte*, 8:278–81.

58. Testimony to the author of François Laudenbach, on the basis of an inscribed copy he had found in his father's library.
59. A typewritten copy intended for performance but bearing the stamp of Éditions Nagel can be found in the Fondo Vigorelli at the Fondazione Biblioteca di via Senato, Milan.
60. Preface to Malaparte, *Les femmes aussi ont perdu la guerre*, 16.
61. Letter of January 22 (29?), 1949, in *Malaparte*, 8:329.
62. Letter of January 31, 1949, in *Malaparte*, 8:339. Aragon and his wife were at the time the most powerful and representative couple of the French Communist intelligentsia.
63. Ambrière, "Das Kapital au Théâtre de Paris."
64. Francis Ambrière, "Monsieur Caméléon," *Le Figaro Littéraire*, February 5, 1949.
65. "La mise au point de Francis Ambrière," with translation of the ballad, *Opéra*, February 23, 1949.
66. The remainder of the documentation is collected in *Malaparte*, vol. 8, part 2: Daniel Halévy, "Qui est Malaparte?," *Réforme*, February 12, 1949; "Francis Ambrière et Malaparte se lancent des injures en attendant d'échanger des balles...," *Paris Presse*, February 13, 1949; "M. Malaparte sans témoins: Un procès-verbal de carence," *Le Figaro*, February 15, 1949; "M. Francis Ambrière répond à Daniel Halévy," *L'Époque*, February 19, 1949; R. Beauvais, "Les Épées à l'ombre du Paradis," *Le Matin*, February 19, 1949, etc. Piovene, a senior official at UNESCO at the time, would later collect his correspondence in *Madame la France* (Milan: Mondadori, 1966), without citing the episode. San Lazzaro, who was among other things director of the *Cahiers d'Art xxe siècle*, left a lovely book of memories, *Parigi era viva* (Milan: Mondadori, 1976), in which he makes a few rather discreet mentions of Malaparte.
67. See *Malaparte*, 8:675–707.
68. See "Le Amazzoni," in *Malaparte*, 7:737–77.
69. "Anche le donne hanno perso la guerra: 'Burlesque' in tre atti di C.M.," in *Malaparte*, 10:225–81.
70. "Sesso e libertà," in *Malaparte*, 9:600–601.
71. Letter from Salvini to Malaparte, dated Rome, January 27, 1952, in *Malaparte*, 10:19–21.

72. Close to Salzburg, in an earlier version; cf. *Malaparte*, 9:51–71.
73. See *Malaparte*, 9:377–80 and 563–91.
74. An extensive selection of reviews can be found in *Malaparte*, vol. 10, part 4.
75. Letter from Borelli to Malaparte of August 3 or 4, 1954, in *Malaparte*, 10:771. Review from *L'Unità*, signed AG.SA. (probably Aggeo Savioli), of April 21, 1955, in *Malaparte*, 11:287–88.
76. Vergani, *Misure del tempo*, 297–300.
77. Testimony of Maltini's son, Fulcieri, to the author.
78. Malaparte, "Io a Cannes," *L'Europeo*, April 29, 1951. He doubled down in a new attack on the festival in the French press: "Il paraît que je viens de faire une gaffe," *Opéra*, May 30, 1951; cf. *Malaparte*, 9:701–3, 720–21.
79. A. W., "The Screen in Review: Curzio Malaparte's 'Strange Deception,' Filmed in Italy, Opens at Normandie," *New York Times*, May 27, 1953.
80. Letter to Tamburi, dated Capri, April 18, 1950, in Tamburi, *Malaparte come me*, 158–60.
81. The film's screenplay has been published in an annotated edition by Luigi Martellini (Naples: ESI, 1992), which also includes preliminary versions of the script and dialogue. See also Martellini's contribution, "Malaparte fra letteratura e cinema," in *Chroniques italiennes*, no. 44 (1995), and the fragments contained in *Malaparte*, 8:713–35.
82. See Giovanna Finocchiaro Chimirri, "Malaparte autore musicale?," in *Malaparte scrittore d'Europa*, 257–63.
83. Le Gant de velours, "Malaparte, compositeur de musique," *Cette semaine*, September 18, 1950.
84. Malaparte, "Come ho composto la musica de 'Il Cristo proibito,'" fragment in *Malaparte*, 8:749–49.
85. Letter dated Capri, April 21, 1950, in *Malaparte*, 9:195–209 (original in French).
86. Later he would devote an article in his column in *Tempo*, on March 4, 1954, to the fate of the Italian prisoners still detained in the USSR, despite Soviet government assurances to the contrary; see "Prigionieri e operai," in *Malaparte*, 10:616–18.
87. See *Malaparte*, 9:705–6. At the Cannes Film Festival, though, after the

showing, he was embraced by the great, highly orthodox Soviet director Vsevolod Pudovkin.
88. M.-C. T., "Malaparte lance au monde un message, 'Christ Interdit,'" *Cinémonde* (Paris), 1950.
89. "La morte," in *Malaparte*, 9:745–49. We find this theme in *The Hunt* (1966), by Carlos Saura, a film that displays considerable affinity with *The Forbidden Christ*, aesthetically as well, in the masterly use of black and white. The massacre of rabbits, defenseless victims, heralds the settling of accounts between hunters, erstwhile brothers in arms during the Spanish Civil War.
90. Ferdinando Castelli, SJ, "Curzio Malaparte di fronte a Cristo," in *Curzio Malaparte, il narratore, il politologo*, 1:118; see also Castelli, "Il Cristo Proibito di Malaparte," *La Civiltà Cattolica*, no. 3423 (1993): 220–32.
91. Letter from Berlin, June 10, 1950, in Joxe-Halévy Archives (original in French).
92. Fabbri, *Schiava di Malaparte*, 42.
93. Fragments reproduced in *Malaparte*, 11:785–95.
94. It was published first in *Malaparte*, vol. 12, then in book form: *Lotta con l'angelo* (Naples: ESI, 1997). In his preface, the volume's editor, Luigi Martellini, explains that the work was supposed to represent a final abandonment of neorealism in favor of a positive conception of human existence, in which Christ would no longer be "forbidden."
95. Letter to Nantas Salvalaggio dated Rome, November 18, 1952, in *Malaparte*, 10:200–201.
96. Testimony to the author.
97. Fabbri, *Schiava di Malaparte*, 21, 25, 67, 74, 100–101. Fabbri also devoted "to Curzio, whom I hope to find again in a better world," a poignant tale, "Giorni da buttare," dated 1980, whose manuscript, along with that of *Schiava di Malaparte*, and with various photographs, is held in the Fondo Vigorelli at the Fondazione Biblioteca di via Senato, Milan.
98. Herbert Van Leisen, "À Paris avec Malaparte," in *Malaparte*, 7:482. Notice, once again, the cliché of a Malaparte who is German or Slavic, not truly Italian.
99. Roger Boussinot, "Visite à Malaparte," *Oural*, May 17, 1947, in *Malaparte*, 7:598–601.
100. Le Gant de velours, "Malaparte, compositeur de musique."

101. Testimony to the author.
102. Testimony to the author.
103. Testimony to the author.
104. Letter to Charles Orengo, dated Paris, March 23, 1949, in *Malaparte*, 8:468.
105. Novella, *Du rocher aux sept collines*, 145.
106. Irene Brin, "Mercantessa in fiera," in *Malaparte*, 7:266–67.
107. According to Tamburi, who claims to have been there, they met for the first time in Florence, through a mutual friend (*Malaparte come me*, 69–70).
108. Fabbri, *Schiava di Malaparte*, 30.
109. "Malaparte raconte la fin tragique de son grand roman d'amour," *France Dimanche*, August 6, 1950 (original in French).
110. "Rentrée di Malaparte a Capri," *La Voce di Napoli*, February 12, 1955, in *Malaparte*, 11:184–85.
111. Letter from Cocteau to Malaparte of November 5, 1950, in *Malaparte*, 9:351–52. An amusing reference to the landing of a flying saucer on the roof of Casa Come Me can be found in Cocteau, *Le Passé défini, Journal III, 1954*, ed. Pierre Chanel (Paris: Gallimard, 1989), 39–40.
112. Unpublished handwritten letter dated Forte dei Marmi, October 3, 1951, in Grossin Archive. The handwriting is Malaparte's; also his is the habit of writing "etc." in the French manner (as opposed to "ecc.," in the Italian). The word rendered here as "dimensions" is a guess based on what looks like the nonsensical *imenzioni* in the original.
113. V. Foschini, "Malaparte in bicicletta da New York a San Francisco. Di notte si allena correndo a piedi per l'isola," *Il Mattino Sera*, September 17, 1955, in *Malaparte*, 11:563–69.
114. Letter dated Capri, September 16, 1955, in AM, Borelli correspondence.
115. V. Foschini, "Lucertole per la Monroe, profumo per Grace Kelly," *Corriere Lombardo*, October 22, 1955, in *Malaparte*, 11:608–9.
116. Curzio Malaparte, "Lettera aperta a Moravia," in an appendix to Pardini, "Malaparte, Moravia e 'Prospettive,'" 126–28.
117. Testimony to the author.
118. Letter to Carla Rulli, from Santiago, January 27, 1953, in Rulli Archive.
119. Some fragments of the screenplay can be found in *Malaparte*, 11:9–22.
120. Anecdote recounted by the journalist Enrico Emanuelli, who was also present that evening in Montevideo, in Pellegrini, "Le guerre di Malaparte," 60.

121. These texts would be collected posthumously, along with a selection of writings from Germany, by Enrico Falqui, in *Viaggi fra i terremoti*.
122. Favalelli, "Sur les bords de l'Arno," in *Malaparte*, 10:338 (original in French).
123. "Intervista a Malaparte," *Settimana Radio TV*, January 2, 1955, in *Malaparte*, 11:120.
124. See *Malaparte*, 12:594–99.
125. For the electoral campaign, see *Malaparte*, 12:437–43, 447–48.
126. See *Malaparte*, 11:127.
127. Furio, "Malaparte e la moda 'virile,'" *Arbiter* (Milan), January–February 1955, in *Malaparte*, 11:164–66.
128. Ibid.
129. G. Capuano, "Malaparte scatena il putiferio alla RAI," *La Notte*, October 8, 1955, in *Malaparte*, 11:588–89.
130. "Non la spada ma il cucchiaio ha risolto la vertenza fra Malaparte e la RAI," *L'Isola di Catania*, October 13, 1955, in *Malaparte*, 11:596–97.
131. "Voci bianche, e maschi," *Tempo*, October 27, 1955, in *Malaparte*, 11:618–20.
132. Testimony to the author.
133. Testimony to the author.
134. "Gli stivali di Churchill," *Tempo*, March 4, 1954, in *Malaparte*, 10:618.
135. "Scrivetemi, e avrete giustizia," in *Malaparte*, 12:417–18, 425–26, etc.
136. Letter from the editor, Arturo Tofanelli, dated Milan, January 4, 1955, in *Malaparte*, 11:121–22, in which he hastens to clarify that "in administrative terms, it will be as if this week's Battibecco had appeared" (i.e., it will be regularly paid for).
137. Testimony to the author.
138. Notes for Battibecco, in *Malaparte*, 10:979.
139. He had given the name "Sexophone" to a text quite different in tone, dated Paris 1932, which opened with these words: "'Sex' has its voice, like blood, the heart, reason, conscience. At times singsong, hoarse, sweet, weak, serious, sharp, childlike, the voice of 'sex,' the sexophone, speaks to us from the deepest part of ourselves" (see *Malaparte*, 3:131–33). He then used the title again in a series of reflections written in Regina Coeli, in October 1933, and later in some fragments in *Malaparte*, 9:713–61.
140. "Malaparte sera la vedette de sa propre revue," *Le Sud-Ouest* (Bordeaux), June 21, 1955, in *Malaparte*, 11:354–55.

141. Fabbri, *Schiava di Malaparte*, 38.
142. I. Mormino, "'Sexophone' Kaputt! Fischi alla rivista di Malaparte," *Film d'oggi*, July 28–August 4, 1955, in *Malaparte*, 11:478.
143. *Malaparte*, 11:412–14.
144. Letter dated Capri, September 20, 1956, in *Malaparte*, 12:633–34.
145. Fabbri, *Schiava di Malaparte*, 70. Alfredo Signoretti recalls that, before the war, Malaparte had driven him around the south of England in a shiny sports car (*"La Stampa" in camicia nera*, 150).
146. Novella, *Du rocher aux sept collines*, 144.
147. Fabbri, *Schiava di Malaparte*, 64.
148. Ansaldo, *Anni freddi*, 429, dated March 13, 1950. See also the grotesque affair of the "contested bed" at the residence of the publisher Gaspare Casella, recounted by Giuseppe Marcenaro, "Malaparte e la fiera un po' noir delle sue vanità," *Il Foglio*, September 3, 2011.
149. Testimony to the author.
150. Testimony of the Chilean writer and diplomat Jorge Edwards to the author.
151. Letter from Rome, March 23, 1951, in *Malaparte*, 9:655–57.
152. See letters from Malaparte to Bompiani of January 2 and March 2, 1949, and conciliatory but firm replies from the latter of, respectively, January 11 and March 10, in *Malaparte*, 8:312–13, 320–23, 428, 450.
153. See Daria Guarnati's letter of October 13, 1939, in *Malaparte*, 4:609.
154. Testimony to the author.
155. Letter dated Paris, March 1949, in *Malaparte*, 8:473–74. He also insisted on a royalty rate as high as 18 percent, after fifteen thousand copies.
156. Letter dated Jouy-en-Josas, April 26, 1949, in *Malaparte*, 8:494–96. He would go so far as to threaten her with legal action; she was shrewd enough not to heed the "sulks" of this "spoiled child." See the letter from Guarnati to the lawyer Carnaroli of April 20, 1950, in *Malaparte*, 9:194–95.
157. As underlined by Giampaolo Martelli, *Curzio Malaparte* (Turin: Borla, 1968), 181–82.
158. Text published in *Malaparte*, vol. 12, parts 2 and 3. Whereas the novella had been abandoned in 1946, the screenplay was complete down to shot sequences.
159. Letter to Borelli dated Capri, September 20, 1956, in *Malaparte*, 12:633–34.

160. Letter to Borelli from the Grand Hôtel, Stockholm, October 13, 1956, in AM, Borelli correspondence.
161. "Ma è possibile?," *Corriere d'Informazione* (Milan), August 26, 1956, in *Malaparte*, 12:580.
162. Davide Lajolo, *An Absurd Vice: A Biography of Cesare Pavese*, trans. Mario and Mark Pietralunga (New York: New Directions, 1983).
163. See his article in *L'Unità* of August 7, 1955, in *Malaparte*, 11:501–2.
164. Lajolo, preface to Fabbri, *Schiava di Malaparte*, 9.
165. Letter dated Rome, May 26, 1956, in AM, Macciocchi correspondence. I was unable to meet Macciocchi, who had died in 2007 after a long and painful illness. Father Castelli, who assisted her to the end, told me they talked frequently about Malaparte, whom she remembered with affection.
166. Letter dated Rome, August 30, 1956, in AM, Macciocchi correspondence.
167. "Malaparte e i giudici," open letter to the editor of *Tempo*, June 27, 1950, in *Malaparte*, 9:278–80.
168. Letter to the editor of *Il Tempo*, in *Malaparte*, 9:283. In 1954 he dedicated the third edition of *Fughe in prigione* to Pavese and added a moving preface, which nevertheless involved a bit of cunning, in which he equates their respective experiences of *confino*, so different in reality.
169. I am grateful to Olga Strada and Maurizio Cabona for this detail.
170. See Macciocchi's contribution to the conference proceedings of *Malaparte scrittore d'Europa*, 27. There is, however, a small factual error here, because Macciocchi situated this dialogue on Capri in January "of the year he died": now, at this time, Malaparte was already in the Soviet Union. More likely, this was January 1956, when the PCI began to take steps to arrange the trip.
171. To tempt him further, Macciocchi added: "But if you want, from Samarkand you could return to Moscow, and cover the distance between Moscow and Peking in eight hours, in a jet plane. (Naturally you like these emotions)." Letter dated Rome, August 30, 1956, in AM, Macciocchi correspondence.
172. Letter from Peking, October 30, 1956, in *Malaparte*, 12:674.
173. Page discovered in the baggage from his China trip, in *Malaparte*, 12:736.
174. Telegram of November 24, 1956, 11:07 p.m., in AM, Borelli correspondence.

175. Letters to Macciocchi of January 6 and to Borelli of January 21, 1957, in *Malaparte*, 12:759–63.
176. Testimony to the author of Laura Ronchi Abbozzo.
177. Telegram of January 31, 1957, to Angiolillo, in AM, Angiolillo correspondence. The telegram must have been dictated before the letter referred to in the next note. Malaparte entrusted his letters to Nuova Cina, the Italian branch of the Chinese press agency, which retransmitted them from Peking.
178. Letter from Hankow, January 26–29, 1957, in AM, Angiolillo correspondence.
179. Letter to Borelli dated Hankow, January 21, 1957, in AM, Borelli correspondence.
180. Ibid.
181. On his deathbed, he allegedly reiterated to Maria Antonietta Macciocchi his intention to leave the Capri house to the Chinese; see her contribution to *Malaparte scrittore d'Europa*, 27.
182. Vegliani, *Malaparte*, 169–81.
183. Giuliano Abbozzo, "Rélation du séjour de Malaparte en Chine" (original in French), published as an appendix to Malaparte, *Les femmes aussi ont perdu la guerre*, 211–21.
184. Letter from Hankow, February 1, 1957, in AM, Macciocchi correspondence.
185. "Ho chiesto a Mao la liberazione di tutti i preti," *Tempo*, November 1956, in *Malaparte*, 12:719–21.
186. Malaparte was evidently accustomed to this kind of treatment: "The government placed a military aircraft at my disposal so that I could visit the great north of Chile, as far as Arica, and along the Peruvian and Bolivian frontiers" (letter to Guglielmo Rulli from Santiago, January 23, 1953, in Rulli Archive).
187. U. De Franciscis, "Il ritorno di Malaparte," *Tempo*, March 28, 1957, in *Malaparte*, 12:799–800.
188. "Saluto," March 28, 1957, in BA2, 615–16.
189. At the time Malaparte wrote a moving homage, which was not published, to one of the rare colleagues of the preceding generation with whom he felt a connection; see *Malaparte*, 3:754–60.
190. Testimony of Beatrice Monti von Rezzori to the author.

191. Letter dated Thursday the fourth (month?), 1957, in AM, Cendrars correspondence.
192. Letter dated Rome, May 8, 1957, attributed to Albert Camus, in *Malaparte*, 12:813.
193. "Malaparte dicte au magnétophone la fin de sa vie: 'Il n'y a plus rien dans ma poitrine qu'un trou et rien d'autre,'" June 19, 1957, in *Malaparte*, 12:826–27. Neuvecelle, pseudonym of Dimitri Ivanov, was the son of the poet and theologian Vyacheslav Ivanov, who had left Soviet Russia for Rome, where he lived until his death, in 1949. I had the privilege of knowing and spending time with Jean Neuvecelle, who was for decades one of the best experts on Vatican issues and a great friend of Cyprienne del Drago Charles-Roux.
194. Igor Man, "La conversione di Malaparte," *La Stampa*, February 6, 2008.
195. Fabbri, *Schiava di Malaparte*, 23.
196. Vegliani, *Malaparte*, 14–15.
197. In 1958 Vegliani published, with Edizioni Daria Guarnati, the lovely novel *Processo a Volosca* (new ed. Palermo: Sellerio, 1989).
198. Guglielmo Peirce, *Il Borghese*, August 14, 1958. Other witnesses recounted a similar scene: the name of the person who "has to die" before him varies: Moravia, Alvaro, etc. As far as Montanelli is concerned, it should be noted that in a satirical novel of 1945, *Qui non riposano*, he had narrated the imaginary biography of the "quasi actor" Folco Ferrasco, who had come through unscathed all the Italian regimes of the twentieth century. Montanelli avoided a formal visit to the Sanatrix but sent a friendly message to the patient (*Malaparte*, 12:779). However, as he confided to Fernando Mezzetti, who kindly told me, he ended up going to the clinic at the request of Malaparte, who at the last minute refused to see him. The hostility between Malaparte and Montanelli, as noted in these pages, was tenacious. Montanelli's judgment, still full of resentment thirty years later, can be found in a July 17, 1987, reply to a reader of his column in *Il Giornale*, in which he describes his frenemy as a "foolish servant of Ciano" and a "chameleon masquerading as Narcissus." A few years earlier he had appeared somewhat more generous, or condescending, in his introduction to Tamburi's book *Malaparte come me*. Malaparte, for his part, limited himself to repeating to Biancamaria Fabbri and others: "He wants to imitate me, but he'll never be like me. He's from Fucecchio [a suburb of Florence]" (*Schiava di Malaparte*, 67).

NOTES TO CHAPTER 5

199. Guérin, *Du côté de chez Malaparte*, 28.
200. Guillaume Hanoteau, "Malaparte: Dialogue avec la mort," *Paris Match*, July 13, 1957.
201. *Malaparte*, 12:808.
202. Letter dated Rome, April 23, 1957, in AM, general correspondence.
203. Gianni Preda, *Il Borghese*, May 24, 1957. This neo-Fascist weekly followed Malaparte's agony closely, as did all the Italian press.
204. Ridomi, *La fine dell'Ambasciata a Berlino*, 124.
205. Testimony of Gianni Letta to the author. There are indications, but no proof, that Togliatti had provided for admittance to a clinic close to the PCI, in the event that Malaparte had to leave the Sanatrix.
206. In *Malaparte*, 12:807.
207. Letter sent from Capri on October 16, 1948, to W. H. Guiton, in *Malaparte*, 8:219 (original in French).
208. Pellegrini, "Le guerre di Malaparte," 56, 65.
209. *Malaparte*, 12:851.
210. According to the testimony of Tadeusz Breza, then the press attaché for the Polish embassy in Rome, who devoted a long note to Malaparte's death in his very well informed diary *La porta di bronzo*, trans. Vera Petrelli (Milan: Feltrinelli, 1962), 187–203.
211. Carlo Testa, *Padre Rotondi: Le battaglie di un gesuita* (Milan: Rusconi, 1992), 119–27.
212. Breza, *La porta di bronzo*, 200.
213. To Guerri's critical reconstruction (*L'arcitaliano*, 258–60, 282–85, and testimony to the author) we can add that of Vegliani (*Malaparte*, 263–68), who, while mentioning Father Rotondi's activity around the dying man, carefully avoids confirming the latter's version of events.
214. Testimony of Daniele Rulli to the author.
215. Letter to Borelli from Forte dei Marmi, January 18, 1954, in *Malaparte*, 10:575–76.
216. Trans. Edoardo Petri.
217. Testimony to the author.
218. Testimony to the author.
219. Testimony to the author.
220. Sister Carmelita furnished her version of the writer's last hours in a moving testimony, collected in 1998 in *L'ultimo viaggio di Malaparte*.

221. The text can be found in *L'ultimo viaggio di Malaparte*. With respect to the story Father Rotondi would later tell the journalist Carlo Testa, there are differences in the last words attributed to Malaparte and some imprecision in the dates. Also absent from the first version is the dying Malaparte's destruction of the PCI membership card.
222. Testimony to the author of Father Castelli.
223. "Die letzte Reportage vom Totenbett," *Die Zeit*, July 25, 1957. Also in Germany, Vegliani's biography was immediately translated.

Conclusion

1. Chatwin, "Among the Ruins," in *Anatomy of Restlessness*, 166.
2. The building has been extensively studied from an architectural point of view. See the documentation gathered in Marida Talamona, *Casa Malaparte* (New York: Princeton Architectural Press, 1993), as well as Sergio Attanasio, *Curzio Malaparte: "Casa come Me," Punta del Massullo, tel. 160, Capri* (Naples: Arte Tipografica, 1990), and Silvia Micheli, "Curzio Malaparte architetto: Villa Malaparte a Capri 1938–1942," *Settentrione* 17 (2005): 17–28.
3. *Malaparte*, 4:24.
4. Originally, the loan was to cover the expenses for *Prospettive*; see *Malaparte*, 4:10.
5. See the letter from Ms. Pellegrini to Amitrano of October 8, 1940, in *Malaparte*, 5:344.
6. See the letter from Ms. Pellegrini to Casini of May 3, 1941, in *Malaparte*, 5:632–33.
7. See *Malaparte*, 6:638.
8. "Con quali fondi ho costruito la mia casa di Capri," in *Malaparte*, 6:706–8.
9. Nonetheless, in his January 1939 trip to Ethiopia, he had confided to his escort that "he was constructing a villa on Capri in a stunning area, on land already declared monumental, which in his telling he could acquire for a paltry sum, thanks to the influence of the Foreign Affairs Minister" (see Conte's report, in *Malaparte*, 4:489). What is striking is that Malaparte attached this far-from-entirely-favorable report to his 1946 statement of defense.

NOTES TO CONCLUSION

10. Written testimony of Daniele Rulli to the author.
11. Leading to confusion, because if you ask local tourism workers, nine times out of ten they will indicate another villa nearby, in front of a famous beach resort, whose frescoes were also painted by Hildebrand, but which did not, alas, belong to Malaparte. For this information I am grateful to Flavia Giorgi Cabona. See also *Malaparte*, 10:655, 981.
12. Orfeo Tamburi, *Malaparte à contre-jour*, trans. Nino Frank (Paris: Denoël, 1979), 23. (Here I cite the French edition of *Malaparte come me*; the anecdote is missing from the Italian edition.)
13. Testimony of Alessia Rositani Suckert to the author. The good taste and shrewd acquisitions on display seem at odds with one of Tamburi's sharpest barbs: "He never understood a thing about painting" (*Malaparte come me*, 24).
14. Guérin, *Du côté de chez Malaparte*, 15.
15. But not as small as he claimed in his letters. According to the efficient Finnish intelligence services, in May 1942 Malaparte sent to Italy eighteen packages containing ceramics, works of art, *ryijy* (local rustic tapestries), and even gymnastics and sauna equipment. To export them, he had to pay seven thousand marks in customs surcharges, the equivalent of the salary of a middle manager (see Ahvonen, "Malaparte in Finlandia," 12).
16. See also his article "Casa Malaparte" in the magazine *Arkkitehti*, no. 4 (1998).
17. See the website of the Fondazione Il Vittoriale degli Italiani, in Italian and English: https://www.vittoriale.it. The estate, visited every year by tens of thousands of tourists from Italy and abroad, presents an important program of cultural events and performances, under the very dedicated direction of his president, Giordano Bruno Guerri, as it did under his predecessor, Francesco Perfetti, both eminent specialists of D'Annunzio and Malaparte.

Index

Abbozzo, Giuliano, 583, 586, 694n183
Accetto, Torquato, 146, 308
Aeschylus, 251
Akhmatova, Anna, 472n
Adamov, Arthur, 508
Adenauer, Konrad, 461
Adloff, Renée, 205
Agnelli (family), 274, 278, 279, 287
Agnelli, Edoardo, 268, 269, 271–72, 657n63
Agnelli, Gianni, 161, 272, 274, 276, 278, 554
Agnelli, Giovanni, 161–63, 171, 172, 185, 187, 190, 191, 192, 218, 257, 269, 271, 273–74, 280–82, 283, 284, 286, 646n62, 647n73, 654n29, 657n66, 658n75
Agnelli, Susanna (Suni), 278, 278n, 284n
Agnelli, Umberto, 272
Agnelli, Virginia, 9, 44, 192, 247, 268–271, 272, 273, 274–281, 284, 284†, 285–86, 339, 536, 617, 654n29, 655n43, 657n62, 657n66, 658nn73–76, 660n97, 660nn99–100
Agnelli Teodorani Fabbri, Maria Sole, 50n, 273–74, 280, 285, 657n63, 658nn73, 660n99

Ahvonen, Jonne, 670n220, 698n15
Aimone, Prince (4th Duke of Aosta), 351
Alberti, Rafael, 312, 450
Albricci, Alberico, 68, 71
Aldington, Richard, 64
Aleramo, Sibilla, 291
Alexander I (king of Yugoslavia), 349, 351
Alexander, Harold George, 392, 422n
Alfieri, Dino, 283, 359, 522, 641n5, 662n113
Alfonse XIII (king of Spain), 82
Alvaro, Corrado, 165, 181, 181n, 290, 318, 441, 457, 475, 695n198
Ambrière, Francis, 459, 486, 515, 687n66,
Amendola, Giovanni, 85, 85n, 117, 124, 234n, 237, 388
Amicucci, Ermanno, 162, 162n
Amitrano, Adolfo, 615, 616, 617, 618
Anfuso, Filippo, 339, 664n151, 678n59
Angiolillo, Renato, 461, 566, 584, 588, 591, 593, 601, 604, 604n, 608, 609, 694n177
Aniante, Antonio, 141, 142, 153, 169, 195, 211
Anne H. (associate of Malaparte's), 537, 672n13

699

NOTES

Ansaldo, Giovanni, 170, 265, 265n, 266, 285, 288, 394, 565, 645n48, 660n97, 674n31
Antinori, Maria Giuseppina, 462
Antona-Traversi, Camillo, 635
Apollinaire, Guillaume, 359
Apponyi, Geraldine. *See* Geraldine, Queen
Aquinas, Thomas, 451
Aragon, Louis, 13, 95, 472, 490, 515, 547, 687n62
Arban, Dominique, 683n10
Aregai, Abebe, 306
Arendt, Hannah, 413, 676n40
Aretino, Pietro, 572
Ariberto (marquess of Tuscany), 268
Aron, Raymond, 56, 491
Attolico, Bernardo, 359
Auden, W.H., 556
Audisio, Emmanuel,159
Audisio, Walter, 143n
Augustine of Hippo, Saint, 308

Babel, Isaac, 374
Baccara, Luisa, 627
Bacchelli, Riccardo, 290
Bach, Johann Sebastian, 622, 626, 677n56
Bacon, Francis, 4
Badoglio, Pietro, 300, 326, 329, 335, 336, 378, 382, 384, 386, 389
Baer, Karl Ernst von, 426
Bagnoli, Duchess of, 557
Bainville, Jacques, 73, 219
Bakunin, Mikhail, 173
Balabanoff, Angelica, 129, 173–74, 259
Balbo, Italo, 9, 108, 147, 221–24, 226–27, 227n, 228–229, 229n, 230–31, 234–239, 241–244, 266, 279, 284, 306, 338, 651n130, 652n142
Balbo, Paolo, 227n, 229n, 284*
Baldi (family), 29, 35, 52, 561
Baldi, Baldo (Jacques), 29, 618
Baldi, Milziade (Mersiade), 29, 31, 34, 59, 151, 166
Baldi, Giacomo, 491
Balla, Giacomo, 289
Baltus (Villa Hildebrand owner's son-in-law), 257, 655n45
Balthus. *See* Baltus
Balzac, Honoré de, 310, 315
Baracca, Francesco, 565n
Barbo, Pietro. *See* Paul II, Pope
Barbusse, Henri, 7, 64, 74, 85, 359, 637n58, 638, 649n100,
Bardot, Brigitte, 613
Barrès, Maurice, 2, 122, 502
Barrett, William, 676n48
Bartali, Gino, 496
Barthou, Louis, 349
Barzini, Luigi, Jr., 287, 288, 660n102
Barzini, Luigi, Sr., 287, 574, 574n
Bassani, Giorgio, 290, 443, 542n, 597
Bastianini, Giuseppe, 261–62
Baudelaire, Charles, 3, 311, 398
Baudouin, Yvan, 508n
Beauvoir, Simone de, 490
Beckett, Samuel, xiii, 508
Beethoven, Ludwig van, 411, 622
Below, Otto von, 66
Benedetti, Arrigo, 310
Benedetti Michelangeli, Arturo, 554
Benelli, Sem, 30, 113, 117, 291
Benn, Gottfried, 312, 412, 478
Bérard, Christian, 511
Bergery, Gaston, 492, 514

Berio, Luciano, 289
Bernanos, Georges, 208, 295
Berthelot (family), 184
Bertolucci, Bernardo, 317
Bertrand, Juliette, 195, 215, 455, 491
Bessand-Massenet, Pierre, 231–32, 248, 250, 254
Bettelheim, Bruno, 413
Bibesco, Emmanuel (prince of Romania), 514n, 686n56
Bibesco (family), 492
Bibesco, Princess, 212
Bilenchi, Romano, 290, 297
Binazzi, Bino, 31, 37, 55
Bismarck, Mona Williams von, 558
Bissolati, Leonida, 57
Bizet (family), 184
Blasetti, Alessandro, 91, 113n, 289
Bloch, Jean-Richard, 208
Blok, Aleksandr, 7, 120
Blum (family), 184
Blum, Léon, 499
Bobet, Louison, 559
Boccaccio, Giovanni, 39, 398, 572
Bocchini, Arturo, 236, 247, 276
Böcklin, Arnold, 257
Bogdanov, Alexandre, 173
Bolloré, Gwenn-Aël, 494, 495, 538
Bombacci, Nicola, 149
Bompiani, Valentino, 368, 526, 567, 650n119, 671n2
Bonaccorsi, Arconovaldo, 101, 295–96, 297, 662n120
Bonaparte, Louis Napoleon (Napoleon III), 32
Bonaparte, Napoleon (Napoleon I), 112, 146, 147, 216, 258, 269n, 511
Bonnard, Abel, 208, 208n
Bonomi, Oreste, 671n240
Bonomini, Ernesto, 103

Bonservizi, Nicola, 103, 104, 105, 640n88
Bontempelli, Massimo, 131, 133, 134, 135, 159, 165, 290, 311, 642n22
Bonuomo, Michele, 664n149
Bordiga, Amadeo, 174
Borelli, Aldo, 164, 194, 196, 197, 198, 199, 211, 213, 219, 220, 227, 231, 232, 235, 236, 237, 239, 242, 243, 244, 251, 252, 255, 277, 278, 280, 283, 284, 288, 289, 294, 301–2, 304, 306, 321, 330, 333, 342, 346, 350, 352, 355, 356, 357, 364, 367, 376, 521, 522, 549, 565, 574, 582, 583, 605, 609, 647n79, 649n127
Borges, Jorge Luis, 47, 474, 552
Borgese, Giuseppe, 478
Borghese, Scipione (10th Prince of Sulmona), 287
Boris III (king of Bulgaria), 344
Bottai, Giuseppe, 94, 127, 148, 152, 229, 244, 450, 617
Bouissounouse, Janine, 458, 459, 482, 516, 681n115, 684n23
Bourbon del Monte, Carlo, 269
Bournbon del Monte
Bourbon del Monte, Ranieri, 271
Bourbon del Monte, Virginia. *See* Agnelli, Virginia
Bourbon del Monte di Pesaros, Francesco Maria, 269
Bourbon del Monte di Pesaros, Guidobaldo, 269
Bourbon del Monte di Santa Maria, Pietro, 269
Boussinot, Roger, 536
Bradley, William A., 209
Bragaglia, Anton Giulio, 83
Bragaglia, Arturo, 83
Bragaglia, Carlo Ludovico, 84

NOTES

Brahms, Johannes, 411
Brancati, Vitaliano, 647n78, 290
Brantôme, Pierre de Bourdeille, 339
Brasillach, Robert, 45
Brasini, Armando, 289
Braun, Eva, 428
Braun von Stumm, Gustav, 462
Brecht, Bertolt, 7, 430, 476
Breguet (family), 184
Breker, Arno, 376
Bresson, Robert, 529, 531
Breton, André, 7, 313, 325, 482*, 489
Breza, Tadeusz, 696n210
Briand, Aristide, 532
Brignone, Lilla, 521
Brin, Irene (Maria Vittoria Rossi), 539
Brion, Marcel, 483
Brun, Louis, 653n15
Bucard, Marcel, 292, 661n105
Buffarini Guidi, Guido, 95
Bulgakov, Mikhail, 374
Bulganin, Nikolaj, 590
Bunton, Lesly, 508n
Buñuel, Luis, 523, 551
Burns, John Horne, 398n
Buzzati, Dino, 288, 290, 302, 342, 346
Byron, Lord George Gordon, 3, 39, 254

Cadorna, Luigi, 61, 65, 75
Caesar, Julius, 102, 112, 145, 307
Cagliostro, Count Alessandro di, 572
Calamai, Clara, 113n
Calvino, Italo, 571
Calzabigi, Ranieri, 30
Camerini, Mario, 289
Campana, Dino, 37, 84

Campbell, Jane. *See* San Faustino, Jane di
Campigli, Massimo, 17, 18, 133, 289, 620
Campolonghi, Luigi, 210
Camus, Albert, xiii, 13, 381, 396, 433, 493, 507, 512
Camus, Clément, xiii, 493, 595, 685n31
Canali, Mauro, 640n87, 640n88, 640n94, 643n23, 657n62
Cape, Jonathan, 230
Capote, Truman, 5
Cappello, Felice Maria, 604, 604*, 605, 605n, 609
Caravaggio (Michelangelo Merisi), 269
Carco, Francis (F. Carcopini Tusoli), 359
Cardarelli, Vincenzo, 83, 290, 291
Cardinale, Claudia, 423n
Carducci, Giosuè, 58
Carli, Mario, 107, 139
Charlemagne, 268
Carmelita (Sister), 609, 696n220
Carnaroli (lawyer), 692n156
Carné, Marcel, 543*
Carnera, Primo, 166
Carrell, Ghitta, 82
Casanova, Giacomo 339, 572
Casella, Gaspare, 290, 393, 692n148
Casertano, Raffaele, 395
Casini, Gherardo, 661n103
Casorati, Felice, 289
Castelli, Ferdinando, 562n, 693n165
Cavallero, Ugo, 336
Cavani, Liliana, 399n, 423, 434*, 679n77
Cayatte, André, 524
Ceccatty, René de, 316n

Cela, Camilo José, 488, 550
Céline, Louis-Ferdinand, xiin, 10n, 12, 397, 442, 456, 487, 493, 595, 685n31
Cellini, Benvenuto, 572
Cendrars, Blaise, 13, 133, 455, 493, 494, 595, 685n33
Cerio (family), 558
Cerio, Edwin, 625
Cervantes, Miguel de, 340
Cervi, Gino, 525, 542n
Cervi, Mario, 666n171
Chagall, Marc, 534, 408, 410
Charles I (emperor of Austria and king of Hungary), 66
Charles V (emperor), 518
Chateaubriand, François-René de, 3, 39, 499, 515
Chatwin, Bruce, 33, 558, 614
Chiavolini, Alessandro, 219
Chiang Kai-shek, 587
Chimichi, Alberto, 662n115
Chopin, Frédéric, 411, 412n, 677n49
Churchill, Winston, 230, 230n, 400, 559
Cianca, Alberto, 85, 210, 388
Ciano, Costanzo, 258, 260, 274
Ciano, Edda. *See* Mussolini, Edda
Ciano, Galeazzo, 84, 139, 146, 169, 188, 229n, 249, 251, 258, 260, 261–66, 266n, 267, 270, 274, 275, 283, 285, 287, 288, 289, 295, 296, 299, 321, 322, 323, 324, 329, 330, 333, 334, 336, 337, 338, 339, 339†, 340, 340n, 341, 342, 343, 344, 347, 359, 455, 557, 569, 616, 617, 656n49
Ciano, Maria, 258
Cini, Vittorio, 522
Cione, Edmondo, 679n76

Cioran, Emil, xiii, 481
Clark, Mark Wayne, 422, 422n
Clausewitz, Carl von, 61
Clemenceau, Georges, 72
Clermont-Tonnerre, Duchess of, 212
Coccioli, Carlo, 539
Cocteau, Jean, 13, 251, 443, 493, 534, 547
Colli, Giorgio, 644n39
Colli, Giuseppe, 163, 191, 644n39
Comisso, Giovanni, 290, 443n
Conrad, Joseph, 315
Conte (inspector), 302, 303, 304, 360, 654n28, 655n44
Conti, Ettore, 161
Cooper, Gary, 270, 657n61
Coppi, Fausto, 497, 548, 559
Corbigny, Marie-José de, 538
Corso, Gregory, 83, 541
Costa, Paolo, 171
Coty, François, 218, 516
Crémieux, Benjamin, 159, 214
Croce, Benedetto, 57, 116, 118, 146, 388
Cumming, Henry H., 389, 433
Cuny, Alain, 507, 525
Curtiz, Michael, 447

D'Amico, Aristide, 535n36
D'Annunzio, Gabriele, 3, 5, 7, 13, 19, 30, 31, 39, 46, 57, 93, 149, 160, 223, 254, 277, 300, 303, 320, 359, 456, 481, 488, 503, 546, 553, 592, 623, 624, 627, 686n55, 698n17
D'Annunzio, Mario, 529
Dallapiccola, Luigi, 290
Dalser, Ida, 259n
Damiot, Jacques, 507n
Dante Alighieri, 53, 58, 406, 407, 474, 607, 613

Darwin, Charles, 426, 491
Daudet, Léon, 103
Déat, Marcel, 661n105
De Benedetti, Giacomo, 662
De Begnac, Yvon, 148, 291
Debussy, Claude, 416
de Chirico, Giorgio, 83, 289, 336, 683n10
De Felice, Renzo, 95n, 301n
de Feo, Italo, 680n91
Defoe, Daniel, 396
De Gasperi, Alcide, 479, 497, 685n39
de Gaulle, Charles, 151, 252n, 329, 485, 494
Delacroix, Eugène, 532
Delcroix, Carlo, 244
del Drago, Cyprienne Charles-Roux, 339, 695n193
Delfini, Antonio, 290, 297
Del Mancino, Amos, 62n
Del Monaco, Mario, 606
De Marsanich, Augusto, 314n
De Nicola, Francesco, 651n133
Denoël, Robert, 487, 487n
Dentice di Frasso, Countess (Dorothy Caldwell Taylor), 270
Déon, Michel, 494,
de Pisis, Filippo, 83, 210, 289, 442, 496, 594
De Santis, Giuseppe, 526
Descaves, Pierre, 456
De Sica, Vittorio, 439n, 441, 523, 526, 566
Destrée, Jules, 59
Devillers, Renée, 507n
Diaz, Armando, 77
Dickinson, Emily, 252, 352
Dietl, Eduard, 366
Dior, Christian, 511

Dolfin, Giovanni, 645n51
Donegani, Guido, 161
Donoso, José, 551
Doriot, Jacques, 661m105
Dos Passos, John, 7, 144n, 251, 548, 682n119
Dostoevsky, Fyodor, 315, 398, 463
Douglas, Norman, 558
Dowling, Constance, 544
Dreiser, Theodore, 161
Drieu La Rochelle, Pierre, 48, 101, 184, 208, 294, 395, 471, 492, 535, 546
Dufy, Raoul, 620, 689
Dumas, Alexandre (père), 451
Dumini, Amerigo, 100–5, 107, 108, 115, 296, 639n86, 640nn87–89
Duse, Eleonora, 254
Dutton, Edward, 488
Dux, Pierre, 507n

Edward VIII (king of England), 230
Edwards, Jorge, 550
Ehrenburg, Ilya, 7, 133, 374n, 550
Eichmann, Adolf, 402, 403
Eisentein, Sergei, 91, 359
Ekberg, Anita, 270
Eksteins, Modris, 637n61
Eliade, Mircea, xiii, 116, 481
Eliot, T(homas). S(tearns)., xi, 7, 311
Elkann, Alain, 278, 319
Éluard, Paul, 13, 311, 325, 352, 450, 472, 489, 490
Emanuelli, Enrico, 690n120

Fabbri, Biancamaria (Bianca Maria), 42, 44, 45, 83n, 277, 443, 526n, 533, 537, 564, 565, 596, 627, 633n15, 660n100, 664n144, 689n97, 695n198

Fabius Maximus Verrucosus, Quintus, 269n
Facchinetti, Cipriano, 210
Falkenhayn, Erich von, 66
Fallaci, Bruno, 633n9, 651n130
Fallaci, Oriana, 538
Falqui, Antonello, 524
Falqui, Enrico, 223, 315, 465, 466, 558n, 573
Fanfani, Amintore, 583, 600, 601, 604, 609
Farinacci, Roberto, 107, 107n, 108, 127, 147, 158, 222, 229, 230, 266, 299, 338
Farouk, king of Egypt, 618
Fassbinder, Rainer Werner, 624
Fath, Jacques, 511
Fattore, Fabio, 667n180
Faulkner, William, 548
Favalelli, Max, 632
Fazzini, Pericle, 620
Fejtö, François, 675n37
Fellini, Federico, 396, 563, 580
Feltrinelli, Carlo, 161, 287
Feltrinelli, Carlo Jr., 660n102
Feltrinelli, Giangiacomo, 287
Feltrinelli, Giannalisa, 287, 574
Fernandez, Ramon, 214
Ferrari, Enzo, 535
Ferrarin, Arturo, 271
Ferrero, Anna Maria, 526, 526n
Ferrero, Guglielmo, 57
Ferretti, Lando, 167, 197
Fersen, Jacques, 558
"Flaminia," 44, 186, 187–88, 195, 199, 209, 225, 226, 246, 247, 248, 249, 267, 268, 272, 273, 536, 654, 658
Flaubert, Gustave, 40, 315
Josephus, Flavius, 396
Fleischmann (Sergeant), 346

Foligno, Cesare, 457
Ford, Henry, 191
Förster-Nietzsche, Elisabeth, xii
Foscolo, Ugo, 3
Fouchet, Max-Pol, 488
Foxá, Agustín de, 401, 402, 402n, 433, 675n38, 676n39, 676n41
Franco, Francisco, 91, 297, 402, 488
Frank, Hans, 343, 361, 362, 393, 408, 411–19, 421, 517, 590, 676n48, 677n49, 677n51, 677n57
Frank, Nino, 135, 159, 169, 643n24
Franz Joseph I (emperor of Austria), 66
Frassati, Alfredo, 161, 165
Fresnay, Pierre, 494, 495n, 507, 507n, 525, 526, 527
Freud, Sigmund, 309, 313, 341, 477
Frignani, Giuseppe, 383
Frugoni, Cesare, 583
Furmanski, Adam, 416
Furtwängler, Wilhelm, 415

Gabrea, Radu, 668n193
Gadda, Carlo Emilio, 42n
Gaddi, Agnolo, 51
Gaetani, Paolo, 558, 663n125
Gallegos, Adrian, 388
Galli, Carlo, 383, 385
Gallimard, Gaston, 498, 499
Galtier-Boissière, Jean, 438n
Gambetti, Fidia, 657n66, 663n135
Gamelin, Maurice, 326
García Lorca, Federico, 450, 311
Garibaldi, Bruno, 58
Garibaldi, Costante, 58
Garibaldi, Ezio, 60
Garibaldi, Giuseppe, 58, 62
Garibaldi, Peppino, 58, 59, 60, 62
Garibaldi, Sante, 60

NOTES

Gary, Romain, 25, 44
Genet, Jean, 45, 407, 476
Genina, Augusto, 289
Gentile, Giovanni, 115, 116, 116n, 119, 127, 149, 452, 641n13
George II (king of Greece), 329
Geraldine, Queen, 322n
Géricault, Jean-Louis Théodore, 358
Germi, Pietro, 523–24
Gershwin, George, 207n, 606
Gaddafi, Muammar, 322n
Giacomozzi, Ugo, 525
Giannini, Guglielmo, 560
Gibault, François, 685n28
Gide, André, 444, 448, 543*
Giolitti, Giovanni, 53, 57, 161, 165
Giorgi, Paolo, 53
Giotto, 524
Giraudoux, Jean, 208, 492, 532
Gischia, Léon, 508
Giuliotti, Domenico, 129
Gluck, Christof Willibad, 30
Gobetti, Piero, 85, 117, 117n, 118–21, 121n, 122–26, 128, 130, 141, 142, 143, 154, 155n, 156, 169, 234n, 237, 271, 383, 384, 642n15
Godard, Jean-Luc, 613
Goebbels, Joseph, 620
Goethe, Johann Wolfgang von, 32, 39, 251
Gogol, Nicolai, 173
Goll, Yvan, 133
Gorky, Maxim, 173
Goya, Francisco, 358, 397, 441, 456
Gramsci, Antonio, 85, 88, 117, 118, 120, 122, 174, 237, 451, 521
Grandi, Dino, 148, 225, 229, 230, 230n, 231, 244, 261, 262
Grasset, Bernard, 141, 159, 183, 184, 185, 189, 195, 196, 204, 205, 215, 218, 240, 254, 455, 514, 532, 650n119, 653n15
Graves, Robert, 64
Grazzi, Emanuele, 330, 331, 333, 334, 335
Gréco, Juliette, 525
Grigorcea (ambassador), 669n195
Grimm (Brothers), 32
Grossman, Vasily, 374n, 397n
Grunewald, Michel, 532
Gualino, Riccardo, 271
Guareschi, Giovannino, 454
Guarnati, Daria, 568,
Guéhenno, Jean, 195
Guérin, Raymond, 41, 45, 505, 556, 598, 620, 685
Guerri, Giordano Bruno, 9, 241, 539, 605, 661n103, 698n17
Guevara, Che (Ernesto), 201
Guicciardini, Francesco, 219, 238, 239
Guidi, Rachele. See Mussolini, Rachele
Guillaumat, Louis, 71
Gustav V (king of Sweden), 128n, 377
Guth, Paul, 491n
Guttuso, Renato, 604
Guynemer, Georges, 359

Haedens, Kléber, 456, 488
Haile Selassie I (emperor of Ethiopia), 307
Haile Selassie, Imru, 621
Halévy, Daniel, 6, 183, 184, 185, 189, 195, 196, 204, 205, 208, 212, 228, 244, 252, 254, 266, 455, 492, 500, 504, 514, 517, 520, 595, 654n24
Halévy, Jacques Fromental, 184
Halévy, Ludovic, 184

706

Halévy, Marianne, 212, 225, 255, 256, 257, 268, 405, 468, 492, 500, 504, 506, 532, 595, 654n24,
Hamerman, Israel, 416
Hannibal, 269n
Heidegger, Martin, 411, 463
Heller, Gerhard, 312, 312n, 461, 463, 495n, 538
Hemingway, Ernest, 7, 64, 66, 343, 455, 457, 548, 557, 628
Hengl, Georg Ritter von, 367, 367n
Herriot, Édouard, 208
Harrison, Barbara, 209
Hildebrand, Ernst, 698n11
Hildebrand, Sylvia, 655n45
Himmler, Heinrich, 403, 404
Hindemith, Paul, 416
Hindenburg, Paul von, 66
Hitler, Adolf, 2, 11, 91, 92, 93, 97, 108, 127, 174, 175, 176, 183, 202, 203, 204, 206, 212, 213, 237, 238, 264, 297, 301, 301n, 322, 322n, 323, 324, 326, 328, 333, 336, 342, 345, 346, 347, 348, 349, 359, 360, 362, 365, 373, 375, 376, 377, 387, 394, 424, 428, 461, 462, 463, 483, 503, 518, 653n9
Hofmannsthal, Hugo von, 311
Hogarth, William, 456
Hölderlin, Friedrich, 613, 614, 624
Honegger, Arthur, 416
Horace, 241
Horowitz, Vladimir, 412n
Horthy, Miklós, 91
Hoxha, Enver, 581
Hughes, Howard, 626
Humboldt, Wilhelm von, 73

Imru. *See* Haile Selassie, Imru
Ingrao, Pietro, 583
Interlandi, Telesio, 139, 240, 240n
Ionesco, Eugène, 508
Istrati, Panait, 251
Ivancich, Adriana, 557
Ivanov, Dimitri (pseud. Jean Neuvecelle), 695n193
Ivanov, Vyacheslav Ivanovic, 695n193

Jacob, Max, 133
Janès, José, 580
Jimenéz, Juan Ramon, 312
Jouve, Pierre Jean, 312, 352, 352*
Joxe Halévy, Françoise, 504, 655n42
Joyce, James, 7, 133, 313
Jünger, Ernst, 7, 47, 64, 69, 75, 76, 201, 339, 358, 394

Kállay, Miklós, 557
Kaplan, Alice, 679n86
Kapuściński, Ryszard, 5n
Karajan, Herbert von, 415
Katz, Robert, 399n
Kawabata, Yasunari, 20
Keats, John, 540, 544
Kelly, Grace, 14, 549
Kemp, Robert, 456
Kempff, Wilhelm, 622
Kerensky, Alexander, 182
Kesselring, Albert, 673
Kessler, Harry, 349
Koestler, Arthur, 230, 445, 455, 490
Komonen, Markku, 622
Korène, Véra, 492, 537
Khrushchev, Nikita, 295, 580, 581, 590
Kuliscioff, Anna, 174
Kun, Béla, 202
Kundera, Milan, 419
Kurosawa, Akira, 482†

NOTES

Labiche, Eugène, 497
Lacretelle, Anne de, 538
Lacretelle, Jacques de, 514n
Lajolo, Davide, 297, 576
Lambron, Marc, 320
Lampedusa, Giuseppe Tomasi di, 423
Landolfi, Tommaso, 30, 290, 315
Lang, Fritz, 248n, 613, 613n
Lanza, Raimondo, 285
Lanza, Michele (Leonardo Simoni), 671n241
Lanzmann, Claude, 413
Lapauze Guarnati, Daria. *See* Guarnati, Daria
Larbaud, Valery, 349
Laudenbach, Roland, 50, 487, 491, 494, 495, 511, 514, 595
Laurencin, Marie, 620
Lauro, Achille, 436
Lautréamont, Comte de (Isidore Lucien Ducasse), 398, 663n137
Lawrence of Arabia (Thomas Edward Lawrence), 230, 322n, 626
Le Bon, Gustave, 128n
Le Corbusier (Charles-Édouard Jeanneret), 620
Le Grix, François, 292
Le Moal, Frédéric, 665n156
Lebesque, Morvan, 482*
Lee, Belinda, 542, 542n
Lemaire, Philippe, 525
Lenin, Vladimir, 11, 56, 149, 172, 173, 177, 178, 182, 183, 202, 203, 205, 207, 213, 215, 216, 217, 218, 221, 224, 590
Leonardo da Vinci, 510
Leppo, Jaakko, 365, 676
Letta, Gianni, 566, 604†

Levi, Carlo, 246, 457, 579
Levi, Primo, 405, 411, 413, 472
Lévy, Paul, 488
Lewis, Norman, 397, 398
Lewis, Sinclair, 161
Libera, Adalberto, 289, 615
Lilli, Virgilio, 288
Lippi, Filippo, 51
List, Wilhelm (general), 344, 349
Lloyd George, David, 72, 73
Lombardi, Riccardo (Father), 604
Longanesi, Leo, 46, 130, 131, 166, 170, 570, 640n89
Lorca, Federico García. *See* García Lorca, Federico
Loren, Sophia, 441, 604
Medici, Lorenzo de' (Lorenzo the Magnificent), 113
Lowry, Malcom, 230
Lu Xun, 580
Lucifero, Falcone, 599
Luciolli, Loredana, 340n
Lucretius, 28
Ludendorff, Erich, 66, 68, 70
Ludwig, Emil, 202
Ludwig, Hellmut, 461
Louis Philippe I (king of France), 226
Lunacharsky, Anatoly, 173
Lussu, Emilio, 78n, 209
Luther, Martin, 121

Mac Orlan, Pierre (Pierre Dumarchey), 133
Maccari, Mino, 129, 130, 131, 164, 166–69, 188, 193, 663n135
Macciocchi, Maria Antonietta, 576, 577, 579, 581, 583, 586, 588, 693n165, 693nn170–71, 694n181
Machado, Antonio, 312

Machiavelli, Niccolò, 183, 219
MacLeish, Archibald, 311
Maderna, Bruno, 289
Magistrati, Massimo, 258, 344, 345
Magnani, Anna, 604
Magni, Riccardo, 154n
Magris, Claudio, 597
Maistre, Joseph de, 122
Malclès, Jean-Denis, 507n
Malipiero, Gian Francesco, 290
Maloney, Jim, 166
Malraux, André, 13, 47, 75, 151, 184, 205, 208, 250, 313, 448, 455, 465, 493, 524, 532, 547, 589
Maltini, Roberto, 523
Mameli, Francesco Giorgio, 395
Man, Igor, 596
Mangano, Silvana, 537
Mann, Klaus, 478
Mann, Thomas, 73, 204, 255, 414, 418, 425, 499
Mannerheim, Carl Gustav, 365
Manzoni, Alessandro (novelist), 43
Manzoni, Gaetano (count), 224, 330
Mao Tse-tung, 2, 11, 16, 249, 581, 587, 589, 601
Marais, Jean, 443, 534
Marceau, Félicien, 556
Marcel, Gabriel, 514n
Marconi, Guglielmo, 149
Margerie, Diane de, 538
Marghieri (lawyer), 283
Marinelli, Giovanni, 100, 105, 235
Marinetti, Filippo Tommaso, 7, 42, 57, 64, 76, 93, 124, 149, 300, 503, 522, 592
Mario, E.A. (Giovanni Ermete Gaeta), 439n
Maroni, Gian Carlo, 623
Martellini, Luigi, 689n94

Marx, Jenny, 511, 512, 513, 520
Marx, Karl, 173, 507, 511, 512, 513
Masaccio (Tommaso di Ser Giovanni di Mòne di Andreuccio Cassai), 524
Masier, Roberta (Titti), 44, 187, 277, 538
Massimo, Leone, 269n
Mastroianni, Marcello, 399n
Matisse, Henri, 450, 534, 620, 680n90
Matteotti, Giacomo, 89, 99, 104, 105, 106, 107, 108, 109, 115, 117, 124, 142, 147, 151, 161, 229, 234n, 237, 258, 297, 651n130
Maulnier, Thierry, 514
Mauriac, François, 208, 493
Maurois, André, 208
Maurras, Charles, 12, 103, 121, 502, 639n85
Mazzetti, Augusto, 311, 316, 609
Mazzini, Giuseppe, 58, 173
Menuhin, Yehudi, 412n
Messe, Giovanni, 553
Metaxas, Ioannis, 329, 330, 332, 333, 334, 335
Metternich, Klemens von, 73
Mezzasoma, Fernando, 452
Mezzetti, Fernando, 695n198
Mihailescu, Titu, 676n41
Milhaud, Darius, 416
Miller, Henry, 111, 372, 373, 548, 641n1, 650n121
Miłosz, Czesław, 381, 420
Mishima, Yukio, 146, 339
Mitropoulos, Dimitri, 606, 606n
Moll, Giorgia, 613
Molotov, Vyacheslav, 347
Moltke, Helmuth von (the Younger), 57

NOTES

Moltke, Helmuth von (the Elder), 58
Mondadori, Alberto, 310, 324, 336, 362, 558
Mondadori, Arnoldo, 310, 359
Monroe, Marilyn, 549
Montale, Eugenio, 118, 290
Montanari, Nilo, 114
Montanelli, Indro, 302, 364, 598, 640n89, 695n198
Monteverdi, Claudio, 352n
Montgomery, Bernard, 422n
Montherlant, Henry de, 66, 208, 250, 493
Monti, Egle, 537, 538, 538n
Monti von Rezzori, Beatrice, 50n, 303, 450, 557, 568, 595
Montico, Maria, 50, 248
Morand, Paul, 7, 208, 349, 492
Morante, Elsa, 316, 558
Moravia, Alberto (Alberto Pincherle), 165, 290, 309, 314, 315, 316, 316n, 317, 318, 319, 319n, 320, 339, 355, 384, 441, 457, 489, 507, 549, 550, 558, 562, 571, 613, 662n115, 664n144, 664n149, 695n198
Morelli, Rina, 526
Morlion, Félix, 603
Mozart, Wolfgang Amadeus, 412n, 416, 626, 677,
Mudra, Bruno von, 69, 70, 306
Munthe, Axel, 389, 401, 558
Murat, Joachim (king of Naples), 434
Mussolini (family), 255, 263
Mussolini, Arnaldo, 140, 140n, 192, 199, 214, 261n
Mussolini, Benito, 2, 4, 9, 10, 11, 12, 42, 57, 79, 86, 87, 89, 90–93, 97–108, 112, 113, 116, 118, 120, 122, 124, 127, 128, 128n, 129, 131, 132, 135, 137, 139, 140, 140n, 141, 142–43, 143n, 144–45, 145n, 146–52, 152n, 153, 153n, 154–62, 162n, 163–65, 168, 169, 172, 174–76, 183–85, 188–93, 196–200, 202–4, 206, 209, 211, 212, 213–22, 224–31, 233–43, 245, 247, 249, 255, 255n, 256, 258, 259, 259n, 260, 261, 261n, 262, 266, 271, 273, 275, 276, 279, 281, 282, 283, 284, 285, 287, 288, 290–93, 295–97, 301, 301n, 302, 308, 309, 316, 322–26, 328, 329, 332–337, 338n, 339, 340, 341, 347–49, 351, 354, 360, 361, 376–78, 382, 384, 387, 391, 427, 428, 443, 446n, 452, 456, 457, 458, 469, 470, 470n, 473, 480, 482, 483, 484, 484n, 486, 495, 496, 500, 503, 529, 551, 590, 592, 593, 619, 620, 624, 627, 628, 652n142, 653n9, 655n44, 657n66, 658n66, 662n113, 665n163, 671n242
Mussolini, Benito Albino, 259n
Mussolini, Bruno, 260, 261, 261n
Mussolini, Edda, 188, 258, 259, 260–64, 267, 274, 275, 284, 284†, 323, 338, 339, 339†, 340, 340n, 428
Mussolini, Rachele, 255, 259, 259n
Mussolini, Vittorio, 260, 482

Nabokoff Joxe, Claude, 492
Nabokov, Vladimir, xiii
Nadeau, Maurice, 456
Nagel, Louis (Lajos Nemès), 484
Napoleon I. *See* Bonaparte, Napoleon

Napoleon III. *See* Bonaparte, Louis Napoleon
Napolitano, Giorgio, 371, 448, 608, 679n87
Natale, Gaetano, 165
Navarra, Quinto, 213
Neruda, Pablo, 550, 552
Nervi, Pier Luigi, 289
Neuteikh, Marian, 416
Neuvecelle, Jean. *See* Ivanov, Dimitri
Nicolardi, Eduardo, 439n
Nicolson, Harold, 74, 209
Nietzsche, Friedrich, xii, 185, 644n39
Nimier, Roger, 494
Nitti, Francesco Saverio, 210
Nivelle, Georges, 65
Noailles (countess de), 212
Nono, Luigi, 289
Novella, René, 492, 539, 565, 660n100, 684n26

Offenbach, Jacques, 184
Ojetti, Paola, 217
Ojetti, Ugo, 159, 164, 217, 225
Olry (general), 326
Orengo, Charles, 491
Orlando, Vittorio Emanuele, 72
Orsini, Filippo, 542
Orwell, George, 445, 491

Pacelli, Eugenio. *See* Pius XII
Page, Giorgio Nelson, 270n
Pajetta, Giancarlo, 521
Palance, Jack, 613
Palandri, Curzio, 114
Palazzeschi, Aldo (Aldo Giurlani), 37, 84, 290
Pampanini, Silvana, 538
Pannunzio, Mario, 310

Pansa, Mario, 286n
Paul, Prince of Yugoslavia, 349
Paul II, Pope (Pietro Barbo), 619
Papini, Giovanni, 7, 37, 129, 130, 290, 320, 455, 603
Pardini, Giuseppe, 107n, 648n94, 651n130, 664n139, 671n1
Pasolini, Pier Paolo, 12, 15, 130n, 407, 453, 470, 471, 476, 532, 542n, 546, 561, 571, 572, 579, 593, 604
Pasternak, Boris, 472n
Paul II, Pope, 619
Paulhan, Jean, 214
Paulus, Friedrich, 376, 671n237
Pavelić, Ante, 351, 419, 678n59
Pavese, Cesare, 12, 14, 48, 246, 252, 290, 320, 544, 576, 578, 593, 693n168
Pavlova, Tatiana, 506
Pavolini, Alessandro, 95, 145n, 339, 340, 354, 355, 665n163
Paxinou, Katina, 579
Peck, Gregory, 447
Peirce, Guglielmo, 578, 597, 695n198
Pellegrini (editorial assisatant), 290, 310, 383, 616
Pellegrini, Lino, 46, 343, 344, 345, 353, 354, 354*, 354†, 365, 367, 367n, 393, 395, 402n, 539, 602, 608, 616, 667n180, 674n30,
Pellizza da Volpedo, Giuseppe, 34
Penna, Sandro, 443n
Perelli Suckert, Elvira. *See* Suckert, Elvira
Perfetti, Francesco, 214, 647n75, 650n117, 650n119, 698n17
Perotti, Benedetto, 275
Petacci, Clara, 143n, 427, 628
Pétain, Philippe, 65, 70, 77, 92, 184, 326

711

NOTES

Petrassi, Goffredo, 290
Phillips, William, 390
Piacentini, Marcello, 289
Piaf, Édith, 555
Picasso, Pablo, 133, 534
Piccoli, Michel, 613
Piero della Francesca, 524, 573
Peter I (king of Serbia), 349
Pietromarchi, Antonello, 50n, 672n5
Pietromarchi, Luca, 672n5
Pilnyak, Boris, 358, 374
Piłsudski, Józef, 81, 202
Piovene, Guido, 288, 290, 518, 573, 687n66
Pirandello, Luigi, 36, 83, 84, 113, 128, 149, 210, 252, 488, 546, 591
Pirelli, Alberto, 161
Pisano, Giovanni, 51
Pitigrilli (Dino Segre), 210
Pitocchi, Nino, 210
Pius IX, Pope (Giovanni Maria Mastai Ferretti), 269
Pius XI, Pope (Achille Ratti), 81, 562n
Pius XII, Pope (Eugenio Pacelli), 441, 542, 603
Plievier, Theodor, 397
Plutarch, 306
Pogány, Gábor, 524
Polevoy, Boris, 579
Pöllänen, Minna, 622
Polverelli, Gaetano, 219, 376, 383
Ponti, Gio, 289, 568
Potente (Aligi Barducci), 452
Pound, Ezra, xi, 7, 12, 149, 313, 314
Pragnito, Duke of, 171
Praz, Mario, 309
Preziosi, Giovanni, 129
Prezzolini, Giuseppe, 7, 37, 84, 135, 136, 148, 159, 160, 457

Primo de Rivera, Miguel, 202
Printemps, Yvonne, 492, 507, 507n, 511
Proudhon, Pierre-Joseph, 128n
Proust (family), 184
Proust, Marcel, 44, 188, 339, 507, 509, 510, 511, 519, 686n56
Pucci, Emilio, 264, 596, 625
Puccini, Giacomo, 606, 607
Pudovkin, Vsevolod, 91, 689n87
Puglionisi, Camillo, 650n117
Pullmann, Simon, 415

Quilici, Folco, 229n
Quilici, Nello, 222, 223, 226, 227, 228, 229, 230, 235, 238, 239, 242
Quisling, Vidkun, 92

Radiguet, Raymond, 339
Ratoff, Gregory, 447
Rebatet, Lucien, 412n, 487, 502
Récamier, Juliette, 364
Reich-Ranicki, Marcel, 409, 415, 416
Remarque, Erich Maria, 7, 64, 499
Rembrandt (van Rijn), 532
Respighi, Ottorino, 149
Revelard, Adrienne, 655n45
Reynaud, Paul, 492
Ribbentrop, Joachim von, 323
Ridomi, Cristiano, 671n241, 671n242
Rigoni Stern, Mario, 328
Rilke, Rainer Maria, 47, 311
Rimbaud, Arthur, 25, 96
Rimbaud, Isabelle, xii
Rizzoli, Angelo, 310
Robert of Anjou (king of Naples), 52
Robespierre, Maximilien de, 216
Röhm, Ernst, 108, 204

Rojas, Waldo, 47n
Romains, Jules, 208, 208n
Rommel, Erwin, 463
Ronchi, Giorgio, 459, 460
Ronchi Suckert, Edda, xii, 26, 28, 59, 223, 603, 609, 633n14, 638n75, 647n81, 651n138
Roosevelt, Franklin D., 140n, 175, 447, 559
Rosai, Ottone, 129, 133, 289, 442
Rosi, Francesco, 78n
Rositani Suckert, Alessia, 619, 621, 622, 628, 629
Rositani Suckert, Niccolò, 619
Rosselli, Carlo, 209, 210
Rosselli, Nello, 316
Rossellini, Roberto, 434†, 445, 482, 482*, 526
Rossi, Cesare, 100
Roth, Philip, 44
Rothermere, Harold, 166
Rotondi, Virginio (Father), 600, 604, 604†, 605, 605n, 606, 609, 610, 696n213, 670n221
Rulli, Carla, 545n, 659n94
Rulli, Daniele, 50n, 616
Rulli, Guglielmo, 102, 317, 363, 366, 383, 385, 387, 605, 609, 684n21
Ruskaja, Jia, 235

Saba, Umberto, 22, 662n114, 662n115, 683n10
Sacchetti, Franco, 398, 572
Sade, Donatien-Alphonse-François, marquis de, 412, 572
Sadoul, Georges, 528
Sage, Katherine (Kay), 271
Saint-Exupéry, Antoine de, 47, 455
Saint-Just, Louis-Antoine, 216
Saint-Simon, Louis de Rouvroy, duc de, 3, 39, 656
Salazar, Antonio de Oliveira, 91
Salerno, Enrico Maria, 542n
Salinger, Jerome David, 626
Salomon, Ernst von, 456
Salvalaggio, Nantas, 539, 543n
Salvemini, Gaetano, 118, 141, 142n, 153, 195, 196, 212, 225, 478, 650n117
Salvini, Guido, 519
San Lazzaro, Gualtieri di (Giuseppe Papa), 518, 687n66
San Faustino, Jane di, 268, 269–70, 270, 274, 277–78, 339, 658n73, 658
Sanfelice, Luisa, 681n109
Sant'Elia, Antonio, 7
Santuccio, Gianni, 521
Sarfatti, Margherita, 129, 168, 240, 557
Sartori (diplomat), 395
Sartre, Jean-Paul, 13, 40, 56, 407, 472, 484, 490, 507, 510, 512, 684n23
Saura, Carlos, 689n89
Savinio, Alberto (Alberto De Chirico), 83, 210, 289, 336, 465n, 620
Savoia, Giovanna di, 344
Savoia Genova, Maria Adelaide di, 269n
Scarfoglio, Edoardo, 160
Schmeling, Max, 408
Schmitt, Carl, 411
Schobert, Eugen von, 353, 354†
Schumann, Robert, 411
Sciascia, Leonardo, 571
Scipione (Gino Bonichi), 289
Scola, Ettore, 443

NOTES

Sebastian, Peter, 673n17
Secchia, Pietro, 600, 605, 606
Segarra Lagunes, Maya, 622
Segre, Dino. *See* Pitigrilli
Semprún, Jorge, xiii
Senise, Carmine, 663n125, 672n5
Serao, Matilde, 160
Serena, Adelchi, 283
Sernas, Jacques, 507n
Serra, Teodorico, 62
Sessa, Pietro, 176
Settanni, Ettore, 313
Settimelli, Emilio, 107, 139
Shakespeare, William, 310, 655n41
Sharkey, Jack, 166
Sheehan, Vincent, 456, 681n109
Shelley, Percy Bysshe, 254, 540, 544
Shirer, William, 408, 676n48
Sieburg, Friedrich, 462
Siegfried, André, 208, 208n
Signoretti, Alfredo, 171, 190, 288, 692n145
Silone, Ignazio, 174, 457, 478
Silvestri, Carlo, 168
Simon, Michel, 508
Simoni, Leonardo. *See* Lanza, Michele
Simpson, Wallis, 230
Sirignano, Princess of, 557
Sironi, Mario, 289
Soca, Susana, 551
Soffici, Ardengo, 37, 84, 129, 130, 606
Solari Bozzi, Giuseppe, 678n59
Solari Bozzi, Onofrio, 50n, 517n, 607
Sontag, Susan, 679n86
Sorel, Georges, 128n
Sorel, Jean, 526n
Soro, Diego, 395

Sorrentino, Lamberti, 362, 669n215
Shostakovich, Dmitry, 416
Soupault, Philippe, 133
Spielberg, Steven, 677n56
Sprigge, Cecil J., 209
Staël, Germaine de, 147
Stalin, Josef, 2, 11, 16, 56, 91, 127, 174, 175, 177, 178, 202, 205, 207, 213, 217, 347, 356, 371, 375, 445, 447, 449, 451, 454, 529, 559, 580, 581, 604
Starace, Achille, 284, 309, 310, 338
Steber, Eleanor, 606
Steinbeck, John, 548
Stendhal (Marie-Henri Beyle), 45
Stirling, 322n
Stockmann [Stöckmann, Stokman], 360
Strauss, Richard, 328, 607
Stravinsky, Igor, 416
Suckert, Claudia, 609
Suckert, Elvira, 43–45, 242, 467, 634n20, 653n18
Suckert, Erwin, 26, 27, 29, 31, 32, 33, 34, 43, 121, 151, 460, 564
Suckert, Ezio, 26, 28, 31, 243, 303, 528, 603, 605, 609, 662n117, 662n120
Suckert, Kurt (uncle of Malaparte), 426
Suckert, Maria, 28, 59, 603, 608, 609
Suckert, Sandro, 26, 28, 30, 61, 63, 242, 355, 357, 543†, 594, 608, 609
Sweigard, Jane [Jana], 44, 523, 526n, 541–45, 545n, 594, 598, 625
Swift, Jonathan, 153†, 456

Talleyrand-Périgord, Charles-Maurice, Prince de, 73

Tambroni, Fernando, 583, 588, 596, 604
Tamburi, Orfeo, 45, 154n, 467, 489, 496, 498, 517n, 524, 529, 536, 548, 563, 643n24, 690n107, 698n13
Tamburini, Tullio, 95, 102, 296, 453
Tanguy, Yves, 271
Tanizaki, Jun'ichirō, 20, 44, 423
Tarchiani, Alberto, 388
Tasca, Angelo, 211, 225, 649n110
Tasso, Torquato, 352
Taubman, Howard, 45
Tavernier, René, 456
Taylor, Robert, 447
Teodorani Fabbri, Anna, 284†, 340n, 533
Terragni, Giuseppe, 289
Testa, Carlo, 697n221
Thorez, Maurice, 451
Tiberius, 626
Tito (Josip Broz), 112n, 453, 485, 592
Tobino, Mario, 290
Tofanelli, Arturo, 691n136
Togliatti, Palmiro, 13, 105, 108, 174, 276n, 319, 449, 450, 451, 452, 453, 454, 477, 497, 500, 501, 576, 579, 581, 583, 600, 601, 605, 608, 609, 610, 620, 640n97, 680n89, 680n91, 681n98, 683n6, 685n39, 696n205
Toller, Ernst, 7
Torre, Andrea, 163, 647n73
Torrecuso, Cito di, 171
Toscanini, Arturo, 57, 456
Tosi, Guy, 429, 455, 486, 487, 491, 493, 681n102, 681n115
Tourneur, Jacques, 447
Trakl, Georg, 64

Traverso, Leone, 337
Trenker, Luis, 328
Treves, Emilio, 195, 217, 240
Trilussa (Carlo Alberto Salustri), 290
Triolet, Elsa, 515
Trotsky (Lev Davidovich Bronstein), 202, 205, 206, 207, 215, 216, 217, 224, 447
Troubetzkoy, Paolo, 43, 634n20
Trulla (colonel), 62n
Tukhachevsky, Mikhajl, 79
Turati, Augusto, 158, 159, 160, 162, 163, 164, 165, 190, 191, 194, 273, 644n40, 657n66
Turati, Filippo, 158n
Tvardovsky, Aleksandr, 294
Tzara, Tristan (Sami Rosenstock), 7

Uccello, Paolo, 51
Umberto I (king of Italy), 97
Umberto II, king of Italy, 187, 246, 478, 599
Ungaretti, Giuseppe, 7, 64, 290, 291, 292, 636n51

Vailland, Roger, 442, 505
Valcini, 676n47
Valéry, Paul, 487n
Vallecchi, Enrico, 218, 567, 569, 588
Valletta, Vittorio, 275, 276, 276n, 286
Vallone, Raf, 524, 525, 526, 527
Valois, Georges, 103, 639n85
Vancini, Florestano, 542n
Varzi, Elena, 524, 526
Vegliani, Franco, 597, 598, 609, 695n197, 696n213, 697n223
Verde, Ferdinando, 617
Verdi, Giuseppe, 111, 607, 681n109
Verga, Giovanni, 252

NOTES

Vergani, Orio, 159, 265, 266n, 522, 656n49
Verne, Jules, 302
Veronesi, Sandro, 319, 561
Vidal, Gore, 556
Vigorelli, Giancarlo, 1, 33, 316, 317
Vilar, Jean, 508
Vilmorin, 492
Visconti, Luchino, 378, 444, 444n, 554
Visconti Prasca, Sebastiano, 329, 335, 336
Vita-Finzi, Paolo, 645n52
Victoria, Queen, 515
Vittorini, Elio, 98, 165, 223, 238, 239, 290, 297, 318, 457
Victor Emmanuel II (king of Italy), 187
Victor Emmanuel III (king of Italy), 97, 344, 378
Vlaminck, Maurice de, 534
Voilier, Jean (Jeanne Loviton), 487, 487n, 537, 538
Volpe, Gioacchino, 127, 415, 641n13
Volponi, Paolo, 571

Wagner, Richard, 606, 677n49
Wallace, Edgar, 310

Welles, Orson, 494
Wilde, Oscar, 519
Wilhelm II (emperor of Germany and king of Prussia), 66
Williams, Tennessee, 556
Wilson, Thomas Woodrow, 72, 73
Winner, Percy, 390, 457, 673n22
Witkiewicz, Stanisław Ignacy (Witkacy), 396
Woller, Hans, 454n
Woolf, Virginia, 133

Yáñez, Rebequita, 44, 47n, 537, 551, 552, 567
Yeats, William Butler, 311

Zachariae (doctor), 338n
Zangrandi, Ruggero, 663n135, 670n226, 675n32
Zoshchenko, Mikhail, 472n
Zog I (Ahmed Zogolli), 321–22, 322n
Zola, Émile, 315
Zweig, Arnold, 74, 349
Zweig, Stefan, 34
Zweigart, Phyllis Jeane. *See* Sweigart, Jane

MAURIZIO SERRA is a diplomat, historian, and writer. Following postings in West Berlin, Moscow, and London, he served as the Italian ambassador to UNESCO in Paris and to the United Nations in Geneva. Among his many books are biographies of Curzio Malaparte, Italo Svevo, and Gabriele D'Annunzio, and two novels. The recipient of numerous awards, in 2020 he became the first Italian elected to the Académie Française.

STEPHEN TWILLEY is an editor and translator. His translations include Curzio Malaparte's *Diary of a Foreigner in Paris* and Giuseppe Tomasi di Lampedusa's *The Professor and the Siren*, both published by NYRB Classics. He lives in Chicago.